APPROACHES TO GREEK MYTH

THE JOHNS HOPKINS UNIVERSITY PRESS

BALTIMORE AND LONDON

APPROACHES
TO GREEK MYTH

Edited and
Introduced by
LOWELL EDMUNDS

This book has been brought to publication with the generous assistance of
the David M. Robinson Publication Fund.

The Johns Hopkins University Press
701 West 40th Street   Baltimore, Maryland 21211
The Johns Hopkins Press Ltd., London

LIBRARY OF CONGRESS CATALOGING-IN-PUBLICATION DATA
Approaches to Greek myth / edited and introduced by Lowell
Edmunds.
        p.   cm.
   Bibliography: p.
   ISBN 0-8018-3863-0.—ISBN 0-8018-3864-9 (pbk.)
   1. Mythology, Greek.   I. Edmunds, Lowell.
BL790.A66   1990
292.1′3—dc20   89-45482
                                                        CIP

The paper used in this publication meets the minimum requirements of American
National Standard for Information Sciences—Permanence of Paper for Printed Library
Materials, ANSI Z39.48—1984.

CONTENTS

PREFACE AND
ACKNOWLEDGMENTS

The title of this collection should imply both that Greek mythology admits a plurality of approaches and that those represented here may not be the only ones. I chose these eight approaches because they seemed to me the most viable of those now in use. Everyone is familiar with at least one of them. Here is a whole panoply. Invitations to contributors followed the decision as to the plan of the collection. I was lucky to get the cooperation of an expert in every case. By chance, four were American and four were European.

The sequence of the approaches is roughly from the tried and true to the innovative. The four categories are almost self-explanatory. In the first, you have historical methodologies, in the second comparative ones. In the third, you have two approaches that emerge from highly developed bodies of theory, Greimasian semiotics and Freudian psychoanalysis. The final category is iconography. I took pleasure in working with all of the contributions. If I could choose a favorite, it would be the last, the methodology of which holds much promise. Vase paintings become readable *as myths* (instead of illustrations of verbal myths), and a large corpus of long silent evidence finds its discourse. Further remarks on each of the contributions will be found at the end of the introduction.

From the beginning of the project, Eric Halpern, humanities editor of the Johns Hopkins University Press, bore a large share of the burdens, and I here record my gratitude to him. And to Susan T. Edmunds, who spent many hours working with me on galley proofs.

L. E.
Highland Park, New Jersey

INTRODUCTION: THE PRACTICE OF GREEK MYTHOLOGY

The definition of "myth" has changed again and again as theories of myth have come and gone. Marcel Detienne offered a radical solution to the problem in *L'invention de la mythologie*, published in 1981.[1] Myth, he said, does not exist. It is nothing but an intellectual or scholarly construct that can be traced to mythology, to the scientific study of myth, beginning with Fontenelle in the eighteenth century. And what then created mythology was the sense of the scandalous in myth. Myth was the Other of religion, reason, or civilization. Mythology arose to explain scandal. Furthermore, given the nonexistence of Greek myth *in particular,* Greek mythology in the sense of a homogeneous system of myths did not exist either. This system was fabricated in the modern period by the science that arose to explain Greek myths. This science had a small-scale precedent in antiquity, however. Certain Greeks—Hecataeus, Pherecydes, and Herodotus are the key figures—began to systematize oral traditions and reduce them to writing. With Plato came a more systematic effort to purge and reform the traditional culture. Plato is, in fact, the first to use the word "mythology" as a collective expression for the culture he repudiates, as he is the first to compose his own myths—improved myths—which he integrates into the philosophical dialogues. Plato is the founder of mythology in antiquity. Such is Detienne's argument.

If in antiquity Greek mythology came into existence only in the perspective of writing and philosophy, as something negative, was it in the first place completely without substance, so that it had to be invented *ex nihilo?* Detienne would concede that the oral culture was rife with proverbs, riddles, stories, and the like. These, however, did not have the status of myth; or, if you like, they were all "myths." The word *mythos* is a floating signifier, and not even in Plato, Detienne maintains, does "myth" mean narrative.[2]

Detienne argues his case in a complex, metaphoric style, apparently owing to his sense of the lack of a discourse that could express the collapse of the distinction between *mythos* and *logos*. Detienne's metaphors for what we—not Detienne—call Greek mythology are repeatedly spatial. Greek mythology does not have "an autonomous territory." Myth is everywhere and thus nowhere. Detienne's evidence is mainly semantic: the Greek word *mythos* did not refer to what we call "myth." He concludes, as said, that there was neither the concept of myth as story nor the concept of a body of myths, a mythology.

In order to investigate Detienne's claims, one must, for reasons to be given below, abandon the semantic approach and try to discover who told myths, on what occasions, and for what purposes. In other words, one must attempt to get at the practice of *mythos*. Besides the explicit statements *about* myth on which Detienne concentrates, Greek literature of the archaic and classical periods contains many references to and examples of the *use of* myth, on the basis of which it can be shown that the Greeks did in fact have a category of discourse or narrative corresponding to "myth" in the sense of traditional tale.[3]

THE PRACTICE OF *MYTHOS*

Aristophanes' *Wasps* is about the conflict between an old man, Philocleon, and his son, Bdelycleon. The old man's ruling passion is love of jury duty, which fills him and his cronies with a sense of power. The son, through force and persuasion, attempts to bring the father to his senses and to set him on a new path. As the final part of this attempted conversion, Bdelycleon dresses the old man up in new clothes and instructs him in the behavior appropriate at an upper-class dinner party. When he comes to the matter of conversation, he asks Philocleon if he knows how to tell elevated stories (*logoi*) in the company of learned and clever men. Philocleon assures his son that he is able to do so and then gives two examples that show that he has failed completely to grasp what Bdelycleon meant. The examples are: how Lamia farted when she was caught and how Cardopion . . . his mother (Bdelycleon interrupts his father before the verb linking subject [Cardopion] and direct object [mother] comes out) (1174–78). Bdelycleon says: "Don't tell me myths [*mythoi*], but some [stories] of the human kind, the kind we usually tell, I mean at home" (1179–80). Philocleon misunderstands the last phrase, taking it to mean stories about things that happen at home. He therefore now proposes: "Once upon a time there was a mouse and a ferret . . ." (1181). Again Bdelycleon interrupts. Philocleon must tell elevated stories, Bdelycleon says, and he gives two examples: how he went as state ambassador with Androcles and Cleisthenes; how well Ephydion

fought against Ascondas in the pancratium. "That's the way," says Bdelycleon, "clever people are accustomed to tell stories" (1186–96).[4]

This scene in *Wasps* distinguishes, then, between two classes of story,
one human and the other mythical. Of the stories branded as *mythoi,*
one is about Lamia, a bogey woman who stole children, and the other
is about the unknown Cardopion, who, to judge from the context, was
probably not another Oedipus but an example of unusual lust and de-
pravity. Philocleon's third attempt, which we can call "The Ferret and
the Mouse," is clearly a fable.

The distinction between the human and the mythical also had a
chronological dimension that was already well established in the earliest
Greek poets. Homer and Hesiod are in broad agreement: first, the period of theogony, ending in the reign of Zeus; then the age of heroes,
with whom the Olympians interact; then the age of mortals. In the
Myth of the Ages in Hesiod's *Works and Days* (106–201), the fourth
age is that of the heroes, who are "the previous generation" (159–60),
the one before Hesiod. The distinction is articulated by the historian
Herodotus this way: "Polycrates is the first Hellene of whom we know
who intended to become master of the sea, except for Minos the Cnos-
sian and anyone earlier than he who had a thalassocracy. In the so-
called human age (*geneē*), Polycrates is the first" (3.122). The distinction, explicitly articulated in Hesiod and Herodotus, between the age of
humans and a previous age or ages, shows the chronological dimension
of Bdelycleon's distinction between the human and the mythical. That
which is human takes place in our time, human time—Bdelycleon prefers contemporary anecdotes, which are more dignified than myths. But
nonhuman mythical stories in hands other than Philocleon's could be a
source of prestige. The poet Pindar confers glory on athletes and their
families by linking them with the heroes of the earlier time. Hecataeus
and Pherecydes, even as they attempt to rationalize the family trees of
their contemporaries, reinforce the chronological division between human and mythical, and reestablish the heroic forebears of the leading
families of their own times.

The series of comic misunderstandings in *Wasps* begins with Bdelycleon's use of the word *logoi* (1174), which can refer to several kinds of
discourse, including *mythos,* the sense in which Philocleon takes it. *Logos* and *mythos* are in fact interchangeable synonyms for "story" until
Plato reorganizes the semantics of these words, with the result that *mythos* is opposed to *logos* in the senses both of verifiable discourse and of
argumentative discourse.[5] Plato's task was made easier, however, by the
fact that *mythos,* and *logos* when used as a synonym thereof, already

had a pejorative connotation, as is evident in Bdelycleon's dismissal of Lamia and Cardopion as *mythoi*. As I show later, myths are never neutral but always have some point in the context in which they are told, and thus in principle they demand an answer. The one who gives an answer (cf. Bdelycleon) brands what he has just heard as a *mythos*, even if his answer consists of what is, from our point of view, another *mythos*. In the First *Olympian*, Pindar repudiates *mythoi* for their untruth; they exceed the true *logos* (28–29). He then proceeds to give another version of the particular *mythos* he has repudiated. On the other hand, Hecataeus refers to his own writing in terms of *mythos* (using the verb *mytheomai*) and to the stories of which he is critical as *logoi*. Given this fluctuation, the semantics of *mythos* alone cannot tell us much about the existence or practice of *mythoi* in the sense of oral narratives.

Philocleon's preference for Lamia and Cardopion not only characterizes him as a myth-loving old man but also places him on one side of a central division in Greek myths between those that were panhellenic and canonical and those that were local or in the nature of folklore. This division is implicit in a well-known statement of Herodotus, which occurs in the context of his argument that Greek religion is for the most part derivative from Egyptian religion and that Greek religion is therefore much younger than the Greeks believe.

> Whence each of the gods came and whether they all existed always and of what sort they were in appearance, they [the Greeks] did not know until yesterday or the day before, so to speak. For I think that Homer and Hesiod lived four hundred years before my time. These are the ones who created a theogony for the Greeks and gave the gods their names and distinguished their honors and arts and indicated their appearances. (2.53)

Herodotus goes on to state that the poets said to be earlier than Hesiod and Homer are in fact later. Hesiod and Homer are the first and the originators. We today think of Hesiod and Homer not as originators but as the shapers of received traditions, and we conceive of the origins of Greek religion in different terms.[6] But Herodotus's sense of the Homeric and Hesiodic theology as determining for the Greeks, for all the Greeks, is accurate and indisputable. The Homeric *Iliad* and *Odyssey*, Hesiod's *Theogony* and *Works and Days* show that narrative and genealogy were the means to this end. Of what else could Herodotus be thinking? It is therefore fair to interpret him as saying that Homer and Hesiod established a canonical Greek mythology consisting of these stories and genealogies.[7] Herodotus attests the sense in the fifth century B.C. of a canon, of *a* mythology. Only, indeed, because they had established a canon could Homer and Hesiod be attacked, as by Xenophanes (frag. B11 DK), for the immorality of the stories they told.[8]

As against the canon, Philocleon represents localism. To illustrate this point, I use an ancient commentator on Thucydides, Dionysius of Halicarnassus (end of first century B.C.). It was still necessary in Dionysius's time to explain Thucydides' avowed goal of excluding the mythical (adj. *mythōdes*) from *The Peloponnesian War* (1.22). Dionysius interprets this goal as a principled refusal to deceive the many with certain kinds of stories. He gives three examples: Lamias; Naiads; and demigods born of unions of gods and mortals. (The first example happens to coincide with one of Philocleon's preferred mythical subjects. Philocleon is thus the sort of person whom, according to Dionysius, Thucydides will refrain from misleading.) Dionysius goes on to characterize such stories in a particular way: "Amongst all men, in common at the local level and in private in cities, some traditions of such things [Lamias, etc.] were preserved, which children inherited from their fathers and took care to hand on to the next generation, and they required that those wishing to publish them [these traditions] write them up in the same way" (*Thuc.* 6–7; cf. Strabo 1.2.35 sub fin.). Philocleon's tastes in mythology can, then, be called local. Although Dionysius speaks of the local traditions as written, because he wants to compare Thucydides, a writer, with other writers—i.e., of local histories—these traditions were still alive in oral form for Pausanias (second century A.D.) to hear long after the time of Dionysius.[9]

The existence of these local traditions necessarily means that there will be differing versions of the same myths, variations between local and canonic and between local and local. Medea is an example. In Hesiod's *Theogony*, she seems to have lived happily in Iolcus with Jason at the end of their adventures (992–1001). The epic version included the rejuvenation by boiling of Jason's father, Aeson (*Nostoi* frag. 6 Allen), and presumably also the homicidal boiling of Pelias, the hubristic king of Iolcus. How else could Jason have succeeded him?[10] Medea's presence in Corinth and her murder of her children there are a variant already within archaic epic.[11] The manner of the children's death, at the hands of their mother, as in Euripides, or at the hands of the Corinthians, also varies.[12] Euripides' tragedy ends with Medea leaving her children to be buried in the temple of Hera in Corinth. This allusion to a contemporary Corinthian ritual is thus specifically local. In her contribution to this volume, Christiane Sourvinou-Inwood has shown how in Athens in the fifth century Medea, as the hostile stepmother of the Athenian hero Theseus, came to represent, among other things, the Eastern menace that the Greeks had withstood in the Persian Wars.

Even the canonical theogony of Hesiod had rival versions, which are now clearer, thanks to the Derveni papyrus. This papyrus roll, dating from the fourth century B.C., was found at a pass called Derveni 12 kilometers northwest of Thessaloniki in January 1962. It is a commentary on an Orphic theogony, of which it quotes several passages.[13] These passages, combined with other ancient sources, enable us to see that the Orphic religion had its own theogony, differing in many ways from the Hesiodic one.

A multiplicity of conflicting versions was always the state of affairs in Greek mythology. It could seem troublesome to the Greeks themselves, and we find it denounced by Hecataeus in the preface to his genealogical treatise: "Hecataeus of Miletus speaks [verb *mytheomai*] thus. I write the following, as it seems to me to be true. For the stories [*logoi*] of the Greeks are many and laughable, as they appear to me" (*FrGHist* frag. 1). When Hecataeus says "many" he means multiple,[14] and he proceeds to try to reduce the stories of the Greeks to order. The multiplicity of different versions of the same story has never ceased to be an embarrassment (cf. Strabo 1.2.35 init). Thus Mark P. O. Morford and Robert J. Lenardon, the authors of the textbook of Greek mythology most widely used in the United States, say of Medea: "It is enough to observe the variations in her legend and to see how the genius of Euripides stabilized the tradition."[15] In other words, we should reduce the variants to a single official version, consecrated by the name of a poet, a version that can then perhaps be interpreted as something other than a myth. The irony is that the compilers of this textbook inevitably create new versions of the myths[16] and a new system of myths and thus participate in the very process they disdain.

The storytelling impulse of old Philocleon indicates yet another fundamental distinction in the practice of Greek mythology—the distinction between different kinds of sources for myths, different kinds of transmission. Lamia and Cardopion, who do not belong to epic, are outside the canon. And yet both Euripides and Crates (of whom no work survives) wrote a *Lamia*—perhaps a satyr play.[17] Just as symposiasts like the ones admonished by Xenophanes (cited below) might retell stories from epic, so a Philocleon might retell a story from a tragedy or a satyr play or from some oral source. This popular retelling of stories is remarked by the scholiast on Euripides, *Alcestis* 1, apropos of the plot of this tragedy. Euripides' version of the story—Apollo's servitude in the house of Admetus—is, says the scholiast, the "oral, popular" one; it is also, he says, to be found in Hesiod (frag. 54c MW). Thus the epic stories or myths did not depend for their survival upon fixation in writing and reiteration by rhapsodes, professional reciters, at public festivals. These myths also belonged to popular oral storytelling. There was a parallel operation of poetic sources and the popular retelling of these sources.

Another sort of parallelism of sources is between poetic and oral but nonpoetic transmission. Thucydides traces the history of Sicily at the beginning of his narrative of the Sicilian Expedition. The earliest inhabitants of the island were the Cyclopes and the Laestrygonians, about whom Thucydides knows nothing and therefore has nothing to say. "Let it suffice as poets have said and as each person somehow has information about them" (6.2.1). "Somehow" means: from some other source than the poets.[18] These two alternative, parallel sources—poetry and nonpoetic oral tradition—appear also in Pindar, who twice distinguishes between poets and tellers of tales as the two sources of immortal fame,[19] and again in Plato (*Rep.* 392D).

Philocleon's Lamia and Cardopion are not only local and not only examples of popular storytelling (whether or not derivative from poetic sources) but belong to a different order of story, which one can call folklore, provided that one recognizes that the Greeks had no taxonomy of narratives corresponding to the ones we use, e.g., the tripartite scheme of myth, legend, and folktale,[20] all of which the Greeks called *mythoi.* Here is a fourth fundamental distinction, between two different orders of story. The one I have called folklore can be subdivided into four kinds.[21]

The only named kind was the *ainos* or 'moral fable,' of which Hesiod's Hawk and Nightingale (*Works and Days* 202–212) and Archilochus's Eagle and Fox (frag. 174 W) and Monkey and Fox (frag. 185 W) are examples. A collection of these fables was made by Demetrius of Phalerum (fourth–third century B.C.)[22] and attributed to Aesop (sixth century B.C.). Another sort of folktale, for which, to repeat, the Greeks had no name except *mythos,* is represented by the stories told by each of the semichoruses in Aristophanes' *Lysistrata.* The chorus of old men begins: "I will tell you a story [*mythos*] which I heard when I was yet a boy" (781). They tell the story of the misogynist Melanion. The women then reply: "And I want to tell you a story [*mythos*] counter to yours about Melanion" (805). They tell the story of the misanthrope Timon. These are stories, which, like the *ainos,* "draw a moral pointing out the connection with the immediate situation."[23]

Two other kinds of story appear to be distinct categories to us, but, again, the Greeks had no names for them. One is the anecdote. It typically concerned a famous historical person and ended with a clever remark or apothegm. In fact, "apothegm" is as close as we come to a name for this type of story.[24] This name is used for the first time in the fourth century B.C. but does not become standard until much later. A typical anecdote goes as follows: Alexander the Great pays a visit to the famous Cynic philosopher Diogenes in Corinth. Diogenes is sunbathing. Alexander says: "What can I do for you?" Diogenes answers: "Get out of my sun" (D.L. 6.38). The other kind of story is the joke. Greek jokes concern generic types, usually Sicilians or Abderites, who for some reason were considered to be stupid. A Sicilian, for example, is told by his friend that the friend's wife has just hanged herself from a fig tree. The Sicilian says: "Could I have some cuttings from that tree? I'd like to plant one for myself" (*Philogelos* 33).[25]

PURPOSES OF STORYTELLING

Jokes indicate one of the purposes of storytelling: entertainment. Thus the dinner party was one of the settings in which, *pace* Bdelycleon, people liked to tell myths. Xenophanes (in the sixth or early fifth century B.C.) chastizes what must have been a customary practice:

> Praise the man who, when he drinks, brings genuine [or noble] things
>   to light,
> in order that there may be memory and exertion over achievement,—
> do not treat the battles of Titans and Giants
> nor of Centaurs, fictions of earlier men,
> or violent seditions. In these there is nothing useful.
>   (Xen. frag. 1.19–23 W = B 1.19–23 DK)

The battle of Titans and gods is an episode in Hesiod's *Theogony* (617–719) and a similar battle of Giants is alluded to (954). Xenophanes' advice presupposes a fondness for the retelling of these canonical stories after dinner, when the drinking began. In Xenophon's *Symposium*, Socrates states that, in order to make a point, he will tell stories (verb *mythologeomai*) (8.28), and one might mention also the speeches in Plato's *Symposium*, some of which have a mythical character. The precedent for the telling of epic narratives had been set by Odysseus himself. On the island of Phaeacia, in the palace of Alcinous, he regaled the dinner guests with an hours-long account of his wanderings and adventures (*Odyssey* 9–12). One can compare the exchange of *mythoi* by Nestor and his guest Machaon after they have returned from the battlefield and have restored themselves (Machaon has been slightly wounded) with a wine-based potion (*Il.* 11.642–43).

The fact that "a tale of Alcinous" became proverbial for a long story[26] implies that an awkwardness was sensed in Odysseus's behavior, though in the poem he was, at a certain point, invited to continue (*Od.*

11.328–84). A code of propriety would have evolved with the practice of after-dinner storytelling. In fact, Philocleon violates particular aspects of the code. At the dinner, he gets drunk and insults the other guests, "making boorish jokes and, what's more, telling stories [*logoi*], in a completely uncultivated fashion, which had nothing to do with the situation" (*Wasps* 1320–21).

It has been observed that every myth in Greek poetry serves as an exemplum[27] and what is true of poetry is undoubtedly true of life, as in the examples from *Lysistrata* cited above. The semichorus of old men tell their myth to make a point against women, and the semichorus of old women reply in the same style. This sort of applied story is clearest in the form of the Aesopic beast fable. Once again, *Wasps* provides an illustration. One of the aspects of jury duty that especially pleases Philocleon is that in court rich men have to supplicate the jurors. Philocleon gives a list of the defendants' various strategies. Sometimes to cajole the jurors they "tell us stories [*mythoi*]; others tell us something laughable of Aesop; others make jokes" (566–67). Later, when Philocleon is worried about having to pay a fine because of possible drunken behavior after the dinner party, Bdelycleon reassures him: either his fellow gentlemen will dissuade the victim, or "you yourself tell some witty story [*logos*], something laughable of Aesop or a Sybaritic tale,[28] which you learned at the symposium" (1256–60). (Bdelycleon here goes against his earlier assumption that such stories would not be told at the high-class dinner for which he was preparing his father.) Philocleon does indeed get drunk and into trouble. He assaults a bread seller, who appears on stage with a witness. Old Philocleon remembers his son's advice, at least to the extent of telling a story *about* Aesop (1401–5).[29] Likewise, when another of his victims appears, he tells two rather underdeveloped stories, which he at least locates in Sybaris (1427–40). Bdelycleon now starts to carry his father into their house, and Philocleon tries to defend himself by introducing another event in the life of Aesop, the one connected with the story, which Philocleon does not have a chance to complete, of the Beetle and the Eagle (1444–48).[30] Aesop told this story, Philocleon says, when he was accused by the Delphians of having stolen a libation bowl. The further details of the story are found in the *Life of Aesop* (*Vita* G 124–42 Perry). Suffice it to say that Aesop was on trial for his life and the story or fable was part of his self-defense. As Gregory Nagy has shown, the narrative frame for the fable is itself archaic and traditional; in the *Fables* as we have them, the moral at the end is a compensation for the loss of the frame.[31]

But the use of a fable in the context of a trial belongs also to historical reality.[32] As a juror, Philocleon enjoys hearing the defendants tell Aesopic tales. The practice to which Philocleon refers is in fact recommended by Aristotle in the *Rhetoric*. In Book 2 of this work, he analyzes the various sorts of oratorical argument. One of these is the example, which he divides into two varieties: historical parallels and stories or fables (*logoi*), which he specifies as Aesopic or Libyan.[33] As an example of an Aesopic tale, he recounts what Aesop said before the Samian assembly in defense of a demagogue who was on trial for his life (*Rhet.* 1393b23ff. = *Fab.* 427 Perry). Aristotle (who obviously regards the narrative frame as part of the fable) in fact prefers the historical parallel to the fable as a means of persuasion (1394a3ff.), but he discusses both of these kinds of example as feasible.[34]

Other kinds of rhetoric than dicastic employed stories. Before the battle of Plataea (479 B.C.), the Athenians and the Tegeans both laid claim to the honorific left flank in the battle line, and both, to support their claim, told stories from what we would call the mythical past (Hdt. 9.26–27). The Athenians' examples—which were or became standard in funeral orations (Lysias 2.4–16; Plato *Menex.* 239a6–246b2; Dem. 60.6–11) and panegyric oratory (Isoc. *Paneg.* 54–70, *Panath.* 168, 193)—concern their alliance with the Heraclids against the Peloponnesians, their recovery and burial of those who died in the campaign of the Seven against Thebes, and their defeat of the Amazons.

These various historically attested competitive uses of stories have their ideal precedent in Homer. Richard Martin, in a forthcoming study of the *Iliad*,[35] has shown that in this poem *mythos* always refers to the performance (as opposed to the product) of speech by someone in power or by someone who lays claim to power. Martin finds that the genres of speech called *mythos* are only three: command, boast or insult, and recitation of remembered events, and he argues that the third of these underlies the first two. The god or hero who commands or boasts or insults will rely on a narrative of what has been, or could be, or should be, or should not be, done. Sometimes he will use genealogy to make his case. Further, such speeches usually take place in public, before an audience that is to be convinced of the status and authority of the speaker. Such Homeric *mythoi* were probably already felt as idealized in the eighth century B.C., even though they were still close, as Martin argues, to actual genres of discourse. But by the fifth century, when genealogy, for example, had become a subject for research, surely the Homeric state of things, in which every *mythos* is a living, powerful speech-performance, seemed to lie on the far side of the divide between men and heroes.

The use of myths by poets, as distinguished from the use of myths by characters in poetry, has the same competitiveness that we see in a crude form in the case of Philocleon. Pindar is the best example, though choral odes in Greek tragedy could also be cited. Most of Pindar's surviving poems consist of odes for victors in athletic competitions, which the Alexandrian scholars arranged in four collections, according to the place where the competitions were held—Olympia, Nemea, Delphi, and Corinth. A typical feature of the victory ode is a myth that somehow contributes to the praise of the victor. In the interpretation of Pindar, the main problem, all Pindarists would agree, is the myth. In particular, the problem is the relation of the myth, which is likely to be briefly and idiosyncratically told, to the rest of the ode, all of which is presumably encomiastic. We often fail to grasp the relation of the myth to the situation—the particular victory, the age and other characteristics of the victor, the victor's home town and family, and the like. One of the reasons for this uncertainty is that adequate sources for the myth independent of Pindar, which would provide perspective on Pindar's use, are lacking.[36] Pindar probably assumes, however, knowledge not only of the story line but also of other applications of the same story.

By tracing the use of Sisyphus as an exemplum in several poets, including Pindar, we can see why any single myth in any single ode of Pindar, or for that matter in any poet, may present difficulties. What this survey of the Sisyphus exemplum will show is the broad range of applications of a relatively simple story in which the protagonist has a single, clearly defined, dominating trait.[37]

Odysseus' storytelling on the island of Phaeacia, to which I have already referred, included an account of his visit to the Underworld. There he saw Sisyphus, among other great sinners. Odysseus describes him, covered with sweat and dust, rolling his stone up the hill, in an ever-losing battle with the force of gravity (Od. 11.593–600). The seven-line description is implicitly negative and does not include the epithet "crafty" that is applied to Sisyphus elsewhere in archaic poetry. We find this epithet, for example, in the Iliad, where the Trojan Glaucus recounts his ancestry, which came from Corinth. "There," Glaucus says, "was Sisyphus, craftiest of mortals, / Sisyphus son of Aeolus" (6.153– 54). Contrary to what the picture of Sisyphus in the Underworld might have led one to expect, Glaucus is proud of this ancestor. Likewise Pindar, in an ode addressed to a Corinthian, praises Sisyphus, the founder of Corinth, as "god-like in his extreme cleverness" (O. 13.52)

This, his principal trait, also appeared laudable to Theognis. In a characteristically pessimistic mood, Theognis states that wealth is now all that matters. Nothing else is of any use. He gives four examples of virtues that you might have thought were superior to wealth, and one is the cleverness of Sisyphus

who came up even from Hades through his great resourcefulness,
having persuaded Persephone with wily words,
the one who gives forgetfulness to mortals, sapping their wits;
and no one else ever yet contrived this thing,
no one whom the dark cloud of death had covered,
and who had entered the shadowy place of the dead,
passing through the dark gates that
restrain the souls of the dead, object though they may.
But Sisyphus the hero came back from there
into the light of the sun, with his great shrewdness.

(702–12)

The return from the dead was in fact the prime example of the cunning intelligence of Sisyphus. Our earliest source for the story is Pherecydes in the fifth century genealogical work already mentioned:

When Zeus was carrying Aegina, daughter of Asopus, from Phlius to Oinone, through Corinth, Sisyphus, at the request of Asopus, showed him how to steal her by trickery. Thus Sisyphus drew upon himself Zeus's anger. Zeus sends Death against him. But Sisyphus, perceiving the approach, binds Death in heavy chains. For this reason no mortal was dying, until Ares released Death and handed Sisyphus over to him. Before Sisyphus died, he instructed his wife Merope not to send him down to Hades with the customary rites. After a time, when the wife did not render [what was due], Hades took notice and released Sisyphus who was to [go and] rebuke her. When Sisyphus reached Corinth, he never returned [to the Underworld] until he died of old age. For this reason, Hades compelled the dead Sisyphus to keep rolling a stone, so that he would never run away again.[38]

This is the story that Homer and Theognis have in mind. But Homer focuses on the punishment, Theognis on the virtue that enabled Sisyphus to return from the dead. Alcaeus for his part focuses on the futility of that virtue. He says to a drinking companion:

Drink and get drunk, Melanippus, with me. Why do you suppose that when you have crossed over whirling Acheron . . . you will see the pure sunlight again? Come, aim not at great ends. King Sisyphus, the son of Aeolus, shrewdest of men, claimed to be master of Death: but for all his cunning he twice crossed over whirling Acheron at the command of fate; and the King, the son of Cronus, . . . him to have great labour under the black earth.[39]

I digress for a moment on one detail of the story as it is found in Pherecydes. Sisyphus bound Death in chains. How he did so is left unsaid but is easy to imagine. In Aarne-Thompson, *The Types of the Folktale*,[40] Number 803 is "Solomon Binds the Devil in Chains in Hell." Solomon, a hero in Baltic, Finnish, and Russian folklore, tricked the Devil by asking him to try on chains meant for Solomon. No doubt the wily Sisyphus used a similar ruse.[41]

To return to ancient sources, the wiliness is culpable also in Hesiod's *Catalogue of Women*. This poem, popular in antiquity, is known to us only through quotations in other ancient authors and from papyrus fragments. We know that Sisyphus had his usual epithet, "crafty" (*aiolomētēs* frag. 10.2), and that his craftiness got him into some legal trouble. He had a dispute over a contract with the father of Mestra, whom he hoped to marry to his son Glaucus (the ancestor of the Glaucus in the *Iliad*), and Athena had to intervene to settle the case.[42] Mestra and Glaucus married. She had a son by Poseidon but none by Glaucus (frag. 43a.52–59 MW). Glaucus next married Eurynome, and the same thing happened. This time, Poseidon fathered Bellerophon (81–82).

Hesiod observes that Sisyphus "did not know the mind of Zeus" (76–77), presumably meaning that Sisyphus was ignorant that he was destined to have no grandchildren of his own to continue his bloodline. The Glaucus in the *Iliad* was descended from the union of Eurynome and Poseidon. So in *The Catalogue of Women*, as in Alcaeus, Sisyphus appears as a figure of mortal futility.

Finally, Sisyphus also bears some resemblance to the resourceful Odysseus, and in a minor tradition he was said to be the natural father of Odysseus (schol. Soph. *Ajax;* schol. Lyc. 344). Again like Odysseus he could be a comic figure, and in the fifth century he was the subject of satyr plays by Aeschylus, Sophocles, Euripides, and Critias. An allusion in Aristotle's *Poetics* indicates the plot of these plays: the cunning knave is in the end tricked himself (1456a21–23). Once again the futility of his cleverness.

SUMMARY AND DEFINITION

The opposition between Philocleon and Bdelycleon articulates the central division in Greek narrative between narrative about humans and narratives of other sorts, which may be concerned with the divine, the heroic, the supernatural or with beasts or even with ordinary folk who have become paradigmatic, like Timon the misanthrope. Human narrative, in virtue of this opposition, refers to what real people do or have done in a time frame measured by human generations or other human chronologies, as distinguished from another, earlier period or a timeless "once upon a time."[43] Bdelycleon's preference for human narrative is

not based on its superior truth or on the falsity of *mythoi* but upon
social norms that repudiate the one and esteem the latter. Only with
Plato would the opposition between true or reasoned *logos* and false or
irrational *mythos* arise. This opposition became, in modern times, the
foundation of the scientific study of myth, of modern mythology, as Detienne affirms. He errs, however, in concluding from the earlier nonexistence of the Platonic opposition that myth did not exist. The pre-
Platonic Greeks were quite able to distinguish different kinds of discourse, and some of them correspond to what we call myth. Greek myth
or mythology was not created by Plato. Indeed, the Platonic opposition
between *mythos* and *logos* was already present in the very form of the
opposition between the human and the other. We could say that Plato
stands in the same relation to myth as to *mētis*, 'cunning intelligence.' It
was Detienne who, with Jean-Pierre Vernant, described *mētis* as a
sphere of praxis whose mental basis escaped and vexed philosophy.[44]
Greek myth was another such praxis, though, for particular reasons, it
underwent, especially in the *Republic*, a certain formalization at Plato's
hands.

Within *mythoi* or *logoi* there was a broad division. Philocleon's preference for a certain kind of story points to this division, clearly attested
in the fifth century in Herodotus and Hecataeus, between panhellenic
and local. While variation seems to belong to the definition of Greek
myth, it comes into play, for obvious reasons, especially at the local
level.

As for the sources of storytelling, the Greeks clearly recognized a distinction between poetry and oral narrative derived from poetry. Philocleon's assumption that myths can be told at dinner parties points to a
practice of retelling stories already established in poetry—in epic or, as
in the case of Lamia, in tragedy or satyr drama, though we cannot say
what his source was. Presumably, like the old men in *Lysistrata*, he had
heard stories when he was a child, and Lamia may have come into his
repertory in this way.

The Greeks also recognized a distinction between poetic and oral
nonpoetic sources. To some extent, this distinction overlaps with the
one between the canonic and the local.

Finally, as the example of Sisyphus showed, Greek myths were never
told without a motive, which was often competitive. Pindar says that
the version of the Pelops myth which he is repudiating was started by
"malicious neighbors" of Pelops' family.[45] His version displaces the
other. No wonder, then, that references to *mythos* in Greek literature
are often negative. My version is the truth, but yours is a *mythos*. We
saw the twentieth century form of this competitiveness in the textbook

mentioned above: Euripides' version is *the* version. The others are negligible.

The traits just summarized might be brought together in the following definition of a Greek myth. A Greek myth is a set of multiforms or variants of the same story, which exist either as written texts, prose or verse, or in oral form, or in both written and oral form, or in vase painting or plastic art as well or independently. The story concerns the divine or the supernatural or the heroic or animals or paradigmatic humans living in a time undefinable by human chronology. Each retelling or application produces a new variant, which stands in some degree of antagonistic relation to other variants or other myths and thus takes its place in a system constituted by the proliferation of such relations. This definition can incorporate the now current definition of myth as "traditional tale,"[46] provided that the difficult word "traditional" means "without an identifiable author." A variant can thus be more precisely defined as the encounter of traditional tale and unique, individual, motivated retelling or artistic reuse of that tale.

THE SYSTEM AND THE POSSIBLE APPROACHES

This system, for the purposes of research and interpretation, appears differently in its two dimensions, synchronic and diachronic. In the former, it is, in the first place, a vast, remarkably consistent geographical and genealogical mapping of the gods and heroes. This consistency is indeed the presupposition of meaningful variation and of the sort of embroidery on the myths to be found in the poets.[47] Unfortunately, the synchronic system presents itself to us as a jigsaw puzzle of which many pieces are missing. To some extent, these can be filled in by the comparative study of modern folklore, as in William Hansen's contribution to this volume.[48] Such studies also help to define the specificity of the Greek realization of a story pattern.

Greek myths can also be usefully studied on the synchronic plane by the structuralist method of Lévi-Strauss: a stable matrix is established of logically contrasting elements, with which all variants can be coordinated. This approach is not represented in this volume simply because it is already so well known. The fundamental article by Lévi-Strauss has been reprinted, paraphrased, and discussed innumerable times.[49] Structuralism is represented in this volume by the Greimasian approach of Claude Calame, who (in fact repudiating the notion of a system of myths) studies the narrative signs and codes by means of which a myth is told in a particular poet. This approach shares with Lévi-Strauss's the assumption of a certain autonomy of the narrative itself, which has an underlying structure distinguishable from the surface features of its presentation. The psychoanalytic approach (here represented by Richard Caldwell's essay), too, though its primary emphasis is on the origin and function of myths, has observations to make on the construction of the narrative. For example, condensation and displacement, two of the hallmarks of "primary process" thinking, are characteristic of mythic narrative.[50]

The synchronic system is not coextensive with Greek poetry. The relation between myth and poetry is complex. The consequence of Milman Parry's demonstration of the oral character of the Homeric poems was a growing and still growing sense of the orality of Greek literature, the sense that performance is what we should be trying to understand. Down to the time of Plato, Greek literature consists of scripts. Even Thucydides, we know, was read aloud. To understand Greek literature, then, is to understand it in the contexts of its performance. What, then, of the relation of Greek mythology to Greek literature thus conceived? It seems that we have to reckon, in the realm of Greek myth, with a rather vast field of reference and one to which reference is in fact being constantly made. We can sometimes see the interaction of the stylistic codes of the various poetic genres with the givens of this mythology. Sometimes not, as in the fourth choral ode of Sophocles' *Antigone,* an especially dense and hitherto unexplained group of mythical references. In short, just as Greek literature is already, in its very nature, densely intertextual, since each performance stands on the affirmation and denial of other scripts or performances, so Greek myth extends the range of this intertextuality into another system. For example, the story of Meleager in *Iliad* 9, whether or not it has a folktale origin, seems to presuppose knowledge of the Meleager folktale.

In the diachronic dimension, Greek mythology might appear to lose its systematic character. On the one hand, it might lose its specificity altogether if, as is proposed by H. S. Versnel in his contribution to this volume, Walter Burkert is right and Greek myths can be reduced to sociobiological "programs of action" presumably shared by many other peoples.[51] On the other hand, with its density of Indo-European (cf. the contribution of J. F. Nagy in this volume) and Near Eastern (cf. that of Robert Mondi) inheritances and borrowings, further worked upon in various ways by the historical experience of the Greeks (cf. that of Carlo Brillante), Greek myth might seem an incoherent amalgam. The systematic character would disappear, however, only if each of the approaches just mentioned were pushed to an extreme, in a way that none of the contributors to this volume and perhaps no contemporary scholar of Greek mythology would propose. Each of these approaches yields some part of the truth, and none, furthermore, seriously threatens the synchronic aspect of the system.

The condition for diachronic change and, at the same time, for the relative stability of the synchronic system, is the foundation of Greek myth in Greek society. The structuralism associated with the names of Marcel Detienne, Jean-Pierre Vernant, and Pierre Vidal-Naquet—arguably the most important of current approaches to Greek mythology—demonstrates the relation of forms of thought, including mythical thought, to social and political forms.[52] To cite the best-known example, Vidal-Naquet showed the interrelations of the Athenian institution of the ephebeia, the myth of Melanthus, and the figure of Melanion mentioned above.[53] This volume contains no example of this approach, because, as in the case of Lévi-Strauss, it is already so well known. It should count, however, as a ninth possible approach, or as a tenth, if Lévi-Strauss is the ninth.

Ten approaches? The number seems foolishly, unscientifically large. Would not a smaller number, if possible one, be more effective, provided that it were the right one? Unfortunately, that provision cannot be satisfied under present circumstances, and, in fact, previous attempts to establish what G. S. Kirk called "monolithic theories" impeded progress in this field. Perhaps the most important contribution of his *The Nature of Greek Myths* (1974) was his argument that the main fault of modern research on myth was the quest for a single universal theory. "Myths," he said, "constitute an enormously complex and at the same time indefinite category, and one must be free to apply to them any of a whole set of possible forms of analysis and classification."[54] The ten approaches just mentioned, of which eight are represented in this volume, seem to be the ones now viable.

NOTES

1. Detienne 1981.

2. Brisson 1982, 124–25, 179–80 has demonstrated the contrary; see also his general critique of Detienne, pp. 168–73.

3. Burkert 1979, 1–5 and Gual 1981, 9–13 on myth as traditional tale.

4. He uses the verb *diēgeisthai,* 'to narrate.'

5. Brisson 1982, 114–43.

6. Burkert 1985, 10–53.

7. Cf. Detienne 1986, 51 on this passage.

8. Cf. Heraclitus frag. B42 DK; Pythagoras D.L. 8.21. Also Pindar O. 1.35–36 and context (the myth of Tantalus and Pelops); O. 9.37–38; Eur. *IT* 391.

9. E.g. 10.33.9–10. Cf. Hansen 1987, 1126.

10. The decoction of Pelias is first attested in Pindar, *Pythian* 4.250.

11. Page 1964, xxii–xxiii.

12. Page 1964, xxvii-xxix.

13. West 1983, 77–79

14. See note 9 in Brillante's contribution to this volume.

15. Morford and Lenardon 1977, 423.

16. For example, Morford and Lenardon 1977, 24, where Ge, Tartarus, and Eros are the offspring of Chaos.

17. Schol. *Ecclesiazousae* 77 is the source for Crates' play, in which "she carried a staff and farted."

18. Thucydides himself sometimes reports oral tradition concerning mythical times. He concludes an uncharacteristic excursus on Alcmaeon as the founder of Acarnania thus: "Such are the reports [verb *legō*] that we have received" (2.102.6). Cf. "Charybdis . . . is said [verb *legō*]" (4.24.5). Cf. Westlake 1977.

19. *P.* 1.92–94, *N.* 6.29–30. The word *logioi* in these contexts does not refer to written histories. Cf. *N.* 6.45–46: "Broad avenues open on all sides to tellers of stories [*logioi*] to grace this glorious island." Cf. also *O.* 7.54 concerning the origin of the island of Rhodes: "the old-time sayings of men report [verb *phēmi*, base *phā-pha-*]"; *P.* 1.96: "a hostile report [noun *phatis*, base *phā-/pha-*] everywhere oppresses Phaleris"; *N.* 3.52–53 on the exploits of the young Achilles: "I have this tale [*epos*] as told [verb *legō*] by men of old."

20. Bascom 1965.

21. Hansen 1987.

22. Perry 1962, 287–346.

23. Henderson 1987, 169, with references.

24. Another word for a clever, pointed remark, *chreia,* was also later used.

25. Foundation legends (one of which is studied by Calame in this volume) might be a fifth distinguishable kind of story: cf. Plato *Hipp. Maj.* 285d.

26. Tümpel 1894, 523–26.

27. Slater 1977, 195.

28. Sybaritic tale is obviously a genre recognized by Aristophanes' audience. Unfortunately this is the only reference to the genre in classical Greek literature and its nature is obscure to us.

29. Although he may be remembering the traditional narrative frame of an Aesopic tale: cf. below.

30. This story is also alluded to at *Peace* 129–34 and *Lysistrata* 695 and is told by the scholiast on *Peace* 130. The scholiast's version is a variant of Aesop *Fab.* 3 Perry 1952.

31. Nagy 1978, 281–83.

32. Cf. Jedrkiewicz 1987.

33. For Libyan tales, the character of which is obscure to us, see Testimonia 85–93 Perry.

34. Stories could have, besides this didactic function, an immediate psychological one. They could be used to soothe (Euripides, *Heracles* 98–100) or to scare children, as the Lamia was often used (Duris *FrGHist* 76 frag. 17; D.S. 20.41; schol. *Pax* 758), or to while away the hours at work (Euripides, *Ion* 197, 506, *IA* 788).

35. Martin forthcoming.

36. Slater 1977, 196,n. 1: "We often cannot see what point Pindar is making because we cannot tell how he is altering the accepted myth."

37. The recent structural analysis of the myth of Sisyphus by Sourvinou-Inwood 1986 provides an excellent background to the varying surface or "enunciative" (cf. Calame in this volume) features of the myth in various texts. In his contribution to this volume, Caldwell provides another, psychoanalytically oriented structural interpretation of the Sisyphus myth.

38. Pherecydes *FrGHist* frag. 119. Cf. Apollod. 1.9.3; Paus. 2.5.1.

39. Page 1955, 300. Ellipses reflect lacunae in the papyrus.

40. Aarne-Thompson 1961.

41. And not, *pace* Sourvinou-Inwood 1986, 48–49, force.

42. Frag. 43a.36–43 MW; West 1985, 169.

43. *Lys.* 784, *Wasps* 1182, Pl. *Phdr.* 273b2, Theoc. 11.7.

44. Detienne and Vernant 1974.

45. cf. Köhnken 1974 and Fuhrer 1988.

46. Cf. note 4 above.

47. Cf. Willcock 1964.

48. In a work provisionally entitled "International Narratives in Greek and Roman Literature," he will show that there are more than two hundred narratives that share story patterns with narratives of other cultures. The opportunities for comparative folklore studies are therefore vast.

49. Lévi-Strauss 1955.

50. Cf. Caldwell's forthcoming book, *The Origin of the Gods: A Psychoanalytic Study of Greek Theogonic Myth.*

51. Cf. the thesis of Blumenberg 1985 on the function of myth: the overcoming of early man's despair in the face of the forces of nature. For both Burkert and Blumenberg, myth is a controlling and ordering medium.

52. For the similarities and differences in the structural approaches of Detienne, Vernant, and Vidal-Naquet, see Buxton 1981.

53. Vidal-Naquet 1986, 106–28.

54. Kirk 1974, 38.

WORKS CITED

Aarne, Antti, and Stith Thompson. 1961. *The Types of the Folktale.* 2nd ed. Helsinki.

Bascom, William. 1965. "The Forms of Folklore." *Journal of American Folklore* 78:3–20.

Blumenberg, Hans. 1985. *Work on Myth.* Tr. Robert M. Wallace. Cambridge, MA. Original 1979. *Arbeit am Mythos.* Frankfurt am Main.

Brisson, Luc. 1982. *Platon: Les mots et les mythes.* Paris.

Burkert, Walter. 1979. *Structure and History in Greek Mythology and Ritual.* Berkeley-Los Angeles.

———. 1985. *Greek Religion.* Tr. John Raffian. Cambridge, MA.

Buxton, R. L. Introduction to Gordon 1981.

Detienne, Marcel. 1981. *L'invention de la mythologie.* Paris.

———. 1986. *The Creation of Mythology.* Tr. Margaret Cook. Chicago.

———, and Jean-Pierre Vernant. 1974. *Les ruses de l'intelligence: La mètis des*

Grecs. Paris. Tr. Janet Lloyd, 1978. *Cunning Intelligence in Greek Culture and Society* Atlantic Highlands, NJ.

Fuhrer, Therese. 1988. "A Pindaric Element in the Poems of Callimachus." *AJP* 109: 53–68.

Gentili, Bruno, and Giuseppe Paioni, eds. 1977. *Il Mito Greco*. Rome.

Gordon, R. L. 1981. *Myth, Religion, and Society: Structuralist Essays*. Cambridge.

Graf, Fritz. 1985. *Griechische Mythologie: Eine Einführung*. Munich.

Grant, Michael, and Rachel Kitzinger, eds. 1987. *Civilization of the Ancient Mediterranean*, vol. 2. New York.

Gual, Carlos García. 1981. *Mitos, viajes, héroes*. Madrid.

Hansen, William F. 1987. "Folklore." In Grant and Kitzinger 1987, 1121–30.

Henderson, Jeffrey. 1987. *Aristophanes' Lysistrata*. Oxford.

Jedrkiewicz, Stefano. 1987. "La favola esopica nel processo di argomentazione orale fino al IV sec. a.C." *QUCC* NS 27: 35–63.

Kirk, G. S. 1974. *The Nature of Greek Myths*. Harmondsworth, UK.

Köhnken, A. 1974. "Pindar as Innovator: Poseidon Hippios and the Relevance of the Pelops Story in *Ol.* 1." *CQ* NS 24: 199–206.

Lévi-Strauss, Claude. 1955. "The Structural Study of Myth." *Journal of American Folklore* 68: 428–44.

Martin, Richard P. Forthcoming. "The Language of Heroes: Speech and Performance in the *Iliad*."

Merkelbach, Reinhold, and M. L. West. 1967. *Fragmenta Hesiodea*. Oxford.

Morford, Mark P. O., and Robert J. Lenardon. 1977. *Classical Mythology*. 2nd ed. New York.

Nagy, Gregory. 1978. *The Best of the Achaeans*. Baltimore.

Page, D. L. 1955. *Sappho and Alcaeus: An Introduction to the Study of Ancient Lesbian Poetry*. Oxford.

———. 1964. *Euripides' Medea*. Oxford.

Perry, B. E. 1952. *Aesopica*. Urbana, IL.

———. 1962. "Demetrius of Phalerum and the Aesopic Fables." *TAPA* 93: 287–346.

Slater, W. J. 1977. "Doubts about Pindaric Interpretation." *CJ* 72: 193–208.

Sourvinou-Inwood, Christiane. 1986. "Crime and Punishment: Tityos, Tantalos and Sisyphos in *Odyssey* 11." *BICS* 33: 37–58.

Tümpel, K. 1894. "'Αλκίνου ἀπόλογος." *Philologus* 52:523.

Vidal-Naquet, Pierre. 1986. *The Black Hunter: Forms of Thought and Forms of Society in the Ancient Greek World*. Baltimore.

West, M. L. 1983. *The Orphic Poems*. Oxford.

———. 1985 *The Hesiodic Catalogue of Women*. Oxford.

Westlake, H. D. 1977. "*Legetai* in Thucydides." *Mnemosyne* 4: 345–62.

Willcock, M. M. 1964. "Mythological Paradeigma in the *Iliad*. *CQ* NS 14: 141–54.

PART ONE

MYTH, RITUAL, AND HISTORY

1

MYTH AND RITUAL

In the context of theory of mythology, the expression "myth and ritual" usually refers to the theory of the ritual origin of myth. This theory is associated with the Cambridge school, comprised of Jane Harrison, A. B. Cook,[a] Francis Cornford, and Gilbert Murray, an Oxford man from Australia. These scholars drew their inspiration from Sir James G. Frazer's *The Golden Bough*, which, in crucial respects, had absorbed the influence of W. Robertson Smith's *Lectures on the Origins of the Semites* (1894). The term "Cambridge school" has, at least in the United States, the ring of an epitaph for a completely outmoded approach to Greek myth. The views and the works of this school, except perhaps for Cook's *Zeus*, which is still valuable for reference, seem to belong to the past. Joseph Fontenrose, attacking in *The Ritual Theory of Myth* Lord Raglan and Stanley Hyman, the two main popularizers of the myth and ritual theory,[b] was only driving nails into the casket. Even when Fontenrose was writing, Americans could hardly imagine a Cambridge, an England, in which classics and anthropology had seemed to be almost the same field.[c]

And yet the fundamental importance of sacrificial ritual is one of two contributions of the Cambridge school that are still very much alive today.[d] Both are to be found in Jane Harrison's *Themis*. In Chapter 8 of this work, Harrison showed the relation of the *daimon* of her theory, which was "the representation of collective emotion,"[e] to the hero, and Gilbert Murray added to this chapter an "Excursus on the Ritual Forms Preserved in Greek Tragedy."[f] Murray showed that a six-part ritual underlay the dramatic action and that the second of these parts was "generally a ritual or sacrificial death."[g] In "collective emotion" and "sacrificial death," we have the main ingredients of Walter Burkert's important article, "Greek Tragedy and Sacrificial Ritual" (1966),[h] which reintroduced sacrifice into the discussion of Greek tragedy. Later, in *Homo Necans* (1972),[i] Burkert developed the idea of sacrifice as sanctioned expression and control of aggression and applied it to other

rituals and myths, notably the myth of Prometheus's deception of Zeus
at Mecone.

The relation of Burkert to Harrison is probably not, however, as
close as it seems. Other influences, some of which H. S. Versnel indicates
in the following essay, must be considered.[j] Of these, the most important
may be Karl Meuli, who had traced the origins of animal sacrifice to
Paleolithic hunters' rites intending a regeneration of the slain prey.[k]

The second contribution of the Cambridge school to contemporary
discussion of myth and ritual is initiation. In her discussion of "savage"
initiations in *Themis,* Harrison drew upon not only Frazer but also the
French school now associated with the name of Emile Durkheim[l]
(whom she cites)—Henri Hubert, Marcel Mauss, and above all, Arnold
van Gennep. "As Monsieur van Gennep has well shown in his suggestive book," she wrote, "the ceremonies that accompany each successive
stage of life, ceremonies, i.e. of birth, of marriage, of ordination as a
medicine-man, and finally of death, are, no less than the ceremonies of
adolescence, one and all *Rites de Passage,* ceremonies of transition, of
going out from the old and going in to the new."[m] As in the case of
sacrifice just discussed, the decade of the sixties saw a return of Harrison's view, though of course in a modified form. Versnel singles out an
article by Burkert on the Arrephoria[n] but recognizes that initiation "was
in the air." There was also Pierre Vidal-Naquet's article on the "black
hunter" (1968),[o] continuing a long-interrupted French interest in this
theme: H. Jeanmaire's notable *Couroi et Courètes* (1939)[p] and Louis
Gernet's article "Frairies antiques" (1928),[q] which harked back to
Durkheim and Mauss.[r] The sixties also saw the publication of Angelo
Brelich's *Paides e parthenoi* (1969) and of the English translation of van
Gennep (1960).[s]

Versnel shows, in effect, that there was some prophetic truth in the
cyclic nature of Frazer's sacral king and the Cambridge school's year
god. In the intense recent concern with initiation, he argues, the same
myth-ritual complex has come back again, in another form. He is able
to provide a full list of data that could be, and in fact have been, explained on the basis of either complex, initiation or the dying and reborn king or god. Thus "what is sauce (evidence) for the goose (sacral
kingship) is sauce (evidence) for the gander (initiation)." He then tries
to answer the question: why do the same data have this range of fungi-
bility? He opts for Burkert's explanation: prehistorically rooted sociobiological "programs of action," to which both myths and rituals are
genetically related, at least in their typical features. In other words, as
further examples will show in the introduction to Carlo Brillante's essay

"History and Historical Interpretation in the Analysis of Myth," Burkert's answer lies in the prehistory of mankind.

What's Sauce for the Goose Is Sauce for the Gander: Myth and Ritual, Old and New

H. S. VERSNEL

   The primary aim of this essay is to give the reader some insight into
the debate, which is exactly a century old now, on the complex of problems concerning the interrelation of myth and ritual. I have found that
it is impossible to gain an adequate impression of the present state of
theory in this field if its previous history is overlooked or is sketched
along too rudimentary lines. Naturally, a survey of the evolution *in toto*
means entering an already well-plowed field. There is no lack of historical and critical surveys of earlier views, and I have made grateful use of
them.[1] The emphasis here is on those aspects of the theories of myth and
ritual that relate to the ancient cultures of the Mediterranean world, a
feature that distinguishes this essay from, for instance, a survey like the
one by Kluckhohn (1942) or the papers by Kaberry (1957), Penner
(1968), and Segal (1980), all of them studies offering a broader, notably
anthropological, perspective. I have tried, moreover, to prevent the critical element from dominating: Bascom (1957) and Fontenrose (1966)
contain many valuable thoughts but, because of their strongly negative
bias, are not the appropriate tools for an introduction to the subject. In
plan and approach my introduction is closest to the survey by Burkert
(1980), which, however, does not go beyond a very summary view. Although it is not my aim here to present a complete bibliography of this
much discussed subject, I cannot refrain from mentioning the interesting chapter "La ripetizione mitico-rituale" in A. M. di Nola, *Antropologia religiosa* (Florence 1974), which treats the subject from the perspective of "repetition phenomena."
   What distinguishes the present effort from its predecessors is that it
does not stop at those theories that, until now, have been associated
with the phrase "myth and ritual," but pays special attention to the
newest trends in classical studies. The main task I have set myself is to
show where the roots of the recent approach are to be found; to what

extent there is a connection between the old and the new points of view; and, finally, to pose the question whether the gap separating them is as unbridgeable as is commonly believed. The way I have arranged the material is unorthodox and some aspects of the disposition are no doubt debatable. The two phases are characterized by two names: J. E. Harrison and W. Burkert. The overall structure of my approach, moreover, is based on Miss Harrison's suggestions about the various ways in which myth and ritual may be connected.

The lavish supply of bibliographical notes, finally, has an additional purpose; it is meant to guide interested readers, especially in the study of specific themes in the subject matter treated here. Myth and ritual are, after all, the main materials of religion, and research into them, as we shall see, has been exemplary for the development of the study of ancient religion.

QUESTIONS

Myth was the dominant factor in nineteenth century studies of the history of religion until a change took place somewhere in the last quarter of the century. Textbooks that nowadays would carry *Religionsgeschichte,* 'history of religion,' in the titles were then classified regularly as mythology, as witness the well-known works by Gruppe, Preller, and Roscher.

Ritual dominates the scene in practically all the textbooks on Greek and Roman religion during most of the twentieth century. This is what M. P. Nilsson says when speaking about the protagonists in this field from around the turn of the century, H. Usener[2] and A. Dieterich[3]: "Der Umschwung war vollendet: statt der Mythen waren die Riten in den Vordergrund getreten" ("The reversal was complete: instead of myths, rites had come to the fore"). Nilsson, author of the two monumental volumes of *Geschichte der griechischen Religion,*[4] "that masterpiece of patient brilliance," as it has been called,[5] died in 1967, the year in which the third edition of Volume 1 was published. On the same page I quoted from, Nilsson continues: "Seitdem ist keine durchgreifende oder grundsätzliche Änderung der Methode und der Richtung der Forschung eingetreten" ("Since then there has not been any radical or essential change in method and direction of research"). In this nonagenarian's view, then, rite, cult, and ceremonial action had carried the day, once and for all. Only recently, nonetheless, an American scholar, B. Lincoln, complained that "ritual [is] a neglected area for study, . . . for most scholars have tended to give far more attention to myth than to ritual," and "there still exists a grievous imbalance in favor of myth."[6]

What actually happened, then, in the interval between Nilsson's complacent statement, dating from the middle of this century, and Lincoln's complaint in 1977? Has the evident shift of interest from myth to ritual around 1900 been followed by a reverse movement in recent decades? In a way, this is indeed what has happened, as can be seen from a comparison of Nilsson's work referred to above with W. Burkert's textbook of Greek religion (Burkert 1985) or his more explicit study of myth and ritual (Burkert 1979). Burkert has given myth its due once again. A theory of myth and ritual worthy of the name should focus on myth *and* ritual; it is therefore no coincidence that both the myth and ritual complexes we plan to discuss were discovered at a time when—precisely because of the shift of interest—both elements were topics of debate: the last quarter of the nineteenth and the last quarter of the twentieth century. A qualification might be in order, though: myth, of course, has never been supplanted completely by ritual. Some scholars have set great store by myth, such as Freud, Jung, and Kerényi from a psychological viewpoint; Dumézil, whose comparative mythology, as far as the classical cultures are concerned, focuses especially on Rome—a subject that I shall leave out of account here—and Mircea Eliade, whose phenomenological school includes Lincoln, quoted above. Furthermore, myth takes pride of place in the studies of the Paris school of Vernant, Vidal-Naquet, and Detienne.[7]

It may not be too adventurous to say that the concept of myth *and* ritual was engendered by the tension that sprang from having to choose: myth *or* ritual. That, however, is not the only kind of tension. Here is another instance: in his popular *Myth: Its Meaning and Functions in Ancient and Other Cultures* (1971), G. S. Kirk states categorically: "Therefore it will be wise to reject from the outset the idea that myth and religion are twin aspects of the same subject, or parallel manifestations of the same psychic condition just as firmly as we rejected the idea that all myths are associated with rituals" (p. 31). Incidentally, both in this book—embodying his Sather lectures—and in his still better known *The Nature of Greek Myths* (1974), one of Kirk's explicit aims is to refute all general theories of the origin, meaning, and function of myth. One of the five overall theories he eliminates is the one that there is always (at least originally) a link between myth and ritual—the minimum definition of the myth and ritual theory.

In 1979, however, W. Burkert's Sather lectures appeared in print: *Structure and History in Greek Mythology and Ritual*. He had certainly read Kirk, but still he states: "And it was in this way that the complex of myth and ritual, though not indissoluble, became a major force in forming ancient cultures, and as it were, dug those deep vales of human tradition in which even today the streams of our experience will tend to flow" (p. 58). This has quite a different ring. Indeed, to refer to the evident contrast between the views of these two scholars as a tension would be rather a euphemism. Both views will be discussed later on. For present purposes, it may suffice to ask two obvious questions, to be dealt with consecutively:

a) How and when did the idea arise that myth and ritual might be closely related, a view that was evidently so successful that Kirk thought it worthwhile to oppose it emphatically?
b) How is one to explain the fact that practically simultaneously two eminent scholars entertain such totally different views of this interrelation?

THE RISE AND GROWTH OF MYTH AND RITUAL THEORY

Interest in ritual in primitive cultures arose in Germany and Britain more or less simultaneously. In a period in which Max Müller's theories[8] reigned supreme and every single myth was thought to be an allegory of meteorological and atmospheric phenomena, W. Mannhardt[9] dispatched questionnaires all over Europe in search of traces of belief in vegetation, grain, and wood spirits and related manners and customs. About the same time E. B. Tylor[10] managed to interest the Anglo-Saxon public in the peculiar features of primitive cultures outside Europe. Darwin[11] published his *Origin of Species* in 1859 and evolution and progress were in the air. Might not Mannhardt's rye wolves and stalk hare be the very archetypes from which, much later, the radiant figures of Demeter, Dionysus, or Adonis emerged? Might not religion have had its origin in spirit worship? Tylor himself professed a straightforward evolutionism. Unable to understand nature around him, primitive man tried to influence his environment. To achieve this he practised magic rites (which did not work, but he did not realize this), and in a later stage he tried to explain this no longer understood ritual and other riddles by means of some myth (which did not fit in, but he did not realize this either)—a twofold misinterpretation, therefore, for which only Germans could have invented a term such as *Urdummheit* ('primeval stupidity'), a phrase that did not fail to find a comfortable niche in anthropological jargon.[12]

Certain vague relations between myth and ritual can be glimpsed, but credit for the first clear-cut theory is due to the Scottish Semitist and theologian W. Robertson Smith, whose famous and influential *Lectures on the Religion of the Semites* (1889) introduced his well-known theory of sacrifice.[13] His interest in "ritual institutions" as *social* instruments influenced both Durkheim and Freud; of fundamental importance for our subject is the fact that in his view, sacrifice as communion—man shares in the vital force of the consumed animal—acquires an additional mythical dimension: as a totem, the sacrificial animal is raised to divine status, so that myth arises from a social rite.

These are the indispensable preliminary stages. It was, after all, Robertson Smith who pointed out the road taken by his student and friend James Frazer.[14] The twelve volumes of Frazer's *The Golden Bough*—next to the Bible and Kitto's *The Greeks*—still adorn many a British upper-middle-class drawing room.[15] The work has been praised as "perhaps the greatest scientific Odyssey in modern humanism" (Malinowski) and disparaged as "part of what every schoolboy knows, and what every gentleman must at least have forgotten" (Marett). In a book published in London in 1961 that reported experiences of ecstasy, one person answered the question, "What has induced ecstasy in you?" as follows: "Reading *The Golden Bough* for the first time." And this informant was not such a fool either, for he had also gone into ecstasies "finding ten chromosomes when I knew they ought to be there." So it must surely be a marvelous book.

In the definitive version (there had been earlier, shorter editions), the first two volumes are called *The Magic Art and the Evolution of Kings,* and this title provides the code words: magic lay at the roots of religion, and the most important means with which primitive man tried to control nature and vegetation lay in magic-sacral kingship. Just as nature goes through an annual cycle of budding, flowering, bearing fruit, withering and dying, so each year the "aged" king had to be supplanted by a new vigorous successor, for it is the king's magic power that sympathetically influences and even controls vegetative life. Nature's death has to be overcome by a new, young king who defeats the old one in a ritual fight—or somehow supplants him. *The King Must Die* is the title of a best-seller by Mary Renault, a book one might read as a kind of romanticized "Frazer abridged." So much for rite. There is, however, also a mythical representation or transposition of the natural cycle, dealt with by Frazer in other parts of his series: *Adonis, Attis, Osiris,* published originally in 1906 as a separate volume; *The Dying God, Spirits of the Corn and of the Wild* (with thanks to Mannhardt); and *Balder the Beautiful.* A great many cultures, notably those of the Mediterranean world and the Near East, have their "dying and rising gods." They represent grain, green plants, and trees. Their myths tell of menace, downfall, sojourn in the underworld, and death, but also of resurrection. During the

annual New Year festivities lamentations are heard bewailing the god
who has died, but it is not long before they are replaced by hilarious joy:
the god has risen or has manifested himself again, heralding a promise
of new life.

There thus emerges an almost ideal parallelism of myth and ritual,
both reacting to or reflecting the vegetative cycle of nature:

Rite	*Myth*
Sacral year king guarantees	Year god represents
fertility of nature;	natural vegetative force;
suffers ritual death;	dies, is imprisoned in
	underworld;
a new, vigorous king succeeds.	rises again, is reborn.

This scheme is a fundamental one: it is invoked by all myth and ritual
theories of the first phase. As a matter of fact, until a few decades ago
the twentieth century remained in the shadow of the golden bough. We
shall concentrate, primarily, on two schools: the Cambridge school,
which in the area of classical studies applied itself above all to the Greek
material, and the Myth and Ritual school proper, which centered on the
pattern of the ancient Near East. Before dealing with these schools,
however, we must focus on one specific figure, even though she herself,
without any doubt, belongs to the former school. The reason for this
preferential treatment will soon become evident.

Jane Harrison

Robertson Smith and Frazer both taught in Cambridge. So did Jane
Ellen Harrison.[16] "Bloody Jane" to friends, a "blasphemous Kêr" as she
said herself,[17] and the last living maenad according to many others, she
led an unorthodox life, which gave rise to rumors with such standard
ingredients as libertinism in matters of sex and religion, more or less
pronounced feminism, and the extremes of esthetic refinement on the
one hand and "ye Beastly Devices of ye Heathen" on the other. I note
this for the sole reason that later criticism seems to have been inspired,
at least partly, by the aversion aroused by these in themselves less relevant features of her life. Additional information about her may be
gleaned, for instance, from her *Reminiscences of a Student's Life* (London 1925). From her best-known and most important works, *Prolegomena to the Study of Greek Religion* (Cambridge 1903) and *Themis*
(Cambridge 1912),[18] she emerges as someone who boasts a vast knowledge of Greek material, above all archeological (archeology had been
her starting point), who has an unmistakable tendency to follow and
practise the most recent trends uncritically (she herself mentions—in

chronological order—Frazer, Durkheim, Bergson, and Freud),[19] and who is criticized by Kirk (1971, 3) for being "utterly uncontrolled by anything resembling careful logic." "Her customary lack of consistency"[20] is a virtually unanimous finding. Still, I should like to show that at least part of the inconsistencies found in her studies may be caused, to a certain extent, by the unmanageable and intrinsically contradictory subject she chose.

A year after the publication of Robertson Smith's major work and in the very year in which the first two-volume edition of Frazer's *Golden Bough* was published, Harrison's *Mythology and Monuments of Ancient Athens* appeared (London 1980). In the introduction she says (p. iii): "My belief is that in many, even the large majority of cases *ritual practice misunderstood* explains the elaboration of myth." In the last analysis, even the most beautiful, the loveliest Greek myths derive from "always *practical* ritual." A quite telling phrase in an 1891 paper—"a solution I believe to be wholly novel"[21]—shows that she expects to be the first to offer this solution. Without doubt, she is being sincere in this respect. Frazer, who, as we have seen, had opted for the very same starting point, did not feel any forceful urge to put the presumed interrelation of myth and ritual on a solid theoretical basis, and Robertson Smith was publishing at practically the same time. It just so happened, as is often the case, that either direct or indirect mental contact gave rise, almost simultaneously, to related viewpoints. However, a glance in modern surveys and textbooks of anthropology and the history of religion will show that, in this broad perspective, the other two scholars have ousted Jane Harrison. It is not a matter of giving honor where honor is due nor of trying to be original at all costs, but solely in pursuit of my subject, myth and ritual, that I want to show that Harrison, in this domain at least, deserves more credit than she was given and that in her works *all* the problems were touched upon that later authors dealt with in *their* way.

In the *Prolegomena* Harrison still adheres to the view, quoted above, that myths were created in order to account for rites. In line with nineteenth century ideas, the gods are supposed to belong to the domain of myth. They arise as a kind of personification from rites, especially apotropaic ones, meant to protect crops and settlements. These *daimones* are products of an almost intellectual explanatory process, and in *Themis* Harrison systematizes these numerous demons into one prototypical, genuinely Frazerian year god, denoting him, for the occasion, by a homemade Greek term as the *eniautos daimon*.

In the same *Themis*, however, there is a sudden, strong emphasis on the social component of the myth-making process: "Strong emotion collectively experienced begets this illusion of objective reality; each worshipper is conscious of something in his emotion not himself, stronger than himself. He does not know it is the force of collective suggestion, he calls it a god" (*Themis*, pp. 46–47). Dionysus, for instance, who was first a typical *eniautos daimon*, is now called "his thiasos incarnate" (p. 38). Here Durkheim has been substituted for Frazer.[22]

It is necessary to realize the implications of this step. In the Frazerian scheme, man is the *manipulator:* he believes he can control *external processes* by means of specific, above all magical, methods—rites. Myth, then, is a kind of verbal account of these rituals. In the new interpretation, on the other hand, man is *the one who is manipulated:* however the ritual may relate to external data like fertility of the soil, what counts is *what the participant himself experiences,* his own emotion. The mythical images, therefore, are products, first and foremost, of *spontaneous, collective emotions.*[23] I do not think it an exaggeration to maintain that the seeds of one of the great controversies in twentieth century approaches to ancient religions can be detected here. The two lines may be illustrated by comparing two types of approach: that of such scholars as Deubner, Nilsson, and Latte, in which rites are studied primarily with regard to their external functions and aims, and in which there is hardly any room for myth, except as an etiological explanation of the ritual acts; and the approach of a very disparate group of modern scholars, guided by Vernant and Burkert, on the other; here myth and rite are considered to be, in the first place, forms of expression that identify or integrate the cultural community itself. I shall come back to this subject.

Just as the year king-god scheme represented Harrison's first approach, for which she used the term *eniautos daimon,* so she illustrated her second approach with a hymn from Palaikastro in eastern Crete that had recently been discovered.[24] The inscription probably dates from the third century B.C., but certain elements of the text indicate a much older period. In this hymn the *megistos kouros,* identified as the young Zeus, is invited to come to Mount Dikte, heading the *daimones* for this year, and "to spring into the wine vats, the herds, the crops, the cities, the ships, the young citizens and Themis." Here she is at last: Themis. Now, no true Frazerian would hesitate to recognize the year god in this *megistos kouros,* especially not one who accepts the most recent interpretation by M. L. West of a corrupt fragment of the text which says, in his view, that the god first "has gone into the earth."[25] Harrison, however, thinks otherwise.

In her view, the hymn points to the mythical Curetes,[26] who perform a war dance at the birth of the Cretan Zeus. As such, it reflects a social event of central importance in all primitive communities: the rite of initiation that turns boys into men, admitting them to the community of adult men. The elements of threat, torture, and death that often play a role in initiatory rites (see below) can be recognized, she believes, in the myth of the Titans, by whom the Dionysus-Zagreus infant (closely related to Zeus Cretagenes) is torn to pieces. They are the mythical reflections of the elder members of the tribe, disguised as spirits of the deceased, who "kill" the initiation candidate, reduced to the status of a baby, so that a new human being may arise. The *Megistos Kouros* that is invoked "is obviously but a reflection or impersonation of the body of Kouretes" (p. 27), who in their turn are mythical reflections of the human ephebes. In other words, the mythical characters "arise straight out of a social custom" (p. 28) and this amounts to saying (p. 29) that "the ritual act, what the Greeks called the *drômenon*, is prior to the divinity" (in other words: "myth").

That much we knew already, but now we are in for a surprise: in a related discussion a dozen pages earlier, Harrison maintained that investigation of the ritual is a primary condition in order to fathom the religious intention of a particular complex. She then continues: "This does not, however, imply, as is sometimes supposed, that ritual is prior to myth; they probably arose together. Ritual is the utterance of an emotion, a thing felt in *action*, myth in words or thoughts. They arise *pari passu*. The myth is not at first *etiological*, it does not arise to give a reason; it is representative, another form of utterance, of expression" (p. 16). When she returns to this relationship at greater length later in the book (pp. 327ff.), she describes myth as the words uttered by the participants in a ritual, originally probably no more than cries and interjections. In fact, this explains their simultaneous occurrence: "[myth] is the spoken correlative of the acted rite, the thing done; it is *to legomenon* as contrasted with or rather as related to *to drômenon*" (p. 328).

This may suffice to explain the irritation felt by many a reader used to more consistent reasoning; in particular, the parenthetical clause, "as is sometimes supposed," would have given offense. But at the same time she has outlined another serious possibility: that of the simultaneous origin of myth and ritual in certain situations. And Harrison even appears to introduce yet a third possibility when she writes: "When we realize that the myth is the plot of the *drômenon* we no longer wonder that the plot of a drama is called its 'myth'" (p. 331). Actually, the suggestion that myth can also function as the scenario of a (dramatic) ritual seems to be formulated here *in nuce*. I do not know whether this was her intention, as she never exploited the possibility that myth may also serve as a model that is imitated in dramatic action. That was done by others, who sometimes used an almost identical terminology.

To sum up: in sometimes rudimentary form and with often dubious argumentation, Harrison offered three suggestions on the interrelation of myth and ritual. These are:

1) Myth arises from rite.
2) Myth and rite arise *pari passu*.
3) Myth is the scenario of a dramatic ritual.

Moreover, she tested these theoretical possibilities in two cases of a specific myth and ritual complex:

a) the Frazerian complex of year king, year god, and New Year festival;
b) the initiation complex.

We shall now see that for decades to come it was only types 1 and 3 of these theoretical possibilities that attracted any attention, and that in the initial phase interest was focused almost exclusively on the New Year myth and ritual complex. The remaining two suggestions (2 and *b*) did not receive much credit or attention until very recently. As stated earlier, I shall structure my remarks according to the patterns of interrelation put forward by Harrison.

Myth Arises from Rite: The Cambridge School

Two genuine classical philologists, G. Murray and F. M. Cornford, each contributed a chapter to *Themis*. In his "Excursus on the Ritual Forms Preserved in Greek Tragedy" (pp. 341–63) Murray explains the rise of tragedy from a dancing ritual around the *eniautos daimon* Dionysus. In tragedy, Murray holds, the following underlying pattern may be discovered: (1) *agon*, a fight between the year god and his enemy; (2) *pathos*, the year god suffers sacrificial death; (3) *messenger* arrives, bringing word of the god's death; (4) *threnos*, lamentation; (5) *anagnorisis*, the killed god is recognized; (6) *theophany*, the god's resurrection and manifestation.

The very next sentence in Murray's paper is: "First, however, there is a difficulty to clear away" (p. 344), and that is precisely what the reader had already suspected. After all, we are always told that a tragedy that ends well is not a good tragedy, and that this is the reason why the rare tragedies with happy endings run the risk of being assigned a place among the satyr plays. In order to solve his difficulty, Murray assumed that the positive final chords had become detached from the tragedy proper and ended up as a separate theme in the satyr plays. This is one of the first explicit invocations of the "disintegration of the pattern," a stereotyped plea in the myth and ritual debate.

In later works Murray repeatedly returned to the myth and ritual notion,[27] for instance in the initial chapters of his popular *Five Stages of Greek Religion*.[28] He also wrote the preface to T. Gaster's comprehensive book *Thespis: Ritual, Myth and Drama in the Ancient Near East* (1950), discussed below. Here at last a connection emerges between Greece and the ancient Near East which had been exploited hardly or not at all in the Cambridge school since Frazer. It was F. M. Cornford who went farthest in this respect. In *The Origin of Attic Comedy* (1914) he held the rather surprising view that comedy, no less than tragedy, arose from a ritual New Year festival around the death and rebirth of the god. He had already adumbrated this theory in his contribution to *Themis*, in which he discussed the origin of the Olympic games: the winner in the contest, the *megistos kouros* of the year, is led in a wild *komos* and celebrates a sacral marriage with the king's daughter. These, he held, are also the ingredients of comedy. In his later work, however, Cornford[29] extended his vision further: man evolves from the magical (Frazer) through the mythical (Frazer/Harrison) to the philosophical/ rational stage, the stage to which Cornford in fact devoted the bulk of his studies. The contacts with the cultures of the Near East were specified by Cornford in a posthumous publication, *The Unwritten Philosophy* (Cambridge 1950), in which he linked motifs from Hesiod's *Theogony* with seasonal myths from the Near East, an initiative that has had a highly productive sequel in the last twenty years or so.[30]

This means that the Cambridge school[31] was eventually posthumously freed from a certain Greece-oriented position of isolation, partly under the influence of another Myth and Ritual school which—in similar isolation—directed attention to the Near East. I now turn to this other school.

Myth as a Scenario for Dramatic Ritual: The Myth and Ritual School Proper

In 1933 the Old Testament scholar S. H. Hooke edited a volume of studies to which many scholars contributed: *Myth and Ritual: Essays on the Myth and Ritual of the Hebrews in Relation to the Culture Pattern of the Ancient East* (London 1933), and twenty-five years later he edited another volume titled *Myth, Ritual and Kingship* (Oxford 1958), in which both opponents and supporters had their say—an ideal state of affairs for later historians.[32] It was this school of myth and ritual theorists that gave this complex its characteristic name and content.[33] The titles of these books are programmatic, pointing as they do to cultures of the ancient Near East, including the Israelite one, and the theme is the interrelation of myth and ritual in a context in which kingship plays an important role. The thesis is that in these areas there existed an endemic, widespread "cult pattern." What did this pattern look like, and how was the idea conceived?

It all began with the Babylonian New Year festival, the so-called Akitu ceremony.[34] All the gods, headed by Marduk, come to Babylon to this festival to celebrate the New Year in ceremonies that include a sacred marriage. The king is subjected to a curious ritual: the insignia of his dignity, his scepter, ring, and crown, are taken from him and laid down in front of Marduk's statue. The king kneels down, and the priest pulls one of his ears; the king professes his innocence and is given the promise that his kingship will prosper. The insignia are returned to him, and he is struck by the priest, which makes the king cry. From other sources we learn that the king then rides through the city in a kind of triumphal procession, together with Marduk.

That is, in itself, already more than enough for a Frazerian scheme, as Frazer himself had not failed to notice.[35] Here we seem to have a variant of the ancient regicide, toned down into abdication, humiliation, and reinvestiture. So much for the rite. As for the myth, the *Enuma Elish*, the Creation Epic, was recited during these New Year festivals. It told how Marduk (originally, of course, an older god) led the gods to war against Tiamat, the chaos monster of the primeval flood; how he defeated Tiamat's forces, sliced her in two, and fashioned heaven and earth from the two pieces. What we have here, then, is a case of perfect parallelism: the rite performed by the king is a reflection, in human terms, of what happened to the god in primordial mythical times, *in illo tempore*.[36] Creation of the cosmos after a victory gained over chaos corresponds to the regeneration of kingship after a period of chaotic anarchy during the king's absence, a correspondence confirmed by the mention of the king's sacred marriage.[37]

For the correspondence to be perfect, the myth would have to start with a description of the god's downfall, too, as is fitting for a "dying and rising" god and as is told, for instance, of other Near Eastern gods (notably Tammuz). Did Marduk, too, perish first? In the *Enuma Elish* this is not the case, but on a sorely damaged tablet from the sixth century B.C.[38] it is recorded that Marduk is imprisoned, beaten, and wounded: "People are looking in the streets for Marduk. Where is he held captive? . . . The *Enuma Elish* they sing in Nisan is about him who is in prison." This, then, completes the myth and ritual pattern, the "cult pattern":

Rite	Myth
Crisis situation between old and new	Threat by primeval chaos in the shape of a monster
King is dethroned and humiliated	Marduk taken prisoner
King is reinstated	Marduk gains victory, becomes king
Triumphal pageant	Triumphal pageant
Sacred marriage	Sacred marriage (celebrated on new year's day).

Numerous scholars, especially in Britain and the Scandinavian countries, (for instance, C. J. Gadd, E. O. James, A. R. Johnson, K. I. A. Engnell, and G. Widengren) have tried to discover this New Year complex in other Near Eastern cultures as well.[39] According to Hooke and others, *his* theory is not to blame for the unavoidable problems that arise. In many cultures, only the mythic component has been preserved; everywhere we have to allow for disintegration of the pattern due to migration, retouching, or theological intervention.[40] As for Israel, one could already hark back to the fundamental studies by S. Mowinckel, who had recognized in some psalms mythic-ritual texts accompanying the king's enthronement as Yahweh's representative.[41]

As stated earlier, this myth and ritual school had hardly any contact with the earlier Cambridge school.[42] Frazer, who was honored by the Cambridge group,[43] is virtually ignored by Hooke and his followers. One sometimes gets the impression that they feel embarrassed when reminded of the unmistakably Frazerian aspect of their cult pattern. Hooke even strongly opposes Frazer's "non-historical method of the purely comparative approach," and this leads to several other characteristic differences between Hooke and Harrison, to take only these two scholars. As Harrison saw it, in the last analysis everything had started with magic and had developed gradually.[44] Hooke, on the other hand, was not interested in the magical origins of sacral kingship, if any. Whereas Frazer and Harrison held that all over the world rite and myth developed in comparable ways through spontaneous evolution, Hooke was not interested in development, but adopted a diffusionist view. He thus betrayed his own origin, the Pan-Egyptian diffusionism advocated by Grafton Elliot Smith and W. J. Perry and the Pan-Babylonian version defended by A. Jeremias and others.[45] (The strongly astral emphasis in these positions may be considered a late offshoot of Max Müller's astral mythology.[46]) There are further differences, such as the stronger emphasis on kingship, which is understandable against the background of the

culture of the ancient Near East. By far the most significant one, however, is the fact that in the relation of myth and rite the order is reversed,
or at least given a slightly reversed bias. Whereas the Cambridge school
in general, in spite of variants, believed in the rise of myth from rite, the
new Orientalist myth and ritual theorists shifted the emphasis. Hooke
did not exactly exclude the rite-myth sequence, but he sidestepped the
question of origin. Taking a synchronic viewpoint, he regarded royal
ritual as a dramatic representation of the mythical scenario. In his first
volume of papers he writes: "In general the spoken part of a ritual consists of a description of what is being done, *it is the story which the
ritual enacts*. This is the sense in which the term "myth" is used in our
discussion. The original Myth, inseparable in the first instance from its
ritual, embodies in more or less symbolic fashion, the original situation
which is seasonally reenacted in the ritual" (p. 3). The passage is not
free from ambiguity,[47] but it does give a clear indication of what the
author does and does not accept. It is at any rate the shortest statement
of this myth and ritual approach[48] and as such a direct heritage from the
Pan-Babylonian Jeremias,[49] who wrote in 1929 that "alles irdische Sein
und Geschehen einem himmlischen Sein und Geschehen entspricht"
("everything that exists and happens on earth corresponds with something that exists and happens in heaven") and that the earthly king is an
"Abbild des himmlischen Königs" ("an image of the heavenly king").
Thus the flock of the faithful need not worry: whatever was said of Him,
God came first and had always done so. Those who preferred to think
that He Himself might have arisen from some earlier social ritual were
always welcome in libertine Cambridge.

THE FUSES BLOW: OUT-AND-OUT MYTH AND
RITUAL THEORISTS[50]

In one of her later works, with the appropriate title *Epilegomena to
the Study of Greek Religion* (Cambridge 1921), Jane Harrison threatened to prove that the well-known legend of Don Juan had arisen from
a fertility ritual (p. xlii n. 1). Murray had already preceded her by applying the myth and ritual scheme to Shakespeare's works.[51] It was to be
expected—why should diffusion be confined to the Near East? Why
would evolution obtain only in Greece? *Patet mundus*. One of the contributors to another volume of essays edited by Hooke, *The Labyrinth*
(London 1935) was A. M. Hocart. The final sentence of his paper,[52]
which also concludes the book, is: "Thus we have gone round the world
in search of the true myth, the myth that is bound up with life. We have
found it in India, beneath the Southern Cross, in the plains of North

America. We have come to find it at our doors." We would not be wrong
to think of Hocart as the founder of what we might call "out-and-out
myth and ritualism." In an earlier work, *Kingship* (London 1927), he
had already discovered a coronation ritual that had spread all over the
world, starting from Mesopotamia (!). It was based completely on the
New Year scheme but consisted of a much greater number of elements,
twenty-six in fact, which are consequently arranged from *a* to *z*. This
opened the floodgates. L. Raglan, in a book that became very popular,
The Hero: A Study in Tradition, Myth and Drama (London 1936),[53]
maintained that *all* myths in the whole world, without exception, were
based on a single primordial rite, sacral regicide, and had their origin in
Mesopotamia. And soon Guy Fawkes, William Tell, Robin Hood, and
Thomas à Becket came to follow suit.[54] It looks like a serious application of the witty argument that proved irrefutably that G. Murray himself must be a dying and rising god. Jane Harrison, by contrast, is honest
and cautious in her pious wish: "It would be convenient if the use of the
word *myth* could be confined to such sequences, such stories as are involved in rites" (*Themis*, p. 331). S. E. Hyman,[55] a forceful advocate of
the myth and ritual theory and admirer of Harrison's *Themis*, "the most
revolutionary book of the 20th century,"[56] not only asserted that myth
was always concomitant with rite, "like a child's patter as he plays," but
also showed that Darwin's evolutionary theories followed the myth and
ritual pattern:[57] the "struggle for life" is the *agon*, the "survival of the
fittest" the theophany of Murray's tragic scheme.

The wildest excesses were due to Murray's namesake, the well-
known Margaret Murray,[58] with her theories about witches as later
priestesses of ancient pagan rituals. She demonstrated that "at least in
every reign from William the Conqueror to James I the sacrifice of the
incarnate God was consummated either in the person of the king or in
that of his substitute."[59] I prefer the explicitly romanticized fictions of
Robert Graves, Shirley Jackson (Hyman's wife), and J. B. Vickery,[60] who
introduced the theme in literature.

When I first became acquainted with myth and ritual theory about
twenty years ago, I had not the faintest notion that I would ever call
Gaster's comprehensive work *Thespis* (see above) a moderate book.
This study gives a concise survey of what is known about the "seasonal
pattern" of the Near East and discusses the related Canaanite, Hittite,
and Egyptian myths, with a few excursions into Greek drama and English mummery play. After our voyage across the seething waters of
much wilder seas, I am inclined to consider this book a relatively calm
and clear fairway and to recommend it—as an introduction to a limited
part of the myth and ritual approach—to those interested readers who

are firmly resolved not to take the author's word for everything he claims.[61]

As far as myth and ritual theory in anthropological literature is concerned, a few remarks will suffice, from which it may become clear that some anthropologists have not wholly unjustly been included under the heading of out-and-out myth and ritual theorists.

Here we should especially mention B. Malinowski,[62] who found his source of inspiration in Frazer and Robertson Smith and also quoted Harrison approvingly. A practising anthropologist himself, he gave a definition of myth as, above all, "charter," an explanation providing legitimation and foundation of customs, rules, moral codes, and rites: "There is no important magic, no ceremony, no ritual without belief; and the belief is spun out into accounts of concrete precedent. The union is very intimate, for myth is not only looked upon as a commentary or additional information, but is a warrant, a charter, and often even a practical guide to the activities with which it is connected." [63] This is one of the monolithic theories of myth attacked by Kirk and others. In this respect Malinowski still betrays the influence of his mentors, without being a genuine myth and ritual theorist: other phenomena besides rites also find their legitimation in myths, and he later speaks of "myth as a dramatic development of dogma," [64] thus following a different course.

Nevertheless, it is remarkable to see how other anthropologists venture very far-reaching statements about the interrelation of myth and rite. C. Kluckhohn, in his paper "Myths and Rituals: a General Theory," mentioned above, claims that we cannot speak of priority in the relation between myth and ritual: "The myth is a system of word symbols, whereas ritual is a system of object and act symbols. Both are symbolic processes for dealing with the same type of situation in the same affective mode" (p. 58). That is why they are interdependent, and the task they have in common is to "reduce the anticipation of disaster" (p. 69). E. Leach puts it in an even less equivocal way: "myth, in my terminology, is the counterpart of ritual: myth implies ritual, ritual implies myth, they are one and the same." [65]

Such statements can be explained if we think of the functionalist perspective from which these anthropologists operated. Both myth and ritual were considered primarily as symbolic means of giving sense, form, and definition to the social universe within which man functions as a social being. In *Natural Symbols* Mary Douglas maintains that "ritual is the institutionalized rhetoric of symbolic order," [66] an absolute condition for the identification of the group and the integration of the individual in the group. Substitute "myth" for "ritual" in this statement and the truth value remains the same.[67]

Many objections have been raised[68] against the generalizing and totalizing claims of the statements quoted above. In anthropological circles the discussion is still in full swing, offering many scholars ample opportunity to prove their skills in matters of jargon, analysis, and polemics. Let us hasten back to our own limited territory, where, for that matter, we shall meet with the very same discussion.

CRITICISM

There is a story that Bertrand Russell once proposed to get Jane Harrison a bull on condition that she and her lady friends would demonstrate how maenads managed to tear such a beast to pieces with their bare hands. Russell, the logician, simply could not believe that the unaided human hand was capable of such an act. His proposal is a mild form of criticism, but matters could be different, as witness the judgment of the Plato specialist P. Shorey:[69] "Professor Murray has done much harm by helping to substitute in the minds of an entire generation for Arnold's and Jebb's conception of the serene rationality of the classics the corybantic Hellenism of Miss Harrison and Isadora Duncan and Susan Glaspell and Mr. Stark Young's 'Good Friday and Classical Professors,' the higher vaudeville Hellenism of Mr. Vachel Lindsey, the anthropological Hellenism of Sir James Frazer, the irrational, semisentimental, Polynesian, free-verse and sex-freedom Hellenism of all the gushful geysers of 'rapturous rubbish' about the Greek spirit." That is how "real" classical scholars judged the Cambridge school, and E. R. Dodds, therefore, with his irrational Greeks was not taken seriously either. Indeed, Cambridge was in such bad odor that M. I. Finley,[70] by far the best-known ancient historian there, saw fit to point out *en passant* that he wrote his *World of Odysseus* before he ever set foot in Cambridge, and Kirk his *Myth* after he left his Cambridge post for Yale. Both books were said to exude a Cambridge odor. Murray, by the way, was an "unregenerate Oxford Australian."

From all this one can perhaps imagine the emotional responses the other myth and ritual school theorists elicited in contemporary orthodox clerical circles. Robertson Smith had already had to listen to this:[71] "His mind is like a shop with a big cellar behind it, and having good shelves and windows. . . . But he doesn't grow his own wool, nor does he spin the thread, nor weave the webs that are in his cellar or on his shelves. All his goods come in paper parcels from Germany." Behind all this is the aversion to ethnological comparativism, especially if this refuses to stop short at Genesis 1.1. And Robertson Smith did not stop. A notorious "Robertson Smith case" resulted, partly in reaction to his blasphemous conviction that Moses could never have written the entire Pentateuch. This led to his dismissal from the chair of Old Testament studies of Free Church College in Aberdeen in 1881. Two years later he moved to Cambridge, where he came to hold a chair of Arabic.

I have not heard about any early retirement among later myth and ritual theorists, but the accusation of having "recklessly imposed their pattern" on Judaism[72] is only a mild version of what has also been voiced in stronger terms. This kind of emotional criticism is highly interesting from the point of view of cultural history, but it does not allow of any reasonable discussion, in contrast to other forms of critical approach.

For example, the building blocks of a theory can be tested for hardness: the tablet on which Marduk's downfall is described may be interpreted as Assyrian war propaganda against the hostile supreme deity;[73] the hymn of the Curetes itself hardly contains any reference to initiation elements (in many ways it seems rather to refer to the New Year complex);[74] and in tragedy there are simply no traces of Murray's theophany and resurrection.

Or we can tackle the pillars of the building: P. Lambrechts[75] was the first to aver that some alleged dying and rising gods, such as Attis or Adonis, *did* die in the myth but did not *disertis verbis* rise again. A similar statement was made about Tammuz by Yamauchi,[76] and it has been suggested that a christological perspective imposed a pattern upon the gods of the Near East, only half of which has actually been attested. Moreover, it has been pointed out that for Greece we do not know anything about either sacral kingship or coherent complexes of myth and ritual.[77] Even the actual existence of sacral regicide, so often recorded in anthropological literature, has been questioned. Informants too often refer to former times: "We ourselves do not practise this any more, but our grandparents chopped up a king."[78] We might consider introducing a category, "mythic ritual," to describe this frequent and highly interesting phenomenon.

Anyone who wants a survey of such instances of specific and detailed criticism should consult J. Fontenrose,[79] who stated categorically as early as 1959 in *Python: A Study of Delphic Myth and Its Origins,* "The rituals did not enact the myth, the myth did not receive its plot from the rituals" (pp. 461–62), and who, responding to opposition from the myth and ritual quarter, devoted a book to *The Ritual Theory of Myth* (1966). The annoying thing is that criticism like Fontenrose's, however useful and even necessary it may be, will never tip the scales. Raglan, Hyman, and Margaret Murray spoke the language of the initiated, which does not require a book to defend or to attack it. There is no convincing the initiated: they see a great light in which all the pieces can be fitted into the big jigsaw puzzle. As for the noninitiated, they thought it all nonsense anyway. And in any case even detailed criticism among reasonable people usually has only marginal effects. Even if it is conceded that the tablet recording Marduk's imprisonment has another background—itself an arguable point—there is still a mass of data left. It is thus essential to ask how many data we need before we feel justified in speaking of a pattern, and that is where opinions differ widely.

Refuting theories in a genuinely scientific way is only possible when the theories claim to have general validity. As the Dutch essayist Karel van het Reve says,[80] popularizing Popper: if a scientific theory claims that all redheads are alcoholics, we can refute this proposition by pointing to one redhead who is not an alcoholic—and whoever came up with that general proposition simply has to hold his tongue henceforth. This neatly sums up G. S. Kirk's approach in his works mentioned above.[81] In *The Nature of Greek Myths* he proves that the five monolithic theories of the origin and essence of myth—theories claiming to possess general and exclusive validity—are untenable because we can always find some myth that does not fulfill the conditions stipulated. As regards the interpretation of myth and ritual, he reasons as follows: if an interrelation could be proved, it would not provide the one and only explanation for the rise of myths, for we know many myths that cannot possibly have any ritual connection, such as myths explaining why a snake has no feet and walks on his belly. And in so far as there really are demonstrable relations between ritual and myth, their nature varies widely. There are instances in which the myth arises from the ritual or is invented for the occasion as an etiological explanation—the types we have dealt with for the most part so far. Then there are forms in which myth and ritual arose independently but were compounded—for instance, again, as an explanation of the rite. And there are few myths that generate rituals. Certain dramatic actions in the mysteries imitate the myth of Demeter and Kore, which in its turn may have been based on an older rite. And it may also happen—but such cases are extremely rare—that ritual and myth arise simultaneously as parallel responses to some critical situation, in Kluckhohn's words: "to reduce the anticipation of disaster."

We can hardly accept this as the last word on this matter. Kirk's skeptical approach has already provoked serious criticism. Was not the baby thrown out with the bath water? Moreover, granted that the redhead is not an alcoholic *now;* does that imply that he has never been one? Perhaps he was *forced* in some way to leave the bottle alone? Or, being an alcoholic at heart, did he switch to drugs as a substitute? Is his red hair

natural? Or could it be that all redheads were indeed originally alcoholics, but that migration and acculturation have led to the disintegration
of their way of life?

It is time, I think, for a very brief conclusion. Frazer is a fallen giant:
that is the *communis opinio* nowadays. "There have been no answers
because there were no questions," says one of his wittiest critics, J. Z.
Smit,[82] thus paraphrasing Gertrude Stein as well as Frazer himself, who
in the introduction to the third edition of *The Golden Bough* writes: "It
is the fate of theories to be wasted away . . . and I am not so presump-
tuous as to expect or to desire for mine an exemption from the common
lot. I hold them all very lightly, and have used them chiefly as convenient
pegs on which to hang my collection of facts"—which we might call the
understatement of the century. However, the giant who once wrote in a
poetical, visionary vein: "The dreamland world of fancy. There is my
own true home,"[83] remains a colossus, albeit a fallen one. Evolution of
religion from magic is an outdated notion by now. Nor should we, as
many epigones used to do, maintain the myth and ritual complex connected with the year king and the year god as a scheme for anything and
everything, outside of which there is no salvation. Setting aside, however, such notions as original regicide, we cannot very well deny that in
many cultures the time around the New Year is experienced as a period
of transition, of crisis, or of threat. The old must be "finished off," the
new joyfully hailed; in between there is no-man's-land. This notion is
often represented ritually through signals of anarchy, lawlessness, and
anomia and mythically as the menace of the chaos from which the cosmos must be created. Mircea Eliade, for one, has given an excellent
sketch of all this in *The Myth of the Eternal Return* (Princeton, NJ,
1954). Let us leave it at that for the moment.

A farewell, equally, to the monolithic explanation of myth as a
stereotyped companion to rite. On the other hand, there *are* certain
links, such as Jane Harrison's types 1 and 3, which we have dealt with.[84]
That one variant—very rare, according to Kirk—in which myth and
rite emerge *pari passu* (Harrison, type 2) we have only *mentioned* so far.
Like the specific second myth and ritual complex, the initiation scheme
(Harrison, type *b*), this variant has not come into the limelight until
recently.[85] A name is associated with this combination of initiation and
myth and ritual in a new key: Walter Burkert.

INITIATION, A MODERN COMPLEX

Harrison's *Themis,* though valued more highly by the writer herself,
was generally much less appreciated than her *Prolegomena.*[86] There is

no need to ask why. The strongly utilitarian and ritualistic approach to the ancient religions in particular might, at a pinch, swallow an occasional *eniautos daimon*—the term is even found once in Nilsson's handbook, and Nilsson was surely not one of Harrison's admirers—but could not sympathize with apparently "aimless" myth and ritual complexes in which the much sought-after element of fertility was not paramount. It might appear surprising at first sight that *Themis* was not enthusiastically received in Durkheim's circles either, which took offence—not unfairly—at the erratic, associative, and intuitive nature of the book. Durkheim's maxim that as soon as a psychological explanation is suggested somewhere you may be sure that it is a wrong one proved to be ominous in this context.

What we can see now is that as the New Year myth and ritual complex came under ever more violent critical fire, attention switched to the initiation complex: the initiation candidate arose from the dying god's ashes. Before the sixties H. Jeanmaire's *Couroi et Courétes* (Lille 1939, reprinted 1978) was the only major study in the classical field in which the initiation scheme was applied to Greek myths and rites in a consistent manner, to which we might add G. Dumézil, *Le problème des centaures: Etude de mythologie comparée indoeuropéenne* (Paris 1929) and L. Gernet 1928. The proviso *in the classical field* is important, however, for outside that domain, notably in the germanic and Old Persian contexts, numerous studies were devoted to *Männerbünde, Jungmannschaften*, and *Geheimbünde*, which were generally recognized as historical reflections of groups of youths in the initiation phase.[87] However, contacts between these studies and those dealing with the Greco-Roman field—in which A. Alföldi is the most prominent figure—were not made until very recently.

Any attempt to ascertain which scholar might have given the initial impulse to the renewed interest in the initiation pattern is bound to be arbitrary. No doubt A. Brelich may be credited with having encouraged the interest in this subject in the sixties, with such studies as *Le iniziazioni* I, II (Rome 1960–61), which remained rather obscure, and above all with *Paides e parthenoi* I (Rome 1969), which was already in manuscript in 1960 (Volume II was never published). In an extensive introduction Brelich presents an anthropological typology of initiation customs, which he then applies to Greek situations. It was precisely in this period that anthropological interest in initiatory rites was given a new incentive.[88] Eliade's *Birth and Rebirth* (1958; reprinted as *Rites and Symbols of Initiation*, 1975) has done much to make the typical characteristics of initiation more widely known. In the same decade of youthful elan and student protests P. Vidal-Naquet published "Le chas-

seur noir et l'origine de l'éphébie athénienne,"[89] a study in which he
maintained that it was not only the Spartan but also the Athenian
youths that were subjected to initiation rites of a strongly archaic type
well into historical times.

Initiation was again in the air, and if I insist on choosing W. Burkert
as a starting point, it is partly because a few younger specialists owe
their inspiration primarily to Burkert and partly because, in my view, it
was Burkert, more than anyone else, who placed the initiation complex
in the context of the myth and ritual approach. Burkert is, after all, the
most innovative scholar of Greek religion.[90] His *Weisheit und Wissenschaft: Studien zu Pythagoras, Philolaus und Platon* (Nuremberg
1962)[91] had already drawn attention to initiation symptoms, but a basic
application was presented in "Krekopidensage und Arrhephoria"
(1966b), an ideal case of myth and ritual. The rite prescribes that each
year the *Arrhephoroi,* two girls between seven and eleven years of age,
are to be secluded on the Acropolis, where they have to weave the *peplos* for Athene. They are assigned the task of taking an object, the nature of which must remain unknown to them, to Aphrodite's garden
through an underground passage, and returning with an equally invis-
ible object wrapped in cloths. The myth tells of two of the daughters of
Cecrops, Athens's most ancient king, Aglauros and Herse, to whom the
goddess Athena gave a *kiste* that they were forbidden to open. However,
they disobeyed and what they discovered inside—(one or) two snakes
and the Erichthonius child—frightened them so much that they threw
themselves down from the Acropolis. The myth ends halfway—at the
tragic low point—whereas the rite ends in a positive way with the girls'
return. The cost in terms of girls would have been prohibitive anyway—
respectable girls, too, for they came from upper-class circles. Apart
from that, there is splendid parallelism along the lines of a scheme that
has been exploited everywhere as a narrative pattern in myths or tales
of "the girl's tragedy":[92] prohibition, seclusion, violation of the prohibition, girl threatened with punishment or death, liberation. As a rule,
the subject is a virgin, who is enjoined (prohibition) to remain a virgin,
is locked in (seclusion) for that purpose, becomes pregnant (violation of
prohibition), is threatened with death by a wicked father or relative, but
is saved, ultimately, by her son, for instance. This, however, as had long
been recognized,[93] is the typical pattern of the girl's initiation, which is
supposed to turn the girl at puberty into a young woman. In this process
two components—apart from all kinds of symbols of leavetaking and
new beginning, which in the much better known initiation rites for boys
have often been elaborated more fully—play an important role: during
the period of seclusion the girl has to learn to demonstrate the truly

womanly skills—the "work-complex" in the words of a specialist[94]—
and her female sexuality will have to be unsealed. Many frightening
means are available for this purpose, such as painful circumcision, mass
deflorations, sexual humiliations, and so forth.[95] Fokke Sierksma's book
De roof van het vrouwengeheim (1962), which deals with this subject
among others, was renamed *Religie, sexualiteit en agressie*—and justly
so—when it was reprinted in an academic edition (Groningen 1979).[96]
This is the explanation Burkert gave for the secret in the *kiste* which the
girls were not allowed to know and yet had to discover: we have here
the symbol of woman's fertility, notably the child, which may also be
recognized in the object, swaddled in cloths, that is returned after the
girls' stay in Aphrodite's garden.

All this started long ago with the research into the better-known
boys' initiation. For her theory Harrison could consult *Les rites de passage* (Paris 1909) by A. van Gennep,[97] the first to make a systematic
study of rites of transition. The distinction he makes among *rites de
séparation*, *rites de marge*, and *rites d' agrégation*, with which the youth
took leave of the old situation, went into seclusion for some time, and
entered his new status, respectively, is still exemplary. Later anthropologists have added many typical features to the ones gathered by Van
Gennep, the second stage (the marginal period) having increasingly become the center of interest.

It is not always easy to distinguish the three constituent elements
clearly; they tend to merge smoothly. Frequent examples of the elements
are: the boy gives up his childhood by withdrawing from his mother,
giving up his old name, banishing his origin from his memory, leaving
the old status behind by amputation of limbs, having a tooth knocked
out, and so forth. As a member of the male community he is accepted as
a new human being. He is often actually reborn—the mother sometimes
being allowed to reappear only once before being consigned to permanent absence—is given a new name, and receives the dignities and insignia of a full-grown man. In between these two situations his existence
as a social being has been suspended. Everywhere the marginal period is
felt to be a period of threat, chaos, and death. The symbol of the labyrinth is often staged literally, as the boy is led around in the labyrinth in
the dark or blindfolded, loses his orientation and identity, and has to be
aided to escape, the labyrinth being seen as the realm of death but also
as the womb: "birth and rebirth." During this time the young boy is in
exile, locked in an initiation house or expelled from the tribe into the
marginal territories where culture and society are no longer valid and
other laws prevail. This is—as in the case of the girls—the time of tests
and trials: torture, (sexual) humiliation, trials of strength, matches, the

struggle to survive outside the tribal community. It is also the time of instruction: threatened by death—a great god or a monster is coming to devour him, to tear him to pieces, or to roast him, after which he will be restored to life as a new human being—he is taught the secret myths of the tribe, the ritual customs, and the use of men's weapons.

This nonsocial, marginal situation is marked or "signaled" by a great number of external features. Virtually all such marginal signals reflect some opposition to normal social features.[98] In matters of dress, role reversal is often obligatory, boys having to wear girls' clothes, or we find status reversal, clothes being used to mark complete social degradation. In a reversal of food habits, novices may be forced to partake of the very kinds of food and drink that are socially taboo. Communication sometimes takes place by means of a private language, a corrupted form of everyday social language. the boys have their hair shaved off, walk on one shoe, or paint their faces white or black. In other ways, too, the verkehrte Welt may become manifest: the boys are permitted to do what is never allowed under normal circumstances. They are free to steal, to demand food under threat, to give the whole tribe a fit by staging night raids and even demolishing the entire roof of a house.[99] Obviously, there is a resemblance here to other "periods of licence" or legale Anarchien such as Carnival or Saturnalia, to which I shall return.

Looking for remnants of these initiatory elements is a fascinating pursuit and Jeanmaire's book mentioned above makes for absorbing reading. In point of fact he already adumbrated virtually all that later scholars were to deal with at greater length and in greater detail, the references to rituals still in use in Greece often being the most convincing part of the argument. That the Spartan krupteia with all it entails is a vivid example of an initiatory situation needs no argument, of course.[100] And that forms of pederasty which were found in Crete and Athens are relics of the sexual humiliations mentioned above is also an arguable thesis.[101] Sometimes there is also evidence of mythical references to initiatory motifs. In 1893 Crawley[102] had already pointed out that Achilles, who hides in the isle of Skyros disguised as a girl and who has been reared, moreover, outside the domain of civilization by a centaur, represents the typical initiation candidate. The same may be said of Philoctetes, who is banished, with a stinking wound in his leg, to a lonely island.[103]

Once again it is interesting to find a ritual accompanied by a myth, as was the case with the Arrhephoria: the Theseus myth and the Oschophoria festival.[104] A characteristic feature of this festival is a procession of young men carrying bunches of grapes from Athens to the temple of Athena Skiras in Phaleron headed by two boys in women's clothes;

there is a sacrifice accompanied by lamentations. The youths are served dishes, namely beans and greens (the *pyanepsia*), by special cooks or waitresses, the *deipnophoroi*, who also tell them stories (*muthoi*). There is a foot race of the ephebes, the winner being offered a draught of a *panspermia*. Plutarch links this festival with Theseus and his exploits, and the reader who is prepared to view the Oschophoria as a ritual reflection of the initiation of ephebes might now also follow Jeanmaire when he recognizes in Theseus the mythical reflection of the initiation candidate. Theseus, too, is an ephebe: he puts on girls' clothes, plunges to the bottom of the sea, has to enter the labyrinth, threatens to be annihilated by a divine monster, but escapes and returns to assume kingship. The theory that in the *muthoi* those women tell the boys the seed might be hidden from which these myths finally developed is highly suggestive, and from there, of course, it will not take long before Heracles' labors are interpreted as the mythical reflection of a phase of initiation as well.

We can go even further: just as in the New Year complex king and god are supposed to be one another's reflection in fall and rise, so here the search has been for mythic-divine—and not only heroic—reflections of the initiation candidate. Harrison's *megistos kouros* was an example, but in the Greek pantheon there is another prototypical *kouros*, whose long hair is a signal of the ephebe on the eve of his initiation, to whom the boys dedicate their locks of hair on attaining manhood, and who remains unmarried, an archer, the god from afar. As early as 1895 T. Homolle[105] was aware that the Spartan *apellai*, notably those celebrated in the initial month of the year, *Apellaios*, were the rite during which the young men were admitted into the community of adults, and with thanks to Homolle (and Van Gennep) Harrison concludes (*Themis*, 441): "Apellon [this is the older form of Apollon] is the projection of these rites; he, like Dionysos, like Herakles, is the arch-ephebos, the Megistos Kouros."

As I have pointed out, nearly everything has already been said— often as a brief suggestion—and the reason why many things have been said once again in recent times is twofold: first, they had been brushed aside during several decades, and second, our store of information has increased to such an extent that, thanks to a wealth of comparative material, that which was formerly no more than a hypothesis may be, if not proven, at least made more plausible. Hence a paper by W. Burkert: "Apellai und Apollon" (Burkert 1975)[106] followed by another by one of his pupils, F. Graf, about Apollo Delphinius,[107] the god that is more immediately concerned with the young man's admission into the official political and social roles. Here and elsewhere a good deal of research remains to be done. Burkert's synthesis is pure "Harrison": Achilleus, fast ein Doppelgänger Apellons.

In the instances mentioned above it is always a matter of ritual relics,[108] mythical references to evident initiatory elements, or in the most interesting cases, longer mythical-narrative sequences, where the ritual counterpart has been given by the ancient authors themselves, the protagonist is at least a typical ephebe, or several elements refer unmistakably to initiation. A case in point is the Theseus myth, which seems to satisfy all three requirements. Apart from that, however, we can make a great stride forward by research in myths and legends that do not so evidently and immediately fit into this frame in order to see whether they do not go back, after all, to a similar initiation scheme. There are precedents in various fields; certain fairy-tale types were believed to contain recognizable initiation elements. Tom Thumb and Snow White, for instance, turn out to be something quite different from that which some of us believed in even up into old age. Robin Hood once more puts in an appearance, not as a year king or year god this time, but as the leader of a *Jungmannschaft,* and in the classical field Odysseus, the Argonauts, Oedipus, and others have long preceded him.[109]

What we perceive here is the shaping of a pattern, a process that may be compared, fundamentally, to the former myth and ritual approach. Instead of the "dying and rising" complex of gods and kings around the New Year festival, the frame of reference is now the initiation candidate, banished, sorely tried, sometimes doomed to death, coming off triumphant, returning. With Frazer and his followers the myth and ritual complex had its function within the larger frame of vegetative fertility, which could be influenced by means of magic. The initiation complex has been embedded in a wider frame, too, that of "marginal existence." We have thus left the realm of nature and have entered upon the domain of culture and society. An evaluation of the most recent myth and ritual explorations in the classical field is incomplete without first taking a critical glance at modern anthropological research on marginality, by which classical studies have been decisively influenced. I shall do this first, briefly adding a few examples of significant applications of marginality theory to classical problems. With the help of another example I shall go on to show that the methodological dangers we find looming here are comparable to—and no less impressive than—those that were inherent in Frazer's theory.

Anyone coming across terms such as "marginal" or "liminal" nowadays should know that Van Gennep's scheme underlies these concepts, but that in more recent studies, notably under the influence of the anthropologist V. W. Turner, these terms are taken in a much wider sense.[110] It was found that the eccentric existence in the margin of society, the asocial or antisocial way of life, is marked by a whole range of phenomena. In this context we may distinguish, in a purely systematic fashion, *marginal groups or individuals,* which find themselves in the eccentric situation either for some considerable time or permanently, from *marginal situations,* in which individuals or groups withdraw from social pattern temporarily, often by way of ritual demonstration. In either case the atmosphere of marginality is marked by *stereotyped marginal signals.*[111] A few examples follow.

Marginal groups or individuals[112] that have their whereabouts, literally, on the outskirts of society are—apart from the juvenile groups of the *Jungmannschaft* type—monks, anchorites, pirates, bandits, as well as, in a sense, animals, and from a certain point of view also the gods and the dead. In this context those people who have a more than normal contact with the gods, the dead, or animals also rank as marginal: the possessed, lunatics, godly men, prophets, seers, shepherds. Groups that, socially speaking, live in the margin of society without taking part in the social process: beggars, cynics, hippies, tramps. Groups that oppose society above all in a political sense: anarchists, revolutionaries, millenarians, messianists. Strangers are fundamentally marginal, especially when of a different color, but also groups within a society that nonetheless are felt to be strange somehow: migrant workers, metics, immigrants, slaves. Groups or individuals that do not function fully in society: children, adolescents, sick, poor, unemployed, and those that, while functioning fully, do so within some specific area only: women, priests, kings.

Marginal situations are situations that tend to remove individual persons or groups temporarily from a normal social existence. Initiation— and in particular the period of the "margin"—is the example we have discussed, but no less exemplary are festivals of an exceptional character, during which things that normally are forbidden are tolerated, roles are reversed, and people generally kick over the traces.[113] Instances of such *Ausnahmefeste* are the Carnival and its predecessors such as the Saturnalia and the Cronia,[114] but also women's festivals such as the Thesmophoria, Dionysiac festivals, the Roman festival of Bona Dea, giving women in seclusion an opportunity to indulge in excesses in their own way. Other marginal situations are periods of mourning, disease, especially epidemics, or famine, and social phenomena of acculturation and disintegration accompanied by crises of identity.[115]

Obviously, there are a great many cross-relations and overlaps between the groups and situations mutually as well as between the concepts of "marginal group" and "marginal situation": members of messianist movements or utopians may be viewed, of course, as temporary marginals but also as groups "in permanent transition."[116]

People in marginal situations are outside normal society; they are asocial, but that does not imply that they necessarily lead a totally atomized existence. On the contrary, more often than not a new, different, nonstructural relationship develops, for which V. W. Turner coined the term *communitas*. There is a feeling of fellowship, of solidarity, that distinguishes this group from the structured society. This communication is brought about among other things by *marginal signals,* which, as a rule, are nothing but opposites to the current cultural signs.[117] People in liminal situations shave off their hair or, on the contrary, wear it long, paint their faces, wear a felt hood or women's clothes, or dress in a strange, eccentric way, abstain from sexual acts or, just the reverse, indulge in perversions or abolish sex distinctions. They speak a different language or remain totally silent. They follow deviant habits in matters of food and drink, change their names, perform acts of self-mutilation or tattooing, and so forth.

Let us now, with the help of a few examples, demonstrate how this concept of marginality can be used to elucidate puzzling problems in the ancient religions. For this purpose I select some suggestions from studies by F. Graf and J. N. Bremmer, who both, more than others, and following in Burkert's footsteps, use the concept of marginality as a tool in their research.

The ancient libation (Gr. *spondai,* Lat. *libatio*), a drink offering that is poured out on the ground or on an *eschara,* may consist of the following basic ingredients: milk and honey, wine, water, oil. In a paper entitled "Milch, Honig und Wein" F. Graf [118] made a study of the frame of reference of these ingredients. He found that milk and honey in particular are the liquid signals of marginal and unusual situations and groups.[119] According to the Hellenic conception, Greek men drink wine mixed with water. Milk and honey, on the other hand, are characteristic of women and children, of marginal groups such as the Pythagoreans, but also of barbarian nations, who are typified as milk drinkers (Teutons, Scythians), and of utopian, "natural" man of both prehistoric and eschatological times.[120] Graf's thesis is fully demonstrable: "Honig und Milch ... waren also abnorm, marginale Flüßigkeiten." With a little more trouble a case could also be made for water, oil, and even wine, if undiluted, but if this *libatio* wholly consists of ingredients that refer to the margin, the question arises of why. The answer is that the *libatio* of this composition is itself used specifically in marginal situations, for instance in contacts with the dead, with heroes, with the underworld: in the liminal sphere, therefore, between death and life. There is an ideal correspondence here between *signifiant* and *signifié*.

In a paper on the Greek *pharmakos* J. N. Bremmer[121] sheds new light on the scapegoat and the related rites from the point of view of "the margin." The fact, for instance, not understood hitherto, that the *pharmakos* is beaten with "squills or twigs of the wild fig tree" is convincingly explained by the fact that these plants, being sterile, belonged to the "marginal" sphere. He can easily interpret the persons who served as *pharmakoi* in historic times as marginal because, on the whole, it was marginal characters such as criminals, paupers, and riffraff generally that were cast in that role. Here too, therefore, there is an excellent correspondence between *signifiant* and *signifié*, both clearly belonging to the margin. When, however, he also defines the kings who acted as scapegoats in the myths as "the lonely marginal at the top," we see tension looming ahead between these two categories of *signifiant* and *signifié*. This is one of the dangers inherent in a general sense in the theories of marginality described so far. These dangers might be classified as follows:

1. There is no need to be a structuralist to conclude that within any conceivable society it must be possible to point to binary oppositions in which one member is unusual or marginal, as compared with another, central or normal member. It is a well-known fact, moreover, that people tend to declare their own group the center and all others outsiders. If we take the—very incomplete—list of imaginable marginals quoted above, it is hard to avoid the conclusion that virtually everybody, depending on the comparison, is or may be marginal, with the exception of a roughly forty-year-old, diligent, healthy, native, non-hunchbacked man with close-cropped hair, entitled to carrying arms and in possession of full civic rights, wife, and children. That I am not exaggerating may be apparent from the results of a study in astrology and marginality by R. Wuthnow,[122] which concludes that "it was the more poorly educated, the unemployed, non-white, females, the unmarried, the overweight, the ill, and the lonely, who were most taken with astrology."

Even those who hold that this statement does prove something will understand that, at the same time, it verges dangerously on tautology. Armed with such a definition, you could take practically any category of person and prove that it is a marginal one, with the exception of the "normal" family man with all the normal characteristics mentioned above. A criminal as a marginal *pharmakos* is not a debatable point: any criminal is marginal by definition. A king as a scapegoat is much more interesting but at the same time less easy to explain if you start from the margin model. In my opinion, the power and the tragedy of the ultimate sacrifice, in this case, are effected not because the king *is* a marginal person but because the king as the *center* of society is *made* a marginal person, through his expulsion from that which society considers the position of highest prestige. It is understandable, therefore, that the king as scapegoat belongs virtually exclusively to the mythical imagination.[123]

Nearly all (groups of) people, then, are marginal in some respect or another, or are potentially so, and so also are most situations. In various studies that I consulted the following ancient people and territories were labeled "marginal": Scythians, Teutons, India, Southern Italy, Thracia, Lemnos, Troy, Lycia, Scheria, Ithaca, Skyros, Boeotia, Euboia, certain regions in Attica. True, such statements will always be tenable with regard to a certain period and a carefully selected center, but there is an obvious danger of arbitrariness and generalization. The same applies to gods and demigods discussed in these various studies, such as Apollo, Dionysus, Hermes, Pan, Poseidon, Athena, Artemis, Heracles, Theseus, who are either called marginal in a more general way or labeled outright "initiation gods."[124]

2. Whereas we can try to escape the preceding danger by using precise definition and careful argumentation, the following objection cannot be met successfully because it does not depend on the researcher's skill: the marginal signals are seldom specific. An exemplary illustration of this phenomenon is found in the *libatio* signals, which, as we have seen, implied *general* references to highly divergent marginal situations and groups and could only be specified thanks to the fact that the context referred to *was known to us*. In my country, when you see a man in an entirely black suit, you at once assume that he is in a marginal situation. Which situation that is, however, requires additional information: he is walking behind a coffin, he carries a prayer book (on Sunday), or he is serving refreshments. When you observe a man wearing a long white or orange robe, with a curious hairdo or a clean-shaven head and a painted face, you have to pay attention to the context before you can tell whether this is a religious marginal or someone from the sphere of carnival or the circus.[125] In other words, the traffic is unimpeded in one direction only: from the situation to the signals. Only the former (the *signifié*) is specific; the signals (the *signifiant*) usually are not, and cannot in themselves, therefore, be related with certainty to any one marginal situation, not even when they seem to fit into an orderly pattern.

3. Here we touch upon a third point. The protagonists of the initiation myth and ritual theory seldom fail to play what they consider their trump card, the "internal coherence" of the pattern in which all the

pieces neatly fall into their proper slots. A characteristic passage, for instance, is the following: "In this way all the different motifs which, taken separately, may of course occur in different contexts, are explained by one hermeneutic key which is, from a methodic point of view, to be preferred to all kinds of supposed influences." [126] Now it cannot have escaped anybody's notice that those two essential dangers mentioned so far—the *general* applicability of the marginality concept and its inherent fatal elasticity, on the one hand, and the lack of specificity of marginal signals, on the other—are, *mutatis mutandis*, in general a threat to any theory that tries to recognize a pattern within a diversity of phenomena. These objections were raised repeatedly, notably to the old myth and ritual advocates, Frazer among them, not least by those scholars who have recently discovered a different pattern.

So let us finally evaluate the "coherence" trump card in this light. In the *Times* (London) obituary, Tylor's work was eulogized as follows: "He held that the enumeration of facts must form the staple of the argument, and that the limit of needful detail was reached only when each group of facts so displayed its general law that fresh ones came to range themselves in their proper niches as new instances of an already established rule." [127] Those words were written by a believer: automatically all the threads fall just right, weaving the pattern of Tylor's animism. One small matter, though: nobody believes in this pattern any more, no more than anybody believes in Frazer's general theories. And yet the latter had filled many hefty tomes chockfull with "facts, facts, facts," which all—so he maintained—fell exactly into their proper places.[128] All the same, even if all the pieces were to fit brilliantly in one single pattern, that still does not guarantee the "truth" of that pattern: "The accepted truths of to-day are apt to become the discarded errors of to-morrow," as Dodds once put it.[129] The researcher is not to blame for this, and fortunately nobody seems to mind this horrible truth too much, for even those who agree with me that "all kinds of supposed influences" as a notion is, in point of fact, an absolutely viable and general factor in constructing cultural realities, cannot do without theory, pattern, or scheme if they want to get on with their research.

Bearing in mind the three dangers mentioned, let us now look at a specific theory in which—unlike the case of *libatio* and *pharmakos*, which remained practically entirely within the realm of the rite—our only information derives from a mythical story that, moreover, does not deal at all with a young man and has nonetheless been interpreted as a literary reflection of the ritual initiation scheme.

In a paper entitled "Heroes, Rituals and the Trojan War" (*Studi Storico-Religiosi* 2 [1987] 5–38), J. N. Bremmer[130] discusses a number of heroes who figure in the epics, concluding that the traditions "designate their protagonists as young men in the transition from boyhood to adulthood' (p. 35). When, in this context, Achilles, Pyrrhus/Neoptolemus, Philoctetes, and Paris are discussed, this will surprise nobody after what we remarked before, but there are already complications. Anyone who writes, "For our purpose we deduce from this interpretation that Achilles' arrival at Troy fell in the ephebic period of his life," must needs keep silence about the equally pseudohistoric context of the equally ephebic son of Achilles, Neoptolemus, who, from the historical point of view, cannot very well have arrived at Troy as an ephebe ten years later than his father. What should worry us much more, however, is the fact that the author includes in his list not only the young men mentioned but also Hector and Odysseus: Hector above all because of his special haircut, the *Hektoreios kome,* Odysseus on account of a number of elements in his history.[131] The fact that Odysseus, on whom we are going to focus from now on, was already a king and had a little son when he sailed from Ithaca may not be a decisive difficulty. All the same, it is apt to rouse the reader's suspicion. The author himself may have had some misgivings, too, witness the fact that, having started out to show that several heroes found themselves "in a transitional state," he finally concludes that all the heroes mentioned, including Odysseus, are described as young men in the transition from boyhood to adulthood (see quotation from p. 35 above), whereas, on page 23, he had inferred from Odysseus's tale that his was "an evident case of royal initiation," which, though doubtlessly related, is a different thing.[132]

What are the narrative elements that turn Odysseus into an ephebe in the initiatory period or, in other words, typify the narrative scheme of Odysseus's wanderings as the mythical reflection of initiation rites? Let me quote the author himself (p. 23): "What conclusion can we draw? It will be clear that we recognize an evident case of royal initiation in the tale of the prince, who has to leave home, wanders around, is present at cannibalistic activities, visits the underworld, has a wound in the thigh, is an archer, is sexually very active, returns as a beggar, restores the cultural order as a symbolic survivor of the Flood and finally becomes king." In support of this thesis a number of parallels had been listed before, showing, for instance, that cannibalistic performances, the notion of the primeval flood, sexual activities, and so forth are typical of the atmosphere of initiation and transitional rites. This is not enough, however, to dispel any doubts we may feel: the presumption that Odysseus is a typical archer is only evidenced by his shot through the axes, whereas everywhere else in the epic he is the adult warrior with the normal equipment; his leg wound is a *scar,* possibly a relic from his time as an ephebe, but only by way of a memento; and as for that sexual appetite, we are equally justified, or even more so, in maintaining that the texts depict Odysseus, despite his enforced contacts, as a faithful and above all married hero. There are many more details that call for some reservations,[133] but that is not what I am concerned with now.

The issue at stake is rather the essential dangers, as formulated above, inherent in the method. That the protagonist of the *Odyssey* finds himself in a Turneresque "transitional state" is, in the case of an adventurous wanderer, as yet no more than a tautology.[134] It is here, therefore, that the problem of the general applicability of the "marginality"concept reveals itself. Now the question arises if and how a more specific "transitional state" can be demonstrated. The argumentation needed to turn Odysseus into an initiation candidate has to be based entirely—because there is no ritual counterpart available and the protagonist, moreover, as a forty-year-old father, cannot very well be depicted as an ephebe—on a bunch of marginal signals, but such signals, in this case too, are practically without exception nonspecific (the second problem pointed out above). In the list of signals quoted above I can detect only one specific initiatory element: the scar on the thigh, but that, of all things, goes back *disertis verbis* to Odysseus's youth and is as such beyond the scope of the pseudohistorical narrative sequence the pattern is believed to be based on.[135] All the other signals that have been suggested, such as, notably, the elements of (man-eating) monsters and survival after a primeval flood—if we may interpret Odysseus's adventures at sea in this fashion at all—also fit smoothly into other schemes that are not necessarily initiatory. In point of fact, they are the stereotyped elements of this type of adventure story. There is a striking parallel in a debate between A. Henrichs and J. Winkler.[136] The former, basing himself on, among other things, cannibalistic elements in a recently discovered Lollianus fragment, discovers a ritual background in the context of secret cult societies, whereas the latter shows in detail that all the elements belonged to the stock in trade of classic fiction. There is some affinity between Henrich's approach and that of R. Merkelbach,[137] who defended the theory that virtually all remaining classical novels are based on some initiation pattern, but this time initiation into the Hellenistic mysteries. Everything fits perfectly: "This book only [!] intends to prove that the novels are really mystery texts" (from the preface).

This discussion is fully comparable and endless, because the thesis is, at best, plausible but incapable of proof. It could not be proven until an immediate ritual counterpart went with it, the signals pointed specifically to one type of ritual, or the story could solely and exclusively be interpreted as the reflection of this specific (and not of any other) ritual. That this is not the case as far as the *Odyssey* is concerned is a fact for which, in the nature of things, we cannot blame the interpreter, who is, in fact, fully entitled to give a maximalist interpretation with the help of his key. He has this right above all because elsewhere and under more favorable conditions he has drawn attention to initiatory elements in later myth or rite more convincingly. Nonetheless, the reader has the right to assess each interpretation critically; I, for one, tend to shy away from reducing the *Odyssey* to an initiatory scheme in such a drastic and rather mechanistic way for two reasons.

The first reason is that this would mean squeezing a great number of elements into one straitjacket, whereas we have a wider and more natural interpretive model at our disposal.[138] Nobody, however, should accept this critical remark without having read the article itself, in which more arguments are advanced than those briefly quoted here—the wooden horse as the hobbyhorse of initiation rites, for instance. The second reason is that by following this course we might be tempted (once again) to reduce mechanically all myths of this genre from the whole world to one relatively narrow ritual scheme. "It would be possible, and indeed easy, to find parallels in myth and ritual for every incident in the *Odyssey*," says Lord Raglan in *The Hero*, referring to sacral kingship. The upshot of such statements and their underlying arguments has been that practically nobody believes in his theory any more. An identical kind of reasoning is now applied to the *Odyssey* and initiation, and now, too, everything always seem to tally. Here, as an illustration, is my contribution: Penelope is a girl in the initiatory phase. As we know, in this period girls are generally locked up in secret rooms to practice, *by night,* women's handicrafts (spinning in the first place). Mythical relics of aggressive men bursting in upon women and destroying their handwork are known from various cultures, prenuptial licence occurring as well in this context: the girls are assaulted and have to give in.[139] Q. E. D. In the same way, however, it might be proved that Alexander the Great is a super initiation candidate: young, unmarried, adventurous journey in far-off lands, homosexual appetite, war, danger, victory, (mass) marriage. And it would be even more perfect if we were allowed to include the Alexander romances with their fairy-tale elements.

Meanwhile a problem comes into view. How *are* we to explain that an "*Odyssey* pattern" shows itself in so many myths, fairy tales, and stories if we are not prepared to trace this pattern invariably back either to the New Year complex or to the initiation complex or even to any ritual whatsoever? In order to look for a tentative answer to this question we now turn to Walter Burkert for the second time. It is he who can guide us, by way of an approach we have not yet discussed.

EPPURE SI MUOVE: MYTH AND RITUAL PARI PASSU

In 1970 Burkert published a paper entitled "Iason, Hypsipyle and New Fire at Lemnos: A Study in Myth and Ritual" (CQ 20 [1970] 1–16). Kirk's critical studies had not yet appeared at the time, but monolithic myth and ritual theories had already been sufficiently subjected to criticism. Burkert, too, conceded wholeheartedly that there exist myths without a rite, and rites without a myth, that we know of etiological myths of the tritest variety, and that it is out of the question, therefore, that myth should always be connected with ritual. Still, there exist complexes—such as the Arrhephoria complex he had discussed before—in which the connection is so close that the observer feels spurred on to consider the matter afresh. One such complex is that of the women of Lemnos.[140] According to myth, Aphrodite inflicted them with an unbearable stench as punishment for some offense. The result was that their husbands refused to have intercourse with them and took Thracian girls as concubines. Not a little vexed at this behavior, the women—all except one—murdered the men in their immediate surroundings. The Argonauts put in at the island on their return voyage and having met nothing much but dragons for some time restored order: thereafter the demographic balance was set right again. The ritual orders all Lemnian fires to be extinguished once a year; during the period of nine days without fire, offerings are to be made to subterranean gods, after which new fire is to be brought by ship from Delos and all fires may be lit again.

A brief note in a later gloss links myth and rite emphatically: once a year the women of Lemnos are said to keep men off by chewing garlic. This is a striking parallel indeed, and the "message" is clear in both: lack of fire means disorganization of social life (no hearth fire, no bread, no work for blacksmiths and potters, no burnt offerings and, therefore, no communication with the gods); it is a period of standstill and stagnation, typical of the transition to the New Year, and the myth represents this sterile, asocial aspect in its own way. In both myth and ritual there is an atmosphere of menace and death.

How are we to explain this parallelism (which even Kirk[141] was later prepared to acknowledge)? What came first, myth or ritual? Burkert refuses to answer this question, since in his words, it "transcends philology, since both myth and ritual were established well before the invention of writing" (p. 14). In his conclusion, though, he hints more than once that myth and ritual, in the final analysis, derive from one single origin, for instance when he maintains that myth may *become* independent of ritual (p. 14) or when he stresses the importance of myths for the reconstruction of rites: "Myth, being the plot, may indicate connections between rites which are isolated in our tradition" (p. 14). Anyway, rite is considered a necessary means of communication and solidarity within a social group. Feigned fear and aggression may prevent real disaster. Myth, however, does the same with different means. Here, too, the theme is menace and death, but now the victims are human beings, whereas the ritual confines itself to animals: "only the myth carries, in phantasy, to the extreme what, by ritual, is conducted into more innocent channels" (p. 16).[142] This is a theme Burkert has elaborated in a fascinating way in his theory of the origin of tragedy, which I am not going to discuss here.[143]

At the same time and above all we recognize here guarded, tentative phrases that immediately remind us of Harrison's second myth and ritual relationship—"they arise *pari passu*"—notably in the shape it was given by some of the anthropologists quoted above, Kluckhohn above all. This impression is confirmed when we turn to Burkert's "Griechische Mythologie und die Geistesgeschichte der Moderne," a treatise published in 1980,[144] and find that with regard to the myth and ritual relationship Harrison and the anthropologists are quoted emphatically and with approval, criticism is relegated to a footnote, and Kirk—in this connection, that is—is not even mentioned. It is a succinct, albeit extremely scholarly and informative survey, and the reader has the feeling that the author has more to say. He did so indeed in the 1977 Sather lectures mentioned above, which were published in 1979 and came on the market more or less simultaneously with this treatise. Here for the first time the essence of myth and the essence of rite were investigated and described in a way that had not been pursued in this context ever before.

In dealing with myth Burkert takes as a starting point the structural approach to the fairy tale narrative inaugurated by V. Propp and simplified and transformed later by others.[145] According to Propp, all Russian fairy tales of a certain category were found to consist of sequences of thirty-one elements (functions, motifemes), a number that strikes us as sufficiently arbitrary to have been discovered, not imposed.[146] In point of fact A. Dundes, in his introduction to the latest edition, points out that Propp follows an empirical, inductive method (which Dundes calls syntagmatic) that stands in stark contrast to the speculative, deductive (paradigmatic) approach of the structuralist *par excellence* Claude Lévi-Strauss. Whereas the latter starts from hypothetical polar oppositions,

trying to place everything within this structure, Propp simply describes
the *linear* order of narrative elements he perceives again and again. The
final twenty elements of Propp's collection have been summed up by
Burkert as follows: there is an instruction, a task, to go in search of
something (something lost) and to get it; the hero gathers relevant information, decides to set out upon the quest, starts on his way, meets with
others, either helpers or enemies; there is a change of scenery; the object
is found and taken possession of by force or by cunning; it is brought
back, the hero being chased by the adversary; success is there; the hero
comes off triumphant.

It is this linear aspect in particular that strongly appeals to Burkert,
who has no use for Lévi-Strauss's algebra[147] and, therefore, does not
show any appreciable affinity with the approaches of Vernant or Detienne either. Numerous other schemes have already been suggested as
an organizational principle of fairy tales and the like,[148] but none as
short as Burkert's proposal. In point of fact Propp's entire scheme may
be summarized in one verb: "to get." What have we got, after all? Nothing but a program of action, elaborated into a narrative and varied
through a number of transformations—a program derived directly
from life, from biology. For what the hero does in Propp's schema is
essentially similar to what the rat does when—driven by hunger—it
goes in search of prey and returns with the spoils, having escaped the
street urchin's stones, the cat's jaws, and envious fellow rats. The identical pattern may be transposed to the world of the primates in that
stage in which food could only be obtained by way of long marches,
hunting, or gathering, which involved the most horrible dangers outside
the relative safety of the settlement. It is not possible, even approximately, to do justice to the very scholarly discourse, which shows a definite receptiveness to the new doctrine of sociobiology. I note the conclusion: "Tale structures, as sequences of motifemes, are founded on basic
biological or cultural programs of action" (p. 18).

This is only the first chapter. The second deals with ritual. Here Burkert has already been preceded by several others on the road that he
wants to take himself and that proves to lead to biology once more.
From other scholars, ranging from Julian Huxley to Konrad Lorenz,[149]
he borrows the definition of ritual: "Ritual is action redirected for demonstration." With many animal species living socially it has been found
that certain types of group behavior possessed an evidently biological
function originally, but became detached from their origin and acquired
a new function: that of a communication signal, the effect of which is
binding on the group.[150] These ritual acts are highly stereotyped,
repeated[151] and exaggerated, often manifested in theatrical and dra-

matic forms, and preeminently social actions. K. Meuli[152] had already
observed that with humans, too, ritual behavior might become divorced
from its original roots and acquire some new function fostering solidarity, such as mourning behavior. Sociologists and anthropologists in their
turn have said repeatedly and in various contexts that the integration of
the group is maintained primarily by ritual means.

A great number of ritual customs are interpreted by Burkert as ritualized, therefore stereotyped and "degenerate" biological actions. We
knew that the Olympian sacrifice should be understood as a relic from
palaeolithic hunting customs,[153] but it may come as a surprise to many
a reader to learn that the ritual of pouring out oil on to a sacred stone
derives, in the final analysis, from the canine habit of demarcating territory. Whether such detailed interpretations are convincing or not,
what is interesting is the consequences of these two views for myth and
ritual.

If we consider them in the light of Burkert's recent theories, we will
soon notice that we are dealing with a single phenomenon with two
aspects: both are "programs of action," both have a biological background involving transformations of action patterns bearing immediately upon the most essential needs, crises, and dilemmas of both animal
and primitive human existence, both have become detached from their
origins, both now primarily serve communication and solidarization.
Myth is the verbal expression, rite a reflection in action, of essentially
identical situations and their inherent psychic emotions. For the first
time an impressive attempt has been made to underpin Harrison's second option theoretically. There are myths and rites that are so closely
connected that many of us had already been under the impression that
these, at any rate, must have originated simultaneously. This is by no
means true of all myths and rites, and it may even hold only for a small
minority. But where there *is* such a plausible connection we now have at
least a soundly based theory as to roughly how this parallelism might
have arisen.

PROSPECTS

So far I have essentially done no more than arrange, describe, and to
a lesser degree, evaluate. The fact that the critical aspect was emphasized more forcibly in the latter part of the discussion may be explained
by the fact that the first phase of the myth and ritual theory had long
been concluded and assessed, whereas the most recent approach is still
in full swing. That is why critical observations can certainly be useful,
but never definitive. I do not want to conclude, however, without once

more gathering in the lines we have observed so far. The resultant synthesis may no doubt strike the reader as sweeping. To make matters worse, lack of space prevents me from arguing more specifically or illustrating it in greater detail with the help of an extended case such as I have published elsewhere.[154] What I have to offer is thus nothing but a tentative, somewhat intuitive suggestion that enables me to return to those complexes that up to now have been felt, more often than not, to be mutually exclusive: the myth and ritual complex of the New Year–sacral king–dying and rising god, on the one hand, and that of initiation, on the other, in order to view them from the perspective offered by Burkert.

Let us concentrate exclusively on the two complexes we have discussed—we might conceive of others, but not many nor such easily recognizable ones—and consider the following questions:

What might be the reason that in the head of one person, Jane Harrison, the notions of two complexes could exist one after or beside the other, the divine protagonists changing effortlessly from one complex into the next (*Megistos Kouros,* Dionysus)?

How can we explain that some enthusiasts trace back the entire world wide mythology to one myth and ritual complex, whereas others reduce a considerable number of myths to the other complex?

How is it that some New Year specialists time and again point out resemblance, affinity, or relation with initiation ideology, and initiation specialists are repeatedly drawing parallels with New Year elements?[155]

What do we infer from the fact that a myth and ritual theorist of the old stamp, A. M. Hocart, wrote a book about coronation rites of kings, whereas a representative of the recent trend is seen to waver between boys' initiation and royal initiation?

Why is it that both types of approach claim primeval images like the flood[156] and man-eating monsters,[157] besides numerous other elements such as role and status reversal, experience of anarchy, and so forth, for their own complex?

How is one to explain that both can refer to worldwide materials? Finally, how is it that so much attention was and still is paid to these two myth and ritual patterns and relatively little, if any, to others?

Now let us just give specific form to these questions once more. In the sequence of the epic of the *Odyssey* and the story of Troy connected with it, the hero leaves his country, has to wander, to wage war far from home, takes Troy by means of a stratagem, is threatened by water (sea), by man-eating and other monsters, returns home, is menaced again, is finally triumphant, and becomes king (again).

If we had been obligated to decide, after reading the second section of this paper, which pattern had been transformed into a myth in this case, would not the New Year pattern of fall and return of the sacral king and the battling god have been the obvious choice? It was this choice that was made long ago by Raglan (and others); witness the way he manages to fit all details into his pattern. And if we had been asked the same question after reading section five, would we not have hesitated to answer the question, because the story, when we come to think of it, fits very well into the initiatory scheme as well?

Meanwhile, the reason for all this has become abundantly clear, and so the questions asked above have been essentially answered. Both situations, that of the New Year and that of initiation, have a firmly related ritual and social function and follow, in essence, identical basic patterns: the old situation has to be taken leave of (symbol of death, fall, farewell: the *séparation*); there is a period of transition between old and new (sojourn in death, underworld, labyrinth, flood, foreign countries, a monster's belly: the *marge*); the new situation is accepted (rebirth, resurrection, reinvestiture, return and reintegration: the *agrégation*). That one complex shows associations with a process of nature, the other with a social passage, is not immediately relevant. What matters is the relationship in the typically transitional situations and the mythical symbols in which they find their expression.

This argument has its starting point in the similarity of the two myth and ritual complexes. While the old one seemed outdated, the new one is not as new as it seems. Burkert's most recent work has not yet been taken account of in the discussion. So let us now take the ultimate step: suppose we had not been asked the question about the interpretation of the Odysseus story until after reading section six. Would we not be inclined to class it under the head of Propp's narrative structure and—as the next step—to consider, with Burkert, whether the story reveals references to deep-rooted biological and cultural schemes of action? If one checks it, everything fits. That would mean that we have reached a deeper level of interpretation, which supports and envelops the two other levels. We might conceive of it in this way: the most elementary and primordial scheme of (originally biosociological) functions has been conserved and transformed, in ritualized and mythicized form, at precisely those points where human society still experiences primal crisis most intensely. Apart from incidental calamities like epidemics, wars, earthquakes, and floods, these are precisely the critical and painful moments of transition that are experienced nowhere more keenly than during initiatory periods and the advent of the New Year. In this way the structural relationship between these two "crises" and their mythical-ritual representation is now placed in an historical evolutionary per-

spective. This seems to be implied in Burkert's clearly evolved view.[158]
The author of "Kekropidensage und Arrhephoria: Vom Initiationsritus
zum Panathenäenfest" now writes (1979, p. 57): "The pattern called
'the girl's tragedy' *can* [my italics] be interpreted as reflecting initiation
rituals; but these, in turn, are demonstrative accentuations of biologically programed crises, menstruation, defloration, pregnancy, birth."
Odysseus and the Cyclops no longer have anything to do with initiation.
Instead, they are related to very remote reminiscences from even palaeolithic action patterns (cf. the lance tempered in the fire). When Burkert
discusses phenomena of role reversal and sexual submission (pp. 29–
30), initiation is found to play only a marginal role in the predominantly
biologically oriented argument (apes also offer themselves in an act of
submission).[159]

No doubt not everybody who *is* perhaps prepared to acknowledge
the structural affinity of the two complexes is willing to take this ultimate step. After all, it is nothing but a suggestion. Still, there are reasons
why it deserves serious consideration. In a book that has come in for a
good deal of discussion, *The Hero with a Thousand Faces* (New York,
1949, London, 1975²), J. Campbell deals with a mythical complex, "the
adventure of the hero," whose structure he outlines as follows: (1) departure, (2) initiation, (3) return. This is a familiar scheme by now, but
what is interesting is that Campbell proceeds totally independently of
the scholars referred to above. He interprets the entire scheme with the
help of Freud and Jung above all in terms of depth psychology, citing
material from dreams. How these images get into our dreams is not
explained, at least not explicitly, and here the recent movement of sociobiology, despite the criticisms it has received might well be revelatory.[160]

As regards our two myth and ritual complexes we thus find that what
is sauce for the goose is sauce for the gander, probably owing to the fact
that both sauces are prepared by the same cook, who works with only
one recipe. His "biodynamic" recipe can be summarized in the verb "to
get." In a given situation, this simple verb is qualified by a number of
indispensable, successive actions that are also reflected in our two complexes *and* in fairy tales and myths of the *Odyssey* type. Equating the
sauces of goose and gander does *not* disqualify either of them. Nor does
it entail a depreciation of the remarkable progress made in our field
through the recent shift in our model of interpretation, as I hope to have
made abundantly clear. While in the natural sciences some implications
of Kuhn's concept of "paradigm" are liable to criticism,[161] the concept
has proved helpful in analyzing developments in the social sciences.
However, it has been pointed out recently that in this sector paradigms
are, as a rule, not radically exclusive. This tolerance has awarded an-

thropology the qualification, "polyparadigmatic." [162] And this is exactly my point.

Though the new paradigm introducing the social interpretation of myth and ritual has cleared the way for explanations that were unheard of in the first half of this century—I am especially referring to the application of the concept of the "margin," both in the rites of initiation and in the festivals of reversal—the new model by no means completely eradicates or replaces the old one. First, I would not (and did not) deny that the presence of the two patterns described by the myth and ritual theorists can actually be demonstrated. What I oppose is the totalitarian, one-sided interpretation of such mythical patterns from the point of view of just one of the complexes. Secondly, I do not doubt that there are myths that, in the final analysis, go back to some New Year scenario, nor that there are myths that derive from initiatory schemes. However, I think it unlikely that all the stories with the scenario described above have developed in either one of these ways. Anyone who goes to such lengths, while still acknowledging that everywhere—in both complexes and in a great mass of myths, fairy tales, stories (and dreams) from all over the world—we can discern a more or less identical basis pattern, has the right if not the duty to try to find an explanation for this phenomenon. Perhaps this can be done without the help of recent ethological and biological insights, but it would be better to try to incorporate them. In any case—and that was my chief aim—this phenomenon explains why the champions of the two complexes have so often encroached upon each others' territories.

To return to the Odysseus story, I, for one, think that an origin in some New Year scenario is less plausible than a descent from some initiatory scenario. Much more plausible than either, though, is the interpretation of this story as a variation on the biological-cultural program of action, which may have been carried over into both complexes and which, *independently,* has become the material from which dreams, fairy tales, and myths of a certain type have been fashioned. Of course, whoever thinks all this much too vague and prefers to sit down and reread the *Odyssey* itself is right, too.

In *The Golden Bough* IV (1914, p. vii), Frazer signs: "The longer I occupy myself with questions of ancient mythology, the more diffident I become of success in dealing with them, and I am apt to think that we who spend our years in searching for solutions of these insoluble problems are like Sisyphus perpetually rolling his stone uphill only to see it revolve again into the valley."

This is a pessimistic expression of what I found more hopefully phrased by the anthropologist E. M. Ackerknecht:[163] "If anthropology returns to the comparative method" [and as we have seen, recent developments in the borderland of anthropology and the classics tend in that direction], "it will certainly not forget what it has learned meanwhile in general and what it has learned about the limitations of the method in particular. It will return only in that spiral movement, so characteristic of scientific thought, *arriving after half a century at the same point but at a higher level*. It will know better how and what to compare than it knew fifty years ago."

Sisyphus's stone rolling but landing at a higher level each time? Let us hope so, even if the stone turns out to obey Zeno's laws.[164]

NOTES

a. But cf. Versnel's n. 31, below.

b. Fontenrose 1966.

c. In spite of Dodds's *The Greeks and the Irrational* (1951), which was dedicated to Gilbert Murray. For surveys of anthropological work in classics, see Wyatt and Allen 1988 and Humphreys 1978, 17–30.

d. For a survey of the scholarship in the last two decades or so, see Foley 1985, 24–56.

e. Harrison 1927, 260.

f. Harrison 1927, 341–63.

g. Harrison 1927, 343.

h. Burkert 1966a.

i. Burkert 1972.

j. Burkert 1979, in a masterful survey of research on Greek mythology since the turn of the century, modestly limits the discussion of his own contributions to a sentence or two.

k. Meuli 1946. (Burkert 1979 barely mentions Meuli, but the debt is fully acknowledged in Burkert 1966a, 105–6.)

l. On this school see Humphreys 1978, 94–106.

m. Harrison 1927, 20.

n. See the citation in Versnel below.

o. Translation in Vidal-Naquet 1986.

p. See the citation in Versnel below.

q. Gernet 1928. Also the work by Dumézil cited by Versnel.

r. Humphreys 1978, 81.

s. The work of Henri Hubert and Marcel Mauss on sacrifice was also translated in the 1960s: Hubert and Mauss 1964.

1. This is only a selection of titles on the theory of myth and ritual (for literature on specific myth and ritual complexes see below n. 15ff. and n. 32ff.): C. Kluckhohn, "Myths and Rituals. A General Theory," *HThR* 35 (1942) 45–79, reprinted in J. B. Vickery, ed., *Myth and Literature* (Lincoln, NE 1969) 33–44; L. Raglan, "Myth and Ritual," and S. E. Hyman, "The Ritual View of Myth and the Mythic," both in Sebeok 1974, 122–35,136–53; W. Bascom, "The Myth-Ritual Theory," *Journal of American Folklore.* 70 (1957) 103–14; Philip M. Kaberry, "Myth and Ritual: Some

Recent Theories," *BICS* 4 (1957) 42–53; Fontenrose 1966; H. H. Penner, "Myth and Ritual: A Wasteland or a Forest of Symbols?" *H&T* Beiheft 8 (1968) 46–57; R. A Segal, "The Myth-Ritualist Theory of Religion," *Journal of the Scientific Study of Religion* 19 (1980) 173–85. Also important are the relevant passages in Kirk 1971, 8–31; Kirk 1974, 66–68, 223–53; Burkert 1979, 34–39, 56–58; Burkert 1980, 172–82; F. Graf, *Griechische Mythologie* (Munich-Zurich 1985) 43–57. Not all publications are of equal value. The article by Kaberry, for instance, is insignificant; both Penner and Segal fail to draw the necessary distinctions between the theories of Harrison and Hooke. In the otherwise important article by Segal one reads: "According to myth and ritualist theory religion is primitive science," which is, as a general rule, quite mistaken.

2. On this *"heros ktistes* ['founding hero'] der modernen Religionswissenschaft" (thus his son-in-law, A. Dieterich, in *Archiv für Religionswissenschaft* 8 (1905) p. x); see: *Aspetti di Hermann Usener filologo della religione,* Seminario della Scuola Normale Superiore di Pisa (Pisa 1982).

3. There is a bibliography of this "founding father" of the German *religionsgeschichtliche* school in his *Kleine Schriften* (Leipzig-Berlin 1911) 11–42.

4. M. P. Nilsson, *Geschichte der griechischen Religion* I (Munich 1967³, 1940¹), II (Munich 1961², 1950¹). A bibliography of Nilsson's works: E. J. Knudtson, "Beiträge zu einer Bibliographie Martin P. Nilsson," in *Dragma: Festschrift M. P. Nilsson* (Lund 1939) 571–656, reprinted in *Scripta Minora* (Lund 1968) 29–116; C. Callmer, "The Published Writings of Prof. M. P. Nilsson 1939–1967," ibid. 117–39. Cf. Waardenburg 1974, 191–97. Biographical sketches and evaluations of his works are given by E. Gjerstad, "M. P. Nilsson *in memoriam,*" *Scripta Minora* (1967–68) 17–28; C.-M. Edsman, "Martin P. Nilsson 1874–1967," *Temenos* 3 (1968) 173–76; McGinty 1978, 104–40.

5. Thus A. D. Nock, who was honored by his fellow students with the proud title of "the greatest living authority on Pauly-Wissowa," and who was lauded by Nilsson (*GGR* Vorwort) as "der bewährteste Kenner der spätantiken Religion." For an epistolary contact between the two giants see: M. P. Nilsson, "Letter to Professor A. D. Nock," *HThR* 42 (1949) 71–107; 44 (1951) 143–51. There is a bibliography in A. D. Nock, *Essays on Religion and the Ancient World* I, II, ed. Z. Stewart (Oxford 1972) 966–86.

6. B. Lincoln, "Two Notes on Modern Rituals," *Journal of the American Academy of Religion* 45 (1977) 149.

7. A discussion of Kerényi and Dumézil would be beyond the scope of the present article. For M. Eliade see: J. A. Saliba, *'Homo Religiosus' in Mircea Eliade. An Anthropological Evaluation* (Leiden 1976) and I. P. Culianu, *Mircea Eliade* (Assisi 1978). Critical views in: G. Dudley, *Religion on Trial: Mircea Eliade and his Critics* (Philadelphia 1977); L. Alfieri, *Storia e mito. Una critica a Eliade* (Pisa 1978). Cf. Smith 1978, 88ff. Eliade phrases his own preference for myth above rite ("Methodological Remarks on the Study of Religion," in M. Eliade and J. Kitagawa, eds., *The History of Religions* [Chicago 1959], 86–107) as follows: "Symbol and myth will give a clear view of the modalities (of the sacred) that a rite can never do more than suggest." I do not discuss the representatives of the Paris structuralist school, not because their work is of no interest for the study of myths and rituals, but because whenever they try to bring them into a cohesive pattern, they practically never do so

in the usual sense of "myth and ritual." R. L. Gordon, ed., *Myth, Religion and Society. Structuralist Essays by M. Detienne, L. Gernet, J.-P. Vernant and P. Vidal-Naquet* (Cambridge 1981), offers an excellent introduction to their ideas.

8. J. H. Voigt, *Max Müller. The Man and his Ideas* (Calcutta 1976.) Shorter studies: R. M. Dorson, "The Eclipse of Solar Mythology," in Sebeok 1974, 25–63; Van Baal 1971, 20–26; Sharpe 1975, 35–46; Burkert 1980, 166, Cf. also F. M. Turner, *The Greek Heritage in Victorian Britain* (New Haven, CT 1981) 77–134 on "Greek Mythology and Religion" in this period.

9. W. Mannhardt, *Roggenwolf und Roggenhund* (Danzig 1865–66); *Die Korndämonen* (Berlin 1868); *Antike Wald- und Feldkulte* (Berlin 1875–77, Darmstadt 1904–5²); *Mythologische Forschungen* (Strassburg 1884). On his work and influence see Frazer *GB* I, pp. xii-xiii; De Vries 1961, 212–16; Waardenburg 1974, 173.

10. E. B. Tylor, *Primitive Culture* (London 1871). An assessment of his work. Kardiner and Preble 1962, 56–77; F. Gölz, *Der primitive Mensch und seine Religion* (Gütersloh, FRG 1963) 12–40; Van Baal 1971, 30–44; Waardenburg 1974, 288–89; Sharpe 1975, 53–58; U. Bianchi, *The History of Religions* (Leiden 1975) 83–86; Evans-Pritchard 1981, 91–94. Recently, there is a revival of interest in Tylor's evolutionism and its background. See for instance: G. W. Stocking Jr., "Matthew Arnold, E. B. Tylor and the Uses of Invention," *American Anthropologist* 65 (1963) 783–99; M. Opler, "Cause, Process, and Dynamics in the Evolutionism of E. B. Tylor," *South-Western Journal of Anthropology* 20 (1964) 123–44; J. W. Burrow, *Evolution and Society: A Study in Victorian Social Theory* (London 1970²) 228–59. Cf. Smith 1978, 261, n. 58.

11. G. Himmelfarb, *Darwin and the Darwinian Revolution* (London 1959). Interesting on the social and mental context: J. W. Burrow (note 10 above); D. F. Bratchell, *The Impact of Darwinism. Texts and Commentary Illustrating 19th century Religious, Scientific and Literary Attitudes* (Amersham, UK 1981) and R. J. Richards, *Darwin and the Emergence of Evolutionary Theories of Mind and Behavior* (Chicago 1987). A full biography: P. Brent, *Charles Darwin* (London 1981, Feltham 1983²).

12. F. R. Lehmann, "Der Begriff 'Urdummheit' in der ethnologischen und religionswissenschaftlichen Anschauungen von K.-T. Preuss, A. E. Jensen und G. Murray," *Sociologus* 2 (1952) 131–45.

13. W. Robertson Smith, *Lectures on the Religion of the Semites* (Edinburgh 1889, 1894²). The German translation *Die Religion der Semiten* (Tübingen 1899) was reprinted in 1967. Biographical surveys: J. S. Black and G. Chrystal, *The Life of William Robertson Smith* (London 1912); T. O. Beidelmann, *William Robertson Smith* (Chicago 1974). Cf. also: Van Baal 1971, 45–53; Waardenburg 1974, 265; Evans-Pritchard 1981, 69–81. Mary Douglas, *Purity and Danger* (Harmondsworth, UK 1970) 25: "Robertson Smith founded social anthropology."

14. "But for Smith," said Frazer, "my interest in the subject [anthropology] might have remained purely passive and inert" (quoted by Kardiner and Preble 1962, 82).

15. Frazer 1890–1915. An abridged edition appeared in 1922 = New York 1950. Other revisions and abridged editions: Theodor Gaster, ed., *The New Golden Bough* (New York 1959); M. Douglas and S. MacCormack, eds., *J. G. Frazer. The Illustrated Golden Bough: A Study in Magic and Religion* (London 1978). Biographical works: R. A. Downie, *James George Frazer. The Portrait of a Scholar* (London

1940); idem, *Frazer and the Golden Bough* (London 1970). They are all superseded by R. Ackerman, *J. G. Frazer: His Life and Work* (Cambridge 1987). Cf. also: Kardiner and Preble 1962, 78–109; Sharpe 1975, 87–94; Evans-Pritchard 1981, 132–52. A comprehensive list of works on Frazer: Waardenburg 1974, 59–60. A critical account: M. J. C. Hodgart, "In the Shadow of the Golden Bough," *The Twentieth Century* 97 (1955) 111–19; S. MacCormack, "Magic and the Human Mind: A Reconsideration of Frazer's *Golden Bough*," *Arethusa* 17 (1984) 151–76. For more criticism see below section 4.

16. Autobiographical data in her books *Reminiscenses of a Student's Life* (London 1925) and *Alpha and Omega. Essays* (London 1915). Biographical information: *Folk-Lore* 37 (1926) 180–92; J. G. Stewart, *Jane Ellen Harrison. A Portrait from Letters* (London 1959) with a full bibliography; R. Ackerman, "J. E. Harrison: The Early Work," *GRBS* 13 (1972) 209–30; McGinty 1978, 71–103; S. J. Peacock, *Jane Harrison: The Mask and the Self* (New Haven 1988).

17. In a letter to G. Murray in Stewart (note 16 above) 113.

18. *Prolegomena* (1903, 1907[2], 1922[3]), reprinted New York 1955 and London 1961, recently also by La Haule Press. *Themis: A Study in the Social Origins of Greek Religion* (1912[1], 1927[2]), reprinted together with *Epilegomena* by University Books (New York 1962) and Merlin Press (London 1963).

19. In *Epilegomena to the Study of Greek Religion* (Cambridge 1921) p.xxii, she formulates her own scientific achievements thus: (1) Totem, Tabu and Exogamy, (2) Initiation Ceremony, (3) The Medicine-Man and King-God, (4) The Fertility-Play or Year Drama. This is precisely the reverse order of her *Werdegang* from Frazer via "the genius of Durkheim" (ibid., n. 1) toward Freud. McGinty 1978, 79: "As a result, to read her oeuvre in chronological order is almost like reading a multivolume history of the discipline of comparative religion disguised as a series of histories of Greek religion" (and cf. his note 35 on p. 213).

20. McGinty 1978, 96. W. J. Verdenius, in his review of *Epilegomena* and *Themis, Mnemosyne* 4th ser. 16 (1963) 434: "Her principal weakness was the susceptibility which induced her to adopt the latest fashion in philosophy, psychology and ethnology."

21. *JHS* 12 (1891) 350. Actually, this refers to her interpretation of the Kekropides myth, which she was the first to explain from the perspective of myth and ritual. However, Burkert 1980, 174, points out that previous initiatives in this direction had already been taken by C. O. Müller and Wilamowitz.

22. Humphreys 1978, 96, suggests that her attention was drawn to Durkheim by the lectures of Radcliffe-Brown, which she attended at Cambridge in 1909. Humphreys also gives a good assessment of Durkheim's work. See also: Harris 1968, 464–82; S. Lukes, *Emile Durkheim. His Life and Work* (London 1973[1], Harmondsworth, UK 1975); Kardiner and Preble 1962, 108–33; Evans-Pritchard 1981, 153–69. The remarkable similarity appears *inter alia* from the following quotations from Durkheim, *Les formes élémentaires de la vie religieuse* (Paris 1912[1], 1968[5]) 597: "l'expérience religieuse, c'est la société"; 603: "la formation d'un idéal . . . c'est un produit naturel de la vie sociale"; 606: "la religion est un produit de causes sociales." On this aspect of Durkheim's theory see R. N. Bellah, "Religion, Collective Representations and Social Change," in R. A. Nisbet, ed., *Emile Durkheim* (Englewood

Cliffs, NJ 1965) 166–72. On Durkheim's influence on Radcliffe-Brown see Kuper 1985, 49ff.

23. Harrison herself recognized this evolution: "Primitive religion was not, as I had drifted into thinking, a tissue of errors leading to mistaken conduct; rather it was a web of practices emphasizing particular parts of life, issuing necessarily in representations and ultimately dying out into abstract conceptions" (*Themis*, p. xii).

24. M. Guarducci, *Inscriptiones Creticae*, Vol. III, Sect. II, No. 2 (Rome 1935-). Cf. eadem, "Antichità Cretesi," in *Studi in onore di D. Levi* II (Catania, Italy 1974) 36f.; eadem, *Epigrafia Greca* IV (Rome 1978) 128f.

25. M. L. West, "The Dictaean Hymn to the Kouros," *JHS* 85 (1965) 149–59, proposed to replace Harrison's "Lord of all that is wet and gleaming, thou art *come*" by an interpretation that results in: "master of all, who to earth art gone." Later on he recanted his metrical suggestions while maintaining his textual conjectures (*ZPE* 45 [1982] 9ff.). West's reading, which completely ignores Harrison's treatment of the text, seems very improbable to me and has, as far as I know, not provoked much enthusiasm. See Guarducci (note 24 above) and J. M. Bremer, "Greek Hymns," in Versnel 1981, 205f. Cf. also A. Motte, *Prairies et jardins de la Grèce antique* (Brussels 1970) 56–60.

26. There are also historical Couretes: S. Luria, "Kureten, Molpen, Aisymneten," *AAntHung* 11 (1963) 31–36; D. Knibbe, *Forschungen in Ephesos* IX, Fasz. I, 1: Die Kureteninschriften (Österr. Arch. Inst. 1981).

27. For Murray's scholarly achievements see F. West, *Gilbert Murray: A Biography* (London 1984) and D. Wilson, *Gilbert Murray OM 1866–1957* (Oxford 1988). Murray returned to myth and ritual theories in other works: *Euripides and his Age* (New York 1913, Oxford 1946²) 28–32; *Aeschylus, the Creator of Tragedy* (Oxford 1940) 145–60. Criticism in A. W. Pickard-Cambridge, *Dithyramb, Tragedy and Comedy* (Oxford 1927) 185–206. In his re-edition of this book (1962) 126–29, T. B. L. Webster gives a reassessment of Murray's achievement. For other theories on the origin of tragedy, see: H. Patzer, *Die Anfänge der griechischen Tragödie* (Wiesbaden 1962); G. F. Else, *The Origin and Early Form of Greek Tragedy* (Cambridge, MA 1965). Recent theories on the ritual origins of tragedy: W. Burkert, "Greek Tragedy and Sacrificial Ritual," *GRBS* 7 (1966a) 87–121; F. R. Adrados, *Festival, Comedy and Tragedy. The Greek Origins of Theatre* (Leiden 1975); idem, "The Agon and the Origin of the Tragic Chorus," in *Serta Turyniana. Studies A. Turyn* (Urbana, IL 1974) 436–88; J. J. Winkler, "The Ephebes' Song: *Tragôidia* and *Polis*," *Representations* 11 (1985) 26–62.

28. *Four Stages of Greek Religion* originated as a series of lectures at Columbia University in 1912. It was published as *Five Stages of Greek Religion* (London 1935, 1946³).

29. Remarkably, the leading French structuralist in the classical field, J.-P. Vernant, highly appreciates the works of Cornford, whereas his mentor Louis Gernet, a pupil of Durkheim, had little or no appreciation for the works of Harrison and Cornford. See S. Humphreys, "The Work of Louis Gernet," in 1978, 76–106, and cf. on the scholar Gernet: A. Maffi, "Le 'Recherches' di Louis Gernet nella storia del diritto greco," *QS* 13 (1981) 3–54; C. Ampolo, "Fra religione e società," *StudStor* 25 (1984) 83–89.

30. H. Otten, "Vorderasiatische Mythen als Vorläufer griechischer Mythenbildung," *Forschungen und Fortschritte* (1949) 145–47; A. Heubeck, "Mythologische Vorstellungen des alten Orients im archaischen Griechentum," *Gymnasium* 62 (1955) 508–20; G. Steiner, *Der Sukzessionsmythos in Hesiods Theogonie und ihren orientalischen Parallelen* (Diss. Hamburg 1958); P. Walcot, *Hesiod and the Near East* (Cardiff 1966); M. L. West, *Early Greek Philosophy and the Orient* (Oxford 1971); Kirk 1971, 213–20; Burkert 1979, passim, and idem, "Die orientalisierende Epoche in der griechischen Religion und Literatur," *SHAW* (1984) 1–135.

31. I leave aside A. B. Cook with his massive monograph *Zeus* I–III (Cambridge 1914–42). He is perhaps the most typical disciple of Frazer, but he did not contribute to myth and ritual theory.

32. His earlier collection *The Labyrinth* (London 1935) has no bearing on the new ideas. Hooke's tryout was: "The Babylonian New Year Festival," *Journal of the Manchester Egyptological and Oriental Society* 13 (1927) 29–38. The most convenient introduction to his ideas is his *Middle Eastern Mythology* (Harmondsworth, UK 1963). On the scholar Hooke see E. C. Graham, *Nothing Is Here for Tears. A Memoir of S. H. Hooke* (Oxford 1969).

33. Several studies have been devoted to the Myth and Ritual school. In *Myth, Ritual and Kingship* (Oxford 1958), Hooke gives a historical survey of this approach, which he refuses to call a school. There is also a critical essay by S. G. F. Brandon in the same collection. Cf. also: J. Weingreen, "The Pattern Theory in Old Testament Studies," *Hermathena* 108 (1969) 5–13; E. O. James, *Myth and Ritual in the Ancient Near East* (London 1958); H. S. Versnel, *Triumphus* (Leiden 1970) 201–35; J. W. Rogerson, *Myth in Old Testament Interpretation* (Berlin 1973) 66–84; and literature in notes 76ff. below.

34. This festival figures in all myth and ritual studies. There is a very circumstantial treatment by S. A. Pallis, *The Babylonian Akîtu Festival* (Copenhagen 1926).

35. In two volumes of *The Golden Bough* (see note 15 above): *The Dying God*, 111; *The Scape Goat*, 354ff.

36. According to the famous expression coined by M. Eliade. He has certain connections with the myth and ritualists, for instance in his *Le mythe de l'éternel retour* (Paris 1949), Ch. 2; *Traité de l'histoire des religions* (Paris 1964²) 335ff.

37. E. D. van Buren, "The Sacred Marriage in Early Times in Mesopotamia," *Orientalia* 13 (1944) 2ff.; S. N. Kramer, "The Sumerian Sacred Marriage Texts," *PAPhs* 107 (1963) 485ff.; W. H. P. Römer, *Sumerische 'Königshymnen' der Isin Zeit* (Diss. Utrecht 1965).

38. There are ample commentaries by H. Zimmern, "Zum babylonischen Neujahrsfest," *Berichte der Sachsischen Gesellschaft der Wissenschaften* 70 (1918); F. Thureau-Dangin, *Rituels accadiens* (Paris 1921) 127ff. S. H. Langdon, *The Epic of Creation* (Oxford 1923) 20ff. provided another edition under the title "The Death and Resurrection of Bel-Marduk."

39. Most enthusiastically by K. I. A. Engnell, *Studies in Divine Kingship in the Ancient Near East* (Upsala 1943) and G. Widengren, *Sakrales Königtum im Alten Testament und im Judentum* (Stuttgart 1955).

40. This is the most conventional—and convenient—escape for desperate defenders of a pattern, exploited by Murray as well as by the "Pan-myth and ritualists" (see below).

41. S. Mowinckel, *Psalmenstudien* I–IV (1922–24), II: *Das Thronsbesteigungsfest Jahwähs und der Ursprung der Eschatologie.*

42. S. A. Hooke gave one of his books, *Alpha and Omega. A Study in the Pattern of Revelation* (Welwyn, UK 1961), the same title as the one Jane Harrison had chosen for one of her books. In the collections, however, there is hardly any reference to the Cambridge school.

43. Frazer later distanced himself from the Cambridge movement, as is evident from his correspondence with Marett, in which he also belittles the influence of Robertson Smith. See R. Ackerman, "Frazer on Myth and Ritual," *JHI* 36 (1975) 115–34.

44. McGinty 1978, 79: "Harrison depended so heavily on evolutionism that, the general theory of evolution of primitive religion having been overturned, her analysis has lost most if not all of its cogency."

45. G. Elliot Smith, *The Ancient Egyptians and the Origins of Civilisation* (London 1911, 1923²); *Human History* (London 1930); W. J. Perry, *The Children of the Sun: A Study in the Early History of Civilization* (London 1923); *The Growth of Civilization* (London 1924). See A. J. Toynbee, *A Study of History* I (London 1955) 424–46.

46. On astral mythology in Old Testament and related studies: J. W. Rogerson (note 33 above) 45–84.

47. To quote from another collection, *The Siege Perilous* (London 1956) 43: "the ritual myth which is magical in character, and inseparable from the ritual . . . is older than the aetiological myth which has no magical potency."

48. That this order does indeed occur can be documented by the coronation ritual of the Japanese emperor, in which what happened *in illo tempore* is imitated in a ritual form: M. Waida, "Conceptions of State and Kingship in Early Japan," *ZRGG* 28 (1976) 97–112. M. Eliade has unequivocally opted for this view of the relationship between myth and ritual. A. E. Jensen, *Mythos und Kult bei Naturvölkern* (Wiesbaden 1951), translated as *Myth and Cult among Primitive Peoples* (Chicago 1963), gives precedence to myth as well. However, his definition of myth is so broad that it practically covers the concept "content of belief."

49. A. Jeremias, *Handbuch der altorientalischen Geisteskultur* (Leipzig 1929²) 171. His "catechism," *Die Panbabylonisten, der alte Orient und die Aegyptische Religion* (Leipzig 1907), is still worth reading.

50. A survey of the themes discussed in this section minus the anthropological data is given by S. E. Hyman (see note 1 above).

51. *Hamlet and Orestes. The Annual Shakespeare Lecture before the British Academy* (1914).

52. This contribution is incorporated in the collection edited by A. M. Hocart, *The Life-giving Myth and Other Essays* (London 1952, 1970²). A bibliography and assessment: R. Needham, *A Bibliography of Arthur Maurice Hocart* (Oxford 1967) and idem, *Man* 4 (1969) 292. His most influential books are *Kingship* (London 1927) and *Kings and Counselors* (Cairo 1936, Chicago 1970²).

53. The book was reprinted in New York-London 1979. For a short survey of his ideas see his article cited above (note 1). Raglan was a faithful disciple of Hocart. In the introduction to *The Life-giving Myth* (p. xiii) he writes: "Since none of these rites and customs can reasonably be supposed to arise naturally in the human mind, their distribution must be due to historical causes."

54. On Becket and Guy Fawkes see Fontenrose 1966, 14ff.

55. "Leaping for Goodly Themis," *New Leader* 45 (1962), 25f. (cited by Fontenrose 1966, 26). Other works by Hyman: *The Armed Vision* (New York 1948); "Myth, Ritual and Nonsense," *Kenyon Review* 11 (1949) 455–75; and note 1 above.

56. In a review of Fontenrose, *Python*, in *Carleton Miscellany* 1 (1960) 124–27 (cited by Fontenrose 1966, 26).

57. *The Tangled Bank: Darwin, Marx, Frazer and Freud as Imaginative Writers* (New York 1962).

58. M. A. Murray, *The Witch-Cult in Western Europe* (Oxford 1921, many reprints); *The God of the Witches* (London 1933 = Oxford 1981). For a short account of Murray, her followers, and her critics see K. Thomas, *Religion and the Decline of Magic* (Harmondsworth, UK 1973) 614ff. A recent, though quite different, theory on the relationship between witches and Diana: H. P. Duerr, *Dreamtime: Concerning the Boundary between Wilderness and Civilization* (Oxford 1985).

59. M. A. Murray, *The Divine King in England* (London 1954) 13. For an assessment of these and similar theories see E. Rose, *A Razor for a Goat* (Toronto 1962).

60. Robert Graves, *The White Goddess* (New York 1958); S. Jackson, in *The Lottery* (I owe this information to Burkert 1980, 181f.); J. B. Vickery, *The Scapegoat* (New York 1972), 238–45. More data in Hyman (note 1 above).

61. Theodor Gaster is perhaps the last true Frazerian. Besides the abridged *Golden Bough* (note 15 above), he also edited *Myth, Legend and Custom in the Old Testament. A Comparative Study with Chapters from Sir James Frazer's "Folklore in the Old Testament"* I, II (1969, New York 1975²).

62. His most famous book, *Argonauts of the Western Pacific* (London 1922, New York 1961²) contained a preface by Frazer. See on this work: M. W. Young (ed.), *The Ethnography of Malinowski: The Trobriand Islands 1915–1918* (London 1979). On Malinowski's place in anthropology: R. Firth, ed., *Man and Culture. An Evaluation of the Work of Bronislaw Malinowski* (London 1957); Kardiner 1962, 160–86; Harris 1968, 547–67; Waardenburg 1974, 169–72; M. Panoff, *Bronislaw Malinowski* (Paris 1972); S. Silverman, ed., *Totems and Preachers: Perspectives on the History of Anthropology* (New York 1980); Kuper 1985, 1–35.

63. *Magic, Science and Religion and Other Essays* (Glencoe, UK 1948) 85. "Explanation" this time not in the intellectualist sense used by Tylor and Frazer.

64. The essay under this name appeared in *Sex, Culture and Myth* (London 1963).

65. E. R. Leach, *The Political Systems of Highland Burma* (London 1954) 13. Although Kluckhohn, contrary to the tendency of functionalism, paid due attention to the needs of the individual and Leach, later on, dissociated himself from functionalism and embraced structuralism, in this case the functionalist background is clear. This has been convincingly shown by H. H. Penner (note 1 above) 51: "They share one basic assumption. This is the assumption that myths and rituals are to be explained by reference to their function for the solidarity or unity of society and the psyche." In this context he refers to Harrison, Hooke, Gaster, Malinowski, Kluckhohn, Spiro, and Leach. His criticism of this approach, which more often than not confuses goal with effect, is refreshing.

66. M. Douglas, *Natural Symbols* (1970; 1973²). The phrase quoted is by an anonymous reviewer in *TLS* (1970) 535. Segal (note 1 above) 181, rightly points out the difference between Douglas and her predecessors: "The real difference between

Douglas and her antagonists is that she concentrates on the meaning, not the effect, of ritual, if not myth. For Harrison and Hooke, Durkheim, Malinowski, and Radcliffe-Brown, the meaning of myth and ritual is secondary. Its effect, on either society or the individual, is primary. The meaning is at most a means to that effect. For Douglas the reverse is true."

67. Cf. Leach (note 65 above) 15: "ritual action and belief alike to be understood as forms of symbolic statement about social order."

68. In addition to the works cited in note 1 above I mention: H. Baumann, "Mythos in ethnologischer Sicht I, II," *Studium Generale* 12 (1959) 1–17 and 583–97; P. S. Cohen, "Theories of Myth," *Man* 4 (1969) 337–53; J. A. Saliba, "Myth and Religious Man in Contemporary Anthropology," *Missiology* 1 (1973) 282–93.

69. Quoted by Clyde Kluckhohn, *Anthropology and the Classics* (Providence, RI 1961) 20.

70. M. I. Finley, *Anthropology and the Classics* in idem, *The Use and Abuse of History* (London 1975) 105, where the preceding quotation appears again.

71. J. S. Black and G. Chrystal, *The Life of William Robertson Smith* (London 1912) 401.

72. Thus H. Frankfort, *The Problem of Similarity in Ancient Near Eastern Religions* (Frazer Lecture, Oxford 1951) 8, an important criticism.

73. W. von Soden, "Gibt es ein Zeugnis dafür dass die Babylonier an die Wiederaufstehung Marduks geglaubt haben?" *Zeitschrift für Assyriologie* NF 17 (1955) 130–66. Very sceptical also: J. Z. Smith, "A Pearl of Great Price and a Cargo of Yams: A Study in Situational Incongruity," *History of Religions* 16 (1976) 1–19, reprinted in revised form in his *Imagining Religion: From Babylon to Jonestown* (Chicago 1982) 90–101. He argues that the New Year complex was the product of Hellenistic apocalyptic ideas (cf. idem, 1978, 72–74). J. A. Black once more explored the whole Akitu complex: "The New Year Ceremonies in Ancient Babylon: 'Taking Bel by the Hand' and a Cultic Picnic," *Religion* 11 (1981) 39–59. Although he rejects the idea of a dying and rising god, he accepts a parallelism between the enthronement rites of Marduk and those of the king. Cf. also Z. Ben-Barak, "The Coronation Ceremony in Ancient Mesopotamia," *OLP* 11 (1980) 55–67, with new evidence.

74. See West (note 25 above) and Fontenrose 1966.

75. P. Lambrechts, "Les fêtes 'phrygiennes' de Cybèle et d'Attis. *BIBR* 27 (1952) 141–70; idem, "La 'résurrection' d'Adonis," in: *Mélanges I. Lévy* (Annuaire de l'Institut de Philologie et d'Histoire orientales [Brussels] 13 1955) 207–40. Cf. more recently: D. M. Cosi, "Salvatore e salvezza nei misteri di Attis," *Aevum* 50 (1976) 42–71; U. Bianchi, "Adonis: Attualità di una interpretazione *religionsgeschichtlich*," and P. Xella, "Adonis oggi: Un bilanco critico," both in *Adonis. Relazioni del colloquio in Roma 1981* (Rome 1984); S. Ribichini, "Salvezza ed escatologia nella vicenda di Adonis?" in U. Bianchi and M. J. Vermaseren, eds., *La soteriologia dei culti orientali nell' impero Romano* (Leiden 1982) 633–47.

76. E. M. Yamauchi, "Tammuz and the Bible," *JBL* 84 (1965) 283–90. C. H. Ratschow, "Heilbringer und sterbende Götter," in R. Stiehl and G. A. Lehmann, eds., *Antike und Universalgeschichte. Festschrift H. Stier* (Münster 1972) 398ff., argues that the act of dying itself is the symbol of salvation. See also C. H. Talbert, "The Myth of a Descending and Ascending Redeemer in Mediterranean Antiquity," *NTS* 22 (1976) 418–40. There is a reassessment of the problems in S. Ribichini, *Adonis*.

Aspetti 'orientali' di un mito greco (Rome 1981) 181–97. An entirely different position has been taken by Burkert 1979, 99ff.; 129ff. and cf. idem, "Literarische Texte und Funktionaler Mythos: Zu Istar und Atrahasis," in J. Assman, W. Burkert, F. Stolz, *Funktionen und Leistungen des Mythos. Drei altorientalische Beispiele* (Göttingen 1982) 63–82.

77. H. J. Rose, "Myth and Ritual in Classical Civilisation," *Mnemosyne* 3 (1950) 281–87; M. P. Nilsson, *Cults, Myths, Oracles, and Politics in Ancient Greece* (New York 1951) 10–12. On the supposed cohesion of myth and ritual M. Eliade, *Antaios* 9 (1968) 329, says, "Dass wir nicht einen einzigen griechischen Mythos in seinem rituellen Zusammenhang kennen." Cf. S. G. Pembroke, "Myth," in M. I. Finley, ed., *The Legacy of Greece. A New Appraisal* (Oxford 1981) 301ff.: "A one-to-one correspondence between myth and ritual is not to be found in Greece." For a similar discussion on sacral kingship and the myth and ritual theory in the Israelite context: N. Snaith, *The Jewish New Year Festival: Its Origins and Developments* (London 1947); H. Frankfort, *Kingship and the Gods* (Chicago 1948); J. de Fraine, *L'aspect religieux de la royauté israélite* (Rome 1954); A. R. Johnson, *Sacral Kingship in Ancient Israel* (Cardiff 1955); K. H. Bernhardt, *Das Problem der altorientalischen Königsideologie im A.T.* (Leiden 1961); J. Eaton, *Festal Drama in DeuteroIsaiah* (London 1979).

78. Thus for instance Fontenrose 1966, 8ff., but see my remarks in the following note. Moreover, he utterly fails to recognize the importance of what I call "mythic ritual." A short discussion of the implications of this phenomenon in J. van Baal, "Offering, Sacrifice, and Gift," *Numen* 23 (1976) 161–78, esp. 176–77; idem, *Dema: Description and Analysis of Marindanim Culture* (The Hague 1966) 540f. The question of whether the rituals as related in literature were ever actually performed becomes pressing when we have to evaluate the well-known charges against Christians and other sects. See A. Henrichs, *Die Phoinikika des Lollianos. Fragmente eines neuen griechischen Romans* (Bonn 1972); idem, "Pagan Ritual and the Alleged Crimes of the Early Christians," in P. Granfield and J. A. Jungmann, eds., *Kyriakon. Festschrift J. Quasten* I (Münster 1970) 18–35; idem, "Human Sacrifice in Greek Religion. Three Case Studies," in *Le sacrifice dans l'antiquité*, Entretiens Hardt 27 (Geneva 1981) 195–235. Cf. R. M. Grant, "Charges of 'Immorality' against Various Religious Groups in Antiquity," in: R. van den Broek and M. J. Vermaseren, eds., *Studies in Gnosticism and Hellenistic Religions Presented to G. Quispel* (Leiden 1981) 161–70. And cf. the long lists of "cannibals" among western European sectarians in: N. Cohn, *Europe's Inner Demons* (St. Albans, UK 1976) 16ff. For a different approach see J. Winkler (note 136 below). There is a remarkable variant in the early rabbinical laws which provided detailed prescriptions of rituals without ever assuming that they would be performed in reality. Here a system of ideas is expressed not in a mythical but in a ritual literary form. "The ritual *is* myth": J. Neusner, "Ritual without Myth: The Use of Legal Materials for the Study of Religions," *Religion* 5 (1975) 91–100.

79. However, Fontenrose does not excel in anthropological knowledge. There is an abundance of evidence on sacral kingship, which clearly proves that ritual regicide is (or was) a common feature in not a few African cultures. I only mention here: T. Irrstam, *The King of Ganda: Studies in the Institution of Sacral Kingship in Africa* (1944, reprinted 1981); P. Hadfield, *Traits of Divine Kingship in Africa* (1949, re-

printed 1979); L. Mair, *African Kingdoms* (Oxford 1977); M. W. Young, "The Divine Kingship of the Jukun: A Re-evaluation of Some Theories," *Africa* 36 (1966) 135–53. Recently, African sacral kingship, including the issue of regicide, has drawn much attention: A. Adler, *La mort est le masque du roi. La royauté sacrée des Moundang du Tchad* (Paris 1979); L. De Heusch, *The Drunken King, or the Origin of the State* (Bloomington, IN 1982); idem, *Rois nés d'un coeur de vache* (Paris 1982); G. Feeley-Harnik, "Issues in Divine Kingship," *Annual Review of Anthropology* 14 (1985) 273–313; J.-C. Muller, *Le roi bouc émissaire: Pouvoir et rituel chez les Rukuba du Nigéria central* (Quebec 1980). The discussion on the meaning of regicide has received a fresh impulse by the provoking theories of René Girard. See S. Simonse, *De slaperigheid van Koning Fadyet. Regicide en het zondebokmechanisme in de Nilotische Soedan*, in W. van Beek, ed., *Mimese en geweld. Beschouwingen over het werk van René Girard* (Kampen, Netherlands 1988) 172–208. Cf. also the balanced discussion of the pitfalls of terminology by S. Price, *Rituals and Power: The Roman Imperial Cult in Asia Minor* (Cambridge 1983) 235–39.

80. K. van het Reve, *Een dag uit het leven van de reuzenkoeskoes* (Amsterdam 1980²) 117.

81. Kirk 1971, 1–31; 1974, 223–53; "Aetiology, Ritual, Charter: Three Equivocal Terms in the Study of Myths," *YCLS* 22 (1972) 83–102. His sceptical approach has, in its turn, provoked critical reactions: *TLS* Aug. 14, 1970, 889–91 (the anonymous author was the same as the one of *New York Review of Books*, Jan. 28, 1971, 44–45, namely E. Leach); J. Culler, *Yale Review* 60 (1970) 108–14; J. Conradie, "The Literary Nature of Greek Myths: A Critical Discussion of G. S. Kirk's Views," *AClass* 13 (1977) 49ff. A balanced account: R. Ackerman, "Writing about Writing about Myth," *JHI* 34 (1973) 147–53. A structuralist view: C. Calame, "Mythologiques de G. S. Kirk. Structures et fonctions du mythe," *QUCC* 14 (1972) 117–35.

82. J. Z. Smith, "When the Bough Breaks," in idem 1978, 208–39, dismantles the enormous structure of *The Golden Bough* piece by piece. Other important criticism: Fontenrose 1966; E. R. Leach, "The Golden Bough or Gilded Twig," *Daedalus* 90 (1961). On Frazer's literary influence: J. B. Vickery, *The Literary Impact of the Golden Bough* (Princeton 1974).

83. In his poem, "June in Cambridge."

84. Of course, there is room for numerous refinements of the various kinds of relationship between myth and ritual. D. Richard, "Tolerance and Intolerance of Ambiguity in Northern Tai Myth and Ritual," *Ethnology* 13 (1974) 1–24, demonstrates that ritual may function in a conservative fashion while myth may be tolerant toward modern ideas.

85. Of course, there are exceptions. A typical *Einzelgänger* like Walter Otto makes the "Zusammenfall von Kultus und Mythos" the central doctrine of his most celebrated book *Dionysos. Mythos und Kultus* (Frankfurt 1933). This founder of (another) *Frankfurter* school eschewed any contact with anthropological theory or comparativist trends in the history of religions and by no means borrowed his ideas from Jane Harrison. He was strongly influenced by Wilamowitz. See W. F. Otto, *Das Wort der Antike* (Darmstadt 1962) 383–86 (bibliography); McGnty 1978, 141–80; A. Henrichs, "Der Glaube der Hellenen: Religionsgeschichte als Glaubensbekenntnis und Kulturkritik," in W. M. Calder III and H. Flashar, eds., *Wilamowitz-Symposium* (Darmstadt 1984); H. Cancik, "Die Götter Griechenlands 1929: Walter Otto als

Religionswissenschaftler und Theologe am Ende der Weimarer Republik," *AU* 27 (1984) 71–89.

86. Harrison's own opinion: *Arion* 4 (1965) 399. M. P. Nilsson, GGR P, 11, 64, was very reserved. For criticism from the side of the school of Durkheim see: *L'année sociologique* 12 (1909–12) 254–60. See generally: G. Murray, *Jane Harrison Memorial Lecture 1928*, reprinted in: *Epilegomena* and *Themis* (note 18 above) 559 ff.: "I think there was also, in conservative or orthodox circles, rather more dislike of *Themis* as a 'dangerous book' than there had been of the *Prolegomena*." Murray himself was reproached for being "etwas zu entgegenkommend gegenüber manchen Ideen Jane Harrisons": O. Weinreich in his review of *Five Stages of Greek Religion, Philologische Wochenschrift* 46 (1926) 643f. = *Ausgewählte Schriften* II, 205–6.

87. A selection of literature on *Männerbünde*: H. Schurtz, *Altersklassen und Männerbünde* (Berlin 1902); L. Weniger, "Feralis Exercitus," *Archiv für Religionswissenschaft* 9 (1906) 201–47; 10 (1907) 61–81, 229–56; L. Weiser, *Altgermanische Jünglingsweihen und Männerbünde* (Bühl 1927); H. Webster, *Primitive Secret Societies. A Study in Early Politics and Religion* (New York 1908, 1932²); O. Endter, *Die Sage vom wilden Jäger und von der wilden Jagd* (Diss. Frankfurt 1933); O. Höfler, *Kultische Geheimbünde der Germanen* I (Frankfurt 1934); G. Widengren, *Hochgottglaube im alten Iran* (Upsala 1938); S. Wikander, *Der arische Männerbund* (Diss. Lund 1938); J. Przylusky, "Les confrèries de loups-garrous dans les sociétés indoeuropéennes," *RHR* 121 (1940) 128–43; W. E. Peuckert, *Geheimkulte* (Heidelberg 1951); J. de Vries, *Altgermanische Religionsgeschichte* (Berlin 1956²) I, 454–55; G. Widengren, *Der Feudalismus im alten Iran* (Cologne 1969); G. Dumézil, *The Destiny of the Warrior* (Chicago 1970); O. Höfler *Verwandlungskulte, Volkssagen und Mythen* (Österr. Ak. Wiss. Phil-Hist. Kl. Sitz. Ber. 279, Vienna 1973); A. Alföldi 1974, esp. 107–50; J. N. Bremmer, "The Suodales of Poplios Valesios," *ZPE* 47 (1982) 133–48; idem 1987, 38–43.

88. The amount of literature on initiation is overwhelming. Besides the works of Van Gennep, Brelich, and Eliade mentioned in the text, I single out: M. Zeller, *Knabenweihen* (Diss. Bern 1923); A. E. Jensen, *Beschneidung und Reifezeremonien bei den Naturvölkern* (Stuttgart 1933); J. Haeckel, "Jugendweihe und Männerfest auf Feuerland," *Mitteilungen der Oesterreichischen Gesellschaft für Anthropologie* 43–47 (1947) 84–114; V. Popp, ed., *Initiation. Zeremonien der Statusänderung und des Rollenwechsels* (Frankfurt 1969); A. Droogers, *The Dangerous Journey: Symbolic Aspects of Boy's Initiation among the Wagenia of Kisangani (Zaïre)* (The Hague 1980). U. Bianchi, ed., *Transition Rites: Cosmic, Social and Individual Order* (Rome 1986). F. Sierksma, *Religie, Sexualiteit en Agressie* (Groningen, Netherlands 1979) 260ff. has a rich bibliography. A particularly interesting methodological approach to the application of classification and definition in the study of ritual, especially initiation, is J. A. M. Snoek, *Initiations* (Diss. Leiden 1987). Cf. also J. P. Schojdt, "Initiation and the Classification of Rituals," *Temenos* 22 (1986) 93–108. For girls' initiation see below.

89. *Annales ESC* 23 (1968) 947–64, reprinted in idem, *Le chasseur noir. Formes de pensée et formes de société dans le monde grec* (Paris 1981) 151–74. English version in *PCPhS* 194 (1968) 49–64. Reconsiderations and answers to critics in idem, "The Black Hunter Revisited," *PCPhS* 212 (1986) 126–44.

90. See on W. Burkert and the significance of his work: L. J. Alderink, "Greek

Ritual and Mythology: The Work of Walter Burkert," *Religious Studies Review* 6 (1980) 1–14. The most important review of his handbook I have seen is the one by B. Gladigow in: *Göttingische Gelehrte Anzeigen* 235 (1983) 1–16.

91. English edition: *Lore and Science in Ancient Pythagoreanism* (Cambridge, MA 1972).

92. On this scheme: Burkert 1979, 14ff. The scheme was already detected by J. G. von Hahn, *Sagwissenschaftliche Studien* (Jena 1876); see J. N. Bremmer 1987, 26, who gives a survey of the classical instances of the "mother's tragedy" on pp. 27ff. He disputes Burkert's interpretation of this motif as a reflection of girls' initiation on the ground that in some cases the mother of the hero is already married. One may grant him this point but he does not solve the enigma of the origin of the motif. For his solution: "Apparently, great heroes come into being during periods of intense crisis and transition in their mother's lives and they become the more extraordinary thanks to their mother's hardships" (p. 30), though obviously true, fails to do justice to the *stereotyped* nature of the mother's particular hardships. We shall see below that Burkert later changed his frame of interpretation. On the myth of the bad father see also the literature in A. Alföldi 1974, 104, n. 147; D. Briquel, in R. Bloch, ed., *Recherches sur les religions de l'Italie antique* (Paris 1976) 73–97.

93. This was not the first time that the *Arrhephoria* were explained as a relic of initiation ritual: Jeanmaire 1939, 264ff.; Brelich 1961, II, 123–26; cf. idem 1969, 231–38. I can neither entirely grasp nor, as far as I can grasp them, accept the recent views of N. Robertson, "The Riddle of the Arrhephoria at Athens," *HSCPh* 87 (1983) 241–88, any more than I can fathom other myth and ritual interpretations by this author, such as: "The Origin of the Panathenaea," *RhM* 128 (1985) 231–95; "The Ritual Background of the Dying God in Cyprus and Syro-Palestine," *HThR* 75 (1982) 313–59.

94. H. E. Driver, "Girl's Puberty Rites in Western North America," *University of California Publications. Anthropological Records* 6 (1941–42) 21–90; p. 61.

95. Besides the works of Brelich, Eliade, Jeanmaire, and Burkert, there is a vast literature on girls' initiations and their possible relics in women's festivals. See for instance: A. Winterstein, "Die Pubertätsriten der Mädchen mit deren Spuren in Märchen," *Imago* 14 (1928) 199–274; R. Merkelbach, "Sappho und ihr Kreis," *Philologus* 101 (1957) 1–29; J. Gagé, *Matronalia* (Brussels 1963) passim; J. K. Brown, "A Cross-Cultural Study of Female Initiation Rites," *American Anthropologist* 65 (1963) 837–53; J. Stagl, "Die Frauensuque und ihre Stellung zu den anderen Melanesischen Geheimbünden," *Wiener Völkerkundliche Mitteilungen* 14/5 (1967–68) 69–104; B. Lincoln, "The Religious Significance of Women's Scarification among the Tiv," *Africa* 45 (1973) 316–23; J. Prytz Johansen, "The Thesmophoria as a Women's Festival," *Temenos* 11 (1975) 78–87; G. E. Skov, "The Priestess of Demeter and Kore and her Role in the Initiation of Women at the Haloa at Eleusis," *Temenos* 11 (1975) 136–47; D. Visca, "Le iniziazioni femminili: un problema da reconsiderare," *Religione e Civiltà* 2 (1976) 241–74; N. J. Girardot, "Initiation and Meaning in the Tale of Snow White and the Seven Dwarfs," *American Journal of Folklore* 90 (1977) 274–300; C. Calame, ed., *Rito e poesia orale in Grecia* (Rome 1977); C. Calame, *Les choeurs de jeunes filles en Grèce archaïque* (Rome 1977); B. Lincoln, "Women's Initiation among the Navaho: Myth, Rite and Meaning," *Paideuma* 23 (1977) 255–63; Graf 1978; B. Lincoln, "The Rape of Persephone: A

Greek Scenario of Women's Initiation," *HThR* 72 (1979) 223–35; B. Lincoln, *Emerging from the Chrysalis, Studies in Rituals of Women's Initiation* (Cambridge, MA 1981); J. N. Bremmer, "Greek Maenadism Reconsidered," *ZPE* 55 (1984) 267–86.

96. In this book there is also an extensive bibliography on initiation. Cf. also B. Bettelheim, *Symbolic Wounds, Puberty Rites and the Envious Male* (London 1955).

97. Translated as *The Rites of Passage* (London 1960). Bibliography of Van Gennep in Waardenburg 1974, 85–89; K. van Gennep, *Bibliographie des oeuvres d'Arnold van Gennep* (Paris 1964). A scholarly biography: N. Belmont, *Arnold van Gennep, le créateur de l'ethnographie française* (Paris 1974), translated as *Arnold van Gennep, Creator of French Ethnography* (Chicago 1979); H. A. Senn, "Arnold van Gennep: Structuralist and Apologist for the Study of Folklore in France," *Folklore* 85 (1974) 229–43.

98. H. Kenner, *Das Phänomen der verkehrten Welt in der griechisch-römischen Antike* (Klagenfurt, Austria 1970), with too much emphasis on reversal as a symbol of death. See Versnel 1981, 582ff.

99. These raids have been treated by K. Meuli in a series of studies on masks, carnival lore, and charivari, collected in his *Gesammelte Schriften* I (Basel-Stuttgart 1975). Cf. also M. Eliade 1975, 83 with notes 9, 10, 11. Comparable rites can be found in women's initiation: R. Wolfram, "Weiberbünde," *Zeitschrift für Volkskunde* 42 (1933) 143ff.; M. Eliade, "Mystère et régénération spirituelle," *Eranos Jahrbuch* 23 (1955) 81ff. For the continuity in charivari ritual see: J. Le Goff et J.-Cl. Schmitt, eds., *Le charivari* (Paris 1981); H. Rey Flaud, *Le charivari: Les rituels fondamentaux de la sexualité* (Paris 1985).

100. *Krupteia* as a relic of initiation: Brelich 1969, 113–207 with a vast bibliography. But Nilsson had already seen the essential in *Klio* 12 (1912) 308–40 = *Opuscula selecta* 2 (Lund 1952) 826–69. With more emphasis on initiatory elements: H. Jeanmaire, "La cryptie lacédémonienne," *REG* 26 (1913) 121–50. Cf. generally: J. Ducat, "Le mépris des hilotes," *Annales (ESC)* 29 (1974) 1452–64.

101. Pederasty as an act of subjection during initiation: Van Gennep 1960, 171; Jeanmaire 1939, 455–60; Brelich 1969, 84f.; 120f.; J. N. Bremmer, "An Enigmatic Indo-European Rite: Paederasty," *Arethusa* 13 (1980) 279–98. Cf. Burkert 1979, 29f.; H. Patzer, "Die griechische Knabenliebe," *Sitzungberichte der Wissenschaftliche Akademie Frankfurt* (1982). Scepticism in F. Buffiere, *Eros adolescent. La pédérastie dans la Grèce antique* (Paris 1980) 55–59. A serious refutation of homosexual practice as part of Greek initiation: K. J. Dover, "Greek Homosexuality and Initiation," in idem, *The Greeks and Their Legacy: Collected Papers*, II (Oxford 1988) 115–34. Various forms of temple prostitution are also explained as (relics of) initiation ritual: Graf 1978, 73.

102. E. Crawley, "Achilles and Scyros," *CQ* 7 (1893) 243–46, whose views are generally accepted: Bremmer 1978, 7, n. 12.

103. For Philoctetes as the image of the initiate/ephebe see P. Vidal-Naquet, "Le 'Philoctète' de Sophocle et l'éphébie," in J.-P. Vernant et P. Vidal-Naquet, *Mythe et tragedie en Grèce ancienne* (Paris 1973) 159–84, and the literature in Bremmer 1978, 9, n. 33.

104. Theseus and the *Oschophoria*: Jeanmaire 1939, 243–45; 338–63. Additions in Brelich 1969, 444ff. When F. Graf 1979, 17, n. 137, suggests: "Im einzelnen

freilich wären seine Analysen nochmals zu überprüfen," it would be wise to pay special attention to the Salaminioi inscription. Cf. P. Vidal-Naquet, *Le chasseur noir* (Paris 1981) 164ff.

105. T. Homolle, "Inscriptions de Delphes," *BCH* 19 (1895) 5–69.

106. With the remark on p. 11: "Es ist erstaunlich wie diese These, kaum beachtet, aus der Diskussion unversehens wieder verschwunden ist." Cf. also the good discussion in idem 1985, 260–64. I have added some observations in Versnel 1986.

107. F. Graf, "Apollon Delphinios," *MH* 36 (1979) 2–22.

108. Cf. also the recent attempt to trace back the Lupercalia to initiation ritual in C. Ulf, *Das Römische Lupercalienfest. Ein Modellfall für Methodenprobleme in der Altertumswissenschaft* (Darmstadt 1982). Cf. the attempts by M. Torelli to explain the archaeological finds in Lavinium as elements of initiation ritual: *Lavinio e Roma: Riti iniziatici e matrimonio tra archeologia e storia* (Rome 1984)

109. Generally on initiatory evidence in fairy tales and elsewhere: V. Propp, *Le radici storiche dei raconti di fate* (Turin 1946, 1972²); A. Fierz-Monnier, *Initiation und Wandlung. Zur Geschichte des altfranzösischen Romans im 12. Jhdt.* (Bern 1951); J. de Vries, *Betrachtungen zum Märchen besonders in seinem Verhältnis zu Heldensage und Mythos*, F. F. Communications 150 (Helsinki 1954); *Enzyclopädie des Märchens*, s.v. "Archaische Züge," 735; "Brauch," 692; "Brautproben," 953. Eliade 1975, 124ff.; idem, "Wissenschaft und Märchen," in F. Karlinger, *Wege der Märchenforschung* (Darmstadt 1973) 311–19, the sole contribution in this collection that connects the fairy tale with initiation. Nor is there any emphasis on initiatory elements in the rich and balanced account by J. L. Fischer, "The Sociopsychological Analysis of Folktales," *Current Anthropology* 4 (1963) 235–95. On Tom Thumb: P. Saintyves, *Les contes de Perrault et les récits parallèles* (Paris 1923); Propp (this note above) 362; G. Germain, *Essai sur les origines de certains thèmes odysséens et sur la genèse de l'Odysée* (Paris 1954) 78–86 (Odysseus, too, was a dwarf). On Snow White: N. J. Girardot and A. Winterstein in studies cited in note 95 above. On Robin Hood: R. Wolfram, "Robin Hood und Hobby Horse," *Wiener Prähistorische Zeitschrift* 19 (1932) 357–74. On Odysseus, particularly the episode with the Cyclops: Germain (this note above). On the Argonauts: R. Roux, *Le problème des Argonautes. Recherche sur les aspects religieux de la légende* (Paris 1949); on the initiatory references of the Symplegades: Eliade 1975, 64ff. On Oedipus: M. Delcourt, *Oedipe, ou la légende du héros conquérant* (Paris 1944, 1981²); V. Propp, *Edipo alla luce del folclore* (Turin 1975); J. N. Bremmer, "Oedipus and the Greek Oedipous Complex," in idem, ed., *Interpretations of Greek Mythology* (London 1987) 41–59. F. Crevatin, "Eroe," *RSA* (1976/7) 221–35, even contends that the term *heros* originally denoted a youth as member of a *Männerbund* or *Jungmannschaft*.

110. V. W. Turner, "Betwixt and Between: The Liminal Period in *Rites de Passage*," in J. Helm, ed., *Proceedings of the American Ethnological Society for 1964* (Seattle 1964) 4–20; idem, *The Forest of Symbols* (Ithaca, NY 1967) 93–111; idem, *The Ritual Process* (Harmondsworth, UK 1974²); idem, "Comments and Conclusions," in B. A. Babcock, ed., *The Reversible World* (Ithaca, NY 1978) 276–96; idem, "Process, System, and Symbol. A New Anthropological Synthesis," *Daedalus* 1977, 61–80; idem, *Dramas, Fields and Metaphors. Symbolic Action in Human Society* (Ithaca, NY 1974) Ch. 6. See also: M. Gluckman, "The Licence in Ritual," in idem, *Custom and Conflict in Africa* (Oxford 1955); idem, *Rituals of Rebellion in*

S. E. Africa, Frazer Lecture 1952 (Manchester 1954); I. M. Lewis, Social Anthropology in Perspective (Harmondsworth, UK 1976) 131ff.

111. The concept of marginality was already exploited by E. V. Stonequist, The Marginal Man (New York 1937).

112. I am aware that this is a very rough presentation that requires refinements in many respects. In his Dramas Turner makes a distinction between "liminality," "outsiderhood," and "structural inferiority." However, the characteristics of these different categories largely concur.

113. On these periods of licence see, besides the literature in notes 87 and 99 above: V. Lanternari, La grande Festa (Bari 1976²).

114. On the Kronia as a carnavalesque festival see Versnel 1987. The present chapter will be incorporated in my forthcoming book Ambiguities in Greek and Roman Religion, which will also contain a study of Saturnus and the Saturnalia.

115. In Versnel 1981 I paid attention to the anomic aspects of liminality. I noticed there that mourning as a period of liminality for the relatives had scarcely been investigated in modern scholarship. In the meantime several monographs have appeared: R. Huntington and P. Metcalf, Celebrations of Death. The Anthropology of Mortuary Ritual (Cambridge 1979, 1980²), which, however, concentrates on the dead, not on the living. Cf. also: L. M. Danforth, The Death Rituals of Rural Greece (Princeton, NJ 1982); S. Humphreys and H. King, eds., Mortality and Immortality: the Anthropology and Archeology of Death (London 1981); G. Gnoli and J.-P. Vernant, eds., La mort, les morts dans les sociétés anciennes (Paris 1982). For Rome, J. Scheid, "Contraria facere: Renversements et déplacements dans les rites funéraires," Annali dell'Istituto Universitario Orientale di Napoli (Archeologia) 6 (1984) 117–39, has demonstrated the essential meaning of death ritual.

116. I borrow this concept from C. H. Hambrick, "World-Messianity. A Study in Liminality and Communitas," Religious Studies 15 (1979) 539–53.

117. See for the adoption of signals of poverty by modish marginal groups: Turner, Dramas (note 110 above), and the discussion of the felt cap in Bremmer 1978, 19f.

118. F. Graf, "Milch, Honig und Wein. Zum Verständnis der Libation im Griechischen Ritual," in G. Piccaluga, ed., Perennitas. Studi in onore di A. Brelich (Rome 1980) 209–21. Cf., however, A. Henrichs, "The 'Sobriety' of Oedipus: Sophocles OC 100 Misunderstood," HSCPh 87 (1983) 87–100.

119. On various diets as signals of segregation: M. Douglas, Purity and Danger (London 1966, Harmondsworth, UK 1970²) passim; eadem, Implicit Meanings (London 1975) 249–75.

120. On specific types of food as characteristic of marginal civilizations and barbarians, see also: J. N. Bremmer, ZPE 39 (1980) 33. In his comprehensive book Le barbare. Recherches sur la conception romaine de la barbarie et de la civilisation (Brussels 1981), Y. A. Dauge does not pay attention to this aspect.

121. J. N. Bremmer, "Scapegoat Rituals in Ancient Greece," HSCPh 87 (1983) 299–320.

122. R. Wuthnow, "Astrology and Marginality," Journal of the Scientific Study of Religion 15 (1976) 157–68.

123. Albeit "egregious," the king is first and foremost the symbol of the center of society: Lewis, Social Anthropology in Perspective (Harmondsworth, UK 1976), Ch.

9: "The Power at the Center"; Clifford Geertz, "Center, Kings and Charisma," in J. Ben David and T. N. Clark, eds., *Culture and Its Creators* (Chicago 1980) 150–71, with on p. 157 the king as "the center of the center." Cf. for the Greek imagination: J.-P. Vernant et P. Vidal-Naquet, *Mythe et tragédie en Grèce ancienne* (Paris 1972) 99–131; H. S. Versnel, "Self-Sacrifice, Compensation and the Anonymous Gods," in *Le sacrifice dans l'antiquité*, Entretiens Hardt 27 (Geneva 1981) 135–85.

124. I have been so bold as to add the god Mars: Versnel 1986, where one can find literature on the other "initiatory" gods. For Heracles see also F. Bader, "De la préhistoire à l'idéologie tripartie: les travaux d'Héraklès," in R. Bloch, ed., *D'Héraklès à Poseidon: Mythologie et protohistoire* (Geneva 1985) 9–124.

125. A good example in: A. Droogers, "Symbols of Marginality in the Biographies of Religious and Secular Innovators. A Comparative Study of the Lives of Jesus, Waldes, Booth, Kimbagu, Buddha, Mohammed and Marx," *Numen* 27 (1980) 105–21, where it appears that liminal signals such as "nature (versus culture), travelling and provisional lodging (versus sedentary life), nonviolence and solidarity" (the same as Turner's *communitas*) are characteristic of both (religious) innovators "who prosper in the margin of society" and of initiates. Numerous, too, are the similarities with behavior of people in mourning: Versnel 1981. All this does not exclude derivation: sacral kings from central Asia have borrowed their initiatory rites from shamanistic initiations. See: M. Waida, "Notes on Sacral Kingship in Central Asia," *Numen* 23 (1976) 179–90; K. Czeglédy, "Das sakrale Königtum bei den Steppenvölkern," *Numen* 13 (1966) 14–26.

126. Cf. also Graf 1978, 67: "Dass diejenige Deutung eines Rituals der Wahrheit am nächsten kommt, welche möglichst alle Einzelheiten geschlossen erklären kann, ist eine Binsenwahrheit"; W. Burkert 1966, 14: "Betrachtet man die *Arrhephoria*—Riten . . . als Mädchenweihe, so wird das Ganze von Anfang bis Ende durchsichtig, sinnvoll und notwendig." But cf. his reconsiderations below section 6.

127. Quoted by Kardiner and Preble 1962, 63.

128. See on this methodological principle: Smith 1978, 240–64.

129. E. R. Dodds, *The Greeks and the Irrational* (Berkeley-Los Angeles 1968⁶) p. viii.

130. In some respects he was preceded by G. Germain (note 109 above). I am happy that Bremmer in *Lampas* 17 (1984) 141, n. 49 has largely accepted my criticism of his interpretation of the *Odyssey*.

131. On the whole, Bremmer's interpretation of the Homeric *kouroi* with their long hair as a reflection of youthful warriors is liable to serious criticism. See for instance: H. W. Singor, *Oorsprong en ontwikkeling van de hoplietenphalanx in het archaïsche Griekenland* (Diss. Leiden 1988) II, Ch. 6, who argues that the term *kouros* like *iuvenis* denotes the age group between twenty and forty-five or fifty. Matters are highly complicated, of course, by the nature of our "historical" source. Homer freely used such techniques as condensation, displacement, and figuration (*Verdichtungsarbeit, Verschiebungsarbeit, Darstellung* according to Freud). See: P. Wathelet, *Les Troyens de l' Iliade: mythe et histoire* (Diss. Liège 1986). F. Hartog, *Le miroir d'Hérodote* (Paris 1980) 59–79, has made the revealing discovery that Herodotus understands the Scythians as cunning ephebes and P. Vidal-Naquet, "The Black Hunter Revisited," *PCPhS* 212 (1986) 124–44, to whom I owe these references, infers that *ephebeia* has become a semantic category by the fifth century, working as a

"symbolic operator." The problem, however, is that the Homeric descriptions of the *kouroi, being the normal* warriors, precisely lack explicit references to the ephebic situation, in contradistinction to the scarce references to actual initiatory scenes, as for instance the story of Odysseus' hunt with the sons of Autolykos in *Odyssey* 19.

132. See e.g., A. Alföldi, "Königsweihe und Männerbund bei den Achämeniden," *Schweizerisches Archiv für Volkskunde* 47 (1951) 11–16 and the works of Widengren and Wikander mentioned in note 87 above.

133. Such scepticism is for instance expressed by A. Heubeck, "Zur neueren Homerforschung," *Gymnasium* 89 (1982) 441f.

134. Consequently, C. Segal, "Transition and Ritual in Odysseus' Return," *PP* 22 (1967) 321–42, has not the slightest difficulty in interpreting motifs such as sleep, purification by baths, the threshold, or, if necessary, the total *Odyssey*, as one great "transition" from death to life, though, for that matter, without any reference to initiation.

135. On the wound of the thigh as an initiatory signal see in particular: G. J. Baudy, *Adonisgärten. Studien zur antiken Samensymbolik* (Frankfurt 1986) 50ff. There are more initiatory signals in connection with Odysseus' youth: Bremmer 1978, 15f. The same for Nestor: idem, "The Suodales of Poplios Valesios" *ZPE* 47 (1982) 143, n. 43. On Odysseus' initiation via hunting probes: N. F. Rubin and W. M. Sale, "Meleager and Odysseus: A Structural and Cultural Study of the Greek Hunting-Maturation Myth," *Arethusa* 16 (1983) 137–71, with a reply to criticism: *Arethusa* 17 (1984) 211–22.

136. For Henrichs see above note 78; J. Winkler, "Lollianos and the Desperadoes," *JHS* 100 (1980) 153–81.

137. R. Merkelbach, *Roman und Mysterium in der Antike* (Munich 1962). Previous attempts in this direction: K. Kerényi, *Die griechisch-orientalische Romanliteratur in religionsgeschichtlicher Beleuchtung* (Tübingen 1927, Darmstadt 1962²). A different, but not preferable approach: G. Wojaczek, *Daphnis* (Meisenheim, FRG 1969). An excellent critical discussion: A. Geyer, "Roman and Mysterienritual. Zum Problem eines Bezugs zum dionysischen Mysterienritual im Roman des Longos," *WJA* 3 (1977) 179–96; G. Freimuth, *MH* 21 (1964) 93ff. An interesting attempt at mediation between the extreme points of view: R. Beck, "Soteriology, the Mysteries and the Ancient Novel: Iamblichus *Babylonica* as a Test-Case," in U. Bianchi and M. J. Vermaseren, eds., *La soteriologia dei culti orientali nell' impero romano* (Leiden 1982) 527–46.

138. One might, for instance, understand the adventures of Odysseus as expressions of his temporary sojourn outside the boundaries of normal time and place, an "eccentricity" marked by both utopian and dystopian imagery. On this ambiguity see Versnel 1987. As R. Scodel, "The Achaean Wall and the Myth of Destruction," *HSCPh* 86 (1982) 33–50, has shown, the Homeric poems contain quite a few references to the "predeluvial" era, and she even argues that the story of the Trojan war itself may have originated in Zeus's wish to destroy the race of the *hemitheoi*, as the episode of the destruction of the Achaean wall certainly does. In the context of "eccentric" experiences there is quite a difference between the statement that Odysseus represents a youth during his initiation and the well-known theory that both fairy tales and (a specific type of) myths, including the one of Odysseus, go back to shaman tales—the records of their ecstatic experiences in the other world: L. Frobenius,

Kulturgeschichte Afrikas (Frankfurt 1933 = Zurich 1954) 306; K. Meuli, "Scythica," in *Gesammelte Schriften* II, 835ff.; F. von der Leyen, "Mythus und Märchen," *Deutsche Vierteljahrsschr. für Literaturwissenschaft und Geistesgeschichte* 33 (1959) 343ff.; M. Eliade, "Les savants et les contes des fées," *Nouvelle revue française* 3 (1956) 884ff.; M. Lüthi, *Das europäische Volksmärchen* (Munich 1978⁶) 105. On the *Odyssey* in this perspective: H. Petersmann, "Homer und das Märchen," *WS* 15 (1981) 43–68.

139. Handworking during the night and male aggression: A. Slawik, *Wiener Beiträge zur Kulturgeschichte und Linguistik* 4 (1936) 737ff.; Peuckert (note 87 above) 253. Licence: D. Zelenin, *Russische (Ostslawische) Volkskunde* (Berlin 1927) 337ff.; E. Gasparini, *Nozze, società e abitazione degli antichi Slavi* (Venice 1954) 22f. Cf. Eliade 1975, 46. Generally: H. Rey-Flaud, *Le charivari. Les rituels fondamentaux de la sexualité* (Paris 1985). Bremmer reminds me that Burkert 1966 has indeed, in an aside, suggested a connection between the handwork of the Arrhephorae and the *peplos* of Penelope.

140. Here, too, a predecessor had noticed the essentials: G. Dumézil, *Le crime des Lemniennes* (Paris 1924). Cf. M. Detienne, *Les jardins d'Adonis* (Paris 1972) 172–84, who, from a structuralist point of view, arrives at comparable conclusions. For some recent reconsiderations on the Lemnian fire: P. Y. Forsyth, "Lemnos Reconsidered," *EMC* 28 (1984) 3–14.

141. Kirk 1974, 246: "It stands out, then, as the one clear case in the whole range of Greek heroic myths—with the Cecropides tale as a weaker ally—in which the myth-and-ritual theory is vindicated."

142. Cf. idem, *Gnomon* 44 (1972) 227: "Rituale, dramatisch theatralische Mitteilung im Spannungsfeld biologisch sozialer Antinomie. So tritt eine tiefere Parallelität zum Mythos zu Tage."

143. "Greek Tragedy and Sacrificial Ritual," *GRBS* 7 (1966) 87–121; *Homo Necans. The Anthropology of Ancient Greek Sacrificial Ritual and Myth* (Berkeley-Los Angeles 1983). Independently, J.-P. Guépin, *The Tragic Paradox* (Diss. Amsterdam 1968) had arrived at comparable conclusions, although there are important differences as well.

144. Burkert 1980.

145. V. J. Propp, *Morphology of the Folktale* (Austin, TX 1973²). For other works of this scholar see above note 109. I can only give a rough summary of Burkert's ideas and he does not follow Propp in every respect.

146. And, indeed, provided one skips some doublets the Russian alphabet appears to consist of thirty-one letters. However, even in the original Russian edition the thirty-one motifemes are not indicated with letters.

147. See for instance his very amusing treatment of this type of structuralism in Burkert 1979, 10ff. For a recent attack on the imposition of modern Western binary classificatory principles on anthropological data, especially ritual, see S. Tcherkezoff, *Dual Classification Reconsidered: Nyamwezi Sacred Kingship and Other Examples* (Cambridge 1987).

148. For instance in A. G. Dundes, *The Morphology of North American Indian Folktales* (Helsinki 1964): Lack-Lack Liquidated; Task-Task Accomplished; Deceit-Deception; Interdiction-Violation-Consequence-Attempted Escape.

149. K. Lorenz, *Das sogenannte Böse: Zur Naturgeschichte der Aggression* (Vi-

enna 1963, 1970²). English translation: *On Aggression* (New York 1966). Burkert 1979, 35ff.; idem, "Glaube und Verhalten: Zeichengehalt und Wirkungsmacht von Opferritualen," in *Le sacrifice dans l'antiquité* (Entretiens Hardt 27, Geneva 1981) 91–125.

150. M. Douglas, *Natural Symbols* (Harmondsworth, UK 1970, 1973²); K. Lorenz, "A Discussion on Ritualization of Behaviour in Animals and Man," *Philosophical Transactions of the Royal Society London*, Ser. B. 251 (1966) 247–526; J. Eibl-Eibesfeldt, *Der vorprogrammierte Mensch. Das Ererbte als bestimmender Faktor im menschlichen Verhalten* (Vienna 1973, 1976²).

151. Repetition is one of the most essential principles: J. Cazeneuve, "Le principe de répétition dans le rite," *Cahiers internationaux de sociologie* 23 (1957) 42–62; A. M. di Nola, *Antropologia religiosa* (Florence 1974) 94–144.

152. Especially in "Entstehung und Sinn der Trauersitten," *Schweizerisches Archiv für Volkskunde* 43 (1946) = *Gesammelte Schriften* I (Basel 1975) 333–51.

153. K. Meuli, "Griechische Opferbräuche," *Gesammelte Schriften* II (Basel 1975) 907–1021.

154. Versnel 1987. Cf. also Versnel 1986.

155. For these associations see for instance Burkert 1966, 25: "In den Initiationsriten erneuert sich das Leben der Gemeinschaft, in den daraus gewachsenen Neujahrsriten erneuert sich die Ordnung der Polis." Cf. idem on the legend of Romulus in: *Historia* 11 (1962) 356ff.; Bremmer 1978, 33f. on elements of lustration as features of New Year festival and initiation; Eliade 1975 passim, especially Ch. 12, 13, p. 48; idem, *The Myth of the Eternal Return* (New York 1954) 62–73; "Nouvel an, peau neuve," *Le Courier* 8 (1955) 7–32. In Egypt the coronation (initiation) of the new king is seen as the beginning of a new eon and a new year: J. Bergman, *Ich bin Isis* (Uppsala 1968) 212ff.

156. There are relatively few examples of the primeval flood as a signal of initiation. Generally, the deluge theme is preeminently the image of chaos, seen as the obstacle to *kosmos*. The latter can only come into being after the victory over the chaotic deluge, a victory that is generally celebrated on New Year's day. K. Meuli, *Gesammelte Schriften* I (Basel 1975) 283–99, concludes: "Jene *regénération totale du temps* ist von alten Völkern begriffen und dargestellt worden als das Auftauchen einer neuen, reinen Welt aus den Wassern der Sintflut" and he gives a substantiation of this statement in *Gesammelte Schriften* II, 1041ff. The same ideas already in: H. Usener, *Sintflutsagen* (Bonn 1899) 36ff. Cf. also: G. Piccaluga, *Lycaon* (Rome 1968) 69; W. Burkert 1983, index s.v. "Flood"; J. Rudhardt, "Les mythes grecs relatifs à l'instauration du sacrifice. Les rôles corrélatifs de Prométhée et de son fils Deucalion," *MH* 27 (1970) 1–15; idem, *Le thème de l'eau primordiale dans la mythologie grecque* (Bern 1971). The theme has a central function in Near Eastern mythology: J. G. Frazer, *Folklore in the Old Testament* I (London 1918) 104–360, in the revised edition by Theodor H. Gaster, *Myth, Legend, and Custom in the Old Testament* (New York 1969, 1975²) 82–130; A. J. Wensinck, *The Ocean in the Literature of the Western Semites* (Amsterdam 1918); O. Kaiser, *Die mythische Bedeutung des Meeres in Aegypten, Ugarith und Israel* (Berlin 1962²); J. P. Lewis, *A Study of the Interpretation of Noah and the Flood in Jewish and Christian Literature* (Leiden 1968, 1978²). Generally on the symbolism of the Flood: H. Gollob, *Chrysaor. Mit einem*

Anhange über die Sintflutsage (Vienna 1956). Cf. also the literature cited by Smith 1978, 98.

157. On man-eating monsters and anthropophagy as symptoms of initiation: Bremmer 1978, 16f. Cannibalism as a sign of (recurrent) periods of chaos and disturbance of order: A. J. Festugière, *Études de religion grecque et hellénistique* (Paris 1972) 145ff.; M. Detienne, *Dionysos mis à mort* (Paris 1977) 135–60; C. Grottanelli, "The Enemy King Is a Monster. A Biblical Equation," *SSR* 3 (1979) 5ff.; Versnel 1980, 591. On the historicity of cannibalistic rituals: W. Arens, *The Man-Eating Myth: Anthropology and Anthropophagy* (Oxford 1979). Nor can it be said that the fairy tales in which persons are swallowed up by a whale or dragon are necessarily connected with initiation ritual. For the widespread occurrence of this motif see: W. Fauth, "Utopische Inseln in den 'Wahren Geschichten' des Lukian," *Gymnasium* 86 (1979) 49ff.; U. Steffen, *Das Mysterium von Tod und Auferstehung: Formen und Wandlungen des Jona-Motivs* (Göttingen 1963); idem, *Drachenkampf: Der Mythos vom Bösen* (Stuttgart 1984).

158. And indeed one perceives traces of a shift in the frame of interpretation in later works of Burkert. Burkert 1980, 184 discusses the overtly Freudian theory of O. Rank, *Der Mythos der Geburt des Helden* (Vienna 1909), in which the *Aussetzung-und Rückkehrformel* is traced back to the father-son conflict. Burkert considers this "eine der solidesten Leistungen" and states: "dies leuchtet weithin ein." The implications of this assessment are crucial: one of the traditional ingredients of the initiation theory has been detached from this context and is now exploited in a different type of interpretation.

159. This appears to be in accordance with recent theories on the social function of "institutionalized homosexuality." Though no doubt often connected with initiation ritual, its application generally exceeds the strict boundaries of the period of initiation. Homosexual subjection appears to have a broader function as a powerful component of social hierarchy: it supports the status and position of older men over and against women and young men. See: G. W. Creed, "Sexual Subordination: Institutionalized Homosexuality and Social Control in Melanesia," *Ethnology* 23 (1984) 157–76, and bibliographical references there; G. Herdt, ed., *Ritualized Homosexuality in Melanesia* (Berkely-Los Angeles 1984).

160. M. Eliade 1975, 128 (with a very hazy note on p. 165) suggests that the initiation scheme was prior and landed in dreams and myths, whereas at the same time he nevertheless concedes that "every human life is made up of a series of ordeals, of 'deaths' and of 'resurrections.'" But if this is so, it is far more likely that these ordeals common to human life have given shape to both the initiation scenario and—independently—to the materials dreams and myths are made of. See on this and similar questions: H. von Beit, *Symbolik des Märchens. Versuch einer Deutung* (Bern 1952) and *Enzyklopädie des Märchens* s.v. "Aufgabe," where, conversely, the unfeasible assignment known from fairy tales is seen as the reflection of *Alptraumerfahrungen*. Nor is it very likely that Snow White has borrowed her seven dwarfs from initiation ritual: H. Bausinger, "Anmerkungen zu Schneewittchen," in: H. Brackert, ed., *Und wenn sie nicht gestorben sind . . . Perspektiven auf das Märchen* (Frankfurt 1982²) 39–70. What Campbell omits has been made up by G. J. Baudy: *Exkommunikation und Reintegration. Zur Genese und Kulturfunktion frühgriechischer Ein-*

stellungen zum Tod (Frankfurt 1980). He offers a psychoethological explanation of
deep-seated fears, for instance the fear of voracious monsters, interpreting them as
relics of primates' primordial fear of the *Artfeind* (the praedator). On pp. 33f. he
juxtaposes the initiate, who is in danger of being swallowed up, and the fairy tale
hero in the same situation, as I have done, but does not suggest an evolutionary link
between the two. On pp. 250 ff., however, he wishes to trace the fairy tale motif back
to initiation (specifically, the shamanistic scenario), which seems unnecessary to me.
Obviously similar problems of origin emerge in different fields: it is *the* problem of
Freud's Oedipus theory. It plays an important role in the discussion between Henrichs and Winkler (note 136 above), where the latter—I think convincingly—refers
to "patterns of narrative, the basic plots and formulae of popular entertainment,"
without, however, inquiring into the origins of these patterns. It also figures in the
discussion between F. Ranke, *Kleinere Schriften* (Bern-Münster 1971), who explains
the popular fancies of the *Wilde Heer* as "innerseelische Vorgänge des numinösen
Erlebniss" (especially as manifest in hysteria, epilepsy, and so forth) and his fierce
opponent O. Höfler, *Verwandlungskulte, Volkssagen und Mythen* (SAWW 279
[1973]), who traces this "wild army" back to historical, cultic *Jungmannschaften*. It
is also present in the discussion on the origins of the Eleusinian and other mysteries.
See for instance on the ambivalence of human initiation and agricultural fertility as
the ultimate background of the mysteries: G. Casadio, "Per un'indagine storico-
religiosa sui culti di Dioniso in relazione alla fenomenologia dei misteri," I, *SSR* 6
(1982) 209–34.

    161. T. S. Kuhn, *The Structure of Scientific Revolutions* (Chicago 1970²). He has
revised his ideas in *The Essential Tension* (Chicago 1977). Criticism: I. Lakatos,
"Falsification and the Methodology of Scientific Research Programmes," in I. Lakatos and A. Musgrave, eds., *Criticism and the Growth of Knowledge* (Cambridge
1970) 91–196; P. Feyerabend, *Against Method* (London 1975).

    162. Application of the concept, "paradigm," to social theory: B. Barnes, *T. S.
Kuhn and Social Science* (London 1982). On "tolerance": S. Seiler, *Wissenschafts-
theorie in der Ethnologie. Zur Kritik und Weiterführung der Theorie von Thomas S.
Kuhn anhand ethnographischen Materials* (Berlin 1980); P. Kloos, "Culturele antro-
pologie als polyparadigmatische wetenschap," in A. de Ruijter, ed., *Beginselen in
botsing* (Utrecht 1981).

    163. I found this quotation in a book from which I have learned more than I have
been able to account for within the scope of this paper: Smith 1978, 264.

    164. Apart from the notes, this paper has been translated from the Dutch by Dr.
P. P. J. van Caspel, who carried out the difficult job with great meticulousness and
intelligence. Professor L. Edmunds and Mr. P. Mason, classicists and native speakers
of English, read the first translation and offered many suggestions for improving the
text. To all of them I express my sincere gratitude.

WORKS CITED

Alföldi, A. 1974. *Die Struktur des voretruskischen Römerstaates*. Heidelberg.
Baal, J. Van. 1971. *Symbols for Communication. An Introduction to the Anthropo-
    logical Study of Religion*. Assen, Netherlands.
Brelich, A. 1960–61. *Le iniziazioni* I-II. Rome.

————. 1969. *Paides e parthenoi*. Rome.

Bremmer, J. N. 1978. "Heroes, Rituals and the Trojan War." *SSR* 2:5–38.

———— and N. M. Horsfall 1987. *Roman Myth and Mythography* (*BICS* Suppl. 52). London.

Burkert, W. 1966a. "Greek Tragedy and Sacrificial Ritual." *GRBS* 7: 87–121.

————. 1966b. "Kekropidensage und Arrhephoria." *Hermes* 94:1–25.

————. 1970. "Iason, Hypsipyle and New Fire at Lemnos: A Study in Myth and Ritual." *CQ* 20: 1–16.

————. 1972. *Homo Necans: Interpretation altgriechischer Opferriten und Mythen*. Berlin. Tr. Peter Bing. 1983. *Homo Necans: The Anthropology of Ancient Greek Sacrificial Ritual and Myth*. Berkeley–Los Angeles.

————. 1975. "Apellai und Apollon." *RhM* 118: 1–21.

————. 1979. *Structure and History in Greek Mythology and Ritual*. Berkeley–Los Angeles.

————. 1980. "Griechische Mythologie und Geistesgeschichte der Moderne." *Les études classiques aux XIXᵉ et XXᵉ siècles: leur place dan l'histoire des idées*. Entretiens Hardt 26, 159–99. Geneva.

————. 1985. *Greek Religion*. Oxford.

Eliade, M. 1975. *Rites and Symbols of Initiation*. New York. (Reprint of *Birth and Rebirth*. New York. 1958).

Evans-Pritchard, E. 1981. *A History of Anthropological Thought*. Ed. A. Singer. London.

Foley, H. 1985. *Ritual Irony: Poetry and Sacrifice in Euripides*. Ithaca, NY.

Fontenrose, J. 1966. *The Ritual Theory of Myth*. Berkeley–Los Angeles.

Frazer, J. G. 1890–1915. *The Golden Bough*. 12 vols. London.

Gennep, A. van. 1960. *The Rites of Passage*. London.

Gernet, Louis. 1928. "Frairies antiques." *RBG* 41:313–59.

Graf, F. 1978. "Die lokrischen Mädchen." *SSR* 2: 61–79.

————. 1979. "Apollon Delphinios." *MH* 36: 2–22.

Harris, M. 1968. *The Rise of Anthropological Theory*. London.

Harrison, J. E. 1890. *Mythology and Monuments of Ancient Athens*. London.

————. 1927. *Themis*. 2nd ed. Cambridge.

Hubert, H., and M. Mauss. 1964. *Sacrifice, Its Nature and Function*. Chicago.

Humphreys, S. C. 1978. *Anthropology and the Greeks*. London.

Jeanmaire, H. 1939. *Couroi et Courètes*. Lille.

Kardiner, A., and E. Preble. 1962. *They Studied Man*. London.

Kirk, G. S. 1971. *Myth: Its Meaning and Functions in Ancient and Other Cultures*. Cambridge.

————. 1974. *The Nature of Greek Myths*. Harmondsworth, UK.

Kuper, A. 1985. *Anthropologists and Anthropology. The Modern British School*. Reprint of 2nd ed. London.

McGinty, P. 1978. *Interpretation of Dionysos: Method in the Study of a God*. The Hague.

Meuli, K. 1946. "Griechische Opferbräuche." In *Phyllobolia für Peter von der Mühll*. Basel.

Sebeok, T. A., ed. 1974. *Myth: A Symposium*. 6th ed. Bloomington, IN.

Sharpe, E. J. 1975. *Comparative Religion*. London.

Smith, J. Z. 1978. *Map Is Not Territory: Studies in the History of Religions*. Leiden.

Versncl, H. S., ed. 1981. *Faith, Hope and Worship: Aspects of Religious Mentality in the Ancient World*. Lciden.

———. 1980. "Destruction, *Devotio* and Despair in a Situation of Anomy: The Mourning for Germanicus in Triple Perspective." In G. Piccaluga, ed. *Perennitas. Studi in onore di A. Brelich*, 541–618. Rome.

———. 1986. "Apollo and Mars One Hundred Years after Roscher." *Visible Religion 4/5*: 134–72.

———. 1987. "Greek Myth and Ritual: The Case of Kronos." In J. N. Bremmer, ed. *Interpretations of Greek Mythology*, 121–52. London.

Vidal-Naquet, P. 1986. "The Black Hunter and the Origin of the Athenian Ephebia." In *The Black Hunter: Forms of Thought and Forms of Society in The Greek World*, 106–28. Tr. A. Szegedy-Maszak. Baltimore.

Vries, J. De. 1961. *Forschungsgeschichte der Mythologie*. Munich.

Waardenburg, J. 1974. *Classical Approaches to the Study of Religion: Aims, Methods and Theories*. II: *Bibliography*. The Hague.

Wyatt, W. F., and P. S. Allen. 1988. "Anthropology and the Classics." *New England Classical Newsletter 15.3*: 13–22.

2

MYTH AND HISTORY

The topic of myth and history is complex. On the one hand, there is the history *of* Greek myths in the sense of the record of their transmission in poets, genealogists, historians, mythographers, and other sources. This approach to the study of Greek myth is usually called "philological." It is the indispensable preliminary to any study of a Greek myth; it can also, even as it aims to clarify, distort the picture, as Brillante argues in his discussion of Kirk's application of the philological approach.[a] On the other hand, there is history *in* Greek myths—their historical content.

The notion of the historical content of a myth presupposes a distinction between myth and history which is fundamental for us but anachronistic for the Greeks. As Brillante shows, the hero myths *were* what we would call history. For the Greeks, the heroes were great men who had lived in a period long past but continuous with their own times. Critical reflection on myth began in the sixth century B.C., an aspect of the larger movement of Ionian rationalism, but in the case of the hero myths, it did not cut deep. (As distinguished from cosmogonical myth, where anthropomorphic deities were replaced by physical elements and abstract principles).[b] Myth, as a variable thing, had the capacity for self-criticism, as in Stesichorus' self-correction as regards the myth of Helen; and epic aims at a "historical" consistency in omitting reference to the Dorians and in many other archaizing traits. History, for its part, when it first appears, in Herodotus, in the form of lengthy prose narrative, preserves some of the goals and characteristics of epic.

Despite the ancient blurring of our distinction between myth and history, modern research, from the eighteenth century, has used Greek myth as a source of historical data. This approach has, indeed, a Greek forebear in Euhemerus, who in the third century B.C. had already discovered great kings of the (historical) past cloaked in the figures of the traditional Greek pantheon. In the eighteenth and on into the nineteenth centuries, a constant in research on myth (which was for a long time tantamount to Greek myth) was the notion that here the earliest history of mankind could be discerned.[c]

Toward the end of the last century, at about the same time as the new developments in anthropology and linguistics that would lead to structuralism, the archaeological discoveries of Heinrich Schliemann at Troy and Mycenae and of Sir Arthur Evans at Cnossos provided a basis for a stronger sense of the historicity of the myths in Greek epic. Great scholars of the turn of the century, Erwin Rohde (1845–98), Eduard Meyer (1855–1930), Carl Robert (1850–1922), and Ulrich Wilamowitz (1848–1931) believed they could read in epic the history of the second millenium B.C. The most cogent and best-known example of this approach is M. P. Nilsson's *The Mycenaean Origins of Greek Mythology*, first published in 1932 and reissued forty years later—a remarkable feat for a book in a field in which early obsolescence is normal. Brillante has given his own example of the historical "record" of political change in the myths concerning Argos and has indicated other sorts of historical traces to be found in Greek myths—Near Eastern influence; the Delphic oracle; political propaganda. He also states the criteria for the detection and demonstration of these traces: the singularity and noniterability of the trace, and adequate parallel data from archaeology or other historical sources.

Besides the political and military history of Mycenaean and archaic Greece, much earlier evidence is sought in Greek myths. The most prominent exponent of this approach is Walter Burkert, who finds the relation between myth and history not in the particular heterogeneous elements in myth which can be defined by Brillante's criteria but in the narrative structures themselves. These, Burkert finds, represent "programs of action" corresponding to elemental cultural or even biological patterns. While Kirk offers a structuralist reading of the Polyphemus episode in the *Odyssey*,[d] Burkert calls attention to a "remarkable historical clue" in that episode, the wooden spear, with its end hardened by fire, which Odysseus uses to blind Polyphemus.[e] It is, Burkert argues, a Paleolithic weapon. Burkert calls for an approach to Greek mythology which would concentrate on the earliest historical aspects: "This may now be the challenge which Greek mythology poses, that, rather than seeing it in its own distinctive form, we should venture to see it in the greater context of the tradition of humanity, and to perceive through the Greek form the antecedent, dynamic structures of experience which have formed human life and molded the human psyche in the vast realm of the past."[f]

History and the Historical Interpretation of Myth

CARLO BRILLANTE

Questions about the relationship between history and myth date from ancient times (the Greeks began to question their own traditions as far back as the archaic age), and in this ancient dispute history has not always succeeded in asserting its authority over myth. In the pages that follow I do not reconsider all aspects of this long-standing debate. I dwell instead only on several problems of central importance, specifying at the outset that my subject is myth rather than history.

In the first part of this essay I explore the way the Greeks looked at myth, focusing particularly on the elements of truth they believed they recognized there as well as on the emergence of historical thought. In the second part I consider the extent to which historical analysis of myth is feasible today, especially in light of modern scholarship. My chief aim is to determine the adequacy of this kind of analysis. Does it account for the complexity of the subject? Another question inevitably arises: what role can structural analysis play here? The third part of the essay is dedicated to this last question.

THE GREEK VIEW OF MYTH AND HISTORY

The theme of the relationship between myth and history, especially if presented as a global alternative between two forms of tradition—one mythic, the other historical—would not have been clearly understood by the Greeks. This is not to suggest that in ancient Greece the stories handed down through the generations enjoyed unconditional acceptance. On the contrary, these tales were subject to doubt, and the critique of myth is probably as ancient as the myths themselves. The alternative (and the choice) was rather between stories that appeared more or less credible, between stories considered true and others that appeared false or distorted, or else between stories from one's own tradition and those from another's. But if a myth was accepted as somehow credible, it appeared for that very reason historically founded and veracious. The Greek heroes are a case in point. Is the heroic world to be placed in a sphere totally distinct from the day-to-day world in which human beings normally operate, or are the two worlds in some way related?

The problem is related to the nature of the heroes. As is well known, many different theses have been proposed to answer this question, all of them seeking to go back to the presumed original, or prehistoric, nature of these figures.[1] If, however, for the moment we limit our considerations to the opinion that the Greeks held with regard to the historical age, we arrive at the same conclusion as before: they imagined their heroes as men who had actually lived, inhabiting the same cities and regions in which they themselves, several centuries later, continued to reside. Thus it is possible to affirm that the heroic world corresponded approximately in its geographical limits to the world of men.

Nor was the temporal dimension in which the heroes acted very different from that of humans. This fact needs to be considered attentively if one is not to overlook an essential element of the functioning of the heroic world as we ought to imagine it. According to the Greeks this was the most ancient "historical" period of the various *ethne* and of the single *poleis*. We cannot but share the observation made by S. Mazzarino: "We must start from a simple premise, which can never be insisted upon enough: for a reader of the fifth century B.C. 'ancient' history or *archaiologia* was, without qualification, a history of unquestionable truth, woven of myth. . . . Since for the Greeks these 'ancient' *logoi* were as worthy of study and of belief as medieval history is for us, the discussion generally centered on the method of interpreting the various traditions 'scientifically,' by means of a rational selection. To this task were called, without distinction, both the prose writers, the 'historians,' and the 'poets.' "[2] Definitions of this sort are of great use in putting us on guard against certain appraisals dedicated to pointing out the more or less profound differences between the human and heroic worlds.

Whatever the origin—or, more precisely, origins—of the heroes, to the eyes of Greeks of the archaic and classical ages they appeared as men who had really lived in a distant past and who belonged to an older and more powerful race than the one presently inhabiting the earth. Yet because they more closely resembled humans than gods, they could serve as models or guides for people.

Starting from this general assumption, for which Greek experience provides abundant evidence, it is possible to examine the significance of the development, particularly in sixth-century Ionia, of a type of reflection on myth apparently different from that previously in practice. The birth of historical reflection constitutes a significant moment for the cultural future of Greece and of the entire West. In general, one can affirm how this reflection, at times profound, suggested reconsideration of traditions handed down over a long period of time, particularly in epic poetry and in local usage, and in various ways either attributed or attributable to the heroic past of the different cities and races. In this sense, the rationalism and the "myth criticism" at the origins of historical reflection are commonly referred to, or from another point of view, the rationalistic character of the traditional story now becomes more important. The exclusion of the marvelous, the elimination of elements that clash with the fully human setting of the story as object of the historical narrative, represents a salient characteristic. Another criticism probably reflects a reaction against the multiple and sometimes divergent versions in which the "same" story was handed down. "Greek traditions are numerous and ridiculous," said Hecataeus; hence his proposal to narrate them in forms that seemed true.[3] In this way, "myth criticism" came to strike at something fundamental: the "variety" tied to the nature and the form of communication, principally oral, by means of which myth was handed down. On the one hand, the heroic world was even further constrained within a purely human dimension; on the other, the nascent historical reflection, making the most pressing and modern demands for rationality, could more freely appropriate a heroic past that clashed even less with the assumptions of human existence. In this way, then, the "historicization" of the epic poem developed an irrepressible stage in the whole process.[4] In epic poetry a notable quantity of easily accessible traditions flowed together and bestowed a fundamental credibility; yet the reduction of the heroic world to a purely human sphere in the aforesaid sense allowed for the elimination (or revision) of those elements that fit in only poorly with a historical presentation of these same traditions.

Thus, the changes observable in the earliest historical reflection were part of that more general process that included the emergence of philosophical thought in the same period and in the same region, sixty-century Ionia, and that probably experienced similar development in other Greek cities, as the historical work of Acusilaus of Argos demonstrates for the Peloponnesus. The affirmation of philosophical thought, too, presupposes a tendency to reject divine intervention in personal form—and, more generally, of the marvelous as a whole—in the explanation of natural phenomena; instead the search for purely physical causes is privileged, even though in such elaborations the presence of older schemes in which divine intervention and the supernatural play a large part is still recognizable. Nonetheless, what prevailed were rational interpretations, which offered a representation of the natural world and its becoming that saw the reasons for the world's existence and change as generated within itself. The sphere of symbolic representations, the type of mythic presentation (and explanation) of cosmogonal processes with the relative "law of ambivalence" inseparable from such interpretative models, was progressively abandoned.[5] The concerted action of Ionian *historie* and the reutilization of traditions allowed for the emergence of new problems and had as a result a new vision and comprehensive organization of the "ancient" past of the various peoples and cities of Greece. Although this reflection made ample use of the epic traditions, it cast them in a fundamentally new light, in which history was more easily recognizable than myth.

The "search for rationality" recognizable in this process finds one of its most important characteristics in the distanced and "critical" stance toward traditional stories. But this stance is only a part of the process. Considered absolutely, particularly as a static, exclusive alternative, it risks prejudicing a balanced appraisal of this reflection on myth. In philosophy this alternative took the form of an opposition between *mythos* and *logos*. As regards the present discussion, it should be pointed out that a "myth criticism" is not in itself an extraordinary phenomenon. As I suggested at the beginning, the notion of "myth criticism" proves to be inseparable from the other, apparently simpler notion of "myth." As long as this situation maintained its vitality, myths continued to be narrated in different ways, each thus providing a critique of previous versions. In practice this process continued, articulated in ever more diverse forms, during the whole of antiquity, but it probably assumed new dimensions and meanings in archaic Greece, where the traditional and almost only mode of communicating myth was oral.[6] In these circumstances myth criticism, which rightly occupies a significant place in the emergence of historical reflection, constitutes an important but not exactly revolutionary event. The new elements concern in particular the type of criticism practiced on the versions of myth that were traditional in the sense specified previously, and perhaps on the type of written communication by means of which the older versions began to circulate. Since it allowed for more detailed analyses and close comparisons, the use of writing made possible the introduction of new elements of evaluation, as the fragment of Hecataeus mentioned above seems to imply. He first points out the variety of *logoi* among the Greeks, and then from this infers their unreliability (*geloioi*). This aspect was particularly emphasized by Jack Goody, who stressed the dependence of historical reflection on the use of documentary material and thus on the spread of writing.[7] The distinction between myth and history became inevitable the moment writing allowed for the juxtaposition of different representations of the universe and the *pantheon* and hence revealed the contradictions between them. Thence was born the need for univocality and the consequent demand for rationality.

Myth criticism, as practiced in the earliest historiography, does not, however, necessarily entail a definite break with traditional religiosity. Such a decidedly religious man as Epimenides objected to the traditional stories in much the same way as Hecataeus and Herodotus did later.[8] On the other hand, "rationalistic" criticism of myth did not presuppose complete abandonment of the traditional story. "As regards Hecataeus, this 'genealogist'—this scholar, that is, of the heroic world—could not deny the fundamental assumption of the heroic history that he studied: namely, intercourse between gods and men."[9] Similar points could be made concerning Herodotean historiography. "Myth criticism" could also take a different direction and aspire to the recovery of a more profound religiosity, as happened for example in the Orphic movement as well as with thinkers either pursuing a more general requirement of rationality, such as the rhapsode-philosopher Xenophanes, or aiming at a more moralized version of the tale, such as Pindar.

These considerations do not aim to reevaluate the importance of sixth century Ionian thought, or to underestimate its genuinely new elements. Rather they call for a careful appraisal of those elements of continuity that allow us to place the emergence of authentically innovative content in clearer focus. Finally, it should be pointed out how the birth of historical thought appears linked to parallel developments in Greek poetry of the early archaic age, particularly in Ionic elegy. In his *Smyrneis,* for example, as in the fragment on the ancient colonization of Colophon, the poet Mimnermus expressed not only a general historical interest but, for the first time, affirmed the need both to understand the causes of important human events and to narrate and interpret them in the light of the remote past,[10] a motif that we find unaltered in the proem to Herodotus's *Histories.* Thus, on the one hand, the difference in the functions that in the archaic age were assigned to poetry and to history should not be exaggerated, while on the other, history appeared very close to—and at first practically inseparable from—geographic and ethnographic research, as is clearly the case in the works of Hecataeus and Herodotus. The sharp distinctions between different disciplines—customary distinctions for us but unthinkable in the same terms for the pre-Aristotelian age—were not yet operative in the Ionian *Histories.*[11] Limiting ourselves to the relationship between myth and history, we can conclude that the type of "research" progressively realized on this common ground did not presuppose nor require a marked distancing with respect to the ancient traditions. Instead these traditions were considered critically and, when necessary, corrected according to criteria of verisimilitude, of comparison with common experience, and hence of general "credibility."

We need not dwell further on this. The treatments accorded by Hecataeus to such traditions as those concerning Cerberus or Geryon, or to the legend of Io at the beginning of Herodotus's *Histories,* are well known.[12] Rather, to conclude this section, we will recall a case of genealogical systematization carried out by Acusilaus of Argos with respect to the traditional origins of his native city. The following genealogy of the first Argive kings can be reconstructed from two fragments of Acusilaus.[13] Phoroneus, the first king, engendered Sparton and Niobe. Myceneus was born of Sparton, while Argos and Pelasgos were the offspring of Niobe and Zeus. These heroes gave their names to the respective cities. The common descent from Phoroneus, presented as the first man,[14] suggests a common origin for Mycenae, Argos, and Sparta. Myceneus, the son of Sparton, however, appears in a different branch from that of Argos and Pelasgos. The genealogy therefore reflects an intention to connect Mycenae with Sparta and, at the same time, to oppose her to Argos. From this observation one can go back to the general conditions of Argolis in the sixth century, when the hostility between Argos and Mycenae was particularly acute; as a consequence Mycenae naturally sought an alliance with Sparta. Pelasgos, on the other hand, is in this genealogy the brother of Argos. This fact may indicate how the hostility between Doric Argos and pre-Doric or even pre-Hellenic elements, probably symbolized in the figure of Pelasgos, was now considered secondary to the more current enmity between Argos and Sparta.[15] If we consider Acusilaus's arrangement in comparison with the one later provided by Hellanicus, we perceive another type of difference. Here Phoroneus has three sons: Pelasgos, Iasos, and Agenor.[16] The tripartition of the region that we encounter at various later times in the traditions of this city comes here to constitute a primary fact and is placed in the age immediately following that of the origins (Phoroneus). If we compare these with the "traditional" genealogies of the city, dating back at least in part to epic traditions (*Phoronis,* Hesiodic traditions) known principally through Pausanias and the *Bibliotheca* of Pseudo-Apollodorus, significant divergences are evident. A profound intention to rationalize and to "order" the oldest traditions of the Argolid has taken measurable effect.[17]

We must still consider how certain elements that are today recognized as typical of historical reflection were not in fact extraneous to mythic narration. A. Momigliano has appropriately recalled how Herodotean historiography was based on a selection of the events to be narrated and favored a qualitative standard: the historian retold those events he deemed worthy of saving from oblivion.[18] Herodotus, like other historians after him, did not intend to recount the past systematically; rather he carried out a selection based on quality. The work of the historian thus appeared as an operation against time, which tended to cancel the past, in order to safeguard the memory of events worthy of being remembered. It will suffice to quote from the proem to Herodotus's *Histories:* "What Herodotus of Halicarnassus has learnt by inquiry is here set forth: in order that the memory of the past may not be blotted out from among men by time, and that great and marvelous deeds done by Greeks and foreigners, and especially the reason why they warred against each other, may not lack renown."

The similarities between this historiographical procedure and the narrative typical of epic have been emphasized numerous times.[19] The epic singer also professed to narrate the truth, which was often explicitly claimed for his own poem. In a nonliterate society narration remained the customary method of transmitting narratives. It "saved" from oblivion those traditions in which the community recognized itself and which for that reason carried out an important social function in the present.[20] Such traditions might appear more or less truthful and they might undergo more or less profound modifications, but what mattered was that they were held to be credible by the community that accepted them. In a society where memory of past events is entrusted to an oral tradition, choice becomes a necessity, and preference obviously goes to those events considered at any given time the most important and the most deserving of preservation. In Herodotus one perceives a reflection of this procedure, characteristic of an oral epic tradition, which continually renews itself and takes on the burden of transmitting the most important exploits of the past so that they are not canceled by the passage of time.[21] The Herodotean formulation is, however, probably already indebted to a consolidated tradition. In the historical work in particular the criterion of veracity assumes a preeminent role and imposes its own requirements and methodologies on the development of the entire narrative.

Equally noteworthy in the proem of the *Histories* is the need to ensure that the glorious deeds of the past do not remain without renown (*aklea genetai*). It will suffice to recall the decisive importance that the epic heroes attached to the attainment of *kleos,* even to the point of gearing all their actions toward its achievement, as well as the decisive role of the poet in conferring *kleos* upon the hero and his exploits.[22] In order for the deed to become fixed in memory and handed down to later generations, the poet's narration and praise are necessary. In this case as well Herodotus appropriated a traditional requirement of the heroic epic. Thus both the choice of events to narrate and the criterion of "historical relevance," arbiter of the greatness of the narrated events, had illustrious precedents in the epic tradition, even if such affirmations ap-

pear oriented toward different ends, linked to the achievement of an
objectively ascertained truth proper to historiography.

Alongside those elements that make historical narrative similar to
epic narrative, epic reveals other elements generally considered typical
of historical narration. These elements have suggested a deliberate "historicizing" or, more accurately, "archaicizing" on the part of the poet.
The almost total absence of references to the Dorians in the Homeric
poems should be viewed in light of the fact that the world described by
the poet is supposed to be that before the Doric invasion (in the sense
that this invasion was absorbed into the Greek tradition), even if such a
negation is not in fact complete and references to the Doric world and
its institutions occasionally appear in the poems. The most notable case
of this type is represented by the traditions surrounding Tlepolemos at
Rhodes.[23] Similar considerations could be advanced for the catalogue of
ships in the second book of the *Iliad*. Considering the complexity of the
problems that this section of the poem still poses—and for which the
Mycenaean documentary evidence has suggested a broader but incon-
clusive array of references—comprehensive solutions may not yet be advanced. There remain, however, some general reference points that must
always be kept in mind in the examination of this section of the poem.
In particular, the description here offered of the Greek continent and the
Aegean islands is not ascribable to any known period of archaic Greece;
at least some of the localities were not easily identifiable at the time of
the poem's composition; and finally the most noteworthy centers in the
Homeric presentation are generally those that enjoyed an analogous importance in the Mycenaean era.[24] This general tendency to "historicize"
may also be noted in several minor but nonetheless significant passages
of the narrative. Again in the catalogue of ships, it is stated that the
Ionian city of Miletos was inhabited by Carian barbarians (*Il.* 2.687):
Karon hegesato barbarophonon), although archaeology demonstrates
that at the time of the Trojan expedition the region was largely Mycenaean. This passage probably reflects the tradition whereby the first truly
Greek colonies to inhabit Miletos arrived there at the time of the Ionian
migration, that is to say several generations after the Trojan War. For a
previous age only the presence of Carian barbarians is accepted. This
presentation thus suggests a deliberate archaizing, aiming to avoid reference to contemporary reality and to situate peoples and cities in the
age the poet considered theirs.[25] Poetry and history seem to condition
each other alternatively in this more ancient period. The frame of reference is established by the fact that both history and poetry make use of
the same mythic heritage, although with different perspectives and intentions. To the extent to which it presents itself as a truthful story and

as the guardian of tradition, epic cannot avoid a certain tendency toward "historicizing," nor can it in consequence do without a certain temporal dimension that would avoid obvious anachronisms. In this sense it does not seem a matter of chance that, when such constraints lapsed, as in similes, the contemporary world could more freely enter this poetry.

We have recalled several aspects of Greek traditions to which the character of historicity was attributed. A related problem concerns the reliability of such claims. This problem will be dealt with to a limited degree in the second part of this chapter, especially in regard to some results of modern research. Several studies have emphasized the fact that myth carried out much more important and complex functions in Greek society than the transmission of more or less reliable memories of the distant past. In certain cases the similarities between mythic and historical narration are unacknowledged, and in consequence an important feature of the method by which the Greeks represented their heroic past is denied. At times the differences have been exaggerated to the point that myth and history have been presented as two separate, unconnected spheres. Here we must recall some of the more frequent objections put forward:

1) the mythic past, handed down orally, refers to a purely legendary past (what happened "once upon a time"), does not show any interest in either relative or absolute chronological order, and thus is by its very nature without historical interest;
2) myth is a stitching together of heterogeneous elements; a historical analysis can point out its internal seams, helping to illuminate its formation, but the myth itself cannot be used in the reconstruction of historical events;[26]
3) the Greeks clearly distinguished between the mythic age and the age of men; these two ages were felt to be profoundly different, as a well-known passage in Herodotus (3.122) demonstrates.

To the extent that these objections tend to valorize other aspects or functions of myth, they are well taken and they require that we avoid misunderstandings or simplifications. Myth was called on to satisfy various demands in Greek society, and it is not possible to limit its function to the transmission of historical events, even to those of general interest for the community.

What is less acceptable in this formulation is the potential misunderstanding of a dimension that from the Greek perspective (the only one under consideration here) appeared inseparable from their traditions: in their myths the Greeks recognized events that actually happened. In particular, the legends recounted in the heroic epic were situated in a well-defined past; this past was neither identified nor confused with "the age of the gods," which was understood as "the time of origins" and felt to be profoundly different from the historical world of men. Systematic examination reveals even the supposed contradictions in the heroic genealogies to be less numerous and less conclusive than was generally thought, although they present the normal oscillations verifiable in other aspects of the tradition.[27] The ancient sources especially did not authorize a distinct separation between heroic and human worlds. In particular, the passage from Herodotus already cited affirms that Polycrates was the first to think about exercising dominion of the seas, if Minos of Cnossos and any others before him are excluded. It concludes: *tes de anthropeies legomenes genees Polykrates protos, ktl* ('at least as regards the human race Polycrates was the first').[28] This passage from Herodotus does not contain anything substantially different from what was already known from the *Works and Days* of Hesiod (159ff.). Here the heroes are defined as *theion genos, hoi kaleontai hemitheoi, protere genee kat' apeirona gaian.* The qualification *hemitheoi* should be understood in the sense of "descended from the gods," without reference to the supposed semidivine status of the heroes.[29] *Protere genee* defines the heroes as belonging to the race immediately preceding the present one. The heroic world is thus situated in a sphere that is neither purely human nor purely divine, but one that occupies its own dimension in the history of the world. The heroic age immediately precedes the present age of man. Therefore, to the extent to which a mythic sphere tends to be clearly defined and opposed to a human sphere, an essential trait that typified the heroic world for Greek eyes is denied. If we wish to maintain the ambivalence that characterized the heroic world, it is necessary to think that on the one hand the heroic world was "the age of myth"— not however simply identifiable with the era of origins—and on the other hand that it constituted "the ancient history" of the various cities and races. It is in this sense that the human character of the heroes, observed numerous times in modern research, is valorized. The complexity of functions projected by the Greeks into their representation of the heroic world does not allow for simplifications and univocal interpretations; even less does it authorize a sharp opposition between the heroic world and the human world.

From what has been said so far we may conclude that the Greeks did not feel very profoundly the opposition between myth and history, as we might be tempted to believe on the basis of a prevalently modern viewpoint. Rather, from a certain age on they began to question myth and to search for answers both by subjecting their traditions to criticism and by adopting a rational analysis (which to us moderns may appear rationalistic) that left no space for the marvelous. Alongside the developments in the historical and philosophical disciplines we could recall a parallel development in the sphere of epic poetry itself. Xenophanes' attacks on the traditions and the criticisms he applied to Homer are to be considered together with the defense offered in the same period by Theagenes of Rhegium. It does not appear to be a matter of chance that the progressive crisis of epic poetry was accompanied by a parallel process of discovery of the values found in this poetry. The allegorical interpretation of Homer, linked to the name of Theagenes, represents a discovery of the "profundity" of the Homeric text.[30] It permitted the attainment of a veracity that escaped a superficial hearing. One should remember that this practice of "reading" Homer allegorically assumed a certain diffusion of written communication. More thorough examinations and comparisons, as we have already noted in regard to historiography, become easier and more natural in a society where written communication has begun to establish itself alongside the oral tradition. Also dependent on the spread of written communication are the first manifestations of textual criticism of the Homeric poems, attributed to Theagenes and correctly esteemed as the oldest evidence of a philological examination of texts.[31] The search for rationality, allegorical interpretation, the birth of historical reflection, the crisis of the traditional forms of communication and of the values that accompanied them all contributed in different ways to delineate a profound change in late archaic Greece. "Myth criticism" played a decisive role in this change.

If on the one hand in historical narrative the Greeks demanded research aimed at truth, at recovering events worthy of narration, on the other hand they displayed a parallel tendency to detach from history events and persons of particular significance. When contemporary individuals or facts were deemed particularly important they might be idealized and raised to the sphere of myth, almost as if what was really notable could not happen at the simple historical level. If, in the scope of research aiming at the attainment of truth through the critique of traditions, myth was called upon to express historical content, on the other hand the historical event could aspire to the achievement of a mythic dimension. The importance that the process of "heroization" of real persons had in this sphere hardly bears repeating. Chosen individuals could be important men—a colonialist who led an expedition or famous athletes or poets.[32] Yet heroic honors could also be bestowed upon far from illustrious persons who were at times marked by grave faults but in whose human experience could be perceived signs that limits traditionally associated with low status had been overcome. In all of these cases the process of heroization provoked an adaptation of the actual circumstances whence it sprang to the forms imposed by a recognized model, "not so much *deforming* historical reality as *integrating* the individual (who had lived in a contingent reality) into the significant and permanent *form* of the hero." [33] The possibility of these reciprocal adaptations may be explained by the similarities that the Greeks recognized between historical experience and myth. As J. Burckhardt stated: "We cannot argue strongly enough against the widespread error according to which a people as shrewd as the Greeks must have had an acute critical sense. In reality the Greeks dedicated themselves with the greatest zeal to seeking out the single events and geographical details of their antiquity, but their historical sense never went much beyond the mythic viewpoint." [34] And later: "And so where a real and true history could have sprung up, it was suffocated by the ever-living saga, that is to say by invention, which gradually plugged every crack through which historical exactness might have insinuated itself. Even evident reality was seen and talked about only in the spirit of myth; even that which was history fell under the laws of a tradition that remained for a long time solely oral and poetic." [35] While affirmations such as these may today appear excessive, because they seem to deny to the Greeks the notable results they achieved in the field of historiography, they are appropriate if referred to the basic function that myth had in the formation and transmission of the heroic past.

The Greek failure to grant supremacy to history may also be discerned in some of the results of theoretical inquiry. Following the premises from which we set out, we must ask ourselves, for example, to what degree the rationality of Thucydidean historiography, through the search for causes, the insertion of speeches, their use within the overall argumentation results in a selective narration. In this way we are lead to appreciate how these new directions in historiography are associated, as they were in the past, with changes observable in other sectors, especially in philosophical thought (the Sophists and Plato). In each case the simple narration of events, to the extent that it appears unable to reorganize the "facts" within general models of interpretation that would confer upon them a character of rationality, for that very reason leads to a loss of interest and scientific credibility.

The clear and decisive disparagement of history in Aristotle's *Poetics* is characteristic: "Poetry is a theoretical activity and more serious than history (*philosophoteron kai spoudaioteron, poiesis historias estin*). Poetry tends to give general truths while history gives particular facts. General means the sort of thing that a certain type of man will do or say either probably or necessarily (*kata to eikos e to anankaion*); and it is this with which poetry is occupied, even if it adds the names of characters. The particular is instead what Alcibiades did or what was done to him." [36] In a poetical work the events unfold according to a criterion of necessity or probability, that is, they are connected by a logical order and sequence that renders their exposition rationally comprehensible; history is instead the realm of the particular and the casual, in which what follows is not necessarily related to what came before. Thus what happens in history is like what happens in the stories of incompetent poets, who are incapable of offering a coherent plot with a single purpose. "And thus the compositions must not be such that we normally find in history, where what is required is an exposition not of a single action, but of a single period of time, showing all that within the period befell one or more persons, events that have a merely casual relation to each other." [37] In this perspective, which clearly privileges the logical order over the chronological succession of events, mythic thought also comes to assume a more important role with respect to history. In the *Metaphysics* he who devotes himself to traditional stories (*philomythos*) is considered along with those who practice the highest forms of knowledge. In fact mythopoetic activity, like philosophic activity, is born from the sensation of wonder provoked by phenomena that cannot be explained, and myth is an aggregate of marvelous elements (*ho gar mythos synkeitai ek thaumasion*).[38] In Aristotelian thought only the universals constitute secure objects of knowledge, and in this approximation to the universals, myth, like poetry, demonstrates its advantage over history. Myth, however, proposing explanations in personal terms, turns to particular causes in order to interpret particular events. In this sense it distances itself from philosophy and approaches historical narrative, which proceeds by means of particular judgments.[39] Herein lies its weakness with respect to the philosophical interpretation. Still, to the extent that myth aspires to a universal knowledge of the world, it joins up again with philosophy and moves away from history.

IS AN HISTORICAL ANALYSIS OF MYTH ADEQUATE?

Having considered in the first part of this chapter several aspects of the relationship between myth and history from the point of view of the ancient Greeks, in this second part we will examine the same problem with regard to certain results of modern research.

In a study of Greek myth, G. S. Kirk, after rapidly reviewing various theories, noted that by the beginning of the 1930s classical scholars were already sated with myth theory.[40] It was the general impression that the new approaches introduced by the Cambridge school would be sufficient for several generations. Yet it is difficult not to agree with Brelich when, in the preface to *Gli eroi greci,* he noted how the interests of the classicists had from the beginning of the century moved continually away from those of the historians of religion in the name of a specialization (invoked primarily by the former) that would eventually cause serious misunderstandings of even the most basic aspects of ancient culture, not limitable to the religious sphere.[41] On the one hand, interest in religion and myth was almost excessive (at least to the extent that this interest appeared inseparable from a complex theoretical apparatus); on the other hand, a profound incomprehension of even noteworthy cultural facts was revealed, to the extent that classicists failed to assimilate new approaches developed in the anthropological and historico-religious fields. A mediation might have been carried out by the work of M. P. Nilsson, whose youthful anthropological interests and studies dedicated to the religion of the primitives led to the later interest in the origins of Greek civilization.[42] Undoubtedly at least a part of this scholar's production has played a very useful role in this respect. One thinks particularly of his studies of Homer and the heroic age and those on the origins of Greek mythology in relation to Mycenaean civilization;[43] obviously many of his contributions are still an indispensable point of reference for current research. Taken as a whole, however, his analyses today appear insufficient, and indeed Brelich considered Nilsson an illustrious example of a "classicist" scholar in the fields of Greek religion and mythology.

The picture offered by current research, even when limited to the subject of this essay, has been enriched compared to that of several decades ago, but not to the point of canceling the differences between traditionally opposed approaches. According to certain scholars, as is well known, the so-called historical interpretation, not always specifically defined, represents the only form for the understanding of cultural facts. Others instead have asserted that such an analysis is totally incapable of an adequate comprehension of Greek myth. Thus on the one hand historical analysis is seen as the only approach able to offer a satisfying interpretation of myth, while on the other hand the structuring categories of myth are deemed largely insensible to history. Here we will seek to define better those historical queries that are pertinent to the object under consideration (myth), distinguishing them from others that, although equally pertinent, require a different type of analysis.

A first type of analysis considers the mythic tale in the light of particular historical events that might have left traces in the tale. This is not to be understood in a restrictive sense, according to which the myth would be more or less entirely reducible to its historical nucleus, as has indeed sometimes been attempted. Such an analysis aims rather at discovering and considering separately a series of facts referable to determinate historical conditions or events. This analysis thus emphasizes something already considered in the first part of this essay, where I showed that the Greeks recognized in myth, and especially in epic tradition and heroic legend, the presence of historical memories of an ancient past. Even with the reservations expressed above, one may assert that by and large classical scholars have appreciated this aspect of the historicity of myth. They have not found it improbable that with this analysis one can classify traditions, tales, and customs evidenced in myth as echoes of a remote age, the memories of which were to some degree preserved in the "traditions." The approach was indeed adopted in the studies that K. O. Muller devoted to the examination of mythology in relation to the "prehistoric" epochs of the Greek world.[44] The area in which history and myth were summoned to confront one another even afterwards remained that of the "origins," or at least the earliest period for which it was thought sufficient historical information was available. Already from these presuppositions the basic option of every historical interpretation of myth clearly emerges: the comprehension of myth depends on knowledge of the causes that determined first its genesis and then its variations. Later, following Schliemann's discoveries, E. Rohde compared the "Mycenaean" evidence then emerging from Circle A at Mycenae with the traditions and customs present in Homer.[45] Similarly, Wilamowitz saw in the Ionian epic reflections of the power and the splendor of great sovereigns who in a period several centuries before our oldest evidence had dominated the Greek continent.[46] This approach subsequently underwent some well-known developments in the work of Nilsson, who was the first to propose a systematic relationship between the Mycenaean archaeological evidence and the formation of the great epic cycles.

At times it was thought that one could venture much further with this system. Wilamowitz saw the Seven against Thebes as the oldest war preserved in historical memory.[47] He was followed in this hypothesis by Eduard Meyer and by Carl Robert, both of whom inserted this tradition in a series of events involving the Cadmeians in the second millennium.[48] Thus the scholars of antiquity were not indifferent to the valorization of this aspect of myth. If anything they ran the risk, as Nilsson himself noted, of offering an excessively historicist interpretation, given that myth appeared heterogeneous in composition and did not have the support of a truly parallel historical tradition.[49] Here it should be added that the new analytical perspectives on the epic tradition initiated by the studies of M. Parry did not substantially modify this general approach. Parry was not much interested in the problem of the historical reliability of the contents of oral epic. Nilsson, however, found confirmation of his thesis on the Mycenaean origins of Greek mythology both in the comparison with the similar epic tradition of other cultures and in the compositional technique pointed out by Parry. This technique allowed for the efficacious illustration of the forms through which epic poetry conveyed contents and cultural characteristics dating back to a remote past.[50]

Along with the historicity of the mythic tradition, we must recall at the very least a second emphasis on which modern research has been generally insistent: The material of mythology has appeared substantially composite in its nature and origin. We have already seen that the reasons for doubt concerning the historical use of myth are attributable to this very fact. As the object of study does not lend itself to an exhaustive analysis conducted from a single perspective, an explanation that isolates the various components in a temporal succession while simultaneously noting their substantial heterogeneity has been attempted. Thus Nilsson returned to Wilamowitz's distinction between *Religion* and *Mythologie:* the former would be the bearer of the Greeks' authentic religious sentiment, while the latter would be primarily the fruit of poetic elaboration.[51] Mythology in its turn appeared two-faced: it contained on the one hand a confluence of folktale contents (*Märchen*) and on the other hand elements recognized as historical (*Geschichte, Legende*).[52] Fables in the strict sense of the word, which had as purpose simple entertainment, were distinguished from the *Aitia,* which played a precise role in providing explanations of the origins of customs and social institutions. But obviously even this distinction did not appear rigid and various elements from one or the other group could come together freely enough.[53] As the analysis became more exhaustive it became that much harder to orient oneself within a myth. Thomas Dunbabin, a historian, could refer to the Greek traditions as a "confused palimpsest of Greek religion and mythology."[54] In the face of concrete analyses, the distinction among the various levels became problematic; and as anyone who has inquired into such a divided documentation can attest, the results tend to be largely hypothetical.

Therefore, if on the one hand these classifications recall the necessity of keeping in mind the complexity of the evidence under examination, on the other hand to the extent that the classifications are "historicizing" and emphasize content rather than form, they reveal themselves ill suited to the purpose. Brelich, for example, viewed as illusory the attempt to separate the purely folkloristic characteristics from the other authentically mythical ones in a mythical narrative, and urged instead the need to emphasize the use made of the same motif in different contexts.[55] Brelich himself, on the other hand, admitted the possibility that some mythic traditions may have been formed around real facts and added that, in such cases, "the historical element is distinguished in that, and as long as, it preserves its own unrepeatable character;" but in the case where the historical element has been totally assimilated into the traditional forms of myth, it would lose, along with its specificity, also the possibility of being recognized as historical.[56]

Along with the criterion just mentioned—the "singularity" of the element under consideration—other criteria may be useful in orienting ourselves in the historical appraisal of a myth:

1) There must be a series of parallel data, referable if only in part to the same events to which the mythic tale supposedly refers. For the second millennium these data are furnished above all by archaeology and, for particular aspects, by historical linguistics. The thesis according to which the heroic legends of the Greeks date back through an uninterrupted tradition to the Mycenaean civilization in the sense indicated by Nilsson still constitutes a useful reference point, even if evidently not all of the historically usable data may be referred to this age.

2) Such archaeological and linguistic data must be abundant, sufficiently unambiguous, and distributable in a continuous series, if possible. The comparison will then be less uncertain, and it will be possible to have a fairly homogeneous succession in the two series brought into comparison.

3) As regards heroic legend in particular, it must be linked to history in various ways, both in the contents chosen for inclusion and in the narrative procedures adopted. On the one hand, heroic legend uses historical elements, inherited for the most part through the mediation of irretrievably lost epic songs, and on the other, it adopts a historical slant expressed, for example, in the poet's deliberate "archaizing" or through the exclusion of fabulous elements. When the fabulous is present, it figures for the most part in secondary episodes that do not contribute significantly to the general unfolding of the action.

A second type of historical approach analyzes myth by focusing not on possible external references, but rather on cultural elements that figure as an integral part of the narration. The interpretation thus depends on the possibility of defining the material and existential exigencies, both individual and collective, of which myth is made the bearer. Even in this case, however, granted that myth is a traditional tale formed over a long period of time, such exigencies are not always homologous; rather, they are necessarily heterogeneous. Therefore this approach insists upon diachronic succession, which is entrusted with primary responsibility for the interpretation of myth. In the words of Brelich's clear formulation: "in order to understand a myth, it is indispensable to establish from which stratum—or in the frequent cases of successive reelaborations, from which strata—it draws its origin.[57] As is well known, there are various models of this kind of historical interpretation. Here we will refer only to a few of those of particular interest for modern research.

According to one thesis, a model for the history of myth follows the general evolution of human societies. A first level of mythic elaboration is made to date back to the phase of hunting and gathering; a subsequent reelaboration would have taken place with the introduction of agriculture ("the neolithic revolution"); and a still later phase with the advent of the "higher civilizations." In Greece, this phase was already reached in the Mycenaean age, as is demonstrated by the existence of a polytheistic *pantheon* in this period.[58] Other analyses have preferred to make a distinction in myth between an older component referable to the so-called Aegean substratum and a more recent one that became established with the arrival of the Indo-European peoples.[59] In these diverse analyses, the relationships between myth and history have been strongly emphasized. Myth appears directly connected with the profound changes predominant from time to time in the social and political structures.

A similar history-inspired analysis, which assumes a stratified formation of myth, is that of Walter Burkert, though it stands out as having certain aspects of particular interest.[60] Of these, the most conspicuous is the emphasis on the profoundly violent nature of human action and the accompanying sensation of anguish. The author's primary referent is the work of Karl Meuli, but significantly he also attempts a recovery of the Freud of *Totem and Taboo*.[61] Man, in the earliest era that we can go back to (Paleolithic), appears as *Homo necans*, but the aggressive character of the human action that leads man to kill animals for food at the same time produces a feeling of guilt. The tension of these opposed needs engenders sacrifice. The historical dimension is here linked to a functional analysis. A process of guilt coupled with denial and exoneration initiates a series of cultural processes that would find wide testimony in the myths and rites of the Greeks.

Finally, along with these theories of a general character, to which we could easily add others, we should recall those historically more verifiable events that are normally considered to play a significant role in the history of myth and sometimes also in its formation. In this sphere the influence exerted on the Greek continent by the Near East played an important role in at least two historical moments: in the final phase of the Mycenaean age and later in the seventh and eighth centuries (the Orientalizing period). Also of notable importance were the Delphic oracle, rationalism in the era of late archaism (sixth century), and especially for a later age, political propaganda. All of these aspects should be attentively considered in the historical examination of a myth.

In *Paides e Parthenoi* Brelich has offered a very interesting analysis, illustrating how traditional tribal initiations came to be adapted to the new structures of the historical *polis*.[62] This work also contains analyses that could be defined as structuralist, but the historical approach, with constant use of comparisons, is far more prevalent. On the whole one cannot escape the impression that there is a general tendency both to qualify the primitive institutions as "original" and to differentiate them from the institutions that in Greece already appear historically conditioned but, because of their "antiquity," could only be understood as originating from the primitive institutions. Brelich's analysis has provoked some well-founded perplexity.[63] The notion of archaism as an interpretive category to define institutions of the oldest phase of Greek culture recalls the parallel attempt to define the "heroic ages" by means of a group of characteristics—for the most part relating to the type of these societies and to the historical epoch in which they were established—that distinguished them with respect to primitive societies, wherein nonetheless they found their natural terms of comparison.[64] This tendency enjoyed its moment of favor when the attempt was made to define a general morphology of the heroic ages. A more extensive examination proved that, even in the literary field, the production of these periods was generally more varied and diversified than had been thought.[65]

A third point to consider regarding the historical use of myth concerns the particular alterations that myth has been subjected to in relation to political reality. Politically motivated introduction of innovations was always possible, but its ascertainment is far from easy. As is well known, myth lives by variants; the possibility of change represents not only one of the conditions of survival, but also myth's primary form of expression. If "myth criticism" was born alongside myth itself (in the sense indicated in the first part of this paper), it follows that the ascertainment of alterations for political purposes (propaganda) requires an even greater prudence than in the cases previously considered. The case discussed in the first part, Acusilaus of Argos's systematization of the Argive genealogies, also represents an interesting political use of myth:

in particular circumstances and for particular requirements even genealogies that had an acknowledged tradition in epic poetry could admit significant changes. This feature of Acusilaus' narrative stood out precisely because of its singularity with respect to other, "traditional" versions; some doubts emerged even in the source to which we are indebted for the information (Pausanias). In order to avoid abusing this sort of reading of a myth several things are necessary: (1) that various narratives of the same myth be available; (2) that the historical circumstances indicated as the more or less proximate causes be relatively clear; and (3) that we possess a series of parallel stories that show the originality of the "altered" version. Given the nature of the evidence, it will not always be easy to bring these ideal conditions together. In this respect, Nilsson's study, *Cults, Myths, Oracles and Politics in Ancient Greece*, appears on the whole convincing. He proposes a systematic analysis of myths for which we possess an ample series of versions; from this it would be relatively easy to ascertain the nature and the meaning of the changes introduced.

Of a somewhat different nature are the reservations that may arise from a unilaterally "philological" reading of myth. The inability of this approach to comprehend even fundamental aspects of the ancient world was pointed out by Brelich numerous times. More recent orientations of research have contributed to a more pragmatic understanding of Greek culture, particularly in the archaic age, through recognition of the role played by oral communication.[66] Here we will dwell upon a number of misunderstandings that may arise even from a largely acceptable vision of Greek literature and culture, such as that which acknowledges the significant role of oral communication and hence also the importance it had in the transmission of myths.

In the general framework proposed by Kirk, the change from oral to written communication, dating back to the sixth century, would have profoundly restructured the myths and significantly altered their nature and meaning.[67] Thus Kirk proposed an orientation somewhat different from Brelich's when he emphasized the fact that we should not consider Greek myths on the same level as those of primitive peoples.[68] His reminder not to underestimate the importance that the passage to written transmission had for Greek mythology is surely appropriate. A story born to be narrated orally loses some of its characteristics when it becomes part of a literary tradition. Such a loss, however, primarily affects the particular forms of the performance or the role of recitation on particular occasions (a religious holiday, for example). In the state in which the mythic tale has come down to us, it is isolated both from the ethnographic context and from the pragmatic conditions that proclaimed its success in the past. All this has certainly had importance as regards the religious valorization of myth, but the loss appears less serious if we limit ourselves to considering the myth as a story. It would be excessive to conclude that myth, once it becomes part of literature, is dominated by the individual and unique aesthetic requirements of which the author is himself the bearer. Kirk in particular tends to differentiate rather sharply between the age of Homer and Hesiod and that which begins with Stesichorus, in which the most markedly reproductive phase of the tradition had its start.[69] It is easy to recognize in this succession the scheme put forward by the same author for the stages of the oral epic tradition. The reproductive stage and the "degenerate" stage, which follows it, constitute the last two links of a poetic tradition now moving toward disintegration.[70] In this perspective, the original and authentic traditional story is reduced to the simplest narrative scheme. Authenticity, a primitive and happy phase in the evolution of myth, is inseparably linked to the oral tradition, whereas the written tradition functions by means of a manipulation of the traditional story.[71] "A distinction needs to be drawn between the instinctive use of a tale for the expression or refinement of an attitude, and the conscious choice of a familiar fictitious situation as a means of representing a deliberate and personal analysis."[72] The oral tradition effects a "type of organic modification," respecting the logic and the meaning of the story, while written communication initiates a phase of the distortion of meaning, an illicit use of the tradition to achieve the most diverse aims.

This interpretive model is open to some reservations:

1. For our knowledge of Greek mythology we possess only traditions known from literature. As a consequence, it is often impossible to distinguish between older and more recent variants: the late source of a story does not attest to its recentness,[73] even if in the most fortunate cases (which, in any case, are few) we possess various parallels that can provide us with clues as to the recentness of a story or some of its features.

2. As regards oral transmission, on the one hand orality has been called upon to guarantee the genuineness of the mythic story, while on the other it is considered easier in an oral culture to intervene in the tradition, which in this perspective appears more changeable and susceptible to corruption. Writing then becomes the guarantor of reliability. Neither option appears decisive: obviously, alterations are possible in either case. In particular, a mechanical parallelism between the progressive stiffening and degeneration of oral epic and the perversion and impoverishment of the mythic tale seems unacceptable. In tracing back the history of a myth we must recognize that the narratives of Homer

and Hesiod already presuppose a long tradition whose precedents are indicated in various poems of the Near East, not only in the contents but also in recurrent stylistic elements and expressive forms.[74] In the case of the myths related by Hesiod, it is well known that similar narratives already circulated in written versions in the Near East in the second millennium.[75]

3. The traditional story is not reducible to a sort of neutral presentation of the facts, assimilable to the simple narrative nucleus. Whether it depends on oral or written, literary or popular sources, every story is the result of a selection and organization of facts, within which certain relationships are established or privileged in preference to others. This characteristic is noticeable in every literary elaboration: in consequence it should be possible to note the presence of such "alterations" already in Homer. But is it really certain that the Homeric narrative is always older and, from this point of view, more "authentic" than those known from later sources? We may also consider a widely known case in which Homer seems to mirror a particularly ancient narrative, perhaps referring to events of the Mycenaean age. In the only place in the *Iliad* in which Oedipus is mentioned, many have wanted to see a reference to the hero's violent death in combat against the neighboring Minyans of Orkhomenos (*Il.* 23.679: *dedoupotos Oidipodao*). This interpretation was already offered in antiquity by Aristarchus.[76] The tradition did not take hold and was later abandoned in favor of that known from the tragedies of Sophocles. That notwithstanding, is it permissible in this case, even if only from a mythic perspective, to consider the tragic version as less authentic or of lesser interest than the version, of venerable tradition, known from Homer? To exclude this possibility it is enough to recall the ending of *Oedipus at Colonus* and the interest that these verses offer in the unfolding of a central thematic of the Oedipus myth. In the case of the Oedipus myth and in many similar cases, it is always possible to invoke the role played in the transmission of myth by local traditions; these serve as the collectors of the "genuine" traditions on which the literary versions drew, revising them in the process.[77] But in this case, and whenever the authenticity of a narrative is argued from the absence of a literary elaboration, it becomes necessary to establish how many of these "ancient" traditions have come down to us solely through "late" sources. Thus one is lead to question the not always easily resolvable history and fortune of a myth. In fact, these are precisely the problems that a historical examination of myth has the greatest difficulties in solving. To get around them, Brelich invoked the ethnological method, which he declared preferable to the "philological" method and which is based on comparison.[78] The evidence is considered on the basis

of the data it offers before it is considered in relation to the sources from which it is known. Some reservations are possible concerning the general efficacy of this method of analyzing myth: in particular, the proposed diachronic grid within which the data are considered (hunting and gathering society, introduction of agriculture, affirmation of a polytheistic *pantheon,* and so forth) appears too broad and does not take sufficient account of the great richness of Greek mythology, of the diversified narrative situations to which it has given birth, or of the no less significant variants. Nonetheless this method represents a marked progress beyond a textual analysis based on the recovery of the narrative's presumed antiquity. A general limit of this latter approach is in fact its claim to draw near to the original nucleus of the narrative in a manner substantially similar to that adopted by a long tradition of study that searched for other myths lying behind those for which we have direct testimony, in the vain quest for a first or original meaning. Not only did this type of analysis often prove illusory, but it also resulted in the introduction of a dichotomy between older and more recent myth, which is at bottom also a distinction between true myth and false myth.

The recognition of the literary character of our sources for myth remains an important fact, even though it ought not to lead to a general disparagement of those sources most deeply influenced by such a reelaboration. However subjective the literary version of a myth may be, the traditional story must still have been recognizable in its essential lines, and that is sufficient to guarantee the reliability of a version, even one known only from a late source. On the other hand, the cases are not very frequent and normally we possess more than one narrative for the same myth. The invitation to consider the specific characteristics of the literary source employed would appear more useful. It is well known that the various modes of communication, especially the literary ones, impose their own forms on the contents of the narrative. Every successive elaboration contributes in various ways, through the conditions imposed by the literary genre or else by the particular circumstances of its execution, to accentuate a certain narrative program only partially implicit in the chosen mythic material. The general proposal of Charles Segal regarding Greek tragedy is particularly interesting because it calls for the valorization of the literary medium through which myth is narrated. By examining this specific mediation, one can appreciate the peculiar character of the story or of the tragic version under consideration.[79] The example of tragedy, as compared with other, older changes introduced by literary treatment, probably represents a limit case, considering the profound influences to which the narration was exposed in such circumstances. In the tragic elaboration—so it has been claimed—

it is the myth itself that disintegrates; the poet's thematic reorganization would thus reach the very mechanisms of myth.[80] These hypotheses appear on the whole excessive. One may note that if the new requirements and values appropriated by tragedy threaten to submerge the organization of the traditional narrative, they encounter some objective limitations in the very nature of the story intended for the stage. New exigencies were able to foster the use of previously neglected diverse or secondary aspects of myth; in some cases they arrived at the creation of new myths, but on the whole they had to express themselves in renewing, or what is the same, in "criticizing," earlier narratives and thus in valorizing previously unexpressed potentialities.

As is well known, the term *mythos* also indicates the plot of a tragedy in Aristotle's *Poetics*.[81] This usage may certainly be explained by the indefiniteness inherent in the term itself (to be understood in the broad sense of "traditional story"), but it should also lead us to avoid too marked distinctions between literary and other versions, even though in the case of the former we ought to pay particular attention to the rules of hypercodification operating in the genre. While the reduction of the mythic tale in tragedy to the level of *fabula* may be useful for the appraisal of the story's general structure, it nevertheless appears untenable whenever one intends to propose an exhaustive analysis of a myth. The literary version is not characterized solely by the fact that it presents a series of additional elements from which the narrative must be liberated; it also represents a more complex version that can offer the modern interpreter useful evidence for the understanding of the myth under consideration.

Before concluding these reflections on the relationship between history and myth it seems opportune to recall the proposal contained in a recent work, which moves in a different direction from the one followed here. Paul Veyne's *Les Grecs ont-ils cru à leurs mythes?* would seem to offer a one-sidedly ideological reading of Greek myth, if the work itself did not reject the primary support on which such a reading traditionally relied, namely the historical and social referent of myth. In this study, the variety and inventiveness usually attributed to mythic creation is revealed to be substantially similar to that which we find in history.[82] According to the author, "If one arrives at elaborating a doctrine for which beliefs can be neither true nor false, it follows from this that even the supposedly rational sectors such as social and economic history must also be considered as neither true nor false." [83] Any possibility of an autonomous elaboration of the human experience is denied to reason. Any reflection, whether qualified as mythic or rational, is shown to be the creation of an *imagination constituante,* that is, of a reason that need not account for its own affirmations, except to itself. Under the impulse of interests that are objective but related only to their own individual choices, historical interpretation, ideology, and myth are united in a single mythopoetic activity. If other analyses have shown themselves either too optimistic in drawing historical elements from mythic stories or simply too inclined to individuate reflections of contemporary events in myth, Veyne's proposal adopts precisely the contrary option: it is not myth that is interpreted historically, but rather it is history that is assimilated to myth. Myth is seen not as the manipulator of collective representations, but rather as the product of man's creative imagination, capable of a divinatory power able to create without a preconstituted model.[84] The complexity and peculiarity of the mythic tale, however, do not permit a general acceptance of Veyne's reading. His radical proposal can be seen, however, as a useful counterbalance to some panhistorical interpretations of myth. In fact, if myth can be interpreted historically, even history can be read in a mythic way, as the Greeks already knew.

The relationships between history and myth examined to this point appear, indeed, rather complex, whether viewed from the perspective of the ancients or from that of certain results of modern research. Their reciprocal limits do not appear clearly definable, but rather from time to time changeable and complicated. This is so because the subject matter of Greek myth cannot be easily reduced to a rigid opposition between myth and history. Euhemerism and hypercritical skepticism, with their respective risks, face each other as two contrary possibilities. In Greek myth many heterogeneous contents—distinguished by nature, origin, and age—have evidently come together. To become oriented in this heterogeneous body of traditions and data has not been easy and has often lead to largely hypothetical results. I have here sought to focus attention on the type of question to which the analysis of myth is capable of offering a response. Some considerations on the Oedipus myth may serve to exemplify what has been said thus far.

We have already seen how the figure of Oedipus was surrounded by a series of stories that presented him in a very different light from that of the tragedies of Sophocles. From the *Odyssey* one learns that the hero did not die together with his mother Epikaste but rather survived her (*Od.* 11.271–80). There is no mention of his exile or of the hospitality offered him by Theseus in Attica. The hero, although amidst great sufferings, continued to rule Thebes according to the disastrous counsel of the gods. From a passage in the *Iliad* (23.677–80) one gathers that Oedipus ruled Thebes until his death; moreover, there is also an allusion to his violent death in combat (23.679: *dedoupotos Oidipodao*).[85] Thus the Homeric version deviates from the better-known tradition on several points. Other events of Oedipus's story must have been narrated in other epic poems—the *Oidipodea* and the epic of Peisandros—but little is known of these works.[86]

The hypothesis has been advanced that these other events could be referred to the Mycenaean age. The information regarding the hero's violent death has been interpreted in this sense, and it is thought that his enemies were the Minyans of Orkhomenos or the Phlegyans, traditionally hostile to the Thebans. In particular, the first of these hypotheses would seem to be confirmed by a fragment of Pherecydes in which it is related that two sons of Oedipus and Epicaste, not known from other sources (Phrastor and Laonytus), perished at the hands of the Minyans lead by Erginos.[87] We learn of this conflict between the Thebans and Orkhomenians from other sources,[88] and in this tradition as in others events of the Mycenaean age might be reflected, probably handed down through the medium of epic. For this reason, Nilsson's thesis, which saw Oedipus as a folktale character and denied the existence of recognizably historical elements in the traditions surrounding this hero, may appear reductive.[89]

In other respects, too, this hero has been related to customs and traditions dating back to the second millennium. In a noted work on Oedipus, Marie Delcourt has interpreted the union of Oedipus and his mother as a sort of hierogamy, related to the hero's taking possession of the land; thus the entire Oedipus story is characterized as that of a conquering hero.[90] Along this same interpretive line is the thesis that sees in Oedipus a primitive figure of the *paredros* (consort), dating back to the Mycenaean age, whose dependence with regard to the mother would be expressed by a relationship of filiation.[91] More recently, Edmunds has demonstrated how other elements of the Oedipus story may be easily interpreted in light of a general model that both in Greece and in the Near East we find in the myths of royal succession.[92] Thus on the whole it appears that a "historical" analysis of the Oedipus myth may lead to very interesting results. On the one hand, it allows us to go back to traditions that probably had their origin in the second millennium; on the other, to recover mythical models tied to definite thematics and historical epochs.

In a parallel fashion, we must recognize the notable importance that the folktale (in the sense indicated by Nilsson) had in the formation of the same mythic event. In this way the story of Oedipus brings us back to the stories of other characters who suffer similar misadventures, such as abandonment after birth (Moses, Cyrus, Romulus, and others). This genre of stories had a lasting appeal, which continued even into the Middle Ages.[93]

Similar considerations might also be offered for many other Greek myths. It will suffice to recall another famous story from which every trait of historicity would seem to be absent: Zeus and Amphitryon. In this story Alcmene, the mother of Heracles, lay both with Zeus and with her husband Amphitryon on the same night. The birth of Heracles and the myth surrounding the birth of the Egyptian pharaoh show significant affinities: in both cases the king of the gods assumes the aspect of the husband of a mortal woman in order to enjoy her love.[94] According to Egyptian belief, it was Ammon himself who appeared before the queen with the features of her husband. To what extent the Greeks of the Mycenaean age appropriated this conception remains in doubt because of the uncertainties that still surround the nature of the Mycenaean monarchy.[95] Nonetheless, this parallelism remains noteworthy and will have to be attentively considered in a historical examination of myth.

THE ROLE OF STRUCTURAL ANALYSIS IN UNDERSTANDING MYTH

In this third part we will dwell on some aspects of the structural analysis of the mythic tale, with the sole intention of considering the points at which the two approaches might appear mutually exclusive. In particular, we will try to clarify in what sense structural and historical types of analysis may usefully be combined.

If one considers some definitions of myth (including recent ones), generality is their distinguishing characteristic. Kirk noted that for the Greeks *mythos* meant simply a story, something narrated in a wide range of senses: an affirmation, a history, the plot of a tragedy.[96] Even more general is Wilamowitz's definition, which sees myth as spoken discourse; "myth" was both the sentence of a judge (as the expression of judgment, without reference to content) and the fable told to children.[97] These generalizing definitions were certainly imposed by the legitimate need not to exclude anything that the Greeks had designated with such a term. But such prudence was also due to the fact that in the mythic tale one had to recognize the simultaneous presence of several, often heterogeneous, components that required recourse to different types of analysis: fairy tale, folktale, history. Thus one finds reflected in these definitions the widespread opinion on the heterogeneity of Greek mythology.

Now if historical analysis allows for the individuation of certain components of the mythic tale (and, in the most fortunate cases, also for the determination of the era to which the tales date back) in the sense specified above, structural analysis still represents today the type of approach most capable of doing justice to the wealth of particular renderings of stories, each of which reveals partial potentialities inherent in the narrative. As we mentioned earlier, myth finds in variety one of its primary qualities of expression; hence an adequate appraisal of the variants appears indispensable in comprehending the meanings of myth. The variants cannot be explained solely by placing them in a chronological succession and referring them to particular exigencies and social spheres. Such constraints are, on the contrary, limited to bringing out the peculiarities that generally inhere in mythic narration. Other, nonstructural approaches offer interpretive categories in which various elements are at times excluded from the analysis as being irrelevant, and it is precisely those particular narrative realizations that, constrained to conform to generalizing models, are often sacrificed. If such analyses seem legitimate when one intends to write the history of a myth, considering the times and manner of its formation and pointing out the external influences that it encountered in particular epochs, they no longer appear sufficient when we consider the myth in relation to a single epoch as a sphere of symbolic representation in which the entire community recognizes itself. A purely historical examination of myth needs to be reshaped for another reason as well. Precisely in its quality as a "traditional story," Greek myth, although undergoing continual modifications and adaptations, did not substantially alter its character during the entire period of antiquity. For this reason, myths can be seen as creations of "long duration" in which subsequent modifications do not substantially compromise the general foundation. In fact, the same myths continued to be narrated throughout antiquity, although in different forms. But a single myth was narrated in a different manner even during the one epoch, in one community, on different occasions. And this is of supreme interest for structural analysis.

A historical analysis, in the various senses previously indicated, is interested in what we might define as the "superficial" level of the mythic tale. We may compare this reading with Greimas's "practical" or "figurative level," opposed to the properly "mythic" level that presupposes the superficial reading but intends to arrive at a more profound understanding attainable through a complex analysis of the tale.[98] Myth is presented as a form of metalanguage in which the first level of communication, of a denotative type, refers back to a higher level of organization of meaning belonging to the order of connotation.[99] This more complex level of meaning does not correspond to (nor is it identified with) the superficial level, although it finds its form of expression there. One must thus operate on the plane of a connotative semiotic that presupposes a denotative semiotic and constantly refers back to it as its level of expression. Obviously, myth shares this characteristic with other forms of communication, especially with poetic language. In fact, poetic language, too, represents the type of particularly "dense" message that in its ambiguity and autoreflexivity, whether functioning on the level of expression or on the level of content, offers a richly descriptive message. In both cases the task of the interpreter could be reduced to an apparently simple operation: to translate onto the level of denotation contents that are traceable on the level of connotation. This would involve explicating contents and functions not immediately emerging in the text, but nonetheless determining in the structure of the message.

An analysis based on the general assumptions indicated in the previous section allows for the consideration of both the specificity of individual myths and the various narrative renderings through which they are expressed. It enables us to examine a series of relations, and indeed contents, that by its very nature historical analysis is incapable of pointing out.

This articulation on two levels is also present in the structuralism of Lévi-Strauss. Here historical analysis is not set up as an alternative to the structural analysis, for in the analysis of myths the recourse to the ethnographic context is indispensable. It alone is able to illustrate the meaning of various narrative elements (mythemes) found in myth. For the purposes of a structural analysis it also appears impossible to exclude the historical dimension in which all societies are inevitably inserted. Rather, what is denied to history in Lévi-Strauss's structuralism is the possibility of offering an exhaustive interpretation of the phenomena observed. On the other hand, even if ethnology and history are brought back into as reciprocal solidarity, only the former is acknowledged to have a real capacity for understanding cultural facts. History appears rather as a first, though necessary, stage of the research. For the rest, however, history plays a role similar to that played by ethnography in the anthropological field, to the extent that ethnography is concentrated on the study of particular aspects of particular societies.[100]

History, however, is relegated to the sphere of the contingent, the variable, the event, whereas ethnology represents the sphere of structural constants through which it is possible to arrive at the cultural presuppositions upon which society and, in a broader perspective, the whole human experience is founded. The highly critical perspective on historical knowledge presented in The Savage Mind spares the effectiveness of the method "which experience proves to be indispensable for cataloguing the elements of any structure whatsoever, human or nonhuman, in

their entirety. It is not therefore far from being the case that the search
for intelligibility comes to an end in history as though this were its terminus. Rather, it is history that serves as the point of departure in any
quest for intelligibility." [101] Consequently, if historical and structural
analyses are called upon to collaborate in the investigation of a single
reality, they do not operate on an equal plane, because only the structural analysis can attain intelligibility.

Yet history turns out to be present in myth for another reason as well.
The various traits that figure in myth provide the basic material used in
the construction of the tale, according to a logic that remains fundamentally extraneous to historical understanding. [102] Considered from such a
perspective, Lévi-Strauss's distinction between the respective attributes
of historical and structural analyses recalls in part the distinction defined by Aristotle in the *Poetics*. As we have said, according to Aristotle,
historical events belong to the sphere of contingency, they can be placed
within precise chronological limits, but they escape a real rational
understanding. On the contrary, the events narrated in poetry are pre-
determined according to precise criteria, the actions unfold according to
the verisimilar and the necessary; [103] poetry must have a recognizable
beginning, middle (development), and end. [104] These may not be freely
changed without compromising the outcome of the composition.
Chronological proximity of events, which may be widely used in poetry,
hardly appears meaningful in history, as Aristotle affirmed with regard
to the battles of Salamis and Himera, which occurred on the same day
but did not converge on a single result. [105] Simple chronological succession, in Aristotle as in Lévi-Strauss, does not appear able to provide
adequate interpretive instruments capable of subtracting events from
their contingency.

In conclusion, we may observe how in Lévi-Strauss's examination of
myth, history has a dual function: on the one hand, it provides indispensable support to structural analysis, offering a detailed examination
of observed phenomena; on the other, it provides crude, heterogeneous
material of various origins that culture uses for its own symbolic representations. Although in both cases history is seen as having limited but
indispensable functions, it is never the real protagonist in the examination of phenomena. In attributing limited functions to historical analysis, Lévi-Strauss may have referred to a particular kind of history, closer
to ethnography and to traditional *événementielle* history (Aristotle's
"facts:" *ta genomena*) than to a sort of "global" historical knowledge.
In any case, the respective fields of historical investigation and structural
analysis do not enter into conflict except insofar as both aspire to an
exhaustive interpretation of myth. Now it is just such a demand that no

historical analysis has thus far been able to satisfy. Similarly, the structural analysis cannot avoid considering the various aspects of the historical dimension of the culture in question. For ancient Greece this principle must be understood in a broad sense, given the particular nature of the evidence, which presupposes a thorough historical and philological investigation. It would be foolish, however, to pretend to explain the variety and the complexity of the mythic tale by using solely these kinds of analysis. The contribution of structural analysis may be decisive for a higher level of investigation, in the above mentioned sense, when the fundamental categories on which the mythic tale is organized are the object.

From what we have said thus far it should be clear that the two approaches do not significantly interfere with one another. All that regards the prehistory and the formation of a myth, as well as the presence, if any, of historical elements, is of no concern to structural analysis. But it should be reaffirmed that structural analysis has never denied the historical character of the cultures it has set out to consider. Lévi-Strauss has drawn attention to this possible mistake numerous times. The so-called primitive societies like all the others operate in temporality, but unlike modern Western societies, "they refuse history and they try to sterilize inwardly whatever might constitute a sketch of an historical becoming." [106] On the other hand, we should recall that structure is capable of a recovery of history because even the new elements, which may be the result of historical becoming, are susceptible of being received into the preexisting system through reciprocal adaptations: thus variants of the same myth or new myths appear as transformations of one another and are re-formed within the system.

We will conclude with some considerations suggested by Marcel Detienne's recent study, *L'invention de la mythologie*.[107] Beginning with an examination of the notion of myth in Greece between the sixth and fourth centuries B.C., Detienne seeks to demonstrate that "mythology" as a discipline in the modern sense was born in ancient Greece, by a process that can be traced form the poetry of Xenophanes and Anacreon onwards.[108] Thus the Greeks would be the creators not only of their myths, but also of that reflection on myth that is still accorded a scientific soundness. In fact, this reflection would represent the most enduring legacy left to us by the Greeks. In reality, however, even this legacy is illusory. "Myth, far from conferring on mythology the identity that seems to belong to it, reveals itself, by oscillating from one meaning to another, to be a signifier available for various uses." [109] Myth does not represent the model of an autonomous system of thought, nor does it denote either a literary genre or a particular type of story; rather it appears as "an unfindable form," ready to be dissolved in the waters of mythology.[110] In this regard, one can observe that the vagueness of the term "myth," called upon to encompass a series of different meanings, had already emerged from an examination of the uses of the term carried out in many previous studies. Of greater interest is the proposal to date the diffusion of the term, in reference to tales declared to be unfounded, back to the late archaic period, when the first questions concerning the reliability and the meaning of myths began to arise. As I tried to clarify in the first part of this chapter, it is possible that in this period in various circles a different use of myth was established; moreover, that the advent of important changes in the use of tradition dates to this epoch. Must one then conclude, as Detienne proposes, that with Pindar and Herodotus *mythos* began to designate a sort of neutral zone that appeared ever more illusory and discredited to the eyes of those who still made use of myths?[111] A conclusion in this sense is not easily drawn from the various occurrences of the term: among the authors considered, *mythos* did not constantly denote an illusory and false discourse, as Detienne himself admits. Innovation might thus appear less general and significant than has been proposed. One must rather consider the possibility that among these authors the term was not yet qualified in relation to a criterion of veracity, even if in different contexts it is possible to use now one aspect, now another contrary one of deceptiveness and falsity. In this sense the Platonic affirmation, according to which children are told myths that are lies but that also contain some truths appears perfectly legitimate and not at all novel.[112]

But perhaps it is not in this direction that Detienne's most stimulating proposals lie. In his analysis the very notion of myth is placed in doubt and practically dispelled. According to Detienne, myth does not present its own specific characteristics, nor is it distinguished from other kinds of narrative otherwise than by deceptiveness and falsity. This drastic negation, certainly excessive in Detienne's formulation, has recently prompted an indirect response from Claude Calame, who revived a series of facts that repropose the legitimacy of a sphere proper to the mythic tale.[113] What nevertheless appears impoverished in the wake of Detienne's analysis is one of the aspects that structural analysis has most emphasized in its examination of myth: myth's capacity of representation, that is, its symbolic function. Lévi-Strauss's entire corpus is addressed to the understanding of various aspects of social organization, with regard to the meanings they assume in the culture that produced them. Probably, as compared with other manifestations of culture, myth is distinguished by its intensified ability to represent such meanings. The traditional questions that we raise in the analysis of myth, however, always tend to involve other aspects of the culture under examination. The anthropological interest becomes predominant; myth tends to dissolve into the same network of relationships that we easily recognize in other aspects of the organization of culture. In this sense the claims of comparison appear weaker, and ever more decisive is the knowledge of the various aspects of the culture of which myths are the expression and which myths are called upon to represent. It is in this perspective that new and more profitable areas of collaboration between historical research and structural analysis could be created.

NOTES

a. For a recent defense of the philological approach see Henrichs 1986.
b. Graf 1985, 94.
c. Graf 1985, 15–38 for a survey of this period.
d. Kirk 1970, 162–171.
e. Burkert 1979, 33.
f. Burkert 1979, 141–42.

I thank Professor Lowell Edmunds and Messrs. Craig Frisch and Eric Halpern, to whom I am indebted for the translation of this essay.

1. On this "classic" problem of Greek religion, see Brelich 1958, 11–22 (in which the history of the problem is also traced, beginning with the theses of Usener and Rohde). A special role is often attributed to those heroes who become established in heroic legend and therefore in epic: see Farnell 1921, 19, 280–85; Nilsson 1967, 184–91 and, most recently, Burkert 1977, 306–19. On the heroes of epic in relation to those who were the object of a heroic cult, see Nagy 1979, 115–16.

2. Mazzarino 1966, 93.

3. *FrGHist* 1 frag. 1; see in this regard Nenci 1951; idem 1964; in addition see Mazzarino 1966, 70–83; Fränkel 1962, 390–95; Von Fritz 1967, 72–76; see also note 9 below.

4. On the relationship between epic and historiography, which were at the foundation of the development of a truly historical narration, especially in the Ionian region, a general consensus has been reached: see for example Schwartz 1928, 15–16; Jacoby 1956b, 76; Strasburger 1968, 62–64; Canfora 1972, 21–28; and, most recently, Hunter 1982, 93–115. On the other hand we should note that epic poetry appeared by its very nature, to the Greeks as well as to other peoples, as the closest to historical narrative: see Bowra 1952, 41. Thus the epic traditions appeared as the first natural sphere of comparison between the poetic tradition and nascent historiography.

5. For similar proceedings at the origins of both philosophic and scientific thought and of historical research, see above all Von Fritz 1952, 201–3; 211–20. More generally: Vernant 1962; idem 1965, 95–124; Kirk, Raven, and Schofield 1983, Ch. 1; cf. Burkert 1977, 452–60; see also, although their interests are different, Thomson 1961, 131–172; Gernet 1968, 415–30. An important role in the redefinition of the relationships between religion and philosophy was played by Cornford's work

(1912; idem 1952). For the relationships between Ionian science and the development of historiography, see Jacoby 1956b, 73–80; more recently Pascucci 1978. On the relationships among nascent historiography, religious movements, and civically committed contemporary poetry, see especially Mazzarino 1966, 23–52; with regard to the new possibilities offered to rational analysis by the diffusion of writing: Goody 1977, 44; 47–48.

6. Here we have left out of consideration the role that may have been played in the birth of history by local chronicles, according to a controversial passage in Dionysius of Halicarnassus (*De Thuc.* 5–7). As is well-known, the thesis that claims that the "great historiography" derived from local chronicles was tenaciously opposed by Jacoby (for example, 1956a, 51–57); more recently, see Gozzoli 1970–71; Verdin 1970. In any case Jacoby's thesis, in which he holds that the works of the first historiographers, Herodotus in particular, drew directly from local oral traditions through the narratives of the *logioi andres,* is to be accepted. For a different interpretation, see Lasserre 1976, 134–35.

7. Goody 1977, 14–15; 36–51. In this study the author takes up again and broadens several fundamental theses put forward in a previous contribution: Goody and Watt 1963.

8. Mazzarino 1966, 27.

9. Mazzarino 1966, 79. Cf. also in this sense Nenci 1951, 55–56; idem 1964, who holds that the objective of Hecataeus's polemic must have been not so much myth itself as rather the plurality of versions. Momigliano (1966) attributes a more radical critique of myth to Hecataeus; see also De Sanctis 1933. Reservations regarding Nenci's thesis have been expressed by Tozzi 1966, 45–46, and by Pascucci 1978, 624–25, both of whom, however, prove only that Hecataeus's critique also concerned other aspects of the narrative. For a more balanced judgment of frag. 1 see Musti 1973, 21–22. Even if the multiplicity of versions was not the only feature to attract the criticisms of a rational analysis, it must have played an important role in the justification of myth criticism. Such multiplicity must have been even more conspicuous when one considers that in the Ionian sphere numerous versions were circulating and that a systematic examination of these versions, inseparable from the use of writing brought about by the nascent historiography, necessarily called forth those contradictions that were henceforth noted as peculiar features of the tale.

10. Mimn. frag. 3 Gentili-Prato; Mazzarino 1966, 37–42; Gentili 1984, 44–45. For an analysis that uses the historiographical aspect of Ionian elegy, see also Lasserre 1976, 120–27, who, however, does not always arrive at persuasive conclusions, at least to the extent to which, moving away from Jacoby's thesis, he brings the affirmation of Herodotean historiography back to the use of local sources, whether poetic or prosaic (118–19; 134–35). The disposition to emend traditional tales with a moralizing perspective is visible also in Pindar's *Epinicians;* see Brelich 1958, 39; Huxley 1975, 14–22.

11. See Mazzarino 1966, 132–33; 564, n. 143; Cassola 1984, 20–21. This may find indirect confirmation in the theses proposed for the genesis of Herodotus's work. Jacoby saw a progressive turn in the historian's interests from geographical and ethnographical research to more purely historiographical research (1913, 353), a thesis substantially accepted by Von Fritz, according to whom Herodotus would have begun as a critic of the geographical system of his predecessor Hecataeus (1967, 442–

43). In general the similarity of interests between ethnography and historiographical research was valorized by Jacoby, who already recognized in Hecataeus, author both of a *Genealogiai* and of a *Periodos ges,* the apparent duplicity of interest that would later encounter diverse fortunes in distinct spheres of historiographical research (1956a, 26–34).

12. *FrGHist* 1 frag. 26, 27; Her. I 1.

13. *FrGHist* 2 frag. 24, 25.

14. *FrGHist* 2 frag. 23a.

15. For this interpretation see Mazzarino 1966, 61–70. The hostility between the Argives and the Spartans also had repercussions on the internal struggles of the Argolis. Mycenae, until its destruction by the Argives (468 B.C.), found a natural ally in Sparta: in Acusilaus's genealogy Myceneus is the son of Sparton. A similar situation is evinced for the era around 700 B.C. by the case of Asine. This city of Dryopes, hostile to Argos, was supported by Sparta until its destruction by the Argives around 700 B.C., when the inhabitants were transferred by the Spartans to the new city of Asine in Messenia: see Paus. 2.36.4–5; 3.7.4; 4.34.9–11; Strab. 8.6.11 (373). This policy of support (in conjunction with a notable anti-Argive function) for the smaller cities of Argolis—which could often boast a glorious past—probably contributed to Sparta's appropriation of ancient "Mycenaean" traditions. For the problem in general, see Janni 1970, 103–26.

16. *FrGHist* 4 frag. 36ab.

17. Cf. in general Paus. 2.14.4–16.1; [Apollodorus] *Bibl.* 2.1.1–5; Brillante 1981, 90–93, cart. 1. Indeed Pausanias, who also related the information on Sparton and Myceneus, attributing it to Acusilaus, declared that he could not accept it and that not even the Spartans accepted it (2.16.4).

18. Momigliano 1969, 29–31; Canfora 1972, 9–19, passim.

19. See for example Schwartz 1928, 19; Jacoby 1956b, 80–83; Gomme 1954, 1–48; Snell 1952, 4–12; Strasburger 1968, 54–55; Canfora 1972, 21–28; on the Herodotean proem in particular: Erbse 1956; Calame 1986a, 71–73.

20. See for example Jakobson-Bogatyrëv 1973, 61–62; Bowra 1952, 40–41, passim; Goody-Watt 1963; Goody 1977, 36–51; Vansina 1976, 290–297; Skafte-Jensen 1986, 22–26.

21. The phrase used by Herodotus to describe the risk to which those events that did not find a narrator would be subject (*tōi chronōi exitēla genetai,* literally: "with time they become faint, they are extinguished") effectively expresses the progressive cancellation leading up to the total extinction of memory: cf. Her. 5.39; Powell 1938, s.v. *exitēlos.*

22. See Detienne 1967, 20–21; Nagy 1979, 16–18; Calame 1986a, 72. The assistance of the muse is indispensable to the poet's undertaking (Hom. *Il.* 2.484–93; *Od.* 8.62–74). According to Nagy, the root of Mousa would be the same as that of the verb *mimnēsko* (**men*); cf. however Chantraine 1968 s.v.; *kleos aphthiton* represents an ancient Indo-European formula; cf. also Vidal-Naquet 1983, 72; Skafte-Jensen 1986, 26–27; most recently, Calame 1986a, 55–67.

23. Hom. *Il.* 2.653–70 (Rhodes); 676–80 (Kos); *Od.* 19.175–77 (Crete); cf. Page 1959, 147–49; Prinz 1979, 76–97; Brillante 1981, 131–134; Musti 1985c, 56–60.

24. Among the various works in which these subjects are dealt with, it will suffice to cite the following: Page 1959, 118–77; Hope Simpson and Lazenby 1970; Nilsson

1932. For a summary of the Homeric poems in relation to the historical elements recognizable within them, see most recently Stella 1978; Heubeck 1979.

25. Mazzarino 1966, 45. In the Greek tradition the Mycenaean settlements in Asia Minor are not really neglected, but are considered together with colonies from Crete; these settlements are kept distinct in the traditions from the first Greek settlements established by Ionians coming from the continent: see Eph. *FrGHist* 70 frag. 127; Paus. 7.2.5; [Apollodorus] *Bibl.* 3.1.2; cf. Prinz 1979, 107–8; 326; n. 33. For a different interpretation see Cassola 1957, 308–10.

26. Finley 1965, 15–16, 18; see also, although in a different perspective, Van Groningen 1953, 47–61. An even more radical critique of any form of historical use of myth is Hampl 1975. It inspired Prinz's 1979 study, which on the whole, however, represents a useful contribution to the systematic reexamination of the foundation legends. For a more balanced judgment on the Greek traditions, Musti's considerations (1985b, 1985c) appear particularly apposite.

27. Brillante 1981, 54–77.

28. This passage, correctly interpreted by Jacoby (1956a,37, n. 63), was subsequently interpreted in a less convincing way: Vidal-Naquet 1983, 81; Finley 1965, 18; Brelich 1977, 20; and most recently Hunter 1982, 18–19.

29. Correctly understood by West 1978 at v. 160.

30. Theag. *VS* 8 A 2. Svenbro 1976, 77–138. This notable study, distinguished above all for the perspicacity with which it analyzes epic poetry's functions in archaic Greek society, shows some uncertainties in the definition of the changes undergone by the same epic tradition in the late archaic period: Gentili 1981, 37–38; Musti 1981, 43–47.

31. Pfeiffer 1968, 9–12; Svenbro 1976, 111. The documented interest in etymology shared in the late archaic Greek world by a "rhapsode" like Theagenes, a "historian" like Hecataeus, and a "theologian" like Pherecydes of Syros is to be considered in this perspective: *VS* 7 A 9; 8 A 9; *FrGHist* 1 frag. 15; Pfeiffer 1968, 12; cf. for example Untersteiner 1972, 245–48. The tendency to etymologize is connected to a traditional use of myth. Thus even in this case the particular use made of etymology for the purposes of scientific inquiry will be exploited.

32. Nilsson 1967, 190–91; 717–19; Brelich 1958, 132; 314–22.

33. Brelich 1958, 315–16. When Vansina, with reference to the structural analysis, objected that a "structured" story is not for that reason alone the fruit of invention, his affirmation was wholly acceptable but not decisive. Thus it is possible to utilize the opposite process: the fact that historical elements figure in a story does not preclude that it has been subjected to "structuring" action, which broadens its references and meanings (1976, 303).

34. Burckhardt 1955, 32–33.

35. Burchhardt 1955, 39.

36. Aristot. *Poet.* 1451b6–12 (tr. Fyfe); cf. for example Else 1957, 301–7; 573–80; Finley 1965, 11–12; Mazzarino 1966, 415–16. Worthy of note is Gomme's attempted rereading of the historians, in particular Herodotus, in light of this Aristotelean formulation (1954, 49–115). Most recently see Funke 1986, who is predominantly interested in the influence exercised by the Homeric epic on historiography. To be considered with some reservations, however, is the role attributed here to Thucydides. In particular, he was not "the first to drift away from poetry on principle"

(1986, 80). In the Archaiologia the historian used Homeric epic, considering it in light of his personal views on the historical evolution of primitive Greece. Cf. for example Mazzarino 1966, 296–97; Musti 1985b, viii.

37. *Poet.* 1459a21–24 (tr. Fyfe).

38. Aristot. *Met.* 1.982b11–19; cf. *Met.* 12.1074b1–14, where the ancient narratives are similarly valorized, inasmuch as they preserve elements of truth under mythic form.

39. Aristot. *De an.* 434a16–21; Guthrie 1962, 40–41.

40. Kirk 1974, 16.

41. Brelich 1958, viii–ix; idem 1972b.

42. See Nilsson 1960, 345–46.

43. Nilsson 1932; idem 1933.

44. On the work of K. O. Müller, see most recently Burkert 1980, 164–65; Momigliano 1983; Sassi 1984; Musti 1985b, xii–xv. We may trace the appreciation of the "historical narrative" (*Sage*) contained within mythic narrative back to Müller, whose systematic examination of Greek traditions allows us to go back to the age of "origins" of the Greek races.

45. Rohde 1988, 32–36.

46. Wilamowitz 1937b, 79; idem 1959, 54.

47. Wilamowitz 1937a, 75; idem 1959, 59. Cf. Chadwick and Chadwick 1932, 14.

48. Meyer 1931, 258; Robert 1915, 120–21; Nilsson 1932, 100–107.

49. Unlike what had happened for the traditions of early medieval Christianity. Nilsson 1967, 25.

50. Nilsson 1932, 18–23; idem 1933, 179–83. "In order to explain how the transmission of epic poetry through many centuries, which its origin in the Mycenaean age presupposes, was possible, it is necessary to see how epic poetry is made and preserved through the lapse of time" (1933, 184); see also Parry 1971, xliii–xlvii; cf. most recently Hoekstra 1981, 59.

51. See Wilamowitz 1959, 40; Nilsson 1967, 13–16. With such an appraisal of "religion" and the ritual aspects connected to it, Nilsson refers, even through the mediation of Usener and Dieterich, to formulations developed by the Cambridge school (Burkert 1980, 177).

52. Nilsson 1967, 16.

53. Nilsson 1967, 17–18; 26–27. The scholar admitted that folktale elements might also have flowed into myth either through the process of humanization or through the presence of rationalized versions originally belonging to the province of the folktale (1967, 18). According to Snell this process did not concern only particular cases, but rather represented a general tendency. He did not acknowledge a substantial difference between *Märchen* and *Sage*. A story takes on the guise of "saga" when it is connected with a definite time and place and is made the object of song by epic singers (1952, 3–4). On the traditional distinctions among myth, legend, and folktale, see for example Frazer 1921, xxvii–xxxi; Carpenter 1958 (with particular reference to his notion of "fiction"); Kirk 1970, 31–41; with reference to studies in the area of folklore and to ancient and medieval literary versions: De Vries 1954, 71–179. In spite of several not always acceptable reconstructions, one sees in this study

how the motifs present in the various genres are substantially the same (1954, 86; 154–55).

54. Dunbabin 1957, 15.

55. Brelich 1958, 59–60.

56. Brelich 1958, 69; cf. also in this sense Calame 1972, 128–29.

57. Brelich 1977, 22.

58. Brelich 1968. Obviously, this does not entail that the religious datum find a direct correspondence in the social and institutional datum: see for example Brelich 1977, 19–20; also see Detienne 1977, 39–40, regarding the historicist interpretation of myths.

59. See Lévêque 1972; idem 1973; idem 1985. The presence of a functional tripartition, traces of which have been sought especially in Roman, Germanic, and Indian mythologies, does not appear easily demonstrable in Greece, as Dumézil himself recognized (for example: 1977, 153). Cf. most recently Sergent 1980.

60. Burkert 1972; cf. idem 1979.

61. See Meuli 1975; cf. Burkert 1972, 20–21, 85–89.

62. Brelich, 1969.

63. Calame 1971, in particular 32–44. Still more recently, Murray holds that it is possible to distinguish between archaic and pseudo-archaic societies, and that "the truly archaic state is a coagulation of contradictory realities" (1980, 172). Finally, it should be noted that in his last phase Brelich strongly insisted on the "popular and oral" character of Greek mythology, which renders it similar to that of ethnologically documented peoples (1977, 11–12; idem 1985, 42).

64. For this view of heroic societies, in which the role played by epic poetry is especially significant, see in particular Chadwick 1912; Chadwick and Chadwick 1932, especially pp. 13–63; cf. Kirk 1962, 56–59. To this tradition belong the contributions of Bowra 1957; idem 1952; see also Bowra 1972, 79–96; Huxley 1976.

65. Finnegan 1977, 244–77.

66. Havelock's 1963 study has had a particular importance in this area; see also Havelock 1982. The role played by oral communication in archaic Greek societies, especially in its pragmatic aspects, has been extensively considered in Gentili's contributions (principally 1969; idem 1984). Among the numerous recent studies on important aspects of Greek culture in relation to the role played by oral communication, see for example Svenbro 1976; Pavese 1981; Longo 1981; and most recently Gentili and Paione 1985.

67. Kirk 1974, 95–112; idem 1977; idem 1986.

68. Kirk 1974, 95.

69. Kirk 1974, 99–100.

70. Kirk 1962, 95–98; idem 1966.

71. Kirk 1974, 105.

72. Kirk 1974, 106. In this sense, see also Pucci 1971, 109–10. Reservations of this type have often been advanced in the attempt to bring out the presumed insufficiencies of structural analysis.

73. Cf. in this sense Brelich 1958, 22 ("a variant handed down solely by a scholiast or by a lexicographer may be more ancient than another that is found in Pindar"), 44–45; idem 1972b, 623; idem 1977, 11–12.

74. See for example Webster 1964, 64–90; Stella 1978, 351–372. Recently, in

regard to likely connections between Greek and Near Eastern myths, Burkert has pointed out that it is impossible to establish precise connecting lines between the two areas and that a truly historical diffusion must be kept distinct from the notion of "migrating myths." In many cases it is possible to demonstrate only a broad and indistinct communication (1987, 12, 17).

75. Walcot 1966; West 1966, 18–31; most recently Burkert 1987.

76. Lehrs 1882, 103–4; Hesych. s.v. *doupēsai*, I 474 Latte; Robert 1915, 115.

77. See for example Jebb 1928, xxvi–xxix.

78. Brelich 1972b, 623; idem 1977, 22.

79. Segal 1981, 1–42; idem 1983; idem 1986, 21–109.

80. Vernant 1972, 24–26; Detienne 1977, 32–35; Kirk 1970, 250; idem 1974, 103–6. Somewhat different is Segal's position (see the previous note). On the one hand, he observed that in the tragic rendering myth's traditional function of representation and mediation is dissolved, and on the other hand, he admits that such a progressive dissolution and negation of the oppositions is observable in the course of the same dramatic action.

81. Aristot. *Poet.* 1450a5: *mythos* as *synthesis ton pragmaton;* see most recently Bompaire 1977; Cessi 1985. The latter study correctly recognizes the variety of uses Aristotle makes of the term; however, it does not seem that this is to be explained by primitive religious values, but rather by the indefiniteness inherent in the term from the earliest examples of its use.

82. Veyne 1983, 50

83. Veyne 1983, 129.

84. Veyne 1983, 137, passim.

85. See Robert 1915, 115; Nilsson 1932, 108–9; Huxley 1969, 41; Brillante 1980, 334–35; most recently see Masaracchia 1986, who, however, is skeptical that *dedoupotos* may refer to the hero's death in battle.

86. See Kinkel 1877, 8–9; Peisandros *FrGHist* 16 frag. 10.

87. *FrGHist* 3 frag. 95. In this narrative Pherecydes probably corrupted the narrative of the *Oedipodeia* with another source (Jacoby, *ad loc.*).

88. See [Appollodorus] *Bibl.* 2.4.11; Paus 9.37.1–3; Diod. Sic. 4.10.3–5; Strab. 9.2.40 (414); Bethe 1907, 433–34; idem 1891, 1–28.

89. Nilsson 1932, 103.

90. Delcourt 1944.

91. Pötscher 1973. This thesis recalls Robert's, in which Oedipus is perceived as a primitive divine figure connected with the vegetative cycle (1915, 44–47); similarly Untersteiner 1972, 42, 62–63. Opposed to Robert's thesis is Nilsson 1951b.

92. Edmunds 1981, 23–25, passim; idem 1986.

93. See for example Zuntz 1967; Propp 1975; Edmunds 1985.

94. See Walcot 1967.

95. See most recently Dietrich 1974, 37–42; 183–85; Thomas 1976. One may also consider the analogous case of the Spartan king Ariston, as it is related in Herodotus (6.69): the substitution of the hero Astrabakos for the legitimate husband Ariston (Walcot, 1967, 57).

96. Kirk 1970, 8; similarly Burkert 1979, 1–2; cf. LSJ s.v. *mythos.*

97. Wilamowitz 1959, 40. For the two cited cases see Hes. *Op.* 263; Plato *Rep.* 377a.

98. Greimas and Courtés 1979, 288–89 s.v. "Pratique"; cf. Greimas 1966, 120.

99. See most recently Calame 1986b. As is well known, this formulation assumes the Hjelmslevian model of a double semiotic, denotative and connotative, linked to and interfering with one another: Hjelmslev 1961, Ch. 13. It has been widely received into a semiotic definition of culture: Barthes 1974, Ch. 4; idem 1957, 221–22; Eco 1975, 82–85.

100. Lévi-Strauss 1966, 14–15. On the relationships between structural and historical analyses, considered as two diverse but fundamentally united aspects, see once again Lévi-Strauss 1966, 31–38; idem 1964, 277–90. On the not always univocal role bestowed by Lévi-Strauss on historical and structural analysis, see Remotti 1971, in particular 38–42, 183–93, passim; more recently Miceli 1983, 36–39. For Brelich's position on structural analysis, see 1972a. Cf. Kirk 1970, 42–83; see also Pucci 1971.

101. Lévi-Strauss 1964, 283.

102. Lévi-Strauss 1964, 48; Remotti 1971, 222–24.

103. Aristot. *Poet.* 1451a36–38.

104. *Poet.* 1450b25–34.

105. *Poet.* 1459a25–29. On the "Aristotelianism" of Lévi-Strauss, see for example Remotti 1971, 97–101. Cf. also Bompaire 1977, 33–36.

106. Lévi-Strauss 1978, 364. This is what happens in every mythic representation, understood in its modern (ideological) dimension as well, to the extent that it tends to isolate specific cultural traits and presents them as "natural." Through such a process it is possible to frustrate the individual and interested historical character of the system of values accepted (or that is intended to be accepted) by the community: see for example Lévi-Strauss 1966, 234–35; Barthes 1957, 237–38.

107. Detienne 1981; see also idem 1980.

108. Detienne 1981, 92–96; Anacr. frag. 21 Gentili, regarding the rebels (*mythiētai*) of Samos; Xen. frag. 14–19 Gentili-Prato (= *VS* 21 B 10–16).

109. Detienne 1981, 235.

110. Detienne 1981, 238.

111. Detienne 1981, 96.

112. See Plat. *Rep.* 377a. It hardly bears repeating that the possibility that untruthful narratives may also have figured in the stories inspired by the muses was already known from Hesiod's *Theogonia:* vv. 26–28; cf. Hom. *Od.* 19.203; Theog. 713, and one might also recall Stesichorus's palinodes; see Detienne 1967, 75–79.

113. Calame 1986a, 150; 1986b.

WORKS CITED

Barthes, Roland. 1957. Mythologies. Paris.
———. 1964. *Eléments de sémiologie*. Paris.
Bethe, Erich. 1981. *Thebanische Heldenlieder*. Leipzig.
———. 1907. *RE* VI 1, s.v. Erginos, 432–34.
Bompaire, Jean. 1977. "Le mythe selon la *Poétique* d'Aristote." In *Formation et survie des mythes* (Colloque de Nanterre), 31–36. Paris.
Bowra, Cecil M. 1952. *Heroic Poetry*. London.

———. 1957. "The Meaning of a Heroic Age." *Earl Grey Memorial Lecture*. Newcastle 1957 (= G. S. Kirk 1964, 22–47).

———. 1972. *Homer.* London.

Brelich, Angelo. 1958. *Gli eroi greci. Un problema storico-religioso.* Rome.

———. 1968. "Religione micenea: osservazioni metodologiche." *Atti e Memorie I Congresso int. di Micenologia*, 919–928. Rome.

———. 1969. *Paides e Parthenoi.* ("Incunabula Graeca" 36). Rome.

———. 1972a. "Perché storicismo e quale storicismo (nei nostri studi)?" *R & C* 1: 7–28.

———. 1972b. "Ad Philologos." *R & C* 1: 621–29.

———. 1977. "La metodologia della scuola di Roma." In Gentili and Paione 1977, 3–29.

———. 1985. *I Greci e gli dei.* Naples.

Bremmer, Jan, ed. 1987. *Interpretations in Greek Mythology.* London.

Brillante, Carlo. 1980. "Le leggende tebane e l'archeologia." *SMEA* 21: 309–40.

———. 1981. *La leggenda eroica e la civiltà micenea.* Rome.

———. M. Cantilena, and C. O. Pavese, eds. 1981. *I poemi epici rapsodici non omerici e la tradizione orale.* Padua.

Burckhardt, Jacob. 1955. *Storia della civiltà greca* (tr. it.). I. Florence.

Burkert, Walter. 1972. *Homo necans.* Berlin.

———. 1977. *Griechische Religion der archaischen und klassischen Epoche.* Stuttgart.

———. 1979. *Structure and History in Greek Mythology and Ritual.* Berkeley-Los Angeles.

———. 1980. "Griechische Mythologie und die Geistesgeschichte der Moderne." Entretiens Hardt 26, 159–99.

———. 1987. "Oriental and Greek Mythology: The Meeting of Parallels." In Bremmer 1987, 10–40.

Calame, Claude. 1971. "Philologie et anthropologie structurale: à propos d'un livre récent d'Angelo Brelich." *QUCC* 11: 7–47.

———. 1972. "Mythologiques de G. S. Kirk: structures et fonctions du mythe." *QUCC* 11: 117–35.

———. 1986a. *Le récit en Grèce ancienne. Énonciations et représentation de poètes.* Paris.

———. 1986b. "Mythique (discours, niveau)." In Greimas and Courtés 1986, 148–49.

———. 1987. "Spartan Genealogies: The Mythological Representation of a Spatial Organisation." In Bremmer 1987, 153–86.

Canfora, Luciano. 1972. *Totalità e selezione nella storiografia classica.* Bari.

Carpenter, Rhys. 1958. *Folktale, Fiction and Saga in the Homeric Epics.* Berkeley-Los Angeles.

Cassola, Filippo. 1957. *La Ionia nel mondo miceneo.* Naples.

———. 1984. "Introduzione" in *Erodoto. Storie*, 5–65. Milan.

Cessi, Viviana. 1985. "*Praxis* e *mythos* nella *Poetica* di Aristotele." *QUCC* 48: 45–60.

Chadwick, Hector M. 1912. *The Heroic Age.* Cambridge.

———— and Nora Kershaw Chadwick. 1932. *The Growth of Literature*. I. Cambridge.

Chantraine, Pierre. 1968. *Dictionnaire étymologique de la langue grecque*. Paris.

Cornford, Francis M. 1912. *From Religion to Philosophy*. London.

————. 1952. *Principium Sapientiae*. Cambridge.

Delcourt, Marie. 1944. *Oedipe ou la légende du conquérant*. Paris.

De Sanctis, Gaetano. 1933. "Intorno al razionalismo di Ecateo." *RFIC* 61 (1933) 1–15 (= 1951. *Studi di storia della storiografia greca*, 3–19. Florence).

Detienne, Marcel. 1967. *Les maîtres de vérité dans la Grèce archaïque*. Paris.

————. 1977. *Dionysos mis à mort*. Paris.

————. 1980. *Enciclopedia*. Vol. VII, 348–63, s.v. Mito/rito. Turin.

————. 1981. *L'invention de la mythologie*. Paris.

Dietrich, Bernard C. 1974. *The Origins of Greek Religion*. Berlin.

Dumézil, Georges. 1977. *Les dieux souverains des Indo-Européens*. Paris.

Dunbabin, Thomas J. 1957. *The Greeks and Their Eastern Neighbours*. London.

Eco, Umberto.1975. *Trattato di semiotica generale*. Milan.

Edmunds, Lowell. 1981. *The Sphinx in the Oedipus Legend*. Königstein/Ts.

————. 1985. *Oedipus. The Ancient Legend and its Later Analogues*. Baltimore.

————. 1986. "Il corpo di Edipo: struttura psico-mitologica." In Gentili and Pretagostini 1986, 237–53.

Else, Gerald F. 1957. *Aristotle's Poetics: The Argument*. Leiden.

Erbse, Hartmut. 1956. "Der erste Satz im Werke Herodots." *Festschrift Bruno Snell*. Munich.

Farnell, Lewis R. 1921. *Greek Hero Cults and Ideas of Immortality*. Oxford.

Finley, Moses I. 1965. "Myth, Memory and History." *H & T* 4(1965): 281–302. A slightly amplified version appears in 1975. *The Use and Abuse of History*, 11–33. London.

Finnegan, Ruth. 1977. *Oral Poetry. Its Nature, Significance and Social Context*. Cambridge.

Fränkel, Hermann. 1962. *Dichtung und Philosophie des frühen Griechentums*. 2nd ed. Munich.

Frazer, James G. 1921. *Apollodorus. The Library*. Loeb Classical Library. London.

Fritz, Kurt von. 1952. "Der gemeinsame Ursprung der Geschichtsschreibung und der exakten Wissenschaften bei den Griechen." *Philosophia Naturalis* II 1:200–23.

————. 1967. *Die griechische Geschichtsschreibung*. I. Berlin.

Funke, Hermann. 1986. "Poesia e storiografia." *QS* 23: 71–93.

Gentili, Bruno. 1969. "L'interpretazione dei lirici greci arcaici nella dimensione del nostro tempo. Sincronia e diacronia nello studio di una cultura orale." *QUCC*: 7–21.

————. 1981. "La parola e il marmo: una discussione." *DArch* n.s. 2. 32–38.

————. 1984. *Poesia e pubblico nella Grecia antica*. Rome.

————, ed. 1985. *Oralità. Cultura, letteratura, discorso*. Rome.

———— and Giuseppe Paione, eds. 1977. *Il mito greco*. Atti del convegno int. di Urbino. Rome.

———— and Roberto Pretagostini, eds. *Edipo. Il teatro greco e la cultura europea*. Rome.

Gernet, Louis. 1968. *Anthropologie de la Grèce antique*. Paris.

Gomme, Arnold W. 1954. *The Greek Attitude to Poetry and History*. Berkeley-Los Angeles.

Goody, Jack. 1977. *The Domestication of the Savage Mind*. Cambridge.

———— and Ian Watt. 1963. "The Consequences of Literacy." *Comparative Studies in History and Society*, 5: 304–45.

Gozzoli, Sandra. 1970–71. "Una teoria antica sull'origine della storiografia greca." *SCO* 19–20: 158–211.

Graf, Fritz. 1985. *Griechische Mythologie: Eine Einführung*. Munich.

Greimas, Algirdas J. 1966. *Sémantique structurale*. Paris.

———— and Joseph Courtés. 1979, 1986. *Sémiotique. Dictionnaire raisonné de la théorie du langage*. I (1979); II (1986). Paris.

Groningen, Bernhard A. van. 1953. *In the Grip of the Past. Essay on an Aspect of Greek Thought*. Leiden.

Guthrie, William K. C. 1962. *A History of Greek Philosophy*. I. Cambridge.

Hampl, Franz. 1975. "Die Ilias ist kein Geschichtsbuch." *Serta Philologica Aenipontana* I. Innsbruck 1962. (An amplified version appears in *Geschichte als kritische Wissenschaft*. II, 51–99. Darmstadt.)

Havelock, Eric A. 1963. *Preface to Plato*. Cambridge, MA.

————. 1982. *The Literate Revolution in Greece and its Cultural Consequences*. Princeton, NJ.

Heubeck, Alfred. 1979. "Geschichte bei Homer." *SMEA* 20: 227–50.

Hjelmslev, Louis. 1961. *Prolegomena to a Theory of Language*. Madison, WI.

Hoekstra, Arie. 1981. *Epic Verse before Homer. Three Studies*. Amsterdam.

Hope Simpson, R., and Lazenby, J. F. 1970. *The Catalogue of the Ships in Homer's Iliad*. Oxford.

Hunter, Virginia. 1982. *Past and Process in Herodotus and Thucydides*. Princeton, NJ.

Huxley, George L. 1969. *Greek Epic Poetry from Eumelos to Panyassis*. London.

————. 1975. *Pindar's Vision of the Past*. Belfast.

————. 1976. "Distinguishing Characteristics of Heroic Ages." *The Maynooth Review* 22:3–12.

Jacoby, Felix. 1913. *RE*. Suppl. 2, s.v. Herodotos, 205–520.

————. 1956a. "Über die Entwicklung der griechischen Historiographie und den Plan einer neuen Sammlung der griechischen Historikerfragmente." *Klio* 9: 80–123 (= *Abhandlungen zur griechischen Geschichtsschreibung*, ed. H. Bloch, 16–64. Leiden.

————. 1956b. "Griechische Geschichtsschreibung." *Die Antike* 2 (1926) 1–29 (= *Abhandlungen*, 73–99).

Jakobson, Roman, and Bogatyrëv, Pëtr. 1973. "Le folklore, forme spécifique de création." In Roman Jakobson, *Questions de poétique*. Paris.

Janni, Pietro. 1970. *La cultura di Sparta arcaica. Ricerche*. II. Rome.

Jebb, Richard C. 1928. *Sophocles. The Oedipus Coloneus*. Cambridge.

Kinkel, Gottfried. 1877. *Epicorum Graecorum Fragmenta*. I. Leipzig.

Kirk, Geoffrey S. 1962. *The Songs of Homer*. Cambridge.

————, ed. 1964. *The Language and Background of Homer*. Cambridge.

————. 1966. "Formular Language and Oral Quality." *YClS* 20: 155–74 (= *Homer and the Oral Tradition*, 1976, 183–200. Cambridge.

————. 1970. *Myth. Its Meaning and Functions in Ancient and Other Cultures.* Berkeley-Los Angeles.

————. 1974. *The Nature of Greek Myths.* Harmondsworth, UK.

————. 1977. "Methodological Reflexions on the Myths of Herakles." In Gentili and Paione 1977, 285–97.

————. 1986. "Myth and Artifice in the Sophoclean Oedipus." In Gentili and Pretagostini 1986, 11–19.

————, John E. Raven, and Martin Schofield. 1983. *The Presocratic Philosophers.* 2nd ed. Cambridge.

Lasserre, François. 1976. "L'historiographie grecque à l'époque archaïque." *QS* 4: 113–42.

Lehrs, Karl. 1882. *De Aristarchi Studiis Homericis.* 3rd ed. Leipzig.

Lévêque, Pierre. 1972. "Formes et structures méditerranéennes dans la genèse de la religion grecque." *Praelectiones Patavinae,* 145–79. Rome.

————. 1973. "Continuités et innovations dans la religion grecque dans la première moitié du Ier millénaire." *PP* 148–49: 23–50.

————. 1985. "I Dori e la religione delle età buie." In D. Musti 1985a, 259–76.

Lévi-Strauss, Claude. 1964. *Il pensiero selvaggio* (tr. it.). Milan.

————. 1966. *Antropologia strutturale* (tr. it.). Milan.

————. 1978. *Antropologia strutturale due* (tr. it.). Milan.

Longo, Oddone. 1981. *Tecniche della comunicazione nella Grecia antica.* Naples.

Masaracchia, Agostino. 1986. "La morte di Edipo in Omero." In Gentili and Pretagostini 1986, 529–39.

Mazzarino, Santo. 1966. *Il pensiero storico classico.* I. Bari.

Meuli, Karl. 1975. "Griechische Opferbräuche." *Gesammelte Schriften,* 907–1021. Basel.

Meyer, Eduard. 1931. *Geschichte des Altertums.* II, 2. Stuttgart.

Miceli, Silvana. 1983. "Mito e storia. Le manipolazioni del tempo." *Annali della Facoltà di Lettere della Università di Palermo* 1: 31–59.

Momigliano, Arnaldo. 1966. "Il razionalismo di Ecateo di Mileto." In *Terzo contributo alla storia degli studi classici e del mondo antico.* I, 323–33. Rome.

————. 1969. "Time in Ancient Historiography." In *Quarto contributo alla storia degli studi classici e del mondo antico.* Rome.

————. 1983. "K. O. Müller's *Prolegomena zu einer wissenschaftlichen Mythologie* and the Meaning of 'Myth'." *ASNP* sez. III, 13: 673–89.

Murray, Oswyn. 1980. *Early Greece.* Glasgow.

Musti, Domenico. 1973. *Società antica. Antologia di storici greci.* Rome.

————. 1981. "La parola e il marmo: una discussione." *DArch* n.s. 2: 43–49.

————, ed. 1985a. *Le origini dei Greci. Dori e mondo egeo.* Rome.

————. 1985b. "Introduzione." In 1985a, vii–xxv.

————. 1985c. "Continuità e discontinuità tra Achei e Dori nelle tradizioni storiche." In 1985a, 37–71.

Nagy, Gregory. 1979. *The Best of the Achaeans.* Baltimore.

Nenci, Giuseppe. 1951. "Ecateo da Mileto e la questione del suo razionalismo." *RAL* 6: 51–58.

———. 1964. "Una risposta delfica alla metodologia ecataica." *CS* 3: 269–86.

Nilsson, Martin P. 1932, 1972². *The Mycenaean Origin of Greek Mythology*. Berkeley-Los Angeles.

———. 1933. *Homer and Mycenae*. London.

———. 1951a. *Cults, Myths, Oracles and Politics in Ancient Greece*. Lund.

———. 1951b. "Der Oidipusmythos." In *Opuscula Selecta*. I, 335–48. Lund.

———. 1960. "Letter to Professor Arthur D. Nock on some Fundamental Concepts in the Science of Religion." In *Opuscula Selecta*. III, 345–464. Lund.

———. 1967. *Geschichte der griechischen Religion*. 3rd ed., Vol. I. Munich.

Page, Denis L. 1959. *History and the Homeric Iliad*. Berkeley-Los Angeles.

Parry, Adam. 1971. "Introduction." In M. Parry, *The Making of Homeric Verse*, ix–lxii. Oxford.

Pascucci, Giovanni. 1978. "Il sorgere della prosa ionica: storiografia e scienza." In *Storia e civiltà dei Greci*. 2, 613–44. Milan.

Pavese, Carlo O. 1981. "Poesia ellenica e cultura orale." In Brillante et al. 1981, 231–59.

Pfeiffer, Rudolf. 1968. *History of Classical Scholarship*. Oxford.

Pötscher, Walter. 1973. "Die Oidipus-Gestalt." *Eranos* 71: 12–44.

Powell, J. Enoch. 1938. *A Lexicon to Herodotus*. Cambridge.

Prinz, Friedrich. 1979. *Gründungsmythen und Sagenchronologie* ("Zetemata" 72). Munich.

Propp, Vladimir J. 1975. *Edipo alla luce del folclore*. Turin.

Pucci, Pietro. 1971. "Lévi-Strauss and Classical Culture." *Arethusa* 4: 103–17.

Remotti, Francesco. 1971. *Lévi-Strauss. Struttura e storia*. Turin.

Robert, Carl. 1915. *Oidipus. Geschichte eines poetischen Stoffs im griechischen Altertum*. I. Berlin.

Rohde, Erwin. 1898. *Psyche. Seelencult und Unsterblichkeitsglaube der Griechen*. 2nd ed. Freiburg.

Sassi, Maria M. 1984. "Ermeneutica del mito in Karl Otfried Müller." *ASNP* sez. III, 14: 911–35.

Schwartz, Eduard. 1928. "Geschichtsschreibung und Geschichte bei den Hellenen." *Die Antike* 4: 14–30.

Segal, Charles. 1981. *Tragedy and Civilization. An Interpretation of Sophocles*. Cambridge, MA.

———. 1983. "Greek Myth as a Semiotic and Structural System and the Problem of Tragedy." *Arethusa* 16: 173–98.

———. 1986. *Interpreting Greek Tragedy. Myth, Poetry, Text*. Ithaca, NY.

Sergent, Bernard. 1980. "L'utilisation de la trifonctionnalité d'origine indo-européenne chez les auteurs grecs classiques." *Arethusa* 13: 233–78.

Skafte-Jensen, Minna. 1986. "Storia e verità nei poemi omerici." *QUCC* 51: 21–35.

Snell, Bruno. 1952. "Homer und die Entstehung der geschichtlichen Bewusstseins bei den Griechen." *Varia Variorum. Festgabe K. Reinhardt*, Münster.

Stella, Luigia A. 1978. *Tradizione micenea e poesia dell'Iliade*. Rome.

Strasburger, Hermann. 1968. "Die Wesenbestimmung der Geschichte durch die antike Geschichtsschreibung." *Sitzungsberichte Goethe Universität Frankfurt am Mein*. 2nd ed. 5:47–97.

Svenbro, Jesper. 1976. *La parole et le marbre: aux origines de la poétique grecque.* Lund.

Thomas, Carol G. 1976. "The Nature of Mycenaean Kingship." *SMEA* 17: 93–116.

Thomson, George. 1961. *Studies in Ancient Greek Society. 2. The First Philosophers.* London.

Tozzi, Pierluigi. 1966. "Studi su Ecateo di Mileto. IV." *Athenaeum* 44: 41–76.

Untersteiner, Mario. 1972. *La fisiologia del mito.* 2nd ed. Florence.

Vansina, Jan. 1976. *La tradizione orale. Saggio di metodologia storica.* Rome.

Verdin, Herman. 1970. "Notes sur l'attitude des historiens grecs à l'égard de la tradition locale." *AncSoc* 1: 183–200.

Vernant, Jean-Pierre. 1962. *Les origines de la pensée grecque.* Paris.

———. 1965. *Mythe et pensée chez les Grecs. Études de psychologie historique.* Paris.

Veyne, Paul. 1983. *Les Grecs ont-ils cru à leurs mythes? Essai sur l'imagination constituante.* Paris.

Vidal-Naquet, Pierre. 1983. "Temps des dieux et temps des hommes." *RHR* 157(1960), 55–80 (= *The Black Hunter*, 39–60. Baltimore).

Vries, Jan de. 1946. *Betrachtungen zum Märchen* ("FF Communications" 150). Helsinki.

Walcot, Peter. 1966. *Hesiod and the Near East.* Cardiff.

———. 1967. "The Divinity of the Mycenaean King." *SMEA* 2: 53–62.

Webster, Thomas B. L. 1964. *From Mycenae to Homer.* 2nd ed. London.

West, Martin L. 1966. *Hesiod. Theogony.* Oxford.

———. 1978. *Hesiod. Works and Days.* Oxford.

Wilamowitz, Ulrich von. 1937a. "Die Sieben Tore Thebens." *Hermes* 26(1891): 191–242 (= *Kleine Schriften* V 1, 26–77. Berlin).

———. 1937b. "Die Griechische Heldensage I." Sitzungsberichte Preuss. Akad. Wiss. 1925: 41–62 (= *Kleine Schriften* V 2, 54–84. Berlin).

———. 1959. *Der Glaube der Hellenen* I. Reprinted Darmstadt.

Zuntz, Günther. 1967. "Ödipus und Gregorius." *A & A* 4(1954): 191–203 (= *Sophokles. Wege der Forschung*, ed. Hans Diller, 348–69. Darmstadt).

PART TWO

COMPARATIVE
APPROACHES

3

GREEK AND NEAR EASTERN MYTHOLOGY

Several of the most important Greek myths have undisputed Near Eastern parallels—the Myth of the Ages in Hesiod's *Works and Days*[a] and the myths of Prometheus[b] and Heracles.[c] Another is the cosmogony in Hesiod's *Theogony,* where the succession of divine rulers culminates in the everlasting reign of Zeus and the stabilization of the universe. This myth, canonical for the Greeks, belongs to a type that has Hurrian-Hittite,[d] Babylonian,[e] and Phoenician[f] parallels. In the following essay, Robert Mondi extends the range of comparison to Egypt and India. The discovery of a papyrus roll at Derveni near Thessaloniki in 1962, with its quotations from an early (perhaps sixth century) Orphic theogony, has provided an even surer sense of the complex relations of Near Eastern to Greek cosmogonic myths.[g] Thus a statement that seemed paradoxical in 1966 but had come year by year to seem more apt found further confirmation: "Greece is part of Asia; Greek literature is a Near Eastern literature."[h] For "literature," one can just as well read "mythology."

The combative views of Robert Brown, published in 1898 in *Semitic Influence in Hellenic Mythology,* are finally vindicated.[i] They were long unsuccessful: a recent book surveys the history of prejudice in the field of classics against the notion of Near Eastern influence.[j] In usually tacit corroboration of this influence, Indo-Europeanists have recognized that Greek religion[k] and Greek mythology are not easily explained in terms of Indo-European origins. What can be demonstrated of the Greek language—its clear relation to the Indo-European parent language—cannot be demonstrated of Greek mythology, as it can be of the mythologies of other Indo-European-speaking peoples. (The problem is set out by Joseph Nagy in the essay following Mondi's in this volume.)

How are the parallels between the Greek and the Near Eastern myths to be explained? Either by polygenesis of the same motifs and narratives or by diffusion thereof. It is generally agreed that the traces of Near Eastern in Greek mythology are due to diffusion. The question then be-

comes: how and when did the Near Eastern myths reach Greece? Trade
routes are the obvious vectors of transmission, and the two possible periods are the late Bronze Age and the eighth to seventh centuries B.C., a
period of renewed contact between Greece and Asia Minor.[1] Mondi cau-
tions, however, against the assumption that myths arrived in Greece in
the form of texts the same as or very like the Near Eastern texts we
happen to have. The medium in which transmission took place was
surely oral, and the process was piecemeal and gradual.

The notion of the diffusion of myths presents yet another problem.
The Greek and Near Eastern myths here at issue seem to be behaving
like folktales, which are held to be more "footloose" than myths.[m] This
peregrine quality is in contradiction to the accepted concept of myth as
possessing particular validity for the society that tells it.[n] On that principle, a myth ought to be tied to a particular society and thus fixed. How
could that society's beliefs, embodied in that myth, become another society's beliefs?[o] The solution to the problem may lie in the determination
of what it is in myths that is diffused. Mondi proposes that we think of
myths not primarily as narratives but as conceptual foci that may be,
but are not necessarily, expressed in narratives. He sometimes refers to
these foci as "mythic ideas." In the case of gods, for example, their
names are conceptual foci or nuclei to which are attached various functions, narrative themes, and relationships to other divinities in their
pantheon. What is diffused from one people to another is not the whole
parcel but only that aspect or those aspects which at a given time are
wanted and acceptable.

Greek Mythic Thought in the Light of the Near East

ROBERT MONDI

Promoting what he called an "Aryo-Semitic school" of mythological
study, the late Victorian mythologist Robert Brown summed up his arguments with an expansive and grandiloquent confidence characteristic
of his age:

> But enough has been said to show an unprejudiced reader that our sys-
> tem is not dependent upon this or that etymology, is not a chain whose
> strength is but that of some dubious and fragile link. It is held together
> by the three-fold cord of history, mythology, and philology, supported in

a most valuable manner by art and archaeology; which latter studies can give no assistance to the maker of Greek and Vedic comparisons. It is not a bygone system, resting upon an exploded philology, or upon complete ignorance of modern discoveries. It is thoroughly up to date; and every newly translated cuneiform tablet, every fresh Phoenician inscription, every Hittite find, every further relic of antiquity laid bare by the spade, Mykenaean civilization, Kretan pictograph, Egyptian papyrus, will but confirm and strengthen it. (1898, 202)

This pronouncement may strike us as overbold—especially because the methodology on which it is based would today be considered dubious and fragile in the extreme—but it is no less than we might expect from a man who had the temerity to take on both Max Müller and Andrew Lang. Its prophetic promise has, however, only partially been fulfilled. In fact, the comparative study of Greek and Near Eastern myth, a pastime at least as old as Herodotus, has in the modern era waxed and waned, with scholarly attitudes alternating between the extremes of excessive and undisciplined exuberance and inevitably reactionary, parochial, and often equally unwarranted negativism. It is only in the last two decades or so that the cause of Orientalism in Greek mythic studies has begun to recover from the unwitting disservice done it by the enthusiasms of the post-Frazerian Myth and Ritualists. (For a historical overview, see Burkert 1984, 7–14.)

There is all the more reason, therefore, to guard jealously ground so grudgingly yielded, and to try to steer clear of some of the methodological abuses to which comparative study is susceptible. Remonstrating against the unbridled zeal of those who "overshoot the mark of comparative research" (specifically Engnell, Hooke, James, and Hocart), Henri Frankfort once provided what might still be taken as the ideal toward which any comparative study should strive: it should, he wrote, "counteract the narrowness of viewpoint entailed in devotion to a particular field but should not in any way infringe upon the individuality, the uniqueness, of each historical actuality" (1948, 405). Cultural patterns, as he warns elsewhere, must be discovered, not imposed (1951, 7–8). When such methodological restraint is wanting, and a variety of mythic representations, on the basis of even the slightest or most general similarities, can be declared to be in some essential way the "same myth," there is a virtually irresistible tendency toward the erection of great transcultural monomyths. The attempt has generally foundered either because the similarities involved are so general and intuitive as to be without compelling significance, or because the patterns and parallels have been "discovered" through a naive or highly idiosyncratic interpretation of some of the texts involved—an interpretation often based more on predisposition than on honest and critical analysis. Hocart once expressed the unassailable sentiment that "imagination must always keep ahead of proof as an advanced detachment to spy out the land," but the main body of critical argument must not be allowed to drop back totally out of sight.

It must also be recognized at the outset that comparison is not in and of itself an autonomous strategy for the interpretation of myth. The comparison of a particular myth with an analogue in another mythological system cannot replace the interpretation of that myth within its own system; it can at best contribute toward the elucidation of its significance or functional role in its own system. Origin ought not be construed as explanation. One must be wary of statements like that, for instance, of Walcot that the Hesiodic birth of Aphrodite from Uranus (as opposed to Zeus) *can only be explained* by the fact that the Mesopotamian Ishtar is the daughter of Anu (1966, 5–6). In the first place, the claim that an explanation is the only one possible is always arbitrary. But even if, for the sake of argument, we assume that this is in fact the origin for the Hesiodic genealogy of Aphrodite, what would it *explain?* Although the genealogy would thereby be removed from the Greek to the Mesopotamian milieu, the question of what it means, if anything, for the love goddess to be genealogically linked with the sky would remain unanswered. The attribution of oriental provenance to an element of Greek myth is thus never a final explanation of the myths, but merely one piece of the puzzle; comparative study is therefore not properly used *instead of* the other methodological approaches discussed in this volume, but only in conjunction with one or more of them.

If it is to contribute anything toward the understanding of Greek myth, the ultimate goal of comparative study should be synthetic rather than analytic. Its task ought not be the dismemberment of the corpus of Greek mythology into ethnically pure elements and foreign contaminants, but rather should lie in the opposite process of placing Greek mythology—in its entirety—in a larger mythology of shared themes and concepts. Like its counterpart in comparative Indo-European studies, comparison of Greek myths with Oriental analogues can help uncover ideological structures and conceptual relationships otherwise latent in the Greek mythological sources by making possible the study of Greek myth not only within the confines of its own closed system, but also in a more extensive nexus of mythic themes and ideology common to Greek and Near Eastern thought. In essence, it increases for our consideration the number of realizations of a mythic idea. The following discussion is consequently concerned less with the historical reconstruction of direct lines of transmission between elements of Greek myth and specific Oriental sources than with exploiting Oriental analogues for an enhanced understanding of Greek myth in its own cultural and intellectual setting.

Any discussion of the diffusion of myth, either within or between cultures, must be premised upon some well-defined notion of just what myth is—or, more precisely, what the units of mythic thought are in which diffusion might take place. Many would today agree that what we, from an interpreter's standpoint, call a myth should be seen essentially as an abstraction that is not to be exclusively identified with any particular narrative realization. One might go further, however, and question whether the narrative form itself is an essential ingredient in mythic thought. We customarily categorize myth as a species of narrative because alien mythic thought is normally accessible to us only when it is actualized as narrative. In its own cultural setting, however—that is, in the minds of those for whom it represents a real world view—a mythological system might better be seen not as a collection of discrete narratives but as a structured array of conceptual foci (god names, for instance) around each of which cluster various ideas, images, and narrative motifs. "Mythic elements derive their force precisely from the fact that they suggest rather than explain, and that they constitute cores of meaning without having been put together in any definite pattern. They function as foundation stones for certain basic assumptions in the life of a community or a person" (Waardenburg 1980, 55). Such conceptual building blocks can be *consciously* arranged in linear order and actualized as narrative by any member of a society when the occasion demands (allowing, certainly, that some can do this more artfully or professionally than others); and it is of course true that should one such actualization become fixed in a popular and widely known version (traditional or written), this *particular* narrative will then indeed become a permanent part of the cultural memory.[1]

If we thus allow that the narrative does not necessarily form the irreducible unit of mythic thought, then evidence of transmission from one mythological system to another need not take the form of complete narratives common to both, and we might focus our comparative study on conceptual analogues rather than narrative parallels.[2] An example will help make this distinction clear. In the Mesopotamian Gilgamesh epic, the hero, flush with victory over the monstrous Humbaba, incites the desire of the goddess Ishtar. In order to win him over, she offers him a dazzling array of gifts:

> I will harness for thee a chariot of lapis and gold,
> Whose wheels are gold and whose horns are brass.

Thou shalt have storm-demons to hitch on for mighty mules.
In the fragrance of cedars thou shalt enter our house.
When our house thou enterest,
Threshold (and) dais shall kiss thy feet!
Humbled before thee shall be kings, lords, and princes!

                                                    (VI. 10–16)[3]

Gilgamesh rejects her proposal and, literally adding insult to injury, catalogues the devastating transformations that have befallen her previous lovers, who now include among their number a bird endlessly bewailing a broken wing, a lion cast into "seven pits and seven," a stallion bridling under the whip, a shepherd-turned-wolf bitten by his own dogs, and (conjecturally) a mole. Thus rebuffed and insulted, Ishtar hastens lamenting to her parents Anu (sky) and his consort Antum. As her instrument of revenge, she extorts Anu's sanction for the use of the drought-causing Bull of Heaven, and a chain of events is thereby set into motion that ultimately results in the death of Enkidu.

This episode has been called an "astonishing parallel" to the wounding of Aphrodite in *Iliad* 5 (Burkert 1984, 92–95; earlier noted in passing by Gresseth 1975, 14–15). Pierced in the hand by Diomedes while removing her son Aeneas from battle, the goddess is led up to Olympus by Iris, where she is comforted by her mother Dione and, at the end of the scene, admonished by her father Zeus that her proper calling is love and not war. In addition to the narrative parallelism, it is further pointed out that not only does the etymological pair Zeus and Dione have a linguistic analogue in the Mesopotamian parents of Ishtar, Anu and Antum, but moreover that this is the only place in the epic corpus where this genealogy for Aphrodite is explicitly attested. On the basis of this coincidence of parallels, Burkert sees the episode in *Iliad* 5 as bearing the stamp of "transposition from an Akkadian classic."

Such comparison of precise narrative parallels and the subsequent attempt to reconstruct the logistics of transmission are endeavors of primarily historical interest. Our concern here is the interpretation of Greek myth and mythological texts. One problem that frequently bedevils that interpretation is that the texts often presuppose and exploit a popular tradition of mythic ideas, a latent substratum never overtly actualized in the surface narrative. Each literary work has its own unique program, and this thematic overlay often conceals from us the very mythic associations upon which it depends for its meaning and force—particularly in those cases where tension is generated by divergence from an audience expectation based on this underlying tradition. The comparison of conceptual motifs, more so than that of narrative parallels, can provide access to this hidden world of shared mythic thought.

One such idea is that of the sexually aggressive goddess whose human lovers are transformed forever and for the worse. In the example narrated above, Ishtar's former consorts are now animals, and in one way or another incapacitated ones at that. Specifically sexual incapacitation, without formal metamorphosis, is also a possible outcome of mingling of the human and the divine, an idea realized most spectacularly in the myth and ritual of the Great Goddess of Anatolia and her gelded human devotees. In the Greek sphere these ideas are often latent rather than overtly actualized. In the Homeric hymn to Aphrodite, for example, Anchises' reaction when he finds out that the woman with whom he has just copulated is the goddess Aphrodite is horrified shock: "I entreat you by Zeus who brandishes the aegis, take pity on me and don't leave me to live strengthless among men; for the man who has lain with an immortal goddess thrives no longer" (*h. Aph.* 187–90). The language is vague, perhaps politely so, but who could help but think of Attis and the Great Mother? (For a comparative discussion see Barnett 1956, 221–26, Burkert 1979, 99–122.)

The danger posed by the Odyssean Circe is in essence a conflation of both metamorphosis and emasculation, although at the narrative level there are a number of divergences from the Oriental analogues. In the figure of Circe the ability to transform men into animals has been subsumed under a more general propensity toward witchcraft, and sexual congress accordingly is here replaced by the ingestion of a drug as the overt mechanism by which the metamorphosis is activated; also, Circe's victims in the poem are uniformly turned into pigs. But, as has been demonstrated to be the case elsewhere in the *Odyssey,* the text here is tapping a popular vein of mythic ideas, leaving the audience to infer what is left unspoken. So when we hear that supposedly wild animals in the goddess's compound actually fawn on rather than attack Odysseus's men, we know why this is and what they are—or should we say who they were? (That Circe changes men into such wild animal forms as well as into swine is not mentioned explicitly until the end of the episode at 10.433). Furthermore, although Odysseus should logically be out of danger once he has fortified himself against the transfiguring draft with the antidote given him by Hermes, when Circe attempts to lure him into her bed (a crisis that the poet has reserved for Odysseus rather than the anonymous companions, in whom he has little interest) the pattern of sex and transformation immediately comes to mind and is reinforced by Odysseus's vaguely conceived fears about the danger to his manhood lurking in the goddess' embrace. (See Page 1973, 51–69 for a discussion of the episode along these lines.)

We might also note the presence of this idea in the increasing debility and (in some versions) transformation of Tithonus into a grasshopper, in this case as an indirect result of his sexual liaison with Eos. This mythological mismatch also brings up a second conceptual motif activated to a greater or lesser degree in these examples: the goddess's offer or attempt to make her lover immortal, a promise that, in the context of both Greek and Oriental religious thought, must somehow fail to be realized. Rather than attain eternal life, Tithonus is eternally dying. Although Ishtar's remarkable offer to Gilgamesh as related in the passage quoted above seems to place him on a par with the gods themselves, immortality is not explicitly mentioned as one of the benefits, and with good, contextually determined reason: a principal theme of the epic is the inevitability of death for everyone, even for one who is two-thirds divine. But with this whole episode we should compare the use of the identical narrative sequence in the Ugaritic tale of Aqhat and Anat recovered from Ras Shamra. Here it is the mortal hero's bow rather than his person that the goddess Anat covets, and immortality is explicitly part of her offer:

> Ask for life, O Aqhat the youth.
> Ask for life and I'll give it thee,
>   For deathlessness, and I'll bestow't on thee.
> I'll make thee count years with Baal,
> With the sons of El shalt thou count months.
>
> (CTA 17.VI.26–29)[4]

Aqhat is mistrustful of this promise and turns it down, to his ultimate destruction (although in the end it appears that Aqhat gains the return from death that Gilgamesh so desperately longs for).[5] The always circumspect Odysseus, tempted by Calypso with the same inducement, likewise turns the goddess down, a refusal based in this case not so much on suspicion as on nostalgia—that is to say, for reasons that grow out of the narrative and thematic context of the *Odyssey*.

The following discussion is divided into two parts of unequal length and importance. The intent of the first section is merely to illustrate the complexity of the transcultural diffusion of mythic thought by means of an admittedly reductionist analysis of mythic narrative into constituent conceptual motifs as defined above, to which I shall also refer simply as mythic *ideas*. Transcultural diffusion is essentially an extension of the means, applied and reapplied for a variety of contextual purposes, by which such motifs can be propagated *within* a culture by spreading from the orbit of one mythic center to another. The second section will attempt a synthesis of a number of more deeply rooted and systematic Greek and Oriental mythic relationships, with the hope that certain structures in Greek mythological thought can be brought into sharper focus when seen in the wider conceptual context of Near Eastern analogues.

THE DIFFUSION OF MYTHIC IDEAS

One aspect of the conventionally drawn distinction between myth and folklore (and, in most cases, between the people who study them) is that, whereas folklorists have generally concentrated on popular diffusion as the means of propagation of folktales and folktale motifs, those studying myth, especially in the context of the ancient world, have often focused attention more on a comparison of particular mythological texts, and therefore on literary diffusion of material. There is of course some necessity in this, since literary texts are in most cases our most important witness to the myths. But there is a tendency therefore, especially in comparative discussions, to apply philological methods to myth analysis, taking the literary influence of one text on another as a model for the cross-cultural transmission of myth; this tendency is often accompanied by the privileging of evidence derived from earlier poetic texts over that preserved sporadically in the later prose sources. There is often what amounts to an unspoken premise that the Oriental texts that, more or less by historical accident, have come to our attention are the very ones through which the Greeks were exposed to Eastern myth; and furthermore, at least in the case of some scholars, that our texts of Hesiod and Homer were themselves directly influenced by these Oriental models. Such a text-based comparison often entails a hypothetical reconstruction of specific times, places, and circumstances in which the transmission of this material supposedly took place, reconstructions that must in turn satisfy the chronological limits set by the putative dates of composition of the texts being compared.[6] An extreme instance of this type of historical positivism is the not infrequently voiced suggestion that Hesiod's father, upon returning to Boeotia from a sojourn in Aeolian Cyme, was somehow personally instrumental in the transmission of Oriental myth to the Greeks.

To be sure, direct textual transmission of mythological matter throughout the fertile crescent at least as early as the fourteenth century is placed beyond doubt by the discovery of actual material evidence: tablets bearing foreign mythological texts, at times in their original languages and at times translated into the local ones, have been found at a

number of archival sites. Literary hoards uncovered at Tell el-Amarna,
Boghazköy, and Ras Shamra bear witness to a remarkable second millennium literary cosmopolitanism. Ras Shamra in particular has yielded
documents in no fewer than eight languages written in a number of different scripts: in addition to the language dubbed Ugaritic itself, tablets
have been found in hieroglyphic Egyptian, cuneiform and hieroglyphic
Hittite, Hurrian, Akkadian, Sumerian, and Cypriot.

To what extent does early Greek literature enter into this picture?
There have been no discoveries of foreign texts on Greek soil, and no
convincing case has yet been made that any work of early Greek literature is in whole or part a translation, or even an adaptation of a particular Near Eastern text. There are, it is true, occasional literary parallels
between Greek and Oriental texts close enough to be suggestive.
Achilles and Gilgamesh, for instance, while mourning over their slain
companions are at that moment both compared to a lion grieving over
lost cubs (*Il.* 18.318–22, *Gilg.* VIII.ii.17–19); were this mere coincidence it would be a remarkable one at the very least. But such close and
specific parallelism is not common and seldom extends over a substantial narrative sequence. In light of the oral transmission of early Greek
poetry, we can assume that any impact of Oriental literature on Greek
literary activity during this period took the form of a gradual and ongoing absorption of Eastern literary themes and motifs into the poets'
repertoire of compositional elements, where, adapted over time to their
new environment, they became ultimately an ingrained and inseparable
part of the poetic tradition. Since our written texts generally date from
the end of such oral traditions, it is small wonder that repeated efforts
to discover evidence of earlier cross-cultural literary influence through
the direct comparison of texts have not by and large produced exciting
or universally accepted results.[7]

But what we are primarily interested in, in any case, is the diffusion
of mythic ideas. It is important to note at the outset that poetry is not
necessarily, and perhaps not even primarily, the vehicle of transmission
of these ideas, although it undoubtedly could play a significant role.
Systems of mythological thought are not the exclusive property of
poets. They constitute a basic world view shared by all members of society, and components of such a world view can spread from one cultural area to another in any number of ways. As suggested above, the
narrative need not even be seen as the minimal unit in which mythic
ideas spread. The study of dispersion perforce must always consist
largely in the comparison of texts, but in the following discussion the
texts will be treated predominantly as specific realizations of an under-

lying stratum of mythic thought rather than necessarily the actual vehicles of transmission. Each of the major mythological texts is a unique and often tendentious combination of numerous interlocking conceptual motifs found variously combined elsewhere in the ancient world, and in accounting for this we might more profitably take as a model the study of the popular diffusion of folklore motifs than the philological influence of one text on another. This entails an analysis that cuts across the various narratives, rather than a comparison of whole narratives themselves as ordered sequences envisioned synoptically—and at times not without the violence of procrustean methods—in parallel columns of supposedly corresponding events.

As an illustration of these remarks we might consider the relationship between the Hesiodic succession myth and its proposed Oriental sources, one of the most commonly drawn and generally accepted East-West comparisons. A connection is usually made specifically between the Hesiodic myth *in toto* and the so-called Kingship in Heaven narrative, which is recorded in Hittite but whose dramatis personae are predominantly Hurrian and Mesopotamian deities. The alleged Phoenician source for the history of Philo of Byblus is frequently brought into the comparative discussion as well, with the suggestion that the Phoenicians played an intermediary role. At the same time that he was presenting the most comprehensive accounting of comparative evidence to date, Walcot had expressed reservations about the strength of this particular comparison. These went largely unheeded, however, by enthusiasts on both the Greek and the Near Eastern sides, and in a recent reexamination of the problem Burkert has again raised doubts about the simplicity of such direct derivation, finding it "troublesome to identify definite channels in a complicated network" (1986, 20). Instead, he claims to hear a "many-voiced interplay of Sumerian, Akkadian, Hittite and West Semitic texts, all of which seem to have some connection with Hesiod" (p. 22). His starting point, nevertheless, remains the "chronologically parallel correspondences of extremely strange events," which are felt to link closely the Hesiodic and Hittite texts. A fresh look at the evidence in which the Kingship in Heaven text is not given pride of place and which focuses on underlying ideas rather than narrative correspondences will suggest that conceptual analogues to these strange events in the Hesiodic narrative are by no means restricted to—or for that matter even concentrated in—Anatolia or Mesopotamia.

One group of such motifs is based on a conceptual analogy, common in folklore, between the functioning of the alimentary and reproductive systems. It is manifested in myth in a number of ways. The sputum of the gods may be thought to have generative force, rendering the act of spitting a theogonic one; or, alternatively, semen may be ingested orally, followed by gestation in the stomach and ultimately live birth by various means and from various points of exit. As might be expected, mythic realizations of this analogy come into play particularly in those cases where a male figure produces live offspring as a solitary act. In an inscription from the cenotaph of Seti I at Abydos, the primordial Egyptian Atum says of the births of the gods Shu and Tefnut, "This is that which came forth from my lips and what I spat into my hand which was a vulva" (Frankfort 1933, 86). The idea of the generation of these two deities by spitting is as old as the Pyramid Texts (*Pyr.* 1652c, 1871a), but elsewhere in that corpus we read: "Atum created by his masturbation in Heliopolis. He put his phallus in his fist, to excite his desire thereby. The twins were born, Shu and Tefnut" (*Pyr.* 1248.a–d).[8] Semen and spittle are somehow combined in a single passage from the text designated the Book of Overthrowing Apophis, in which Atum proclaims, "I was the one who copulated with my fist, I masturbated with my hand. Then I spewed with my own mouth: I spat out what was Shu, and I sputtered out what was Tefnut" (*ANET* 6; see Brandon 1963, 21–23).

This would all be explicable if we could infer that Atum first swallowed the result of his onanism, thereby in essence impregnating himself, and then gave birth through the act of spitting; this, however, is not explicitly stated. But oral impregnation does play an important role in one of the many mythological skirmishes between the gods Horus and Seth, as narrated in the New Kingdom Contendings of Horus and Seth. The impregnation of one male by another is here seen as a hostile gambit rather than an act in the theogonic drama. Seth first attempts to cause his semen to enter the sleeping Horus, but by placing his hands surreptitiously between his legs the latter gathers up the fluid and prevents it from entering his body. When shown this, his mother Isis screams and cuts off Horus's hands with a copper knife; hands and semen both are thrown into the water (the hands are later restored). In retaliation, Isis takes some of Horus's own semen and smears it on a lettuce leaf that she has reason to believe Seth will consume. This in fact transpires and the scene shifts to the assembly of the gods, where the now unwittingly pregnant Seth lays claim to the divine rulership on the grounds of his imagined violation and humiliation of Horus. To substantiate the charge, Thoth calls to witness the semen of Seth; the response comes not from Horus's body, however, but from the [marsh] waters, and Horus is thereby vindicated. Then, putting his hand on the shoulder of Seth, Thoth calls out to the semen of Horus:

"Come out, you semen of Horus." Then it said to him: "Where shall I come from?" Thoth said to it: "Come out from his ear." Thereupon it said to him: "Is it from his ear that I should issue forth, seeing that I am divine seed?" Then Thoth said to it: "Come out from the top of his head." And it emerged as a golden solar disc upon Seth's head.[9]

An inscription in the temple of the ithyphallic Min at Edfu brings the generational aspect of the act into sharper relief. Accompanying a depiction of the king offering lettuce to Min are the following words:

> Offering lettuces. For recitation. The beautiful plants, the herbage from the district, rejoice thou at seeing it. Cause thy seed to enter the body of the enemy, that he may be pregnant, and that thy son may come forth from his forehead.[10]

These mythic motifs compellingly call to mind the Kingship in Heaven text (Meltzer 1974, 156). In the process of forcibly overthrowing his predecessor, Kumarbi likewise ingests reproductive material, resulting in a grim warning of retribution from the deposed Anu: "*Three* dreadful gods have I planted in thy belly as *seed*. Thou shalt go and end by striking the rocks of thine own mountain with thy head" (*ANET* 120). Presumably in an attempt to evade this fate, Kumarbi immediately spits something out—an action that, depending on the content of a hopelessly broken part of the text, may have resulted in the immediate birth of one or more deities. It would seem, from the reference to counting months, that the weather god at least is brought to term, and although the exact manner of his birth is beyond recovery, there are comprehensible fragments of a conversation about this very problem between Anu and the weather god still in Kumarbi's stomach, a conversation that, if properly understood, closely echoes the one between Thoth and the semen of Horus quoted above:

> "If I come forth from his . . . , it will *derange* (my) mind. If I come forth from his . . . , it will defile me at that spot, . . . it will defile me at the ear. . . . If I come forth from the 'good place,' a woman will . . . me." (*ANET* 121)

Both these ideas, gastric gestation in the male and divine offspring barred from birth, are present in the Hesiodic text, but they are separated in the two discrete narratives into which the succession myth falls. That the Greeks themselves thought of Cronus's regurgitation of the gods in his stomach as a parturition is evident from the designation of Hestia in the Homeric hymn to Aphrodite as the firstborn of Cronus as well as the youngest (cf. also Nonnus's grotesquely descriptive narration of the birth/regurgitation of the children of Cronus at *Dion.* 41.68–76).

On the other hand, it is in the first stage of the succession myth that we see a close parallel to the plotting between the imprisoned unborn and an external advisor concerning a means of attaining birth, in this case in a conversation between the mother Ge herself and the long-overdue children in her womb.

Very similar to this, though seldom cited in comparative discussions, is a myth about the birth of Indra related in typically allusive fashion in the fourth book of the *Rig Veda*. The hymn opens with a conversation between the young Indra *in utero*, where he has been for "a thousand months and many autumns," and his mother, concerning the route through which he might exit from her body (tr. O'Flaherty 1981):

> "This is the ancient, proven path by which all the gods were born and moved upward. By this very path he should be born when he has grown great. He should not make his mother perish in that way."

> "I cannot come out by that path; these are bad places to go through. I will come out cross-wise, through the side. Many things yet undone must I do; one I will fight, and one I will question." (R.V. 4.18.1–2)

Upon birth the child is hidden by his mother for his protection, "as if she thought he was flawed." There is a reference to the infant being swallowed by Kushava, a name explained either as that of a demoness or the river in which the young god is apparently hidden and reared. In the end we learn that it was Indra's own father who represented the threat to the infant, and that Indra killed him upon reaching maturity:

> Who made your mother a widow? Who wished to kill you when you were lying still or moving? What god helped you when you grabbed your father by the foot and crushed him? (4.18.12)

Once again, there are analogous ideas in both stages of the Hesiodic succession myth, but exact narrative correspondence to neither. In addition, the reference to Indra's grabbing his father by the foot and "crushing him" is arrestingly similar to Kumarbi's grabbing hold of the feet of the fleeing Anu before biting off his genitals (euphemistically termed his "knees"). We might also note that the concealment of the young god by his mother out of fear for his safety, as present in both the Greek and Vedic narratives, is also realized in Hittite, but in a slightly different form and a totally different narrative context: the birth of Ullikummi is at first concealed by his father Kumarbi lest the infant be destroyed by the weather god; the diorite child is hidden by the Ishirra goddesses under the earth and nourished until it attains sufficient size to challenge the weather god in combat.

But to return to the Hesiodic narrative, it is not generative matter that Cronus swallows but the newly born children themselves; and before we rush to construe this as typical Hellenic rationalization of a crude Oriental mythic motif, we might take note of analogues to this idea also, once again from Egypt rather than Anatolia. In the context of an injunction against the eating of birds or fish on the twenty-second day of the month of Thoth, a calendar from the New Kingdom briefly relates the following myth (Notter 1974, 96): Re summoned all the gods to his presence, whereupon he had them enter his stomach. Once inside, they began to make a din, so he killed them and spat them out. Their souls then flew upward as birds, while their corpses became fish. Closer to the Greek succession myth, if one is again willing to ignore the superficial order of events, is a mythic representation of the disappearance of the astral bodies in daylight recorded in the above-mentioned cenotaph of Seti I. Each morning the sky goddess Nut is said to swallow her children the stars, and then to give birth to them the following evening after they have traversed the vault of the sky in her interior; for this act she is designated the "sow who eats her piglets." Her consort Geb (the earth) becomes incensed at this destruction of their children and apparently threatens some retaliation. It is at this point that Shu intervenes to separate the sky and earth, driving Nut upwards to her celestial station (see Frankfort 1933, 83, Walcot 1966, 77–78). It is interesting to note in passing a belief about the birth of fish that Herodotus mentions in the context of his description of Egypt (2.93): The male drops milt, which the female eats; thus impregnated, she produces her spawn. Some of these are in turn eaten by the male and perish; those that manage to escape their father's gullet survive and grow to maturity.

Both the Greek and the Egyptian myths thus represent the cosmic separation of earth and sky as the result of strife between this pair over the suppression of their children by the sky. There is even evidence that, at least in some realizations, the separation of the Egyptian sky and earth was, like the Hesiodic, conceived as taking place with the pair *in coitu*. But the concomitant castration of the sky is generally, and rightly, cited as an element that links especially closely the Greek and Anatolian myths. And precisely here it is most clear that the comparison should not be based on specific texts, but on the pool of traditional mythic concepts from which they draw. In the Kingship in Heaven the sky is emasculated orally by his successor, with the idea of separation from earth at best only hinted at by the detail that Anu flies upward after the deed (there is no personification of the earth in this narrative). The text conventionally known as the Song of Ullikummi presents evidence for what is potentially a much closer parallel to the Greek myth in a passing reference to the blade with which the sky and earth were separated, although here there is no mention of castration or of any involvement of Kumarbi. But even in this case it would be wrong to restrict our view to Anatolia, for there is an analogy at least equally relevant to the Greek myth to be found once again in Egypt. Although the attempt is often made to see in the Hittite text a parallel to the Hesiodic birth of various deities from the drops of blood emanating from the severed genitalia of Uranus, the state of that text dictates that this will always remain in doubt. But the seventeenth chapter of the Book of the Dead as recorded on the Ani papyrus contains the following brief narrative of the birth of the gods Hu and Sia: "The drops of blood it is [which] come forth from the phallus of Ra, after he set out to perform the mutilation upon himself. They came into existence as the gods [who] are in the following of Ra, Hu and Sa" (Budge 1895, 35–36; discussed by Meltzer 1974, 155).

A number of conclusions emerge from this exercise. Although most of the narrative and conceptual motifs interwoven in the Hesiodic succession myth are closely paralleled elsewhere, no particular text is so much closer than the others that it merits being singled out as the ultimate "source" of the Greek. Nor does it even seem reasonable to suppose the existence of a single hypothetical protomyth, from which our attested versions have descended. The evidence rather suggests that these various mythic ideas were circulating around the Mediterranean at least as early as the Bronze Age, particularly within the triangle formed by Greece, Egypt, and the eastern Mediterranean coast. As we have seen, some of the closest parallels are actually to be found between the latter two areas, and any historical reconstruction that simply attempts to trace the migration of this mythological material from Anatolia or the Levant to Greece is bound to fall far short of telling the whole story. In fact, we might question why it goes without saying that all of these ideas necessarily moved from East to West, or why Greece is automatically assumed to be the debtor in every case. Most of the individual mythic ideas here discussed are attested earliest, most pervasively, and most organically in Egyptian documents; as one moves eastward their use becomes not only less frequent but often seemingly gratuitous.

Finally, certain striking analogues in Greek, Vedic, and Hittite mythological texts should give pause for thought to those who would claim categorically that the succession myth, seen as an irreducible unit, is non-Indo-European (e.g., Littleton 1970). It is at least worthy of note that the hostility between the currently empowered weather god and his father/predecessor is documented primarily in these three Indo-European languages. It is quite possible that we are dealing here with a fusion of some common Indo-European motifs with mythic structures originally at home in the older cultures, for example the three-stage evo-

lutionary succession from the sky to the weather god, which will be
touched upon in the following section. At the very least, this type of
analysis should call seriously into question the usefulness or validity of
any attempt to separate neatly the Indo-European from the non-Indo-
European in the complex of Greek myth, the "inherited" from the "borrowed."

STRUCTURE AND FUNCTION IN THE
COSMIC ORDER

In a frequently cited statement, Herodotus essentially attributed the
creation of Greek mythology to Hesiod and Homer; and when we consider the postepic literary tradition we cannot deny that the poetry connected with these two names quickly attained a certain canonical status.
At the same time, however, such nonliterary sources as the antiquarian
and ethnological researches of a Pausanias or a Strabo attest to the continuing coexistence of a popular substratum of mythic thought and
expression underlying this literary mainstream, and in some cases
widely differing from it. Although Homeric and Hesiodic poetry has
been lauded as a conservative and unifying force establishing and preserving Panhellenic "social values," as far as the mythological tradition
is concerned it has an innovative and tendentious side as well: in the
(perhaps evolutionary) process of selection and interpretation of mythic
material along strict programmatic lines, the monumental poems have
concealed and distorted as much as they have preserved of this rich popular tradition, and in some cases it is the version of a myth presented by
Homer or Hesiod (and subsequent sources dependent on them) which,
considered in light of other Greek attestation, appears as the exceptional and idiosyncratic one. This circumstance has considerable impact
on the modern student of Greek myth, for whom noncanonical traditions have often been reduced to allusive references and learned margi-
nalia.

The situation emerges quite clearly in the treatment of mythic figures
such as Cronus, Typhon, and Prometheus, all of whom have in common
that an essential part of their mythic essence lies in a contrast or overt
opposition to the divine authority represented in the figure of Zeus. The
first two receive scant attention in the Homeric corpus; the third none
at all. All three, on the other hand, are of considerable interest to Hesiod, at whose hands they are subjected to a highly damning interpretation in which their significance in the overall mythological system is
overshadowed by Hesiod's moralistic orientation, as well as by his in-
discriminately assigning them all to a final cosmic location in the same

underground penitentiary for immortal miscreants. Finally, all three figures act out greater mythological roles in postepic sources, which assign
them different roles from those accorded them by Hesiod and also bear
greater resemblance to the patterns of Oriental myth. One possible explanation for these facts is that in each case the poetry of Hesiod and
Homer does in fact represent an essentially Hellenic tradition and that
the later representations are all attributable to postepic development,
with the increased similarity to Eastern analogues due to subsequent
orientalizing. There is no doubt that in some particular details this is the
case, but on the whole it seems more plausible to suppose that the poetry of Homer and Hesiod, in keeping with its programmatic concerns,
has passed over, distorted, or been unaware of certain traditional
mythic patterns in its presentation, patterns that nevertheless remain
basic to Greek mythic thought and first come to our attention only in
later sources. Pindar, in the first Olympian ode, announces explicitly
that he is distorting the traditional tale of Pelops to suit his religious
sensibility, and there is no reason not to believe that Homeric and, in
particular, Hesiodic poetry issue from a similar type of activity, carried
out in silence and perhaps to some degree over the course of time rather
than as the sudden interpretive insight of a particular poet.

If this be the case, then the comparison of the Greek evidence with
Eastern myth may help uncover a number of patterns and relationships
that might not be immediately apparent in the Greek material when
considered in isolation. I would like to look specifically at a complex of
interrelated mythic ideas concerned with the organization and hierar-
chization of the cosmos, and the means by which it was attained. This
is one area of mythic thought in which evidence for a common Indo-
European tradition seems particularly lacking, and it is not surprising
that here we should find the richest material for comparison between
Greece and the Orient. In particular, the following pages have as their
primary goal an elucidation of the functional roles of Cronus and Typhon in the world view of Greek mythology, both of whom early on
attained a canonical representation in Hesiod's unyielding apology for
the supremacy of Zeus.

A preliminary word of caution is perhaps in order, concerning the
equating or identifying of different gods in the comparison of one religious or mythological system with another. A frequently replicated argument runs as follows: in the account of Philo of Byblus, El is identified
with Cronus; El-Kumarbi has been read as a double name in a
fourteenth-century Hurrian god list found at Ras Shamra;[11] therefore,
Cronus and Kumarbi are to be somehow equated, providing conclusive
evidence for the close historical connection between the Hesiodic

succession narrative and the Hittite Kingship in Heaven. The objection to argumentation of this type has to do with the most basic question of just what sort of entity a god of mythology actually is. The chain of reasoning just cited assumes that such gods are subject to a kind of transitive law of equality—indeed, in one of his numerous comparative articles Lesky justified it explicitly as being based on a "well-known mathematical axiom" (1950, 144–45). But a god should not be seen as a precisely defined and delineated mathematical entity, particularly if one is going to admit all manifestations from across the entire chronological and geographic expanse of a culture's history. If we instead think of each god name, in the manner described above, as a conceptual nucleus around which are clustered a number of narrative themes and functional relationships to other divine figures, then syncretism, of both the ancient and the modern variety, can be said to be based on the overlap of one or more of these functions and relationships in two such ideational constellations. A single god can therefore be involved in as many such identifications as there are conceptual and narrative motifs associated with his name; and if a mathematical model is needed to imagine this, the concept of intersecting sets—envisioned as overlapping circles—is much more realistic than the quantitative axiom cited above.[12]

Philo, for instance, makes numerous identifications of Zeus with Phoenician deities: Zeus = Belos (Baal); Zeus = Beelsamen (i.c., "Lord of the Sky"); Zeus Arotrius = Dagon, the discoverer of agriculture in Philo's Euhemeristic scheme; Zeus Demarous = Adodos (Hadad, the West Semitic weather god); and finally, for reasons known best to Philo himself, Zeus Meilichius = Chusor (cf. Canaanite Kothar-wa-Khasis), the craftsman god whom Philo also identifies with Hephaestus. El shares significant mythological characteristics not only with Cronus, but with Uranus and Zeus as well, depending on which particular functional relations and mythic ideas are under discussion; and, alternatively, our understanding of the mythology of Cronus can be enhanced by comparison with the mythological roles of Baal and Ea as well as that of El. What we are primarily interested in, in other words, is not the comparison of particular god names, but that of structural functions within the pantheon, and of the relationships that exist between gods. This is in accord with the principle established by Dumézil in Indo-European comparative analysis, that priority should be given to function over name, *even in the case of names that are beyond doubt derivationally connected,* such as Jupiter, Zeus, Dyaus, and *Tiwaz, or the Indic Mitra and Zoroastrian Mithra.[13]

The relationships between gods in which we will be interested are not

primarily genealogical relationships, which have often been over-
stressed in comparative studies. Genealogical relationship between deities or even between abstract ideas is but one means of expressing mythically various types of conceptual or structural associations. It happens
to be the one most prolifically applied in Greek mythic thought, especially as manifested in Hesiodic poetry; but it is not the only one. Many
of the same associations and polarities are represented in the Orient, for
example, by relative placement of names in the god lists, with no explicitly stated filiation at all. Furthermore, even when it is explicitly present,
the use of the genealogical relationship means different things in different mythological systems. We see it applied in the Greek system at its
most literal and rigid. Its use in the Eastern sources is quite different:
When the Egyptian Nun is called "father of the gods," the term seems
to denote little more than chronological priority; Baal is called the son
of both Dagan (most commonly) and El; and in a single Sumerian text
narrating her descent into the underworld the goddess Inanna is successively called the daughter of Enlil, Nanna, and Enki (*ANET* 53–54). In
the Kingship in Heaven text there is no explicit filiation at all in the first
three generations, and considering the manner of his conception and
birth, it is a moot point just who the "father" of the weather god actually is.

The Organization of the Cosmos

One of the most significant and distinctive congruences in the Greek
and Near Eastern mythic world view is the manner in which the organization of the world is inseparably linked with a classification and hierarchy of the gods. In the simplest case, a divine name is identical with
that of a cosmic region, such as the Mesopotamian An(u) or the Greek
Ge. More commonly, the relationship between a deity and a cosmic region is conceived of indirectly in metaphorical terms. The god might
reside in a region, as does Ea in the nether waters of *apsu,* and the Titans
in Tartarus; or he might be said to rule in his cosmic quarter, as in the
case of the three sons of Cronus in the *Iliad,* or the Canaanite Baal,
Yamm, and Mot. Sometimes a cosmic region becomes a personified
agent simply to play a role in the cosmogonic myth that narrates how it
came to receive its relative position in the cosmic structure, whereupon
it is relegated to an impersonal status. In cosmological terms, for instance, the Mesopotamian Ea/Enki is said to reside in the subterranean
apsu (Sumerian *abzu*); but in the cosmogonic narrative of the *Enuma
Elish* Apsu takes on a personality, is defeated by Ea in battle, and only
then becomes the locale of Ea's abode in the nethermost part of the cosmos. Similarly, the Greek Uranus is of little mythological significance as

a personal being outside the single cosmogonic myth describing his separation from Ge and allocation to his proper cosmic station.

Mythic cosmogony is essentially a means of expressing a cosmology in narrative form, and similarities in the overall process of cosmic evolution as described in various Greek and Near Eastern texts reveal a shared conception of the basic structure of the universe. As is true in much of the world's mythology, the coming-to-be of the current cosmic order is represented as a process of separation and increasing differentiation. Characteristic of the mythologies here under consideration is what we might call a *politicization* of this process, with the result that cosmic differentiation is conceived of simultaneously on two levels—as the ordering and delimiting of the cosmic masses themselves, and also in terms of the specialization and distribution of divine offices to the members of the pantheon. It is generally a mark of later composite and theologizing texts that these two modes of representation are separated and a "naturalistic" evolutionary cosmogony is adjoined to a more mythic divine history. Because the divine myths themselves represented cosmogonic events, this process often results in a conceptual doubling, such as can be found in the *Theogony*, the *Enuma Elish*, and the first two chapters of Genesis.

A major organizational principle of the Greek and Oriental world view is the conception of the cosmos as a three-tiered structure whose levels can be described, from the anthropocentric viewpoint, as here, above, and below. The imagined symmetry is evident in the Hesiodic statement that the distance from the sky to the earth, measured, as it were, in "anvil-days," is exactly equal to that from the surface of the earth to Tartarus. (The Homeric version of this at *Iliad* 8.13–16 is complicated by an attempt to distinguish Hades vertically from Tartarus, resulting in what is effectively a four-tiered system.) So, too, Marduk in the *Enuma Elish* constructs a Babylon-centered universe along a vertical axis with heaven and his celestial abode directly above the subterranean *apsu*, with both poles equidistant from Babylon and his terrestrial temple Esagil in the center (IV.135–46, V.119–30; for the individual conceptions involved in this composite account, see Lambert 1975, 55–60). This vertical tripartition is manifest in the names of the gods comprising the main trinity of the Mesopotamian pantheon: Anu, the sky; En-lil, whose name literally means "lord of lil," or the atmospheric region between earth and sky; and En-ki, "lord of the earth," who resides beneath the surface of the earth and sends up the fresh waters necessary for life. It is said that, in the progress of her descent to the netherworld, Inanna "abandoned heaven, abandoned earth, to the netherworld she descended" (*ANET* 53); and a Hittite prayer invokes "gods [and] goddesses, . . . dark netherworld, heaven [and] earth, clouds [and] winds, thunder [and] lightning, place of assembly where the gods meet in assembly" (*ANET* 398). This underlying cosmic structure is often manifested in the divine witness lists attached to treaties and oaths: the mid-eighth century Sefire treaty, for instance, between Matî'el of Arpad and a Mesopotamian overlord Bir-Ga'yah calls to witness the cosmic pairs heaven and earth, the abyss and the springs, and night and day (*ANET* 659; Fitzmyer 1967, 13, 38). The Odyssean Calypso similarly summons sky, earth, and Styx to bear witness to her oath (5.184–85), as does Leto in the Homeric hymn to Apollo (84–85); later in that same hymn Hera calls to witness earth, sky, and the Titans in Tartarus (334–36). Vertical structuring also appears to be realized in the Hittite Kingship in Heaven sequence: the first god mentioned, Alalu, goes down below the earth when deposed; his successor Anu flies upward; and the final god in the series, the weather god, is of course operative in the atmospheric space between.

In most of the mythological systems here under discussion, an important conceptual context for stratification of the cosmos is a series of polar oppositions that separate and define the three modes of conscious existence: the currently empowered gods, the living human race, and the defunct of both groups—former gods and the human dead. The polarity between the sky and earth is instrumental in the distinction between the divine and the mortal; that between earth and the netherworld is entailed in the distinction between the human living and deceased; and, taking the two outermost regions, the polarity consisting of the sky and the underworld is involved in the dichotomy between the currently efficacious deities and the former gods, whose current nether location may be the result of either force or choice. This last opposition between uppermost and lowermost, taken a step further, often represents the distinction between cosmos and chaos itself: the divine architects of the present world order keep watch from the celestial regions above, while a remnant of the primal precosmic state is wholly or at least partially confined below—for example, Egyptian Nun, Greek *chaos*, biblical *tehom*, and Mesopotamian *apsu*.

Alongside the conceptual opposition between sky and earth, a cosmological contrast is also commonly drawn between earth and sea. The biblical cosmogony basically consists of an original definition and fixing of earth and sky, followed by the differentiation and delimiting of water and land. When the Corinthian Sosicles, according to an account of Herodotus, wished to express in the strongest possible terms his appalled astonishment that the Spartans would support tyranny on Greek soil, the unnaturalness of such a thing is likened to a cosmic reversal in terms of precisely these oppositions: "Surely the sky will be below the earth, and the earth in the air above the sky; men will inhabit the sea and fish will replace them on land" (5.92). Since the solid earth is a common term in both of these oppositions, they can both be realized *cosmologically* through the designation of the whole of the universe as the triad sky, earth, and sea. (For a collection of comparative data see E. G. Schmidt 1981, although I cannot agree with the genetic cast of his argument.) The use of this triadic designation is common in biblical texts as a representation of the totality of Yahweh's universal domain—for example, Ps. 69.34: "Let heaven and earth praise him, the seas and everything that moves therein" (cf. also 96.11, 89.9–11, Pr. 3.19–20, 8.28–29). With this we might compare the universal power of Aphrodite as proclaimed in the Homeric hymn in her honor, where she is said to excite not only gods and humans, but also the birds in the air and as many animals as are nourished on land and in the sea (*h. Aph.* 2–5; cf. *Il.* 18.483–89, Ap. Rh. *Arg.* 1.496–502). Hesiodic poetry conventionally combines this triadic designation with the three-tiered structure described above to produce a fourfold description of totality: sky, sea, earth, and the netherworld, a scheme itself not without Oriental analogues.[14]

Expressed purely in naturalistic form, the concurrence of these general conceptions of cosmic structure in Greek and Near Eastern sources might not be especially remarkable; the division of the empirical world into sky, earth, and sea seems an obvious one, and both Indic and Norse myth, just to remain within the Indo-European family, have variants of the vertically tripartite cosmic organization. What strikes the attention more forcefully is the politicization of this cosmic structure, attested in both Greek and Oriental sources with similarities in general conception as well as in some rather specific details.

In the Hesiodic and biblical texts, owing largely to the theological orientation in each case, the personalization of the cosmic structure is notably attenuated. Both Zeus and Yahweh are represented as sole universal rulers: Yahweh's cosmic victory is over a generally impersonal sea (*yam* or *tehom*), and the insignificance of Poseidon in the *Theogony* is especially noteworthy. But in other contexts the personal and political mode of representing the organization of the cosmos figures much more prominently. A characteristic feature of these representations is that the earth is diminished in significance and does not share as an equal partner with the male gods of the politicized cosmos. In Sumerian cosmogony, for example, one of the first events is the primordial separation of earth and sky, whose original conjunction is represented by the compounding of their names, An-Ki. Thereafter, An becomes a leading

member of the pantheon, whereas Ki retains little cosmological significance. In the mythic terms in which this is expressed in the text known
as *Gilgamesh, Enkidu, and the Netherworld,* An "carried off heaven,"
Enlil "carried off earth," and Ereshkigal, the queen of the underworld,
was carried off by (or into) Kur "as its prize" (Kramer 1979, 23–24).
The role of Ki as a personification of earth is in some respects filled by
Ninhursag/Ninmah, a significant figure in the mythological system as a
whole, to be sure, but more in the role of giver of life than as a component of the cosmic structure (Kramer 1979, 26–29; Jacobsen 1976,
104–10). Similarly, whereas Ge retains an important narrative role in
the Hesiodic *Theogony,* in the politicization of the cosmos as represented by the Homeric division among the three male children of
Cronus, the earth plays no significant role. Not only is it without personality, but it is not even attributed to any particular cosmic ruler: it is
the common ground of all three.

Narratively, the political distribution of the gross regions of the cosmos among divine personalities can be realized by a number of mythic
devices. In the theologizing texts in which a single god is exalted at the
expense of all others, it is predictably seen as a unilateral delegation of
divine offices. So Marduk in the *Enuma Elish* assigns Anu, Enlil, and Ea
to their cosmic locations in the sky, earth, and nether waters, respectively (IV.146; on the tendentious theology in evidence here, see Brandon 1963, 102–3). In the Hesiodic *Theogony,* Zeus apportions the pre-
rogatives (*timai*) to the other gods (including, presumably, Poseidon and
Hades) after his victory over Typhon and subsequent enthronement (*Th.*
74, 885). There appears to be a historicized reflex of this mythic concept
at Deut. 32.8–9, where Yahweh (designated Elyon) divides the peoples
of the world among the "sons of God," in the process himself receiving
the people of Jacob as his "allotted heritage." So too in the account of
Philo of Byblus the cosmic apportionment has become ethnographic,
when Cronus distributes the cities of the world to their various patron
deities (Eusebius *P.E.* I.10.31–35).

More interesting from the comparative point of view is the idea of
cosmic apportionment by lot. In the *Iliad* we are told that the three sons
of Cronus had divided the cosmos among themselves by means of such
a lottery, the result of which is that Zeus now rules in the sky, Poseidon
the sea, and Hades the netherworld, a myth widely documented
throughout Greco-Roman antiquity.[15] We have seen some sort of voluntary partitioning of the cosmos represented by the Sumerian division
among An, Enlil, and Kur, and in a Hittite text relating the marriage of
Telepinus to the daughter of the sea there is a reference to a primordial
allotment of the sky, earth, underworld, and human race to the appro-

priate gods (Hoffner 1975, 137). Most explicit is the Mesopotamian *Atrahasis* epic, in which it is expressly as the result of a lottery that Anu, Enlil (an almost certain supplement for a textual lacuna), and Enki receive their cosmic stations in the sky, earth, and nether waters of *apsu* (*Atrah.* I.i.11–16, Lambert and Millard 1969, 43; see also Burkert 1984, 86–87).

Although the last-mentioned text provides a close narrative parallel to the Greek myth of the cosmic allotment, a closer structural analogue is found in the Canaanite pantheon as reconstructed from the Ugaritic texts at Ras Shamra. As Hesiod refers to the Olympians collectively as "those born from Cronus," so the council of Canaanite gods is designated as the "sons of El," or the "family" or "circle of El" (Pope 1955, 48–49; Mullen 1980, 15–22). El himself is called the "father of the gods," and his consort Asherah is designated their mother. Of all these gods (who traditionally number seventy), three male figures are singled out for special prominence in the tablets that have come to light: Baal, Yamm, and Mot, manifested, respectively, in the cosmic realms of the atmosphere, the sea, and lower world of the dead. This structure is identical to the Homeric division of the world into the realms of Zeus, Poseidon, and Hades. Although certainty is out of the question owing to the fragmented nature of the texts and the difficulty of knowing the order in which the fragments are to be read (or even if they are all from a single poem or cycle of poems), the main theme of the so-called Baal cycle appears to be the establishment of a permanent and stable division of the cosmos among these deities. It is realized mythically through a series of hostile encounters in which both Yamm and Mot successively attempt to extend their suzerainty at the expense of that of Baal and are rebuffed and thenceforth restricted to their own domains, presumably once and for all. Nowhere in the preserved material is it mentioned explicitly how the allotment was made in the first place, but it is clear that El somehow has the power to grant or withhold these cosmic kingdoms. The term *nḥlt,* 'inheritance' (for a discussion of the meaning see Clifford 1972, 69–73), is used of Mot's underworld kingdom (*CTA* 4.VIII.13–14, 5.II.16), as well as the mountain of Baal (3.III.27 = 3.IV.64) and the throne of the craftsman god Kothar wa-Khasis in Crete (3.VI.16).

Since the notion that even the supreme god of the pantheon received his portion by lot inevitably entails a diminution of his stature relative to the other gods, and considering the pervasiveness in the Greek tradition of the cosmic lottery from the time of the earliest documentation, it is not unlikely that we here have a case in which the Hesiodic tradition has concealed from the comparativist a close association of Greek and Eastern myth. Had it not been for the single reference in the *Iliad,* we might have attributed later Greek references to such a lottery to postepic orientalizing. We have seen that the *Enuma Elish,* a poem whose theological program and compositional methods are much the same as Hesiod's, has done precisely this same thing in representing Marduk as himself appointing the divine offices, in contrast to the lottery tradition manifested in the *Atrahasis* text. And in his hymn to Zeus, Callimachus was later to do with explicit vehemence what I suggest the Hesiodic tradition has accomplished through its silence (58–67):

> The ancient poets were not completely truthful when they said that the sons of Kronos were apportioned the three dwellings by lot. . . . It was not the casting of lots which made you the king of the gods but your physical deeds, that strength and power which you have set beside your throne.

The King of the Gods and the Kingdom of God

Cosmic organization is hierarchical, and it is realized as such simultaneously in physical and political terms: primacy in some form is generally associated with the superterrestrial regions of the cosmos and expressed personally through the concept of kingship. When Zeus draws the sky as his domain in the cosmic lottery, the implication is that, Poseidon's protestations of equality notwithstanding, Zeus is to be the first among equals, the king of the gods.

It is not, however, completely accurate to say that this divine kingship is simply a case of a mythic world view "reflecting" human institutions. Although the divine monarch may ultimately owe his throne to his mortal counterpart, a firm distinction must nevertheless be maintained at all times between the historical institution of human kingship and the mythic use of the *idea* of kingship, particularly when attempting to employ the latter as evidence for reconstructing the former. In some cases it may in fact be the historical that reflects the mythic: it is not unusual for the human king to be represented (or to represent himself) in mythically ideal terms usually associated with divine kingship.[16] Mythic use of the idea of kingship can answer to a variety of conceptual needs and not uncommonly long outlives the historical institution.

As it is actualized in the Greek mythological system, two related aspects of the idea of divine kingship merit attention. On the one hand, there are two divine figures to whom kingship is attributed in this system, Zeus and Cronus, each after his own fashion. On the other hand, from the very earliest literary documentation the throne of Zeus is associated with two cosmic locations: the sky as well as the more immediate Olympus. Each of these observations hints at an underlying conceptual dualism, one that we can see overtly realized in Near Eastern texts. This comparison will suggest that in the Greek mythological tradition *overall* Zeus and Cronus represent two quite different aspects of divine kingship, while the Zeus of Homer and Hesiod is in some ways a coalescence of the two, at the expense of Cronus, in the person of a single universal ruler.

A common feature of religious thought in many and scattered parts of the world is a dual conception of the superterrestrial regions of the cosmos, a differentiation between a divine but passive presence in the calm serenity of the sky and a dynamic force manifest in the meteorological phenomena of the lower atmosphere. As opposed to the fixed and remote celestial locale of a personalized sky, the imminence of the atmospheric deity is often reflected in his having a mythological abode (not to be confused with his actual temples) not only on earth, but within the bounds of real geography—though its immediate locale may be sufficiently unapproachable to lend it the requisite quality of awe. A common actualization of this idea, local topography permitting, is the holy mountain from whose peaks the god is imagined to descend in the progress of his storm theophany.

Mythic thought typically entails a congruence of time and space, a duplication in conception of what was long ago and what is far away. Accordingly, the transcendent sky can also be distinguished from the imminent force of the weather by a temporal projection into a past that is not only remote but prior—on the relative scale of mythic time—to the latter's birth or assumption of power. The result is a synchronic distinction expressed mythically as a diachronic sequence. There is a common Mesopotamian tradition of a temporal sequence at the head of which is the authority represented by a personified sky, and which culminates in a currently active deity in some way manifest in the weather. Most clearly seen in the progression Anu—Ea—Marduk, which provides the narrative structure for the *Enuma Elish,* it is also evident in the Sumerian genealogical sequence An—Enlil—Ninurta, and in the Hittite Kingship in Heaven text (Anu—Kumarbi—Weather God). Superficially, at least, this is identical to the Hesiodic sequence Uranus—Cronus—Zeus. If we are willing to credit Philo with preserving material at this point which really derives from Canaanite tradition and not from Hesiod, it is possible that that tradition likewise had a divine sequence Shamem (sky)—El—Baal (Pope 1955, 55–58; Miller 1967, 414–17; Cross 1973, 40–41; L'Heureux 1979, 48). Common to all these examples, it should be noted, is not only the temporal primacy of transcendence over imminence, but also the presence of a mediating figure between the two, the position occupied by Cronus, Kumarbi, Ea, Enlil, and perhaps El.

It has been widely debated whether or not such mythic succession is a reflection of history—the result either of evolution within a religious system or of such contingent factors as migration and conquest. Eliade has argued on a global scale for the historical evolution of religious feeling from belief in the remote and transcendent to belief in the imminent (e.g., 1958, 38–123), and various diachronic explanations have been brought forward in the special cases. Ultimate origins are not our primary concern here, but we should recognize the possibility that this dualistic representation of cosmic supremacy through the mythic device of temporal succession from one type to the other was present from a very early period and constitutes a conceptual polarity of long standing rather than a mythic reflection of history. In other words, it is possible that the mythic past was always a past, and that certain "former" gods are former *by nature* rather than as the result of historical change.

On the political level, this dualism of transcendence and imminence is realized in a binary representation of divine kingship. In functional terms, it takes the form of a contrast between the hoary *auctoritas* of the wise and aged patriarch and the intimidating physical vigor of a younger executive deity. The influence of the former resides in his wisdom and command of respect; efficacious through verbal utterance rather than physical action, he holds a position of authority in the council of the gods as the ultimate fount of cosmic order and is often accorded a judicial function, especially in the settling of disputes between gods. In the case of the pan-Mesopotamian An(u) this cosmic authority is represented by his possession of the so-called Tablets of Destiny. The younger god, on the other hand, physically manifest in the weather, is mythologically conceived of as the warrior-king: he is both the victor in the cosmic struggle that brought about the current world order and the executive force through which this order is maintained.

It would be overly simplistic, however, to see here merely a distinction between the social functions of king and warrior. The distinction is rather a conceptual one between *status* and *process*, between the static, unchanging, and eternal essence of cosmic governance and the dynamic process by which it is attained and preserved. It is therefore not surprising that there is little mythological interest in how the figure representing the former attained his position: it is his nature to *be* authority, not to come into it. Moreover, the actualization of this duality often results in the synchronic coexistence of more than one "king" in the same mythological system, and we are led astray if we try to impose the historical model of an exclusive human monarchy too rigorously on the divine paradigm. These figures embody different aspects of the idea of kingship which are to be seen as complementary rather than exclusive, and we should not assume that the elder figure must be thought of as having been replaced or deposed by his successor, and hence completely without real function or authority. The common Near Eastern pattern is that they coexist.

The caveat made at the outset about comparing functions rather than gods is particularly germane in this context. In spite of the superficial similarities in these dynastic sequences from sky to weather, we should be wary of mechanically equating gods at the same genealogical level, thereby imposing a common pattern that glosses over the variation in the way in which the differentiation is worked out in each system, to say nothing of variation within each system itself. Two factors in particular complicate the comparative picture.

The first is the functional ambivalence of the intermediary figure. As an example we might consider the mythological roles accorded to Enlil, who occupies a position between the sky An and Ninurta, whose utterance "is a storm." In some cases the pair An/Enlil presents aspects of the duality of authority and executive force, the latter associated with the devastating power in the wind. The destruction of a city, for example, could be theologized as the force of Enlil executing the decree of An (cf. the lamentation over the destruction of Ur [ANET 455–63], and see Jacobsen 1976, 86–104, Frankfort 1948, 231). In other texts, however, it is the pair Enlil/Ninurta that seems to fit this functional dichotomy. In a Sumerian hymn in his honor, Enlil is described as the "judge and decision-maker of the universe," whose "noble word is weighty as heaven" (ANET 575). In combat texts Ninurta is characterized as the "right arm," the "prop," and the "warrior" of his father Enlil, on whose behalf he turns back the cosmic challenge (Sjöberg 1976, 421; van Dijk 1983, 75, 147; Cooper 1978, 59). In the text designated Lugale, Enlil is portrayed as totally dependent on his son to defeat the usurper Asakku (van Dijk 1983, 75); and in the (An)zu myth it is Ninurta who must recover the Tablets of Destiny and with them the "Enlilship" of the cosmic order (ANET 110–18, 515–16).

A second complicating factor is sectarian theologizing, which can willfully blur functional distinctions for the greater glory of a particular divinity. The theology of the god Marduk, for example, accords to that god attributes of both the transcendent authority of Anu and the executive force of an Enlil or a Ninurta. His role as executive agent is, of course, amply in evidence in the cosmogonic warfare of the Enuma Elish; but in the formal pronouncement of his coronation in that same poem he is granted the Anu function as well and with it the authority of that god's inexorable command: "Thy decree is unrivaled, thy word is Anu; from this day unchangeable shall be thy pronouncement" (IV.3–7). In spite of this language, however, it should be noted that when Marduk recovers the Tablets of Destiny from the fallen pretender Kingu, he in fact duly and graciously turns them over to the possession of Anu, "as the first gift of greeting" (V. 70).

Viewed thus in functional terms, the seemingly precise correspondence between the Greek dynastic sequence from Uranus to Zeus and the Mesopotamian examples is specious at best. Uranus is but a pale reflection of Anu: apart from the castration myth he has very little significance as a cosmic personality at all and is not associated with kingship in any systematic way (Detienne and Vernant 1974, 66, Briquel 1980, 248–49). The same holds true for the Canaanite pantheon—at least to the extent that it can be reconstructed from the texts unearthed at Ras Shamra: whether or not the sky Shamem was ever considered in any sense a predecessor of El, he too appears to have had little mythological significance. In both these systems it is rather the *immediate* predecessor of the weather god—Cronus or El—who represents the transcendent function in which we are interested. We have already seen one quite clear indication of the functional equivalence of Canaanite El and Mesopotamian Anu: the corresponding roles played by these two gods in the narrative pattern in which an insulted goddess—Ishtar or Anat—seeks patriarchal sanction for retaliation against an offending human. Just as the division of El's kingship among the gods Baal, Yamm, and Mot is the closest structural analogue to be found to the Homeric division of Cronus's royal legacy, so too the conceptual relationship between El and Baal provides the most illuminating analogue to that between the Greek Cronus and Zeus and for that reason merits further attention. It also provides a key to a number of striking congruences in Greek and Hebrew mythic thought.[17]

Characterized as *malk olam,* the "eternal king" (*Ug.* 5.2.1), El is the essence of kingship. He is consistently depicted as old, just, compassionate, and patriarchal: "Thy decree, O El, is wise: Wisdom with ever-life thy portion" (*CTA* 3.V.38–39 = 4.IV.41–43).[18] The Ugaritic texts have no tale to tell of his rise to power and make no mention of a predecessor. Although he himself is seldom portrayed as engaged in what we might call executive activity, a type of ultimate authority over the cosmic order is associated with the concept of El and it runs throughout the mythological texts. Analogous to Anu's possession of the Tablets of Destiny we hear of unalterable "decrees" which El alone issues (Mullen 1980, 87–88). The executive power of each of the three cosmic regents derives from him: beyond the fact that they are designated as his sons and that at least Yamm and Mot are called "Beloved of El," this dependence is evident in the necessity for the younger gods to secure the sanction of El for the building of their palaces (emblematic, in the Ugaritic texts, of the permanent establishment of each god's rulership), as well as in the apparent ability of El to withdraw his sanction at will, as the warning of the sun Shapsh to Mot suggests:

> Harken, now, godly Mot!
> > Why striv'st thou with Puissant Baal? Why?
> Should Bull El thy father hear thee,
> > He'll pull out thy dwelling's pillars,
> Overturn thy throne of kingship,
> > Break thy staff of dominion!
>
> (CTA 6.VI.23–29)

Whether or not El is ever conceived of as a warrior himself has been a subject of considerable discussion among students of Canaanite myth (evidence collected by Miller 1967, 1973, 48–58); but in any case it is clearly Baal who in the texts published to date is the executive warrior-king *par excellence*. In addition to the cosmic battles waged with Yamm and Mot, there are passing references to a number of chaotic demons defeated by Baal (e.g., CTA 5.I.1–5 = 27–31). Particularized as the West Semitic weather god Hadad, the Ugaritic Baal is also the force of the storm and bringer of rain: designated as the Rider of the Clouds, his temporary death at the hands of Mot results in a seven-year drought. As divine kings, El and Baal well illustrate the complementary concepts of status and process as defined above: "El is king, Baal becomes king. Both are kings over other gods, but El's kingship is timeless and unchanging. Baal must acquire his kingship, affirm it through the building of his temple, and defend it against adversaries; even so he loses it, and must be enthroned anew. El's kingship is static, Baal's is dynamic." [19]

Attempts to impose preconceived dynastic patterns on the relationship between Baal and El—especially patterns derived from Hesiodic myth and Philonic syncretism which portray El as a "former" god violently deposed by his son—are not compellingly supported by the available evidence. Although there may well have been other traditions in which El is himself a warrior who attained his throne by overthrowing his father and perhaps was himself in turn deposed by his son, the texts from Ras Shamra point toward a coexistence, at times perhaps uneasy, of the transcendent authority of El and the executive activities of his three sons, each supreme in his own sphere, with Baal the *primus inter pares* in accord with his higher cosmic station.[20] In an Ugaritic text often cited because of the remarkable parallel it provides to the biblical relationship between the elderly Saul and the young shepherd David summoned to sing in his court (cf. 1 Sam. 16), this relationship between El and Baal-Hadad is crystallized in a domestic vignette:

> El sits enthroned with 'Aṭṭart [i.e., Astarte]
> El sits in judgment with Haddu, the shepherd,
> Who sings and plays upon the lyre.[21]

In the texts narrating the tales of Aqhat and Keret, the two gods are depicted acting in tandem, with Baal functioning essentially as an intercessor for the human kings in the presence of El.

This functional dualism is reflected in the cosmic station of each of these deities. While Baal's kingship is ratified by the construction of his palace on Mount Zaphon in northern Syria, El's mountain abode, the meeting place of the divine assembly over which he presides, is said to lie "at the source of the rivers, in the midst of the sources of the two deeps." The vagueness of this expression has led to an inevitable scholarly debate over precisely where in the cosmic structure El's habitat was imagined to be, and whether or not a particular mountain or mountain range originally provided the inspiration for it (see Pope 1955, 61–81; Kaiser 1962, 47–55; Mullen 1980, 147–68). But what is significant is that wherever or whatever El's mountain abode is, it is conceived of in mythic terms; it is removed from human experience not so much on the basis of its actual location but because of its mythic quality (W. H. Schmidt 1966, 7–8). El is the focus of an array of mythic ideas that properly belong to *him* rather than to any specific cosmic address: "The mythic pattern which couples the cosmic river(s) with the Mount of God, the place where the gates of heaven and the watery passage into hell are found, may be applied to any great mountain with springs at its foot or side where a sanctuary of El (or Yahweh) exists" (Cross 1973, 38).

Just as the Marduk of the *Enuma Elish* is a melding of characteristics realized elsewhere in the figures of Anu and Enlil, both the El and Baal of Canaanite tradition have been seen as contributing to the biblical representation of Yahweh. He is at the same time imminent and transcendent; both the storm warrior and the patriarchal shepherd of his chosen people. Like El he is the "eternal king" (*melek olam*, Jer. 10.10; cf. *el olam* at Gen. 21.33); but like Baal he "rides upon the clouds" (Ps. 68.4). He is located on Mount Zion as well as in the sky: "The Lord is in his holy temple, the Lord's throne is in heaven" (Ps. 11.4; cf. 18.6–9, Mic. 1.2–3). He is represented as the head of the divine council, which meets on the mountain of god, but also as the cosmic dragon slayer, in which role his actions are on occasion described in language so close to that used of Baal and Anat in the Ras Shamra texts that some underlying connection is generally admitted (e.g., Ps. 74.13–14; CTA 3.III. 35–39).

When we turn to the Greek system, we see this same coalescence of transcendent authority and executive imminence in the representation of Zeus that emerges from the poetry of both Homer and Hesiod: Zeus is not only the executive deity manifest in atmospheric phenomena, but he is also the guardian of *themis* and, it will be recalled, drew the sky as his domain in the Homeric lottery. Like El, he is a patriarch, the "father of gods and men"; but at the same time an important part of the mythology associated with his name, like that of Baal, concerns the attaining and defending of this political supremacy and resulting world order through cosmic combat. His ideal embodiment of both aspects of kingship is reflected, as was the case with Yahweh, in his dual abode in the sky and on Olympus.

We must look elsewhere in the Greek hexameter corpus for the crystallization of the dualism under discussion in separate figures. It is salient, for instance, in the characterization of the Hesiodic races, a distinction between the remote "royal" race of gold and the more immediate warrior-kings of the bronze and heroic races. It also forms part of the social ideology of the *Iliad*, a dualism represented ideally by what we might call the Nestor type and the Achilles type. The *Iliad* dramatically exploits this functional duality in the dispute between Agamemnon and Achilles, which is in essence a clash between acknowledged authority and physical force: though each is technically king in his own right, Agamemnon is the "shepherd of the people," by consensus the most "kingly," while Achilles is the acknowledged superior in physical combat. (Note that even Achilles yields to Agamemnon in the end by giving up Briseis, although it is not clear how Agamemnon would enforce his claim if Achilles had simply refused to comply.) The result of this strife is a total and catastrophic social breakdown in which functions that ideally complement each other (as they do, for instance when An and Enlil team up to destroy a city) are set at odds.

Viewed in a slightly different way, this dualism can now help clarify the conceptual relationship between Cronus and Zeus. Given the nature of human experience, the distinction between dynamic process and attained status is in effect the distinction between reality and idealism. According to an ideology common in the ancient world, there are three components of a successful human society: internal justice, security from foreign threat, and agricultural plenty, the last often connected explicitly with a ready sufficiency of fresh water. While the executive king of the gods is associated in his various aspects with the struggle in history to achieve these ends, their complete and perfect attainment is often projected into mythic time or space, realized as an otherworldly *kingdom of god*. Not surprisingly, such an idealized reign can form an important component in the conception of a primordial paradise or of a promised world awaiting the chosen. Characteristic is the eschatological pronouncement of John's Revelation: "The kingdom of the world has become the kingdom of our Lord and of his Christ, and he shall reign for ever and ever" (11.15; cf. Zech. 14.9).

We have already seen that associated with El's abode is an unfailing supply of subterranean water—which is to say a supply of water that does not depend on the vagaries of the weather or the toilsome maintenance of a system of artificial canals. With quite similar mythic imagery, the postdiluvian abode of the Mesopotamian flood hero Utnapishtim is located "far away, at the mouth of the rivers," in a fabulous garden of lush and bejeweled flora (*Gilg.* XI.195, IX.v.47–51).[22] It is precisely because he is removed from executive responsibility that El can be depicted as benevolent, compassionate, and tranquil; never portrayed as angry, he gives blessings rather than curses, rewards rather than punishments. Seemingly averse to strife of any sort, he himself remains aloof in the midst of contention among the younger gods and repeatedly yields to pressure put upon him to sanction their various schemes. This apolitical elevation above the fray is frequently construed as a sign of El's weakness in the current regime but may be regarded rather as an essential and timeless aspect of his character, in contrast to that of Baal.[23]

The similarities between the complex of mythic themes associated with Canaanite El and the biblical idea of Eden have often been noted.[24] In the strife-free state of Eden the uncultivated abundance of food is likewise watered automatically from the subterranean source of fresh water—Eden is itself the source of four great rivers. The absence of strife and injustice is such a defining characteristic of Eden that there is no provision for punishment: the first unjust act brings human participation in the state to an end. It is "an ideal of pre-political existence, and redemption which ends in the garden of Eden is deliverance from the tensions of political life" (Levenson 1976, 33). Accordingly, no executive activity of any sort on the part of God is required.

In accordance with a widespread belief that the eschatological *Endzeit* will be a return to the primordial *Urzeit*, the Day of Yahweh in the prophetic tradition promises to inaugurate the coming together once and for all of these same ideal qualities. After one final conflict in which Yahweh, playing the role of the divine warrior one last time, will descend from Mount Zion in a storm theophany that will make the whole earth tremble (Joel 3.16), the *true* kingdom of god will be inaugurated on Zion, "from this time forth and for evermore" (Mic. 4.7; Zech. 14.9). Streams of "living waters" will flow from this new Jerusalem to the sea (Zech. 14.8; Joel 3.18; cf. Is. 33.21), and after this last outburst of executive activity justice and peace will pertain forever. The ideal will become real. The process of history will finally reach fulfillment and cease.[25]

It is against this background that we can begin to understand ideas associated wth the figure of Cronus in Greek mythic thought. It has long been noted that there is a seemingly irreconcilable breach between the Cronus of the succession myth and the Cronus of the golden age,[26] and the vividness of Hesiod's narrative of the former, coupled with our tendency to privilege older textual sources, has made this conception of Cronus the norm. But it should be noted that there is no subsequent attestation of Cronus's role in the succession myth—the castration of his father and the devouring of his children—which is not essentially identical to the Hesiodic version or clearly derived from it; when mentioned by prose authors it is often attributed to Hesiod himself, or to the literary tradition (i.e., to the "poets"). On the other hand, our witnesses to what we might call the utopian Cronus are much more varied, and the greater variation in those attestations suggests that they do not stem from a single poetic tradition but rather represent a more deeply ingrained ideology that was more widely and popularly diffused among the Greeks for a long period of time (see Philippson 1944, 134–35; Baldry 1952, 84–86).

If we distract ourselves from the unforgettably scandalous events of the Hesiodic narrative, we note that a prominent concept incorporated in the mythology of Cronus from the earliest documentary evidence to the latest is his connection with kingship.[27] But his is not the executive type of kingship associated with Zeus as head of the contemporary pantheon. The kingdom of Cronus is not of this world; like the biblical concepts of Eden and Zion, the proverbially utopian "life under Cronus" (ὁ ἐπὶ Κρόνου βίος) is relegated to mythic time and place. In spite of a generally negative portrayal of Cronus in the *Theogony,* his reign is connected in the *Works and Days* with the golden *genos,* a race for whom the three components of the successful society as described above are not a goal but a reality: as compared with the silver race the gold is free from injustice; as compared with the bronze it is free from war; and as compared with the iron the earth produces its bounty of its own accord, without strife, toil, or meteorological anxiety. In short, there is as little need of divine executive activity in the kingdom of Cronus as there is in Eden; and indeed in most mythological accounts the reign of Zeus is inaugurated only with the subsequent race of silver, congenitally hubristic and impious.

Looking toward the other end of human history, although the idea of an eschatological creation of a new world order never really took root in traditional Greek religious thought, Hesiod's prophetic vision does hint at such a resurrection of the primordial paradise from the social and moral chaos of the coming end of the iron race (W&D 174–75). More productive in Greek religious thought was the idea of an individual eschatology, and here the notion of the kingdom of Cronus comes into play once again: his ideal regency is not only a feature of the primeval golden race, but also of the blessed state awaiting the elect (W&D 173a, Pind. Ol. 2.68–77).[28] The Hesiodic description of these two conditions is in fact virtually the same (cf. W&D 112–20 and 166–73a): like the primordial Eden and the eschatological Zion, they are in essence the same ideal, realized mythically as both lost Urzeit and promised Endzeit.[29]

Prose authors later made repeated use of this popular conception of "life under Cronus." The Euhemerizing history of Diodorus makes Cronus not only the first king, but also the ideal king and benevolent culture hero who "transformed the way of life of the men of his day from wild to civilized; because of this he came into great favor and travelled all over the inhabited world, introducing justice and openheartedness to all" (5.66.4). Plato had earlier exploited this mythic notion of the ideal and idyllic kingdom of Cronus in the exposition of his own conception of ideal governance:

> Recognizing that human nature is in no instance capable of exercising absolute authority over human affairs without becoming filled with hubris and injustice, Cronus . . . placed in charge of us at that time a superior race of daemons, who looked after us with as much ease to themselves as to us. They provided us with peace, reverence, order, and unstinted justice, and made the human race blessed and free from strife. (Laws 713D-E).

Aristotle characterizes Peisistratus as being kindly, mild, and merciful, and his reign as peaceful and leisurely; for this reason, he adds, people at the time likened it to the reign of Cronus (Ath. Pol. 16). In his treatise on the face of the moon, Plutarch's myth of the island of Cronus presents a similar picture of human paradise in the company of Cronus who is remote and tranquil—sleeping in fact—but at the same time the very essence and idealized form of kingship, untarnished by executive activity, a figure in whom "the royal and divine element is all by itself, pure and unalloyed" (Mor. 942A).[30]

As one last example of this concept of Cronus we might consider the characterization of the god in Lucian's *Saturnalia*. Although obviously somewhat tongue-in-cheek and undoubtedly influenced to some extent by a syncretism with the Roman Saturn (although the very fact of such a syncretism attests to the force of the concept of Cronus here under discussion), this composition paints a picture of the Greek Cronus which more than any other invites comparison with the partiarchal El in his transcendent remoteness and in particular in his relationship to the executive activity of his sons. For the two-week duration of this festival the kingdom of god is realized: the fabled "life under Cronus" is in effect, and the presence of Cronus among the revellers brings about a temporary return to the beneficent justice of the golden *genos*. Cronus is represented as easygoing and benevolent, in contrast to Zeus and the tools of his executive enforcement, the terrifying thunderbolt and the gruesome aegis. He is a gray-haired and avuncular figure, who has voluntarily stepped aside, divided his kingdom among his three sons, and now claims to be enjoying a well-deserved retirement (Hesiod is dismissed as a rustic quack spreading scandalous tales):

> I wasn't able to put up with the excessive injustice of the current generation. I constantly had to run up and down waving the thunderbolt, scorching perjurers, temple-robbers or muggers—a demanding job which wanted a younger man. So I stepped aside in favor of Zeus. It seemed high time in any event to divide my kingdom among my sons and devote myself primarily to enjoyment and leisure: no longer dealing with suppliants or being irritated at those making contrary requests; no longer thundering or flashing lightning, or feeling obligated from time to time to throw hail stones. Instead I lead an old man's life of pleasure, drinking my nectar neat and nattering with Iapetos and my other pals from the old days. Zeus is now king and has all the headaches. (*Sat.* 7)

Cronus mingles freely among mortals, reminding everyone he meets what life had been like under his rule, when "wine flowed in rivers, and there were springs of honey and milk; for everyone was good, everyone was gold."[31] All this during the reign of a god whom, giving Hesiod more than his due, Andrew Lang once condemned as an "odious ruffian."

The Enthroning of the Storm Warrior and the Dragon Who Would Be King

The focal theme in the mythology of the imminent aspect of divine kingship is the cosmic struggle by which this executive power was attained, and the consequent establishing of the current world order. The

main players in this event are the currently empowered executive god
and an often monstrous challenger—which will henceforth be referred
to generically as the "dragon"—whose defeat ensures the god's acquisition and retention of the throne. We might take as our own starting
point the following description of this pattern in the context of the
Canaanite-Hebrew tradition, noting in particular with how little change
it could be applied to the Greek conceptualization of the defeat of Typhon and subsequent enthroning of Zeus, especially as narrated in Hesiodic poetry.

> From the several texts cited, two patterns or genres can be discerned
> either in separate or mixed form. The first pattern (1) is the march of the
> Divine Warrior to battle, bearing his terrible weapons, the thunderbolt
> and the winds. He drives his fiery cloud-chariot against his enemy. His
> wrath is reflected in all nature. Mountains shatter; the heavens collapse
> at his glance. A terrible slaughter is appointed. All nature wilts and lan-
> guishes. In the foreground is the cosmogonic struggle in which chaos—
> Yamm or Lotan—is defeated. The second pattern (2), and the most fre-
> quent, is the coming of the Divine Warrior from battle to his new temple
> on his newly-won mount. In the background is his victory over Sea or
> the flood-dragon, though it is often alluded to, especially in his being
> enthroned on the Flood. Primary is his manifestation as Victor and King
> in the storm. The roar of his voice awakens nature. The appearance of
> his radiant storm cloud is both awesome and fructifying. His rule is
> manifest in the fertility of the drenched earth, of seed and womb.[32]

The *Theogony, Enuma Elish,* and the fragmentary Baal epic are primarily devoted to the working out of this narrative sequence, to which we
might also add the Sumerian *Angim,* whose story begins with the return
of the victorious Ninurta to Nippur (Cooper 1978).

The two patterns distinguished in the quotation above can be seen as
two realizations of the same underlying idea: the victory of the divine
warrior, whether it is a precondition of enthronement or the repulsing
of a challenge to an already enthroned regent, represents narratively the
same absolute control over the cosmic order implied by the very concept
of cosmic kingship. The threat posed by this adversary represents the
greatest challenge to that order that could ever be, and once this challenge is turned back and the victorious warrior securely enthroned, it is
clear that there will never be another so great. This close connection
between victory and coronation is crystallized in the final line of the
Enuma Elish, a valedictory salute to Marduk, "who vanquished Tiamat
and achieved the kingship." The two notions likewise coalesce in the
statement that Yahweh "sits enthroned over the flood; the Lord sits en-

throned as king forever" (Ps. 29.10; cf. the founding of the victorious Ea's dwelling on the defeated Apsu at *E.E.* I.71) and the proclamation of victory in the Canaanite Baal epic: "Yamm is dead. Baal will rule"(*CTA* 2.IV.32). As was the case with the original organization of the world, the threat posed to that organization by this force of disorder is realized simultaneously in both cosmic and political modes, each of which will be taken up in turn.

The Threatening of the Cosmic Order. Regarded in broadest terms, the threat posed by the challenger is a reversal or inhibition of the separation and differentiation of the cosmic components that, as discussed above, define the world. Most commonly in the Near Eastern myths the dichotomy in peril is that of land and sea: The challenger might be conceived of as the sea itself, simply personified, or as some species of monstrous demon closely associated with the sea, for example, by dwelling in it, being born from it, or acting in its service.

Both conceptual possibilities are realized in the Ugaritic texts. Yamm's challenge to the cosmic hierarchy and his temporary ascendancy over Baal seem to entail the submission of all other components of the cosmos to the sea, as represented by the accession of all divine members of the council of El—to say nothing of El himself—to Yamm's demands. The so-called Astarte papyrus, dating from the eighteenth or nineteenth dynasty, contains what seems to be an Egyptian rendering of this myth: in spite of the extremely poor state of the text, it can be discerned that Yamm demands tribute from the divine council (the Ennead), Astarte makes efforts to placate him, and Seth perhaps takes the role of Baal in putting an end to the sea's ascendancy.[33] References made in passing elsewhere in the Ugaritic texts point also to an underlying Canaanite tradition of the defeat by Baal (or Anat, or both), of one or more monstrous entities closely associated with the sea. In one fragment Anat catalogues these previous conquests:

> Crushed I not El's Belov'd Yamm?
>> Destroyed I not El's Flood Rabbim?
>> Did I not, pray, muzzle the Dragon?
> I did crush the crooked serpent,
>> Shalyat the seven-headed.

> (*CTA* 3.III.36–39)

Even more varied are the realizations of this idea in the biblical tradition. In its most naturalistic form, the conflict is manifested as the taming of the sea by Yahweh (often through the force of a divine wind)

and its confinement to its allotted cosmic limits, "thus far and no far-
ther":

> Thou didst cover [the earth] with the deep as with a garment;
> > the waters stood above the mountains.
> At thy rebuke they fled;
> > at the sound of thy thunder they took to flight.
> The mountains rose, the valleys sank down
> > to the place which thou didst appoint for them.
> Thou didst set a bound which they should not pass,
> > so that they might not again cover the earth.
> > > (Ps. 104.6–9)[34]

The conflict appears in a historical context in the narrative tradition of
the Exodus, often with the imagery of cosmic battle still dominant:

> When the waters saw thee, O God,
> > when the waters saw thee, they were afraid,
> > yea, the deep trembled.
> The clouds poured out water;
> > the skies gave forth thunder;
> > thy arrows flashed on every side.
> The crash of thy thunder was in the whirlwind;
> > thy lightnings lighted up the world;
> > the earth trembled and shook.
> Thy way was through the sea,
> > thy path through the great waters;
> > yet thy footprints were unseen.
> > > (Ps. 77.16–19)[35]

Finally, there are remnants of a more mythically conceived battle with
the monster of the sea in the allusions to the defeat of Rahab, Leviathan,
and the *tannin*. In many cases these designations are used metaphorically of Israel's enemies, particularly Egypt; but even figurative use presupposes an underlying mythic tradition:

> Thou didst divide the sea [*yam*] by thy might;
> > thou didst break the heads of the dragons on the waters.
> Thou didst crush the heads of Leviathan,
> > thou didst give him as food for the creatures of the wilderness.
> > > (Ps. 74.13–14)[36]

The eschatological vision of the new Jerusalem at Rev. 21.1 makes it
clear that the sea, like darkness, is viewed as an essentially negative and
chaotic component in the cosmic order: "Then I saw a new heaven and

a new earth; for the first heaven and the first earth had passed away, and the sea was no more."

Tiamat is of course the sea herself and is overcome by the winds marshalled at the side of the storm warrior Marduk. Because of the vague terms in which she is described, there has never been a consensus about the form in which we ought to envision Tiamat. But regardless of whether or not she herself is conceived of dually as cosmic element and theriomorphic demon, she produces a brood of "monster serpents" to fight at her side against Marduk. Elsewhere in Mesopotamian sources a fragmentary text describes how the god Tishpak is challenged to face the enormous marine serpent *labbu* in battle (Heidel 1951, 141–43). The sea likewise challenges the gods in the divine assembly in the Telepinus myth discussed above (Hoffner 1975, 137), and elsewhere in Hittite documents there are fragmentary hints that Kumarbi and the sea were in cahoots against the weather god (*ANET* 121–22, Güterbock 1946, 32–33).

Although it is not nearly such an overriding concern, there are scattered manifestations in Greek myth of this negative representation of the sea as a threat to the established order. On the personal level there are indications of a rivalry between the Homeric Zeus and Poseidon much like that between the brothers Baal and Yamm (cf. *Il.* 13.354–57, 15.158–217; *Od.* 13.128–58), and the mythological Poseidon has in general an unpleasant and threatening personality.[37] A general connection of the sea with monstrous entities is amply illustrated by the Hesiodic gathering of all such figures into one genealogical line of descent from Pontus through the mating of Phorcys and Ceto, herself a distillation of all marine monstrosities.

Direct conflict between the warrior god and the demonic forces of the sea has by and large not been drawn into the orbit of Jovian mythology, but it is readily recognized as an element in the legends of human heroic combat, where the monster from the sea is a conventional obstacle to the hero's quest. More interesting is the realization of this underlying idea in the battle in *Iliad* 21 between Achilles and the flood waters of the river Scamander, which has overflowed its banks in pursuit of the warrior. The representation of Achilles on a number of occasions in the poem has drawn upon the mythic ideology surrounding the divine warrior, for example in the manufacture of his divine weaponry by the craftsman god, and in his epiphany at 18.205–29, where, his head cloaked in clouds and flashing fire, his thunderous shout panics the Trojans fighting over Patroclus's body (for the flight of the foe upon hearing the thunderous voice of the storm god, see *CTA* 4.VII.29–39; Ps. 29.3–9, 104.7). The fire and the winds that force the waves of the river back within their proper limits of course do not emanate from Achilles himself, but the idea of cosmic combat between the storm god and the sea is salient nonetheless.

The clearest Greek realization of the conflict between the divine warrior and the serpent from the sea is associated not with Zeus, but with Cronus, in his battle with Ophion(eus) for cosmic supremacy. The challenger's name transparently reflects his serpentine nature, and in addition his wife Eurynome was a daughter of Ocean (*Th.* 358, *Il.* 18.399) who was represented iconographically in an Arcadian sanctuary in the form of a mermaid (Paus. 8.41.6). There is some disagreement in the scattered sources for this myth regarding who ruled first—that is to say, who is challenging whom for supremacy. The conflict is said in one source to be between armies of Cronus and Ophioneus, but an important part of it clearly is some sort of individual combat between the two would-be rulers. The cosmic prize awaiting the winner was possession of the sky, and according to the rules of combat he who fell into the sea would be the loser. This suggests again that the sea is the "proper" cosmic station for the ultimately defeated Ophioneus and Eurynome, the bounds of which they would never again aspire to transgress. The victorious Cronus and Rhea take up, or resume, the rule of the sky, until they in their turn are deposed by Zeus.[38]

It is the figure of Typhon in whom we are primarily interested, however, and although the Philonic triad of Pontus, Typhon, and Nereus may be indicative of a marine association for Typhon in Philo's mind (*P.E.* 1.10.26), the Greek representation of this serpentine demon in the preserved sources does not in general connect him closely with the sea. In fact, the Greek Typhon is as difficult to envision as the Mesopotamian Tiamat, but for the opposite reason that *too many* physical characteristics are attributed to him. The picture is hopelessly composite already in Hesiod, and only gets worse as the later mythographers labor to incorporate every attested characteristic into one preposterous mélange whose physical appearance beggars the imagination. In vase painting the usual iconography is a human torso on serpentine "legs." But the polycephalous nature of Hesiod's Typhon and the prominence of the sickle (*harpe*) in the Apollodoran version of the Typhonomachy suggest that one of the strands woven into the fabric of the Typhon tradition from an early date is the Oriental complex of narrative and iconographic motifs better known to us through its manifestation in the Heracles tradition as that hero's battle with the Hydra.[39] Further complicating the picture is a purely Greek development in which Typhon was connected with volcanic activity, perhaps as a result of the Hesiodic conception of the Typhonomachy as an immense fire storm. Whatever its origin, this incendiary theme determined a new elemental association for the demon and eclipsed any connection there might originally have been between Typhon and the sea.[40]

Instead, the Greek concept of Typhon entails a different danger to the cosmic order, a threatened bridging of the separation of the celestial and lower worlds. This too can be seen against a backdrop of oriental analogues. In one text from Ras Shamra there is a description of a dragon who "swirled the sea, his double tongue licked the heavens, his twin tails churned up the sea" (Clifford 1972, 60). Similarly, in the struggle between Baal and Mot the temporary ascendance of the lord of the netherworld over the god of the upper world is realized in cosmic terms (whatever else its significance) when Baal enters the mouth of Mot, which at this moment of his victory is imagined as circumscribing the whole cosmos:

> One lip to earth and one to heaven,
>> [He stretches his to]ngue to the stars.
> Baal enters his mouth . . .

(CTA 5.II.2–4; cf. 23.61–62)

The similar nature of the threat posed by the diorite monster Ullikummi to the cosmic order is made clear in the description of his phenomenal growth:

> When the 15th day came, the stone had grown high. He [was standing] in the sea with his knees (as) a shaft. It stood out above the water, the stone, and in height it (was) like [a pillar]. The sea reached up to its belt like a (loin) cloth. Like a tower the stone is raised up and reaches up to the temples and the *kuntarra* house in heaven. (*ANET* 123)

Striving to reach from the foundations of the earth to the celestial heights, Ullikummi has no need of mountainous stepping stones, as did the Greek Aloades: the mythic conception is that he assaults the sky simply by growing.[41]

The Apollodoran description of Typhon draws upon the same underlying concept:

> In his size and power he surpassed all the children of Earth. As far as his thighs he had the shape of a man and was of such immense size that he towered above all the mountains, and his head often brushed the very stars. (1.6.3)

Here again, the sky is the goal, which Typhon assaults with "hissing and shouting, spewing a torrent of fire from his mouth." This cosmic siege, in essence an effort to reunite the three tiers of the cosmic edifice, is

described with a baroque profusion of detail by Nonnus: like Ullikummi, his Typhon similarly "stood in the fish-filled sea, his feet im-
planted in the weedy ocean depths and his stomach high in the air,
crowded around with clouds" (1.268–71). The threatened violation of
this most crucial cosmic polarity between uppermost and lowermost
was fully appreciated by Ovid, whose Typhon "rose from the lowest
depths of the earth and filled the celestial gods with fear" (*Met.* 5.
321–22).

These are of course late sources, but the Ovidian passage in particular gives us a clue to a detail that dates back to the earliest source: the
birth of Typhon from Tartarus. It is often noted that this "personification" of Tartarus is unique not only in the Hesiodic corpus, but in Greek
mythology in general. As is so often the case in mythic thought, birth is
here representative of essence: the genealogical metaphor is employed
to express an essential connection between Typhon and the lowest
depths of the world structure, and consequently the cosmic magnitude
of his assault on the very highest—the abode of the overseers of the
present world order. There is a discernible logic therefore in the Hesiodic order of presentation: the long description of Tartarus and its
primordial chaos (*Th.* 720–819) prepares us for the challenge presented
by its champion (820–80), who represents all of the fathomless chaos
of that quarter crystallized into a single animate threat against the ethe-
real guardians of the cosmic order. With the rise and fall of Typhon we
might compare the beast of John's Revelation, who, having ascended
from the "bottomless pit," is seized by an angel who "bound him for a
thousand years, and threw him into the pit, and shut it and sealed it over
him" (20.2–3).

The Challenge to the Throne. Alongside this vision of the adversary's
attack as a threat to the cosmic organization, we see here too a simultaneous political representation: the dragon's nefarious actions are portrayed as an attempt to take over the office of supreme sovereign from
the executive deity or to prohibit him from assuming it. A survey of the
various Oriental realizations of this challenge shows that more often
than not the dragon temporarily attains his goal, a success symbolized
by his taking possession of something that represents either the office of
the divine kingship and the cosmic order itself, or the physical potency
of the young warrior god and king-to-be. We have already had occasion
to note that the Sumerian Asakku usurps the kingship and must be
ousted by Ninurta, and the Akkadian Zu steals the Tablets of Destiny
and himself assumes the "Enlilship" of the gods. In the *Enuma Elish*
Tiamat places her henchman Kingu on the throne and gives him control

over the Tablets of Destiny (I.146–57). In one of the two preserved versions of the Hittite myth of Illuyankas (whose name means simply "dragon"), the monster renders the weather god helpless through the theft of his heart and eyes. The diorite monster Ullikummi likewise had a political agenda: "[Up to heaven] I shall go to assume the kingship. Kummiya [I shall destroy] and the *kuntarra* house I shall take over. The gods I shall [drive out from] hea[ven]" (*ANET* 125). Although the details are by no means clear, in the so-called KAL text a usurper known only by the ideogram KAL is placed temporarily on the throne, having taken the "reins and whip" away from the storm god (Güterbock 1961, 161–64).

The weird appearance of Typhon and the awesome cosmic imagery associated with his battle with Zeus should not blind us to the fact that this is likewise a political struggle for the office of divine kingship. The political nature of the threat is explicit already in Hesiod: had Zeus not taken notice of his machinations, Typhon "would have been king of gods and men," a remark that has given more than one Hesiodic commentator pause for thought. This political ambition of Typhon is in fact one of the few things about him that is fairly consistent throughout the textual sources. Although attributed to different agents with different motives, his very birth is an act of political defiance designed to unseat Zeus: the initiative is variously assigned to Gaia in revenge for the death of the Giants, to Hera out of jealousy over the birth of Athena, or to Cronus, presumably to avenge the loss of his throne.

Although Hesiod is clear about the political nature of the challenge posed by Typhon, he is (perhaps intentionally) vague about its seriousness—i.e., how far it had progressed before Zeus's resurgent theophany and crushing victory. Later sources are not only more explicit, but contain narrative elements that have very close analogues in the Eastern material just surveyed. We hear that Typhon assaulted and took control of the very palace of Zeus; that the Olympians fled and were pursued by Typhon as far as Egypt, where they took the form of animals; that Typhon stole and hid the sinews of Zeus, or, in another version, his thunderbolt. The danger is most extensive, and most extensively described, in the *Dionysiaca*. To mark his cosmopolitical ambitions, Nonnus's Typhon covets both the trident of Poseidon and the scepter of Zeus, to say nothing of Zeus's wife Hera. Temporarily in control of Zeus's thunderbolt, he confides these ambitions to Cadmus:

> I will march on Olympus, with little worry about an unarmed Zeus.
> Being female, Athena with her armor is of no account—what could she
> do to me? Strike up the song of Typhon's victory, herdsman, sing my

praises as the new and legitimate ruler of Olympus, bearing the scepter
of Zeus and cloaked in lightning. (1.475–80)

Is this idea of a temporary defeat for the currently ruling deity, attested in so many Near Eastern examples, a late development in Greek?
It goes without saying that there is every reason why Hesiod would not
want to dwell on this aspect of the myth, even if it were traditional and
known to him and his audience. We can of course never prove that Hesiod was familiar with but rejected anything that does not appear in his
text, nor do we care to. It is important merely to stress again that, as the
case of the cosmic lottery has already demonstrated, the argument from
Hesiodic silence is not a strong one in discussions of the relative antiquity of specific features of Greek mythic thought, especially in cases
where the detail in question is one that would have run counter to the
obvious program of Hesiodic poetry. As we did in the instance of
the lottery, we can point once again to the compositional parallel of the
Enuma Elish. There is as little hint of any defeat of Marduk in our text
of this poem as there is of Zeus in the *Theogony*, and, we might suspect,
for much the same reason. But actualized elsewhere in Babylonian poetry, ritual, and iconography is the idea that Marduk, like Baal, is held
captive in the netherworld (i.e., "killed") and restored to life.[42]

We might take note, in conclusion, of the presence of the victory-
enthronement complex in the mythology of Apollo, particularly as
articulated in the Homeric hymn. Josef Kroll (1956) had seen in the
opening tableau of this poem a scene that is unique among Greek representations of the god, but one having Oriental parallels:

> The gods tremble before him as he goes through the house of Zeus, and
> all spring up from their seats as he approaches, bending his shining bow.
> Leto alone remains at the side of Zeus who wields the thunderbolt. She
> loosens his bow and closes the quiver, and with her own hands she re-
> moves the bow from his mighty shoulder and hangs it from a golden peg
> on a column in her father's house. When she has brought him to his
> chair and bidden him sit, his father welcomes his beloved son with a
> golden cup of nectar; the other gods then return to their seats, and
> queenly Leto rejoices in her son the mighty archer. (*h.Ap.* 2–13)

There is a redistribution of the familiar mythic functions here: Zeus is
represented as the patriarchal El type, with Leto playing the role of his
consort; it is Apollo who is the young and dynamic regent. This allocation of functional roles is confirmed for us in a directly ensuing passage,
where the narrator goes back to the time of Leto's pregnancy and the
prophecy of Delos concerning the executive career of her future child:
"They say that Apollo will be exceedingly impetuous and greatly lord it

over gods and men everywhere on the grain-giving earth" (67–69). The Pythian section of the hymn continues this mythic characterization of the god, adhering closely to the victory and enthronement sequence outlined above. Here Delphi is the microcosm over which Apollo is to be the lord, and that lordship is reified by the construction of his temple. The serpent Pytho presents an immediate threat to Apollo's new realm, and upon her defeat before Apollo's arrows a localized cosmic order is established for all time.[43] This comprehensive picture of Apollo as divine warrior, cosmic architect, and fear-inspiring potentate is indeed unique in the preserved Greek sources, and it is perhaps its Oriental pomposity that seemed to Ovid to be such a tempting invitation to parody.

SOME CONCLUDING REMARKS

In spite of a number of differences attributable, for the most part, to a difference in subject matter and thematic program, Homeric and Hesiodic poetry present an essentially consistent world view as regards basic cosmology and divine classification, and one that remained substantially unchanged throughout the life of Greek mythic thought. It is a frequent premise in comparative studies that the elements common to Hesiod and Homer are by definition "Greek"; these elements in turn become a benchmark, the basis of comparison for ferreting out non-Greek elements. But an overview of Greek myth in the light of the Orient strongly suggests that the world view that emerges from the earliest Greek literary monuments is already a blend of Indo-European mythic thought with elements subsequently derived from contact with the considerably more advanced cultures to the East and South. The result of this contact is a mythological system that, as Dumézil acknowledges, "escapes Indo-European categories" (1973, 37) but lends itself well to interpretation in terms of the categories of Oriental myth.

It might be fitting to conclude this comparison of Greek and Oriental mythic thought with that representation of the early Greek world view par excellence, the Homeric shield of Achilles. The description of the fabrication of the shield is in essence a microcosmic account of creation, with the craftsman Hephaestus cast in the role of Creator:

> And upon it he made the earth and the sky and the sea, the tireless sun and the waxing moon, and all of the constellations which wreathe the sky. (*Il.* 18.483–85)

As noted earlier, this manner of structuring the cosmos accords precisely with that underlying the various biblical accounts, as an example of which we might take an excerpt from Psalm 136, a hymn of thanks-giving:

> to him who by understanding made the heavens,
>> for his steadfast love endures forever;
> to him who spread out the earth upon the waters,
>> for his steadfast love endures forever;
> to him who made the great lights,
>> for his steadfast love endures forever;
> the sun to rule over the day,
>> for his steadfast love endures forever;
> the moon and the stars to rule over the night,
>> for his steadfast love endures forever.
>
>   (5–9)

The shield's subsequent generic depiction of human activity realizes the threefold social agenda discussed above: we see a city at peace in which the elders are dispensing justice in a murder trial; a city under siege endeavoring to repel an external aggressor; and a series of scenes portraying the harvesting and celebration of agricultural produce, while the king stands by watching happily, scepter in hand. This description is often held to be one of the few overt realizations of the Dumézilian tri-functional ideology in a Greek context, but we can as well say that it manifests a social ideology common throughout the Semitic world. We might here compare the representation of the ideal king in the 72nd Psalm:

> Give the king thy justice, O God,
>> and thy righteousness to the royal son!
> May he judge thy people with righteousness,
>> and thy poor with justice!
>
>   (1–2)
>
> May he have dominion from sea to sea,
>> and from the River to the ends of the earth!
> May his foes bow down before him,
>> and his enemies lick the dust!
>
>   (8–9)
>
> May there be abundance of grain in the land;
>> on the tops of the mountains may it wave;
>> may its fruit be like Lebanon;
> and may men blossom forth from the cities
>> like the grass of the field!
>
>   (16)

In evaluating such comparisons we should be wary of taking the familiar to be the universal. Ideas like the three-tiered universe, the divine council, the paradisiacal kingdom of god, and the cosmic battle with the sea or its theriomorphic representative are such a fixed part of our conceptual heritage that they may seem to be the obvious way of seeing the world in mythic terms; it may therefore occasion no surprise that they should play a significant part in both the Hellenic and Semitic world view. But even a cursory comparison with other systems of mythic thought—in both ancient and contemporary cultures—easily proves the contrary, and alerts us to the pervasive similarities, rather than the differences, in the Aegean and Near Eastern ways of seeing the world. Athens does after all have something significant and interesting to do with Jerusalem, in a way that Tertullian never supposed.

NOTES

a. Lines 106–201; cf. West 1978, 29–30, 176–77.

b. Duchemin 1974, 33–46. Further parallels are discussed in a forthcoming paper by Mondi.

c. Burkert 1986, 14–19.

d. For texts, see Güterbock 1946, Hoffner 1975, and Laroche 1968a and 1968b in Mondi's bibliography. Most convenient is Pritchard 1969 (see Mondi n. 3).

e. Texts in Pritchard: see preceding note.

f. Herennius Philo of Byblus (A.D. 64–c. 140) wrote a work known to us from Eusebius's excerpts in the *Praeparatio Evangelica.* Commentary: Baumgarten 1981.

g. West 1983, 100–107.

h. West 1966, 31. For an exploration of various themes, see Burkert 1984.

i. Brown 1898.

j. Bernal 1987.

k. Helios, the sun god, and Eos, the dawn goddess, are the only members of the Greek pantheon who have a certain Indo-European lineage; and they are less important than the Olympians. (I am speaking not of the etymologies of the Greek gods' names but of their relation to the reconstructed Indo-European religion.) See my introduction to the next essay (Nagy) in this volume.

l. West 1978, 176–77.

m. Puhvel 1987, 30.

n. Graf 1985, 9–10 speaks of *Verbindlichkeit.*

o. Burkert 1986, 10–14.

1. Waardenburg uses the term "implicit myth" to designate popular conceptualization beneath the level of narrative and characterizes as a process of objectification the "act of making an implicit myth explicit in the form of a story" (1980, 59). For earlier statements of a similar view of mythic thought see Langer 1957, 196–98 and Smith 1973, 78–84. We might employ as an analogy Saussure's linguistic distinction between syntagmatic and associative relations (1959, 124–27): in the case of the latter, "a word can always evoke everything that can be associated with it in one way or another. Whereas a syntagm immediately suggests an order of succession and a

fixed number of elements, terms in an associative family occur neither in fixed numbers nor in a definite order."

2. There is certainly no intent here to deny that narratives can travel across cultural boundaries; the fact of such transmission in the ancient world is amply attested. But some of the most interesting and compelling comparisons to be discussed below are not between superficially similar narrative sequences, but rather between analogous structural or functional relations.

3. Unless otherwise specified, all translations of nonbiblical Near Eastern texts are taken from *Ancient Near Eastern Texts,* ed. J. B. Pritchard (3rd ed., Princeton, NJ 1969), henceforth designated *ANET.*

4. The notational system for Ugaritic texts employed here is that of A. Herdner, *Corpus des tablettes en cunéiformes alphabétiques* (Paris 1963).

5. The correspondence between the remaining details of the Canaanite tale and the Ishtar episode of the Gilgamesh epic renders this an indisputable example of the cross-cultural transmission of a complete narrative structure: upon rejection by Aqhat the goddess flies off to the house of her father El plaintively seeking permission to avenge this blow to her dignity. As did Ishtar, she resorts to gruesome threats to overcome initial demurral on his part and is ultimately given leave to employ a figure called Yatpan, who kills Aqhat while hunting.

6. For a characteristic example of this approach to comparative data, see Burkert's discussion of the narrative of the Seven against Thebes (1981; 1984, 99–106). He sees the Greek tale as "the epic transposition of a purification ritual of ultimately Babylonian origin" (1981, 42) and uses the date of composition of these Eastern ritual texts to date the Greek tradition of the Seven: "Thus if any connection between the Babylonian and the Theban 'Seven' is accepted, the tale cannot have been created in Greece before 750 B.C." (44–45).

7. In the case of the comparison between *Iliad* 5 and *Gilgamesh* discussed above, what we might call the "Lament of the Wounded God before Zeus" is a compositional theme actualized twice elsewhere in the *Iliad,* when Ares is also wounded by Diomedes later in Book 5 and when Artemis is roughed up by Hera in the theomachy of Book 21. Rather than see, as does Burkert, the realization of this theme with Aphrodite as the original, derived from the Orient, which is "repeated" and "slightly varied" in the theomachy (he makes no mention of the wounding of Ares), we might assume that, regardless of its ultimate origin, at the time of the composition of our *Iliad* this scene type was a productive motif in the epic repertoire, realized three times by the poet of our *Iliad* with three different deities for three different contextual purposes.

8. Translations from the Pyramid Texts are those of S. A. B. Mercer, *The Pyramid Texts* (New York 1952).

9. Simpson 1973, 121; cf. Griffiths 1960, 41–46. There is also a tradition of the sexual mutilation of Seth by Horus attested already in the Pyramid Texts, one of which (*Pyr.* 1463e) refers to a time "before the testicles of Set were torn away"; see Griffiths 34–35.

10. Griffiths 1960, 45. Analogous to the birth of Athena from the head of Zeus, there is a tradition that Thoth was born from the head of Seth. In fact, the idea of the birth of one god from the head of another is realized with a number of Egyptian deities; see Erman 1916, 1142–43.

11. Even this is not as certain as it is sometimes presented. In the document on which this argument is usually based (*CTA 166*) the entry El Kumarbi may as well be two separate names as a single double name. In other Hurrian god lists from Ras Shamra El and Kumarbi appear as separate, and separated, entries. See LaRoche 1968a, 523–24 and 1968b, 148–50; L'Heureux 1979, 39.

12. See Burkert 1986, 16–17 for a discussion along these lines of the various syncretistic identifications involving the figure of Heracles.

13. E.g., Dumézil 1971, 11; 1973, 37–38. Excessive reliance on phonological similarity between names has vitiated a number of previous comparative studies of Greek and Near Eastern myth. Even in rare cases where such an identity of names seems very likely, as for instance that between Iapetos and the biblical Japeth, there is often little to be gained by the comparison (see West 1966, 202–3). To take the extreme case, we might even question the essential identity of deities of the *same* name worshiped in widely different times or places: we might ask, for instance (with Frankfort 1951, 22), in what sense the Isis worshiped in the Roman Empire is the "same" deity as that worshiped in Egypt millenia earlier.

14. Hes. *Th.* 678–82, 736–37 = 807–8, 839–41, 847–51. For other examples of this quadripartite structure of the cosmos see Rev. 5.13, Morenz 1973, 182 (Egypt) and van Dijk 1976, 129 (Sumer).

15. *Il.* 15.187–93; *h. Dem.* 85–87; Pind. *Ol.* 7.54–55; Plato *Gorg.* 523A; Callim. hymn 1.58–67; Verg. *Aen.* 1.139; Apollod. *Biblio.* 1.2.1.

16. For the representation of the human king in mythic terms of ideal rulership in Sumerian royal hymns, see Kramer 1979, 50–70; it is also evident in such royal texts as the preamble to the law code of Hammurabi and the inscription of Darius at Behistun. Frankfort 1948, 338 notes the borrowing of such mythic embellishments from Mesopotamia by the Hittite kings. For a discussion of the reciprocal relationship between the representations of human and divine kingship, see Oemisch 1977, 1–25, esp. 11–12. He rightly stresses that even in cases where characteristics of idealized kingship usually associated with the divine ruler are attributed to his historical human counterpart, there need not be any underlying *belief* in the divinity of the living king; it is a question not of creed but of conceptualization.

17. Although at times exercising less discrimination in his amassing of parallels than one might desire, Cyrus Gordon has been one of the foremost voices arguing for the significance of the texts from Ugarit as the "connecting link between Homer and the Bible" (1955, 46; see especially idem 1962). West Semitic influence on Greek myth in the Mycenaean period is likewise the operating hypothesis in Astour 1965.

18. On the nature of El's kingship and its relationship to that of Baal, see Mullen 1980, 22–45, 84–110 and W. H. Schmidt 1966, 23–32. On the special use of the designation *mlk* with El, see Schmidt 22–25 and Mullen 22–25.

19. W. H. Schmidt 1966, 31. Cf. also Gray 1965, 190; 1966, 178: "Baal's role is to actualize the Order of El the creator by his repeated conflict with, and victory over, the forces of Chaos. Baal but maintains what El has decided and decreed."

20. So W. H. Schimdt 1966, 64–66; Gray 1965, 154–55. For an extreme view of the hostility between El and Baal see Oldenburg 1969, esp. 101–63: he argues that Baal challenges, castrates, and replaces El, who is now in exile in the netherworld; cf. also Pope 1955, 27–32, 94–104, and Cassuto 1971, 42–43. In addition to comparison with the *Theogony*, these arguments rely heavily on the testimony of Philo of

Byblus; for recently renewed warnings about the need for caution in using Philo as evidence for Canaanite myth see Baumgarten 1981, Barr 1974, and Oden 1978. Against these later Greek sources might be held the evidence of Ugaritic liturgical texts in which El is given pride of place over the rest of the pantheon, including Baal; see Cross 1973, 14–15; Mullen 1980, 267–74.

21. *Ug.* 5.2.I.2–4; tr. Mullen 1980, 256. This triad also provides one of the most compelling parallels to Philo's account (*P.E.* 1.10.31): "Greatest Astarte and Zeus Demarous—also called Adodos—king of the gods, ruled the land with the consent (*gnome*) of Cronus."

22. For the thematic association of the life-giving streams with the mountain of god, see Clifford 1972, 158; Levenson 1976, 11–12. In the Sumerian version of the flood story, the survivor Ziusudra is immortalized in the land of Dilmun, a paradise of lush vegetation fostered by Enki's nether waters. A fragmentary Hittite text locates El at the sources of the Mala river (*ANET* 519), and Philo places the castration of Uranus by Cronus-El "near the sources and rivers" (*P.E.* 1.10.22). Cf. also the words of the prince of Tyre: "I am *el*. I sit in the seat of the gods, in the heart of the seas" (Ezek. 28.1–2).

23. Although poorly understood, the Ugaritic text *CTA* 30 would appear to be particularly germane to the discussion of these aspects of El; for translation and discussion, see Gray 1966, 182–85. He sees the duality of El and Baal as an "expression of the eternal paradox of the omnipotence and beneficence of God and the complication of evil and suffering in the world of his creation" (178–79). In quite similar terms, L'Heureux explains the dualism in the kingship of El and Baal as representing belief in a "basic beneficence of the cosmos" in the face of a sometimes contrary and hostile "structure of reality" (1979, 6).

24. For a general discussion of the "garden of God" theme see Wallace 1985, 70–88. On the connections between El's milieu and the Garden of Eden, see also Clifford 1972, 50–51, 158–160; Mullen 1980, 151–54; Cross 1973, 38. On El's association with the moral order (particularly the dispensing of justice), see Gray 1966.

25. Levenson uses this distinction between the historical and the ideal to explicate the fundamental differences in the concepts of Sinai and Zion: the latter "tells of the fundamental cosmic order," while the former "prescribes the kind of society which Israel must build" (1976, 44; cf. also 18, 161). He sees this distinction as underlying a tension between the idea of Yahweh as king of the gods and that of the promised kingdom of the Messiah. For a further development of these ideas, see Levenson 1985.

26. Attempts to reconcile them are as old as *W&D* 173b–c; cf. also Plut. *Mor.* 420A. For the most recent discussion of the problem see Versnel 1986; for a comparative approach similar to that undertaken here, see Schwabl 1960 and Cassuto 1971, 55–56.

27. See Philippson 1944, 119–120; Versnel 1986, 124–26. The priests who offered sacrifice to Cronus on Mount Cronion at Olympia were called "kings" (*basilai*), and local tradition had it that a shrine had once been built on the spot by men actually living during the reign of Cronus in the golden age (Paus. 6.20.1, 5.7.6). The Egyptian Atum-Re was similarly represented as the first king, the prototype and archetype for all subsequent pharaohs, who were said to occupy the "throne of Atum" or the "throne of Re" (Frankfort 1948, 148–51).

28. The authorship of *W&D* 173a is not a pressing concern in the present context, but we might note in passing that, given the pervasiveness of the popular tradition of the utopian kingdom of Cronus, the authenticity of the line should not be questioned on the ground that this aspect of Cronus is secondary, or non-Hesiodic. For a defense of the Hesiodic authorship of 173a–e in this spirit see van der Valk 1985.

29. Later attempts to locate Cronus in real geography associate him with the boundaries of the known world, generally toward the West: one of the designations for Gibralter was the "pillars of Cronus," and Plutarch locates him on an island west of Britain, beyond the already fabulous Ortygia (*Mor.* 420A, 941A).

30. There are sporadic indications of traditions in which the kingship of Cronus was not violently usurped by Zeus, but either peacefully transferred or even in some sense shared. Diodorus reports a tradition of such a peaceful transfer as an alternative to the better-known Hesiodic version (3.61.4, 5.70.1). The Orphic theology, while incorporating the Hesiodic castration myth and in fact extending it so that Cronus is himself castrated by his son, also held that Zeus, upon attaining office and in combination with his consultation of Night, received from Cronus certain principles (*archai*) for his demiurgic activity (*Orph. frag.* 129, 155; a similar statement was apparently in the text employed by the Derveni commentator). For evidence of joint worship of Zeus and Cronus, cf. Pausanias 1.18.7, 9.39.3.

31. Cf. the description of the eschatological Jerusalem in Joel 3.18: "And in that day the mountains shall drip sweet wine, and the hills shall flow with milk, and all the stream beds of Judah shall flow with water; and a fountain shall come forth from the house of the Lord and water the valley of Shittim."

32. Cross 1973, 155–56. Two of the most extensive studies of Greek and Oriental combat myths are those of Fontenrose 1959 and Gaster 1961, although I could not agree wholeheartedly with the conclusions drawn by either from the comparative data.

33. *ANET* 17–18; Kaiser 1962, 81–91. Egypt of course had its own tradition of the battle with the dragon of the sea: the serpent Apophis dwells in the cosmic waters of Nun and is defeated each night by the sun in a repetition of the cosmogonic battle. In the Instruction for Merikare it is said: "Well directed are men, the cattle of the god. He made heaven and earth according to their desire, and he repelled the water monster" (*ANET* 417).

34. Cf. Job 38.8–11, Dan. 7.2, Ex. 15, Job 26.12–13. Also noteworthy in this context is the divine breath or spirit (*ruah Elohim*) hovering over the chaotic waters of Gen. 1.2. The aftermath of the great flood, when Yahweh "made a wind blow over the earth, and the waters subsided" (Gen. 8.1) is essentially a repetition of this primeval ascendance of the wind of God over the waters of the flood.

35. At Is. 17.13 Israel's enemies are themselves represented as the flood waters of chaos, stilled by the divine wind: "The nations roar like the roaring of many waters, but he will rebuke them, and they will flee far away, chased like chaff on the mountains before the wind and whirling dust before the storm."

36. Cf. also the imagery at Ezek. 32.2–8, where the defeat of the pharaoh, who is specifically said to be "like a dragon in the seas," is described in mythic terms very similar to Marduk's netting and dismemberment of Tiamat. Job 26.12–13 provides a good example of the inextricable duality in the conception of the cosmic opponent

as monster and sea: "By his power he stilled the sea; by his understanding he smote Rahab. By his wind the heavens were made fair; his hand pierced the fleeing serpent."

37. Zeus's complaint at *Il*. 15.166–67 that Poseidon alone of the gods does not shudder at his majesty (for the proper attitude of reverence cf. 1.533–35) calls to mind the tone of Yamm's instructions to his messengers when he challenges Baal for supremacy before the council of El: "At the feet of El fall not down, prostrate you not to the Assembled Body. Proudly standing say ye your speech" (*CTA* 2.I.14–16). What happens in fact is that the gods themselves give obeisance to Yamm's messengers by bowing their heads, a deferential act that enrages Baal.

38. This account is based primarily on the fragments of Pherecydes; for a reconstruction along these lines, see Kirk et al. 1983, 66–70 and Fontenrose 1959, 230–32.

39. Of great interest in this connection is the illustrated plate of a Boeotian fibula from the seventh century containing all elements of this complex: the polycephalous serpent, the warrior and his companion, the curved and toothed or serrated weapon, and even the crustaceanlike creature between the feet of one of the warriors. See Levy 1934; Brommer 1953, 12–17, with Plates 8–11; Burkert 1979, 80–83. The toothed sickle appears in the *Theogony* in the castration of Uranus rather than in the Typhonomachy.

40. Two close parallels between the *Theogony* and the *Enuma Elish* suggest that there might originally have been such a connection. The catalogue of monsters accompanying Tiamat at *E.E.* I.132–42 corresponds strikingly with that of the various voices of Typhon at *Th.* 829–35; and the evil winds that inflate Tiamat and, presumably, escape when she is pierced by Marduk's arrow seem *conceptually* very similar to the evil winds that escape from Typhon upon his defeat by Zeus, a curious detail for which nothing previously said by Hesiod about Typhon has prepared us.

41. In a *topos* of Mesopotamian wisdom, the limits of mortal capability are defined in terms of such cosmic aspirations: "Who is so tall as to ascend to the heavens? Who is so broad as to compass the underworld?" (Lambert 1960, 149, 327; cf. also *ANET* 48).

42. See Langdon 1923, 34–59, Frankfort 1948, 318–25, Fontenrose 1959, 161–62. On the "sectarian and aberrant" nature of the preserved text of the *Enuma Elish* and the caveat that it "can only be used safely in the whole context of ancient Mesopotamian mythology," see Lambert 1965, 291. For further argument for the antiquity of the defeat of Zeus in the Greek tradition, see Fontenrose 1966.

43. For Apollo as dragon slayer see Fontenrose 1959, 13–27; on the comparison of Apollo in this role specifically with Marduk, see Walcot 1966, 48–49. Lesky 1954, 14–15 had also pointed out the deference of the gods in council as an Oriental motif. Very similar is the description of the return of the victorious Ninurta to Nippur in the *Angim* text: the gods are unable to face him (line 71), and prostrate themselves (13); even Enlil "humbled himself" (106). The one deity present who is apparently unafraid is the proud mother Ninlil (108–12).

WORKS CITED

Astour, M. C. 1965. *Hellenosemitica*. Leiden.

Baldry, H. C. 1952. "Who Invented the Golden Age?" *CQ* 46:83–92.

Barnett, R. D. 1956. "Ancient Oriental Influences on Archaic Greece." in *The Ae-*

gean and the Near East: Studies Presented to H. Goldman, 212–38. Locust Valley, NY.

Barr, J. 1974. "Philo of Byblos and his 'Phoenician History.'" *BRL* 57:17–68.

Baumgarten, A. I. 1981. *The Phoenician History of Philo of Byblos.* Leiden.

Bernal, Martin. 1987. *Black Athena: The Afroasiatic Roots of Classical Civilization,* Vol. 1 (The Fabrication of Ancient Greece 1785–1985). New Brunswick, NJ.

Brandon, S. G. F. 1963. *Creation Legends of the Ancient Near East.* London.

Bremmer, Jan, ed. 1986. *Interpretations of Greek Mythology.* Totowa, NJ.

Briquel, D. 1980. "La 'Théogonie' d'Hésiode: Essai de comparaison indo-européenne." *RHR* 197:243–76.

Brommer, F. 1953. *Herakles.* Cologne.

Brown, Robert. 1898. *Semitic Influence in Hellenic Mythology.* London.

Budge, E. A. W. 1895. *The Book of the Dead.* London.

Burkert, Walter. 1979. *Structure and History in Greek Mythology and Ritual.* Berkeley-Los Angeles.

———. 1981. "Seven against Thebes: An Oral Tradition between Babylonian Magic and Greek Literature. In C. Brillante, M. Cantilena, and C. O. Pavese, eds., *I Poemi epici rapsodici non omerici e la tradizione orale,* 29–51. Padua.

———. 1984. *Die orientalisierende Epoche in der griechischen Religion und Literatur.* Heidelberg.

———. 1985. *Greek Religion.* Tr. John Raffian. Cambridge, MA.

———. 1986. "Oriental and Greek Mythology: The Meeting of Parallels." In Bremmer 1986, 10–40.

Cassuto, U. 1971. *The Goddess Anath.* Eng. tr. Jerusalem.

Clifford, R. J. 1972. *The Cosmic Mountain in Canaan and the Old Testament.* Cambridge, MA.

Cooper, J. S. 1978. *The Return of Ninurta to Nippur.* Rome.

Cross, F. M. 1973. *Canaanite Myth and Hebrew Epic.* Cambridge, MA.

Detienne, M., and J.-P. Vernant. 1974. *Les ruses de l'intelligence: la mètis des Grecs.* Paris.

Dijk, J. van. 1976. "Existe-t-il un 'Poème de la Création' sumérien?" In B. L. Eichler, ed., *Kramer Anniversary Volume,* 125–33. Neukirchen-Vluyn, FRG.

———. 1983. *LUGAL UD ME-LÁM-bi NIR-ĜÁL: Le récit épique et didactique des Travaux de Ninurta, du Déluge et de la Nouvelle Création.* Leiden.

Duchemin, J. 1974. *Prométhée: Histoire du mythe, de ses origines orientales à ses incarnations modernes.* Paris.

Dumézil, G. 1971. *Mythe et épopée I.* 2nd ed. Paris.

———. 1973. *Gods of the Ancient Northmen.* Eng. tr. Berkeley-Los Angeles.

Eliade, M. 1958. *Patterns in Comparative Religion.* New York.

Erman, A. 1916. "Beiträge zur ägyptischen Religion." *SDAW* 1142–53.

Fitzmyer, J. A. 1967. *The Aramaic Inscriptions of Sefîre.* Rome.

Fontenrose, J. 1959. *Python. A Study of Delphic Myth and its Origins.* Berkeley-Los Angeles.

———. 1966. "Typhon among the Arimoi." In *The Classical Tradition: Literary and Historical Studies in Honor of Harry Caplan,* 64–82. Ithaca, NY.

Frankfort, H. 1933. *The Cenotaph of Seti I at Abydos I.* Egyptian Exploration Society Memoirs 39. London.

————. 1948. *Kingship and the Gods*. Chicago.

————. 1951. *The Problem of Similarity in Ancient Near Eastern Religions*. Frazer Lecture for 1950. Oxford.

Gaster, T. H. 1961. *Thespis. Ritual, Myth, and Drama in the Ancient Near East*. New York.

Gordon, C. H. 1955. "Homer and Bible: The Origin and Character of East Mediterranean Literature." *Hebrew Union College Annual* 26:43–108.

————. 1962. *Before the Bible: The Common Background of Greek and Hebrew Civilizations*. New York.

Graf, Fritz. 1985. *Griechische Mythologie: Eine Einführung*. Munich.

Gray, J. 1965. *The Legacy of Canaan: The Ras Shamra Texts and Their Relevance to the Old Testament*. VT Suppl. 5. 2nd ed. Leiden.

————. 1966. "Social Aspects of Canaanite Religion." *VT* Suppl. 15:170–92. Leiden.

Gresseth, G. K. 1975. "The Gilgamesh Epic and Homer." *CJ* 70.4:1–18.

Griffiths, J. G. 1960. *The Conflict of Horus and Seth*. Liverpool.

Güterbock, H. G. 1946. *Kumarbi. Mythen vom churritischen Kronos aus den hethitischen Fragmenten zusammengestellt, übersetzt, und erklärt*. Zurich.

————. 1961. "Hittite Mythology." In S. N. Kramer, ed. *Mythologies of the Ancient World*, 139–79. Garden City, NY.

Heidel, A. 1951. *The Babylonian Genesis*. 2nd ed. Chicago.

Hoffner, H. A. 1975. "Hittite Mythological Texts: A Survey." In H. Goedicke and J. J. M. Roberts, eds. *Unity and Diversity: Essays in the History, Literature, and Religion of the Ancient Near East*, 136–45. Baltimore.

Jacobsen, T. 1976. *The Treasures of Darkness*. New Haven.

Kaiser, O. 1962. *Die mythische Bedeutung des Meeres in Ägypten, Ugarit und Israel*. ZAW Bhft. 78. 2nd ed. Berlin.

Kirk, G. S., J. E. Raven, and M. Schofield. 1983. *The Presocratic Philosophers*. 2nd ed. Cambridge.

Kramer, S. N. 1979. *From the Poetry of Sumer: Creation, Glorification, Adoration*. Berkeley.

Kroll, J. 1956. "Apollon zu Beginn des homerischen Hymnus." *SIFC* 27/28:181–91.

Lambert, W. G. 1960. *Babylonian Wisdom Literature*. Oxford.

————. 1965. "A New Look at the Babylonian Background of Genesis." *JThS* 16:287–300.

————. 1975. "The Cosmology of Sumer and Babylon." In C. Blacker and M. Loewe, eds., *Ancient Cosmologies*, 42–62. London.

Lambert, W. G., and A. R. Millard. 1969. *Atra-hasis: The Babylonian Story of the Flood*. Oxford.

Langdon, S. 1923. *The Babylonian Epic of Creation*. Oxford.

Langer, S. K. 1957. *Philosophy in a New Key*. 3d ed. Cambridge, MA.

LaRoche, E. 1968a. "Documents en langue hourrite provenant de Ras Shamra." *Ugaritica* 5:447–554.

————. 1968b. "Notes sur le panthéon hourrite de Ras Shamra." *JAOS* 88:148–50.

Lesky, A. 1950. "Hethitische Texte und griechischer Mythos." *AAWW* 87:137–59. Reprinted in *Gesammelte Schriften* (Bern 1966) 356–71.

———. 1954. "Zum hethitischen und griechischen Mythos." *Eranos* 52:8–17. Reprinted in *Gesammelte Schriften* 372–78.

Levenson, J. D. 1976. *Theology of the Program of Restoration of Ezekiel 40–48.* Missoula, MT.

———. 1985. *Sinai and Zion.* San Francisco.

Levy, G. R. 1934. "The Oriental Origin of Heracles." *JHS* 54:40–53.

L'Heureux, C. E. 1979. *Rank Among the Canaanite Gods: El, Baal, and the Rephaim.* Missoula, MT.

Littleton, C. S. 1970. "Is the 'Kingship in Heaven' Theme Indo-European?" In G. Cardona, H. M. Hoenigswald, and A. Senn, eds. *Indo-European and Indo-Europeans,* 383–404. Philadelphia.

Meltzer, E. S. 1974. "Egyptian Parallels for an Incident in Hesiod's *Theogony* and an Episode in the Kumarbi Myth." *JNES* 33:154–57.

Miller, P. D. 1967. "El the Warrior." *HThR* 60:411–31.

———. 1973. *The Divine Warrior in Early Israel.* Cambridge, MA.

Morenz, S. 1973. *Egyptian Religion.* Eng. tr. Ithaca, NY.

Mullen, E. T. 1980. *The Divine Council in Canaanite and Early Hebrew Literature.* Missoula, MT.

Notter, V. 1974. *Biblischer Schöpfungsbericht und ägyptische Schöpfungsmythen."* Stuttgart.

Oden, R. A. 1978. "Philo of Byblos and Hellenistic Historiography." *PalEQ* 110:115–26.

Oemisch, C. 1977. *König und Kosmos: Studien zur Frage kosmologischer Herrschaftslegitimation in der Antike.* Berlin.

O'Flaherty, W. D. 1981. *The Rig Veda.* Harmondsworth, UK.

Oldenburg, U. 1969. *The Conflict Between El and Baal in Canaanite Religion.* Leiden.

Page, D. 1973. *Folktales in Homer's Odyssey.* Cambridge, MA.

Philippson, P. 1944. *Thessalische Mythologie.* Zürich.

Pope, M. H. 1955. *El in the Ugaritic Texts. VT Suppl.* 2. Leiden.

Puhvel, Jaan. 1987. *Comparative Mythology.* Baltimore.

Saussure, F. de. 1959. *Course in General Linguistics.* New York.

Schmidt, E. G. 1981. "Himmel-Meer-Erde im frühgriechischen Epos und im alten Orient." *Philologus* 125:1–24.

Schmidt, W. H. 1966. *Königtum Gottes in Ugarit und Israel.* Berlin.

Schwabl, H. 1960. "Die griechischen Theogonien und der Orient." In *Éléments orientaux dans la religion grecque ancienne,* 39–56. Paris.

Simpson, W. K., ed. 1973. *The Literature of Ancient Egypt.* New Haven, CT.

Sjöberg, Å. W. 1976. "Hymns to Ninurta with Prayers for Šūsîn of Ur and Būrsîn of Isin." In B. L. Eichler, ed., *Kramer Anniversary Volume,* 411–26. Neukirchen-Vluyn, FRG.

Smith, P. 1973. "The Nature of Myths." *Diogenes* 82:70–87.

van der Valk, M. 1985. "On the God Cronus." *GRBS* 26:5–11.

Versnel, H. S. 1986. "Greek Myth and Ritual: The Case of Kronos." In Bremmer 1986, 121–52.

Waardenburg, J. 1980. "Symbolic Aspects of Myth." In A. M. Olson, ed. *Myth, Symbol, and Reality,* 41–68. South Bend, IN.

Walcot, P. 1966. *Hesiod and the Near East*. Cardiff.
Wallace, H. N. 1985. *The Eden Narrative*. Atlanta.
West, M. L. 1966. *Hesiod: Theogony*. Oxford.
———, ed. 1978. *Hesiod: Works and Days*. Oxford.
———. 1983. *The Orphic Poems*. Oxford.

4

INDO-EUROPEAN AND GREEK
MYTHOLOGY

The notion of Indo-European is in the first place a linguistic notion. Indo-European is the name of a family of languages that originated in a parent language, Proto-Indo-European. From the reconstruction of this parent language,[a] it followed that there was an Indo-European people. Although its dwelling place has not been located (the steppes north of the Black Sea are often proposed), on the basis of the linguistic evidence, its social institutions,[b] religion and mythology, and even its poetic language and meters[c] can to some extent be reconstructed.

Greek is an Indo-European language, and certain institutions of the ancient Greeks have an Indo-European look.[d] Greek religion, however, is strangely non-Indo-European. With the exceptions of Zeus, Hades, and Poseidon, at least in some of their aspects, the Olympians are newcomers, and generally "the triumphant Olympian deity has relegated his Indo-European predecessor to the periphery, which usually means that the latter has survived only in outlying areas, the backwoods and boondocks of Greece, and has been secondarily inducted into the fringes of the central pantheon by being passed off as the offspring of the new god."[e] Thus the Indo-European Pan becomes the son of the non-Indo-European Hermes. Whereas Greek "theology" is thus remote from that of the Indo-European forebears of the Greeks, at the level of civic religion, in the distribution of cults and sacrifices, the connection is closer.[f]

If the Greek pantheon is largely non-Indo-European,[g] the stories about the gods are unlikely to be Indo-European, and, in fact, it is not a god but a hero, Heracles, whose myths can lay the best claim to Indo-European origin.[h] For the most part, Greek contributes little to the reconstruction of Indo-European mythology; or to put the matter another way, returning from the reconstruction to the Greeks, one finds less than might have been expected. The reconstruction now generally accepted is based on what C. Scott Littleton called "the new comparative mythology,"[i] by which he meant the work of Georges Dumézil and his followers. The mythologies on which their work is based are mainly four: Indian, Roman, Iranian, and Scandinavian. The reconstructed Indo-European mythology is a reflection of both Indo-European social organization and ideology, which are characterized by three hierarchical "functions," as Dumézil called them. These are, in short, (1) the kingly and priestly, (2) the martial, and (3) the agricultural and life-fostering.

Joseph Nagy here brings the myth of Orpheus into the ambit of the three functions, adding a new piece to the puzzle of Indo-European inheritance in Greek mythology, the solution of which, Bernard Sergent has suggested, is only beginning.[j] Orpheus is a puzzling figure. His myth seems to be a patchwork of separate elements: the story of how he brought his wife back from the underworld; the power of his music to attract animals, trees, and rocks; his death at the hands of maenads or of Thracian women; the vicissitudes of his severed head.[k] Nagy, concentrating on the head, shows how, in its very detachment, it paradoxically serves to harmonize the three classes through the power of persuasion. The head indeed represents the fundamental, integrative beliefs and ideas of the decapitated hero's people. In this way, Nagy completes a hermeneutic circle that begins with Emile Durkheim's notion of myth as a representation of social reality and continues with Dumézil's trifunctionalism. The talking head of Nagy's essay, linked to Dumézil's scheme, comes back precisely to the Durkheimian view from which Dumézil started: the head's own function, in its marginal position, is to harmonize the three functions of society.

Hierarchy, Heroes, and Heads: Indo-European Structures in Greek Myth

JOSEPH FALAKY NAGY

Ever since the pioneering work of the Grimm brothers in the first half of the nineteenth century, the reconstruction of a mythological repertoire of patterns and motifs common to speakers of all or most branches of the Indo-European family of languages (including Greek, Indo-Iranian, Celtic, Germanic, Slavic, and many others) has been the goal of numerous scholars in the fields of philology, comparative religion, and folklore (see de Vries 1977, 80–90; Vernant 1980, 207–33; Littleton 1982, 32–40; Puhvel 1987, 11–15). These attempts at reconstruction are all grounded in the assumption that groups that speak the same kinds of languages have other cultural traits in common. Unfortunately, most early treatments of "Indo-European myth" were informed by the devolutionary model of cultural history, according to which myths, rituals, and customs that were originally meaningful gradually become prey to misunderstanding and distortion in the course of a people's cultural development. Thus, in effect, scholars engaged in the work of reconstruction would mine the sources for our knowledge of Indo-European mythologies (both ancient literary texts and more recent orally transmitted folklore) for some supposedly coherent original essence and ignore the synchronic realities of the texts and traditions themselves: realities that were not viewed as developments but rather as degenerations. For example, in the thinking of the Indologist and pioneer Indo-Europeanist Max Müller, whose analyses of "solar" symbolism generated great controversy in the second half of the nineteenth century, myth itself was already a misunderstanding, the result of a so-called disease of language (see de Vries 1977, 89). It is not surprising, then, that with the triumph of the evolutionary model in the study of religion around the turn of the century, interest in restoring Indo-European mythological structures waned.

In our own century, the work of Georges Dumézil has radically revitalized and reoriented the study of the shared traits of Indo-European mythologies.[1] Unlike their intellectual forebears, Dumézil and those who carry on his scholarly tradition have not aimed at reconstructing a past religious totality. Rather, they have attempted to isolate key structures of relationships that not only recur in the myths of Indo-European peoples but actually generate new myths, and even evolve beyond themselves under pressure from historical circumstances or the weight of the mythological systems themselves. Thus, Indo-European mythology is no longer approached as an inert treasure encrusted with accretions or corroded by later misunderstandings. It is instead recognized as a dynamic process that produces different results in each Indo-European tradition.

At the heart of a mythology, as Dumézil and his mentors Durkheim and Mauss viewed it, lies a collective view of society. The most pervasive of the structures discerned by Dumézil among Indo-European traditions is the system of the three "functions," which forms in effect a paradigm of a society—one that may have never originally existed, but as an ideological reality has proven for the bearers of these traditions to be "good to think with," or even good to model social life after. The three functions (that is, a tripartite hierarchy of values closely connected with particular classes) consist of:

1) sovereignty or religion (rulers and priests)
2) force (warriors)
3) fecundity (producers of food and other goods; women in their sexual capacity)

It is important to emphasize that the three functions form a hierarchical whole, and that any one function implies the other two. Yet this cohesion does not always imply harmonious relations among them; indeed, there is a productive tension inherent within the system, tending to pit its elements against one another.

An exemplary illustration of the three functions and the way in which the system works (or doesn't work, in cases of imbalance) is the myth of the judgment of Paris, as it is to be found in both literature and art (Dumézil 1968, 580–86). Each of three goddesses—Hera, Athena, and Aphrodite—promises a special gift to the Trojan prince in return for his selecting her as the fairest of female divinities: Hera offers kingship over many lands, Athena conquest and glory in war, and Aphrodite the most beautiful of women (Helen). Paris's choice, as we know, proves to be disastrous for him and his people. This outcome, the result of setting the tripartite social model on its head, is typical of the function represented in this case by Helen. In Indo-European traditions, the third function characteristically proves unreliable and paradoxically destructive, unless firmly subordinated to the first and second levels of the trifunctional system.

Dumézil's analysis of this *aition* of the Trojan war features key principles of his method which assure both rigor and flexibility.

1. A structure of relations (in this case, among the three goddesses and what they offer) is to be legitimately inferred only when they are found together (in an attested story, a ritual formula, a pictorial representation)—that is, when they are pointedly linked together by the tradition itself (Dumézil 1961, 280–81). It would be simple enough to discern the system of the three functions in any mythology, Indo-European or not, by simply picking and choosing the appropriate mythological terms at large. Unfortunately, some of the scholars who have been inspired by Dumézil's work to look for Indo-European patterns in ancient Greek culture have engaged in precisely such dubious eclectism (see Sergent 1979, 1158–61).

2. At the same time, the territory of "tradition" (the cultural logic behind transmission, selection, and innovation) must be kept open. "Older," according to Dumézil, is not necessarily "better" for the purpose of finding and studying the Indo-European reflexes within a particular Indo-European mythology. The story of the judgment of Paris does

not appear in full in the Homeric poems, although traces can be found in them of the trifunctional contrast among Hera, Athena, and Aphrodite (Sergent 1979, 1160; Dumézil 1985b, 16–26). The tale does appear, however, in considerably later literary works such as Euripides' *Trojan Women* (lines 924–31), among others. In going from Homer to Euripides, we have crossed the boundary between "oral" and "literary," and even to some extent the boundary between "traditional" and "individual" expression. Yet Euripides and even much later authors can still represent Greek, or Indo-European, tradition. Such continuity is not necessarily a matter of unknowing preservation for preservation's sake. In the case of Plato, for example, Dumézil and others have argued convincingly that the trifunctional ideal society described in the *Republic* constitutes an innovative recycling of traditional concepts (Dumézil 1968, 493–96; Sergent 1979, 1173–76; 1980, 256–72; Pralon 1981).

3. The mythological terms arranged in a "meaningful" system in one particular case (such as that of the myth of the judgment of Paris) do not necessarily adhere together in a similar way elsewhere, or even express the same meanings from appearance to appearance, although such consistencies are possible and, when they occur, helpful to the mythologist. Structures are more important and lasting than the individual components arranged in and through them. Dumézil emphasizes that the three goddesses featured in the Paris myth, given their names of probably non-Indo-European origin and the variety of characteristics they exhibit in Greek religion, are not survivals of the Greeks' Indo-European heritage and that by no means are they fundamentally connected with the three functions they represent in this particular myth (1968, 585–86). Yet it is significant that other trifunctional configurations involving one or more of the three divinities are attested. And Helen herself, with her three husbands (Menelaus the king, Paris the favorite of Aphrodite, and Deiphobos the warrior, who wins her in competition), appears to string together all three functions in the course of her mythological career, as is the wont of the many trifunctional female figures attested throughout the Indo-European world (Sergent 1979, 1169–70). Furthermore, Paris's inability to prioritize the functions properly is echoed in the actions of his ancestor Laomedon, the founder of Troy, who is seen by Dumézil as another Trojan violator of the hierarchy of the three functions (1985b, 31–37).

4. The presence of trifunctionalism or any other structure underlying Indo-European myth is ascertained and confirmed by means of comparison. Dumézil legitimates and strengthens his claim that the myth of the judgment of Paris was generated along the lines of an Indo-European pattern by setting the story alongside examples from Indian, Iranian,

and Germanic traditions, each of which features an analogous narrative situation of a young man's being offered his choice of future destiny in trifunctional terms (Dumézil 1968, 586–601). True, the structures must arise from the individual narratives or other forms of cultural expression themselves; but the structures are not necessarily apparent unless these various data are set side by side. For Dumézil, the limits of this comparability are determined by the historical fact of the existence of an Indo-European group of languages. A linguistic criterion is of course not the only legitimate means available whereby we can circumscribe cultural materials for the purpose of examining to what extent they can be treated as a resonant whole. Some scholars of myth limit themselves to one society, or one segment or epoch of society, while others have compared the myths of societies sharing basic typological features. Dumézil's Indo-Europeanist comparative approach does not contradict or supersede these other approaches, whether parochial or cosmopolitan; it is but one way to begin to understand the semantic riches of myth, which, as Dumézil himself emphasized, should be studied primarily within each individual cultural context.

Nowhere does Dumézil's respect for the individual "personalities" of Indo-European cultures appear more clearly than in his judicious studies of ancient Greek tradition.[2] Greece offers a most conspicuous example of the operations of what Lévi-Strauss has described as *bricolage*,[3] whereby the heritage of a relative past continually fuses with the cultural forces encountered in the relative present and a new synthesis is produced that represents a society's choices of terms with which to express itself to itself. One classical scholar following in Dumézil's footsteps has concluded that—as a result of the dramatic disruption of the post-Mycenaean "Dark Age," the seeming absence of a powerful priestly class among the Greeks in whose interest it would have been to conserve tradition, and Greece's perennial openness to "outside" influences—the Indo-European features of Greek culture, and of Greek religion in particular, were transformed on many levels beyond recognition, and that these features can be easily discerned for the most part only in seemingly "conservative" pockets of the Greek world (e.g., Crete, Boeotia), marginal strands of the Greek tradition (e.g., Pythagoreanism), and minor details of myth and epic—for instance, episodes of the Homeric poems but not their underlying narrative patterns (Sergent 1979, 1176–79; 1980, 272–73; 1984, 22). It has also been argued that, starting in the eighth century B.C., the cultural phenomenon of Panhellenism, which was the driving force behind the ancient Greek epic tradition, reduced the Indo-European element in heroic tale and weakened the functional correspondence between gods and heroes in the process of freeing itself from local cult and isolating the "common denominators" that united the various mythological and religious traditions of the Greek world. Thus, in effect, the Indo-European heritage would have been relegated or reduced to the local level, where it in turn was remolded or even dissolved to suit the needs of the evolving political institution of the *polis* (G. Nagy 1981, 138–39).

This impression of the relatively non-Indo-European nature of Greek culture and myth remains, however, an impression rather than a fact. Perhaps we know Greece too well and are therefore less likely to characterize it as Indo-European—and more likely so to describe some other culture from which we are distanced, or which we are not forced to view in its totality. Again, it should be emphasized that the inconspicuousness of Indo-European patterns (even if we limit ourselves only to those discerned and described by Dumézil) does not necessarily indicate their absence but perhaps only their restricted development, as well as the limits of our knowledge at the present time. In the words of Jaan Puhvel:

> Thus Greece in its inimitable way has managed to meld elements that can be rolled back to components only by the kind of scholarly struggle waged in this chapter. This is a task requiring thorough familiarity with both the immense store of Greek myth and the vast secondary literature as well as the external comparands, a combination rarely possessed by either specialists in classical studies or generalists in mythology. Hence Greece remains an extreme challenge to the comparativist, a hard nut that we have merely dented (1987, 143).

Their protestations of the apparently slim pickings in Greek tradition notwithstanding, Dumézil and other scholars have already built up an impressive dossier of Greek attestations of mythological patterns that can be found in other Indo-European mythologies as well.[4] One of the best attested of these patterns in Greek myth is the mechanism of "the three sins of the warrior" as it informs the mythological cycle centered on Heracles, the most popular of Greek heroes (Dumézil 1970, 96–104), whose life in general conforms to an Indo-European "heroic biography" pattern (Dumézil 1983, 123–34; 1985a, 97–105; 1985b, 71–79). The text Dumézil uses as the basis for his analysis of the Heracles myths is the account given by Diodorus Siculus, although key points of the analysis are reflected in other texts as well (see Davidson 1980). Analogous to the lives of certain other Indo-European second-function figures (Starkaðr of Germanic epic and Śiśupāla of Indian), Heracles' life unfolds as follows:

1) He is the product of reproductive "excess" (Zeus's three nights with Alcmene, during which the hero is conceived).

2) A man of great strength and physical power, he is profoundly affected and driven by the actions of a god who favors him (Zeus/ Athena) and those of a god who hates him (Hera).

3) In the course of his heroic career, he violates or offends the principles of each of the three functions in hierarchical succession (he disobeys the king Eurystheus, treacherously slays Iphitus, and greedily obtains a second wife). Each violation has a significant impact upon his life, and the third terminates it (Heracles is punished for his first two crimes and dies as a result of his last).

4) At his death, however, the hero is "rehabilitated" by being wondrously returned to his divine source and by passing on his martial attributes to a hero directly or indirectly responsible for his death (Heracles bequeathes his weapons to Philoctetes, who lights the funeral pyre that translates the dying Heracles onto Mount Olympus).

The story of Heracles, like those of his fellow Indo-European warriors, reflects an ideology within an ideology: the ambiguous position of the second function in society, the tensions inherent in the use of physical power, and the ambivalent attitude of the warrior toward society and its leaders, whom he both serves/protects and threatens.[5] Warriors are as unreliable and yet as indispensable in their own way as are representatives of the third function.

Not all the heroes of Greek myth are associated primarily with the second function, just as physical force is by no means the only distinguishing feature of Heracles or the only device available to culture heroes in general for balancing (or disrupting) the ideological superstructure. An alternative mode of supernaturally powered action is vividly presented in Lucian's essay on Heracles, which supplies us with a useful example of mythological comparativism as it was practiced in the classical world. Lucian claims that Heracles, whom the Celts "call Ogmios in their native tongue," is depicted among them as an old man. He describes a particular picture:

> That old Heracles drags after him a great crowd of men who are all
> tethered by the ears! His leashes are delicate chains fashioned of gold
> and amber, resembling the prettiest of necklaces. Yet, though led by
> bonds so weak, the men do not think of escaping, as they easily could,
> and they do not pull back at all or brace their feet and lean in the oppo-
> site direction to that in which he is leading them. In fact, they follow
> cheerfully and joyously, applauding their leader and all pressing him
> close and keeping the leashes slack in their desire to overtake him; ap-
> parently they would be offended if they were let loose! But let me tell
> you without delay what seemed to me the strangest thing of all. Since

the painter had no place to which he could attach the ends of the chains, as the god's right hand already held the club and his left the bow, he pierced the tip of his tongue and represented him drawing the men by that means! (*Heracles* 3, tr. Harmon).

Lucian, puzzled by this depiction, is enlightened by a Celt, who corrects the foreigner's false impression that the chains were connected to Heracles' tongue because the artist had nowhere else to lead them. Indeed, this motif, according to the informant, was the very point of the picture:

> We Celts do not agree with you Greeks in thinking that Hermes is Eloquence; we identify Heracles with it, because he is far more powerful than Hermes. . . . This being so, if old Heracles here drags men after him who are tethered by the ears to his tongue, don't be surprised at that, either; you know the kinship between ears and tongue (ibid. 4–5, tr. Harmon).

The surprisingly literal oral/aural chain that forms the focal point of Lucian's lesson in Celtic ideology is indicative of another kind of force in Indo-European mythologies that can be just as constructive, or even destructive, as the martial fury of the warrior: the often magically persuasive power of the spoken word, specifically as it is framed in various traditional forms of verbal expression such as poetry/song, prophecy, and prayer. This force is by no means inconsistent with that of the warrior, just as the Celtic version of Heracles, as described by Lucian, is not totally inconsistent with the Heracles of Greek myth, who is, among other things, a trained poet, associated with the muses (see Dumézil 1983, 137).

In a study of the god Apollo, Dumézil, using Indian, Greek, and Scythian evidence, argues for the existence of an Indo-European ideology of *parole* that reflects the tripartite structure and expresses the importance of speech and other humanly produced sounds for all levels of social action (1982, 11–108). In the ancient Indian collection of hymns known as the *Rig Veda* (10.125.4–6), we encounter the goddess Vāc, 'Voice', declaring herself the patroness of priestly and prophetic utterance (first function), of the bow (a manmade "instrument" of war), and of the well-being of society brought about through verbal communication among its members (third function). In the Homeric Hymn to Apollo (lines 131–39), the young god, who claims for himself the lyre and the bow (second function) as his emblems, promises to convey the wishes of Zeus to humans through oracles (first function), and gratefully covers the isle of his birth with gold (third function). Dumézil, while emphasizing that there is much more to the figure of Apollo than to the divine personification Vāc, nevertheless would see in this and

other descriptions of Apollo's powers an underlying tripartite schematization of the uses to which the human voice and its analogues or ex-
tensions are put. Actually, the tripartition blossoms into a quadriparti-
tion here as in other Indo-European conceptualizations of human
utterance and its accoutrements (see Dumézil 1982, 43–50; cf. Dumézil
1985b, 201–10, and Dubuisson 1985). One of Apollo's domains—music, as represented by the god's lyre—comes to enjoy "independence
within the interdependence" (Dumézil 1982, 48) of the ideological
schema, although in its religious and ritual dimensions music maintains
its original connection with the first function. Thus, according to Indo-
European ideology as reflected in Greek and other traditions, speech in
its various forms embodies and holds together the social fabric, and in
so doing it paradoxically transcends the ideological schema. This holds
true particularly for musically delivered speech, which can appear theoretically apart from the whole, or even drop out of the ideological accounting.

Furthermore, as we can see in Lucian's striking image of Heracles/
Ogmios leading men by the ears, speech (whether simply spoken or
sung) can be a means of "winning" and "obtaining" peacefully, break-
ing down barriers, and establishing continuity without bloodshed. In
these respects, the power of the speaker/singer paradoxically supple-
ments or even rivals the power of the warrior. Hence it is perhaps not
surprising that in Greek mythology Apollo's most distinguished offspring, the singer Orpheus (see Segal 1988a), lives out a mythological
career that presents some pointed intersections with the exploits of martial figures such as Heracles, who is even said to have been Orpheus's
pupil (Pseudo-Alcidimas, *Ulix.* 24 [Kern 1963, 37]; see Linforth 1941,
15–16, and Schoeller 1969, 41–42). The singer's famed involvement in
the Argonaut expedition, alongside Heracles and a roster of warlike heroes, is well established in the epic tradition. There is even a telling of
the story that is actually attributed to Orpheus (the so-called Orphic
Argonautica—see West 1983, 37–38). His participation in this heroic
exploit provoked the following comment from one scholiast:

> It is a question why a weakling (ἀσθενής) like Orpheus sailed with the
> heroes. It was because Cheiron with his gift of prophecy told them that
> if they took Orpheus they would be able to pass the Sirens. (schol. Apol-
> lon. 1.23; Kern 1963, 2; tr. Guthrie 1952, 28)

Of course, the peaceable figure of Orpheus—poet and mystic, the
putative author of so-called Orphic writings—embodies qualities that
make him in crucial respects the opposite of the warrior-hunter of myth
(Robbins 1982, 18–19). Especially in his role as the perhaps too-loving

husband of Eurydice, Orpheus places himself at the opposite end of the mythological spectrum from devotees of a *männerbund* ethos like the Argonauts and poses a risk to the social order with his amorous excess (see Detienne 1981). And yet, in several of the accounts given of Orpheus's postmatrimonial life, he turns into a celibate or even a woman-hater, comparable in his misogynistic intensity and potential for sexual disruption to second-function figures such as the hunter Hippolytus, with whom Euripides pointedly associates Orpheus (see below). The gamut of Orpheus's audiences and of his own dimensions as a mythical figure, ranging from the martial to the domestic, is realized in a painting of the fourth century B.C., in which "we see Orpheus playing in the midst, with two warriors on one side of him, and two women, apparently with no hostile intent, on the other; beneath him is lying a deer, which has also yielded to the spell of his music" (Linforth 1941, 32). Like Heracles (Burkert 1977a, 320), Orpheus is noted for taming wild creatures—although with the power of music, not the power of physical force—and he achieves the seemingly "shamanic" feat of gaining entrance into the world of the dead and, at least according to some strands of the mythological tradition, rescuing the dead (his wife Eurydice) from that world.[6] Perhaps the clearest indication of Orpheus's mediating identity, based upon a close ideological link between hunter/warrior and poet/singer, is the tradition according to which Orpheus trained one of the sons of Jason to be a warrior and the other to be a musician (Linforth 1941, 5–7). The proposed etymology for *Oiagros*, the name of Orpheus's father according to some sources, 'Lone Hunter' (Gruppe 1897–1902, 1112), would appear, if correct, to affirm these second-function connections.

When Orpheus dies—like Heracles and Hippolytus, at the hands of the opposite sex—he is decapitated.[7] This in fact is the fate we could have anticipated for Heracles, given the Indo-European pattern of second-function biography, adumbrated by Dumézil, to which Heracles' life in the main adheres. (Both Śiśupāla and Starkaðr, the Greek hero's Indo-European analogues, lose their heads in spectacular fashion [Dumézil 1983, 74, 78]—an ironic end in light of their having been born with "superfluous organs" that must be lopped off.) But unlike the mythological warrior, for whom the separation of the head from the body necessarily and naturally entails an end to life and heroic individuality, Orpheus, even after being deprived of his trunk, does not die: he lives on as a singing head.

This striking coda to the Orpheus myth has attracted a considerable body of scholarship, but relatively few scholars have paid more than passing attention to its Indo-European resonances. Yet the account of

Orpheus's demise and emergence in a new, "reduced" form can serve us as a paradigmatic mythological expression of the power of the spoken word as it was understood among the Greeks and other Indo-European peoples, whose traditions feature illuminating parallels to the tale of the "death" of Orpheus and its aftermath. To study this myth from a comparative perspective, therefore, is not to lose sight of its uniqueness within its own cultural setting but rather to expand its semantic field and shed light on its internal coherence.

Ovid in the *Metamorphoses*—reacting specifically to Vergil's telling of the story in the *Georgics* (4.315–527; see Anderson 1982), but in the main echoing other accounts extant in classical literature—tells the following version of the story of the grisly death of the greatest singer of Greek mythology (10.78–85, 11.1–60). Having foresworn women as the objects of both his love and his art after the irreversible loss of his beloved Eurydice, the bereaved yet still singing poet has the bad fortune to come across a band of maenads (devotees of Bacchus/Dionysus) who, resentful of his scorn for their sex, tear him apart limb from limb and head from trunk. Tumbling into the river Hebrus and floating along with the poet's still-playing lyre, the head makes its way, mourning all the while, to the isle of Lesbos—which, as we learn from Phanocles and other sources, owes its wealth of poetic talent to the presence of Orpheus's head (Kern 1963, 22–23; Linforth 1941, 129, 134).

We learn the further history of the head from Philostratus:

> And they tell that it was here [Lesbos] that Orpheus once on a time loved to prophesy, before Apollo had turned his attention to him. For when the latter found that men no longer flocked to Gryneium for the sake of oracles nor to Clarus nor [to Delphi] where is the tripod of Apollo, and that Orpheus was the only oracle, his head having lately come from Thrace, he presented himself before the giver of oracles and said: "Cease to meddle with my affairs, for I have already put up long enough with your vaticinations" (*Life of Apollonius* 4.14, tr. Conybeare).

Thus even Apollo, Orpheus's father, ultimately feels threatened by his son's knowledge. Other extant accounts point more explicitly to a rivalry between gods, or between the singer and the gods, as the cause of Orpheus's death. According to what we are told of Aeschylus's lost play *Bassarides,* Orpheus was slain by female worshipers of Dionysus sent by the jealous god, who was angered by Orpheus's faithful worship of Apollo (Kern 1963, 34; see Guthrie 1952, 32, 232–33, Detienne 1979, 91–93; cf. Linforth 1931, 11–17; 1941, 9–10; Detienne 1985).[8] Offering a rather different perspective on Orpheus's relationship with the gods is a tradition recorded by Pausanias, according to which Orpheus was actually slain by a divine thunderbolt in punishment for having divulged divine mysteries to humanity (9.30.3).

There is also a prominent sexual factor behind Orpheus's death, in addition to these divine-human tensions. The close connection between sex and violence in this myth is amply attested in the mythographer Conon's version of the death of Orpheus, which is full of suggestive detail:

> He was torn to pieces by the women of Thrace and Macedonia because he would not allow them to take part in his religious rites, or it may be on other pretexts too: for they do say that after the misfortune he had with his own wife he became the foe of the whole sex. Now on appointed days a throng of armed Thracians and Macedonians used to gather at Leibethra, and come together in a certain building which was large and well adapted for the performance of initiatory rites; and when they entered to take part in the rites, they laid down their arms before the door. The women watched for this, and, filled with anger at the slight put upon them, seized the arms, slew those who attempted to overpower them, and rending Orpheus limb from limb, cast the scattered remains into the sea. No requital was exacted from the women, and a plague affected the land. Seeking relief from their troubles, the inhabitants received an oracle, saying that if they should find the head of Orpheus and bury it, then they should have rest. After much difficulty they found it through a fisherman at the mouth of the river Meles. It was still singing, and in no way harmed by the sea, nor had it suffered any of the other dreadful changes which the fates of man bring upon dead bodies. Even after so long a time it was fresh, and blooming with the blood of life. So they took it and buried it under a great mound, and fenced off a precinct around it, which at first was a hero-shrine but later grew to be a temple. That is, it is honoured with sacrifices and all the other tributes which are paid to gods. No woman may ever set foot within it (*Narr.* 45; tr. Guthrie 1952, 61–62).

Here it seems that the widowed Orpheus attempts to reestablish the distinction between male and female domains (threatened by his previous uxoriousness) with a dangerous zeal. As a consequence of his sexual radicalism, the sexes are polarized; remarkably, their roles are all too easily switched (males lose their arms, women acquire them), and disaster results.[9] However, with the discovery of the singing head, and the head's finding an audience, the continuity of cult (human-divine communication) and the proper relationship between the sexes are restored: the rites of Orpheus are continued from generation to generation of men, without further female interruption.

Except in Philostratus (see above and also his *Heroicus* 5.3), there is no mention in our sources of the head's serving as an oracle, or of any continuation of Orpheus's poetic performance beyond the time when the head was recovered or rescued. In the following local tradition recorded by Pausanias, the head does not appear at all. Nevertheless, here too Orpheus continues to communicate after his death, and he remains an almost natural force to be reckoned with:

> The Macedonians of the city of Dion and the country below Mount Pieria say Orpheus was murdered there by the women. Two and a half miles from Dion on the way to the mountain a pillar stands on the right, with a vase of stone on it. The people of the district say this vase has Orpheus's bones in it. The river Helikon runs for a little under ten miles, then its stream disappears underground, but after three more miles the water rises again, changing its name to Baphyra, and reaches the sea in a navigable estuary. The Dionians claim that this river originally ran entirely above ground, but the women who murdered Orpheus wanted to wash away his blood and the river dived down into the earth for fear its water should purify murderers. I heard another story at Larisa about a city called Libethra on the Macedonian side of Olympos with Orpheus's memorial quite close to it. The Libethrans received a message from Dionysos through an oracle in Thrace, that when the sun saw the bones of Orpheus the city of Libethra would be rooted up by a wild boar. They took little notice of the prophecy, thinking that a wild beast could not be big and strong enough to capture the city, and wild boars are more fierce than strong. When the god thought fit, this is what happened to them. A shepherd was lying against Orpheus's grave during the middle of the day, and he fell asleep: in his sleep he sang the poems of Orpheus in a loud, sweet voice. Of course everyone watching their flocks close by, and even ploughmen, abandoned work and crowded to hear the shepherd singing in his sleep. They shoved and pressed to get closer to him and they overturned the pillar. The urn fell and smashed and the sun saw what was left of the bones of Orpheus. At once the very next night the god poured down water out of heaven, and the river Boar, which is one of the winter streams on Olympos, broke the walls of Libethra, overturned the sanctuaries of gods and the houses of men, and drowned the people and every living thing in the city, all alike. The Libethrans had perished: and so the Macedonians of Dion, according to the story of my friend at Larisa, carried away the bones of Orpheus to their own country (9.30.4–5; tr. Levi 1971, 372–73).

This manifestation of the still-living voice of Orpheus causes a sensational disruption and elicits unwitting irreverence toward the dead. The bones, as seemingly helpless and inert as a decapitated head should be, bring destruction to the town, just as the neglected head of Conon's account is behind the plague that punishes Libethra. Orpheus demands to be heard, just as his bones are tragically fated to be seen.[10] The ambiguous oracle encourages confusion between the real (a boar) and the metaphorical (a river named Boar), while the musical performance of the possessed shepherd, Orpheus's mouthpiece, generates a breakdown of social decorum (the unseemly jostling at the grave site), not to mention a confusion of the categories of dead and living. The finale, prefigured by the oracle and precipitated by the performance, is a terrible overturning of spatial boundaries: rain from the sky overcomes the earth, and river floods land. Speech unheeded (the message of the oracle)—or, in the case of the musical performance, overly heeded—rends the social fabric and creates a cosmic breakdown.

As it does for the above-mentioned warriors Starkaðr and Śiśupāla, the severing of the singer's head from his body creates a supernatural aftereffect of continuity: Orpheus's head, according to some strands of the tradition, continues to sing and becomes an oracle, protected by Apollo, or a cult object. This extension of undying heroic essence, however, does not constitute a return to the divine source (as it implicitly does for Starkaðr and Śiśupāla) or a passing-on of heroic attributes and powers to other heroes (as in the dying Herakles' act of bequeathing his bow and arrows to the young Philoctetes). The singer, rather, continues to live through part of himself—and even through his instrument: Orpheus's lyre is said to continue playing, alongside the singing head, after his death (Ovid, *Metamorph.* 11.51–52; Lucian, *Adv. indoct.* 11). The various modes of final dissolution and reconstitution for the second-function figures (Starkaðr's offering himself to Hoðr/Odin; Śiśupāla's absorption into Kṛṣṇa; Heracles' deification) confirm the existence of a sacred totality into which they ultimately can be subsumed. Orpheus's mode of life after death, however, would seem to indicate that the singer, his performance, and the tradition he represents potentially form a closed system, grounded in an autonomy and invulnerability of music and speech. Orpheus needs no one to revive or succeed him, any more than his instrument is in need of a player.[11] And the head, part of a now absent whole, is almost more effective an exponent of the power of the verbal and musical arts than was the "complete" singer in life. Typologically at least, the power of this singing, self-vivifying head, like that of Orpheus himself, is akin to the power of Lucian's Heracles/Ogmios, which lies very pointedly in the head—not in the body—and is visually expressed with chains attached not to the limbs but to the heads of those enchained. Free to exist apart from the body, Orpheus oracularly continues to address society, just as the verbal and musical arts can stand apart from the ideological whole and yet embody and serve that whole. Orpheus once "concentrated" into his head becomes all the more a mixed, and therefore especially charged, message. He is a source of conjunction—the "chaining together" produced by speech, and the reflection of audience in the person of the performer—and yet also the product and sign of disjunction: the detachment of the singer from society and the head from the body, brought about by alienation between men and women, among gods (as well as the values they represent), and gods and humans.

The resemblance between Orpheus's head and a host of other severed heads in Indo-European traditions has been noted by a variety of scholars (e.g., Kittredge 1916, 147–94; Deonna 1923; Eliade 1964, 391; Avanzin 1970; Colledge and Marler 1981). It has also been observed that the motif of the "vital head" (as it is dubbed in Thompson's *Motif-Index of Folk Literature* [E783]) is by no means limited to the Indo-European world.[12] There is extensive evidence from all phases of human civilization that a fascination with the head or skull detached from the body is virtually a universal element in religion and folklore (Klingbeil 1932; Meslin 1987). Scholarly assessments of the significance of the many heads that live on in Indo-European myth in particular have drawn on available archaeological and ethnographic data indicating the existence of head cults and headhunting among several peoples, including the Indo-Europeans (Sterckx 1981). And it has been stated often enough that vital heads in narrative are an affirmation of a traditional perception of the head as the seat of intelligence, life, potency, or status—qualities which, in sufficient amounts, can, at least in the world of myth, keep the head alive without the body. Very little attention, however, has been paid to what these heads in Celtic, Norse, Greek, Indian, and other Indo-European mythologies actually *do*—for they are usually more than just "vital." Often these heads are verbal, and powerfully so, and they actually manipulate the still-attached heads of their audience through the power of their words or their verbal performances. As we have already seen in the myth of Orpheus, these heads are not only long-lived but also persistent, and their "overmarked" personalities entrance or enchain their auditors, like the Heracles/Ogmios of Lucian's description. It can therefore be argued that a major function of vital heads in Indo-European mythologies is the signification of the oral tradition in its function as a mechanism for establishing a continuity of verbal discourse—that is, for preserving and renewing the spoken word. Furthermore, in Indo-European traditions, heads tend to be severed and rendered miraculously communicative under a set of narrative circumstances that, as we shall see, form a recurrent pattern.

One of the best examples of this verbal tenacity as expressed through the bodiless head is to be found in the episode known as the *Sírrabud Súaldaim*, 'The Persistent Warning of Súaldaim', which is contained in the recensions of the medieval Irish *Táin Bó Cúailnge*, 'Cattle Raid of Cooley' (O'Rahilly 1976, lines 3410–53; 1967, lines 3981–4052).[13] The great warrior Cú Chulainn's strength has been depleted in the course of his single-handed defense of the province of Ulster against the combined forces of all the other provinces of Ireland, who are being led by the Connaught queen Medb. The exhausted hero is approached by his father Súaldaim, who is commissioned by his son to carry word of warning to the Ulstermen in the capital of Emain Macha, where they are recovering from their mysterious debility, the result of a curse laid upon them by a pregnant supernatural female (see Rees and Rees 1961, 58–59). Súaldaim, who is described as only a mediocre fighter (O'Rahilly 1967, lines 3994–97), reaches the men and declares his message to them but is unheeded: the men of Ulster will not speak before the king speaks, the king will not speak before his druid speaks, and the king's druid declares that someone with so unpleasant a message should be executed. In his frustration, the spurned messenger falls off his horse and is decapitated by his own shield. Despite this setback, Súaldaim's message is not lost; instead, it gains new force. His head, lying on his shield, which in turn is on the horse, continues to proclaim the news of impending disaster and finally arouses Conchobar, the king of Ulster, out of his stuporous, druid-ridden hauteur. The head's terse but persistent warning gives way to a lengthy call to arms addressed to the men of Ulster by their king. Finally, the Ulstermen muster their forces and in an extended battle throw back the invasion of their province.

Like Orpheus, Súaldaim presents an alternative to the hero characterized by physical strength, and he is treated by the conventional representative of the first function, the king's druid, as a threat (compare Orpheus's supposedly impious acts of communication that brought divine wrath down upon him). Súaldaim proves to be of little use for the defense or enlightenment of the province until he is "minimized." This diminution in effect "turns up the volume" on Súaldaim's message and highlights his head's communicative function. Thus the narrative presents us with a direct parallel to the paradoxes of the Argonautic Orpheus (a "weakling" whose verbal powers are essential for the completion of warriors' tasks), the severed head of Orpheus, and the aged but irresistible Heracles/Ogmios. All of these figures symbolize the same binding power by which Súaldaim's warning, *rabud*, is indeed *sír*— 'long' or 'lasting', even beyond death—and vital to the interests and functions of kings, priests, and warriors, as well as society at large.

The curious placement of the talking head on the back of a horse reflects a theme to be found in the Orpheus tradition as well. In Ovid's account of the poet's death, we are told that Dionysus punished his murderous maenads by turning them into oak trees (*Metamorph.* 11.67–84), while Apollo stopped a serpent about to eat Orpheus's head, beached on Lesbos, by turning the beast into stone (ibid. 11.56–60). These destinies of immobilization present a stark contrast to the relative freedom and mobility of the severed head, which escapes the scene of the crime and is transported by water to Lesbos. The frantic women and the enterprising snake are rendered static, or even rooted, entities, while the head, seemingly the most vulnerable and helpless of all, proves to be surprisingly locomotive. This defeat of expectations also appears in the climactic scene of the Súaldaim episode, where a mounted head moves about addressing warriors who are normally active, mobile, and mounted, but who at this time are barely moving or responding. Such ability to move and cross boundaries is in fact a typical feature of the vital head as it appears in various mythologies, both inside and outside the Indo-European world. It is yet another sign, operating in another "code," that connotes the persistence and dynamic of the spoken word as it lives on in tradition beyond the individual performance and the individual performer.

Obviously, vital heads do not just exist *a priori* but are made, usually under circumstances of violent hostility between opposed persons and values (cf. Oosten 1985, 62). Súaldaim, not a native of Ulster and hence not afflicted by the Ulstermen's debility (said to be like the pangs of childbirth), loses his head when confronting the unresponsive Ulstermen, still recovering as if *post partum,* and thereby evokes a response from them. The celibate (or homosexual) Orpheus, a devotee or son of Apollo, is attacked and decapitated by female devotees of the god Dionysus, and so Apollo is seemingly deprived of the main exponent of the verbal arts he sponsors. Yet Orpheus's head survives and returns, as it were, to Apollo, who becomes the protector and manager of this performing cult object. A similar pattern of hierarchical and sexual tension underlying a sequence of loss and recovery acted out among a cast of cosmic characters is apparent in the *aition* of another vital head, that of Mímir in Scandinavian mythology.[14]

According to the medieval Icelander Snorri's account of the struggles among the Norse gods (in the *Ynglingasaga,* the first part of the *Heimskringla,* 1.12–13), Mímir, a source of wise utterance for Odin and the other gods of the Aesir family, was one of the hostages delivered over to the other family of gods, the Vanir, when the two groups made peace with each other. Along with Mímir went another god, Hoenir, who was elected chief of the Vanir for his great size and beauty. Hoenir, however, proved to be so dependent on Mímir's advice that, unless he were accompanied by his fellow hostage, he could say nothing of interest or value in the assembly. The Vanir grew angry at the Aesir because of Hoenir's apparent worthlessness as a leader and counselor. In their pique they cut off Mímir's head. The greatly bereaved Odin managed to obtain the head and preserve it by means of pickling, and from that time on Mímir's head would speak to Odin whenever he sought its advice.

In this story, a head (or the contents of a head) becomes an object of contention in a conflict between two opposed cosmic forces: the Aesir, who, as Dumézil has convincingly argued, represent the Indo-European second and first functions (with the second instead of the first predominating, in typical Germanic fashion), and the Vanir, who represent the third (1973, 3–25). Furthermore, in light of the previously discussed analogues of the Mímir story, we should note that the Aesir are a notably more "masculine" pantheon than the Vanir, who are sometimes rather markedly represented by their females and characterized as sexually deviant (see ibid., 7–8, 24, and the tradition recorded in the *Heimskringla* [1.13] that the Vanir, unlike the Aesir, practiced incest). Here, as in the other myths we have examined, the sexual connotations of the image of the severed yet still productive head, especially in these various frameworks of male-female rivalry, are quite obvious. But equally important is the fact that Mímir's head, like those of Orpheus and Súaldaim, functions as a living and productive reminder of its original owner's wisdom-laden verbal performance. Relevant in this regard is the proposed etymology of Mímir's name, according to which it is cognate with Latin *memor* 'remembering' (de Vries 1937, 361; cf. Lincoln 1982b, 28). Equally intriguing are the connotations of the Irish word *rabud*, which appears in the traditional title of the Súaldaim episode of the *Táin*, *Sírrabud Súaldaim*. While it is usually translated as 'warning', *rabud* also has the meaning 'sign' (Royal Irish Academy 1983, s.v. *robud*). Hence it may refer to Súaldaim's ominous speech, which lingers after his death, and *also* to the wondrous epiphany of a talking head: a living memorial that infuses power into the already spoken word.

These three Indo-European stories centered on the vital head construct an opposition between the mortal, normally communicative body, or head attached to the body, and the immortal, abnormally or supernaturally communicative severed head: that is, between an unmarked, vulnerable whole made up of parts that do not "stick together" or cannot communicate adequately (e.g., the unsatisfactory team of Hoenir and Mímir) and a marked, invulnerable part that "sticks with it" and gets the job of communicating done. In Indian tradition, which is replete with severed heads (Coomaraswamy 1944; Heesterman 1967, 23–29), we find the following story, attested already in the *Rig Veda* (1.117.22), in which the poles of this opposition are shifted onto two alternating heads on the same body.[15]

Dadhyañc (a seer, kindler of sacrificial fire, or the son of a priest) is privy to the secret of the whereabouts of mead, or to the esoteric sacrificial technique of reuniting head with body, but is forbidden by the divine warrior-king Indra from imparting this information to anyone: the second-function god (Indra) has assured this first-function possessor of knowledge that if he divulges what he knows, his head—his organ, as it were, of communication and the repository of his wisdom—will be cut off. However, the divine Aśvín twins (characteristically associated with the third function—Puhvel 1987, 58–60) finally prevail upon Dadhyañc to divulge the secret by promising to protect his head. They remove it and put a horse's head upon him while he instructs them. (In so doing, the Aśvínā ['Pair of Horsemen'], who have the heads of horses themselves [O'Flaherty 1975, 56; Puhvel 1970a, 169–70; Frame 1978, 145–52], render their teacher an "honorary Aśvín.") Then, after Indra in his fury cuts off the horse's head (Dadhyañc's temporary head), the twins reinstate their teacher's real head.

The plight of the priestly sage Dadhyañc, which is mirrored in the later myth of Śiva's elephant-headed son Gaṇeśa (Courtright 1985, 62–98), is essentially that of the Norse Mímir, another first-function pawn in another contention between primarily second-function figures and third-function figures. Dadhyañc himself and his restored original head—vital yet not so vital—have no further role to play in mythology, but the horse's head, we are told in later sources, is secreted in a lake and lies dormant until it is found by Indra and used as a weapon to slay Vrtra or other demons challenging Indra's cosmic supremacy (*Rig Veda* 1.84.13–15; O'Flaherty 1975, 57–58).[16] Furthermore, there is a connection made in later Indian tradition between Dadhyañc (or Dadhīca) of the watery horse's head and the fiery androgynous horse that will emerge catastrophically from the ocean at the end of the world (O'Flaherty 1980b, 226–33).

Dadhyañc's temporary head—not just a head on a horse, like Súaldaim's, but actually a horse's head—speaks to the Aśvínā in a way that his regular head attached to his body could not. Thus it falls in line with the other vital heads we have examined. After it is taken off the priest's body, however, the horse's head apparently grows silent, or we only see it used as a vengeful instrument of violence, not as an instrument of verbal or musical expression.[17] Yet the motifs connected with this disembodied, spoken-out instead of outspoken, head—its residence in water, its fieriness, its value to Indra as a means of affirming his sovereignty—are reminiscent of the Iranian *xvarənah,* the divine essence lodged in the waters which, once obtained, confers kingly prestige upon anyone lucky enough to obtain it (see Puhvel 1987, 108–9, 277–83). As Patrick Ford has demonstrated (1974), this *xvarənah* is paralleled in Irish tradition by *imbas,* 'great knowledge', an essence that resides in an otherworldly spring, inspires poetic utterance, and wells up with destructive force. This perhaps not-so-distant Celtic cousin of the priestly horse's head of Indian tradition brings us back to the verbal element that is missing from Dadhyañc's "head for a day" as it exists in its watery semiretirement.[18]

The following are the key elements of what would appear to be the underlying narrative pattern common to these four Indo-European mythological recipes for a productive severed head. Each opens on a note of potentially disastrous discord; the three functions, the sexes, or the pantheon are dangerously disunited, and the "whole" threatens to disintegrate:

Greek: Orpheus, seer (first function) and companion to warriors (second function), is tragically separated from his wife, who remains in the world of the dead. He is alienated from women and their sexuality (third function). Or, revealing the secrets of the gods, Orpheus antagonizes them. Or, Apollo and Dionysus are at loggerheads over Orpheus.

Irish: The Ulster warriors and their king (second and first functions, respectively), as a result of the disrespect they showed toward a supernatural female, are rendered helpless in a "feminine" way during a crisis in which their cattle, women, and children are threatened. The avowed purpose of the invaders, headed by a woman (Queen Medb of Connaught), is to steal the Ulstermen's best bull, for the purpose of breeding, as well as their other prized possessions (that is, their interests lie in the domain of the third function). The warrior Cú Chulainn, unaided by his fellow warriors, is forced to fight virtually alone against these depredators.

Norse: The third-function Vanir, reconciled to the first- and second-function Aesir in a perfunctory manner, are disenchanted with their hostages. Hence the rapprochement of the pantheons is threatened.

Indian: The warrior-king Indra forbids the priestly Dadhyañc from revealing his first-function secrets to the third-function Aśvínā.

The outcome of the problematic situation in each tale is the death of a mediating figure ("mediating" at least in the sense of being caught between the opposing forces), his decapitation, and the survival of his head (or, in the Indian example, the replacement of his head), which proves remarkably mobile and imparts vital information. In each example, this outcome constitutes in effect a solution to the original problem of disjunction:

Greek: Orpheus—ambivalent toward women and half divine—is slain by members of the opposite sex and/or a god and treated as a source of fertility (his body is scattered on the ground—a third-function "application"). Apollo and Dionysus, whose followers were at odds (Orpheus versus the maenads), mutually tidy up the loose ends of Orpheus's murder: Apollo protects the remains, and Dionysus punishes his savage devotees. The slain singer's head floats away and becomes a valued oracle, serving to maintain communication between the divine and the human. The head-oracle is finally closed down lest the other, divinely sponsored oracles be neglected. Women or those who do not respect the living voice of Orpheus are punished for their impious behavior: the maenads are turned into trees, women are excluded from Orpheus's rites, or Libethra is destroyed.

Irish: Súaldaim, neither warlike nor subject to the "feminine" condition of the Ulstermen, is ignored by druid, king, and warrior, and he dies. His head continues to communicate his message. Finally, thanks to Súaldaim's persistence, the Ulster king and his men regroup as an effective social force, and the despoilers of Ulster are driven out of the province.

Norse: The Vanir slay Mímir, who played the role of go-between for the two pantheons. Having thus vented their ire, the Vanir apparently remain at peace with the Aesir. Odin in turn wins back Mímir in the form of his head, which thus manages to "return" to the Aesir. The head becomes a precious source of knowledge for Odin.

Indian: The Aśvínā "slay" Dadhyañc, the sage whose knowledge everyone wants, after obtaining the desired information from him, and confer upon him a semiequine identity similar to their own. Indra "slays" Dadhyañc in punishment. But Dadhyañc's head returns to his body, and he continues his priestly communicative functions, while his temporary head continues to exist on its own, serving Indra as a weapon. Thus the horse's head becomes emblematic of all three functions and symbolically reintegrates them.

Despite the dichotomous turmoil looming in each myth, the force that impels and speaks through the severed head proves not only indestructible but even salvific. A part that acts like a whole, a product of destruction that lives notwithstanding, the speaking head mediates between the various opposed realities featured in these myths (male-female; human-divine; first and second function–third function; living-dead) and reintegrates the totality that originally threatened to disintegrate. In this mythological complex, therefore, we have yet another expression of the concept of the crucial marginality of speech, separate from but inclusive of the entire ideological system, which is saved and sustained through its reflection in the talking head and its utterance.

In the stories examined, the realm of discourse over which the vital head ranges and rules is limited to the oral, as we would expect of a thematic cluster that stems from the prehistoric and preliterate Indo-European past. There are, however, some instances in Indo-European mythologies where the work of the severed head and the act of writing are contrasted or connected. (Indeed, the very presence of the sign of a talking head in literary texts, such as those upon which we based our preceding survey of the motif, draws attention to the tension between the spoken and the written that we may assume was keenly felt by the scribal bearers of these various traditions.) As we shall see, the symbolic baggage of the severed head, the complex of ideas that we have been exploring, can lend itself to an evaluation of the relationship between written and oral communication in those Indo-European cultures where literacy was culturally important enough for there to develop the need for an ideological reckoning of the relationship. This concluding excursion on the "new" applications of the vital head motif in Irish and Greek traditions is conducted in the spirit of Dumézil—that is, the goal is not to retrieve a fossilized *Urmythologie* but to study some of the varieties of specialization and transformation that sustain a protean ideological heritage in Indo-European cultures.

In the medieval Irish collection of lore known as *Cormac's Glossary*, there appears an account of domestic turmoil that features an act of written communication leading to the creation of a severed, singing head (Meyer 1912, §1018; see also Dillon 1932, 48–49, 58–61). The story is set in the days before the arrival of Christianity—therefore, before the era of scribes and literary tradition.

Lomna, the fool (*drúth*) of the great warrior-hunter Finn mac Cumaill, stays at home one day while his master goes off to the hunt. (Lomna, we are told, was a *midlach*, 'weakling'.) Walking about outside, the fool discovers Finn's paramour *in flagrante delicto* with a member of Finn's retinue, the warrior Cairpre. Despite the woman's attempts to dissuade him from giving away her secret, Lomna feels compelled to tell Finn about what he saw. But in order to be as discreet and safe as possible, he gives Finn the message in the form of a cryptic poem written on a stick in ogam (a pre-Christian alphabet used by the Irish for inscriptional purposes). The cuckolded husband deciphers the message and understands the gist of the poem. The paramour, presumably upon being confronted by Finn, instantly realizes who has let the cat out of the bag and instructs her lover to slay Lomna. The fool is killed, and, as an apparent subscriber to the old tradition of Celtic headhunting, Cairpre takes Lomna's head with him on his flight into the wilderness. Finn finds the headless corpse at home, and his men ask him to discover whose it is, through his wondrous power of divination. Finn identifies the body as that of his fool Lomna and goes immediately in hot pursuit of Cairpre. Using his hunting skills, Finn finds his enemy's trail and tracks him to his camp, where he spies on Cairpre and his men as they grill a catch of fish, with Lomna's still-alive head perched on a spit beside the fire. Cairpre proceeds to distribute the cooked fish among his mates, but gives none to the head—an act of niggardliness that, the text informs us, was anathema to Finn and his fellow hunters. Having been thus ignored, Lomna's head utters a poem in which he complains about his ill treatment at the hands of his captors. A second fish course is served, the head is once again snubbed, and so it composes some more plaintive verse. His patience exhausted, Cairpre orders his men to put the head outside the camp—although, he admits, in so doing they will acquire a bad reputation. Even outside, however, the head continues to harangue poetically those within. This all proves too much for Finn, and he surprises his enemy and slays him along with all his men. Unfortunately, we are not told what happened to Lomna.

The fool's head is part of an ensemble in this story, which despite its brevity presents us with a virtual inventory of signs, both visual and verbal. (The text of the tale itself is a citation, framed as a glossarial explication of an obscure word—a difficult verbal sign—that appears in one of Lomna's cited poems.) The opening contrast between hunters and domestics soon becomes a matter of differing objects, and levels, of interpretation: Finn is a successful hunter because he can read signs in nature indicating the presence of prey, but an unsuccessful husband, precisely because he is so preoccupied with hunting. The domestic, on the other hand, is a reject from the hunting band, but he is all too aware of the sexual predation taking place on the home front. From rather straightforward and easy-to-read signs—animal tracks, a couple making love—the story moves on to the doubly difficult sign of Lomna's warning poem to Finn: words that are hard to understand, and that are not even heard but seen, written in the esoteric code of ogam. Finn, however, can read and interpret this sign, and even his paramour can indirectly read it, through its effect on Finn, and identify its author. Curiously, that which proves to be the most difficult sign of all, the one that requires supernatural intervention for its proper reading, is the headless corpse—even though we might think that Finn and his men could easily figure out who had been killed. For the solving of this mystery, Finn must use his special divinatory technique. Once this acephalous sign has been properly decoded (the message being that Lomna has been killed and that Cairpre, his slayer, has fled), all falls into place: the disjunction between the knowledge possessed by the hunter-hero and that by the domestic nonhero dissolves. Finn is once again off on a hunt, but this time on the track of the domestic predator now turned prey.

In the heart of the wilderness, having openly discerned and decoded the inert sign of the headless corpse at home, Finn now furtively witnesses and responds sympathetically to the most active, engaging, and nagging sign in the story: the complement to the anonymous headless corpse, the talking head that is indisputably Lomna's. This appendage, demanding to be heard and satisfied, seals the fate of Cairpre the homewrecker, who in the story had consistently undermined the rules of proper conduct and, along with his mistress, attempted to silence the spoken word. The garrulous head that "roughs it" in the wilderness also succeeds in vindicating the erstwhile homebody Lomna: a seemingly helpless protagonist who in the tale's final scene speaks, as opposed to writes, for the first time—a rather ironic deferral, given that as a *drúth*, he is a member (albeit a lowly one) of the ranks of traditional verbal performers in Irish culture.

Writing is dangerous: the ogam message, written with the best of intentions and meant to defuse the time bomb of infidelity in the domestic realm, instead itself creates a messy explosion. The writer loses his head and his proper sphere of influence (that is, Lomna is removed from his seemingly appropriate milieu). As a head, however, the fool reestablishes the power of the true, specifically spoken, utterance; he reveals the essential unworthiness of his adulterous beheader and thus seals his fate; and he effects a balance between social domains, and between man and woman: Finn, the hunter, avenges the domestic insult of adultery. (We have of course already seen these tensions, and their resolution, in other narratives featuring the severed head.)

There would seem to be a trifunctional dimension to the Lomna tale. The *drúth* who possesses special knowledge (first function) is caught in a struggle between the hunter-warrior Finn (second function) and the wily Cairpre, who adulterously engages the hunter's wife and is marked as niggardly (third-function "sins"). Only when he is decapitated and seemingly rendered helpless does Lomna become powerful or "significant" enough to make a difference in the struggle and bring about a culturally acceptable conclusion to it. In many ways, therefore, the story of Lomna falls in line with the other narratives we have considered.

Ogam, the form of writing that plays such a pointed role in this tale, was viewed in medieval Irish literary tradition as a paradigmatic, and by no means outdated, form of written expression, even though nothing approaching our concept of "literature" has survived in ogam script, nor is there any reason to believe that such ever existed. That the visual sign of the ogam message is superseded in the story by the more striking visual sign of the living head, which is vocal as well as visible, suggests a reactionary hierarchy in the medieval Irish ideology of communication.

Some of the underlying tensions within this hierarchy were uncovered by Dumézil in his study of the continuities and discontinuities between the oral ethos of the Gaulish druids (who, according to Caesar, disdained writing) and medieval Celtic assumptions about writing (Dumézil 1940; see also Le Roux and Guyonvarc'h 1986, 263–69). In a Middle Irish text that plays a central role in Dumézil's argument (Stokes 1891, 199–202), a poet's son held hostage in the court of the legendary Irish king Cormac mac Airt loses his costly sword to the royal steward who covets it, after the latter secretly inscribes his own name on its hilt and then claims the sword by virtue of the inscription. And so in this instance, we are told, the dead bore witness against the living, in that the written word won the case for the devious steward despite the oral protestations of the hostage. Script surpasses utterance in the political arena of Cormac's court, but it is almost inherently devious and a precarious vessel (at best) of the truth. (In fact, the steward does not get to keep the sword but ultimately is forced to return it to the poet's son, who in turn is forced to give it over to Cormac.)

Surely the same invidious comparison underlies the tale of Lomna, with its two strikingly different acts of communication: the delivery of a fateful message in written form, which leads to the revelation (but not the punishment) of wrongdoing as well as to the death of the innocent writer; and Lomna's oral protest that *defies* death and, although seemingly impotent, pinpoints guilt and brings swift punishment upon the story's villain. The ogam inscription is not described as "dead" in this text, but it is doubtless significant that it is contrasted with a bodily part that should be dead and yet is not because it still has something to say.

The paradoxicality of oral "life" and literary "death" is also apparent in the medieval Irish tale of the madman Suibne (O'Keeffe 1913), which has already been explored for its use of the Indo-European "three sins of the warrior" pattern (Cohen 1977). Here, we see the career of an oral poet shaped by his relationship with saints who are presented in the text as users or producers of the written word. At the beginning of the story, Saint Rónán calls madness down upon the feckless Suibne after he gravely offends him by, among other things, throwing the cleric's psalter into the water. In his exile in the wilderness, away from the domain of the literary culture of Christianity, Suibne is inspired: he composes poems in which he both laments his loneliness and discomfort, and extols his vibrant freedom. Finally, Suibne becomes the friend of another saint, Moling, who convinces the madman to come in from the wild every day so as to give Moling the chance to write down the poems Suibne has composed. However, this voluntary acquiescence to the power of the written word and its bearers brings death to Suibne: he dies, like Lomna, a victim of sexual intrigue within Moling's household, at the hands of a jealous husband.

In one of Suibne's wilder adventures, which takes place before the rapprochement with Moling, he encounters a band of rolling, roaring heads. These recognize Suibne and attack him for no apparent reason, both verbally and physically. In the struggle to escape from them, Suibne leaps and flies as he had never done before (O'Keeffe 1913, §64–66). Such feats of restlessness and superhuman mobility punctuate the madman's fall from grace. That this climactic display of these qualities is brought about by vital heads—which clearly exist outside the realm of saints, books, and proper social discourse—is a telling reflection on Suibne's destiny. Orpheus survives a concerted attack upon him as a mobile, talking head because he still has something important to say; Suibne survives an attack launched by talking heads because he himself is metaphorically a talking head: both dead and alive, putatively "cut off" and silenced yet all the more markedly vociferous. Ironically, the saint's curse, which removes Suibne from his community and renders him dead to the world, simultaneously gives him the power to survive where other humans would be overcome by the elements: the curse specifically condemns him to the life of a bird in the wilderness (ibid., §9). Such liveliness, which makes for good poetry and inspired oral performance, gives way to the final utter immobilization of the reformed, transcribed Suibne: he is mortally wounded in the back while he is in a prone position, drinking as was his wont his portion of milk out of a pile of cowdung in Moling's monastic compound (ibid., §79). To reattach Suibne to the social body is ultimately to deprive him of his unique voice—and his life.

Yet, just as in Indian myth, where the head of Dadhyañc must be detached and replaced in order for knowledge to spread and tradition to grow, we find in medieval Irish narrative a key instance of "head recovery," in a tale that may have functioned as the *aition* for the scribal tradition itself (see Mac Cana 1970, 62–66; Slotkin 1977–79, 437–40). The warrior Cenn Faelad ('Wolf's Head') receives a serious head wound in the Battle of Mag Rath, a conflict involving the major kings of Ireland. (This in fact is also the battle in which Suibne goes mad, after the saint's curse takes effect.) Hospitalized next door to three separate schools of learning, Cenn Faelad listens to and remembers the instruction given during the day and writes all of it down at night. And so the practice of writing down both secular (or native) and Christian (or Latin) learning flourished in Ireland. Cenn Faelad's remarkable powers of memorization are attributed to his battle injury, for it was his *inchinn dermait*, 'brain of forgetfulness', that was damaged and excised. Here too, then, we have a "head" that leaves the body as the result of a bitter conflict beyond the control of the head's owner: the Battle of Mag Rath, in which Cenn Faelad is only a follower and not a leader. But in this case, the "head" is an eminently forgettable appendage—the mysterious forgetful brain, to which no other reference can be found in Irish tradition. The remaining head, or part of the head, goes on to share in the wisdom and glory of one of the legendary founders of Irish literature. But this is a silent amanuensis of a head, very much attached to the body and dependent upon its arms and hands for writing. Cenn Faelad's is a vital head co-opted by the new medium of writing. No longer itself a source of original communication, the head has become a conduit and repository for what is orally communicated.

In Greek tradition, the singing head similarly rolls up against the monolithic fact of literacy, but here too the scribe and the head live to learn and even benefit from one another. To understand this ideological innovation, it is necessary to explore the murky connection between the figure of Orpheus and so-called Orphism. Perhaps one of the most surprising aspects of this diverse complex of myths, beliefs, and rituals is that it is grounded in the figure of the oral performer par excellence of Greek myth, and yet Orphism is so markedly based on the written word, to the extent that some scholars have argued that there was no such thing in the ancient world as Orphism but only Orphic writings. These were traditionally attributed to Orpheus, who is even credited with the invention of writing in an epigram of uncertain origin (Linforth 1931, 5–11; 1941, 15–16).[19] Devotees of these mystical texts and the ideology behind them were, like the Pythagoreans, a fringe group (see Detienne 1979, 68–94). Followers of the literary Orpheus "chose writing and the book as an effective symbol of their otherness" (Detienne 1987, 113; see also Burkert 1972, 130, n. 55, and 1977b, 2–3, 15). This bookishness is referred to in Euripides's *Hippolytus*, when Theseus denounces his wrongly accused son:

Your current hero is Orpheus,
your days are spent inhaling the holy aroma
from books of arcane absurdity.

(lines 953–54; tr. Bagg 1973, 62)

The irony of Theseus's remarks is notable. Hippolytus, as celibate and even contemptuous of women as the bereaved Orpheus ever was (Tierney 1937, 72–73), has just been implicated in his stepmother's death by a written message she held in her lifeless hand. For the young hunter-devotee of Orpheus and reader of Orphic literature, as for the famous poet and the oral tradition he represents, writing is both a bane and a blessing (see Svenbro 1987, 31, 40, and Segal 1988b, 355–56).

Ivan Linforth observed that the pointed reference to "books of Musaeus [traditionally Orpheus's son] and Orpheus" in the description of the rhetorical arsenal of itinerant priests in Plato's *Republic* (2.364) sets these poets apart from Homer and Hesiod, also mentioned as sources for these priests' "pitches" to potential clients:

> Observe, first, the prominent use of the word βίβλων. . . . One might expect the new sentence to begin Μουσαίου δὲ καὶ ᾿Ορφέως, contrasting these poets with the preceding ones. There seems to be a false emphasis on "books," because one feels the idea to be already latent in the reference to Homer and Hesiod. What is the cause of this emphasis, which, of course, in the language of Plato cannot be false? Two causes can be discerned. In the first place, whereas the poems of Homer and Hesiod, the great classics, are known to the people by heart or through the recitation of rhapsodes, the works of Musaeus and Orpheus are accessible only to the reader, or to the participant in the teletae [purification rituals, often associated with Orphism], who perhaps heard them read. In the second place, the fact that the persons who conducted the teletae used books in some way means that they depended on the sanctity of the written word (Linforth 1941, 77–78).

That the books produced by Orpheus and his son were not only read aloud but traditionally understood to be the result of transcriptions of mystically inspired performances is perhaps suggested by Plato's characterization of this literature as a ὅμαδος βίβλων 'din' or 'hubbub of books' (2.364e; Linforth 1941, 78). In Euripides's *Alcestis* (lines 967–69) the chorus refers to "Thracian boards inscribed by the voice of Orpheus" (Θρήσσαις ἐν σανίσιν, τὰς/᾿Ορφεία κατέγραψεν/γῆρυς). Here again we see a marked, paradoxical juxtaposition of the spoken and the written in connection with this, the greatest of preliterate poets.

Linforth sees a link between Euripides' curious characterization of Orpheus's compositional technique and the tradition, attested in both

Apollonius's *Argonautica* and the Orphic version, that Orpheus dictated his poetry to Musaeus. He also draws attention to the scene, depicted in classical art from the fifth century onwards, of a severed head speaking or singing to a man who is apparently transcribing the head's utterances (ibid., 119–27; Schoeller 1969, 69–71; Graf 1987, 93–94; in one fourth century scene, the head is identified as that of Orpheus). This tableau, a veritable paradigm of the hypothesis that Greek oral poets dictated their performances to scribes and thus "entered" the literary tradition (Lord 1960, 124–26), may have been a symbol of a continuity between oral and written tradition—the latter represented in the tableau by the shadowy figure of Musaeus, whose name indicates his devotion to the Muses, the oral poet's sources of inspiration. The conceit of Orpheus's living, dictating head may also have legitimated the continued production of Orphic writings: just as the severed head lived on, and its utterances were recorded, so too Orpheus lives on in the Orphic writer, inspired to write down what he mystically receives (Linforth 1941, 127–28; cf. Detienne 1986, 1231–34). Here, as in medieval Irish tradition, the singing head or its "owner," mediating between the categories of living and dead, and part and whole, assumes the task of mediating between utterance and text as well. Dumézil, in the article referred to above, noted that the same uneasiness about written, as opposed to oral, tradition which is evident in medieval Celtic cultures can also be found in the classical world (1940, 326–28). He cites Plutarch's life of the Roman king and religious reformer Numa (22.2), in which we learn that before his death Numa ordered that the books in which he had written down sacred lore be buried with him, since he had already imparted their contents to the priests, and he would not want such information to be preserved in the form of "dead letters" (ἐν ἀψύχοις γράμμασι). The ideological impulses behind such avoidance of inanimate script, which according to Plutarch was part of the Pythagorean ethos as well (22.3), were perhaps akin to the less reactionary impulses that generated the image of the singing head performing for the scribe, an icon that preserves the preeminence of the spoken even while recognizing the seemingly final victory of the written.

NOTES

a. Cowgill 1975; Watkins 1975.
b. Benveniste 1969.
c. See the bibliography in Bremmer 1987, 8, n. 5.
d. G. Nagy 1987.
e. Puhvel 1980, 27.
f. Sergent 1979, 1164–67.

g. See the survey of deities in Puhvel 1987, 128–38.

h. Sergent 1979, 1167; Littleton 1980, 148–49; Puhvel 1987, 250–53.

i. Littleton 1973.

j. Sergent 1979, 1179; cf. Boedeker 1983.

k. For a survey of the evidence, see Graf 1987.

1. In the opinion of many, the best introduction to Dumézil's method and find-ings—among his innumerable publications and the many works that have been writ-ten about his achievements—remains Dumézil's *L'idéologie tripartie des Indo-Européens* (1958; see also Desbordes 1981). His published conversation with Didier Eribon, which took place shortly before his death, is a fitting meditation on his life's work (Dumézil 1987). Here, for the last time (199–211), he responded eloquently to the charge leveled in the recent past by Arnoldo Momigliano and Carlo Ginzburg that Dumézil's Indo-European studies were informed by fascist sympathies. The con-troversy was reignited after Dumézil's death by Bruce Lincoln in his review of Du-mézil 1985b, *Times Literary Supplement,* Oct. 3, 1986, pp. 1107–8; see the letter written by Puhvel et al. in response to Lincoln in ibid., Dec. 5, 1986, p.1375.

2. See his 1953 survey and later publications passim (listed in the Bibliography at the end of this chapter). Much of Dumézil's early work, which he later disavowed, centered on Greek myth and religion—e.g., 1924a; 1924b (especially 84–125, 254–64); 1929, 155–93, 241–50. The most up-to-date and thorough survey of Indo-European elements in Greek myth is to be found in Puhvel 1987, 126–43 (see also idem 1980, and Burkert 1977a, 42–48).

3. "There still exists among ourselves an activity which on the technical plane gives us quite a good understanding of what a science we prefer to call 'prior' rather than 'primitive', could have been on the plane of speculation. This is what is com monly called 'bricolage' in French. . . . And in our own time the 'bricoleur' is still someone who works with his hands and uses devious means compared to those of a craftsman. The characteristic feature of mythical thought is that it expresses itself by means of a heterogeneous repertoire which, even if extensive, is nevertheless limited. It has to use this repertoire, however, whatever the task in hand because it has noth-ing else at its disposal. Mythical thought is therefore a kind of intellectual 'brico-lage'." (Lévi-Strauss 1966, 16–17).

4. An excellent critical survey of such comparative studies is presented in Sergent 1979 (see also Littleton 1979 and Rivière et al. 1979, 103–4). Major relevant works published after that date or not covered by Sergent or Littleton are included in the Bibliography (see especially Dumézil 1983 and 1985b).

5. Sergent perceives an Indo-European significance in the distinction between the "Argive" Heracles, whose twelve labors take place "within the Argive sphere of in-fluence," and the Theban Heracles (that is, the Heracles narrative cycle before and beyond the labors). The latter figure is a leader of men in war—that is, an example of the more sociable, "chivalric" aspect of the second function—while the former is a lone slayer of monsters in the outlands, who thus embodies the more savage, un-cooperative end of the martial spectrum (Sergent 1986, 140–42). On this distinction within the second function in myth and epic, see also Dumézil 1970, 53–64; Vian 1968; and G. Nagy 1979, 322–30.

6. On the traditions concerning the success or failure of Orpheus's mission in the underworld, see Lee 1965 and Graf 1987, 81–82; on the contrast implicit in Euripi-

des's *Alcestis* between Orpheus's musicopoetic methods of persuasion in the under-world (lines 357–62) and Heracles' more direct, forceful approach, see Sansone 1985. Hultkrantz (1957, especially pp. 162–271) offers a comparative study of the many appearances of the theme of the rescue of the dead in the world's story traditions.

7. For an accounting of the sources, see Gruppe 1897–1902, 1165–72, and Ziegler 1939, 1293–96. The extant literary accounts of Orpheus's death and references to it are collected in Kern 1963, 33–42. On the pictorial representations of his death in classical art, see Schoeller 1969, 55–59, and Vermeule 1979, 197.

8. Scholars have noted the resemblances among the violent manner of Orpheus's death, wherein his limbs are torn apart and scattered on the ground, the *sparagmos* of Dionysian cult (particularly as it is described in Orphic sources), and fertility rituals in other religious traditions (Frazer 1922, 38–41; Weber 1932, 14–17; Segal 1966, 319). The motif of Orpheus's animate head has been connected by some to the *myths of the Egyptian death-and-resurrection god Osiris, whose head floated to By-blos* after he was torn to pieces (e.g., Gruppe 1897–1902, 1170–71). There is, however, much more to each myth than the single motif of the head floating in a river. Taken as a whole, the story of Orpheus's death is not traceable to the Osiris cycle. See West's comments on the Osiris material and its connections, or lack thereof, to Greek tradition, in 1983, 140–41.

9. An intriguing connection between the tearing-apart of Orpheus and the failure of his attempt to restore his marriage is proposed in Belmont 1985, 78–79.

10. The parallelism of the traditions of Orpheus's singing head and his bones suggests a connection with the "The Singing Bone" oral story pattern, wherein the remains of a wrongly slain victim are made into a musical instrument that proclaims the murderer's guilt; often the instrument is made from a plant that grows on the victim's grave (see Linforth 1941, 134–36; J. Nagy 1986). Clearly of a kind with this tradition is the pattern evinced in the Grimm tale "The Juniper" and elsewhere in which the murdered human becomes a bird that sings of its fate and thus exposes its enemy (ibid.). Not to be discounted in this regard are the reference in Pseudo-Plutarch, *De fluviis* 3.4 to a plant that springs from the blood of Orpheus and produces a lyrelike sound (Kern 1963, 37; see Linforth 1941, 228), and Pausanias's mention of nightingales that hover over his grave, singing with a special sweetness (9.30.3).

11. We learn from Lucian (*Adv. indoct.* 11–12) that Orpheus's lyre, which had accompanied (in both senses of the word) the head to Lesbos, received its own cult, and that in its temple setting it continued to play beautiful music long after its owner's death. One time, however, the son of a tyrant with the aid of a corrupt priest took away the lyre in hopes of becoming a second Orpheus. His wish was ironically granted, for when he struck the lyre, he produced a sound that aroused the nearby dogs to tear him to pieces. Thus the impostor died an Orphic/Bacchic death but, of course, his head did not live on. The intimate link between Orpheus's floating head and his floating lyre, evident in this story concerning the deceased Orpheus's revenge on a wrongdoer by means of his instrument, once again brings to mind elements of "The Singing Bone" (see above).

12. There is, for example, the motif's appearance in the popular African and Afro-American tale known as "The Talking Skull Refuses to Talk," in which the supernat-

ural skull/head's capriciousness often leads to the death of its discoverer. Clearly related to this narrative are others within the African tradition that tell of talking animals (particularly tortoises) that similarly jeopardize the lives of those to whom they reveal themselves (Bascom 1977). In North and South American Indian folklore, we find the vital head in the numerous accounts of vengeful, sometimes plaintively verbal "rolling heads" (Thompson 1929, 162–63, 343; Lévi-Strauss 1981, 140–41). Interestingly, Lévi-Strauss finds that in many South American Indian myths the severed yet vital head is often associated with an "excessive attitude toward marriage," ranging from incest to celibacy (1978, 105–21). As we have seen, Orpheus is the exponent as well as victim of radical sexual attitudes.

The vital head in the Orpheus myth has been interpreted as yet another indication of the "shamanic" nature of Orpheus's powers (Dodds 1951, 147–49; Eliade 1964, 391). On shamanic elements in Greek culture, see Burkert 1962; Dodds 1951, 135–78; and West 1983, 146–50. There is, however, nothing intrinsically linking the motif of the vital head to the only vaguely definable phenomenon of "shamanism" (see Bremmer 1983, 46–47).

13. The importance of heads in Celtic cults and narrative traditions is discussed in Ross 1960 and 1962, and Mac Cana 1987.

14. The seemingly contradictory references to Mímr/Mími/Mímir in Scandinavian literature are outlined in de Vries 1937, 360–62, and Simpson 1962–65a (see also 1962–65b).

15. On the rather obscure figure of Dadhyañc/Dadhīca, see Macdonell 1897, 141–42, and O'Flaherty 1975, 218–20.

16. This is comparable to a later tradition according to which Indra's weapon was made from Dadhyañc's bones, or from his horse's head (Bhattacharji 1970, 240). The power to destroy inherent in Dadhyañc's remains brings to mind the revenge exacted by Orpheus's exposed bones (see above).

17. Another mythological head removed by Indra proves to be vocal: that of the demon Namuci, which rolls after Indra and accuses him of wrongdoing (Śatapatha Brāhmaṇa 5.4.1.9–10).

18. It should be noted that *imbas* boils up from its subterranean source and creates rivers or other bodies of water when women attempt to obtain it (Ford 1974, 69, 72–73). The same effect is achieved in the medieval Irish story of Loch Rí—a well, created by a horse urinating, that overflows spectacularly when a woman neglects to cover it (O'Grady 1892, 1:234, 2:266)—and in the story of Loch Ríach, which threatens to burst after the heads of slain warriors are deposited in it and finally does overflow once it is left uncovered (Gwynn 1913, 326). Perhaps the frenzied behavior of Irish wisdom-laden waters in reaction to the threat of (mostly female) misappropriation is comparable to that of the river Helicon, which according to Pausanias (see above) went underground in an attempt to escape pollution at the hands of the maenads who murdered Orpheus.

19. Orpheus is indirectly responsible for the presence of "writing" or "prewriting" on the bodies of his slayers: according to Phanocles and Plutarch, the Thracian men punished their women for the crime against Orpheus by tattooing them (Kern 1963, 23; on the pictorial motif of tattooed Thracian women and its relation to the Orpheus myth, see Zimmerman 1980, 167–88). Perhaps there is a connection between the markings on the Thracian women and the remarkable tattoos or writing

said to be on the skin of "fringe" mantic figures such as the Cretan Epimenides and the Thracian Zalmoxis (Dodds 1951, 141–42, 163–64, notes 43–44; West 1983, 45–53).

BIBLIOGRAPHY

Note: works that are cited primarily as contributions to the study of Indo-European elements in Greek myth are preceded by an asterisk.

Anderson, W. S. 1982. "The Orpheus of Virgil and Ovid: *flebile nescio quid.*" In Warden 1982, 25–50.

*Aranovsky, Olga R. 1978. "On the Interpretation of the 'Knowledge by Suffering' in Aeschylus, 'Agamemnon'." *JIES* 6:243–62.

Avanzin, Anton von. 1970. "Bemerkungen zum weissagenden Totenkopf." *Carinthia* 1st ser. 160:974–77.

Bascom, William. 1977. "African Folktales in America: 1. The Talking Skull Refuses to Talk." *Research in African Literatures* 8:266–91.

Belmont, Nicole. 1985. "Orphée dans le miroir du conte merveilleux." *L'Homme* 25:59–82.

Benveniste, Emil. 1969. *Le vocabulaire des institutions indo-européennes.* 2 vols. Paris.

Bhattacharji, Sukumari. 1970. *The Indian Theogony: A Comparative Study of Indian Mythology from the Vedas to the Purāṇas.* Cambridge.

*Boedeker, Deborah. 1983. "Hecate: A Transfunctional Goddess in the *Theogony?*" *TAPA* 113:79–93.

Bonnet, Jacques, ed. 1981. *Pour un temps: Georges Dumézil.* Paris.

Bremmer, Jan. 1983. *The Early Greek Concept of the Soul.* Princeton, NJ.

*———. 1987. "What Is a Greek Myth?" In idem, ed., *Interpretations of Greek Mythology.* Beckenham.

*Briquel, Dominique. 1978. "'Mahābhārata', crépuscule des dieux et mythe de Prométhée." *RHR* 193:165–85.

*———. 1983. "Note à propos de l'article de Daniel Dubuisson, 'L'équipement de l'inauguration royale dans l'Inde védique et en Irlande'." *RHR* 200:67–74.

*———. 1983. "Trois recherches sur les traces d'idéologie tripartie en Grèce. A. A propos du Télephe allaité par la biche d'Herculanum. B. Sur la libation aux morts en Grèce. C. Zeus et les fils du Titan Japet: une série trifonctionelle?" *Etudes indo-européennes* 4:37–62; 5:19–33.

*———. 1980. "La 'Theogonie' d'Hésiode. Essai de comparaison indo-européenne." *RHR* 197:243–76.

Burkert, Walter. 1962. "ΓΟΗΣ. Zum griechischen 'Schamanismus'." *RhM* 105:36–55.

———. 1972. *Lore and Science in Ancient Pythagoreanism.* Tr. E. L. Miner, Jr. Cambridge, MA.

———. 1977a. *Griechische Religion.* Vol. 15 in *Die Religionen der Menschheit.* Stuttgart.

——— et al. 1977b. *Orphic and Bacchic Mysteries: New Evidence and Old Problems of Interpretation.* Center for Hermeneutical Studies in Hellenistic and Modern Cultures, Colloquy 28. Berkeley.

*Cardona, George, H. M. Hoenigswald, and Alfred Senn, eds. 1970. *Indo-European and Indo-Europeans. Papers Presented at the Third Indo-European Conference at the University of Pennsylvania.* Philadelphia.

Cohen, David J. 1977. "Suibhne Geilt." *Celtica* 12:113–24.

Colledge, Edmund, and J. C. Marler. 1981. "'Céphalogie': A Recurring Theme in Classical and Mediaeval Lore." *Traditio* 37:411–26.

Coomaraswamy, Ananda K. 1944. "Sir Gawain and the Green Knight: Indra and Namuci." *Speculum* 19:104–25.

Courtright, Paul B. 1985. *Gaṇeśa: Lord of Obstacles, Lord of Beginnings.* New York.

*Cowgill, Warren. 1975. "Indo-European Languages." In *The Encyclopaedia Britannica* 15th ed., Macropaedia 9:431–38.

*Davidson, Olga M. 1980. "The Indo-European Dimension of Herakles in *Iliad* 19:95–133." *Arethusa* 13:197–202.

Deonna, Waldemar. 1923. "Orphée et l'oracle de la tête coupée." *REG* 38:44–69.

Desbordes, Françoise. 1981. "Le comparatisme de Georges Dumézil. Une introduction." In Bonnet 1981, 45–71.

Detienne, Marcel. 1979. *Dionysos Slain.* Tr. Mireille Muellner and Leonard Muellner. Baltimore.

———. 1981. "The Myth of 'Honeyed Orpheus'." In R. L. Gordon, ed. *Myth, Religion, and Society,* 95–109. Cambridge.

———. 1985. "Un polythéisme récrit. Entre Dionysos et Apollon: mort et vie d'Orphée." *Archives de Sciences Sociales des Religions* 59:65–75.

———. 1986. "L'écriture inventive (entre la voix d'Orphée et l'intelligence de Palamède)." *Critique* 42:1225–34.

———. 1987. "Orpheus." Tr. D. M. Weeks. In Eliade 1987, 111–14.

———, ed. 1988. *Les savoirs de l'écriture. En Grèce ancienne.* Cahiers de Philologie Publiés par le Centre de Recherche Philologique de l'Université de Lille III. Vol. 14. Série Apparat critique. Lille.

Dillon, Myles, ed. and tr. 1932. "Stories from the Law-Tracts." *Ériu* 11:42–65.

Dodds, E. R. 1951. *The Greeks and the Irrational.* Berkeley-Los Angeles.

*Dubuisson, Daniel. 1978. "The Apologues of St. Columba and Solon or the 'Third Function' Denigrated." *JIES* 6:231–42.

*———. 1985. "Matériaux pour une typologie des structures trifonctionelles." *L'Homme* 25:105–21.

*Dumézil, Georges. 1924a. *Le crime de Lemniennes. Rites et légendes du monde égéen.* Paris.

*———. 1924b. *Le festin d'immortalité. Etude de myth comparée indo-européenne.* Paris.

*———. 1929. *Le problème des Centaures. Etude de mythologie comparée indo-européenne.* Paris.

———. 1940. "La tradition druidique et l'écriture: le vivant et le mort." In Bonnet 1981, 325–38. (Orig. pub. in *RHR* 122:125–33.)

*———. 1953. "Les trois fonctions dans quelques traditions grecques." In *Hommages à Lucien Febvre,* 25–32. Paris.

*———. 1958. *L'idéologie tripartie des Indo-Européens.* Collection Latomus 31. Brussels.

———. 1961. "Les 'trois fonctions' dans la Rgveda et les dieux indiens de Mitani." *BAB* 47:265–98.

*———. 1968. *Mythe et épopée I. L'idéologie des trois fonctions dans les épopées des peuples indo-européens.* Paris.

*———. 1970. *The Destiny of the Warrior.* Tr. Alf Hiltebeitel. Chicago. (= *Heur et malheur du guerrier* [1969].)

———. 1973. *Gods of the Ancient Northmen.* Ed. Einar Haugen. Berkeley-Los Angeles.

*———. 1982. *Apollon sonore et autres essais.* Paris.

*———. 1983. *The Stakes of the Warrior.* Tr. David Weeks; ed. Jaan Puhvel. Berkeley-Los Angeles. (= Part One of *Mythe et épopée* 2 [1971].)

*———. 1985a. *Heur et malheur du guerrier. Aspects mythiques de la fonction guerrière chez les Indo-Européens.* 2nd ed. Paris.

*———. 1985b. *L'oubli de l'homme et l'honneur des dieux et autres essais.* Paris.

*———. 1987. *Entretiens avec Didier Eribon.* Paris.

Eliade, Mircea. 1964. *Shamanism: Archaic Techniques of Ecstasy.* Tr. Willard R. Trask. Bollingen Series 76. Princeton, NJ.

———, gen. ed. 1987. *Encyclopedia of Religion.* New York.

Euripides. 1973. *Hippolytos.* Tr. Robert Bagg. New York.

*Evans, David. 1974. "Dodona, Dodola, and Daedala." In Larson 1974, 99–130.

*———. 1980. "Agamemnon and the Indo-European Threefold Death Pattern." *HR* 20:153–66.

Ford, Patrick K. 1974. "The Well of Nechtan and 'La Gloire Lumineuse'." In Larson 1974, 67–74.

*Frame, Douglas. 1978. *The Myth of Return in Early Greek Epic.* New Haven, CT.

Frazer, James G. 1922. *The Golden Bough.* Abridged ed. New York.

Graf, Fritz. 1987. "Orpheus: A Poet Among Men." In Bremmer 1987, 80–106.

*Grégoire, Henri. 1949. *Asklépios, Apollon Smintheus, et Rudra. Etudes sur le dieu à la taupe et le dieu au rat dans la Grèce et dans l'Inde.* Memoires de la Académie Royale de Belgique 40. Brussels.

Gruppe, Otto. 1897–1902. "Orpheus." In W. H. Roscher, gen. ed., *Ausführliches Lexikon der Griechischen und Römischen Mythologie.* Vol. 3, pt. 1, 1058–1207. Leipzig.

Guthrie, W. K. C. 1952. *Orpheus and Greek Religion: A Study of the Orphic Movement.* 2nd ed. London.

Gwynn, Edward, ed. and tr. 1913. *The Metrical Dindshenchas.* Vol. 3. Royal Irish Academy Todd Lecture Series 10. Dublin.

*Haudry, Jean. "Les trois cieux." 1982. *Études indo-européennes* 1:23–48.

*———. 1983–84. "Héra." *Études indo-européennes* 6:17–46; 7:1–28.

*———. 1985a. "Deucalion et Pyrrha." *Études indo-européennes* 11:1–12.

*———. 1985b. "Héra et les héros." *Études indo-européennes* 12:1–51.

*———. 1985c. "Traverser l'eau de la tenèbre hivernale." *Études indo-européennes* 13:33–62.

Heesterman, J. C. 1967. "The Case of the Severed Head." *Wiener Zeitschrift für die Kunde Süd- und Ostasiens und Archiv für Indische Philosophie* 11:22–43.

Hultkrantz, Åke. 1957. *The North American Indian Orpheus Tradition. A Contri-*

bution to Comparative Religion. Ethnographical Museum of Sweden, Stockholm, Monograph 2. Stockholm.

*Jong, J. W. de. 1985. "The Over-burdened Earth in India and Greece." *JAOS* 105:397–400.

Kern, Otto, ed. 1963. *Orphicorum Fragmenta*. 2nd ed. Berlin. (Orig. pub. 1922.)

Kittredge, George L. 1916. *A Study of Gawain and the Green Knight*. Cambridge, MA.

Klingbeil, Waldemar. 1932. *Kopf- und Maskenzauber*. Berlin.

*Larson, Gerald J., ed. 1974. In C. Scott Littleton and Jaan Puhvel, eds. *Myths in Indo-European Antiquity*, 99–130. Berkeley-Los Angeles.

Le Roux, Françoise, and Christian-J. Guyonvarc'h. 1986. *Les druides*. 2nd ed. Rennes.

Lee, M. Owen. 1965. "Orpheus and Eurydice: Myth, Legend, Folklore." *C&M* 26:402–12.

Lévi-Strauss, Claude. 1966. *The Savage Mind*. London.

———. 1978. *The Origin of Table Manners: Introduction to a Science of Mythology* 3. Tr. John Weightman and Doreen Weightman. New York.

———. 1981. *The Naked Man: Introduction to a Science of Mythology* 4. Tr. John Weightman and Doreen Weightman. New York.

*Lincoln, Bruce. 1981. "The Lord of the Dead." *HR* 20:224–41.

*———. 1981. *Priests, Warriors, and Cattle: A Study in the Ecology of Religions*. Berkeley-Los Angeles.

*———. 1982a. "Place Outside Space, Moments Outside Time." In Polomé 1982, 67–84.

*———. 1982b. "Waters of Memory, Waters of Forgetfulness." *Fabula* 23:19–34.

*———. 1986. *Myth, Cosmos, and Society: Indo-European Themes of Creation and Destruction*. Cambridge, MA.

Linforth, Ivan M. 1931. "Two Notes on the Legend of Orpheus." *TAPA* 52:5–17.

———. 1941. *The Arts of Orpheus*. Berkeley-Los Angeles.

*Littleton, C. Scott. 1970a. "The 'Kingship in Heaven' Theme." In Puhvel 1970, 83–121.

*———. 1970b. "Some Possible Indo-European Themes in the 'Iliad'." In Puhvel 1970b, 229–46.

*———. 1973. "Poseidon as a Reflex of the Indo-European 'Source of Waters' God." *JIES* 1:423–40.

*———. 1980. "The Problem That Was Greece: Some Observations on the Greek Tradition from the Standpoint of the New Comparative Mythology." *Arethusa* 13:141–59.

*———. 1982. *The New Comparative Mythology: An Anthropological Assessment of the Theories of Georges Dumézil*. 3rd ed. Berkeley-Los Angeles.

Lord, Albert B. 1960. *The Singer of Tales*. Harvard Studies in Comparative Literature 24. Cambridge, MA.

Lucian. 1927. *Lucian*. Vol. 1. Tr. A. M. Harmon. Cambridge, MA.

Mac Cana, Proinsias. 1970. "The Three Languages and the Three Laws." *Studia Celtica* 5:62–78.

———. 1987. "The Celtic Head Cult." In Eliade 1987, 225–26.

Macdonell, Arthur A. 1897. *Vedic Mythology*. Grundriss der indo-arischen Philologie und Altertumskunde 3 1 A. Strassburg.

*McGrath, W. T. 1975. "The Athenian King List and Indo-European Trifunctionality." *JIES* 3:173–94.

*Melia, Daniel F. 1979. "Some Remarks on the Affinities of Medieval Irish Saga." *AAntHung* 27:255–61.

Meslin, Michel. 1987. "Head." Tr. Kristine Anderson. In Eliade 1987, 221–25.

Meyer, Kuno, ed. 1912. *Cormac's Glossary from the Yellow Book of Lecan. Anecdota from Irish Manuscripts* 4. Ed. Osborn Bergin et al. Halle.

*Miller, D. A. 1977. "A Note on Aegisthus as 'Hero'." *Arethusa* 10:259–65.

*Nagy, Gregory. 1979. *The Best of the Achaeans: Concepts of the Hero in Archaic Greek Poetry*. Baltimore.

*———. 1980. "Patroklos, Concepts of Afterlife, and the Indic Triple Fire." *Arethusa* 13:161–96.

*———. 1981. "Essai sur Georges Dumézil et l'étude de l'épopée grecque." In Bonnet 1981, 137–46.

*———. 1987. "The Indo-European Heritage of Tribal Organization: Evidence from the Greek *Polis*." In S. N. Skomal and Edgar C. Polomé, eds., *Proto-Indo-European: The Archaeology of a Linguistic Problem: Studies in Honor of Marija Gimbutas*. Washington, DC, 245–66.

Nagy, Joseph F. 1986. "Vengeful Music in Traditional Narrative." *Folklore* 95:182–90.

O'Keeffe, J. G., ed and tr. 1913. *Buile Suibhne (The Frenzy of Suibhne)*. Irish Texts Society 13. London.

O'Flaherty, Wendy D., tr. 1975. *Hindu Myths: A Sourcebook Translated from the Sanskrit*. Harmondsworth, UK.

*———. 1980a. "Dionysus and Śiva: Parallel Patterns in Two Pairs of Myths." *HR* 20:81–111.

*———. 1980b. *Women, Androgynes, and Other Mythical Beasts*. Chicago.

O'Grady, Standish Hayes, ed. and tr. 1892. *Silva Gadelica*. 2 vols. London.

*Oosten, Jarich G. 1985. *The War of the Gods: The Social Code in Indo-European Mythology*. London.

O'Rahilly, Cecille, ed. and tr. 1967. *Táin Bó Cúalnge from the Book of Leinster*. Dublin.

———. 1976. *Táin Bó Cúailnge. Recension I*. Dublin.

Pausanias. 1971. *Guide to Greece*. Tr. Peter Levi. 2 vols. Harmondsworth, UK.

Philostratus. 1960. *The Life of Apollonius of Tyana*. Tr. F. C. Conybeare. 2 vols. Cambridge, MA.

*Polomé, Edgar C., ed. 1982. *Homage to Georges Dumézil*. JIES Monograph 3. Washington, DC.

*Pralon, Didier. 1981. "Le modèle triparti dans la philosophie grecque du IVe siècle AC." In Bonnet 1981, 121–36.

*Puhvel, Jaan. 1970a. "Aspects of Equine Functionality." In Puhvel 1970b, 159–72.

*———, ed. 1970b. *Myth and Law among the Indo-Europeans*. Berkeley-Los Angeles.

*———. 1970c. "Mythological Reflections of Indo-European Medicine." In Cardona et al. 1970, 369–82.

*———. 1980. "The Indo-European Strain in Greek Myth." In Stanley M. Burstein and Louis A. Okin, eds., *Panhellenica: Essays in Ancient History and Historiography in Honor of Truesdell S. Brown*, 25–30. Lawrence, KS.

*———. 1982. "The Warrior at Stake." In Polomé 1982, 25–33.

*———. 1987. *Comparative Mythology*. Baltimore.

Rees, Alwyn, and Brinley Rees. 1961. *Celtic Heritage: Ancient Tradition in Ireland and Wales*. London.

*Rivière, Jean-Claude, et al. 1979. *Georges Dumézil à la découverte des Indo-Européens*. Paris.

Robbins, Emmet. 1982. "Famous Orpheus." In Warden 1982, 3–23.

Ross, Anne. 1960. "The Human Head in Insular Pagan Celtic Religion." *Proceedings of the Society of Antiquaries of Scotland* 91:14–43.

———. 1962. "Severed Heads in Wells: An Aspect of the Well Cult." *Scottish Studies* 6:31–48.

Royal Irish Academy. 1983. *Dictionary of the Irish Language*. Compact ed. Dublin.

Sansone, David. 1985. "Orpheus and Eurydice in the Fifth Century." *C&M* 36:53–64.

Schoeller, Felix M. 1969. *Darstellungen des Orpheus in der Antike*. Freiburg.

Schwartz, Ella. 1984. *Aspects of Orpheus in Classical Literature and Mythology*. Ph.D. Diss. Cambridge, MA.

Segal, Charles P. 1966. "Orpheus and the Fourth *Georgic:* Vergil on Nature and Civilization." *AJP* 87:307–55.

———. 1988a. *Orpheus: The Myth of the Poet*. Baltimore.

———. 1988b. "Vérité, tragédie et écriture." In Detienne 1988, 330–58.

*Sergent, Bernard. 1976. "La représentation spartiate de la royauté." *RHR* 189:3–52.

*———. 1977–78. "Le partage du Péloponnèse entre les Héraklides." *RHR* 192:121–36; 193:3–25.

*———. 1979. "Les trois fonctions des Indo-Européens dans la Grèce ancienne: bilan critique." *Annales (ESC)* 34:1155–86.

*———. 1980. "L'utilisation de la trifonctionalité d'origine indo-européenne chez les auteurs grecs classiques." *Arethusa* 13:233–78.

*———. 1984. "Three Notes on the Trifunctional Indo-European Marriage." *JIES* 12:179–91.

*———. 1986. *Homosexuality in Greek Myth*. Tr. Arthur Goldhammer. Boston.

Simpson, Jacqueline. 1962–65a. "Mímir: Two Myths or One?" *Saga-Book of the Viking Society for Northern Research* 16:41–53.

———. 1962–65b. "A Note on the Folktale Motif of the Heads in the Well." Ibid., 248–50.

Slotkin, Edgar M. 1977–79. "Medieval Irish Scribes and Fixed Texts." *Éigse* 17:437–50.

Sterckx, Claude. 1981. *La tête et les sens: la mutilation rituelle des enemis et le concept de l'âme*. Forschungen zur Anthropologie und Religionsgeschichte 6. Saarbrücken.

Stokes, Whitley, ed. and tr. 1891. "The Irish Ordeals, Cormac's Adventure in the Land of Promise, and the Decision as to Cormac's Sword." In Stokes and E. Windisch, eds., *Irische Texte* 3.1, 183–229. Leipzig.

*Strutynski, Udo. 1970. "The Three Functions of Indo-European Tradition in the 'Eumenides' of Aeschylus." In Puhvel 1970b, 211–28.

*———. 1980. "Ares: A Reflex on the Indo-European War God?" *Arethusa* 13:217–32.

Svenbro, Jesper. 1987. "The 'Voice' of Letters in Ancient Greece. On Silent Reading and the Representation of Speech." *Culture and History* 2:31–47.

Thompson, Stith, ed. 1929. *Tales of the North American Indians*. Bloomington, IN.

———. 1955–57. *Motif-Index of Folk Literature*. 6 vols. Bloomington, IN.

Tierney, Michael. 1937. "The *Hippolytus* of Euripides." *PRIA* 44.C.2:59–74.

Vermeule, Emily. 1987. *Aspects of Death in Early Greek Art and Poetry*. Sather Classical Lectures 46. Berkeley-Los Angeles.

*Vernant, Jean-Pierre. 1965. *Mythe et pensée chez les Grecs*. Paris.

*———. 1980. *Myth and Society in Ancient Greece*. Tr. Janet Lloyd. Sussex, UK.

*Vian, Francis. 1952. *La guerre des Géants. Le mythe avant l'époque hellénistique*. Paris.

*———. 1960. "La triade des rois d'Orchomène: Etéoclès, Phlégyas, Minyas." *Hommages à Georges Dumézil*. Collection Latomus 45. Brussels.

*———. 1963. *Les origines de Thèbes. Cadmos et les Spartes*. Paris.

*———. 1968. "La fonction guerrière dans la mythologie grecque." In Jean-Pierre Vernant, ed., *Problèmes de la guerre en Grèce ancienne*. Paris.

Vries, Jan de. 1937. *Altgermanische Religiongeschichte. 2. Religion der Nordgermanen*. Berlin.

*———. 1977. *Perspectives in the History of Religions*. Tr. Kees W. Bolle. Berkeley-Los Angeles. (Orig. pub. as *The Study of Religion: A Historical Approach*.)

*Walcot, P. 1979. "Cattle Raiding, Heroic Tradition, and Ritual. The Greek Evidence." *HR* 18:326–51.

*Ward, Donald J. 1968. *The Divine Twins: An Indo-European Myth in Germanic Tradition*. University of California Press Folklore Studies 19. Berkeley-Los Angeles.

Warden, John, ed. 1982. *Orpheus: The Metamorphosis of Myth*. Toronto.

*Watkins, Calvert. 1970. "Studies in Indo-European Legal Language, Institutions, and Mythology." In Cardona et al. 1970, 321–54.

*———. 1975. "Indo-European and the Indo-Europeans." In William Morris, ed., *The American Heritage Dictionary of the English Language*, 1496–1502. Boston.

Weber, Leo. 1932. "Orpheus." *RhM* 81:1–19.

West, M. L. 1983. *The Orphic Poems*. Oxford.

*Yoshida, Atsuhiko. 1964. "Survivances de la tripartition fonctionelle en Grèce." *RHR* 165:21–38.

Ziegler, Konrat. 1939. "Orpheus." *RE* 18(1): 1200–1316.

Zimmerman, Konrad. 1980. "Tätowierte Thrakerinnen auf griechischen Vasenbildern." *JDAI* 95:163–96.

5

GREEK MYTHOLOGY
AND FOLKLORE

Folktales in the *Odyssey* are an old subject in classical scholarship,[a] and there is general agreement on their presence in the epic. Hansen has found a new one (which he calls a "story"), on which he has already published important articles. His contribution here brings together and extends the previous work. He calls the story, "The Sailor and the Oar," and he has collected twenty-six modern texts of it. On the basis of this collection, he constructs a type and divides it into two subtypes, which he compares with *Odyssey* 11.121–34, where Tiresias gives Odysseus instructions for his return to Ithaca. Upon his return, Odysseus must carry an oar inland until he reaches a people ignorant of the sea. There he must plant the oar in the ground and sacrifice to Poseidon. Then he will return home. Tiresias's instructions are a mixture of injunction and prophecy.

Twelve of Hansen's texts (his Subtype A) are narratives in the past tense. Hansen shows that the Tiresias form of this material can be understood as the transposition of a narrative of a past event into the future. The principal difference between the two forms of the narrative, between the ancient and the modern, is the shift from the dangerous sea to the hostile god as the motive for the inland journey. With this change, the epic poet can adapt the story, or prophecy, to the larger pattern of Odysseus's life, as it was handed down in the epic tradition. Hansen's comparative approach to the passage in the *Odyssey* provides answers to several of the questions classicists have raised.

The point in Hansen's article that may provoke controversy is also the most fundamental one: the modern tradition of the Sailor and the Oar cannot derive from the *Odyssey;* rather, the modern tradition goes back to an old story that Homer knew and adapted, as he is believed to have adapted various folktales.[b] The notion that oral stories recorded in the nineteenth or twentieth centuries can belong to a tradition going back to Homer's times can be difficult or even threatening. Can it be that peasants and uneducated persons in our times are in possession of

the same stories that are consecrated in the great works of Greek literature?

This indignant question rests on two kinds of objections. The first
concerns the apparently exclusive difference between the myths and
hero legends used by the Greek poets and the simpler, less serious modern folktales that are introduced as comparanda. (Here I shall state the
matter in terms of "myth" and "folktale.") This objection disappears,
however, as soon as it is realized that there is no clear dividing line between myth and folktale, that the same narrative elements may appear
in both at the same time among the same people.*c* Robert Mondi's methodological statements (in Chapter 2) may be relevant here.

The fluid relationship between myth and folktale also removes two
other common notions: that folktales are earlier than myths; that folktales are later than myths. Both notions are still current. On the one
hand, scholars identify certain motifs in Greek myths as *altes Märchen-
gut,*d* or even argue for the total reshaping of a folktale into a myth, as
M. P. Nilsson did in the case of the Oedipus myth.*e* On the other, they
regard folktales as one of the "debased forms of originally mythical narrative" which consists of "footloose motifs" that (annoyingly?) have an
international character.*f*

The other objection concerns the lack of evidence for oral transmission of folktales from antiquity up to the present: it is held that such a
transmission is simply indemonstrable. The most adamant exponent of
this view is Detlev Fehling. He sets two (as he says, almost mutually
contradictory) conditions for proof of transmission.*g* First, there would
have to be an old document proving that the material under discussion
existed at a particular time in the past. Second, there would have to be
proof that no one had read this document because a later reader could
have introduced its contents into oral circulation.

At first glance, these conditions seem reasonable, no matter how severe they may be. How else could one be absolutely certain that an ancient story had persisted into modern times through word of mouth?
But reflection will show that the conditions are completely unreason-
able. What is to be demonstrated is an *oral* tradition. To ask for written
documentation of such a tradition at its very beginning is in contradiction to the very nature of the material to be explained. Oral tradition
must be inferred, in the first place, from the material itself, just as Milman Parry did in his argument for the oral background of the *Iliad* and
the *Odyssey*. In the application of modern folkloristic materials to
Greek myths, two procedures are called for: the construction of a typology on the basis of the modern material and the application of that ty-

pology to the ancient myth or text. Hansen has provided a demonstration of these procedures.

Odysseus and the Oar: A Folkloric Approach

WILLIAM F. HANSEN

The comparative method, a classic approach to folk narrative (Dégh 1986), is the principal method of inquiry employed in this essay. But I also draw upon other folkloric methods, especially the contextual approach, which has been little used in the study of ancient oral narratives. As I hope to illustrate, these two techniques have the advantage of bringing the investigator very close to the dynamics of the living story and to the people for whom the story has meaning, and of avoiding some of the snares that occasionally entangle investigators who employ more speculative approaches to oral narrative.

In applying the comparative method to ancient materials, one usually brings together a particular ancient text or story with as many other texts of the same type as are available and compares their contents or structures. Naturally, the comparison is informative only if the comparative texts offer something the target text does not. One may confront an ancient text with similar texts that are known to derive from oral tradition, for instance, in order to demonstrate that the ancient text also reflects an oral story. Wilhelm Grimm compared Homer's narrative of Odysseus and Polyphemus (*Od.* 9.105–566) with nine similar texts from more recent tradition (Grimm 1857). He concluded that Homer's account of Odysseus and the Cyclops represents a version of an oral tale that was current in Homer's time and has survived, independently of Homer, in a widespread, international tradition.

The technique of comparing different versions of the same tale type was eventually systematized into the historic-geographic method, a technique employed by folktale scholars in an effort to learn the origin and history of particular oral tales (Krohn 1971; Goldberg 1984). The Polyphemus legend and its analogues were the subject of a historic-geographic study in which more than two hundred texts from many countries were gathered and summarized (Hackman 1904). The chief monument to the historic-geographic enterprise is Aarne-Thompson's *Types of the Folktale* (1961), which classifies a large number of stories in oral circulation from Europe to India. The Polyphemus story, for example, appears there as Type 1137. Pattern studies are another elaboration of the comparative method. The researcher abstracts the shared features of a group of narratives in order to demonstrate that they are genetically related (Fontenrose 1959; Taylor 1964).

Finally, when one wishes to evaluate the treatment of a folk narrative by a Greek author, the comparative texts can serve as a control, as when Denys Page and Justin Glenn each draw upon comparative studies of the Polyphemus story in their investigations of Homer's use of the story (Page 1955, 1–30; Glenn 1971). Another form of this technique is to fill in the lacunae of a fragmentary narrative, or to clarify the meaning of a difficult one, by comparing it with less problematic texts, as James George Frazer, following Wilhelm Mannhardt, does for the imperfectly known myth of the marriage of Peleus and Thetis (Frazer 1921, 2: 383–88).

THE SAILOR AND THE OAR

In what follows I draw upon a corpus of twenty-six texts of the Sailor and the Oar that I have gathered from published sources and from oral informants. Except for the passage in Homer, the texts were all collected in the nineteenth and twentieth centuries. It is uncommon to come upon many early texts of folk narratives, inasmuch as the systematic transcription of oral stories began only in the nineteenth century. (On the Greek collections see Roderick Beaton [1986].) Since the texts are generally short, many of them will be quoted in full, although there is insufficient space to give them all. A complete list of the texts and their sources appears at the end of this essay.

I begin with a sample of nine texts.

1   They say about St. Elias that he was a seaman and served all his life as a
    captain on ships. He experienced great storms, and in one frightful
    storm his ship sank and all except for him were drowned. Getting hold
    then of the oar of a boat, St. Elias managed to reach the mainland. Disgusted, however, with his sufferings at sea, he withdrew far inland. With
    his oar on his shoulder he began going forward, and whomever he met
    on the road he asked, "What is this?" And whenever they said, "An
    oar," he understood that these people knew of the sea. And he kept
    moving on in order to go further inland. In this manner one day he
    reached a little village built on the top of a mountain. He gathered the
    villagers, showed them the oar, and asked them, "What is this?" With
    one voice they all answered, "A piece of wood." These people had never
    seen the sea, ships, and boats. For this reason he remained with them

forever. And from that time the chapels of St. Elias have always been built on mountain tops.

2 St. Elias was once a seaman. On account of his endless rowing, the man got tired (rowing while eating, that's the way they had it in those days). He put his oar on his shoulder and left to go to find a place where they didn't even know the name of it. He walks to the village, he asks, "What is this called?" "An oar," they say. He walks to another village, he asks, "What is this called?" "An oar." What the devil! He became desperate. Keeping on with his inquiry he finally asks at one village situated at the very top of the mountain, "What is this called?" "A piece of wood." Thank God! He sets the oar straight up, builds a hut, and resolves to remain there for the rest of his life. For this reason they always put St. Elias on mountaintops.

3 Saint Elias was a seaman and lived a dissolute life. But afterwards he repented of what he had done and detested the sea. Others say that because he suffered much at sea and many times came near to drowning, he became disgusted with his voyages and resolved to go to a place where they did not know what the sea was and what ships were. So he puts his oar on his shoulder and steps out onto dry land, and whomever he met he asked what it was he was carrying. So long as people answered, "An oar," he kept moving higher and higher. Finally he reached the top of a mountain. He asks the people whom he found there what it is, and they tell him, "A piece of wood." He understood then that they had never in their life seen an oar, and he remained there with them on the heights.

4 Wishing to explain why on almost every mountaintop there stands a chapel in the name of St. Elias, the folk tell different legends. From many such legends we report one unpublished Paxian legend reported by Dem. Loukatos from the narration of D. Kontares.
   "Are we going fishing?"
   "Hey, I'm not going anywhere. I'm going to do what St. Elias did. I'm going to put my oars on my shoulder.
   "St. Elias was a seaman and got so tired of the seaman's life—at that time they did not have engines and sails, only an oar—that he put his oars on his shoulder and said, 'I'm not coming back to the sea.' And he went to the highest mountain. For which reason, all the churches of the prophet Elias that exist are also on mountains. (I don't remember the conversation with the villagers.)"

5 It is said that an English seaman once became so weary at heart from the dangerous uneasiness of his profession that when he returned to his home port he put an oar on his shoulder and wandered inland in search of people who did not know the wild sea. He went from place to place

with his burden and lingered nowhere until he came to a village where they asked him what kind of strange implement he was carrying; there he settled down. The parable is found here and there in old sea stories, where shipwrecked persons narrate it to their companions as a consolation, and tormented and discouraged seafolk swear to one another to follow its example if they should ever touch foot again on English soil.

6 The story, as I remember it, goes roughly like this, that there was an old sailor in the United States Navy—presumably, since the story took place on the East Coast of the U.S. He put in his thirty years, and took his retirement option, and set out walking down the gangplank with a gunnysack over one shoulder and carrying an oar over the other shoulder, and headed due west inland, and walked somewhere through New Jersey or so, and happened to pass someone standing along the road who waved to him and said, "Where're you going with that oar over your shoulder?" And he just nodded, and barely looked at the person who greeted him in this fashion, and marched on heading westward, and traveled further and further inland.

At some point in the middle of, say, Ohio or Indiana, he passed someone else alongside the road who waved at him, greeted him, and yelled as he passed by, "Hey, where're you going with that rower over your shoulder?" And he just sort of barely met eyes with the person who greeted him in this fashion, and kept on walking.

And sometime further along the way, perhaps around Nebraska somewhere, he passed someone along the side of the road who said to him something to the effect of, "Hey, mister, what on earth are you carrying that piece of lumber over your shoulder for?" And a grin slowly broke across his face, and he stamped his foot and said, "This is where I'm settling down." And that's the end of the story.

7 "I've lived here all my life and I've worked on the water and I'm getting kind of sick of it all. When I retire I'm gonna go and go until somebody asks me what that is I've got in my hand. Then I'll say, 'You don't know what an oar is?' And if he says, 'No,' I'm gonna throw my oars away and let that rowboat go with the tide, and then I'm gonna spend the rest of my life right there."

8 "When this hooker gets to port I'm goin' to put an oar over my shoulder and I'm goin' to start walkin' 'way from saltwater. I'm goin' to keep right on walkin' until some hairlegger says to me, 'What's that funny stick you have on your shoulder, matey?' an' right there I'm goin' to settle down and dig potaters."

9 "I'm gonna put this goddam oar over my shoulder," a weary seine hauler snorts, "and head west, and the first sonofabitch asks me what it is, that's where I stick it in the ground and settle."

The Sailor and the Oar is an international story type with a modest distribution. In my texts the narrators are Greek, British, or American, though of course it is quite possible that additional collecting would reveal a wider distribution.

In the exemplary modern texts given above, a sailor who is unhappy with the sea takes an oar and walks inland with the oar on his shoulder until he finally meets someone who does not know what it is, and there he settles down. This is the essence of the story. Different tellings, including Homer's from around 700 B.C., are elaborations or abbreviations of these basic events, the result of such factors as the form of the story known to the narrator, the narrator's competence, and contextual conditions. For example, the storyteller's competence is a factor in Text 4, in which the narrator knows that he does not recall all the details of the story and acknowledges his omission to the collector.

A close examination of the sample texts reveals that they fall into two groups. On the one hand, Texts 1–6 tell of a past event: after suffering at sea, a mariner one day walked inland carrying an oar (or oars) until he encountered a man (or a community) who did not know what the oar was, and there the mariner settled down. On the other hand, Texts 7–9 promise a future event: the narrator (who is a mariner) says he will one day take an oar and walk inland until he meets a man who does not know what the oar is, and there he will settle down. Stories in the former group are told in the third person about events that already have taken place; stories in the latter group are told in the first person, and the events still lie in the future.

Since this basic distinction characterizes all the texts of this story, each narrative belonging to one group or the other, I shall divide the tale type into two subtypes, labeling the former as A and the latter as B. Approximately half of my texts belong to each group. Perhaps we can learn something of the historical relationship between the two branches of the tradition from Text 4, in which a narration of Subtype A is preceded by the following conversation between folklorist and narrator:

> "Are we going fishing?"
> "I'm not going anywhere. I'm going to do like Saint Elias: I shall put my oar on my shoulder. Saint Elias was a seaman and became so wearied of nautical life. . . ."

The narrator's declaration that he himself intends to follow the example of the protagonist in the legend suggests how a narrative told in the third person preterite might give rise to one told in the first person future. Similarly, we read in another text that tormented and discouraged seafolk swear to follow the example of the sailor who went inland if

they should ever reach their homeland again (Text 5). So it may have
happened that Subtype A gave rise at some unknown time in the past to
Subtype B.

ODYSSEUS AND THE OAR

The story of the mariner and the oar is first mentioned in a passage
in Homer's *Odyssey* (11.121–34), where Tiresias tells Odysseus about
the quest he will undertake after he returns to Ithaca:

10   "Take a well-shaped oar and go
           until you reach men who do not know of the sea
           and who eat food that is not mixed with salt:
           they know neither of red-cheeked ships
           nor of well-shaped oars, which are the wings of ships.
           I'll tell you a very clear sign, and you won't miss it:
           when you come across another man on the road
           who says that you have a chaff-wrecker on your shining shoulder,
           then plant the well-shaped oar in the earth
           and perform a fine sacrifice to lord Poseidon—
           a ram, a bull, and a boar, mounter of sows.
           Then return home and sacrifice holy hecatombs
           to the immortal gods, who dwell in the broad sky,
           to all of them in order."

When Odysseus consults the seer Tiresias about his return from Troy
to Ithaca, the seer reveals that (1) the god Poseidon is angry with Odysseus and will make Odysseus's return difficult; (2) Odysseus will come
to the island of Thrinacia, where he must leave unharmed the cattle of
the Sun, else his companions and ships will suffer destruction; (3) if he
himself survives, he will find his home beset with suitors, whom however he will kill; (4) then he should take an oar and go inland until he
discovers men who are unacquainted with the sea and perform there a
sacrifice to Poseidon; finally (5) he will die away from the sea (11.100–
137).

Tiresias's speech is an oracular catalogue of important events to follow in Odysseus's life. Accordingly, the seer foretells (with a mixture, as
appropriate, of future tenses, conditional sentences, and imperatives)
stories that otherwise would be narrated as past events. Several of the
same stories (1–3) are subsequently renarrated by the poet in the usual
past tense in their proper chronological slots in the epic. The future setting of these stories is therefore an incidental trait of the present passage
rather than an intrinsic property of the stories themselves. Conse-

quently, Odysseus and the Oar is really a past narrative that happens to have a future setting in the *Odyssey*. It belongs with the stories of Sub-type A.

Transformed back into the past, the Homeric passage would read as follows.

> Odysseus took a well-shaped oar and went
> until he reached men who did not know of the sea
> and who ate food that was not mixed with salt:
> they knew neither of red-cheeked ships
> nor of well-shaped oars, which are the wings of ships.
> There was a very clear sign, and he did not miss it:
> when he came across another man on the road
> who said that he had a chaff-wrecker on his shining shoulder,
> then he planted the well-shaped oar in the earth
> and performed a fine sacrifice to lord Poseidon—
> a ram, a bull, and a boar, mounter of sows.
> Then he returned home and sacrificed holy hecatombs
> to the immortal gods, who dwell in the broad sky,
> to all of them in order.

Although the passage can simply enough be put back into its past setting, it is not completely reversible because Homer's recasting the story as a future event undoubtedly involved more than adjusting the tenses. It must also have involved his economizing some details of the legend because incidental details, which are natural enough in a story of the past, can seem awkward when set in the future. For example, Homer mentions no details of Odysseus's quest other than the climactic encounter with the inlander who mistakes his oar for something else.

Brief though it is, the Homeric passage has proven to be a difficult text to understand. Scholars have wondered why Odysseus must undertake a quest for men who are ignorant of the sea. What, moreover, is the point of their eating unsalted food? Why must Odysseus seek them out by means of an oar? And why must he plant it in the ground? Must the inlander call Odysseus's oar precisely a "chaff-wrecker"? Is the adventure connected with the way Odysseus will die? And so on.

Attaching the story of the Sailor and the Oar to a traditional character whose nature or biography is already established in people's minds must inevitably condition the form of the story that results, if only a little. In the case of the etiology that is regularly appended to the St. Elias legend, the effect is palpable though modest; the events of the story are affected only in that Elias must always settle on a mountaintop, for that is where his chapels are in fact located. The established traditions that were associated with Odysseus in antiquity were more complex than those connected with St. Elias or St. Nikolaos (of whom the story is also told, e.g., Text 22) in modern Greece, and their effect upon the form of Odysseus and the Oar was greater. For one thing, Odysseus had a wife, to whom he would wish to return, and a kingdom, which happened to be insular. There could be no inland sanctuary for Odysseus, at least not for the Odysseus of Homer's *Odyssey*.

Furthermore, Homer refuses to leave off his poems without reconciliation, or the promise of it, for his principal characters. Odysseus has angered the god Poseidon by blinding his son Polyphemus. If Odysseus were made to escape from the wrath of the sea deity by seeking out and remaining at a community far removed from the sea, Poseidon's hostility would abide, and the tension between the two would remain unresolved. No, the hero and his divine opponent must come to terms.

And yet they must not come to terms immediately. Homer introduces the idea of Poseidon's hostility toward Odysseus because he wishes to exploit the tension of this relationship in his epic; therefore, it would not serve his purpose to permit Odysseus to placate the marine god straightaway. Homer informs Odysseus in Book Eleven of the god's hostility toward him and of the eventual necessity of his placating Poseidon, but the poet wants to delay this reconciliation until the end of the epic, when the god's anger has served its purpose. Homer accomplishes this by ensuring that Odysseus cannot meet the necessary conditions at the time when he is informed of them. The obligation of undertaking a major mainland journey, implied by the condition that the god must be honored among a people who are totally ignorant of the sea, effectively postpones the sacrifice until after the hero's return to Ithaca and the nearby Greek mainland.

So Odysseus will eventually have to make peace with Poseidon and in the end will return to his island kingdom, whereas the mariner in the Sailor and the Oar seeks to escape, not to placate, the power of the sea and ultimately remains in his inland sanctuary. It might appear that the strategies of the epic poet together with the established givens of Odysseus's biography would make impossible any use of the story of the Sailor and the Oar in connection with Odysseus. But a significant substitution in the form of the story makes it possible: Odysseus's demon takes the form not of the sea but rather of the Sea, personalized as Poseidon, Lord of the Sea. This subtle shift from dangerous sea to hostile sea god is the principal difference between the Odyssean form of the story and the ordinary tradition.

Still, why should Odysseus make a prodigious effort to sacrifice to the Lord of the Sea at a place where men have never heard of the sea or, we assume, of its divine ruler? But that is the very point, as a scholiast long ago observed. He explains that the best way to do honor to a man or a god who is already honored in one place is to bring it about that he also receives honor in another place. Thus, Odysseus brings knowledge of Poseidon, that is, of his cult, to mainlanders who know nothing of the sea, so that Poseidon can be honored also as Poseidon *epeirotes,* 'Poseidon of the Land' (schol. V *Od.* 11.121, 130; Eustathius *ad. Od.,* p. 1675.30–35). It is this gesture that reconciles Odysseus and Poseidon. Having placated the Lord of the Sea, Odysseus need never again fear the sea wherever he may subsequently settle. Like Elias and the rest, Odysseus achieves permanent relief from the threats of the sea, but unlike them he is not bound to his inland sanctuary. Reconciled to the god of sea and storm, Odysseus is free to return home. The consequence of his quest is therefore functionally, but not formally, identical to that of the mariner who settles down away from the sea.

It is then an easy step to infer, as many scholars have done, that what we have here is the foundation legend of one or more inland sanctuaries of Poseidon, an etiological narrative purporting to account for a phenomenon that some might find curious: the existence of shrines of Poseidon out of sight or sound of the sea (Hansen 1977, 32–33). The Greek traveler Pausanias (8.44.4) describes the remains of such a shrine, a temple of Poseidon and Athena said to have been built by Odysseus after his return from Troy. It stood atop Mt. Boreium in Arcadia. Ancient tradition identified Odysseus's inlanders with a number of different inland communities in western Greece. These were located in Arcadia (the land-locked Arcadians had to sail on borrowed ships to get to Troy [Homer, *Il.* 2.603–14] and were the inlanders par excellence of the Greek world), in Epirus (the name means simply 'Land' or 'Mainland'), and in places whose sites are no longer known (Hansen 1977, 33).

SUBTYPE A

The texts of Subtype A usually begin with the introduction of the protagonist, who in modern Greece is regularly St. Elias or St. Nikolaos and in anglophone countries is an unnamed mariner.

The Cause of the Mariner's Departure. Most frequently, the mariner's departure is motivated by the dangers of the seafaring life. Seven texts mention storms, shipwreck, misfortunes, or fear of the sea (for example, Texts 1 and 3). A couple of texts cite instead the hard work that used to be part of the seaman's trade, especially the incessant rowing (Texts 2 and 4), and one text mentions that the seaman had once lived a dissolute life, which he later repented, and as a result detested the sea (Text 3). (Since some texts are defective, we do not always know the mariner's motive.) Although it does not matter what precisely the mariner's motivation is, the meaning of his quest is determined by his reason for leaving the sea. Most commonly he wants relief from the dangers of the sea.

Although Odysseus's enemy is not the sea but the Lord of the Sea, the effect on him is the same, since Poseidon expresses his hostility in the form of sea storms. Angry at Odysseus, he creates a terrible storm expressly for him, wrecking his boat and causing him to spend two days and nights amid the wreckage until he manages to come ashore at the land of the Phaeacians (5.282–493). Storms and shipwreck therefore precede Odysseus's inland journey. Perhaps in some versions of the ancient legend they were the immediate cause of Odysseus's quest, but in our *Odyssey* the immediate cause seems to be Tiresias's informing Odysseus of the god's anger and telling him how to deal with it.

The Oar. The sailor then takes an oar (or two oars), which he is usually said to carry on his shoulder, and proceeds to walk inland.

The Mariner's Goal. Usually the narrator makes explicit what the mariner's intent is. The two favored sites for revealing this information are at the onset of the quest and at its conclusion. Texts 2 and 3 exemplify the former strategy: "He put his oar on his shoulder and left to go to find a place where they didn't even know the name of it" (Text 2); while in other texts the storyteller climactically witholds the explanation until the mariner has successfully completed his quest (e.g., Text 1). The Homeric text exemplifies the former strategy. Odysseus's intent is given from the first: to locate men who are ignorant of the sea, ships, and oars, and who eat unsalted food, which is to say, men who are so removed from the sea that they are ignorant not only of the sea but also of things that people commonly associate with the sea, such as ships, oars, and salt.

Particularly interesting in connection with the Homeric version is the fact that narrators occasionally embellish the idea of the inlanders' ignorance of the sea by giving a brief catalogue of things connected with the sea that are unfamiliar to them. Thus, "These people had never seen the sea, ships, and boats" (Text 1), "He became disgusted with his voyages and resolved to go to a place where they did not know what the sea was and what ships were" (Text 3), and, in a comic version, "He wanted to go back in the country and marry a girl that didn't know nothing 'bout saltwater, nor the boat, nor anything like that" (Text 21).

From antiquity to the present, commentators on the *Odyssey* have accepted with little or no comment that inland peoples may be ignorant of the sea and ships and oars, but for some reason they have felt uneasy about the inlanders' saltless diet. The scholiasts, pointing out that there exist inland salt mines, explain that Homer means not simply "salt" but "sea salt" or perhaps "seafood" such as fish and oysters (BQ on *Od.* 11.123). Stanford mentions that, according to Sallust (*Bell. Iugurth.* 89), the ancient Numidians did not use salt; that hunting and pastoral peoples are said not to need salt; and that Homer does not take into account the possibility of inland salt mines (Stanford 1961, 1: 386). Germain rejects suggestions made by various scholars that the detail about a saltless diet is either an ethnographic allusion or an interpolation or even a joke, for he himself believes that the people who do not use salt in their food must be a supernatural people since food offered to the gods was not salted (Germain 1954, 275–84). The Byzantine commentator Eustathius mentions several familiar explanations before stating his own preference: it is best to take Homer's salt as referring to ordinary salt; the saltless people are simply so rustic that they know salt in no form whatsoever, either from the sea or from mines or from any other source (Eustathius *ad Od.*, p. 1676.22–28).

Eustathius's explanation, as the comparative materials show, is substantially correct. The inlanders' saltless diet is only the narrator's elaboration of the idea of a people who are so removed from the sea, so far inland, that they are wholly ignorant of salt, a common item of which the sea is the usual source. When Homer says salt, he is not thinking of inland salt mines or of seafood or of actual peoples who have saltless diets; rather, he means simply salt, and his intent is to illustrate how thoroughly unconnected with the sea the inlanders are.

One must not be misled by the future form of Tiresias's speech into believing that there is only one particular community for which Odysseus must search, an unnamed people who alone can be characterized as being so ignorant of the sea that they know nothing of ships, oars, and salt. Rather, Odysseus, like other heroes of this story, will proceed until he comes upon any community whatsoever that is ignorant of the sea.

The Oar Test. The central part of the tale is the oar test. The seaman travels inland, carrying his oar on his shoulder. In most texts he asks the people he meets what it is, but in a couple of texts (Texts 5 and 6) the inlanders take the initiative. Homer does not say whether Odysseus, as he proceeds inland, asks people what he has, but if Homer were narrating more fully (as in a different context he might), he would probably represent Odysseus as actively inquiring. For there would be little reason for an inland farmer, seeing a man carrying what looks to him like an ordinary agricultural implement (a chaff-wrecker is a winnowing shovel), to announce unasked that the stranger has a chaff-wrecker on his shoulder. On the other hand, it would make fine sense for Odysseus to ask, "What do I have here?" and for the rustic to reply, "You have a chaff-wrecker on your shining shoulder."

Narrators differ in how frequently they illustrate the encounter of seaman and landsmen, different texts giving one, two, or three encounters, of which only the last, of course, is successful from the viewpoint of the seaman. Poetically most elegant is the gradation from knowledge to ignorance which the inlanders display in a unique text: the first respondent calls the oar an oar, the second calls it a rower (not quite right but not quite wrong either), and the third calls it a piece of lumber (Text 6). Since Homer has recast the story into the future, he provides only the final, successful encounter. That there were fuller ways of telling this part of the story, however, is perhaps implied by a line that Odysseus later attributes to Tiresias: Odysseus is to go "to very many towns of mortal men" (23.267) in the course of his quest.

The Ignorant Inlander. Eventually the sailor locates a person (or a community) for whom an oar is a meaningless object. It makes no difference whether the role of the ignorant inlander is played by one person or an entire village, since the individual inlander is only a representative of the local community anyway. This relationship is clear in the Homeric narrative, in which Odysseus quests for men who are ignorant of the sea, but the sign of his having located them is one man on the road who displays the appropriate ignorance. This man should not be understood as a traveler like Odysseus but as a local person who is using a public road.

The Inlander's Error. The inlander expresses his ignorance of the test object in one of two different ways. Usually he identifies the oar simply as a piece of wood or the like (that is, he does not recognize it as a cultural artifact), as in Texts 1–3; more rarely, he identifies it as an implement other than an oar (that is, he mistakes the marine artifact for a terrestrial artifact that it resembles), as in Texts 10 (Homer), 11 (see below), and 21.

A charming instance of the concrete form of the error appears in a Greek version of the story that we know only from two defective and somewhat inconsistent reports.

11a Mr. Paton tells me that he heard a Folk-tale recounted by a woman from Constantinople with the Odysseus incident included, and in it the *winnowing fan became a baker's peel*! (*phtyari tou phournou*). The shift from the country to the town implement is very natural.

11b In the note in *Folk-Lore* at the reference above, I ventured to dispute the claims of certain modern Greek folk-tales to an ancestry in ancient Greek mythology. Mr. W. R. Paton has since been good enough to draw my attention to an indisputable instance of survival, the case of the sailor who is told to put his oar on his shoulder and march on until he comes to a land where they say that it is a baker's peel. This story Mr. Paton remembers hearing from an old woman in Calymnos some years ago: his notes of it have unfortunately been mislaid.

The baker's peel is a terrestrial isomorph of the sailor's oar, each implement being essentially a wooden tool with a long handle ending in a flat blade.

In Homer the inlander mistakes Odysseus's oar for a "chaff-wrecker," that is, a winnowing shovel (schol. QBHV *Od.* 11.128). The ancient winnowing shovel (*ptyon*) had a long handle and a flat blade and was fashioned from wood. Its shape was quite similar to that of an oar. The winnower employed the shovel to toss the threshed material into the air, allowing the chaff to be carried away by the breeze while the grains, which were heavier, fell back to the floor.

Unfortunately, nearly all Anglo-American translators of the *Odyssey* ruin the point and flavor of the rustic's mistake here by rendering *athereloigos*, not as "chaff-wrecker" or even as "winnowing shovel," but as "winnowing fan" (*liknon*). A winnowing fan (also called a "winnowing basket") strictly refers to a round, shallow wicker basket two or three feet in diameter (Harrison 1903–04; White 1967, 32–35; White 1984, 62). The incident of Odysseus and the oar depends upon the possibility that a man ignorant of oars might, upon seeing one for the first time, mistake it for a winnowing shovel. Although the fan and the shovel are both winnowing implements, they are not visually interchangeable because they do not at all look alike. No inlander, however ignorant of the sea, would ever mistake an oar for a basket, and of course the point of the incident is destroyed if the inland farmer is made to mistake Odysseus's oar for something that has no resemblance to it at all. What is so apt about the winnowing shovel is that, of all the agriculturalists' tools, it is the one most nearly isomorphic to a mariner's oar. Eustathius says as much when he observes that the point of the inlander's misinterpretation is that both implements are called blades: the oar is a blade of the sea, while the winnowing shovel is a blade of the land (*ad Od.*, p. 1675 51–52)

A couple of interpreters have seen the term "chaff-wrecker" as a kind of spell-breaking word that must be uttered in order to disenchant Odysseus and thereby free him of Poseidon and the sea; since the prospect of someone's actually uttering precisely this word is extremely small, Odysseus's journey may be extraordinarily long (Dornseiff 1937, 353; Peradotto 1986, 438). But this interpretation is fallacious because it mistakes the future setting of the Homeric narrative for an intrinsic, rather than an incidental, property of the narrative. Notice that when a past narrative is transformed into a future narrative, unexpected side-effects can arise. A detail that, when narrated in the past tense, is incidental or variable, appears to be obligatory when it is converted into the future indicative or imperative. If one transforms "Odysseus went until he met a man who said his oar was a chaff-wrecker" into the imperative, it becomes "Go until you meet a man who says your oar is a chaff-wrecker." Taken strictly, the command would require Odysseus to disregard all other expressions of ignorance of the sea and look only for that man who will utter precisely the word "chaff-wrecker." This condition is virtually impossible of fulfillment and would be pointless. Nor is the interpretation supported by the comparative materials.

The noun "chaff-wrecker" (*athereloigos*) is a kenning, a kind of substitute expression (Wærn 1951; West 1966, 89), and the word for which it is substituted—its solution, so to speak—is "winnowing shovel" (*ptyon*). It belongs to the same category of descriptive kenning as *ennosigaios,* "earth-shaker" = "Poseidon," and other similar compounds that are familiar in Homer and elsewhere in Greek literature. Homer probably has the speaker say "chaff-wrecker" in this passage rather than the more straightforward "winnowing shovel"—which the poet does use elsewhere (*Il.* 13.588)—in order to characterize him as a man of unusual diction. The question is: whose diction is the poet representing here, the seer's or the farmer's? For it is the agriculturalist who mislabels Odysseus's oar, but it is the seer who reports the mislabeling.

The usual assumption is that the allusive term "chaff-wrecker" lends an oracular atmosphere to the seer's speech (Harrison 1903, 301–2; Dornseiff 1937, 354; cf. West 1978, 289–90); however, this assumption is not supported by the evidence. Homeric seers do not deliberately obfuscate their meaning with obscure allusions or cryptic metaphors; rather, they speak straightforwardly, trying to be understood. Moreover, kennings are actually rare in Greek oracular literature (Wærn 1951, 69, 106). It seems therefore more likely that "chaff-wrecker" is an instance of folk speech, a provincialism. The inland farmer is a man who, like Hesiod, uses popular kennings such as *anosteos* (Hesiod, *Op.* 524), 'boneless one' = 'octopus', *phereoikos* (*Op.* 571), 'carry-house' = 'snail', *hemerokoitos aner* (*Op.* 605), 'day-sleeping man' = 'thief', and *pentozos* (*Op.* 742), 'five-brancher' = 'hand'. Homer characterizes the agriculturalist by making the single sentence he utters one of conventional rustic wit. The charm of the man lies in his ignorantly mistaking an oar for an agricultural tool and doing so with a term countryfolk would regard as clever.

The Mariner's Response. When the mariner finds what he has been looking for, he remains where he finds it. Except for Odysseus.

Here the Odyssean reinterpretation comes full circle, for just as in the beginning it is the Lord of the Sea rather than the sea itself whose hostility drives Odysseus inland, so also here Odysseus seeks safety from the god of the sea rather than from the sea itself. In sacrificing to Poseidon at this inland spot that has had no contact with the sea, that is, by introducing Poseidon to men who have never heard of him, Odysseus enhances the reknown of his persecutor and thereby wins his goodwill. As a result, Odysseus need no longer fear the sea god or, by implication, the sea; he is free to go. Odysseus's inland sacrifice is the functional equivalent of the inland haven, the place utterly removed from the sea where in most versions of the story the harried mariner settles for good.

The implication of the successfully completed quest is that the mariner will be freed of the pain that originally drove him from the sea. If he was in danger, he is now safe; if he was weary, he will have ease; etc. This result is ordinarily left to the hearer's inference, but in the *Odyssey* the seer makes it explicit in the verses immediately following the oar story proper (11.134–37): Odysseus's death will be gentle and unconnected with the sea (Hansen 1977, 42–48).

> "A very gentle death
> will come to you away from the sea and slay you
> in a comfortable old age. And the people around you
> will be prosperous. This is the truth that I tell you."

Sometimes narrators elaborate the conclusion of the oar test or its consequences. In three texts (2, 10, and 15) the mariner is said to stick his oar in the ground, marking the end of his quest and his definitive retirement from the sea (Hansen 1977, 39). Other elaborations are found: the mariner builds a hut (Text 2) or founds a church (Text 9) or, in a ribald text, marries a girl (Text 21).

The detail of Odysseus's planting his oar in the ground has induced several scholars to suppose that the oar was a fetish of the god Poseidon or that it had some other cultic significance (Hansen 1977, 38–42); however, as the comparative data show, the significance of the detail is simply that it marks the end of the mariner's quest and his retirement from seafaring. Although it is natural for the mariner to dispose of the oar once the testing is over, it is just as natural for a narrator to pass over this detail. The comparative texts show that it is not a critical act, one that must be there. The hypothesis of a cultic oar is therefore unnecessary. The planting of the oar in the ground misleadingly takes on an air of importance because the story is told not as it has occurred but as it will occur. An incidental gesture that would ordinarily be related in the narrative past is here transferred to the future, and description is transformed into instruction, thereby giving the impression that the planting of the oar is an obligatory act, a gesture of some unstated importance.

Etiological Coda. Countless mountaintops in present-day Greece are crowned by a chapel dedicated to St. Elias. The reason for this phenomenon is not obvious, and more than one legend purports to give a historical reason for it. Accordingly, almost without exception the Greek texts in which St. Elias is made to play the role of the mariner have him conclude his quest and settle down at the top of a mountain, adding that this is why Elias's chapels are always built on mountaintops. Since, however, the texts of the Sailor and the Oar make equally good sense whether an etiological conclusion is present or not, an etiology is not required by the logic of the story.

There is no explicit statement in the Homeric passage that links Odysseus's task with the establishment of the inland worship of Poseidon, but the Homeric story makes little sense without this assumption, for it would be absurd for Odysseus to seek out a community that is ignorant of the sea merely in order to perform at the site a private sacrifice. A scholiast shows the way here, explaining that Odysseus's missionary work allows Poseidon to be honored also as a god of the land (V on *Od.* 11.130). As we have seen, the extra-Homeric evidence indicates that many communities in western Greece were identified with the sealess inlanders, and in at least one instance Odysseus is said to have founded a mountaintop temple to Poseidon (Hansen 1976, 32–35). Very likely, then, ancient narrations of Odysseus and the Oar sometimes featured an etiological coda of the sort that usually concludes the Elias texts today, alluding to the inland or mountaintop location of a cult site. This inobvious link between the modern Elias tradition and the ancient popular tradition suggests that the ancient popular tradition concerning Odysseus is closely related to the modern popular traditions about Saints Elias and Nikolaos.

In any case the modern tradition can scarcely derive from the passage in Homer, where the narrative is set in the future, the motive for Odysseus's inland journey is implicit, the point of sacrificing among a people ignorant of the sea is not obvious, the inlander's kenning requires interpretation, the hero does not stay but returns to his wife and his island kingdom, and the cult etiology is not explicit. It would certainly be easier to borrow the story of Odysseus and Polyphemus from the *Odyssey* than it would be to borrow the story of Odysseus and Oar, and yet the consensus of scholars is that the modern analogues of the Polyphemus story are independent of the Homeric narrative (Glenn 1971, 135–42). Nor is it plausible that the story of the Sailor and the Oar, which admittedly is fairly simple, has arisen independently at different times in different lands. For if that were the case, we should expect to find the tale here and there throughout the world in no particular pattern, whereas in reality it appears to be a Euro-American story. Consequently, it is best to treat all the texts, including Homer's, as independent realizations of an old story (Hansen 1977, 34–37).

SUBTYPE B

Our main interest in Subtype B is the evidence it provides for narrative embellishment and for the nature of a narrative set in the future.

Unlike the narratives of Subtype A, which, with one or two exceptions, are not related primarily for comic effect (though there is possibly a latent comic element in even the least witty of the tales), the versions of Subtype B are basically jokes.

The Cause of the Mariner's Departure. In this form of the story, the narrator tells the story about himself so that narrator and protagonist are identical. The ego-narration, the teller's desire to achieve a comic effect, and the future setting of the narrative condition its realization in several ways. The narrator does not introduce and characterize the protagonist to his listener(s) because he is there before them, a living text. The narrative skips this element, as it were, and goes directly to the cause of the protagonist's quitting the sea. For example, the man is sick of working on the water (Text 5).

But even this element may be passed over, in some cases because this information has been a part of the conversational context and so is not repeated in the narrative proper (e.g., Text 8) and in others because the narrator, in the interest of comic economy, chooses not to dwell on the cause. So one speaker merely states what he will do (Text 7).

The Oar. As in Subtype A, the usual test object is an oar or, less frequently, oars, which are sometimes said to be carried on the shoulder. But there are several curious departures from this norm. We can wish good luck to the narrator who evidently plans to row to a land where the inhabitants are ignorant of oars, saying that once he finds the place he will throw his oars away and let his rowboat go with the tide (Text 7). Another says he plans to walk inland carrying an anchor (Text 25). As a symbol of seafaring an anchor will do as well as an oar, but the task of carrying it inland will be worthy of a true hero. Both of these oddities probably result from thoughtless narration. More clever is the narrator who declares he will walk inland carrying a binnacle light (Text 17, below).

The Mariner's Goal. Almost no examples of this subtype make explicit the mariner's intent. "I'll know I've got to where they don't know nothing about ships or the sea" (Text 17, given in full below) is the exception. The reason why most versions do not admit this feature is probably that, since Subtype B is told as a kind of witty remark, its tellers strive to recount it as succinctly and quickly as possible in order to achieve maximum humorous effect.

The Oar Test. The mariner will walk inland with his oar (oars, anchor, binnacle light). He does not take the initiative in inquiring, because it would protract his tale uncomically by requiring an inquiry and a response. And the raconteur illustrates only one encounter of seaman and landsman, the final encounter, which of course takes the form of the landsman's ignorant inquiry. For the teller does not wish to spoil the effect by drawing out his tale and, more important, he cannot provide the details since he has not yet undertaken the quest: he does not know how many people he will encounter before he finds his man.

The Ignorant Inlander. As in Subtype A, the mariner will eventually locate a person for whom his oar (or equivalent) is a meaningless object.

The Inlander's Error. The future setting of the joke conditions the form the inlander's ignorance takes. Since the point of the quest is to locate people who are ignorant of the sea, all that is required is that the inlander not recognize the test object for what it is; it is not, of course, important that he mistake it specifically for another cultural object. If a narrator tells of this quest as a past event, he may well relate that the inlander either simply fails to recognize the oar or that he makes the somewhat more interesting error of mistaking it for a specific object that it resembles. But if he foretells it as a future event, he is likely to content himself with the inlander who simply fails to recognize the oar; he is less likely to demand (except perhaps for comic effect) that the inlander make a very particular form of error, for a mariner could wander around for years encountering all manner of inlanders who fail to recognize his oar but do not misidentify it in a prescribed way. In Subtype B, then, the inlander typically expresses his ignorance by asking, "What's that funny thing you've got over your shoulder?" (Text 23). But one sailor plans to search until someone calls his oar a shovel (Text 16), and another will go until someone calls his binnacle light a flashlight (Text 17).

The Mariner's Response. In all but the defective texts the quester's response is to settle down. As in Subtype A, the idea may be elaborated: he will build a house there (Text 16), dig potatoes (Text 8), raise chickens (Text 12).

12

"They'll Do It Every Time." Reprinted with special permission of King Features Syndicate, Inc.

The two subtypes employ basically the same narrative ideas: a mariner who is unhappy with the sea takes an oar (or the like) and walks inland with it until he meets someone who does not know what it is, and there he settles down. But they realize the ideas in somewhat different ways. Since Subtype A is a third-person story set in the past, as most narratives are, it can be told as an event that actually occurred. In Greece it has regularly been told of allegedly historical persons (Odysseus, St. Elias, St. Nikolaos), and it usually includes a cult etiology. But elsewhere it is told as a folktale, and the protagonist is nameless. Moreover, the narrator is free to draw out the story and usually does so, as when he develops the quest as a succession of encounters.

In contrast to this, the texts of Subtype B are ego-narratives, set in the future, and told as jokes. Consequently, the narrator does not describe the protagonist, tends not to include unforeseeable details, does not ground the story in history, and aims in general for comic brevity. The result is a quick tale with a relatively spare development of the ideas.

The legend of Odysseus and the Oar is a form of Subtype A, but Homer's treatment of it resembles some of the spareness of Subtype B because he transposes the story into the future in order to permit it to be foretold by a seer. Thus, there is no description of the protagonist in the passage itself, no explicit statement of Odysseus's motive, no encounters with inlanders other than the final encounter, no explicit etiology.

THE SENSE OF THE STORY

All tellings of the story show a strong structural opposition between sea and land: whatever one realm signifies, the other signifies the opposite. The significance, however, is not constant from text to text, for the meanings of sea and land are determined by the sailor's motive for quitting the sea, which varies from text to text. When, as most frequently happens, the man rejects the sea because of frightful storms or shipwreck, the sea signifies danger, and land therefore signifies safety. When he rejects the sea because of the unrelieved labor of rowing, the sea means weariness, and land means ease. When the sea is associated with immorality, land suggests morality. The meaning of the two realms and therefore of the seaman's quest is always a function of the sailor's motive for departure. Even when his motive is not explicit, there is still the implied opposition of sea (bad) and land (good).

The tale chronicles the mariner's complete rejection of the sea, his exchanging one realm for its opposite. Between the realms of sea and land there is an intermediate realm of land that is tainted by its acquaintance with the sea, and the function of the oar test is to distinguish the inhabitants of all these realms from those of the purely terrestrial realm.

Now, the oar test is a curious strategy. If a man really wanted to discover a community that was entirely ignorant of the sea, he would not walk around with an oar on his shoulder; instead, he would probably make direct verbal inquiries of the people he met as he made his way inland. But what we are dealing with is not an actual quest but a story about a quest, and the difference is important. The key to a proper understanding of the oar test is the observation made by folklorist Axel Olrik that in traditional oral story the attributes of characters tend to be expressed through their actions more than their speech, for oral story prefers the concrete and the visual (Olrik 1909, 8–9). Consequently, in the present tale the mariner is made to *act out* his quest, walking inland with a concrete symbol of the sea. The oar test is a dramatic and visual expression of the man's search. A man carrying an oar far from the sea is a virtual question: Do I make any sense to you? The scene is wonderfully unrealistic and striking. Most of the charm of this story surely resides in the motif of the oar test, the single feature that a hearer is most likely to remember (Hansen 1976, 41–42).

The oar is virtually constant as the test object because it is the basic tool of the mariner and also because it is the most common and easily portable symbol of seafaring. It is safe to conclude that a person who does not know what an oar is does not know anything of the sea. If the realm were different, the symbol would be different, as a related anecdote from Whitehorse, Yukon Territory, illustrates.

13 Some of the boys in a saloon here the other night were talking about
    a local woman who had won $1,800 in a lottery. The consensus was
    that her decision to put the money in the bank showed a sorry lack of
    ambition.
       "What I'd do," said one, "is to tie a snow shovel to the hood of my
    car and drive south until nobody had the faintest idea what the damn
    thing was."
       It is a time-honored sentiment. Robert Service, the gold rush poet,
    wrote that "some say God was tired" when He made the Yukon, which
    Service described as "the cussedest land that I know."

In this variation of Subtype B the hated realm is snow country and the symbol of hardship for its inhabitants is the snow shovel.

In contrast, the form of the landsman's error is variable because it is not crucial for the sense of the story that the test object be mistaken for any particular thing, only that it not be recognized for what it is. Although most often the inlander simply fails to recognize the object as a cultural artifact, several texts have the marine tool mistaken specifically for an isomorphic terrestrial tool, elegantly symbolizing that in exchanging physical realms the mariner also exchanges his means of live-lihood: his oar becomes, so to speak, a baker's peel (Text 11) or, as Homer has it (Text 10), a winnowing shovel.

When the mariner has found his inland haven, the implication is that he has succeeded in escaping from whatever drove him to quit the sea. If he was in danger, he will now be safe; if he suffered from continual labor, he can look forward to rest.

The comparative method can be a productive approach to ancient Greek oral narrative in a number of ways. In the present case, it has been employed to show something that rarely has been recognized, that Odysseus and the Oar is actually a *story* rather than the mysterious in-structions of a seer, the consequences of which are uncertain, or a strange journey into nowhere, the point of which has been lost. More-over, I have used the method to demonstrate that these events constitute a *traditional* story, for it has not been recognized in classical scholarship that the Sailor and the Oar is an international story. Radermacher does not mention the story in his standard survey of tales and legends in the *Odyssey* (1915), nor does Page devote any space to it in his *Folktales in Homer's Odyssey* (1973). And when researchers have now and then happened upon a text of St. Elias and the Oar, they have usually dis-missed it in few words as being of little relevance to the Odysseus tradi-tion.

The comparative method has also been a useful device for getting at the content and structure of the folk narrative, showing what are the constants and the variables in the tradition and so serving as a control in the study of the Homeric version, with its saltless inlanders, oar planted in the ground, chaff-wrecker, and other snares for scholars. It has shown that the story really begins earlier and ends later than is usu-ally thought, for it begins in a sense with the storm that Poseidon sends against Odysseus and it ends with a description of how the hero even-tually will die, once he has made his peace with the sea god. The method puts the elements of the Homeric narration into perspective and makes clearer the relationship of the parts and the coherency of the whole.

But there are some kinds of information that it does not, and cannot, provide. The comparative method divorces narratives from the social situations in which they are employed. The resultant texts do not reveal to us who tells a particular story and who listens to it, nor do they tell us why narrators bother to relate the story at all. Texts alone do not tell us whose story this is and for whom this story has meaning. The mes-sage a narrator wishes to communicate is often different from the struc-tural message of the narrative itself (Hansen 1982). Oral stories do not exist as isolated objects but rather as part of social events (Dundes

1964; Georges 1969; Ben-Amos 1971; Bausinger 1980; Holbek 1981; Bauman 1986). Until recently, however, most collectors of folk narrative have not been much interested in the social context of narration and so have paid little attention to it.

CONTEXT OF NARRATION

Some ancient folk narratives are embedded in real or fictive storytelling contexts that an investigator might profitably examine (Hansen 1988). This is the case, for example, with the mythic novella of Ares and Aphrodite in the eighth book of the *Odyssey*, where Homer represents a character within the story singing this tale for listeners. Unfortunately, the Homeric account of Odysseus and the Oar is not situated in a storytelling context, nor do we have another ancient source in which the legend is represented as being told by a narrator to listeners. However, since something is known about the telling of this story in our own day, I shall consider several representative contexts from the present century. My procedure will not be essentially different from the one I have been applying to narratives; I will simply extend it to narrative situations.

The following text is the first portion of a thoughtful letter that appeared in the *Times Literary Supplement* in 1919.

14 A naval officer tells me that the boatswain of his ship, in speaking of his future retirement, said that he should walk inland with an oar on his shoulder, and when he met with people who asked him what he was carrying should settle there.

This naturally reminded me of the passage in the eleventh book of the Odyssey where Odysseus is told to go inland till he comes to a people which has no knowledge of ships and the sea. The sign of his reaching his destination is to be that a wayfarer meeting him will ask if he is carrying a winnowing shovel on his shoulder. I was also told that the saying was not uncommon with sailors, but I have not had further confirmation of this.

In the excerpt that follows, a classical scholar, W. H. D. Rouse, reports a conversation he had with a Greek skipper, Kapetan Giorgis. The exchange took place one evening around 1905 in the course of a fifty-mile voyage to the island of Astypalaia. Giorgis was, on his own estimation, in his early seventies and had been a skipper for fifty years.

15 "Ah well," says Giorgis, "'tis a poor trade this, as the holy Elias found." "What was that?" I asked. "The prophet Elias," quoth he, "was a fisherman; he had bad weather, terrific storms, so that he became afraid of the sea. Well, so he left his nets and his boat on the shore, and

put an oar over his shoulder, and took to the hills. On the way, who should he see but a man. "A good hour to you," says he. "Welcome," says the man. "What's this, can you tell me?" says St Elias. "That?" says the man. "Why that's an oar." Eh, on he goes till he meets another man. "A good hour to you," says St. Elias. "You are welcome," says the man. "What's this?" says St. Elias. "Why, that's an oar, to be sure," says the man. On he goes again, until he comes to the very top of the mountain, and there he sees another man. "Can you tell me what this is?" asks St. Elias. "That?" says the man. "Why, that's a stick." "Good!" says St. Elias. "This is the place for me, here I abide." He plants the oar in the ground, and that is why his chapels are all built on the hill tops." "Well, well, I didn't know the prophet Elias followed the sea; of course the holy apostles did, we all know that." "Aye, and so they did. You know why they left it, sir, don't you?" "Why?" "Well, you see, Christ and the Apostles. . . ."

In the final two texts, an educated reporter with training in the classics records his feelings as he hears an uneducated narrator relate the story. First, the conversation of an old sailor and a classical scholar, Cedric Whitman, who rode together on a train to New York:

16 The old seaman of my story was a U.S. sailor who sat next to me on a train going to New York many years ago. He was reading a comic book and I was reading *Paradise Lost*. Presently he began to read over my shoulder, then nudged me and asked: "Hey, you like dat stuff?" I said I did, and a conversation began. I asked how long he had been in the Navy, and he said something like twenty-five years. I remarked that he must have liked it to have stayed in it so long. His answer was: "Look, when I get out of dis Navy, I'm gonna put an oar on my shoulder and walk inland; and when somebody says, 'Where d'ya find a shovel like dat?' dat's where I'm gonna build my house." He made no mention of a sacrifice to Poseidon; he was shamelessly secular about it all, but clearly the inland journey spelled release from, and forgetfulness of, the hardships of the sea, peace at last. I didn't ask him if he'd read the *Odyssey,* but I doubt it; he had not read *Paradise Lost*. He seemed, in fact, pretty nearly illiterate—perhaps a bard? Anyway, that's all I remember, except that the experience gave me a pleasantly creepy feeling that I was talking to One Who Was More Than He Seemed.

In the last text, the reporter of the incident is an officer in the U.S. Navy who happened to overhear the tale in a neighboring conversation among enlisted men. The raconteur, as the reporter later ascertained, was a twenty-two-year-old West Virginian who had completed two years of high school before enlisting in the Navy.

17   Although I have long been a Canadian citizen, I was born and raised
in the United States, and was a U.S. Navy flier in World War II. Just
about this time of year in 1945, I was standing in a queue in Providence,
Rhode Island, waiting for a bus to Naval Air Station Quonset Point,
where I was then stationed. Most of the people in line were noncommis-
sioned personnel; I had the rank of Lt., USNR. . . .
      The Japanese had surrendered, and the war was over. Ahead of me in
the line, several enlisted men were talking about what they were going
to do after their discharge from the Navy. One chap expansively declared, in Appalachian accents: "I'm going to get me a binnacle light off
some junked-up boat or ship—they'se lots around—and I'm going to
take and carry that son of a bitch straight in away from the god-damned
ocean. I'll show it to people and when I get to where they say, 'What is
that funny-looking flashlight?' I'll just stop right there. I'll know I've got
to where they don't know nothing about ships or the sea."
      This is from memory, but I think I have it fairly as given. When I say
that I had graduated college with a degree in classics shortly before the
war, you can understand the thrill with which I heard these words.

      The narrators are all males and and seamen by occupation. There is
a British boatswain, a seventy-year-old Greek sea captain, an old sailor
in the U.S. Navy, and a twenty-two-year-old enlisted man in the U.S.
Navy. The educated reporters happen to be familiar with the ancient
literary tradition but are not themselves narrators of the oral tale, while
the narrators are active transmitters of the story but are evidently unacquainted with ancient literature.
      In the present corpus as a whole the narrator, when known, is always
male, with the single exception of the old Greek woman in Text 11. He
is an adult, young or old: this is not a child's tale. We know the vocation
of about eighteen narrators. It always has to do with the sea: he is a
skipper, a fisherman, in the merchant marine, in the navy, for example.
Often the narrator is an uneducated man, as in two or three of the texts
above, but the educated narrator of Text 6 actually learned the story
from an old chief petty officer who assisted the Naval ROTC lecturer at
Columbia University. Even so, when later he read the *Odyssey* for the
first time, he did not connect the tale with that of Odysseus and the Oar.
      The profile of the narrator's typical audience would probably be very
similar to that of the narrator himself, since seafolk, like other people,
tend to spend time with others like themselves. It is not surprising, then,
that in five of the texts we know that the audience consists of seamen.
Special circumstances, however, sometimes bring together persons who
would not ordinarily exchange stories, as when a classics professor and

a sailor happen to sit next to each other on a train, or when a folklorist deliberately seeks out a good storyteller, so that some of the texts in the corpus also reflect conversations between persons who would not typically consort with each other.

What prompts a seaman to narrate the story? In Text 15 we read: "Ah well," says Giorgis, "'tis a poor trade, this, as the holy Elias found." The skipper illustrates this proposition with a narration of the Elias legend in which the beleaguered Elias reaches the same conclusion about his trade and actually leaves the sea. As raconteurs frequently do, Kapetan Giorgis first announces the point of his story and then tells the story. He continues this train of thought by relating next a story about why the Apostles also left the sea. In the following conversation (Text 16), the seaman's narration is touched off by the scholar's remark that the seaman must have liked the Navy to have stayed in it for some twenty-five years. The old seaman's response about what he will do when he gets out is meant to illustrate—seriously or with comic exaggeration—just how much the career sailor dislikes his trade. In Text 14 the boatswain is speaking of his future retirement. Presumably he will have the option at that time to remain near the sea or to go elsewhere, and he states through the medium of the tale that he intends to settle as far from the sea as possible. In Text 17 the conversation concerns what the discussants are going to do upon their discharge from the navy, a topic that is similar to the subject of forthcoming retirement from the sea. One young sailor employs the tale to communicate humorously that he will certainly not choose to continue seafaring.

In these four conversations, which are typical of the corpus to the extent that contextual information is available at all, tellers tell the Sailor and the Oar when the opportunity arises of commenting upon seafaring as a trade, of *evaluating it as a way of life*. The teller's evaluation is unambiguously negative. Indeed, several American informants report that seamen frequently complain about the sea. According to the reporter of Text 23, a former merchant marine who, like Kapetan Giorgis (Text 15), knew two different tales about quitting the sea, seamen always say they are going to stop, but they rarely do. The narrator of Text 26, also a former merchant seaman, describes the life at sea as a lonely life, a cut-off life, saying that the men are there for the money or because they cannot cope, so that it is fashionable among them to belittle the life at sea. Greek seamen are similarly said to have a love-hate relationship with the sea, cursing it while at the same time being tied to it with more than economic bonds (Text 22).

An ambivalent attitude toward the sea as giver both of livelihood and of distress must have been a feature of the mariner's experience from the time of the earliest seafaring careers. The Sailor and the Oar expresses in a simple fashion the purely negative side of the seaman's attitude by describing a disgusted sailor who acts out the mariner's fantasy of walking away from the sea for good. It objectifies the fantasy that every mariner must sometimes have, the desire of quitting the sea.

Other texts in the corpus suggest that the story can support other functions and meanings as well. According to a rather vague report, shipwrecked persons are said to narrate this tale to one another as a consolation in certain sea stories, and tormented and discouraged seafolk say they will follow the example of the sailor who went inland if ever they themselves reach home (Text 5). So also in one account St. Elias, experiencing a rough sea, proclaims that if he ever escapes he will find the highest mountain peak and settle there forever (Text 24). So it may be that seafarers in difficulty sometimes employ the tale to console themselves and others with the thought that if they escape their present plight they will never have to face a similar problem again, for they will have quit the sea forever. In two other texts the story is employed to evaluate seafaring in relation to a particular terrestrial vocation, either farming or herding; but the contextual information is of uncertain reliability in one case since the tale appears in a work of fiction (Text 8), and it is inadequate for our purpose in the other (Text 24). One version of Subtype A, recounted by a retired lobster fisherman in Maine, is a ribald tale of a sailor and a farmer's daughter (Text 21).

Surprisingly, the contextual data do not support the notion that for some narrators the main purpose in telling the story is to provide an *aition* for the mountaintop chapels of St. Elias. Etiology does not appear to hold a high rank in the minds of most narrators of the story, for although all versions of the Sailor and the Oar can express the mariner's fantasy of quitting the sea, only the Odysseus and Elias subtraditions contain the cult etiology, and even so it is not always present (Texts 3 and 10). The educated imagination is inclined to accord too much importance to the formal element of the etiological coda and too little importance to the expressive element of the mariner's fantasy. This is nowhere clearer than in Text 4, in which a Greek fisherman is trying to communicate that he, like Elias before him, is weary of his trade, whereas the scholar who quotes this conversation does so in illustration of the fact that the Greek folk tell various legends to explain why chapels of St. Elias stand on nearly every mountaintop. The scholar, who is interested in folk etiology, simply overrides the narrator's message.

Still, a man may include the etiology even when his point is the misery of his work and not the location of Elias's chapels. Although incidental to his message, the feature may lend force and verity to his narration because, as anyone can see, Elias's chapels are indeed found on hilltops. It would be unwise, moreover, to deny that a narrator's main interest might ever be etiology because the present corpus may not be representative in this regard. In any case I can myself testify that in 1986 when I mentioned to two Athenians that on a mountainside near my residence in Ano Glyphada there stood a little chapel of St. Elias, both immediately began to tell me the legend of Elias and the oar. The incident shows how natural it is to recount the story in such a context.

I conclude, then, that seamen constitute the principal conduit (Dégh and Vázsonyi 1975) for the transmission of the Sailor and the Oar, which offers them a means of expressing implicitly and cleverly a negative evaluation of seafaring as a way of life. These men are the active bearers of the tradition. Other, lesser conduits also exist, but they are not well documented.

It is frequently stated that the stories in the *Odyssey*, especially in Books 9–12, are old sea stories. No one ever presents any evidence for this assertion, probably because it seems like a perfectly safe claim to make; however, I myself do not believe the claim is wholly true, since I doubt that the Polyphemus legend and the Circe legend, to cite two well-known narratives from this part of the poem, are in any true sense old sea stories. Even if it were true, I do not think the evidence to prove it would be forthcoming, since we possess little contextual information about these stories and their analogues. But the modern contextual evidence does suggest that the claim is correct for Odysseus and the Oar, since the Sailor and the Oar *is* indeed a true seaman's story, a story typically told by adult male seamen to other seamen.

In the absence of earlier contextual information, our only guide to the narrative transmission of this story in ancient times is the evidence of the present day. There is no reason to suppose that the working conditions—danger, hard work, and so on—that make the story meaningful to today's seamen would have made it any less meaningful to yesterday's seamen, whose work indeed was even more dangerous and wearisome. Probably the Sailor and the Oar has always been primarily a mariner's story and its principal function has been to give artful expression to one of the mariner's several attitudes toward his profession. As a popular story, it no doubt circulated in antiquity, as now, primarily among men of the sea, but it has perhaps regularly acquired as well a constituency of landfolk who were amused or charmed by the narrative and who became mostly passive bearers of the tradition, recognizing it but not often transmitting it, since in the end it rarely could be so meaningful to them as to seamen. When the story was drawn into the biographical legend of that most beleaguered of Greek sailors,

Odysseus, it was necessarily adapted and somewhat reinterpreted to fit the givens of the hero's life, and yet it must have remained a familiar sequence of events with a familiar resonance to those Greek seafolk who knew the ordinary seamen's story, just as today educated seamen who have heard the oral story of the Sailor and the Oar and subsequently read Homer's *Odyssey* sometimes recognize Odysseus's strange inland quest as a form of the seamen's tale they know.

18

"Captain's Gig," by Virgil Partch. Copyright © Field Enterprises, 1977. Reprinted by permission of North American Syndicate, Inc.

NOTES

a. Page 1973.

b. Again Page 1973.

c. This observation necessarily rests on anthropological data: we do not have the folktales of Greek antiquity. Cf. Kirk 1974, Ch. 2 ("The Relation of Myths to Folktales"), pp. 30–37.

d. The habit persists even in Kirk 1974, 164–65.

e. Edmunds 1981, 2–3.

f. Puhvel 1987, 3, 31.

g. Fehling 1984, 82–83. This article can be taken as his *summa*.

SOURCES OF THE TEXTS

For bringing to my attention texts that I would otherwise have missed, I am grateful to Professors Shirley Arora, Helen Bacon, Mark Edwards, Thomas Jacobsen, Michael Jameson, Betty Rose Nagel, and Warren Roberts. The translations are my own, but I wish to acknowledge the help of Professors Michael Herzfeld, Fred Householder, and George Koniaris, whom I consulted at different times concerning my renderings of Modern Greek.

The first eighteen texts are printed in full or in part in this essay and are listed here in the order in which they appear; the remainder are listed in chronological sequence. I have noted the subtype in brackets.

1. Akes Tamasias. 1951. "Laïkes Paradoseis." *Mathetike Hestia* 1: 129, no. 3. [A]

2. N. G. Polites. 1904. *Meletai peri tou Biou kai tes Glosses tou Hellenikou Laou: Paradoseis.* Vol. 2, 801–2. Athens. [A]

3. Polites, op. cit., Vol. 1, 116, no. 207. [A]

4. Christodoulos B. Syrmakeses. 1964. *Elias ho Thesbites (me laographiko Par-artema) kai ho Mathetes tou Elissaios,* 60–61. Athens. [A]

5. Karl Reinhardt. 1948. "Die Abenteuer der Odyssee." In *Von Werken und For-men: Vorträge und Aufsätze,* 505–6, n. 30. Godesberg. [A]

6. Taped interview with Adam Horvath (July 5, 1975), an editor at Indiana University Press. [A]

7. George Carey. 1971. *A Faraway Time and Place: Lore of the Eastern Shore,* 111. Washington, DC, and New York. [B]

8. Frank Shay. 1930. *Here's Audacity! American Legendary Heroes,* 20–21. New York. [B]

9. Robert Hughes. 1986. Review of Peter Matthiessen, *Men's Lives: The Surfmen and Baymen of the South Fork.* In *The New York Review of Books* (October 23), 21. [B]

10. Homer, *Odyssey* 11.121–37. [A]

11a. Harrison 1904: 246, n. 11. [A]

11b. W. R. Halliday. 1914. "Modern Greek Folk-Tales and Ancient Greek Mythology: Odysseus and Saint Elias." *Folk-Lore* 25: 122–23. [A]

12. Jimmy Hatlo, *They'll Do It Every Time.* © King Features Syndicate, Inc., date uncertain. Reprinted with special permission of King Features Syndicate, Inc. [B]

13. Douglas Martin. 1982. "Wolf at Yukon's Door, in More Ways Than One." *The New York Times* (December 21), 2. [snow shovel]

14. J. E. King. 1919. Letter in *Times Literary Supplement* (September 11), 485. [B] See also response in *TLS* (October 2, 1919), 533.

15. W. H. D. Rouse. 1906. "A Greek Skipper." *The Cambridge Review* 27 (May 24): 414. [A]

16. Personal letter (October 13, 1975) from the late Cedric Whitman, Professor of Classics, Harvard University. [B]

17. Personal letter (October 11, 1977) from Richard Slobodin, Professor of Anthropology, McMaster University. [B]

18. Virgil Partch. 1977. *Captain's Gig.* ©Field Enterprises. By permission of North America Syndicate, Inc. [B]

19. F. W. Hasluck. 1910. *Cyzicus,* 65. Cambridge. [A]

20. A. Erotokritos. 1955. "Threskeutikoi Thryloi." *Mathetike Hestia* 5: 160, no. 15. [A]

21. Richard M. Dorson. 1957. "Collecting Folklore in Jonesport, Maine." *PAPhS* 101 (June): 287. [A]

22. Irwin T. Sanders. 1962. *Rainbow in the Rock: The People of Rural Greece,* 35. Cambridge, MA. [A]

23. Taped interview with Philip Appleman (April 19, 1972), Professor of English, Indiana University, Bloomington. Excerpt published in Hansen 1976, 226. [B]

24. Nicolas E. Gavrielides. 1976. *A Study in the Cultural Ecology of an Olive-Growing Community: The Southern Argolid, Greece,* 167–69. Ph.D. diss., Indiana University, Bloomington. [A]

25. John Gould. 1978. "I name thee so-and-so." *The Christian Science Monitor* (June 9). [B]

26. Written interview with James M. Patterson (February 25, 1987), Professor of Marketing, Indiana University, Bloomington. [B]

WORKS CITED

Aarne, Antti, and Stith Thompson. 1961. *The Types of the Folktale: A Classification and Bibliography.* Folklore Fellows Communications, No. 184. Helsinki.

Bauman, Richard. 1986. *Story, Performance, and Event: Contextual Studies of Oral Narrative.* Cambridge.

Bausinger, Hermann. 1980. "On Contexts." In Nikolai Burlakoff and Carl Lindahl, eds., *Folklore on Two Continents: Essays in Honor of Linda Dégh,* 273–79. Bloomington, IN.

Beaton, Roderick. 1986. "The Oral Traditions of Modern Greece: A Survey." *Oral Tradition* 1: 110–33.

Ben-Amos, Dan. 1971. "Toward a Definition of Folklore in Context." *Journal of American Folklore* 84: 3–15.

Dégh, Linda, ed. 1986. *The Comparative Method in Folklore = Journal of Folklore Research* 23: 77–236.

——— and Andrew Vázsonyi. 1975. "Hypothesis of Multi-Conduit Transmission in Folklore." In Dan Ben-Amos and Kenneth S. Goldstein, eds. *Folklore: Performance and Communication,* 207–52. The Hague.

Dornseiff, Franz. 1937. "Odysseus' letzte Fahrt." *Hermes* 72: 351–55.

Dundes, Alan. 1964. "Texture, Text, and Context." *Southern Folklore Quarterly* 28: 251–65.

Edmunds, Lowell. 1981. *The Sphinx in the Oedipus Legend.* Beiträge zur klassischen Philologie 127. Königstein/Ts., FRG.

Fehling, Detlev. 1984. "Die alten Literaturen als Quelle der neuzeitlichen Märchen." In Siegmund 1984, 52–63.

Fontenrose, Joseph. 1959. Reprint 1980. *Python: A Study of Delphic Myth.* Berkeley-Los Angeles.

Frazer, Sir James George. 1921. *Apollodorus, The Library.* 2 vols. Cambridge, MA.

Georges, Robert A. 1969. "Toward an Understanding of Storytelling Events." *Journal of American Folklore* 82: 313–28.

Germain, Gabriel. 1954. *Genèse de l'Odyssée: Le fantastique et la sacré.* Paris.

Glenn, Justin. 1971. "The Polyphemus Folktale and Homer's *Kyklôpeia.*" *TAPA* 102: 133–81.

Goldberg, Christine. 1984. "The Historic-Geographic Method: Past and Future." *Journal of Folklore Research* 21: 1–18.

Grimm, Wilhelm. 1857. "Die Sage von Polyphem." *Abhandlungen der Königlichen Akademie der Wissenschaften zu Berlin, phil.-hist. Klasse,* pp. 1–30 = *Kleinere Schriften* (Gutersloh, 1887) 4: 428–62.

Hackman, Oskar. 1904. *Die Polyphemsage in der Volksüberlieferung.* Helsingfors.

Hansen, W. F. 1976. "The Story of the Sailor Who Went Inland." In Linda Dégh, Henry Glassie, and Felix Oinas, eds. *Folklore Today: A Festschrift for Richard M. Dorson,* 221–30. Bloomington, IN.

———. 1977. "Odysseus' Last Journey." *QUCC* 24: 27–48.

———. 1982. "The Applied Message in Storytelling." In Egle Zygas and Peter Voorhees, eds. *Folklorica: Festschrift for Felix Oinas,* 99–109. Indiana University Uralic and Altaic Series, Vol. 141.

———. 1988. "Folklore." In Michael Grant and Rachel Kitzinger, eds. *Civilization of the Ancient Mediterranean: Greece and Rome,* 2: 1121–1130. New York.

Harrison, Jane. 1903–1904. "Mystica Vannus Iacchi." *JHS* 23: 292–324; 24: 241–54.

Holbek, Bengt. 1981. "Moderne Folkloristik og Historisk Materiale." In Gun Herranen, ed. *Folkloristikens Actuella Paradigm.* 129–49. NIF Publications, No. 10. Åbo.

Kirk, G. S. 1974. *The Nature of Greek Myths.* Harmondsworth, UK.

Krohn, Kaarle. 1971. *Folklore Methodology: Formulated by Julius Krohn and Expanded by Nordic Researchers.* Tr. Roger L. Welsch. American Folklore Society, Bibliography and Special Series, Vol. 21. Austin, TX.

Olrik, Axel. 1909. "Die epische Gesetze der Volksdichtung." *Zeitschrift für deutsches Altertum und deutsche Literatur* 51: 1–12.

Page, Denys. 1955. *The Homeric Odyssey.* Oxford.

————. 1973. *Folktales in Homer's Odyssey.* Cambridge, MA.

Peradotto, John. 1986. "Prophecy Degree Zero: Tiresias and the End of the *Odyssey.*" In B. Gentili and G. Paioni, eds. *Oralità: Cultura, Letteratura, Discorso,* 429–59. Rome.

Puhvel, Jaan 1987. *Comparative Mythology.* Baltimore.

Radermacher, Ludwig. 1915. *Die Erzählungen der Odyssey. Sitzungsberichte der kaiserlichen Akademie der Wissenschaften in Wien, phil.-hist. Klasse,* 178: 1–59.

Siegmund, Wolfdietrich, ed. 1984. *Antiker Mythos in unseren Märchen.* Veröffentlichungen der Europaischen Märchengesellschaft. Vol. 6. Kassel, FRG.

Stanford, W. B. 1961. *The Odyssey of Homer.* 2 vols. London.

Taylor, Archer. 1964. "The Biographical Tradition of the Hero." *Journal of the Folklore Institute* 1: 114–29.

Wærn, Ingrid. 1951. *GES OSTEA: The Kenning in Pre-Christian Greek Poetry.* Uppsala.

West, M. L. 1966. *Hesiod, Theogony.* Oxford.

————. 1978. *Hesiod, Works and Days.* Oxford.

White, K. D. 1967. *Agricultural Implements of the Roman World.* Cambridge.

————. 1984. *Greek and Roman Technology.* Ithaca, NY.

PART THREE

APPROACHES BASED ON THEORY

6

STRUCTURALISM AND SEMIOTICS

Structuralism has many meanings.[a] The term is used here to refer to theories of myth originating in the structural linguistics of Ferdinand de Saussure, the main statement of which is found in his *Cours de linguistique générale* (1915).[b] Two of the main thinkers who have built theories of narrative on this linguistic model are Claude Lévi-Strauss and A.-J. Greimas. The now canonical statement of the former, in which the Oedipus myth was the example, appeared in 1955 and has been reprinted and paraphrased innumerable times. Since, however, some of the basic principles are shared by Greimas, who avowed the close relation of his work to that of Lévi-Strauss,[c] it is appropriate to review these principles in the form in which they appear in Lévi-Strauss.

For him, the most important distinction in Saussurean linguistics is between the synchronic and the diachronic. Any phenomenon in a language can be regarded either historically, in terms of change, or as part of a system self-sufficient and coherent at any point in the history of that language. Any use of the language will share in both aspects. The unique, irreversible act of speech (called *parole* by Saussure) belongs to the diachronic dimension; indeed, it is the use of the language that causes it to change. The condition of the speech act, however, is the language as a generative system (called *langue*). Furthermore, the components of this system have no independent meaning. They have the capacity to signify only through their differential relations with other components.

Turning to Greimas, the principal concepts at work in Calame's contribution to this volume are three. First, the distinction between utterance (*énoncé*) and enunciation (*énonciation*). Utterance, that which is uttered, is distinguished from the speech act of which it is the result. Since Calame holds that there is no such thing as "Greek mythology," that "myths" are available only as particular texts in particular genres, he shifts the focus from the utterance, which would be the myth as found, say, in a handbook of mythology, to the enunciation, which is, for the purposes of his essay, three odes of Pindar, *Pythians* 4, 5, and 9.

The Pindaric victory ode typically contains a mythical exemplum, but the poet's anfractuous, allusive style makes this exemplum difficult to study as a narrative. In order to perceive the narrative in the difficult Pindaric enunciation, Calame must appeal, paradoxically, to a theory of narrative based on the study of narratives as utterances. This is the theory of the "canonic schema," the second of the key principles in Calame's study.

Greimas developed the schema from an analysis of Vladimir Propp's study of Russian folktales. Propp had reduced the story patterns of a group of these folktales to thirty-one functions: one of the members of a family absents himself from home; an interdiction is addressed to the hero; and the like.[d] Greimas further reduced this number to three basic tests of the hero: qualification or test of competence; realization or performance; and sanction—that is, retribution and recognition. These tests can be further reduced to the following oppositions. (1) Subject versus Object. Neither can be present without the other. The two are related either conjunctively or disjunctively. Typically a story begins with a lack, a disjunction or separation between the hero and a desired object, and ends, after various transformations, with a conjunction, as the hero succeeds in his quest.[e] (2) Sender versus Receiver. The Sender belongs to a transcendent domain. In the odes Calame discusses, Apollo is a Sender. (3) Helper versus Opponent. These three oppositions constitute the "actantial model," in which the actant is that which does or undergoes an act—a person, a thing, or an animal—and is thus far more general than a character; an actant could be two different actors. Greimas diagrams the model thus:

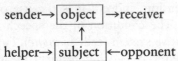

Greimas comments: "It is entirely centered on the object of desire aimed at by the subject and situated, as object of communication, between the sender and the receiver—the desire of the subject being, in its part, modulated in projections from the helper and opponent."[f]

The given content of the schema consists of "figures" drawn from the natural world. The status of these figures is the third principle that Calame's study presupposes. Several figures can express the same theme. For example, "priest," "sacrifice," and "beadle" in a narrative might express the "sacred."[g] In this case, the three figures would constitute an "isotopy" correlative to that theme. Calame refers to the figures he discusses as the "concrete semantic elements." The term "semantic" calls for attention. It is not used in its customary lexical sense but in a technical Greimasian one, according to which the discoursive (*sic*) semantics (*sémantique discursive*) are the stuff of a narrative. So "semantics" in the Greimasian sense is to some degree synonymous with "figures" but more general.

Narrating the Foundation of a City: The Symbolic Birth of Cyrene

CLAUDE CALAME

Contemporary archaeology is agreed: the development of Cyrene, a Greek colony in northern Libya, began in the second half of the seventh century B.C. Doubtless the presence of objects dating from Late Helladic III A and B could suggest even more remote contacts between Greece and the Mediterranean coast of Africa. But nothing indicates, before the middle of the archaic period, the development there of a city in the Greek sense.[1] Such, at any rate, is the interpretation proposed by archaeologists in their efforts to reconstruct, from the ruins left by the passage of time, a chronology conforming to our sense of history: an arithmetic time with double orientation, one that sketches out an accumulation of years after the supposed birth of our own civilization's founding hero, and also the unfolding back of years beyond this date.[2] Nothing is more foreign, however, to the Greek manner of envisioning what constitutes for us the temporal organization of a historic past.

Self-evident proof of this is the multiplicity of events that one poet is apt to place at the temporal origin of the city whose rulers, his contemporaries, he praises: Apollo's rape of the nymph Cyrene and celebration on the Libyan coast of his union with this young lion huntress; occupation of the site by the sons of Antenor, accompanied by Helen, following the destruction of Troy; the clod of Libyan earth transferred by a son of Poseidon to another son of the same god, and its coming to ground at Thera (Santorini) so as to return metaphorically to its land of origin in the colonial expedition of Battus, Cyrene's founder, seventeen generations later. Here then is the earliest chronological reckoning, but no indication is given about the number of generations separating Battus's colonizing act from the time and circumstances of its narration. The enunciative moments of the narrated events in this indeterminate past are, however, amenable to precise dating. I have summarized above, in

order, fragments of the narratives contained in the Ninth, Fifth, and
Fourth *Pythian Odes* of Pindar. The first of these epinicia sings of the
victory obtained at the hoplite race in the twenty-eighth Pythian Games
by Telesicrates of Cyrene in the year 474 B.C. The ode was probably
performed in Cyrene at the time of festivities marking the return home
of the athlete. The second celebrates the success in the chariot race of
the brother-in-law of Arcesilas the Fourth, King of Cyrene, on the occasion of the thirty-first Pythiad, in 462; it was sung in honor of the
king's charioteer near the Garden of Aphrodite, perhaps for the festival
of the Carneia. As for the last of these odes, composed on the occasion
of the same chariot victory, it was performed in the king's palace itself,
most probably during a banquet celebrating this most prestigious of
agonistic victories.[3]

This projection of founding events into a chronologically indeterminate past seems to constitute the touchstone of what we know as myth.
These primordial, exemplary events, fixing the ephemeral present into
atemporal permanence, apparently furnish us with an ideal means of
entry into the very essence of the mythological.

NARRATIVE FORMS OF AN UNDISCOVERABLE
MYTHOLOGY

Illusion! What we call myth, however, has no existence in itself, nor
does it correspond to any universal cultural reality. In essence, myth is
only a concept invented by modern anthropology out of uncertainties
gradually recognized by the Greeks themselves as to the historical reality of certain episodes in their tradition. To this tradition, the epithets
"legendary" and "historic" are equally applicable: for the Greeks, a
narrative's credibility lies not so much in its congruence with factual
truth as in a judgment about its moral coherence. The Greeks invented
a concept called "the mythic" certainly, but their concept differed radically from the version accepted by the *communis opinio* of modern anthropologists. Thus what we call myth has neither essence nor reality
apart from a purely Eurocentric perspective. Each culture possesses its
own taxonomy for the narratives of its historicolegendary tradition. In
the central Himalayas, for example, the Pahari culture possesses a rich
oral tradition, but even within the local taxonomy, the criteria of classification fail to present any kind of homogeneity: they refer variously to
the content of the songs or to the different occasions of their being recited.[4]

A similar situation prevails in Greece. Myth does not exist, except as
a general notion of the mythic, which developed toward the end of the

fifth century, along with the kind of politicomilitary, psychologizing history exemplified by Thucydides. But what we call a legendary history of Greece is made up of a number of narratives, whose contents distinguish them from one another without causing them to be assigned to homogeneous categories: stories of a reigning family in the form of genealogies, narratives dealing with the founding of cities (*ktiseis*), local stories centering on a particular event, biographies of heroically magnified "historic personages." [5] Our knowledge of these "historical" genres depends on fragmentary products coming out of the movement to rewrite a coherent legendary past, a movement whose traces can be made out in the fifth century. Thus the history of primitive Greece is created for us in the prosaic labor undertaken by Hecataeus of Miletus to critically systematize epic legends. It can be seen in the attempt by Acusilaus of Argos to inscribe the legends of the Trojan War and of Heracles in the perspective of a single genealogical line centered at Argos and having its origin in a theocosmogony. It corresponds also to the undertaking of Pherecydes of Athens to synchronize the different legendary genealogies that existed in Greece. All these works, constituting the rewriting of legendary history, were entitled by the ancients *Genealogiai* or *Historiai*. [6]

Moving back in time from the classical epoch to the archaic, one becomes aware that legendary history does not exist as a specific genre. It generally gets confused with literary genres, which are distinguished by the manner of execution. For example, the narratives of Achilles' anger and of the events leading up to the Trojan War in an *Iliad* or *Cypria* are both designated by Herodotus as *epea*, poems in dactylic verse. The genealogy of Orestes written by the Lacedemonian poet Cinaethon is classified in this same literary genre, an epic poem in dactylic hexameters. The struggles of the Smyrnan people against Gyges and the Lydians are told in elegiac verse in the *Smyrneis* of Mimnermus of Colophon. A long narration in lyric verse tells of the destruction of Troy in the *Iliou Persis* by Stesichorus, not to mention the numerous legendary narratives in archaic lyric poetry presented in bits and pieces to illustrate the proposal of a poet composing for a given ritual or social occasion. [7]

The fifth century still, in large measure, pays tribute to these different modes and forms of writing history. It is thus impossible to determine whether the Cyrenean narrative of the founding of Cyrene, presupposed by the famous oath of the founders, was written in prose or in verse, and, if in the latter, in which meter. As for ourselves, we learn of this narrative—or these narratives—only in works whose end purpose is quite different from that of writing a city's history: the epinicia of Pindar, which were intended to eulogize the victor in an event at the Panhellenic games, or the *Histories* of Herodotus seeking to determine the causes of the great confrontation between Greeks and barbarians, not to mention learned works in epic form by the Alexandrian poets Callimachus or Apollonius of Rhodes, with their etiological concerns. Be it lyric verse, *logos* in prose, or poems in epic form, the narrative of the founding of the great Greek colony of Libya exists for us solely in the widest variety of literary forms.

There exists no autonomous narrative of the founding of Cyrene, just a number of legends, or fragments of legends, brought together in genres distinguished by their form, each governed by an individual perspective. Thus the following pages do not treat the legend of founding as an abstract narrative entity, but follow its development through the principal forms in which it is realized—first by Pindar, then by Herodotus in juxtaposition with Callimachus or Apollonius of Rhodes. Our fragmentary knowledge of the authors of *Lybica* or of *Cyrenaica*, works dating generally from the Hellenistic epoch, condemns them to play merely a supporting role: that of clarifying or completing, through information derived from narratives with historical pretensions, the unavoidable abridgments found in texts that are, properly speaking, poetic.[8]

NARRATIVE AND FIGURATIVE DEVELOPMENTS

The complexity of the enunciative situation in the narratives of Cyrene's founding may legitimate the semionarrative approach proposed here. In confronting elaborate literary texts, one must first rediscover the thread of a narrative development that is constantly interrupted, confused, or turned from its direction because of particular generic conditions or its own internal logic. This is especially the case with Pindar, past master of the rupture, the condensation, the retrospective digression, and the light allusive stroke.[9] But beyond reconstituting the logic of the narrative action and the causality linking the individual acts that make it up, we must envisage the values brought into play, which are inscribed in the succession of actions, affirmed or denied by them, transformed by them into new values.

As for the surface discursive structures, it is essential to pay attention to the figurative process of "actorialization" and "spatialization." By figures I mean those concrete semantic elements taken from the natural world in order to be moved about (*vehiculées*) by the actors of the narration or by the spaces where they evolve, giving rise during the course of the narrative's development to its "reality effect." Invested in actors, actions, or spatial trajectories (*parcours*), figures follow one another according to the syntactic dimension that is laid out by the narrative's linear unfolding. In general, this unfolding corresponds to the "canonic schema," which involves four phases—(1) manipulation (prompted by a condition of lack), (2) competence, (3) performance, and (4) sanction (return to a state of narrative equilibrium)—and also the causal link that this schema constructs. Thus the recurrence in the text of allied semantic elements leads to the definition of figurative and generic isotopies that assure the coherence of the text. As for the semionarrative structures, the profoundest stage of that schematization of which every discourse is the location, an attempt will be made to determine the themes that directly underlie the reiterations of figures. The thematic is then understood as the most abstract semantic level, where those concepts manifest themselves which underlie the choice, in the natural world, of surface figures. It is at this level that a discourse can become the location of a culturally and ideologically determined construction; at this moment of thematic and figurative articulation the discourse becomes the object of the process of construction, then of symbolic interpretation.[10]

Being culturally determined, these different expressions of the meaning-production process can never take on any value in themselves. It is invariably necessary to relate them to the conditions of utterance (énonciation). Semantic analysis cannot take place without reference to the conditions of the production and reception of meaning, as understood through the marks and instructions inherent in the discourse itself. The values that the text sets into play, and that a semionarrative analysis attempts to track down, are pertinent only in relation to the interpretive community to which the narrative was originally addressed. We cannot accept the supposed closure of the text or the negation of its richness. Epinicion, logos of inquiry, or learned epic poem, each is a case of a symbolic representation elaborated within the perspective of a unique situation. Whether historical or legendary, the past that is narratively constructed is always a function of the present.

We begin by interrogating Pindar, the oldest witness to the existence of narratives of Cyrene's foundation. And we begin with the most developed of his texts, the Fourth *Pythian*.

THE ARIADNE'S THREAD IN A
NARRATIVE LABYRINTH

At the outset Pindaric narration centers on the occasion of its recitation: the celebration of Arcesilas the Fourth, King of Cyrene. Also at the outset one can designate Apollo the Sender (*Destinateur*) of the king's action, that is to say the one who has enlisted it (manipulation). But then the Pindaric time machine, that appanage of his poetry, sets quickly to work.[11] The hymn evokes the oracular speech, addressed in an indeterminate past (*pote*, 4), to the one who is destined to become the founder of Cyrene; thus Apollo, through the mediation of the Pythia, is set in relation to Battus, designated from this moment as the "oecist of fecund Libya" (*oikistēra karpophorou Libuas*, 6). Whether ode or oracle, a speech of divine origin, put forward by an inspired mediator, brings together the human actor and the divinity who guides his action.

The victory won by the chariot of Arcesilas then places us at the completion of a narrative program in its moment of sanction, whose meaning is inverted because, once incarnated in the poem, it is conceived as an honor paid to the god as Sender (*Destinateur*) of victorious action. In contrast, Battus finds himself at the beginning of a trial into which that same god has enlisted him. This is the initial phase, termed "manipulation" in the narrative program of the "canonic schema." The narrative constructed by Pindar thus seems to make the story of Battus, founder of Cyrene, the narrative beginning of the story of the contemporary king of the city.

Sanction on the one hand, initial manipulation on the other: the narrative is still disarticulated. Now Pindar goes back seventeen generations before the founding act of Battus. Again, it is through the mediation of divinely inspired speech that the narration finally begins to develop, in a prediction articulated by the immortal mouth of Medea, when seized with a prophetic delirium that seems sourceless (*zamenēs*, 10). The first narrative utterance addressed by Medea to the demigod Argonauts on the occasion of their putting-in at Thera refers to the trajectory (*parcours*) of Battus; but this utterance situates the trajectory at an entirely distinct figurative level, in that the utterance brings onto the scene actors who are not anthropomorphic. From the insular land represented by Thera, Libya will give root to future cities consecrated to Zeus Ammon. Here one learns, through an implicit reference to the agonal occasion of the poem, that Theran colonists, instead of seafarers, are destined to become tamers of horses and drivers of chariots.

Medea finally enunciates the performance phase, along with the narrative transformation it signals, in prophesying to the future founders of Cyrene more or less the same future that Tiresias foresees for Odysseus during his encounter with the Homeric hero in the Underworld: that he will return to his city to restore order and journey by foot until the oar he carries is mistaken for a winnowing fan. A sacrifice to Poseidon will then mark Odysseus's leave-taking from the sea's domain and the beginning of a period of earthly abundance in the midst of his own people. For the descendants of Battus this prophecy translates as the transition from mastery of the waves to mastery of horses. Even on land, then, one remains in this case attached to a privileged domain of Poseidon.[12]

To complete this narrative transformation a chronological reckoning is activated by the mention of the seventeen generations that separate Medea's prediction from the founding act of Battus but is carefully effaced by the double *pote*, 'once upon a time,' of lines 10 and 14: both the speech of the girl inspired by Aietes, and the founding event that she announces, are situated in an indeterminate past.

Indeterminate as it might be, this past begins to take on nevertheless the form of a succession of events. Could Thera be considered the capital of a colony? The opportunity arises for Medea to recall an essential precedent, not contemporary with the colonists, but further back in time, in connection with the clod of earth. Once again in an indeterminate past (*pote*, 10), the narrative action referred back to its nonanthropomorphic foundation discovers at last its beginning, anticipating from afar the manipulation whose object will be Battus the founder.

Pindaric narration, however, fulfills the canonic schema only in terms of its most formal aspect. First, in place of the condition of lack that generally drives every narrative plot by inserting it into a causal sequence, the narrative of Medea creates a situation of paradox. Attempting to reach the Mediterranean Sea from Ocean, the Argonauts have just pulled their vessel for twelve days "across the back of a barren land" (26). They come to the mouth of Lake Triton, that body of water in the interior; Jason's "chariot"—from the synecdoche (with two meanings) 'beam' (*doru*, 27)—then reacquires its maritime character, and its "bridle" reacquires its use as anchor.[13] In this way, categories of navigation and equitation are mingled though they are carefully distinguished in the later phase of the narrative. In this singular situation Triton-Poseidon appears alone to the Argonauts.

In the absence of a true condition of lack, the meaning of the manipulation phase of the narrative ensemble remains hidden at first. Assuming mortal shape, Poseidon gives to Euphemus, first of the Argonauts to disembark upon the shore of Lake Triton, a handful of earth: it is his "gift of hospitality" (*xeinia*, 22; *xenion*, 35).[14] Should this be read as a simple act of welcome? Not at all, since the gift is accompanied by a clap of thunder sent by Zeus himself. Described as *aisios* (23), as responding therefore to the will of destiny, the sign from Zeus marks, within the narrative frame of the Argonauts' expedition, the point of departure for a new narrative action. The new subject will not be the

Argonauts as a group, but Euphemus, king of the holy city of Taenarum, *anax* (45) and *hērōs* (36), the son of Europa and Poseidon, the one who masters horses (*hipparkhos*, 45), the child born in the center of continental Greece near Cephisus but who reigns over the extreme reaches of the Peloponnesus. It is definitely, then, to his equal that this Poseidon, who takes the form of Eurypylus, speaks. Eurypylus himself, the scholia tell us, is the incarnation of Triton; but we are concerned principally with another son of Poseidon, of this god who, Pindar says, embraces the earth and has the power to shake it (*gaiaokhos, ennosidas*, 33).[15]

In so far as it does not arise from a condition of lack and is consequently not the object of a demand, the miraculous clod of earth appears as a spontaneous gift, without causal provocation. If the doubly divine intervention could be said to institute this gesture of hospitality as the manipulation phase of narrative action, this first step leads to a competence (*compétence*) and then to a performance that are both negative. As envisaged in Medea's prophecy, the same narrative program would have led Euphemus, on his return to Taenarum, to throw the clod of earth into the mouth of Hades, which was believed to open near the cape of the same name. By the fourth generation, the descendants of Euphemus of Taenarum, along with Danaans emigrating from Sparta, Argos, and Mycenae, would have taken possession (*ke . . . labe*, in the unreal mode; 47ff.) of the Libyan continent.[16]

Here, comparison with an analogous narrative in the fourth book of the *Argonautica* by Apollonius of Rhodes seems in order. In this work, produced three centuries after Pindar's, narration finds a temporal unfolding and a linear causality: the Argonauts' encounter with Triton-Poseidon now represents nothing more than a stage in the sequence of trials imposed on the voyaging heros; it corresponds to any one of a number of divine interventions aiming to assure their return to Iolcus. Even if this encounter is later revealed in the *Argonautica* as assuming the role of manipulation phase in the story of the founding of Thera (and not of Cyrene), this narrative will hold a position entirely subordinate to the unfolding of the principal plot. Pindar, to fulfill his eulogistic task, has completely reversed this subordination.

The manipulation phase of a secondary narrative, I would say, is activated in Apollonius by a condition of lack. Owing to a lack of *mētis* (1539), the Argonauts are unable to find the "passes" (*poroi*, 1538), the likely means, that would lead them out of Lake Triton.[17] Hence the offering that is made—to the gods 'of the locality' (*engenetai*, 1549)—of Apollo's tripod, hence also the countergift by Triton of a clod of earth. As ruler of this "littoral," Triton is soon revealed to be not only the avatar of the Eurypylus who is born in Libya (*engegaōs*, 1561) but, most important, the incarnation of Poseidon. Raised by a sacrifice intended for aquatic divinities (1600ff.), the god manifests himself fittingly in a shape at once equine and marine to guide the Argonauts' vessel toward the high seas. In a quest for knowledge, the Greek heroes thus acquire the power that enables them to complete an additional step along the return route out of the "confines" of the Libyan land (*peirata*, 1567). The characteristics of these confines—they nurture savage beasts (1561); terrestrial and aquatic paths intermingle there (1566ff.)—are found also in the Fourth *Pythian*.[18] But Triton's prophetic words, which announce the future stages reached in the Argonauts' success—Crete, the Peloponnesus—do not evoke at any point the coming to ground of the clod of earth at Thera. Furthermore, Apollo and Poseidon, whose respective interventions the Pindaric legend takes great care to distinguish, now appear together! The syntactic linearity of the narrative of Apollonius produces as its corollary a kind of semantic flattening; it aims above all at reintegrating the line of the principal narrative.

REORIENTATION OF THE NARRATIVE

Even while projecting into a later phase of his narration the consequences of the Libyan episode, the Argonauts' tribulations, Apollonius neglects to mention the unrealized narrative program evoked by the Pindaric Medea in the Fourth *Pythian*. Against this program, uttered in the unreal mode, Medea sets the one that will be substituted for it in reality, though some features of the latter appear negative on first inspection. Euphemius, as it turns out, has just lost control of the clod of earth, whose guardians let it fall into the sea instead of bringing it to the mouth of Hades. But this disjunction between the Subject and its Predicate in no way prevents the divine gift from undergoing a change of status: in coming to ground on the island of Thera, where Medea and the Argonauts are presently to be found (*en tāide nasōi*, 42), it is promised as the eventual "indestructable seed" of Libya. But in order for the realization and the sanction of this transformation to operate, the intervention of an anthropomorphic actor is indispensable.

Through such an intermediary, the negative narrative program, activated by the coming-to-ground of the clod and substituted for the unrealized program, will not delay in taking on a positive inflexion. This narrative reorientation is perfectly marked on the temporal level. Granted, the miraculous clod of earth arrives at Thera "out of season" (*prin hōras*, 43); but now (*nun*, 50), at the moment of Medea's prediction, an anthropomorphic actor will take the destiny of the divine gift back into his hands, to inflect its course. On reaching Lemnus, a point

that Pindar locates, contrary to the subsequent tradition, at the end of
the Argonauts' expedition, Euphemus and his companions will unite
with the women of the island.[19] And in anticipation of the seventeen
generations that will pass after the time contemporary with the utterance of Medea's words, one learns that the *genos* born of this fleeting
union will emigrate to Thera, "in this island" (line 52 takes up line 43).
There will be engendered the future lord (*despotas,* 53) of Libya. The
performance resulting from Apollo's manipulation of Battus (5), and
that which results from the manipulation of Poseidon (37), finally reach
a complete convergence.

The rectification of the conduct of the narrative program has as its
corollary not only the indicated temporal deviation but, more important, a displacement in the line of descent of Cyrene's founding hero.
Battus is not the direct, legitimate descendant of Euphemus, in that his
ancestor was born of an extramarital union between the king of Taenarum and a woman from another country. Added to this genealogical
displacement, there occurs a change in the Sender (*Destinateur*) of the
heroic action: it is no longer Poseidon but rather Apollo who, according
to the oracular words, is destined to guide Battus toward those regions
of the Nile reigned over by Zeus, son of Cronus (55f.).

Medea's Theran prediction situates itself spatially as well as chronologically at the center of the narrative. The phase of Euphemus's manipulation by Poseidon and of his failed performance thus actually locates
itself beyond the place and after the time of the prediction. The clod of
Libyan earth is lost at that time and subsequently reappears at Thera, in
the very place of Medea's prophecy. Starting from this point, and extending in the future, the bastard race engendered from the passion of
Euphemus and the Lemnian woman is guided from Lemnus to Thera
that it may take charge of its abandoned root. Hence the second phase
of manipulation already mentioned: Apollo presents to Battus, descendant of Euphemus, the oracle that will permit the seed to return to Libya,
there to bear fruit. At the realization of this performance, there lacks
nothing to complete the narrative program but the phase of sanction.

Medea the vaticinator is no longer in a position to prophesy the sanction of the narrative action, but she is the object of the narration enun-
ciated by the poem itself. Taking up again the projective narrative of the
sorceress, Pindar on two counts doubles it even as he completes it.

First, in an address to Battus, the son of Polymnestus, the narrator
insists on the manipulation phase of the Theran hero's colonial undertaking by showing that the oracular order from Apollo is the object of a
triple repetition. Given in response to a question on an entirely different
subject (the stammering that afflicts the future founder), this oracle is

additionally said to be "spontaneous" (*automatos*, 60); it makes of Battus a predestined king (*peprōmenon*, 61). As for the sanction of Battus's colonizing act, it is not yet made explicit in these lines; but the narrator situates it in the prosperity of Arcesilas, who lives "now" (*nun*, 64[20]), in the present of the poem's recitation, which is also favored by the Delphic god.

Interrupted by the longest narrative attested in a poem by Pindar—a narrative devoted to the adventures of the Argonauts—the address to Arcesilas is taken up again toward the end of the poem, at 250. It is repeated at the exact moment when the unfolding of actions of which the Argonauts are protagonists begins to become confused with the events leading up to the founding of Cyrene: their diversion by way of the Ocean (and thus by way of Libya) and their lingering with the Lemnian women, who, we learn, have killed their husbands (252). The union of the Greek heroes with these homicidal women takes place upon the outcome of a foot race that could be thought of as a prematrimonial trial, despite the fleeting character of the Argonauts' stay in Lemnus.[21] This union is finally a fortunate one because from it will be born the privileged "race" of Euphemus, destined to rediscover Libyan ground: from Lemnus to Lacedemonia, whence they will adopt Spartan culture, from there to Calliste-Thera, which they will colonize, and finally, through the intervention of Apollo, to Libya, where they will administer with prudent intelligence (*mētin*, 262) "the divine city of Cyrene" (*astu theion Kuranas*, 261). The narrative finishes by rediscovering its own logic!

A SEMANTIC LABYRINTH

The complexity of semantic development in the Fourth *Pythian* loses nothing in comparison to that of its syntactic articulation. The interlacing of recurrent isotopic figures, which assures their coherence, is so dense that a commentary on the entire poem would require, from this point on, a book in itself. Now the different semantic strata within the narrative tissue of the Fourth *Pythian* depend intimately upon the enunciative voices that support them. Thus the monograph recently devoted to this attractive Pindaric poem emphasizes the skillful polyphony that interlaces the voice of the narrator addressing *hic et nunc* its Receiver (*Destinataire*) Arcesilas, the prophetic words of Medea reported in direct discourse, and the oracles of Apollo relayed by the voice of the Pythia and cited indirectly, not to mention the individual voices of the Argonauts, protagonists of the narrative, to whom Pindar willingly surrenders the floor, such as Mopsus the soothsayer of Zeus. All of these voices are prophetic in a context in which the clod of Libyan earth itself becomes an oracular portent (*ornis*, 19).[22]

Attention has yet to be paid to the hierarchic relations that, from the perspective of the legend of Cyrene, orchestrate the three voices mentioned above. These take shape, at first, through the mediation of the narrative's temporal organization: Medea's prophecy, inspired (*anepseuse*, 11) perhaps by Aphrodite (cf. 216ff.) occurs in the *pote*, the "once upon a time," chronologically the furthest back. Seventeen generations later, one finds the oracles of the Pythia inspired by the god of Delphi; finally, in the "today" (*sameron*, 1) of the poem's execution, the narrator is the one who speaks, relayed to Arcesilas's side by the muse.[23] But undoubtedly the spatial arrangement of these different voices is the most important. I have already referred to the central position assured in the narrative itself by Thera, the location of Medea's prediction. To this we can now add Delphi, explicit origin of the Apollonian oracles; yet it belongs to the voice of the poet, from Thebes onward (222) and through the mediation of the Muse, to set Delphi and then Thera in relation with Cyrene. The spatial order of the utterance of the poem's different voices ends by inverting the temporal organization of these same voices. The most originary is also the most decentralized, and it is the most recent voice that can designate, after Thebes, the hitherto uncharted course between Thera, Delphi, and the land of Libya. To the temporal mark "today," which opens the poem, there responds the spatial mark that concludes it, closing it upon itself to create a ring-shaped structure: *Thebai*. Thebes is the source of ambrosial songs (299), that is to say, songs of divine origin.[24]

Having considered the narrative's modes of utterance and the homologies that organize its space, time, and shared reference to divine inspiration, we move on to the actual tissue of utterances woven by these voices. Before teasing out the complex spatial image that the narrative constructs, we can try to define the isotopies that arrange its contents. We know that in classical Greece, as in other societies, the moment of matrimonial union is readily compared to labor. The metaphoric relation is frequently between a field made fertile by being plowed and sown and the essential goal of the Greek institution of marriage: the production of handsome children, themselves conceived, in a vegetal image, as offspring or as new shoots. But agricultural activity, and particularly grain-centered culture, serve, for their part, as the metaphorical expression of the achievement of civilization. Agriculture and the production of grain are situated at the center of Greek representation of social life, while political activity is itself the birthright of offspring born of legal marriage between citizens.[25]

Precisely upon these three levels—of agricultural production, foundation of a family, and the development of civic life, according to a vegetal isotopy and a doubled human isotopy—Pindar, playing all the while upon their reciprocal metaphoric relations, articulates the semantic values of the narrative of founding Cyrenaica. The clod that Euphemus receives from the hands of Eurypylus-Poseidon as hospitality gift is in origin a handful of earth (*gaia*, 26). But at the very moment when it is presented to Euphemus it becomes a fragment of "plowed earth" (*aroura*, 34), only to transform itself into a "divine clod" (*bōlax daimonia*, 37) when the hero sets foot on the ground of Libya to receive it. Incidentally this encounter with the human incarnation of Poseidon occurs after the Argonauts' long journey across a region of earth (*gaia*, 26) that is entirely barren. Arriving in Thera, the clod becomes the "indestructible seed" of Libya (*sperma aphthiton*, 43). Then, Medea's prediction gives two complementary images of the clod's return to its land of origin: the return is conceived as an act of transplantation (*phuteuesthai*, 15) by Libya, granddaughter of Zeus, and as the pulling of a root (*rhiza*, 15) from the "land battered by floods" (*haliplaktos ge*, 14) that Thera represents, a root destined to produce the trunk for numerous cities upon ground already prepared for its coming, the land consecrated to Zeus Ammon (*themethla* in 16 implies in its etymology the founding act expressed by the verb *tithenai*). But the gardener for this transplantation would be Battus, the future master of these plains covered with clouds and rain (*kelainephea pedia*, 52), the fertile territory (*pion*, 56) controlled by the son of Cronus. In the same way as the plays upon time, the metaphor drawn from the fecundation of the earth contributes to the conjoining of two acts, the two narrative performances that, at the poem's beginning, distinguished their respective phases of manipulation. At the beginning of the ode Libya was already seen as a "productive" land (*karpophoros*, 6), and within this frame the hill forming the acropolis of Cyrene could be defined as a breast (*mastos*, 8).[26] Having served as relay for the fecund clod, Thera can henceforth figure, in the proper sense of *matropolis* (20), as the "mother city." The fecundation of the soil thus—simultaneously—results from and produces nurturing cities.

But this manipulation of earth is incapable, in its strictly feminine character, of fully accomplishing the act of founding a city. The absent masculine principle will be supplied by the *genos* of Battus, by way of the narrative displacement that has been described. This *genos*, conceived in the bed of foreign women (*allodapai*, 50) becomes the object, at the end of the poem, of an important reinterpretation: it becomes a "predestined seed" (*sperma moiridion;* the term *sperma* being a correction by Hermann), planted in "foreign fields" (*arourai allodapai*, 254). Euphemus's "race" takes on, in turn, a plantlike sprouting (*phuteuthen*, 256).[27] Its action bears as much upon the administration of the divine city of Cyrene (261) as upon the mastery and fecundation of Libya's well-watered plains, which are made to "swell" (*ophellein*, 260) by the god's benediction. Euphemus's offspring will end, in fact, by controlling both the city's political activity and the agricultural production of its *chōra*.[28] The success of this transplantation will deploy its full effects at the very moment when the poem by Pindar is uttered, in that its blossoming (*thallei*, 65) is attributed to Arcesilas the Fourth, the eighth offshoot (*meros*, 65) of Battus the founder.

The imbrication of these three metaphoric levels, no one of which is hierarchically superior to another, fails, however, to account sufficiently for the specificity of the founding of a colonial city. There is yet missing a properly cosmogonic dimension. The spatial trajectories (*parcours*) followed respectively by the clod (the feminine element) and by the race of Euphemus (the masculine) are, in this respect, particularly important.

The famous clod issues from the shore of the Libyan Lake Triton. Variously described as a lake, a sea, even a river, this strange stretch of water is hemmed in by solid land even while remaining in communication with the sea, but the Argonauts—as has been said—reach it by a land route. Neither sea nor earth, Lake Triton is also distinguished by its shallows. From Herodotus onward this lake was renowned for the worship the inhabitants of its banks were reputed to offer up to Triton, Poseidon, and above all, Athena. In point of fact, one of the numerous versions of the birth of Athena locates the event on the shores of Lake Triton; Tritogeneia is one who is "born of the earth" (*gēgenēs*).[29]

But this terrain—propitious for chthonic births—is not in itself sufficient to assure the fertility of the clod, hospitality gift of Poseidon. Its first destination, as we have seen, is one of the extremities of the Greek continent, the Peloponnesian Cape Taenarum with its mouth of Hades (44) and the sanctuary of Poseidon associated with it.[30] Through this opening, explicitly associated with "extremities," Heracles is said to have dragged Cerberus into the light of day. Bacchylides describes the Hades visited by the heroic son of Zeus as the dwelling of Persephone, and Euripides produces a version of the legend according to which Heracles would have been initiated into the Eleusinian Mysteries to permit his descent into hell. It is, besides, in the sacred wood consecrated to the chthonian Demeter, next to Hermione, that the hero would have buried the captured canine monster.[31]

To throw the clod of Libyan earth into the mouth of Hades at Cape Taenarum is thus to cause it to reach the kingdom of Persephone through a gesture of consecration characteristic of communication with the world of the dead. This act is perhaps to reproduce the gesture, made by legitimate wives in Athens, of placing young pigs in pits at the time of the Thesmophoria; the pigs' dead bodies are not intended to remain inactive in the bowels of the earth. Recuperated in the period of plowing and sowing and mixed with crop seeds, these evil-smelling remains represented the promise of an abundant harvest. We know that the exemplary act reputed to legitimate this strange rite is none other than the myth of Core's shared sojourn between Hades and the earth's cultivated surface. But the Libyan clod is not destined to know the revivification traced by the myth of Core and Demeter. As there is no fall into Hades, there is also no Calligeneia, no "Beautiful Birth." In fact, on the occasion of this rite, within the frame of the Athenian Thesmophoria, were associated the growth of agricultural products and the generation (*spora*) of men; as Epictetus teaches it, the seed (*sperma*) must rest buried for a time in the earth in order to bear fruit.[32]

Now, through the neglect of Euphemus and his guards, the clod of Libya disappears into the sea instead of being swallowed up into the bowels of the earth. An island, a bit of anchored earth in the vast sea stretches, then receives it. The mediating role played by Thera is marked as much by its geographical position midway between Libya and the Peloponnesus as by its hybrid status as island, a status that many Greek insular lands share with Santorini.

Delos, for example, "battered by the waves" like Thera, is itinerant until the moment when the hospitality it accords Leto and Apollo finally fixes it in one place. Asteria becomes Delos the same way that Calliste becomes Thera, at the moment of its colonization by the descendants of Euphemus (258). The civilizing intervention of Apollo becomes all the more indispensable in that, according to the Greek representation, the islands are first the product of a cosmogonic act by Poseidon, who, in order to form them, threw rugged mountains down into the sea and caused them to take root there, acting at a purely geological level. Thus, before the birth of Apollo, Delos offered a topography more propitious to seabirds than to horses, and is described by the *Homeric Hymn to Apollo* as devoid of herds and of vegetation, a stony land threatening to disappear beneath the waves.[33] Rhodes plunges its roots directly into the sea and emerges through the action of Poseidon Genethlius, the "Generator," to satisfy Helius, neglected by Zeus in the distribution of the *timai*. In contrast to Delos, it is a nurturing land for men and favorable to herds. The reason, Pindar adds in the Seventh *Olympian,* is that it benefited from the shower of gold that Zeus made fall on the occasion of Athena's birth, who, for her part, hastened to grant to Rhodes that it would excel in all artistic techniques. Like Delos, however, Rhodes will only know the achievement of urban civilization when it is colonized by Tlepolemus at the injunction and under the protection of Apollo.[34]

A MYTH OF AUTOCHTHONY

For some time no doubt the word "autochthony" has been on the reader's lips. It is a strange autochthony nevertheless for these islands, which themselves undergo autochthonous births that generally benefit the founding heroes of continental *chorai*. And again, it is a question of birth out of the ocean depths and not out of the bowels of the earth. So, for example, at Sparta, the very first king of the land, founder of its aboriginal dynasty, was believed to have been born from the earth and consequently to have reigned upon his mother's ground.[35] We know, too, the double myth of Athenian autochthony. The first king of Attica, Cecrops, is not only born from the earth—this is the fate of any number of primordial beings—but issues from the earth belonging to the city over which he will extend his sovereignty. Like Triton, he is *diphuēs,* a being half-man, half-serpent. As with the other colonizing heroes, his intervention signifies a change of name for the land over which he reigns: "Acte" becomes "Cecropia" before bearing the name "Attica." But, more important, the autochthonous birth of Cecrops coincides with the moment the gods reapportion the Greek cities among themselves, the *timai* of Zeus, from which each receives in turn a share of *timai*. Hence the famous struggle between Athena and Poseidon. Thanks to the olive tree, Athena is able to extend her power over Attica, while Poseidon pretended to the same control by inverting the gesture of founding islands: under the blow of the god's trident the sea rises up in the center of Athens, upon the rock of the Acropolis.[36] As in primordial Libya, early Attica is marked by a mixture of earth and water.

The second legendary narrative of Athenian autochthony reverses the terms of the vegetal graft metaphor. No longer is the idea of germ and root transposed into the geological domain to figure the creation of a territory and to anticipate, by this image, the birth of a *genos*. Instead, the sperm of a man is literally planted into an already existing soil to engender the first king of a long dynasty. This marks a reversal, but also an impoverishment: human generation is invested in the vegetal figure, certainly, though it abandons its geological and cosmogonic expression. The reason for these modifications in the functioning of the symbolic process can be sought in two different directions: first, from the side of an underlying historic reality. According to the evidence, Attica was never founded by a colonizing act and was never so represented. But consideration must also be given to the narrative medium: the rationalized mythological account, attributed to Apollodorus, that gives us the Athenian legend does not lend itself to the constant game of metaphorical cross-checkings proper to the Pindaric epinicion.[37]

A mythic and metaphorical situation analogous to that explaining the birth of Attica concerns Thebes. The autochthony to which the Cadmeans can lay claim is founded upon the tilling and seeding of the motherland, from which are born the Spartoi, literally the "sown men." Aeschylus in the *Seven against Thebes* reappropriated this metaphor—of the generation of a *genos*—to illustrate the incestuous act of Oedipus, the parricide who inseminated the sacred furrow of his own mother and inserted there a blood-stained root (*rhiza*). With the dramatic poet, we reencounter the three levels—mineral, vegetal, and human—of the metaphoric expression of a reigning family's birth, accursed as it might be.[38]

There are then autochthony myths whereby continental cities give root to their inhabitants in the ground of the motherland. But there also exist "marine" autochthony myths that aim to give terrestrial roots to islands floating at sea, before causing continental peoples, capable of founding human civilization, to emigrate there. If Santorini occupies an intermediate geographical position between the continent and Libya and if its foundation by Theras confers upon it, in all likelihood, the status of a hybrid autochthony like Delos or Rhodes, Libya itself assumes an even more marginal position, exemplifying a third class of possible representations of autochthony. Centered on Lake Triton and placed under the control of Poseidon, Libya is indeed truly neither earth nor sea. To acquire an "autochthonous" value, its roots would most fittingly originate on the outside, in the bowels of the continent, near Cape Taenarum. But in an additional confusion of separate categories, the Libyan earth comes to ground upon the island of Thera and can only there acquire the generative force of a germ; this also is the moment when human actors can intervene in a positive way.

Autochthony, therefore, cannot be realized without anthropomorphic actors. Of course, even before its arrival in Thera, the piece of Libyan earth has been manipulated by Euphemus, but the lack of care taken by the son of Poseidon causes the divine clod to fall short of its original destination. Should we be surprised when Apollonius of Rhodes, seconded by a commentator on Pindar, tells us that Euphemus has precisely the ability to synthesize, through his gift of walking upon the ocean waters, the categories of sea and land? Conversely, does he not reach Lake Triton by a land route and yet on a boat? This capacity to confound semantic categories is inscribed even in the genealogy of the Taenarian king. His mother, Europa, is in fact the daughter of Tityus, a Giant born from Earth.[39] Doubtless these qualities can make of Euphemus the king of a port city attached to the continent, but not the founder of an essentially continental colony.

Reclaimed by a descendant of Euphemus, the Libyan clod could not have fallen into better hands. Not only has the union of which this bastard is the offspring taken place on an island, but, in addition, the Lemnian woman, the Taenarian king's bride during his stay, has killed her legitimate husband.[40] However, before establishing themselves at Thera, the descendants of Euphemus and the murderess "mingle" with the Lacedemonians, as in a sexual union (line 257).[41] And the emigration to Thera would, for its part, have as its frame the colonial enterprise led by Theras the Lacedemonian, the eponymous hero of the island.

I will attempt to shed light on the convergence at Sparta between the descendants of Euphemus and the founding hero Theras when I discuss the text of Herodotus. For the moment, I will limit myself to filling in the Pindaric allusions by specifying that Theras, Cadmean in origin and consequently from Thebes, comes from a continental city, though he lives as a foreigner in Lacedemonia. He is in fact only the maternal uncle of Eurysthenes and Procles, the Heraclids who carry on in Sparta the autochthonous dynasty that founds the two dynasties exercizing political power over the city. Like the descendants of Euphemus, Theras is an outsider in relation to the political legitimacy of Lacedemonia. But on the island of Calliste, which his arrival transforms into Thera, he recovers his own. While in search of Europa, Cadmus had in fact left one of his parents there, not without having founded a sanctuary consecrated to both Athena and Poseidon. Hence, explain the scholia, Pindar's qualifier for the island: "holy" (*hiera,* 6). And Hierocles adds—no doubt much later—that the worship of Apollo would have taken root there only consequently, on the occasion of settlement there by colonists originally from Lacedemonia.[42] The colonial undertaking launched toward Calliste-Thera thus finds itself in the hands of two lines with ties that are in part continental and with royal ancestry, but both strangers to the *genos* that holds political power in the capital. We rediscover these different aspects in the genealogy of Battus, and we will see that the narrative of the founding of Tarentum inserts its protagonists into much the same kind of ancestry. But in founding a colony of continental character, Battus enjoys an additional quality: he maintains a privileged relationship with Apollo, a point upon which Pindar insists (lines 5ff., 50ff., 59ff., 259ff.).[43] The Sender (*Destinateur*) in this respect plays a central role.

APOLLONIUS OF RHODES: NARRATIVE RECTIFICATIONS

Before dealing with the qualities invested in the Senders (*Destinateurs*) of the action, we should compare the lot that the anthropomorphic actors reserve for the clod of Libya in the narrative by Apollonius of Rhodes. Some eloquent variations appear.

Inserted into a simple exchange of hospitality gifts when the Argonauts seek to escape from the shallows of Lake Triton, the clod of earth that Triton-Eurypylus-Poseidon offers Euphemus does not seem destined for any narrative future whatsoever. Only toward the end of the last book of the *Argonautica* and Euphemus's dream on the island of salvation (Anaphe from *anaphainō*, 1730) is the clod enlisted in a narrative program, one that remains secondary to the principal action. The reason the secondary program remains unresolved is that, upon reaching Anaphe, practically at the end of the Argonauts' itinerary, it is essentially a question of presenting the *aition* of creating the neighboring island of Thera. At this point in Apollonius's scholarly narrative, the founding of Cyrene is no longer pertinent. But particularly in the four interpretations it receives, this Hellenistic text still, in large measure, pays tribute to the classical representation of the colonization process.

We begin, then, with Euphemus's dream, which substitutes recollection for the forgetting of an object that, in the Pindaric version, was the handful of earth. Divine (*daimoniē*, 1734) as in the Fourth *Pythian*, the clod is nurtured by Euphemus himself; the king of Taenarum is then cast in the role of its mother before becoming a lover when it transforms itself into a beautiful young girl. Through inversion of sexual roles and incest, all family roles are thus confused. But on a second interpretive level, for which the young girl herself is responsible, she reveals herself to be the daughter of Triton and Libya and destined to nurture the offspring of Euphemus, having first been entrusted to the Nereids.[44] The distinction between the family roles that devolve on each gender is reestablished by negating the incestuous relation and by a woman's assumption of the nurturing function. In addition, the young girl will mediate between the domain of the sea and the surface of the earth, following the same course as the island of Anaphe, which rises from the bottom of the sea at the will of Apollo. Entrusted for her rearing to the sea daughters of Nereus, the young girl will receive the descendants of Euphemus in the light of day. But the oneiric memory of Euphemus has for its double, at a third level, the waking memory of Jason. Thus, Apollo's oracle as given to the leader of the Argonauts at the beginning of the expedition ends up conferring on the dream and its interpretation a third meaning; the oracular speech, even while remaining figurative, transports us beyond the narrative's anthropomorphic surface. Euphemus must throw the clod into the waves so that, with the aid of the gods, it might become the island of Thera, future abode of his descendants: this handful of mud is indeed nothing other than a fragment of the terra firma (*ēpeiros*, 1753), which Libya represents, gift from Poseidon. Little remains for Apollo's prediction, at this point, but to receive its realization, in a narrative reality that forms a fourth interpretive level. Mineral, anthropomorphic, and divine actors now behave in concert. Euphemus throws the clod into the sea's abyss, whence Calliste subsequently rises. Sacred (*hierē*, 1758), the island becomes nurturer to the children of the Taenarian Argonaut, of whose migratory course we proceed to learn: to Lemnus, whence they are driven by the Tyrrhenians; then to Sparta, where they are accorded the privileges of the city; and finally to Calliste, to which they are led by Theras, who gives his name to the island risen from the waves—but of Battus, not a word.[45]

The hierarchic inclusion of four enunciative and semantic levels seems to furnish the contemporary interpreter with unexpected hermeneutic confirmations. It is enough to privilege for explication one of the levels that the narrative proposes in order that the psychoanalyst, the narratologist, the theologian, and the historian may each profit. I limit myself here to a brief comparison with the parallel narrative of Pindar, avoiding a reduction to any single level that would become the explicator of the others.

From a syntactic point of view, the narrative of Apollonius, with its etiological aim, no longer presents the deflected program manifested by the Pindaric narration. Memory has replaced forgetting and made Thera into the direct creation of Euphemus, who is manipulated by Poseidon and enlightened by Apollo. Instead of existing before his arrival, the island is born of the clod and changes its name when the descendants of Euphemus, led by the descendant of Polynices, come from Sparta to colonize it. The convergence, in the generation of Thera, of the explicit course of the clod, the itinerary of Euphemus's descendants and that of Theras as well corresponds to the joint interventions of the two divinities that the Pindaric narrative, for its part, works to distinguish. In its syntax, the narrative of Apollonius is thus "rectified," as is—we will see—that of Herodotus. From a figurative viewpoint as well the different enunciative levels of the narrative all tend to deny and to counteract the deviations that are revealed, at the first level, by Euphemus's dream.

On the other hand Apollonius does not succeed in completely effacing certain figurative values belonging to the Pindaric narrative. The clod retains its generative power; it retains also its metaphoric capacity to be the nurturer of the *genos* of Euphemus. It is in addition the locus of the transition between the sea's domain and the terrestrial surface that is characteristic of the cosmogonic aspect of insular myths of founding. Also significant from this perspective is the collaboration between Poseidon's demiurgy and Apollo's founding intervention, even if Apollonius's narrative tends to superimpose them. In its syntactic dimension, the Hellenistic narrative can still be considered a myth of (insular) "autochthony," but its different levels of metaphoric expression are made explicit by the interpretations that have been integrated into the narrative itself to increase its verisimilitude.

THE TRIAD OF FOUNDING GODS

As Senders (*Destinateurs*) of human actions, the gods in the Pindaric version of Cyrene's colonization play precisely the determining role one would expect. The foundation phase, which manipulates even the ground of the colony, is placed entirely under the control of Poseidon, a "terrestrial" Poseidon, let us call him, to avoid the over-used term, "chthonic," whose action is indispensable for creating and stabilizing the foundations of any city. Even at Thera the above-mentioned worship is offered to Poseidon *Gaieokhos,* "who holds the earth." The sons of the earth god are then naturally the first kings of those cities newly established on firm ground.[46] But on islands and in the colonies, the primordial act of demiurgic foundation accomplished under the auspices of Poseidon remains without effect if it is not followed by an immigration of men originally from the continent and guided by Apollo. Even Delphi does not escape this scenario. Chthonic Gaia and Poseidon are the ones who utter the oracles before Apollo takes the prophetic function back from these primordial divinities. The avowed aim of this divine succession is nothing less than civilization (*hēmerotēs*).[47]

After Poseidon the founder and Apollo the colonizer, we have yet to deal with the third Sender (*Destinateur*) of Greek civilizing action, as narrated by Pindar, upon the Libyan continent. Every phase of this action is favored by the presence, albeit discreet, of Zeus, the father of the Olympian gods, who marks by an auspicious clash of thunder (*aision,* 23) the gift of Libyan earth by one son of Poseidon to another. After its diversion through Thera, this terrestrial root will emerge from the ground that already serves as foundation for the worship of Zeus Ammon (line 16). Beneath the gaze of Zeus's eagles, protectors of the *omphalos* of Delphi, Battus receives from Apollo the oracle enlisting him in the colonizing effort (line 4).[48] Apollo alone is capable of assuring the fertility of Libyan soil, to make of it the "rich sanctuary" that is consecrated to him (line 56).

This appurtenance of Libya to Zeus is not expressed merely in the worship of Ammon but also, in legend, by the ancestry of Libya, the granddaughter by Epaphus (line 14) of the son of Cronus, ancestor of the Danaans, and by the characteristic climate of the region around Cyrene, where black clouds gather to fecundate the ground (line 56).[49] Zeus's presence in Libya is required as much because he is the imposer of order over the terrestrial surface as from his being keeper of the fecundating water from "on high." The god of the heights thus orchestrates his action with that of the god of the depths to constitute, through their separation, the terrestrial surface, the world that nurtures mankind.[50] But under the control of Poseidon and Zeus, the African continent yet exists merely as the land of Libya. Only with the foundation of Cyrene under the auspices of Apollo will it be marked by the seal of civilization (Greek, of course!). By simplifying, no doubt in the extreme, we can represent the collaboration of these three divinities in the colonizing act as a distribution of the isotopies that run through the narrative: to Poseidon the mineral, to Zeus the vegetal, and to Apollo the human!

SEMANTIC REVERBERATIONS OF THE ODE

The theme of generation/germination takes upon itself, by turns, figures organized in isotopies: mineral, vegetal, and human; attachment of masculine political legitimacy to an earth-motherland; complementarity of Poseidon, Zeus, and Apollo, and so on. These lines of semantic development assure the coherence and richness of the Pindaric narrative. Guaranteed by the assimilation of the different enunciative voices that carry the narrative, this play of semantic reverberations and reciprocal metaphors recurs in the two other narrative sections of the Fourth *Pythian* that focus on the Argonauts' expedition and on the fate of Damophilus, contemporary of Arcesilas the Fourth.

Relying on Segal's recent study, we here need only recall that the Pindaric version of the Argonauts' expedition presents the capture of the Golden Fleece as the root (*phuteuthen,* 69) of fame for the Minyans who accompany Euphemus, the ancestor of Battus. Jason's arrival at Iolcus is predicted by an oracle uttered near the Delphic *omphalos,* at the center of the earth mother (line 74). Under Apollo's protection, the hero comes to recover the power accorded his great-grandfather Aeolus (line 107): thus he merely returns to the land of his fathers (lines 97ff. and 117ff.), whose rule was overturned by Pelias, son of Poseidon, a descendant, like Jason, of Zeus (lines 138ff. and 167). As for the quest for the Golden Fleece, it is placed under Zeus's protection in an episode that inverts the gift of Libyan earth to Euphemus. It is at the stern of the ship, once the anchor has been raised, that Jason receives the favorable sign from the father of the gods (lines 191ff.). Arriving at the Euxine Sea, the Argonauts pass into the domain of Poseidon (line 204). In this untamed land Jason succeeds in accomplishing an incredible labor, after having yoked the raging oxen of Aietes and having promised marriage to his daughter Medea (lines 218ff.). Finally, the dragon that guards the Golden Fleece submits under Jason's blows to the same fate as Python beneath the sword of Apollo.[51] As for the heroes' return to Greece, it was anticipated by the adventures of Euphemus, with which it partly coincides. Pindar breaks, then, Jason's circular course into two segments, whose order of succession he inverts. But reestablished in its circularity, this itinerary repeats, with the aid of adjacent figures, the course of the miraculous clod that—with its autochthonous value—becomes in Libya the foundation of a city after its long diversion by way of Thera.

And an analogous course is desired by Pindar for Damophilus, the Cyrenean exiled to Thebes: the same circular scheme, but with its second portion projected into the future in relation to the moment of utterance. After having frequented the palace of Battus (line 280), and although he has learned to hate hubris (line 284), this just heart lives far from "the land of his fathers" (line 280). He is at that point compared to Atlas, the son of a Titan and an Oceanid who—other texts add—is banished to the limits of the earth to assure, from his place at the bottom of the sea's abyss, the cosmological separation of sky and earth. To free the Cyrenean from this assimilation with the quasidemiurgic role of the Titanid and to reestablish the order desired by Zeus, Pindar asks Arcesilas, who enjoys the protection of Apollo Paean, to intervene as a doctor would (line 270). Damophilus hopes, in effect, to recover his "house," that is to say, the neighborhood of the spring of Apollo, with its joys of the banquet and of poetry amid citizens living in harmony (hēsukhia, 296).[52]

In short, it is always the same passage that is in question, circular yet transformational, from a state in which civilization is merely latent to a state of realized civility, through an intermediate stage in which the protagonist grapples with primordial forces that, once dominated, give rise to culture.[53] The terrestrial germ of Libya becomes a Greek city after having sunk beneath the ocean waves; Jason, a king in strength, will reign over Iolcus after having imposed tillage, yoke, and marriage upon the untamed forces—geological, theriomorphic, and anthropomorphic—of a fringe territory; Damophilus will return to the activities of civilization and of the political community of men after having purged his presumption by undergoing the primordial punishment of Atlas. But, in a reversal that belongs exclusively to Pindar, Damophilus's Titanesque sojourn in Thebes is transformed *in extremis* into an initiation into poetry in the vicinity of a welcoming and inspirational spring (line 299, compared with lines 21ff.). Subtly, the poet inserts into the domain of civilization the place of his enunciation even while taking up again the poetic itinerary that, leading from Delphi to Cyrene by way of Thebes, opens the poem. The ode hence ends as it began, as the banquet understood as the location of literary inspiration. But this most skillful movement of recuperation belongs to the constraints that the occasion imposes upon the Pindaric narrative of Cyrene's founding.

The Cyrenean myth told in in the Fourth *Pythian* thus takes as its figure the manipulation of the earth of Libya, in an action that, though the intermediacy of a vegetal growth gradually humanized, ends by assuming the nearly historical person of Battus, thereafter centering on the city of Cyrene.

The Ninth *Pythian* leaves to one side the metaphoric echoes of these three interwoven isotopies of generation (autochthonous), in order to fix the listener's attention on the colonial city. Returning again to metaphoric expression, the foundation narrative builds itself around another theme, and in pursuance of a completely different isotopy, takes the figure of the biography of the city's eponymous nymph.

THE SYNTAX OF A BIOGRAPHY

It is undoubtedly easier to reconstitute this narrative plot than that of the previous ode. In the mountainous confines of Thessaly, the young Cyrene guards the herds of her father, defending them from the attacks of wild animals. Apollo is taken with the young girl in the course of her athletic struggle against a mighty lion (situation of lack provoked by the desire for amorous fulfillment). The advice asked by the god of the Centaur Chiron with regard to the realization of his desire allows, in a typically Pindaric procedure, the anticipation of the outcome of the intrigue at the same time that the manipulation phase is provided. Paradoxically, it is the wise Chiron who, in revealing the oracular god's future to him, appears as the Sender (*Destinateur*) of Apollo.[54] The union of the nymph and the god, probably the latter's first experience of love, will have Libya as its frame. To accomplish the transformation proper to every narration, the performance realized in the form of conjunction must be accompanied by a spatial disjunction. The promised sanction: the birth of a son destined to reunite divine qualities in his own immortality.

Undoubtedly the prophetic counsel of Chiron is only a narrative artifice intended to break the linearity of the narrative. In any case, with the competence that is his by virtue of his divinity, Apollo immediately realizes in performance the Centaur's prophecy. He joins in love with Cyrene in the palace of Libya, which, for this occasion, also takes the figure of a woman. Reserved exclusively for Cyrene is a second sanction in addition to the promised son: control of a city distinguished by its beauty and excellence in the games. The pretext for the narrator to advert at this point to the occasion of the poem is the brilliant Pythian victory of Telesicrates of Cyrene.[55] *Epinicie oblige!*

It has often been said that the heart of Pindar's narrative is matrimonial union, doubled by the young couple's transportation to Libya. There has been little analysis, however, of the figures assumed by this simple narrative transformation. It has been considered a punctual event, and critics have been insensitive to the change in status it implies for Cyrene.

Cyrene is a virgin hunter (*parthenos agrotera*, 7). But, unlike Atalanta, for example, her rejection of labor and of conviviality with her companions (18f.) is not the corollary of a rejection of marriage. If Cyrene battles with wild beasts, she does so because she is the shepherdess of her father's cows (21ff.).[56] Just as the young Theseus fought barehanded the monsters that infested Attica, she struggles with the lion (26ff.). Like that adolescent hero, she is armed with javelins and a sword (20f.).[57] These masculine qualities of strength and courage (32ff.) attract Apollo, who is himself represented as an adolescent with long hair (5). In addition, the young woman's genealogy singles her out as being close to the founding gods of the Hellenic cosmos. Her father Hypseus, king of the Lapiths, issues from the union of the river Peneus, son of Ocean, and the naiad Creusa, daughter of Ge. Their union is sheltered by the dales of Pindus, the great mountain chain separating Thessaly from the west.[58]

Cyrene, with Apollo, takes advantage of Aphrodite's hospitality after having been transported to Libya in the god of Delos's divine chariot. Soon, she becomes sovereign (*despoina*, 7) of this territory, mistress of a veritable city (*arkhepolis*, 54). When she reaches adulthood, the nymph returns to a protective role in which she is likened to a man. But the fact that the wedding of Cyrene and Apollo marks the installation of the young woman in a political role does not prevent the marriage from assuming its traditional role as a passage to maternity, the function that characterizes the status of the married woman. In Libya, Cyrene gives birth, as we have said, to a son who will be brought up and immortal-ized by the Seasons, as well as by his great-grandmother Ge. There is nothing surprising in such a destiny for a son who will take up sheep-herding, his mother's former task. He will also assume roles (by way of interposed *epicleseis*) that will identify him with both Apollo and Zeus: Agreus, "the hunter," Nomius, "the shepherd," Aristaius, the "excel-lent" or the "benefactor"(65).[59] Hunting and herding open up the per-fect order, established by Zeus.

The contrast between the two poles of spatial displacement accom-panying Cyrene's transformation into both an adult woman and a man simultaneously repeats this transformation. Apollo notices the young Cyrene, an inhabitant of "the thickets of shadowy mountains" (33ff.) in the wind-battered Pelion range (5) lying at the eastern limit of Thes-saly.[60] Apollo wants to bring the huntress into the "extraordinary gar-den" kept by Zeus in Libya (53). It seems, on this occasion, that Aphro-dite rules there.[61] The young woman who had refused to take up domestic chores is conjoined with Apollo is a golden palace (56 and 69). Now sovereign, Cyrene has part of the land at her disposal (*khthonos aisa*, 56). It is a land of "vast prairies" whose produce would still be called remarkable. According to an image used in the Fourth *Pythian*, the land is the "flowering root" (8) of the third continent, which was Libya in the Greek image of the inhabited world.[62] Libya is not simply *chora*, without an urban center, however. This center, built on top of a hill where Cyrene will assemble "an island people" (54f.), will be the city that bears her name.[63] The Thessalian woman's reign over this fer-tile soil in no way prejudges its future colonization by the Therans.

ISOTOPY AND NARRATIVE VARIATIONS

The myth of the union of Apollo and Cyrene stages a transformation that assumes the different figures of the theme of matrimonial union. Now the Ninth *Pythian* reproduces the process that determined the whole narration in the Fourth *Pythian*, renewing the same theme with different figurative variations in different narratives.

The legitimate marriage introduced by the conquest of the fiancée (manipulation and competence), which results in procreation (sanc-tion), is an isotopy that, far from being reduced to a mere reiterated unity, finds a syntactic articulation in the narrative's development.[64] Al-exidemus's marriage with the daughter of the Libyan king of Irasa, modeled on the wedding of Danaus's forty-eight daughters; the wedding of Telesicrates, the ode's Receiver (*Destinataire*), with the young woman of Cyrene; and the usually forgotten union of Alcmene with Zeus and

Amphitryon, which produces the hero par excellence, introduced by the evocation of his own nephew Iolaus, are all figurative variations. All these unions have well-marked antecedents and consequences in their narrative development.[65]

Anteus is the king of Irasa and the father of the young Libyan woman offered in marriage. The son of Poseidon and Ge, he is a giant with whom Heracles will do battle according to Pindar to prevent him from offering his hostages in sacrifice to his divine father.[66] The monstrous traits that link this king to a Polyphemus or a Cercyon do not hinder him at all from organizing races (that most Greek of competitions) to decide among those aspiring to the hand of his daughter. The swiftest, Alexidemus, will enter a just marriage (*gamos,* 112 and 114) with this exceptionally beautiful girl. The *xenos* leads his fiancée before the assembled crowd of nomadic cavaliers. Even if some scholiasts hesitate to identify the Anteus of the Ninth *Pythian* with Heracles' adversary, there is little doubt that the union of the Libyan daughter and the noble Cyrenean symbolizes the integration of the indigenous population with the first group of Greek colonists under the sign of patriarchy. Irasa was of course the most beautiful region of Libya according to Herodotus. And in later tradition Anteus's daughter bears the name Barce, the name of the city founded under Arcesilas the Second by dissident aristocrats who seem to have depended upon the support of the indigenous population for their political undertaking. This is a discreet Pindaric allusion to the political conditions that obtained at the time of the poem's enunciation.[67]

Yet, according to the scholia on this passage, Alexidemus is an ancestor of Telesicrates (line 105), the Pythian victor celebrated by Pindar. During the course of the celebration of different Cyrenean games, the young athlete wins the admiration of young women (line 99) who dream of making this brilliant conqueror their husband or son, thus becoming women capable of assuring their city's fame (line 74). This is a situation that inverts the relation between the lovestruck Apollo and Cyrene, the admired athlete, according to one contemporary interpreter,[68] who perhaps forgets that the suitors' contest (in which Alexidemus, ancestor of Telesicrates, participates) plays a mediating role and acts as a narrative pivot.

Through these interlocking narratives, man progressively becomes the subject of the central action: the feminized Apollo is subjected to the advice of Chiron, eventually kidnaps Cyrene, and takes her to Libya to make her its queen. Alexidemus takes the Libyan daughter of Anteus to Cyrene, thus integrating indigenous legitimacy with Greek power. Telesicrates soon marries—at least this is what the imbrication of the three

narratives suggests—one of the young Cyrenean women whose admiration and love he has aroused.[69] Husband or son? This is one way to
sum up the twofold narrative consequence, made explicit in the two
other narratives, of the conquest of the fiancée (manipulation and competence) in a single formula. Telesicrates will be the Apollo or the Alexidemus of the chosen Cyrenean woman (performance), but he will also
be likely to engender a descendant worthy of him (sanction), just as
Cyrene and Apollo's love produces the immortal Aristeus, and his own
genos issues from the marriage of Alexidemus and the beautiful native.
What varies, on the other hand, are the secondary antecedents and consequences proper to each of these unions: transfer to Libya of a Greek
woman who fights wild animals and who under the control of a Greek
god will reign over a city; transfer to Cyrene of a native woman, belonging to a nomad people, who will become the wife of a Greek colonist;
the union in Cyrene of a Cyrenean woman with a Cyrenean man who
has just competed victoriously in games held in honor of the god who
initiated the whole series of events.

   In these interlocking, echoing actions, each performance becomes the
manipulation phase of the one that follows. And each of these transformative matrimonial unions is the site of a modification that tends toward progressive Hellenization and masculinization of Libya. The
Ninth *Pythian*'s narrative development is hence to be read not only hor-
izontally, but also in its vertical dimension.

NATURE AND CULTURE

   Doubled by a spatial transference, these different marriages introduce their respective protagonists to a new status: a passage from nature
to culture, as the most recent interpreters (clearly influenced by Lévi-
Strauss) have affirmed, moving from the figurative isotopy to the theme
of the ode. But things are much more complex, and we must distrust
binary logic—too often applied without nuance in the field of anthropology.

   It is hardly a controversial point that Pelion, where Apollo falls in
love with Cyrene, corresponds to the Greek representations of savagery.
But within this framework, Cyrene defends a pursuit that may be said
to be the first stage on the road to civilization: the activity of herding.
Wild animals (line 21) are contrasted with the "paternal cows" (23).
Without taking fruit production into account (7 and 58, cf. *Pyth.* 4.6),
this is exactly the activity to which the vast plains of Libya, especially
the Cyrenean region, are best suited. Cyrene is said to be "rich in herds"
(*polumēlos,* 6).[70] The installation in Libya of the Greek Cyrene results

in the creation of the most beautiful of cities (69) surrounded by a *chōra* devoted essentially to pasturage, not agriculture. Troy's founding, as described in the *Iliad,* follows an analogous model. Zeus generally supervises operations, while Poseidon builds the walls of the city, and Apollo opens Ida's valleys to grazing.[71] When Cyrene enjoys a complementary state of civilization by way of Alexidemus's marriage with the native king's daughter, the activities of the natives—those nomad cavaliers (123)—are integrated into the colonized domain and undergo a transformation. Under the influence of Greek technical knowledge, native equitation becomes the art of driving a horse-drawn chariot, an art destined to bring fame to the city (4).[72] As for the future marriage of Telesicrates, it will plant on the soil of Cyrene one who, as hoplite, is distinguished at the greatest games of Greece.

HELLENISTIC VARIANTS

The establishment of this first stage of civilization in Libya corresponds exactly to the function imparted to Apollo in the episode in the *Hymn to Apollo* which introduces the Callimachean version of the founding of Cyrene. The Alexandrian poet, after defining Apollo's general attributes (archery, song, divination, medicine), specifies his function as "shepherd" (*nomios*): he looks after (*etrephe,* 48) oxen, goats, sheep, and mares. And on this same function of "melotrophia" (cattle-raising) the shepherd-god's capacity to found cities depends. Apollo "weaves" (*huphainei,* 57) the first foundings (*themeilia,* 57, 58, and 64) at Delos by establishing the first altar there; the famous Ceraton is formed by intertwining (*epleke,* 61) the horns of the goats of Cynthus, which were hunted by Artemis, sister of the founding god. The horned altar's construction, with its foundation (*edethlia,* 62) and the walls that enclose it, appears figuratively to represent the passage from the savagery that reigned in Delos before Apollo's intervention to the civilized state signified by the god's edifying weaving. This founding transformation constitutes a supplementary aspect of the Apollonian *tekhnē* (42).[73]

The Callimachean prelude, narrating Cyrene's foundation, tallies, in its broad outline, with the version Pindar gives in the Fifth *Pythian.* Then the narrative goes back in time to deal with an episode predating the installation of the Greeks in Cyrene. In this episode, which already figures in Herodotus's *logos,* the Theran colonists live for seven years on the site of Aziris. This substitutes for the contest for the hand of the daughter of the king of Irasa, while still carrying out an analogous intermediary function. Callimachus tells us that under Apollo's watchful eye the Greek warriors celebrated the Carneia with Libyan women, in this wooded spot, before reaching the waters of Cyre. In this place, intermediate between Thera and Cyrene, the native women's participation in one of the most widespread Apollonian festivals, which become the pivot of Cyrene's future festival calendar, displays the same will to integrate on the part of the autochtonous population as does the wedding of Alexidemus and Anteus's daughter.[74]

Apollo and his consort, without respect for spatial likelihood, admire the Greek dances from the Mont of Myrtes, Cyrene's future center.[75] This spatial displacement is a pretext for a new leap in temporal origins. The narration becomes that of the rape of Cyrene and of her struggle to defend the indigenous king Eurypylus's herds, no longer those of her father. This displacement of the young woman's heroic battle with the beasts, from Thessaly to Libya, has not failed to preoccupy philologists. At least as far back as Acesandrus's *History of Cyrene,* the displacement served simply to situate the exploits of the city's eponymous nymph in a wholly Cyrenean perspective. This manipulation of the founding myth should not be thought surprising because it brings the triumph of the first state of civilization, represented by the Thessalian's victory over a wild beast, back into Libyan territory.[76] By making Eurypylus, that hypostasis of Poseidon, the aboriginal ruler of Libya and the lion's head the price of his realm, Acesandrus's version presents Cyrene's great fait accompli in Libya as the advent of a new royal power that imposes herding and grazing in a region menaced by savagery. By means of different figures, both Callimachus's and Acesandrus's narratives serve to confirm the underlying theme in the Ninth *Pythian.*

Likewise we can understand the role of mediators, who in this case include Chiron, Aristeus, and Heracles, in the context of the transition from savagery to pastoralism. One recent analysis has shown well that Cyrene will excel in precisely those arts that Chiron teaches: hunting and fighting. In his roles as prophet, pedagogue, healer, and cavalier, the Centaur is close to the god he is called upon to advise. No doubt his double nature—human and equine—defines him from the first as the mediator. Nevertheless, he is a mediator between the wildness of the mountainous forest in which he lives (line 30) and the pastoral domain, guarded by Apollo and Cyrene, not between "nature" and "culture." [77]

The hunter and the shepherd are the two poles that designate Aristeus's *epicléseis,* "Hunter" and "Shepherd" (65). The son of Apollo and Cyrene is endowed with these qualities also by Apollonius of Rhodes in the *Argonautica,* in which Aristeus's brief gesture is not a mere insertion in the Argonaut's voyage to Libya but the action that explains the origin of the etesian winds. This is proof of the narrative function's malleabil-

ity in Greek myths. The Hellenistic version of the legend retains its semantic values and is not hindered by the narrative detour. Aristeus,
born in Libya, is brought to Thessaly, where he is handed over to Chiron
for his education. Once adult, he becomes Apollo's double, endowed
with the arts of healing, divination, and herding. He tends the herds on
the plain of Phthia, between mountains and river. Then he is called to
Ceos, where he assumes another of his father's functions, saving the island from the scourge of drought. The methods Aristeus uses evoke
both the moisture necessary to the exercise of his pastoral function and
also Zeus Icmaeus, "the moist," by offering a sacrifice to him and to the
burning Sirius. In answer, Zeus sends the etesian winds to refresh Ceos
from that time forward.[78] Cyrene's soil similarly owes its fertility to
Zeus's benevolence; he favors the climate by accumulating black clouds
above it.

Heracles, Panhellenic in his notoriety, is ably introduced by the evocation of Iolaus, his local homologue. The Theban hero Iolaus, related
to Heracles, recalls the place of the poem's composition and perhaps
that of Telesicrates' victory, Thebes itself. Like Telesicrates and his
ancestor Alexidemus, Iolaus and Heracles are athletes. The son of the
Theban Alcmene liberates Greece from its monsters in the course of his
athletic struggles, so that it can welcome civilization.[79] His combat with
the Nemean lion closely resembles that of the nymph, Cyrene, while as
the exemplary son (lines 84f.) he evokes Aristeus. The young woman's
transformation into a masculine, heroic figure might be brought about
in this assimilation.

No doubt the different myths in play in the Ninth *Pythian* aim to
heighten the praise of Telesicrates' brilliant victory. For this Cyrenean
athlete's force, by a pun on his own name, culminates in victory, just as
marriage culminates in the birth of a legitimate son.[80] But through this
metaphorical assimilation of agonistic victory and matrimonial union,
the legend of Cyrene's founding gains from Pindar's "serializing" of different legends. Their figures, articulated according to the matrimonial
isotopy, show the more abstract thematic passage from savagery to
herding, which informs the classical representation of the flourishing
colony's birth and its singular civilization.

In order to sing for a second time the praises of the victory won by
Arcesilas the Fourth's chariot at Delphi, the Fifth *Pythian* no longer has
recourse to the metaphorical entanglements of different isotopies developed in the same narrative, as the Fourth did. Nor does it go back to the
superpositioning of narrative transformations on the homologous figurative content as in the Ninth. The ode's development organizes a por-

trait gallery into a route that advances and then retreats in time, in a constant spatial traffic between different sites in continental Greece and Cyrene itself. The narrative action of the poem consists of these displacements. As for the actors, the sequence in which they appear springs from common enjoyment of the *olbos* (lines 14, 55, 102) given by the gods, a prosperity that always has Cyrene as its setting.

We start with Arcesilas, the victor celebrated at the time of the poem's enunciation. Arcesilas, through the power accorded him by the gods (lines 12ff.), is the just ruler of many cities. Next, there is the narrator, who has confided his song to a chorus of men under Apollo's authority (lines 20ff.; spatial link between Thebes and Cyrene). And Arcesilas's brother-in-law, Carrhotus, the charioteer, artisan of the victory celebrated in Cyrene, consecrated his chariot to the god of Delphi (lines 25ff.; connection of this site with Cyrene). Carrhotus's return to the Libyan plain, in the city of his fathers (*patrōïa polis,* 53, recalls the city and the *chōra* surrounding it), evokes the memory of the *olbos* of Battus, founder of Cyrene by Apollo's order (lines 55ff.; reiteration of the route Delphi–Cyrene). Apollo also favored the installation of the Heraclids, founders of the continental Greek cities' definitive state in the Argolid, Messenia, and Laconia (lines 69ff.; route from Thessaly to the Peloponnesus).[81]

Having reached back to the most distant point in legendary history, the narrator moves quickly along the chronological line while developing the isotopy of the favorable welcome reserved for all the protagonists who have suffered a spatial displacement. To evoke the work of the city-states' refounding by the Heraclids is also to recall the itinerary followed by the *genos* of the Aegids, which in its mythical origin traces a very opportune supplementary relation between the place of the poem's composition (Thebes) and that of its enunciation/execution (Cyrene). Pindar enumerates the stages of migration, willed by the gods and by destiny (*moira,* 76), of those who are ancestors of both himself (*emoi pateres,* 76) and the Cyrenean colonists: Thebes, Sparta, Thera, and Cyrene, the "well-built" city (*agaktimena,* 72ff.). The beginning of the future Aegids' migration is paralleled by the arrival of the Trojans in Libya. Sons of Antenor, they were driven away by their city's destruction and were accompanied in their flight by Helen (lines 82ff.; link Troy–Cyrene). The coincidence of these two *genē* in Cyrene allows for the effacement of temporal distance that, in fact, separates the Trojans' arrival in Libya from that of Battus. In this respect, repetition of the isotopy of hospitality makes a double return to the present possible and contributes to the reinforcement of the impression of the two interventions' simultaneity. In fact, though, they are altogether separate in time. In effect the evocation of the Theban Aegids' emigration, willed by the gods (*hikonto* in the aorist, 75), entails that of the present Cyrenean celebration (*sebizomen,* 80; celebration assumed by the narrator) of the Apollonian festival of the Carneia, which was received (*anadeksamenoi,* 78) in the past from these immigrant Spartan heroes. The Carneia's evocation in turn recalls the older migratory movement of the Trojan foreigners (*xenoi,* 82) descended from Antenor (*melon,* in the aorist, 85). The Cyreneans now receive and greet this "horse-loving" race, in the time of the poem's enunciation (*dekontai,* in the present, 86), probably on the occasion of the Carneia's celebration.[82] This double passage from past to present takes the figure of a transition from myth to rite, and everything happens as if it were finally the Theran colonists, descendants of the Aegids, who had received the Antenorids in Cyrene!

The movement back in time can occur through the reprise of the isotopy of hospitality, now figured by the honors that proceed from it. Thus Battus, after his founding work, is honored by the people as a hero (lines 89ff.). The same can be said for Battus's successors, the kings of Cyrene, who become "saints" (*hieroi,* 97) in the burial they have received in front of their palace. The succession of Battus's descendants leads us naturally to Arcesilas the Fourth, the celebration of whom represents an offering to Apollo (lines 100ff.). Doesn't he, along with his fathers, benefit from *olbos,* and also from a communal and justified recognition? Hospitality, ritualized, is transformed into honors addressed to a divinity as one moves back into the present. Thus the Ninth *Pythian* is logically dedicated to Battus's *genos* as a whole, in a desire for an Olympic victory by the sovereign act of Zeus. This desire moves the narrative's time, just brought back into the present, into the future (line 123).

THE AGE OF HEROES

The mythological version of Cyrene's colonization presented by the Fifth *Pythian* complements the one played out in the Fourth. For the purposes of praise this poem used a narrative of origins and the act of a land's foundation by human manipulators and divine protectors. The epinicion that follows centers on the ancestry of a *genos* in conformity with the temporal movement and spatial trajectory (*parcours*) that organize the poem. Certainly in the Fourth *Pythian* the integration of the magical clod's itinerary with the narrative of the Argonauts already gave precise indications of Battus's family origin, and consequently that of

Arcesilas the Fourth, the ode's Receiver. The trajectory (*parcours*) from
Sparta to Cyrene by way of Thera, covered by Battus's ancestors, is already expressed in the Fourth *Pythian*.

In the Fifth *Pythian* this itinerary no longer starts from the same
point—no longer Lemnus, but Thebes. Profiting from the mixed composition of the Theran founders, widely attested elsewhere, the Fifth
Pythian has the Aegids, who issue from Oedipus's Theban family, take
the place of the bastard descendants of Euphemus's union with one of
the homicidal women of Lemnus. As has already been said, the Aegid
lineage represents the collateral line of the double family of Heraclid
origin which holds royal power in Sparta. Illegitimacy it thus replaced
by a matrilineal legitimacy from a Spartan point of view: Theras,
Thera's founder, is Heraclid only through his mother Argeia, while
Autesion, his father, descends from Polynices, King of Thebes, of Cadmean ancestry.[83] To refer the *genos* of Arcesilas and Battus to the Theban and Labdacid origin of Thera's other coloniziers inserts this family
in the age of heroes, and no doubt the much-discussed mention of the
Antenorids must be understood in this context. In the Hesiodic myth of
the races, the heroic class is defined by two components: those who
fought for a share of Oedipus's herds in Thebes, and the soldiers who
died under the walls of Troy for Helen's beauty. The Thebaïd and the
Trojan War correspond precisely to the content of the heroic poems that
form the famous epic cycle.[84] It should be no surprise, then, to find a
myth that tends to attach the Libyan colony not only to the Labdacid
ancestors of the Cyreneans but also to the past of the Trojan War. I have
just described the play of space and time by which Pindar ably succeeds
in making two perfectly distinct colonizing interventions coincide, while
at the same time slipping Battus's ancestors into the colonists of Labdacid origin.

Does this mean that before the arrival of the Therans Cyrene was the
object of a Trojan colonization reaching back to the Mycenean epoch?
We can imagine that historians have separated what Pindar purposely
confused, in order to reestablish the linearity of a legendary chronology
meant to be transformed into history: first, in the twelfth century, the
Trojan (or another "pre-Dorian" population) arrived, then, in the seventh century, Battus and his companions of Spartan origin.[85] But a historicist argument of this type does not take into account the heroization
process that demonstrates its effects from the archaic epoch's very beginning. From the end of the eighth century onward, every renascent
city tried to attach its present to Greece's legendary past. In a movement
of double commemorative manifestation, which tends to establish a
bond of continuity between the archaic epoch's political reality and that

of the heroic age, the traces left by the Mycenean kingdoms become the places of ritual celebration of these legendary figures, exalted as heroes. Thus they receive the honors of a mixed *mnēma:* the tomb, object of commemorative cult practices, and the epic song, reactivating the memory of their lofty deeds.[86] The mention of a mound of the Antenorids, with respect to Cyrene, could attest to the existence of this type of cult, rendered to the Trojan heroes of legend.[87]

THE HEROIZATION PROCESS

In the Fifth *Pythian,* the evocation of the Trojan Antenorids' stay in Cyrene opens up into praise of Battus—which, by design, leaves the date of his arrival in Libya extremely hazy. Battus is, above all, the founder of the city; he is its architect; he organizes its space to receive the festivals of Apollo. But the line Battus imposes on the city's central axis is shown to be autotelic, since this Apollonian way leads directly to the stern of the agora, where the founder's tomb stands. Battus is a hero twice over: he lives among men as blessed (*makar,* 94)—that is, like a god—and is also the object of his people's cultic veneration (*hērōs laosebēs,* 95).[88]

The whole semantic articulation of the legend of Cyrene's founding, as presented in the Fourth *Pythian,* developed the theme of the "autochtonous" generation of a foreign soil, destined to become Greek. In the Ninth *Pythian,* the semantic articulation defined the civilization of this land, employing the different figures implicated in the matrimonial transformation. The Fifth concentrates on the founding's different heroic protagonists and on the Cyrenean land's civilization while displaying the permanence conferred upon their figures by the cult devoted to them.[89] Its semantic coherence is assured by the theme of heroization.

This perspective clarifies the narrative emphasis placed on the Aegid branch, as opposed to the Lemnic one, of Cyrene's Theran founders. Battus and his colonists are situated in the perspective of the Heraclid ancestry through the intermediary of the Aegids. However, the reigning families who claim Heraclid or Heraclean ancestry are innumerable. They thus attempt to attach their legitimacy to either the Dorians or even to the Achaens.

Aside from the three regions of the Peloponnesus that are, strictly speaking, Heraclid, the Bacchiads, the great aristocratic family of Corinth, takes its origin back to Aletes, a "Dorian" descendant five generations removed from Heracles. In Sicyon, the Dorian and Heraclid dynasty merely substitutes itself for Cacestades, a sovereign whose ancestor is also Heracles. As for the islands, Tlepolemus, founder of

Rhodes, previously mentioned, is a son of Heracles who claims to have been driven from the continent by Heraclid pressure. The Catalogue of Ships confers Heraclid ancestry upon Cos, through the intermediary of Thessalus. From the Homeric through the classical epoch, this heroization process is at work: even at the margins of Greece, King Candaules of Lydia linked his *genos* to an eastern branch of the numerous descendants of Alcmene's son, and Alexander the First of Macedonia, the philhellene, claimed descent from the Heraclid Temenus of Argos.[90]

But in the Cyrenean tradition evoked by Pindar, the Heraclid ancestry is explicitly attached to the figure of Aigimius and, consequently, to the control exercised by the Dorians over the Peloponnesus (line 72) through the intermediary of Theras and the Aegids.[91] This in no way excludes a second lineage, aiming to attach the colony to Greece's Achaean past, especially because the mention of the Trojan line of origin is not explicitly grounded in a genealogical relation. Pindar limits himself to inscribing the Antenorids' arrival in Cyrene in the context of a *nostos*, 'return,' without directly indicating that the Trojans had founded a family in Libya. Why Trojans rather than Greeks? The colonial city of Cyrene seems to share this peculiar character of its alleged Achaean past with other cities situated at the geographical limits of the hellenized world. Samothrace refers to Dardanos; Sarpedon, who battles at the Trojans' side, passes for having found Miletus; and in Salaminian Cyprus, from the fifth century onwards, Teucrus's descendants are mixed up with the Trojans.[92] No doubt the Antenorids were welcomed all the more warmly into Cyrene because Antenor distinguished himself from other Trojans by receiving the Greeks with all the honors due them as guests; their mention in the Fifth *Pythian* takes part in the isotopy of hospitality that parallels the heroization theme and assures the semantic coherence of the whole poem.[93] In addition, they are accompanied by Helen, whose figure leads us back to the Spartan origins of certain of the colonists of the Greek city of Libya.

Pindar did not choose the Carneia—out of all the Cyrenean festivals—by chance, to reinforce the genealogical and historical bond between the city's present and the heroic Greek past. From remote antiquity onward, the Carneia constituted the most characteristic festival of Dorian cities. Imported by the Aegids, fathers of Pindar and the Cyrenean Greeks, and instituted in the city by the heroized oecist (lines 74ff., 89ff.), the sacrifices of the Carneia were destined for the Trojan Antenorids (lines 85ff.). This path of the rite, with the temporal confusion it masks, is no doubt made possible only by the duplicity of the legend that explains its institution: it is either a ritual expiation of the involuntary murder of Carnus, the soothsayer who accompanied the

Heraclids in the conquest of the Peloponnesus, or a ritual expiation to appease the anger of Apollo, whose chosen cornel-wood trees (*kraneiai*) had been destroyed to build the Trojan horse.[94] There is every reason to think that the worship of the oecist, confused with Apollo in his colonizing and apotropaic (if not his oracular) functions, coincided with the celebration of the Carneia, the greatest festival in those cities whose culture hailed from Sparta.[95]

Whatever the case may be, Battus's heroization, and that of his successor kings of Cyrene, could only be accomplished by the double reference to the Heraclid ancestry and to the heroes of the Trojan War.[96] This heroization process, through the shift in the mythological perspective, and also by cult acts, left its traces in Cyrene's spatial organization: Battus's tomb, vestiges of which have been found "at the poop of the agora" (line 93) just where Pindar indicated and perhaps the Hill of the Antenorids.[97] The circularity of the temporal path sketched out by the portrait gallery in the Fifth *Pythian*, and the spatial reciprocity between Cyrene and the Greek continent, have as their only goal the submission of Arcesilas the Fourth to the cultic and legendary heroization of the founder of the colony. While waiting to be able to assimilate himself to Olympia with the sovereign qualities of Zeus, Arcesilas, the Fifth *Pythian*'s recipient, appears as a second Apollo through the intermediary of his ancestor Battus. Here, in Pindar's demonstration, the superpositioning of heroic destinies has replaced the play of metaphorical echoes among many intertwined isotopies.

HERODOTUS AND THE CHRONOLOGY OF HISTORY

The whole of Herodotus's prose narrative of Cyrene's foundation, nearly contemporaneous with the Pindaric version in the Fifth *Pythian*, is imbued with this heroizing aim. After having narrated Darius's disappointment in his expedition against the Scyths, Herodotus turns toward the south, to study in a symmetrical way the events that determine the history of that part of the world during the same period. The expedition undertaken by the Persian governor of Egypt against Barce at the request of Arcesilas the Fourth's mother, furnishes Herodotus with a pretext to show, once again, the double perspective, historical and ethnographic, of his *Inquiry*.

An exhaustive history of the Greeks's immigration into a land that they believed formed a third continent precedes a long description of the peoples of Libya. There we find all the stages that are dispersed by Pindar ordered in a linear chronological succession. In addition, Herodotus puts the technique of synchronization into motion, while occasionally

still leaving some incoherencies. This story of the antecedents of the Cyrenaica expedition clearly distinguishes the two genealogical lines that
will coalesce at Sparta in the form of the mixed contingent sent from
Thera as colonizers.[98] The first part of Herodotus's narrative is quite
compatible with our modern conception of history inasmuch as it is
stripped of all divine intervention: the narrative action's motives are to
be found in men, more particularly in men moved by political considerations.

At the origin are the Argonauts' grandchildren and the women of
Lemnus, who have been driven from the island by the Pelasgians (situation of lack). The exiles seek refuge in Sparta, where they claim their
Minyan origin (phase of manipulation and competence) in order to demand from the Lacedemonians the rights of the city, which are cohabi-
tation with the citizens, access to political functions, the assignment of
portions of land, and repartition among the tribes. The Spartan's acceptance (performance) in the name of the active role taken by the Dioscuri in the Argonauts' expedition, is sanctioned by an exchange of
women: the Minyans' descendants marry the citizens' daughters, while
the Lemnians are given to the Spartans in marriage.[99] The Minyans, not
content with obtaining citizen's rights, make excessive demands for the
royalty reserved to the two dynasties descended from the Heraclids.
This lands them in prison (rupture of the contract and of the narrative
equilibrium). A performance that reverses the terms of the matrimonial
exchange saves them from prison. The Minyans' wives, daughters of the
most prominent Spartan citizens, take their husbands' places at the end
of a nocturnal travesty scene, and the Minyans take up their marginal
positions on the wild spurs of the Taygetus once again (new situation of
lack).

These events coincide chronologically with the (voluntary) margin-
alization of another clan, which, although possessing the rights of the
city, is not authorized to assume royal power. This family's Theban ancestry, however, brings it closer to the two reigning Spartan families: as
has been said before, Theras, their representative, is descended through
five generations from Polynices; he is thus the maternal uncle of the
Spartan royal families' two Heraclid initiators.[100] After having assured
the regency, Theras prefers exile in Calliste–Thera, an island which, according to Pindar, was colonized eight generations previously by Cadmus, founder of Thebes. Both the Minyans' refuge in the Taygetus and
Theras's exile to Calliste allow them to return to their own, while not
going back to the lands of their ancestors. This common destiny allows
a group of Minyans to follow Theras and the group of Spartan citizens
he chose and to converge on the neighboring island, which then takes

the name of its second founder. Only in this way will the son of Theras who remained in Sparta find himself at the origin of the Aegids, named after his own Aigeus. It is notable that in the heroization process undertaken in the Fifth *Pythian* Pindar did not hesitate to anticipate this familial denomination. All the same, this' influential family will remain marginal in Sparta, marked by the malediction that will weigh on its offspring.[101]

Compelled to start from the destinies of these two lineages, the history of Thera will be confused in Herodotus with the preliminaries of the legend of Cyrene's founding. I have already analyzed the two Herodotean versions of the foundation elsewhere.[102] Here, I will limit myself to emphasizing that the first one leaves the initiative with the Therans as much as possible, confining Battus's role to that of executor of orders pronounced by the oracle at Delphi and relayed by the people of Thera. In this Theran light, Battus, as in Pindar's poem, is the descendant of the Argonaut Euphemus, who was widely considered to be a Minyan. The second version is oriented entirely toward Battus, and although it undoubtedly gives him a marginal origin, it no longer marks him as bastard. Battus is, rather, the son of a Cretan sovereign's daughter, who was saved by a Theran merchant, and of an important citizen of the island. Battus, as a political leader, is not the only one to enjoy a double ancestry of this type.[103] In the Cyrenean version the Delphic oracle is consulted directly by Battus, while in the Theran version, the oracle is addressed to the king of Thera, Theras's descendant. The Cyrenean narrative is at pains to erase the Spartan origin of the colonization of Cyrenaica. But the two versions converge just as soon as Battus touches Libyan soil, at first the island of Platea, then the continental coast at Aziris; finally he is led toward the interior by the indigenous people.

The syntactic and semantic contacts between these politicized, if not historicized, versions of Cyrene's founding and the narrative of Tarentum's founding (also of Spartan origin) are striking. The latter narrative, which also goes back to a fifth century source, places dissensions arising between Spartan citizens and the Partheniae at the origin of the colonists' departure for Tarentum.[104] Whether these were the sons of Spartan traitors, considered to be helots, or descendants of illegitimate unions between female citizens of Sparta and young men, they represent a group denied the rights of the city by Spartans. Their position is all the closer to that of the Minyans in that their aborted attempt at rebellion took place outside Sparta, at Amyclae. The conquest of Amyclae was the appanage not of the Heraclids, but of Timomachus, a Theban, who belonged to the *genos* of the Aegids.[105]

Thereafter in this narrative the chief of the Partheniae, like Battus, consults, in the absence of the intermediary Thera stage, the oracle at Delphi, which advises emigration to "rich" Tarentum. Like the Theran colonists, the Partheniae are welcomed there by the native population and by the Cretans, who are supposed to have arrived there during the same epoch that the Antenorids arrived in Cyrene. Unlike the Herodotean narrative of Cyrene's founding, however, the Tarentine legend does not erase the theme of autochtony. The Tarentines find a second oecist, Phalanthus, who is transformed from the negative status of a Parthenian into a true Spartan hero in Tarentum. Taras, the eponymous hero of the city, was believed to be the son of Poseidon and a local Nymph.[106] Thus the historicization process of the legend of Tarentum's founding manages to integrate at once the Poseidon-Apollo polarity, the autochtony theme (as figured in the Cyrenean legend by Poseidon's manipulation of the clod), and also the figure of fertilizing moisture (as incarnated in the Cyrenean narrative by the nymph whose name is finally assimilated to that of the spring Cyre).[107]

Herodotus does without the marvelous clod, swallowed up by waves only to reappear transformed into an island, and without the hunter-nymph kidnapped by a traveling god to found a Greek city.[108] On the contrary, there is an attempt to develop a new discourse, answering to two of the criteria that, for us, define historical discourse: the chronological reckoning, and the staging by protagonists of a political action, embodied in peoples or their governments.

From a chronological point of view, Herodotus's narrative tries to fill the gaps left by Pindar. The methods of nascent historiography help in this. They keep accounts of generations and their genealogical corollaries and, when possible, they keep track of years.[109] Computation of generations goes with the coherence of the narrative: Minyan refugees in Sparta and Lacedemonians led by Theras can converge at Calliste since the former are descended from the Argonauts through an interval of two generations, and the latter go back to Polynices through more than four generations. The island of Thera was colonized by the Cadmeans eight generations earlier. At Thera, the computation of years makes the next shift: seven years of drought after the first oracle, two years in Platea, seven in Aziris, then to Cyrene where Battus reigns for forty years, thus beginning a new balance that follows the number of years of each king's reign. On the other hand, Herodotus gives no indication of the temporal space separating Theras's arrival in Thera from the first oracle given to King Grinnus, his descendant. Consequently there is no reference to the Fourth *Pythian*'s unique "historical" fact—that seventeen generations intervene between Euphemus and Battus. This lacuna corresponds precisely to the transition from the Spartan narrative to the narrative, properly speaking, of Cyrene's founding in its two versions.

As for the narrative's protagonists—kings of Sparta, sovereigns of Thera, or chiefs of colonial expedition—they behave like politicians with respect to the people they lead, granting the privileges of the city or establishing their power over new territories. By relying on the legitimacy established by a genealogy, their action casts the civic order into such high relief that Herodotus attempts a rationalizing interpretation of Battus's name. He makes Battus into the "king," *battos* in the native language of Cyrene, instead of the "stutterer." This is also how one of the essential figurative transformations that manifest Battus's colonizing is projected onto the political isotopy. In the Fifth *Pythian,* Apollo provides Battus with a voice that "coming from across the sea" (line 59) terrified the lions infesting Cyrene's site. This is the realization of the oracle pronounced by the god at Delphi, whose pejorative allusion to the founder's stuttering is silenced by Pindar. What the nymph Cyrene realizes through her athletic struggles in the tradition after Pindar, Battus obtains through the effect of his refound voice. To drive away the lions infesting Cyrene is, as has been said, to introduce Greek civilization into Libya. But on the narrative level, Herodotus prefers to abandon the animal isotopy of the theme of passage to civilization in order to express the same transformation through the figure of royalty, which develops through the political isotopy. Stutterer and bastard, Battus becomes the strong-voiced sovereign of Cyrene. Although earlier he is clothed in the attributes of a tyrant because of his physical deficiency, in Cyrene Battus takes the figurative marks of the legitimate king upon himself. As they are staged by Herodotus, the vocal figures refer us once again to the political theme of the establishment of Greek civilization through the figure of sovereignty.[110] Herodotus's narrative also effaced marriages from the number of figures assumed by the passage to a civilization theme. Furthermore, he silences completely the autochtonous generation theme, with its figurative development in birth from the earth's entrails.

MYTH AND HISTORY

In the Theran and Cyrenean parts of Herodotus's *logos* the gods' repeated manipulation of the human protagonists subsists even though it is absent from the first, Spartan part of the narrative. Battus is led by the founder god Apollo from Delphi. This mythologizing aspect of the historical narrative, frequent in Herodotus, is called upon to double the

heroic worship accorded Cyrene's founder. With the gods' intervention
we find, once again, the theme of the heroization process. This serves
the historian of Halicarnassus as the model for the figure of the narrative's principal protagonist.

Now it is precisely in these injunctions addressed by Apollo to the
civic actors, through interposed oracles, that the figures of the Cyrenean
land's fertility and of the pastoral activity it permits emerge in the Herodotean narrative. Apollo leads the Greek colonists toward Libya,
which "nourishes herds" (*mēlotrophos*, 4.155.3 and 157.2), toward
Aziris "with beautiful dales" (*napai kallistai*, 4.157.3) bathed by a river,
and finally toward Cyrene with its spring and its "pierced sky"
(4.158.3). The drought that struck Thera is thus transformed into moisture that favors herding, by the act of colonization ordered by a god.

We can thus distinguish three distinct semantic levels in the Herodotean narrative. Vegetal and animal figures, which refer to the civilization
theme, are limited to the actions of the gods who occupy the position of
the Sender (*Destinateur*) of human action. The same can be said for
figures that refer to the heroization theme. On the other hand, in the
unfolding of human action itself, the figures set in motion by the narrative constitute the political isotopy that will penetrate the entire history
of Cyrene.

We possess indirect testimony to this legendary action, transferred to
the political level and at the same time corresponding to our own idea
of history, in a summary drawn from the *Libukai Historiai* by Menecles
of Barce. This third century historian finds the cause of the Cyrenean
colonial expedition in the sedition at Thera, not in an oracular consultation about the voice of the future oecist. The first oracular response
(which, parrying the question posed, leaves all the power to Apollo's
intervention) will be situated henceforth in the realm of the "mythic"—
the mythic that, from then on, will be the base of our own anthropological concept of myth as fabulous narrative. Opposite the *aitia muthikō-
tera*, the "mythical motive," we find the *aitia pithanōtera*, to which we
can accord more credence. Indeed, there is interrogation of the oracle in
Menecles' version, though in secondary fashion, concerning the stasis.
Apoikia, colonial expedition, is preferable to political sedition; it is necessary to abandon a maritime (hence unstable) territory to settle on the
continent.[111] With Menecles of Barce's narrative, the political motivation invades the whole causal chain of narration, relegating both the
gods and the fertilizing force by which they manifest themselves to the
second rank of importance.

Thus the concept subjacent in Herodotus's *logos* covers our modern
category of historical discourse as well as our concept of myth. From

the historical point of view, nonanthropomorphic figures and isotopies are erased and the events explaining Cyrene's founding are inscribed in a linear, genealogical chronology, even if the time thus defined is still largely "disengaged" ("*débrayé*") in relation to that of the *logos*'s enunciation. From the point of view of myth, the primary role is accorded to oracles and consequently to divine modes of action and intervention in the vegetal and animal domains.

This happens first in Callimachus and next in Apollonius of Rhodes, in texts that have already been partially discussed. The foundation narratives of these two Hellenistic poets are inscribed in a larger ensemble, which has its own enunciative objective: first an etiological and literary hymn to Apollo and, second, a learned epic that relates the Argonaut's expedition. Now they both follow a chronological development. But respect for a trait proper to the syntactic articulation of historical discourse does not in any way prevent the reappearance of the isotopies put in place by "mythic" versions on the semantic level.

CALLIMACHUS: BETWEEN THE LEGEND AND THE CULT OF APOLLO

In the *Hymn to Apollo*, the enunciator is not a Theban, as in the Fifth *Pythian*, but a veritable Cyrenean. The address to Apollo and the Cyrenean point of view confer a precisely oriented enunciative conditioning upon the narrative. This explains why the god's different *epiclēseis* are brushed aside through the rhetorical form of *praeambulum* in the Cyrenean part of the *Hymn* in order to affirm only one; Carnean Apollo is the god of the narrator's fathers (*patrōios*, 71).[112] It is a welcome *epiclēsis*, since it allows the chronological development of the stages of Cyrene's founding to be linked to Apollo himself, the builder of *edethlia*. The first foundation (*edethlon*, 72) is Sparta, then Thera, and finally the city of Cyrene. The foundation is relayed to Thera by Theras, who belongs to the "sixth generation" from Oedipus; in Cyrene it is relayed by Aristotle the oecist, whose other name has been silenced because it indicates stuttering. This series of founding acts culminates in the construction (*deima*, 77) of a temple dedicated to Apollo the oecist, and it is accomplished in the worship rendered him in this place. There was an earlier celebration in the provisional stage at Azilis or Aziris, which I have already discussed.

If at the outset of this development the figure of the profundity and fertility of Cyrenean soil reappears (*bathugeios*, 65), it is in order to better fix the foundations foreseen there by Apollo.[113] The manipulation of the very soil of Cyrene in the Fourth *Pythian* through the legend of the clod is subordinated here to Apollo's founding activity. The moment of an autochthony's establishment under Poseidon's authority is effaced in favor of the civilizing action of the god of Delos and Delphi.

The figurative isotopy of florescence substitutes for that of germination through the intermediary of the cult devoted to the founder god, and expresses itself principally through the ever-favorable seasons. But as in Pindar, henceforth the flourishing seasons attached to the cult of Carneius Apollo in wooded, moist places are simply a metaphor for human sexual fecundity. Thence, retracing time on the path already indicated, the Dorian dances with the blond natives in Azilis's wooded dales, and Apollo and Cyrene's union by the Mount of Myrtes. In addition, this union recapitulates two complementary aspects of the foundational act: Cyrene's assurance of the protection of the native king's herds, and Apollo's construction of a city with walls (*teichea*, 67; *astu*, 73, *polis*, 94). Roles are much more clearly separated than they are in Pindar; the woman's pastoral activity is in the *chōra*, and the masculine god founds the polis.

Callimachus abandons Pindar's long sequences of interlaced metaphors in favor of a subtle play of finer touches. Callimachus reformulates the themes developed in the *Pythian* poems, in a narrative whose syntax conforms to the model of historical discourse. The themes correspond to those of the founding of a land and its passage to civilization, but there is also reformulation to the extent that the "mythic" isotopy based on the process of heroization is replaced by the ritual isotopy of cult devoted to Apollo. Callimachus's *Hymn* is clearly no longer destined to vaunt the agonistic exploits of a descendant of Battus.

The figurative continuity introduced by Callimachus allows him to inscribe in the same perspective the Theban hero's foundation of Thera, Battus's historic foundation of Cyrene, and Cyrene's "mythic" founding by Apollo and the eponymous nymph, through a repetition of the semantic in the syntactic articulation. The versions Pindar treated separately have become one legend. This is another reason not to take them as historical testimony of the different phases of the colonization process. In the authors of local histories one already finds traces of this work of setting in perspective the episodes belonging to the legend of Cyrene's founding.[114] If Herodotus's politicization of the legend could be connected to the first gestures toward the writing of history, the transfer of the act of foundation from Poseidon to Apollo in the Callimachean legend might have as much to do with the destination of the Alexandrian poet's work as with the gradual predominance of the cult of Apollo at Cyrene.

The Alexandrian epic poet Apollonius of Rhodes gives himself over entirely to the same play Callimachus did. He respects the narrative's chronological syntax and some of its figures, but he reformulates them into a single theme. In addition, from the perspective of the Argonaut legend, the foundation narrative—which will end, as we have seen, with Thera's creation—originates in the gift of the marvelous clod and not in Apollo's rape of Cyrene. But the quadruple semantic interpretation of the divine clod carries the most importance. Thus we find human, vegetal, and mineral figures, no longer organized in interwoven isotopies as in Pindar, but rather divided into four interpretive levels expressing the generation theme. The coincidence of the fourth of these levels with that of the narrative's realization specifies the generation theme as a veritable cosmogonic act. The Hellenistic legend of Cyrene's foundation, rationalized somewhat by this reductive operation, paradoxically reveals the subjacent representation better than the different Pindaric approaches had.

From Pindar onward different versions of the legend of Cyrene's founding set the stage for many cosmogonic acts—cosmogony in the Greek sense, since it culminates in the establishment of civic order in a place whose geology, flora, and fauna are transformed. This order is distinguished from that of the continental Greek cities to the extent that it establishes, under Apollo's supervision, a pastoral civilization that will prolong the monarchic model, already obsolete elsewhere, well into the fifth century.

Thus in the narratives of the Cyrenaic creation we find all the traits that characterize the products of the symbolic process. Starting from a more or less locatable historical transformation—the Greek colonization of Cyrene—the narrative borrows figures of different orders from the natural world (mineral, vegetal, animal) to inscribe them in a narrative program of anthropomorphic actions. Regrouped around certain focalizing themes—autochthony as manifestation of the generation of a cultured land, herding as a stage in the civilization process, matrimonial union in reference to the institution of a civic order, and legendary portraits as the incarnation of the process of heroization—these figures, which the syntactic articulation of the narrative disseminates in the linear sequence of its actions, form isotopies, those semantic levels of expression that the play of metaphor puts in reciprocal relations. Hence these symbolic products that transfigure reality in the direction of fiction, at the same time manifesting themselves in the most diverse literary forms; hence these pages of subtle flavors that vary according to the palaces for which they are destined![115]

NOTES

a. Derrida 1976, liv-lvii (G. C. Spivak in her translator's preface.)
b. Saussure 1959.
c. Greimas 1983, xv.
d. Propp 1968.
e. Courtés 1977, 330, 333.
f. Greimas 1983, 207.
g. Greimas and Courtés 1982, 118.

May Claude Bérard, Danielle Maeder, and Manuela Ryter find here the expression of my thanks for their documentary support.

A draft of this translation was prepared by Susan Maslan and Samuel Schmidt.

1. These same rare objects, however, have brought back into consideration the possible validity of the most ancient date attributed by Eusebius to Cyrene's colonization, that is to say 1336 (as opposed to 761 and 632: cf. *Chron.* VII 52.18; 87.16ff.; 96, 19 Helm): cf. Sandro Stucchi, "Aspetti di precolonizzazione a Cirene" in Musti 1985, 341–47. This thesis was rejected in its time, upon the basis of less substantial documentation, by Chamoux (1952): 69–91.

2. This "arithmetic" time, oriented within the perspective of Christian culture, enters into the larger category of "chronical (*chronique*) time" defined by Benveniste 1974, 67–78; Ricoeur 1985, 154–60, takes it up again to make of it a "calendrical" time. But neither of these two authors analyzes the material aspect of the time of physical events.

3. On the occasion of the Ninth *P.*, cf. Carey 1981, 65–66 and 93. On that of the Fifth *P.*, cf. Lefkowitz 1985, 37 and note 96 below. On that of the Fourth *P.*, cf. Giannini 1979, 35–36.

4. Cf. Marc Gaborieau, "Classification des récits chantés: La littérature orale des populations hindoues de l'Himalaya Central," *Poétique* 19 (1974): 313–32. The situation in archaic Greece is very similar: see my remarks in "Réflexions sur les genres littéraires en Grèce archaïque," *QUCC* 17 (1974): 113–28.

5. See, in this connection, the reflections of François Lasserre, "L'historiographie grecque à l'époque archaïque," *QS* 4 (1976): 113–42; strangely enough, the author omits from his list the local genealogical history, which is well represented, however, from the archaic epoch, by the *Corinthiaca* of Eumelus of Corinth: cf. notably Paus. 2.1.1 = *Cor.* frags. 1 and 4 Bernabé.

6. On this work of systematization of genealogy by Hecataeus, cf. Lionel Pearson, *Early Ionian Historians* (Oxford 1939) 96–106. On the later phase of rewriting legend in the form of mythography properly so-called, cf. Albert Henrichs, "Three Approaches to Greek Mythography" in Bremmer 1987, 242–77, with the references given in note 2.

7. Hdt. 2.116f.; Paus. 2.18.6; Mimn. frags. 21 and 22 Gentili-Prato; Stes. frags. 196–205 and S 88–132 Page. On the role of myth in lyric poetry, see now Gentili 1984, 153–202.

8. This signifies that one does not, in general, take into consideration sources later than the Alexandrian epoch. On these texts, see Malten 1911, 26–41 and Chamoux 1952, 78–79.

9. On Pindar's narrative technique in the perspective of plays upon time, cf. now

André Hurst, "Aspects du temps chez Pindare" in Hurst 1985, 155–97, with the bibliographic references that he gives in note 1.

10. On these concepts, see the corresponding entries in Algirdas J. Greimas and Joseph Courtés, *Sémiotique: Dictionnaire raisonné de la théorie du langage,* vol. 1 (Paris 1979). Of the recent critiques presented in regard to certain of these concepts by François Rastier, *Sémantique interprétative* (Paris 1987) 117–19, 172–75 and 177–211, we will retain especially the vanity of wanting to use a distinction between "figurative" and "thematic" isotopies and the refusal to introduce a hierarchy among the different isotopies: the metaphorical relations that set them up in a reciprocal echoing forbid it. Without entering into the subtle distinctions used by Rastier, we have substituted for the notion of "thematic isotopy" that of "generic isotopy," which rests on the reiteration of general traits like "animal" or "human." On the other hand, we have retained the notion of "theme," even if, not manifested on the text's surface, it is by definition the object of a reconstruction on the part of the interpreter. Themes seem to be nevertheless at the basis of the particular semantic orientation of each text.

In an effort at simplification, we have, however, also substituted for the notions of "path" or "process" (*parcours*) and "narrative programs" that of a narrative program understood as particular realization, concrete or potential, of the canonic schema.

11. Cf. André Hurst, "Temps du récit chez Pindare (Pyth. 4) et chez Bacchylide (11)," *MH* 40 (1983): 154–68.

12. Hom. *Od.* 11.118ff. (= 23.268ff.) with the commentary by William F. Hansen, "Odysseus' Last Journey," *QUCC* 24 (1977): 27–48. On the difficulties of close interpretation that this complex passage poses, see Alfred Heubeck, *Omero. Odissea,* vol. 3 (Milan 1983), 270–73.

On Poseidon's modes of intervention in marine and equine domains, cf. Detienne and Vernant 1974, 176–200 and 221–41.

13. Even while designating the wood of a weapon and consequently a lance, *doru* refers, in its primary sense, to wood that is squared for construction—whence its triple sense of "frame of a ship" (Hom. *Il.* 15.410 or *Od.* 9.198), of "armature of a chariot" (Hes. *Op.* 456), or of a tower (Hom. *Il.* 12.36) and, through synecdoche, of "ship" (Aesch. *Pers.* 411 and *Suppl.* 846).

The function of dominating the savage forces of the horse assumed by the bit is well defined by Detienne and Vernant 1974, 183–91.

14. It may be observed that the words of hospitality accompanying this gift are explicitly assimilated by Pindar to the banquet offered to a foreigner (29ff.). It is precisely in the frame of a banquet that Arcesilas the Fourth receives Pindar's song (2): the originary *xenion* that Euphemus receives from the hands of Poseidon is then nothing other than the prefiguration of the hymn that the king of Cyrene, his descendant, receives from the author!

15. Sch. Pind. *P.* 4.61 (II, p. 105, 20ff. Drachmann); cf. also ad 4.51 (104.17f.; from here on, scholiasts will be cited in this abridged form), where Eurypylus is presented as indigenous king of Cyrene (cf. below). The attribution of this quality of Eurypylus goes back, in any case, to the historiographers of Cyrene: Acesandrus *FrGHist* 469 frag. 3, cited by the scholiast A.R. 4.1561c (p. 322.4ff. Wendel); cf. also frag. 4 and Phylarchus, *FrGHist* 81 frag. 15. The scholiasts insist twice over upon

the family tie that connects Eurypylus and Euphemus: cf. also ad 4.36a (102.14ff.). The sch. ad 4.57 (105.4ff.) recall the equivalence that Apollonius of Rhodes (4.1552 and 1561) establishes between Triton and Eurypylus; cf. as well the sch. A.R. 4.1551 (p. 32.21ff. Wendel), who attributes this equivalence to Pindar!

The Pindaric scholiasts also cite a fragment of Acesandrus (*FrGHist* 469 frag. 1); according to this historian of the fourth century, Eurypylus would be the son of Poseidon and of Celaeno, the daughter of Atlas; he would thus be the brother of Triton. On Triton, see note 29 below.

Significantly, the Cephisus near which legend causes Euphemus to be born empties into Lake Copais, a sort of Greek homologue to Lake Triton, near Orchomenus, the capital of the Minyans, to whom the Argonauts belong.

16. According to the sch. ad 4.85 (109.4ff.), the emigration of the Danaans originating from Sparta, Argos, and Mycenae is provoked by the return of the Heraclids, whom one habitually associates with the "Dorian invasion"; cf. Giannini 1979, 41, n. 30.

The narrative analysis shows that it is a question in that case of the nonrealized program of the same legend, and not of a different legend, as affirmed by Burton 1962, 152, following other experts.

17. On the mastery by *mētis* of marks that represent the *poroi* over an indistinct expanse, cf. Detienne and Vernant 1974, 140–57.

18. On this type of sacrifice, see the numerous parallels cited by Paul Stengel, *Die Griechischen Kultusaltertümer*, 3rd ed. (Munich 1920) 135–36.

On the reading *thērotrophos* that the manuscript offers to qualify Libya, cf. note 70 below. In relation to the mixture of earth and sea, note that if the Argonauts erect the tripod on the earth (*en chthoni*, 1550), Triton will cause it to disappear into the lake (1590).

19. The sch. ad 4.455b (160.25ff.) attribute to the Lemnian woman with whom Euphemus unites the name of Lamache or Malache. The same commentary distinguishes, relying notably on Didymus (frag. II.5.25 Schmidt), four different bearers of the name Euphemus: the founder of the *genos* of the Cyrenean colonists and consequently of the Battiads; the descendant of this first Euphemus, son of Samos; a third Euphemus who would have accompanied Battus in the foundation of Cyrene; and the contemporary of Arcesilas the Fourth, whom Pindar indirectly eulogizes in the Fifth *Pythian* according to the sch. ad 5.34 (175.21ff.) = Theotim. *FrGHist* 470 frag. 1 (cf. note 89 below). It will be noted that the scholiast designates the first Euphemus with the term *archēgos*, which is equally applicable to the author of the act of founding a *genos* as to the oecist of a colonial city: Casewitz 1985, 246–48.

The sch. ad 4.447a (159.6ff.) stresses once again the inversion to which Pindar's poem submits the traditional succession of stages in the voyage of the Argonauts.

20. This *nun* seems to pick up again the *nun* that in line 50, in the prediction of Medea, designates the moment of the birth of the race of Battus and thus of Arcesilas.

21. According to the sch. ad 4.450a (160.3ff.), it is a question of the funeral games in honor of the missing husbands or of Thoas.

22. Segal 1986, 27, 30–51, 136–45, 171, cf. also 183; a good part of my study was already drafted before I could see Segal's work; its views show a welcome convergence with those I develop here.

23. On this reversal in lyric poetry of the traditional roles held respectively by the inspired poet and by the inspiring muse, cf. Calame 1986, 47–50.

24. On the springs that give forth water of divine origin, by which the poet calms the poetic thirst of his patron, cf. Gianotti 1975, 110–14.

25. These representations of the foundations of civilization have been successively analyzed by Detienne 1972, 215–20 and by Jean-Pierre Vernant, *Mythe et société en Grèce ancienne* (Paris 1974) 148–53.

26. It will be noticed that to this nurturing *mastos* there corresponds the *omphalos* of Delphi, center of a "well-wooded mother" (74), that is to say of a fertile earth. Near this navel of the earth the prediction is put forward that will be at the vegetal origin (*phuteuthen*, 69) of the honors that will fall to the Minyan Argonauts, but also, through Euphemus, to the ancestors of Cyrene's founders.

On the other hand, according to the sch. ad 4.14 (98.5ff.), Aristarchus in his commentary on Pindar compares the image of the *mastos* to the Homeric expression *outhar arourēs*, which designates "the breast of the field," that is to say its most fertile part (Hom. *Il.* 9.14f.; cf. also *HCer.* 450); is it also in this sense—of the double fertility, vegetal and civic—that the sch. ad 4.25b and 27 (100.6ff. and 22ff.) understand this entire passage.

27. Segal 1986, 68–71 has shown the ties that align the metaphoric labor of Battus's ancestor with that undertaken by Jason to capture the Golden Fleece (224ff.). But in the legend as Pindar treats it, the labor of Jason does not bear fruit but leads implicitly to the reconquest of legitimate power over a city (105ff.) and not to the foundation of a new city. Jason is, in some sense, already in possession of a "root."

28. Segal 1986, 81–82 has been sensitive, as well, to the "citizen" isotopy that runs through the entire ode (cf. 7, 19f., 56, 260, and 272), but he neglects its "terrestrial" counterpart. The myth of Cyrene's foundation does not bring us to civic life from the desert, but from a virtually fertile ground to its products: a fecund *chōra* and a well-administered city.

29. Hdt. 4.179 and 188; Diod. Sic. 3.70.2 as well as sch. ad 4.36a (102.7ff.) and sch. A.R. 4.1311 (p. 313.14ff. Wendel); cf. also Diod. Sic. 5.70.4 and 72.3. Athena is born from the umbilical cord of Zeus fallen near the river Triton in Crete in a spot called, ever since, *omphalos* (cf. Call. *Jov.* 42 ff.).

On the place of Lake Triton in the Greek representation of the inhabited world and on the aspects of the Golden Age which are associated with it, cf. Ballabriga 1986, 216–21.

30. On the gate to Hades at Cape Taenarum, cf. Men. frag. 842 Kock cited by the sch. ad 4.76d (108.1ff.), Strab. 8.5.1, sch. Aristoph. *Ach.* 510 (I.1B, p. 71.19ff. Koster) and sch. Lyc. 90 (II, p. 50.5ff. Scheer).

31. On Heracles and Cerberus: Bacch. 5.56ff.; Eur. *HF* 23ff., 612 ff., and 1277ff.; version confirmed by Apoll. 2.5.12 as well as by Diod. Sic. 4.25.1 and 26.1; Paus. 2.35.10 as well as 3.25.5, who, to nurture his skepticism in regard to the cavern he visits at Cape Taenarum with its path of communication to Hades, cites the attempt at a rationalizing explanation by Hecat. *FrGHist* 1 frag. 27. On the possibly Peisistratid origin of the version that makes of Heracles an initiate in the Eleusinian Mysteries, cf. Godfrey W. Bond, *Euripides: Herakles* (Oxford 1981) 218–19.

A propos of the worship of Demeter Chthonia at Hermione, cf. Burkert 1977, 308 as well as Detienne and Vernant 1979, 203–8.

32. Clem. *Protr.* 2.17, sch. Luc. p. 275.23ff. Kabe, with the parallels of analogous gestures given by Burkert 1977, 365–70 and the interpretation proposed by Detienne and Vernant 1979, 191–99. Epict. 4.8.36, with the commentary by Detienne 1972, 215–20.

33. Call. *Del.* 11ff. and 30ff.; *HAp.* 53ff. and 72f.; for the cosmogonic action of Poseidon, see W. H. Mineur, *Callimachus: Hymn to Delos* (Leiden 1984) 77–78. On the change of name from Calliste to Thera, cf. also Hdt. 4.147.4, A. R. 4.1763, sch. ad 4.455c (161.12ff.) as well as Call. frag. 716 Pfeiffer, with the numerous references this scholar gives in the apparatus to this fragment.

34. Hom. *Il.* 2.653ff.; Pind. *O.* 7.27ff., with the commentary by Angeli Bernardini 1983, 170–85. Version of the foundation of Rhodes rationalized in Diod. Sic. 5.56.1ff.; for Apoll. 1.4.5, Rhode, daughter of Poseidon and Amphitrite, would be the sister of Triton; cf. Prinz 1979, 78–97.

It will be noted that the island of Syme, inhabited from the origin, is the object of a first colonization on the part of the men who accompany Triops under the guidance of a certain Chthonios, son of Poseidon and of Syme: Diod. Sic. 5.53.1.

A semantic analysis of the verb *ktizō* in its archaic usage shows that, particularly for the islands, this verb designates the activity of cultivation after the clearing of terrain as well as the civilizing construction of a civic establishment: Casewitz 1985, 21–34.

35. Paus. 3.1.1; on other autochthonous heroes and founders of cities, cf. Brelich 1958, 137–39.

36. A propos of Cecrops, see notably Aristoph. *Vesp.* 438 and Philoch. *FrGHist* 328 frag. 93, Marm. Par. *FrGHist* 239 A 1 and Apoll. 3.14.1. For the dispute between Poseidon and Athena, cf. Hdt. 8.55, Plut. *Them.* 19, Paus. 1.26.5 and 8. 10.4, etc.

If the double nature of Cecrops (half-man, half-serpent) attaches this figure to the earth, that of Triton (half-man, half-dolphin) attaches him to the sea, as does also his descent from Poseidon and Amphitrite: cf. Hes. *Theog.* 930f., A. R. 4.1602ff. as well as sch. A. R. 4.1619 (p. 324.7f. Weidmann) and sch. Lyc. 886 (II, p. 287.5ff. Scheer). By his family lineage, Triton is, incidentally, the brother of Rhode: cf. note 34 above! But Lyc. 886 and 892 cause this *dimorphos* god to descend from Nereus.

Libya herself is termed *autokhthōn:* Hdt. 4.45.3. In relation to the birth from the earth expressed by the concept of *gēgenēs,* autochthony has the added implication of residence on the ground where one was born: cf. Enrico Montanari, *Il mito dell'autoctonia* (Rome 1981) 31–37 and V. J. Rosivach, "Autochthony and the Athenians," *CQ* 81 (1987): 294–306.

37. On Erichthonius born from the seed of Hephaestus scattered on the ground of Athens without having touched Athena the *parthenos,* cf. Apoll. 3.14.6 as well as Hom. *Il.* 2.546ff., Eur. *Ion* 266ff., and *Erechth.* frag. 65.55 Austin; other versions of the birth of Erichthonius/Erechtheus in Robert Parker, "Myths of Early Athens" in Bremmer 1987, 187–214, with the impact that this birth in a nurturing earth has upon the representation of the standing of the Athenian citizen; see also in this regard Loraux 1981, 41–72. For figured representations, cf. Claude Bérard, *Anodoi: Essai sur l'imagerie des passages chthoniens* (Neuchâtel-Rome 1974) 34–38.

38. Aesch. *Sept.* 752ff.; on the myth of the autochthonous birth of the Cadmeans, cf. Vian 1963, 158–76.

39. A.R. 1.182ff. who, in his catalogue of the Argonauts, attributes to Euphemus the same ancestry as Pindar does; see also Paus. 5.17.9, who indicates that on the chest of Cypselus Euphemus was presented as the winner of the chariot race in the games for Pelias, Hyg. *Fab.* 14.15, sch. ad 4.61 (106.3ff.) and sch. Lyc. 886 (II, p. 287.17f. Scheer).

It is true that the Hesiodic tradition makes Euphemus into a son of Poseidon and Mecionice, the daughter of Eurotas: Hes. frag. 253 Merkelbach-West as cited by the sch. ad 4.36c (102.16ff.) and developed by the sch. ad 4.15b (99.1ff.). In addition, Euphemus is taken to have married one of Heracles' sisters: ibid. and sch. ad 4.79b (108.7ff.).

On Tityus born of Ge, cf. Hom. *Od.* 11.576. One will remark that the Trojan king Erichthonius (!), mediator between Dardanus (a son of Zeus), the founder of a first city in the Troad, and Tros, the founder of the city of Troy properly speaking, possessed mares capable of running upon the "nurturing glebe" as well as upon "the back of the sea": Hom. *Il.* 20.219ff. and Diod. Sic. 4.75.1f.; this capacity to run upon the surface of the sea with a team also belongs to Poseidon himself: Hom. *Il.* 13.17ff.

Apart from the suppositions given by the scholiasts to explain the placement of Euphemus at the prow of the boat when the Argonauts arrive in Libya, one could wonder if this explicit indication from Pindar (line 22) cannot be put in relation to this special faculty of Euphemus of walking upon the water; cf. sch. ad 4.36c and 61 (102.11ff., 105.18ff. and 106.5ff.), who cites Theotim. *FrGHist* 470 frag. 2. In any case, these respective functions attributed to the two pilots of Theseus show that the *proreus* is the second of the *kubernētēs*: Philoch. *FrGHist* 328 frag. 111.

40. These are, in any case, the qualifications Pindar attributes to the Lemnian women even if their unions with the Argonauts mark, in other versions of the legend, their return to marriage under the sign of the good odors dispensed by Aphrodite; see in this regard Detienne 1972, 172–84.

41. On the polysemy of this expression in Pindar, cf. Thomas J. Hoey, "Fusion in Pindar," *HSCPh* 70 (1965): 236–52 and Segal 1986, 64 and 71. On its particular meaning here, cf. below.

42. Hdt. 4.147, in a text analyzed below; cf. equally the sch. ad 4.10b (citing Hierocles), 10f, and 88c (97.14ff., 98.1ff., and 110.10ff.). As for the second, it mentions taking its information on the sanctuary of Poseidon and Athena founded by Cadmus at Thera from Theocrestus of Cyrene (and not Theophrastus): *FrGHist* 761 frag. F 3. On other analogous insular foundations attributed to Cadmus, cf. Vian 1963, 60–64.

43. This ascertains that the function traditionally attributed to the Fourth *Pythian*, that of affirming the legitimacy of the Battiad dynasty, and in particular of Arcesilas the Fourth (Giannini 1979, 37, 39, and 42–43), passes along a tortuous path, destined to designate the singular quality of founding hero that distinguishes the figure of Battus (cf. below).

44. Despite the doubts of interpreters in this regard, the term *nepodes* (1745) is particularly adapted to the designation of the descendants of Euphemus. Taken from Homer (*Od.* 4.404), where it designates the baby seal offspring of Halosudne, the "Daughter of the Sea," this term readily designates in Alexandrian poetry the de-

scendants of a river god: Call. frag. 66.1 and 533 Pfeiffer (but in the frag. 222, the aquatic meaning of the term is no longer active; the same holds in Theocr. 17.25). Here, the usage of this term to designate the descendants of Euphemus can point back as well to the capacity of their ancestor, the son of Poseidon, to walk on water (cf. note 39 above) as to their own insular destiny as mediators between the sea and the earth.

On the representation of the seal as amphibious animal and mediator, cf. Detienne and Vernant 1974, 244–52; on the etymology of the term *nepodes*, cf. Pierre Chantraine, *Dictionnaire étymologique de la langue grecque,* vol. 3 (Paris 1974) 747.

45. The scholia have not failed to complete the narrative of the Alexandrian poet by mentioning his Cyrenean issue: sch. A. R. 4.1750/57 and 1760/64d (pp. 327.7ff. and 328.3ff. Wendel), who mark the difference between the neglect of which the clod is the object in the Pindaric version and the voluntary gesture by Euphemus in Apollonius.

46. Poseidon as divinity of the ground, in particular of its continental bowels, and as god of the sea depths: Burkert 1977, 217–19. On the origin and the nature of the worship of Poseidon in Thera, cf. note 42 above.

47. Mus. frag. 2 B 11 Diels-Kranz cited by Paus. 10.5.6, cf. also 24.4 and Ephor. *FrGHist* 70 frag. 150 and 31b; see the commentary by Christiane Sourvinou-Inwood, "Myth as History: The Previous Owners of the Delphic Oracle" in Bremmer 1987, 215–241, who enumerates the different versions of the succession from Ge to Apollo at Delphi while showing the vanity of a historicist analysis; epigraphic attestations in Georges Daux, "The *Poteidanion* of Delphi," *BCH* 92 (1968): 540–49.

48. On the intervention conjugated in the Fourth *Pythian* of Zeus and Apollo in relation with Metis and Themis, cf. Giannini 1979, 42 and 49–53.

49. The Libyan cult of Zeus Ammon is already placed in connection with that of Dodona by Hdt. 2.54ff., who attributes to them a common Egyptian origin: see the commentary by Alan B. Lloyd, *Herodotus Book II: Commentary 1–98* (Leiden 1976) 251–64. According to the sch. ad 4.28 (100.25ff.), all of Libyan earth was consecrated to Zeus.

For the forebearers of Libya, cf. sch. ad 4.25 (100.11ff.), but also Aesch. *Suppl.* 315ff. and Apoll. 2.4.1f.

50. On the organizing and fertilizing functions of Zeus, cf. Burkert 1977, 200–203; Segal 1986, 171–79 places these functions in relation to the "patriarchal" role of the god. The tradition includes elsewhere, as well, in relation to the fecundity of the ground, a Zeus Chthonius: Hes. *Op.* 465, cf. also 379, 474, and 488.

51. The subtle play of echoes that refer the Pindaric version of the quest of the Golden Fleece back to the foundation legend of Cyrene has been highlighted by Segal 1986, 72–85 and 92–93. Segal insists essentially upon the passage, across the interchange between sea and land, from instability to the establishment of civic roots. But he does not see that the principal protagonist of the foundation legend of Cyrene is neither Euphemus nor Battus, but the miraculous clod.

52. Parallelism glimpsed by Segal 1986, 84–85 and 160–61; on the cosmogonic echoes of the same episode: 103–5 and 144. The same scholar puts forward the hypothesis (p. 91) that, in his turn, Pindar follows an itinerary articulated as a depar-

ture and eturn. On the *mētis* that Pindar exercises with regard to Demophilus, cf. Giannini 1979, 60–62.

On the genealogy of Atlas, hero of hubris, cf. Hes. *Theog.* 507ff.; cosmogonic role of Atlas in relation to the sea: Hom. *Od.* 1.52ff. and Aesch. *Prom.* 348ff.: cf. Martin L. West, *Hesiod: Theogony* (Oxford 1966) 311 and Ballabriga 1986, 75–91.

53. Those who interpret the circularity of this course as a simple return omit its transformative aspect. Such is the case with Burton 1962, 168, Kirkwood 1982, 163, and even Segal 1986, 89–93.

54. This paradox has been pointed out many times, most recently by Woodbury 1982, 245–46. Köhnken 1985, 94 likewise offers a solution at the level of the narrative. In the poetry of Pindar, the figure of Apollo varies according to the receiver of the poem: Angeli Bernardini 1983, 64–67.

55. Köhnken 1985, 78–79 has well illuminated the divergences within the structure of Pindaric narrative in relation to chronological succession.

56. The two nymphs who guard the cattle of the Sun on a remote island are also the daughters of the cattle's proprietor: Hom. *Od.* 12.131ff. On the other hand, in Call. *Dian.* 206ff. Cyrene appears as the companion of Artemis. The nymph is honored by the goddess after an athletic victory as an *eromenos* would be: cf. Fritz Bornmann, *Callimachi Hymnus in Dianam* (Florence 1968) 97–98.

In assimilating Cyrene and Atalanta (cf. most recently Woodbury 1982, 251–53), the commentators have effaced the positive character of the former's hunting activity as well as the note of *aidōs* that marks her union with Apollo. It is never said that Cyrene *phugei gamon*, as in the case of Atalanta: Hesiod frag. 73 Merkelbach-West, Theognis 1287ff., Aristoph. *Lys.* 785ff.; other sources and pictorial documentation in John Boardman and Giampiera Arrigoni, "Atalante," in *LIMC* II.1 (Zurich-Munich 1981) 940–50.

57. On the armament of the adolescent Theseus in his combats against monsters, cf. Frank Brommer, *Theseus: Die Taten des griechischen Helden in der antiken Kunst und Literatur* (Darmstadt 1982) 3–34.

58. Slightly different versions of the genealogical origin of Hypseus in Pherecydes *FrGHist* 3 frag. 57 and in Acesandrus *FrGHist* 469 frag. 2, who are cited by the scholiast on 9.27b (233.12ff.); cf. also sch. on 9.104 and 105 (230.7ff. and 13ff.).

59. In *O.* 6.29f. Iamus, the son of Apollo and Evadne (herself a daughter of Poseidon) has a destiny similar to that of Aristeus. He, too, ends by sharing with his father one of his essential functions, in this case the oracular art. The analogy is pointed out by Crotty 1982, 116–17.

On the *epiclēseis* of Aristeus, cf. note 78 below.

60. Even if the sch. on 9.6a (221.12ff.) asserts that Pindar draws the legend of Cyrene from an *Ehoiē* of Hesiod, frag. 215 Merkelbach-West, cited in this scholium, attributes to Cyrene a place of sojourn more suitable to the ascendancy of her father (cf. note 58 above): the grandchild of Peneus and Creusa stays in the country of Phthia beside the waters of the river Peneus, which flows down from Mt. Pindus.

Pindar's geographical displacement of Mt. Pindus to the Pelion range, while presenting a place equally marked by savagery, shows the liberties the poet takes with regard to his supposed source (Diod. Sic. 4.81.1 follows the Pindaric version). This fact ought to contribute to the subversion of the historicist hypotheses that have been drawn from the scholiast's information: cf. Malten 1911, 154–63 and Chamoux 1952, 84–88 and 171.

On the other hand A.R. 4.500 brings back the Hesiodic version of the presence of Cyrene by "the marshes of the Peneus."

As for the transfer of Cyrene from Thessaly to Libya, the versions differ just as much. The nymph is carried to Libya by the swans of Apollo (Pherecydes *FrGHist* 3 frag. 98 and Ariaethus of Tegea *FrGHist* 316 frag. 3); she makes a stop in Crete (Agroitas, author of *Libyca, FrGHist* 762 frag. 1); she emigrates to Libya of her own free will (Mnaseas the Periegete, *FHG* frag. 3, III p. 156 Müller); cf. also Phylarchus of Athens, *FGrHist* 81 frag. 16. All these fragments are cited by the sch. A.R. 498/ 527a (p. 168.13ff. Wendel).

In myths of topographical foundation that present the rape of a nymph by a god, islands and mountains take their name from a nymph seduced by Poseidon: thus Mt. Rhodope (sch. Theocr. 75d, p. 98.17ff. Wendel) or Corcyra (Diod. 4.72.3), while continental colonies are reserved to a beloved of Apollo, for example, Sinope on the Black Sea (sch. A.R. 2.946c, p. 196.15ff. Wendel).

61. Here the power Aphrodite usually wields over flower gardens is limited by that of Zeus, who, a habitué of these same gardens, turns them into areas productive of civility. Aphrodite brings the power to seduce and to fertilize necessary to the paradigmatic matrimonial union that takes place there. References for gardens of Aphrodite and Zeus in Motte 1973, 121–36 and 207–28. These gardens are opposed to Adonis's sterile one; cf. Detienne 1972, 191–201.

In the fifth *Pythian,* Aphrodite's garden where Arcesilas is celebrated is included in Apollo's sanctuary; cf. below.

62. The parallelism Pindar establishes between the florescence of the land of Cyrenaica and the blossoming of Cyrene is highlighted by Rubin 1978, 359 and 365.

During the fifth century the question of whether Libya and therefore Africa formed a third continent after Europe and Asia was hotly debated. Cf. Hdt. 4.16.

63. On the geographical identification of this hill, cf. note 75 below.

64. Köhnken 1985 throughout his study explains that the victorious conquest of the fiancée and the marriage form the common denominator of the myths staged by the Fifth *Pythian.* Procreation in the poem takes the figure of florescence traced by Kirkwood 1982, 216.

65. This union is omitted in the otherwise stimulating narrative analysis of Rubin 1978, 358–63.

66. Pind. *I.* 4.52ff. with sch. ad loc. (III p. 235.14ff. Drachmann), who emphasizes the *apanthrōpia* and the *asebeia* of the giant. Cf. Angeli Bernardini 1983, 58–62. See Phryn. *TrGF* 3 frag. 3a, Diod. Sic. 4.17.4, Apoll. 2.5.11, etc.; other sources and iconography in Ricardo Olmós and Luis J. Balmaseda, "Antaois I," in *LIMC* I.1 (Zurich-Munich 1981) 800–811.

67. For chronological reasons, two distinct Anteuses are thought to have existed, according to the sch. ad 9.185b, 185d, and 217 (238.5ff., 16ff., and 240.16ff.). On the circumstantial reasons for the text's refusal to accept the doubling of the figure of Anteus, cf. Chamoux 1952, 281–85 and Robbins 1978, 103, n. 37; the young native would thus be the daughter of the king of Anteus's city.

The sch. ad 9.185a (237.19ff.) attributes the name of Barce to Anteus's daughter; according to the epic poet Pisander (frag. 6 Kinkel), she is named Alceis.

A propos Irasa, "the most beautiful of the regions of Libya," which the natives prevent the Greek colonists from seeing in the version of Hdt. 4.158.2, cf. Pherec. *FrGHist* 3 frag. 75 (cited by the same scholium). The latter situates the Libyan city near Lake Triton: cf. Ballabriga 1986, 216–17. On the modern attempts to find the locale of Irasa, cf. Goodchild 1971, 17–18 and Stucchi 1975, 5. For the founding of Barce, cf. Hdt. 4.160, with Chamoux's commentary (1952): 136–38. We notice that Barce seems to have had a native king named Alazir; Arcesilas III marries his daughter, perhaps repeating the legendary gesture of Alexidemus: Hdt. 4.164.4.

68. Woodbury 1982, 254–55. See the intelligent commentary this author gives (246–47 with notes 8 and 9) on the line discussed (100), which describes the double object of the desire of Telesicrates' admirers. Also cf. Segal 1986, 187–88.

69. Cyrene itself is progressively feminized in proportion as man takes precedence over woman. Finally Cyrene, as the "country of beautiful women," receives Telesicrates (line 74), just as Aphrodite received Apollo at the beginning of the narrative (lines 9 and 56).

70. The reference to grazing is constant in the qualification of Cyrenaica; it is green in the middle of a wild, desert Libya (Hdt. 2.32.4); the oracles given to Battus telling him to colonize this well-watered soil especially recall this quality: Hdt. 4.155.3 and 157.2 (*mēlotrophos* qualifies Libya at this point). Cyrene itself benefited both from water from the sky (4.158.3) and from the earth (Apollo's spring: ibid.; river: 4.164.3); they assure the *Kurēnaiē khōrē*'s extraordinary fertility and productivity: 4.199. See also later testimonia of Arr. *Ind.* 43.13 and of Strab. 17.3.21.

In A.R. 4.1561 the reading *thērotrophos* must be retained, in spite of its concurrence with *mēlotrophos*, to qualify Libya in its primordial state. In this vein, we remark that Libya was supposed to nourish golden goats (not sheep), who were watched over by a dragon, called *agrios*: Agroitas, *FrGHist* 762 frag. 3a and b. In addition in Lyc. 893 the Libyan people who receive the Argonauts are presented as a pastoral people. Homer had already mentioned the marvelous animals that situate pastoral Libya between savagery and the Golden Age, attributing to this region ewes that furnish milk abundantly all year long: *Od.* 4.85ff.; cf. also Hdt. 4.29. Undoubtedly the qualities accorded silphium should be evaluated in this context. cf. Aristoph. *Plut.* 925 and sch. Aristoph. *Eq.* 894 (p. 66.22ff. Dübner); further documentation in Chamoux 1952, 246–63.

71. Building of Troy: Hom. *Il.* 21.441ff.; the complementarity of constructing a city with houses, walls, and temples, and the constitution of the *aroura,* the cultivated territory that surrounds it, is manifested in the act of the foundation of Scheria: *Od.* 6.8ff.

72. Also cf. *P.* 4.2 and 5.32 ff., 85, 92, and 115, as well as Call. frag. 716 Pfeiffer. Even if Pindar does not seem to have used it here, it is useful to recall the image of the domestication of mares, the metaphor that represents the effects of marriage; cf. the remarks made about this subject in my *Les choeurs de jeunes filles en Grèce archaïque,* vol. 1 (Rome 1977) 413–20. Alexidemus's marriage with the native princess could receive a metaphorical expression in the domestication represented by the passage from nomadic equitation to maneuvering chariots.

73. Call. *Ap.* 43ff. As for the origin and the placement of the horned altar of Delos, see the references given by Williams 1978, 59–60.

In the form *themethla,* the first term Callimachus used for the foundations established by Apollo, designates in *P.* 4.16 those of the sanctuary of Zeus Ammon and consequently those of the Libyan soil. The same term is used again to designate Apollo's foundation of the temple at Delphi: *HAp.* 254 and 294. On the use of the verb *huphainein* to denote the construction of an edifice, cf. Williams 1978, 56–57.

74. Hdt. 4.158, Call. *Ap.* 85ff. On the probable geographic location of Aziris (orthography "Azilis" in Call. *Ap.* 89), see Goodchild 1971, 19–20. On the warrior aspect assumed by the Spartan-Theran colonists celebrating the Carneia, cf. Williams 1978, 75–76. On the military character of the Carneia itself, cf. Burkert 1977, 354–58. The Carneia's implantation in Libya also constitutes an organizing theme in the version of the Greek migration to Cyrenaica as it is presented in the Fifth *Pythian.* Cf. below.

75. The "Mount" of Myrtes is also mentioned by A.R. 2.505, where it also designates the site of Cyrene before its colonization, and by Steph. Byz. s.v. *Murtoussa* (p. 464.17f. Meineke). For its geographic identification, cf. Chamoux 1952, 268 or Stucchi 1975, 117, who collapses the Myrtoussa of the legend with the ground on which the sanctuary of Apollo was built. In this case the "breast" Pindar speaks of in *P.* 4.14 corresponds to the entire hill of the Acropolis as well as the "eminence" surrounded by a plain mentioned in *P.* 9.55.

76. Acesandrus *FrGHist* 469 frag. 4, cited by the sch. A.R. 2.498/527a (p. 168.25ff. Wendel). In conformity with this version, A.R. 2.509 indicates that Apollo made an *agrotis,* a "huntress" of Cyrene in Libya. On Eurypylus, native king of Cyrene, cf. note 15 above.

On the supposed opposition between this version and the Pindaric version, cf. Chamoux 1952, 77–83, who also mentions later sources. Malten 1911, 51–55 would like to see the versions of Acesandrus and Callimachus as purely local narratives. Different reasons have been alleged to justify this divergence. They are enumerated by Paola Radici Colace, "Cirene e Artemide *potnia therōn* nell'Inno secondo di Callimaco," *GIF* 27 (1975): 45–59, who herself advances a ritualist thesis that is difficult to defend.

77. Robbins 1978, 96–104, who, in an explicitly structuralist reference, confuses the second term of the opposition with that of cultivation (agricultural); more prudence with respect to this subject is found in Kirkwood's commentary 1982, 223 and 226.

For an analysis of the Centaur's double nature, cf. G. S. Kirk, *Myth: Its Meaning and Function in Ancient and Other Cultures* (Berkeley-Los Angeles 1970) 152–62.

78. A.R. 2.498ff., with the sch. ad loc. (pp. 168.4ff., 169.10ff. and 24ff. Wendel). Aristeus is already defined as the guardian of flocks, along with Hermes, by Hes. frag. 217 Merkelbach-West (cf. also frag. 216 and *Theog.* 977). Call. *Aet.* frag. 75.32ff. Pfeiffer attributes the name Aristeus to Zeus Icmaius, making of this name an *epiclēsis* of the god of the etesian winds. In this connection, one remarks that in Hom. *Il.* 13.154 and 14.213 as well as in *Hhom.* 23.1, Zeus is qualified as *aristos.* No doubt this *epiclēsis* facilitated the assimilation of Aristeus to the god of the celestial water. In addition, Pindar probably uses the name Aristeus in a play of mythological assimilation manifested in the Ninth *Pythian;* the hero's name is found once again in the designation of the suitors for Aristeus's daughter's hand, among whom figures Alexidemus (*aristēes* 107). Cf. Köhnken 1985, 105.

On Aristeus's essentially pastoral function, see Woodbury 1982, 255–58. Brelich

1958, 171 has seen that the alimentary inventions attributed to Aristeus do not include the cultivation of cereals: cf. Diod. Sic. 4.81.2f. and sch. ad 9.112 and 115b (231.1ff. and 13f.); other sources in Malten 1911, 77–85. We also note that according to the sch. ad 4.4 (94.26ff.) Aristeus himself would have been honored by the Cyrenians as oecist.

79. Amphitryon and Iolaus were both objects of heroic cults in Thebes: cf. Pind. O. 9.98f., I. 5.32f., N. 4.19ff. and frag. 169.47ff. Snell-Maehler; see Albert Schachter, *Cults of Boiotia*, vol. 1 (*BICS* 1981 Suppl. 38.1) 30–31 and vol. 2 (1986, 38.2) 64–65, who cites all the other evidence on the tomb shared by the two heroes.

Heracles, whose brother Iphicles is the father of Iolaus, is attached to this hero by a double relation, familial and amorous: cf. ibid., 15–18. The uncle and the nephew were probably both honored in the same Ioleia/Heracleia festival; Pindar seems to situate another of Telesicrates' agonal victories there; cf. for this subject Laura Nash, "The Theban Myth in *Pythian* 9, 74–103," *QUCC* 40 (1982): 77–97, with references given by Kirkwood 1982, 228–29, and discussion of the syntactic articulation of this passage in Burton 1962, 45–50 and in Carey 1981, 90–91.

On the founding and civilizing character of Heracles' athletic exploits, cf. Brelich 1958, 193–96.

80. This metaphorical relation is highlighted by Köhnken 1985, 108–10, who, however, does not perceive that the *telos* of both battle and marriage apply to Telesicrates (cf. line 99f.!). In the same vein, see Crotty 1982, 95, Emilio Suarez della Torre, "El mito de Cirene y la victoria de Telesicrates (Pind. *Pyth.* IX)," *EC* 26 (1984): 199–208 (with an abundant bibliography on the subject in note 2), and Segal 1986, 187–88. More subtly done is Anne Carson, "Wedding at Noon in Pindar's Ninth *Pythian*," *GRBS* 23 (1982): 121–28. She shows that Telesicrates' victory is only effective to the extent that it is integrated into the community through the civilizing ritual of marriage.

Since Elroy L. Bundy, *Studia Pindarica* I, (Berkeley-Los Angeles 1962) 17–18 and Burton 1962, 48–50, we have found allusions in lines 79–103 to different victories carried off by Telesicrates not only at Thebes, but also at Aegina, Megara, and finally Cyrene in the local festivals cited in lines 97–103; cf. especially Jacques Peron, "Pindare et la victoire de Télésicratès dans la IXe Pythique (vv. 76–96)," *RPh* 50 (1976): 58–78 and Nash's article cited in note 79 above.

81. On the Heraclids' intervention in the Peloponnesus, cf. Prinz 1979, 277–313, who considers the insertion of Delphic influence to be rather late (p. 278, n.82). On the tripartite division of the Peloponnesus confirmed by the Heraclid legacy, see my remarks in "Spartan Genealogies: The Mythological Representation of a Spatial Organization" in Bremmer 1987, 153–86.

82. These different movements along the time line have not aided the comprehension of this passage. One wonders particularly how "the gift-bearing men whom Battus brought on the ships" could receive "the drivers of horses," those descended from Antenor the Trojan (85ff.). Making *dekontai* into an historical present only reinforces the contradiction; this however is the solution proposed by Chamoux 1952, 71 and 279, n.5 (but cf. 389) and Jean Brunel, "Les Anténorides à Cyrène et l'interprétation littérale de Pindare, *Pythique* V, v. 82–88," *REA* 66 (1964): 5–21, who proposes making *to ethnos* the subject of the verb *dekontai*, following various paraphrases of the passage given by the sch. ad 5.113. Francis Vian, "Les Anténor-

ides de Cyrène et les Carnéia," *REG* 68 (1955): 307–11, argues that the verb under discussion, specified by *thusiaisin* and by the expression *oikhneontes sphe* (allusions to the movement of a procession), refers to an act of cult devoted to the heroes. On the other hand, as we shall see, it is impossible to envision as probable the real installation of the Antenorids in Cyrene before its colonization by the Thereans. Menelaus himself passes as having stopped in Libya: Hdt. 2.119.2.

83. Thera's family ancestry and his political destiny are unfolded in Hdt. 4.147ff. in a *logos* that will be commented upon below (cf. note 102). For the attempts to connect the figure of Theras to the herding protected by Apollo, cf. R. Holland, "Theras," in *Ausführl. Lexikon der gr. u. röm. Mythologie,* vol. 5 (Leipzig 1916) 640–52. We note that historians after Herodotus will attempt to suppress the Aegid line in the history of Cyrene's founding by substituting Samus, a descendant of Euphemus, for Theras, the founder of Thera: cf. note 114 below.

84. Hes. *Op.* 156ff.; on the content of the *Cyclia* (in the broad sense) see especially the introduction to *Cypria* frag. 1 Bernabé: the Theban War and the Trojan War are inscribed in the same plan by Zeus; for a reconstruction of the epic cycle's plot, cf. Albert Severyns, *Le cycle épique dans l'Ecole d'Aristarque,* (Liège and Paris 1928) 163–425.

85. The ancient historians had already arrived at the thesis of Cyrene's precolonization by Antenor's descendants who fled Troy's destruction: Lysimachus, *FrGHist* 382 frag. 6, a historian of the second century B.C., is cited by the sch. ad 5.110 (186.3ff.). Cf. also sch. Lyc. 874 (II p. 283.20ff. Scheer). See also Timach. Rhod. *FrGHist* 532 frag. 17 with the commentary of Chamoux 1952, 72; this hypothesis justifies the early date of 1336 attributed to the colonization of Cyrenaica (cf. note 1 above). Among modern historians the hypothesis of a "pre-Dorian" or "Mycenean" colonization of Cyrene has been advanced by Alfred Gercke, "Die Myrmidonen in Kyrene," *Hermes* 41 (1906): 447–59, and taken up again recently in an article cited in note 1. In addition there have been attempts to identify the Antenorids with the Tritopatores or the Acamantes cited in *SEG* IX.72.21ff. Cf. Malkin 1987, 209–12, and Leschhorn 1984, 68. There is a more prudent historicist thesis in Malten 1911, 112–51. A refutation of the various precolonization hypotheses can be found in Chamoux 1952, 71–91. Lorenzo Braccesi, "Antenoridi, Veneti e Libyi," *Quaderni di archeologia della Libya* 12 (1987): 7–14 gives an interesting historical explanation for the insertion in the fifth century of the Antenorids in Cyrenean legend.

86. On the institution of cults, on Mycenean sites, devoted to the heroes of the Trojan War during the archaic epoch, cf. Claude Bérard, "L'héroïsation et la formation de la cité" in *Architecture et société: De l'archaïsme grec à la fin de la République romaine* (Paris and Rome 1983) 43–59. For something more specific on the "invention of the mythic founder" and the cult devoted to him, cf. François De Polignac, *La naissance de la cité grecque* (Paris 1984) 132–38. For Sparta, cf. the remarks cited in note 81. The problem posed by the founding of Rome is identical. Built, in legend, by heroes of the Trojan War, Rome has existed from the archeological point of view only since the eighth century B.C.! Other colonies wanted to have a heroic past: cf. Malkin 1987, 153.

87. The existence of the Hill of the Antenorids is pointed out by Lysimachus in the frag. cited in note 85. For an attempt to locate it, cf. François Chamoux, "Les

Anténorides à Cyrène" in *Mélanges d'archéologie et d'histoire Charles Picard,* vol. 1 (Paris 1949) 154–61. This article contains some of the arguments developed by the same author (cf. the work cited in note 85) in order to refute the historical existence of a pre-Battiad colonization of Cyrene.

88. *Makar* essentially denotes the happy condition gods enjoy living in the ideal regions: Martin L. West, *Hesiod: Works and Days* (Oxford 1978) 193–94; heroes accede to this after mortal existence: Brelich 1958, 352–53. Traces left in legend by the process of Battus's heroization have been studied by Calame 1988, 118–23.

89. If we follow Theotimus, Cyrene's historiographer, we can affirm that even the charioteer Carrhotus is inscribed in the sequence of founders/civilizers, since on Arcesilas the Fourth's demand he is substituted for a certain Euphemus (cited in note 19) to take charge of a colonial expedition to the Hesperides: *FrGHist* 470 frag. 1 cited by the sch. ad 5.34 (175.16ff.); cf. Chamoux 1952, 173–75.

90. Corinth: Paus. 2.4.3; Sicyon: Paus. 2.6.7. We must not forget that Heraclean or Heraclid ancestry was used as a means of attaching a dynasty to either an Achaean or a Dorian ancestry: cf. Domenico Musti, "Continuità e discontinuità tra Achei e Dori nelle tradizioni storiche" in Musti 1985, 37–71; the state of the question in Prinz 1979, 212–16.

Rhodes: Hom. *Il.* 2.653ff., also Pind. *O.* 7.20ff. with sch. ad loc. (I p. 208.17ff. Drachmann); Cos: Hom. *Il.* 2.677ff.; cf. G. S. Kirk, *The Iliad: A Commentary,* vol.1 (Cambridge 1985) 225 and 228, who shows that the Achaean continuity implied by this genealogical projection does not have an archeological correspondence. Lydia: Hdt. 1.7; Macedonia: Thuc. 2.99.3 and Diod. Sic. 7.15.3ff.

91. On Aigimius as representative of the Dorians cf. Pindar, *P.* 1.62ff. and Strab. 9.4.10. The legend of the encounter of Heraclids and Dorians for the conquest of the Peloponnesus, pretext for a first Aegid emigration from Thebes, is made explicit by sch. ad 5.101b (184.12ff.), who cite Eph. *FrGHist* 70 frag. 16. Cf. note 101 above.

92. On these legends cf. Prinz 1979, 187–205, 97–111, and 56–78, without forgetting Rome's founding by Aeneas!

93. Antenor's favorable, conciliatory attitude vis-à-vis Menelaus and Odysseus is described by Hom. *Il.* 3.205ff. and 7.348ff.; cf. also Bacch. 15, Paus. 10.27.3 and commentary by sch. ad 5.110 (186.3ff.), who cite the frag. of Lysimachus already mentioned in note 85 above.

Antenor himself founds Patavium in the Veneto: Soph. *TrGF* p. 16f. Radt, Strab. 5.1.4, Liv. 1.1 and Verg. *Aen.* 1.242ff.; other evidence in Mark Davies, "Antenor I," *LIMC* I.1 (Zurich and Munich 1981) 811–15. The hospitality isotopy is also actualized in the Fourth *Pythian*: cf. note 14 above.

94. On the "Dorian" character attributed to the Carneia since antiquity, cf.Thuc. 5.54.2 and Paus. 3.13.4. The festival is best attested in Sparta; sources in Samuel Wide, *Lakonische Kulte* (Leipzig 1893) 63–87; cf. also Burkert 1977, 354–58. Double *aition* of the Carneia: Paus. 3.13.3 and 5; also see Alcm. frag. 52 Page, Theop. *FrGHist* 115 frag. 357, Con. *FrGHist* 26 frag. 1.26 and sch. Call. *Ap.* 71 (II p. 48.20ff. Pfeiffer).

This game of temporal effacement through a probable reference to the double origin of the Carneia leads me to consider the Carneia cited in line 80, the welcome sacrifices offered to the Antenorids (86), and the festival designated in line 90 by the general term "Apolloniai" as all one festival. Analogous interpretation in Lefkowitz 1985, 45 and 50. See, however, sch. ad 5.121 (188.1ff.). On the Cyrenean celebration of the Carneia, see again Call. *Ap.* 77ff., a text commented on below.

95. On the Apollonian cult whose object was Battus in Cyrene, cf. Chamoux 1952, 285–87 (with an error in the location of the tomb of the hero: cf. note 97 below) and Calame 1988, 118–23.

96. The assimilation of these two heroic references is facilitated not only by the double return to the present and the common celebration of the Carneia already evoked, but also by the subtle enunciative play Pindar exploits in the poem. The "I" of the narrator that expresses his kinship with the Aegid heroes (*emoi pateres* 76; cf. I. 7.12ff.) returns in line 80 with "we" (*sebizomen*), which may also refer to the Cyrenean choreutai who sing the Fifth *Pythian* for Arcesilas as well as to those who celebrate the Carneia, which honors also the Antenorids. On the referential suppleness of the Pindaric "I/we," see the indecisive remarks in Lefkowitz 1985, 45–49 and "Who Sang Pindar's Victory Odes?" *AJP* 109 (1988): 1–11, and the more precise ones made by Gordon M. Kirkwood, "Pythian 5.72–76, 9.90–92 and the Voice of Pindar," *ICS* 6 (1981): 12–23. Burton 1962, 146–47 attempts to reduce the contradiction represented by this double enunciative reference by imagining that Pindar himself participated in the celebration of Arcesilas the Fourth at Cyrene!

Perhaps the occasion for the Fifth *Pythian*'s recitation is to be found in the Carneia, cf. Burton 1962, 135–37 and Christian Froidefond, "Pittoresque et idéalité dans la Ve Pythique de Pindare," *REA* 80 (1981): 217–27. This hypothesis finds confirmation in the recommendation that, after the evocation of the festival's introduction in Cyrene, the narrator makes to Arcesilas to celebrate Apollo "by the song of young people" (103; announced by the *komoi* of 100); this song is none other than the Fifth *Pythian*. This means that Aphrodite's garden, where the execution of Pindar's ode takes place (24), is part of Apollo's sanctuary, not next to it (as Chamoux argued 1952, 267–69). A small temple of Aphrodite seems to have been part of the sanctuary, at any rate: Stucchi 1975, 53 and 54 with n. 3. Perhaps the Ninth *Pythian*'s matrimonial isotopy recurs here; on the qualities of Aphrodite's garden, cf. Motte 1973, 121–37. In Delos, also, the statue of Aphrodite brought by Theseus probably stands in Apollo's sanctuary: cf. Philippe Bruneau, *Recherches sur les cultes de Délos à l'époque hellénistique et à l'époque impériale* (Paris 1980) 19–21 and 333–34.

97. The identification of the tumulus corresponding to Battus's tomb is not yet certain; cf. Goodchild 1971, 94 and Stucchi 1975, 12 and 104, n.4. An attempt at reconstitution in Büsing 1978, 66–75. On the cult of the oecist, see Malkin 1987, 204–12.

On the Hill of the Antenorids, cf. note 87 above.

98. Hdt. 4.145–57 (the ethnographic part of the Herodotean introduction to Libya extends from 168 to 199). This Herodotean version of the antecedents of Cyrene's founding is at the same time recapitulated and completed by the sch. ad 4.88b (109.14ff.); cf. also sch. ad 5.99b (184.3ff.).

The coincidence of these two lineages at Sparta at the moment of the decision to found Thera is also emphasized by Paus. 7.2.2, who dates this colonization one generation after that of Ionia.

As for Herodotus's practice of synchronic historical writing and its defects, cf.

Catherine Darbo-Peschanski, *Le discours du particulier: Essai sur l'enquête hérodo-téenne* (Paris 1987) 30–32.

On Libya as a third continent, cf. note 62 above.

99. The Minyans' claim to consider their return to Sparta as a return to the land of their fathers (Hdt. 4.145.4) is marked by a fire lit on the slopes of the Taygetus, which may be interpreted as a sacrifice to Hestia: cf. Francesco Prontera, "I Minii sul Taigeto (Erodoto IV 145): genealogia e sinecismo in Sparta arcaica," *AFLPer* 16 (1978/79): 159–66. Prontera's interpretation is confirmed in A.R. 4.1761, who shows Euphemus's descendants coming to establish themselves "by the hearth" (*ephestioi*) of the Spartans; this term is glossed by "colonists" (*epoikoi*) in the sch. ad loc. (p. 327.71f. Wendel).

According to Herodotus, Pindar's use of the enigmatic expression *meikhthentes* (P. 4.257) to qualify Euphemus's descendants' stay in Sparta may be taken in its direct sense of matrimonial union and its secondary signification of incorporation into the civic body of Sparta.

100. The same genealogy, going back to Oedipus, is recalled by Call. *Ap.* 74; cf. sch. A.R. 1760/64c (p. 327.25ff. Wendel).

101. On the Spartan destiny of the Aegids, cf. Pind. *I.* 7.12ff. with the sch. ad loc. (III p. 263.1ff. Drachmann), who cite Androt. *FrGHist* 324 frag. 60b, with the complex commentary of Franz Kiechle, *Lakonien und Sparta* (Munich and Berlin 1963) 82–95. The reference to Sparta in the Fifth *Pythian* by means of the mention of the Aegids is part of the process of heroization that traverses this ode; cf. Nafissi 1985, 378 and 380.

102. Calame 1988, 108–18.

103. As far as bastardy is concerned, legend makes Penthilus, founding hero of Lesbos, the offspring of the unmarried union of Orestes and Erigone, who herself is born of the unsanctioned union of Clytemnestra and Aegisthus: cf. Paus. 2.18.6 and 3.2.1 and Alc. frag. 70.16ff. Voigt. On the other hand, the destiny of Agamemnon's mother strangely resembles that of the mother attributed to Battus in the Cyrenean version. She, too, a Cretan, granddaughter of Minos the Second, is taken away by her father and confided to Nauplius to be sold abroad, at Argos she marries Pleisthenes the Atreid: Eur. *Cressai* p. 501f. Nauck² and Apoll. 3.2.2.

104. The two versions of Tarentum's colonization, cited by Strab. 6.3.2 and 3, go back to Antiochus of Syracuse, *FrGHist* 555 frag. 13 and to Ephorus, *FrGHist* 70 frag. 216, respectively. Other sources in Marinella Corsano, "Sparte et Tarente: le mythe de fondation d'une colonie," *RHR* 196 (1979): 113–40, who furnishes, following an abundant bibliography, the best analysis of this legend.

105. Sch. Pind. *I.* 7.18c (III p. 263.18ff. Drachmann), who cites Arist. *Resp. Lac.* frag. 532 Rose.

106. Dion. Hal. 19.1; Paus. 10.10.4; other sources in the article cited in note 104.

107. Call. *Ap.* 88, Steph. Byz. s.v. *Kurēnē* (p. 396.17f. Meineke); Chamoux 1952, 126–27 cites the moderns' epistemologizing attempt to give a meaning to this toponym.

108. The silence of Herodotus on the subject of the clod received by Euphemus in no way prevents the historian from Halicarnassus from knowing the forced march of the Argonauts in Libya. But the version he gives thereof a propos of his description of Lake Triton (4.178f., cf. note 29 above) mentions only the exchange of the tripod,

which Jason destined for Delphi, contrary to the information transmitted by Triton; this gift of a tripod is the promise of numerous Greek foundations in Libya. Undoubtedly it is an echo of a narrative found in an especially enigmatic passage of Lycophron (886ff.): having become a mixing bowl and been transmitted to Triton by Medea, the gift of the Greeks, too, presents itself as the presage of Greek control over Libya. Completely detached from the Cyrenean context, this Herodotean narrative cannot be considered a Libyan version intended to be opposed to the Theran version of the founding of Cyrene found in the Fourth *Pythian:* the theme of autochthony carried by this ode forbids this interpretation, which has been proposed by Jutta Kirchberg, *Die Funktion der Orakel im Werke Herodots* (Göttingen 1965) 53–55. It has been forgotten that the clod lost at Thera is of Libyan origin!

109. On the chronological system Herodotus put in place cf. Hermann Strasburger, "Herodots Zeitrechnung," *Historia* 5 (1956): 129–61 and Darbo-Peschanski (see note 98 above) 25–32. For an attempt (illusory) to bring together the chronology of the Herodotean narrative and that of the narrative of the Fourth *Pythian* by thus making Theras the one who, in the fourth generation, should have founded Cyrene, cf. Büsing 1978, 62–66.

With regard to generational succession as a chronological principle of historiography, cf. Ricoeur 1985, 160–71.

110. The attribution of the battle with the Libyan lions to Battus is inscribed within the framework of the spatial displacement of the nymph Cyrene's hunting activity from Thessaly to Cyrenaica to civilize the native king Eurypylus's territory: cf. notes 15 and 76 above. Aristarchus, cited by the sch. ad 4.76b (181.11ff.), understood perfectly the civilizing action attached to the effect of Battus's voice, whatever interpretation one may give: cf. sch. ad 78a, 80a, and 83 (181.2 ff., 182.11ff., and 18f.).

The version given by Pausanias (10.15.7; cf. also sch. Call. *Ap.* 65; II p. 51.61ff. Pfeiffer), far from representing the myth of origin as supposed by Burton 1962, 145, is, no doubt, a later development. The transference of the fear displayed by the wild animals to Battus himself only rationalizes the legend. There is another attempt of the same type in Acesandrus (*FrGHist* 469 frag. 6), who talks about a transformation *apo tautomatou* of the voice of Battus, who becomes from then on an *anēr rhētorikos!* Cf. also Call. *Ap.* 76, who terms the oecist an *oulos,* a term to which the sch. ad loc. (II p. 52.81ff. Pfeiffer) give the meaning "healthy in language"; see the commentary by Williams 1978, 69–70. For the double name Battus-Aristoteles, cf. Leschhorn 1984, 61, n. 2.

For Plutarch, *Pyth. Or.* 405b, there is no incompatibility between Battus's stuttering voice and the fact that he is *basilikos, politikos,* and *phronimos!* Henceforth, the legend is rationalized and the passage from stuttering to strong voice is no longer seen as the affirmation of sovereignty. The Fourth *Pythian* is unambiguous in this regard: the oracular interrogation concerning a voice's clumsiness opens up onto the institution of a royalty still prosperous through the eighth generation.

The central character of the transformation undergone by Battus in the process of the heroization of an oecist has been made explicit by Maurizio Giangiulio, "Deformità eroiche e tradizioni di fondazione: Batto, Miscello e l'oracolo delfico," *ASNP* III.9 (1981): 1–24.

Segal 1986, 145–50 has also pointed out that Battus represents the inverse of Oedipus the tyrant; other bibliographical references in Calame 1988, 122n. 14.

In a late version of the legends concerning Athenian Thesmophoria (Ael. frag. 44 Hercher) Battus is taken to be emasculated because he has seen that which he ought not to have seen or understood: cf. Detienne and Vernant 1979, 184–209. I will leave the exegesis of the stuttering hero's impotence to a psychoanalytic interpretation.

111. Menecl. *FrGHist* 270 frag. 6 with commentary by Calame 1988, 105–6. Unfortunately, the text of the oracle given by Menecles is corrupt: cf. Herbert W. Parke and Donald E. W. Wormell, "Notes on Delphic Oracles," *CQ* 43 (1949): 138–40. It is still possible to see a metaphorical play there: the passage from an unstable maritime country to a continent glossed as "terra firma" (*sterros gē*) undoubtedly echoes the transition from stuttering, to which the name Battus refers, to the accomplishment of the Theran oecist's enterprise.

112. Callimachus claimed Battiad ancestry for himself: cf. test. 1, 4, 6, and 87 Pfeiffer, with commentary by Williams 1978, 65 and 67. As the latter suggests, it is not impossible to see in the term *patrōïos* an explicit reminder of the "Aegid" ancestry Pindar claimed in *P.* 9.76.

113. On the meaning of this term cf. Williams 1978, 63.

114. Especially in the case of Acesandrus, who, in his treatise on the history of Cyrene, makes the eponymous nymph's combat with the lions under the reign of Eurypylus follow the episode of Battus's stuttering: *FrGHist* 469 frag. 4 and 6. This historian attempted to rationalize the legend by attributing the founding of Thera directly to Samus, a descendant of Euphemus, and not to an Aegid: frag. 5; cf. also Theocr. *FrGHist* 761 frag. 1, and sch. ad 4.88b (110.5ff.). There are echoes of another "historicization" of the legend in Strab. 17.3.20f.

115. Bruce Karl Brasswell, *A Commentary on the Fourth Pythian of Pindar* (Berlin-New York 1988) appeared after the redaction of this study.

WORKS CITED

Angeli Bernardini, Paola. 1983. *Mito e attualità nelle odi di Pindaro. La Nemea 4, l'Olimpica 9, l' Olimpica 7.* Rome.

Ballabriga, Alain. 1986. *Le soleil et le Tartare. L'image mythique du monde en Grèce archaïque.* Paris.

Benveniste, Emile, 1974. *Problèmes de linguistique générale*, II. Paris.

Brelich, Angelo. 1958. *Gli eroi greci. Un problema storico-religioso.* Rome.

Bremmer, Jan, ed. 1987. *Interpretations in Greek Mythology.* London.

Burkert, Walter. 1977. *Griechische Religion der archaischen und klassischen Epoche.* Stuttgart.

Burton, Reginald W. B. 1962. *Pindar's Pythian Odes.* Oxford.

Büsing, Hermann. 1978. "Battos." In T. Lorenz, ed. *Thiasos: Sieben archäologische Arbeiten*, 51–79. Amsterdam.

Calame, Claude. 1986. *Le récit en Grèce ancienne. Enonciations et représentations de poètes.* Paris.

———. 1988. "Le récit hérodotéen de la fondation de Cyrène: mythe, récit épique et histoire." In C. Calame, ed. *Métamorphoses du mythe en Grèce antique*, 105–25. Geneva.

Carey, Christopher. 1981. *A Commentary on Five Odes of Pindar. Pythian 2, Pythian 9, Nemean 1, Nemean 7, Isthmian 8.* Salem, MA.

Casewitz, M. 1985. *Le vocabulaire de la colonisation en grec ancien. Etude lexicologique: les familles de* κτίζω *et de* οἰκέω-οἰκίζω. Paris.

Chamoux, François. 1952. *Cyrène sous la monarchie des Battiades.* Paris.

Courtés, Joseph. 1977. "Sémiotique et théorie actantielle du récit dans la perspective d'A. J. Greimas." In Gentili and Paioni 1977, 323–47.

Crotty, Kevin. 1982. *Song and Action. The Victory Odes of Pindar.* Baltimore.

Derrida, Jacques. 1976. *Of Grammatology.* Tr. G. C. Spivak. Baltimore.

Detienne, Marcel. 1972. *Les Jardins d'Adonis. La mythologie des aromates en Grèce.* Paris.

——— and Jean-Pierre Vernant. 1974. *Les ruses de l'intelligence. La mètis des Grecs.* Paris.

——— and ———. 1979. *La cuisine du sacrifice en pays grec.* Paris.

Gentili, Bruno, and Giuseppe Paioni, eds. 1977. *Il Mito Greco.* Rome.

———. 1984. *Poesia e pubblico nella Grecia antica da Omero al V secolo.* Rome-Bari. Translated as *Poetry and Its Public in Ancient Greece.* Baltimore, 1988.

Giannini, Pietro. 1979. "Interpretazione della *Pitica* 4 di Pindaro." *QUCC* 31: 35–63.

Gianotti, Gian Franco. 1975. *Per una poetica pindarica.* Turin.

Goodchild, Richard G. 1971. *Kyrene und Apollonia.* Zurich.

Greimas, A.-J. 1983. *Structural Semantics: An Attempt at a Method.* Tr. D. McDowell, R. Schleifer, and A. Velie. Lincoln, NE.

——— and J. Courtés. 1982. *Semiotics and Language: An Analytical Dictionary.* Tr. L. Crist and D. Patte. Bloomington, IN.

——— and ———. 1986. *Sémiotique: Dictionnaire raisonné de la théorie du langage,* II. Paris.

Hurst, André, ed. 1985. *Pindare. Entretiens sur l'Antiquité classique XXXI.* Vandoeuvres-Geneva.

Kirkwood, Gordon. 1982. *Selections from Pindar.* Chico, CA.

Köhnken, Adolf. 1985. "'Meilichos orga'. Liebesthematik und aktueller Sieg in der neunten pythischen Ode Pindars." In Hurst 1985, 71–111.

Lefkowitz, Mary R. 1985. "Pindar's *Pythian V.*" In Hurst 1985, 33–63.

Leschhorn, Wolfgang. 1984. *"Gründer der Stadt." Studien zu einem politisch-religiösen Phänomen der griechischen Geschichte.* Wiesbaden.

Loraux, Nicole. 1981. *Les enfants d'Athéna. Idées athéniennes sur la citoyenneté et la division des sexes.* Paris.

Malkin, Irad. 1987. *Religion and Colonisation in Ancient Greece.* Leiden.

Malten, Ludolf. 1911. *Kyrenen. Sagengeschichtliche und historische Untersuchungen.* Berlin.

Motte, André. 1973. *Prairies et jardins de la Grèce antique. De la religion à la philosophie.* Brussels.

Musti, Domenico, ed. 1985. *Le origini dei Greci. Dori e mondo egeo.* Rome.

Nafissi, M. 1985. "Battiadi e Aigeidai: Per la storia dei rapporti tra Cirene e Sparta in età arcaica." In Barker, Graeme et al. *Cyrenaica in Antiquity,* 375–86. Oxford.

Prinz, Friedrich. 1979. *Gründungsmythen und Sagenchronologie.* Munich.

Propp, Vladimir 1968. *Morphology of the Folktale*, 2nd ed. Trans. Laurence Scott. Austin and London.

Ricoeur, Paul. 1985. *Temps et récit*, III. *Le temps raconté*. Paris.

Robbins, Emmett. 1978. "Cyrene and Cheiron: The Myth of Pindar's Ninth Pythian." *Phoenix* 32: 91–104.

Rubin, Nancy Felson. 1978. "Narrative Structure in Pindar's Ninth Pythian." *CW* 71: 353–67.

Saussure, Ferdinand de. 1959. *Course in general linguistics*, tr. W. Baskin. New York.

Segal, Charles. 1986. *Pindar's Mythmaking: The Fourth Pythian Ode*. Princeton, NJ.

Stucchi, Sandro. 1975. *Architettura cirenaica*. Rome.

Vian, Francis. 1963. *Les origines de Thèbes. Cadmos et les Spartes*. Paris.

Williams, Frederick. 1978. *Callimachus. Hymn to Apollo*. Oxford.

Woodbury, Leonard. 1982. "Cyrene and the *teleuta* of Marriage in Pindar's Ninth Pythian Ode." *TAPhA* 112:245–58.

7

PSYCHOANALYSIS

The apostasy, as Sigmund Freud perceived it, of Carl Jung in 1912 led to a major division within the psychoanalytic movement and thus to a major division in the psychoanalytic interpretation of myth. Although Freud often referred to myths, he rarely interpreted them, and even in the canonic statements of the Oedipus complex his emphasis alternates between the form of the Sophoclean tragedy and the mythical story.ᵃ Even when they were still on good terms, he was sceptical of Jung's interest in mythology.ᵇ Jung, however, who turned to the notions of "collective unconscious" and inherited, instinctual "archetypes," believed that myths had therapeutic value.ᶜ Some of his best-known followers became scholars and retellers of myths—Erich Neumann, C. Kerényi, and Joseph Campbell.ᵈ

The first prominent mythologist among Freud's followers was Otto Rank, who published *The Myth of the Birth of the Hero* in 1909. In 1912, Rank became a founding editor of the journal *Imago*, which regularly published articles on mythology. Though interpretation of myth was thus from early days an offshoot of Freudian psychoanalytic theory, in view of the vastly different premises of the two schools, it never had the same vital, almost religious importance for Freudians that it had for Jungians. According to the particular orientations of analysts or scholars, Freudian interpretation of myth pursued various paths, which sometimes crossed with psychoanalytic interpretation of literature. As Richard Caldwell implies at the beginning of his chapter, these two objects of interpretation, myth and literature, ought to be distinguished. In fact, much "Freudian" interpretation of myth has focused on the motivations of characters in myth, as if they were characters in a novel. Mythical characters do not have great psychological depth, and psychoanalytic interpretation properly focuses on other aspects of myth.

Caldwell's chapter shows that what must be interpreted is the myth as a whole in relation to the teller and audience of the myth. Myths are "about" not the unconscious of the heroes but that of the people to whom the myths are meaningful. For this reason, as Caldwell stresses, psychoanalytic interpretation uses historical and anthropological data whenever possible. Sometimes branded as "reductive," the psychoanalytic approach is in reality cooperative, and its results may corroborate and be corroborated by the results of other approaches. For example, Caldwell uses the Sphinx and Jocasta in the Oedipus myth as an example of the dream mechanism called "decomposition." The figure of the mother is divided into two representatives, one positive, the other negative. This observation concerning the close connection between Jocasta and the Sphinx, who are as unconnected as possible at the narrative level, is confirmed by comparative folkloristic analysis.[e]

The psychoanalytic approach is not limited to analysis of the origin (childhood fantasy) and function (representation of unconscious ideas) of myth, but also offers interpretation of narrative. Caldwell outlines a psychoanalytic version of Lévi-Straussian structuralism that preserves the notion of groups of synchronic units having a capacity to signify only in virtue of their relations to one another. But he replaces the notion of binary opposition with that of emotional conflict. He demonstrates this psychoanalytic-structuralist approach with four myths or groups of myth: those of Oedipus; of Tiresias; of the great criminals Ixion, Tantalus, Sisyphus, and Tityus; and of Orestes and the Pelopids.

Caldwell thus contributes to an ongoing controversy between structuralism and psychoanalysis. Sporadically in the volumes of *Structural Anthropology* and now more systematically in the final chapter of *The Jealous Potter*, Lévi-Strauss has challenged Freudian interpretation of myth, arguing that Freud is himself a mythical thinker who creates new versions of myths when he attempts myth analysis.[f] Lévi-Strauss challenges in particular the Freudian concentration on the sexual, which Lévi-Strauss regards as only one of several codes that any myth may deploy simultaneously. Further, the sexual code is not obligatorily employed. It may be absent, and, when it is present, its value or function is relative to other codes that are present. Here is a cardinal difference between the structuralist and the psychoanalytic approaches to myth. For the structuralist, the characters, the actions, in short the content of a myth does not have any one-to-one relation with the reality about which the myth is speaking. On the contrary, the various components of the myth are able to signify something only because of their relation to one another. (Cf. my introduction to Calame's contribution to this volume.) The psychoanalytic approach sometimes finds a one-to-one relation between myth and reality. If Caldwell's psychoanalytic adaptation of structuralism succeeds in preserving the structuralist criterion of signification, then Freud has to some extent been vindicated against Lévi-

Strauss. I would call attention especially to the closing pages of Caldwell's chapter, in which he suggests that Freud's concept of dreamwork recognizes the importance of contextual relationships for the interpretation of any individual element in a dream. Since dream interpretation is the basis of Freudian myth interpretation, this suggestion would find an important point of rapprochement between the structuralist and psychoanalytic approaches to myth, at least in a tentative form, in Freud's thought.

The Psychoanalytic Interpretation of Greek Myth

RICHARD CALDWELL

The aim of this essay is to provide a practical demonstration rather than a theoretical defense.[1] I will therefore assume what is in any case unprovable at this length: that psychoanalysis, whatever its merits as a scientific theory or as a therapeutic method, provides a valid model of unconscious mental functioning (which of course implies the further assumption that unconscious mental functions exist). I will also assume that the usefulness of this model in generating a methodology for myth interpretation depends not on prior theoretical considerations but rather on the usual tests of methodological utility (general applicability, coherence, economy of explanation, and so on).

MYTHS, DREAMS, AND CHILDHOOD

Psychoanalytic interpretations of both Greek myth and Greek literature have often met skepticism and outright hostility. In the case of psychoanalytic literary criticism this reaction is understandable and sometimes justified, but in the matter of myth it would seem that a psychoanalytic method should have an a priori claim to legitimacy. If a native informant in a tribal society is asked the meaning of his culture's myths, the answer typically given resembles nothing so much as the attempts a dreamer makes to understand his dream (or a phobic to explain his phobia). In the case of ancient Greece, these native informants whose comments have survived are mostly late and mostly scholarly, but even they share with the dreamer and the phobic a tendency toward naive rationalization and an almost willful failure to see the point.

We tend to think of Greek myth in the same way we think about literature, probably because most of the familiar myths have come down to us in literary versions (and this fact of transmission helps to explain some of the aforementioned hostility to psychoanalytic interpretation). But myths are not thereby literary phenomena, any more than the Industrial Revolution is a literary phenomenon because it is the context of Dickens's novels. Myths have much more in common with dreams than with (nonmythic) literary works, as Freud asserted when he described myths as the "dreams of youthful humanity" (1908, 152). There are significant differences between myths and dreams, as we shall see, but far more important is their fundamental similarity in regard to both function and form (that is, the mechanisms that govern their formation and the structures in which they appear).

Before turning to the relationship between myths and dreams, however, we should stop for a moment to ask what general category we can put myth in, if it is not literature. The answer, I think, is obvious: myth is a religious phenomenon, and myth and ritual are the two primary components of Greek religion. This concept, most recently prominent in the work of Walter Burkert, is not entirely accurate if it implies the inseparability of myth and ritual; as Burkert acknowledges (1979, 56–58), myths may be unconnected with ritual and rituals unconnected with myth, and the verbal component of ritual may contain nonmythic elements. Nevertheless it is crucial to recognize that myth is an aspect of religion; like other religious entities it may take on a life of its own and be used for nonreligious purposes, but its essential function is to fulfill religious needs (that is, to explain the unknown and to respond to wishes and fears that cannot be dealt with satisfactorily by nonreligious means). This function of myth, like that of religion itself, is therefore both intellectual and emotional.

Myths, of course, have other functions in addition to the religious one. They entertain, they inform, they instruct, they justify, they remember, and so on. But two related functions seem to be operative in nearly all myths: the expression of unconscious fantasies and the satisfaction of curiosity. The first of these, almost predictable in a religious phenomenon, connects myth with the primary function of dreams, and the second connects it with childhood development and fantasy life.

It might be objected that the satisfaction of curiosity could hardly be a general motive of myth, since it is essential that myths be repeated over and over, whereas curiosity would presumably be exhausted after the first telling. To answer this objection, we need only recall the universal demand of small children that their favorite stories be told again and again, their insistence that they be repeated faithfully and accurately, and also the mixture of exasperation—and delight—with which they greet any deviation. It may be that a compulsion to repeat is present here; that is, the pleasure of curiosity's initial satisfaction is so great that the experience can be repeated many times. But it is probably better to assume that the satisfaction (and resatisfaction) of curiosity is combined with another function related to the child's emotional needs. In other words, there are two simultaneous satisfactions, one intellectual and the other emotional, that work together; the first achieves its purposes by answering questions, and the second succeeds in a number of ways—by mastering fear, resolving emotional ambivalence, providing identification with a relevant character, and so forth. When the evil stepmother disappears and the fairy godmother returns in the nick of time, the child learns two things: on an intellectual level, he learns how the story ends; on an emotional level, he realizes that the bad mother (who is in reality the punishing, disappointing, denying, or merely absent mother) is only temporary and that the real mother is the good mother who will surely return.

Myths also satisfy curiosity of many different kinds, although the underlying question is always, "What was it like in the past?" In the case of a theogony, the object of curiosity is how the world began, how things started, how the cosmos and its gods came to be the way it is believed they are. But this intellectual goal is inseparable from an emotional goal, just as the child's question, "Where do babies come from?" is really an expression of concern over the circumstances of his own conception, birth, and status.

Whatever other functions myth may perform, its most important and characteristic functions are psychological, and may be briefly stated:

1) Myths allow the expression of unconscious, usually repressed, ideas in a conventional and socially sanctioned form.
2) Myths use the emotional content attached to these ideas to energize other, nonemotional functions of myth.
3) Myths provide a societal response to psychological needs, whether universal or culture-specific.

Since these psychological functions seem to be present in all (or nearly all) myths, the relationship between psychological and nonpsychological functions is reciprocal: the former provide emotional energy for the latter, and the latter provide an opportunity for the emergence of the former. No matter what the nonpsychological functions of a given myth may be, the pervasive presence of psychological functioning has a determining effect on the form of myths, since nonpsychological concerns must be formulated in a structure that allows the expression of psychological needs. In the Greek theogonic myth, for example, cosmological and theological matters are presented and defined in terms of familial configurations, especially the relationships between father and son and between son and mother. The intellectual question, it seems, must be phrased in such a way as to allow the emotional question to be asked simultaneously.

It is certainly possible that a specific myth (or, more frequently, a part of a myth) may have a purpose or motive completely apart from emotional needs; some genealogical myths, for example, seem to have as their sole purpose an attempt to answer the question, "Why do these people with these names live in these places?" (but even this question may well have a psychological, as well as political, motive). Nevertheless, it seems that a model based on psychological or emotional function best explains myths in general, large and recurrent mythical patterns, and the majority of puzzling and anomalous details in individual myths.

It is not necessary to know all, or even most, of psychoanalytic theory in order to use the theory to interpret myth, since the aspects of psychoanalysis most relevant for this purpose are the fundamental discoveries of Freud's early career, especially those contained in *The Interpretation of Dreams* (1900), which revealed the workings of unconscious mental processes, and *Three Essays on the Theory of Sexuality* (1905), which studied the nature and influence of childhood psychosexual development.

As Freud and the other early analysts soon perceived, the study of dreams opened a window both on the meaning of myths and also on the ways in which we think unconsciously. In Freud's famous phrase, the interpretation of dreams is the "royal road to a knowledge of the unconscious" (1900, 608). Most importantly, since dreaming is something every person regularly does, what we can learn from dreams is applicable to a general psychology, not just to a psychology of neurotics or children or primitives.

Every dream exists, for the purposes of analysis, on two levels: its manifest content and its latent content. The manifest content is the dream as it is remembered, typically a brief visual narrative that may be quite sensible, or quite nonsensical, or anything in between. The latent content is the collection of ideas that are combined together and transformed into the manifest content. Freud calls the process of transformation from latent content to manifest content the "dreamwork," and it is perhaps helpful to compare this process to translation from one language to another (although this is not quite accurate, since the manifest content is often a severely compressed abridgement of the latent thoughts). The reason why any dream may be viewed as existing on two levels, as well as the necessity of transformation in the relationship between the two levels, is that a kind of "censorship" operates in dreams, a particular instance of the general function of repression in mental activity. Because of the special conditions of the state of sleep, especially its lack of motility—its requirement that all action take place in hallucination rather than in reality—dreams allow certain repressed ideas to enter consciousness momentarily. Nevertheless, repression is lifted only partway; because full expression of these unconscious ideas would threaten anxiety, a partial repression or censorship disguises them, a function facilitated by the modalities of unconscious thinking.

Just as myths may contain material of different kinds, serving a variety of purposes, dreams also incorporate elements from a variety of sources: people, objects, events, wishes, and fears, some from the recent past, some from the remote past, even some that occur during the actual time of the dream, some from preconscious memories, and some from unconscious fantasy.[2] A number of possible reasons explain why any one element may appear in a dream: it may be something the dreamer was thinking of during the waking time preceding sleep, it may be something from long ago that the dreamer wants (or doesn't want) to remember, it may be a chance stimulus like the unwanted ring of a telephone or alarm clock or a physical pressure like hunger or pain, it may be an object of curiosity or intellectual concern, or it may simply provide a connection between other elements in the dream. But for dreams in general, and for almost any individual dream, there are only two principal functions, both of them conducive to the health of the dreamer: to guard against the interruption of sleep, and to allow some kind of expression, usually disguised or distorted, for repressed ideas.

Research experiments in which people who are systematically prevented from dreaming (but not from sleeping) become very nervous and anxious and within a week or so acquire a kind of artifical psychosis (depression, hallucination, and so forth) would seem to indicate that an important function of dreams is the preservation of mental health through the allowable expression of repressed ideas. After a week or so, the nondreamers begin to display quasipsychotic behavior, symptoms that can be "cured" by allowing dreaming to resume. This phenomenon is not so surprising or anomalous as it may seem, but is merely the correlate on a "normal" level of the function of neurotic and psychotic symptoms on an "abnormal" level; symptoms, like dreams, are the disguised representation of psychic conflict and express a person's attempt to attain health and protect against a greater danger.[3]

This discovery has little practical value for therapy, since we all dream on a regular basis, but it has large and important implications for the study of the function of myth. If dreams are in fact of the same nature as myths, it would then follow that myths perform the same function for a society that dreams fulfill for the individual. And just as every individual must dream, every society must have its myths, whether religious, political, or cultural, to maintain its collective mental health.

The unconscious fantasies represented in myth are also found in dreams, but only a small percentage of dream fantasies appear in myth. There are several reasons for this disproportion, the most obvious and necessary being the requirement that the myth be communicable and that the wishes and fears embodied in it be shared by the majority of its audience. The latent content of the myth must be sufficiently general to elicit an emotional response from the group, not just from one or a few individuals, whereas a dream requires no psychic relevance beyond the individual dreamer. Another important difference between myths and dreams is that myths are typically set in a distant, or virtually timeless, past, while the context of dreams usually comes from the immediate past. This separation of myths from the recent past removes them at the same time from the experiences of present and recent members of the society who might challenge their credibility. A shared trust in the truth of myths would seem to be necessary for their full psychological effect to be realized. A dreamer also usually believes in the reality of his dream while dreaming, but there is no requirement, nor virtually any likelihood, that the dreamer when awake or any other person will believe that the events of the dream actually took place. Myths, however, require a waking consent to their reality, and so must be far enough removed from any past or current reality against which they could be tested and falsified.

Despite these differences, the primary function of myth is identical to that of dreams: the conscious representation of unconscious (that is, repressed) wishes and fears. The presence of this material, usually connected with childhood and sexuality, gives the dream its motive and energy, and the virtual necessity of this presence led Freud to regard the dream itself as the disguised fulfillment of an unconscious wish (1900, 160). Even anxiety-provoking dreams such as nightmares or punishment dreams, which seem far from expressing a wish, are only apparent exceptions; the wish would not be repressed were it not for a corresponding fear or opposing wish, and it is this conflict that is represented in such dreams (and in neurotic symptoms as well).[4]

The unconscious fantasies embodied in virtually all myths and dreams rarely achieve conscious representation without being subjected to at least an attenuated censorship; since repression cannot be entirely undone, unconscious ideas typically appear in a disguised or distorted form. The most common means by which these ideas are simultaneously expressed and concealed is displacement, the transfer of emotion or meaning from one idea to another. A good nonmythic example of how displacement operates is the case of phobias, excessive and inappropriate anxiety transferred from a repressed idea to a conscious idea. In myth displacement occurs most frequently in three mechanisms—symbolism, decomposition, and projection—that play a major role in transforming a simple unconscious fantasy embodying a repressed wish or fear into an enlarged and elaborated narrative.

Despite the existence of symbols that retain the same meaning across individual or even cultural barriers, Freud always insisted on the dangers of "automatic" interpretation and sought wherever possible an explanation of the symbol in the context of the dreamer's associations. These associations are lacking in the study of ancient myth, of course, although the very presence of a symbol in myth is usually sufficient warrant that the symbol has meaning, albeit unconscious, for the members of the society in which the myth occurs; a completely idiosyncratic symbol would probably not become, and certainly not remain, part of a myth. Nevertheless, even if we cannot produce associations to the elements in a myth, we can and should use as a substitute for these associations anything we can learn about the mythical, cultural, and historical context of any given mythic element. We should be especially careful to explain the reciprocity between the symbol and its immediate context in a specific myth; any symbol affects, and is affected by, the other elements of the myth.

An example of the need for contextual interpretation of a symbol appears in the Greek myth of Melampus, a mythical shaman or healer who is called on to cure the impotence of Iphiclus, prince of Phylace (Apollodorus 1.9.11–12).[5] Melampus learns that the ailment is related to a childhood incident in which Phylacus, Iphiclus's father, frightened the boy with a bloody knife (he had been gelding rams) and then stuck the knife in a tree. Since "knife" and "tree" appear in Freud's list of dream symbols (1916–17, 154, 156) as representing, respectively, the male and female sexual organs, one might assume that the episode represents a child's imaginary version of parental intercourse (a "primal scene" fantasy), that sexual intercourse was seen by the child as a bloody and violent act, and that impotence was the result of this traumatic sight. This interpretation is valid, but another interpretation is suggested by what happens to the knife after it is stuck in the tree; the tree's bark grows over the knife and conceals it, and Iphiclus cannot be cured until the knife is found and uncovered. A second interpretation would see the knife as representing not the phallus but the idea of castration at the hands of the powerful father, a fate transferred from the rams to the child. The insertion of the knife into the tree, which hides it, would represent the repression of this idea, which in turn will have to be brought back into the open if the patient is to be cured. This interpretation is reinforced by the fact that the tree is identified as a "sacred oak"; another sacred oak in Greek history and myth is the oak at the center of the oracle of Dodona, whose rustling leaves brought a message from Zeus. Mythical oracles regularly tell those who consult them of their unconscious wishes and fears (for example, the oracle that tells Oedipus that he will kill his father and marry his mother), and the oak of Phylace contains the hidden castration fear of Iphiclus. The two interpretations are not mutually exclusive but complementary, just as castration anxiety and a primal scene fantasy may be interrelated.

Another form of displacement that is very important in myth is decomposition or splitting, the representation of one idea in the latent content of myth, as in a dream, by several ideas in the manifest content. Since the manifest ideas typically represent partial aspects of the latent idea, decomposition is metonymic in the traditional sense of the term as representing a whole by one of its parts. Decomposition occurs frequently and familiarly in fairy tales, where it clearly serves the tales' function of helping children deal with the problems of growing up. One of the major problems of childhood is emotional ambivalence; children tend to oscillate between emotional extremes in regard to the significant persons in their lives, and a great maturational achievement is the ability to maintain a consistent affective stance in relationships. A three-year-old with his mother in a supermarket grows livid with rage when his mother refuses to buy him candy; if she relents, his anger immediately subsides, only to reappear when she refuses to buy him something else. In psychoanalytic terminology, the childhood problem is the instability of object relations; in the child's view, how can his mother, the most important person in his life, the one on whom he depends for love, security, and the gratification of his wishes, also be this hated woman who denies and frustrates him? The fairy tale helps resolve this conflict by attaching the good (loved) aspects of the mother to one imaginary figure and the bad (hated) aspects to another. The good mother often appears as a fairy godmother, the bad mother as a wicked witch or evil stepmother, and the final victory of the former over the latter allows the child to exorcise his feelings with the assurance that the good mother is the real mother.

The closest counterpart in Greek myth to the fairy tale plot is the story of Athamas and Nephele (Apollodorus 1.9.1): they had two children, Phrixus and Helle, and then Athamas married Ino and had two children by her; Nephele's children were hated by their stepmother Ino, who used a complicated scheme to compel Athamas to sacrifice Phrixus; at the last second Phrixus and Helle were snatched from the altar by Nephele, who gave them a flying ram with a golden fleece on which to escape. The fact that Nephele's name means "Cloud" perhaps explains her ability to disappear and appear at will throughout the myth. Her sudden arrival out of a clear sky to save her children, like the magical appearance of the fairy godmother at the last moment, answers every child's anxious question, "When will my mother return?"

Decomposition, like symbolization, occurs everywhere in myth, as a few examples typical of many myths will show. Future heroes frequently are separated from their parents at birth and raised by foster parents (usually, but not always, of low or even subhuman status), and upon attaining manhood set out to find their true parents.[6] Often it is the struggles of this search for identify and family which confer upon the searcher his heroic reputation (Theseus, for example). This mythical pattern of true and foster parents appears in the fantasies and play of children, who create imaginary parents of great wealth and kindness; someday, they fantasize, they will be discovered to be the long-lost children of Rockefellers or DuPonts.

This fantasy, which constitutes a virtual genre in Hellenistic, Roman, and Shakespearian comedies or the "foundling" novels of Fielding and Dickens, is not just another example of the child's ingratitude toward the parents who raised and love him, but instead results from the child's overvaluation of his parents. To the young child his parents are perfect and omnipotent (ask any four-year-old who the smartest man in the world is, or the most beautiful woman), but inevitably the child learns that his parents will not or cannot give him whatever he wants whenever he wants. Unwilling to relinquish his former belief, the child subverts a reality he does not want to face by inventing new parents who are simply a continuation of the old, idealized parents. Thus, if we compare reality to myth, the true parents of reality correspond to the foster parents of myth and the fantasized parents of reality correspond to the true parents of myth.

In the myth of Bellerophon (Apollodorus 2.3.1–2; see below), the hero, after denying any desire for the amorous Stheneboea, then kills the monster Chimaera and subsequently marries Stheneboea's sister. Both women represent the mother as object of desire, but in the case of Stheneboea desire is opposed by fear, both of the mother's sexual demands and of the father's vindictive anger. By overcoming representations of the feared father (Proetus, Iobates and his armies) and the feared aspect of the mother (Chimaera, the Amazons), Bellerophon is enabled to overcome fear, admit desire, and win the double of the woman he had earlier rejected.

A more complicated version of this pattern is found in the myth of Perseus (Apollodorus 2.4.1–4), who kills the female monster Medusa and then marries the Ethiopian princess Andromeda, whom he finds and rescues in exactly the same situation his mother Danae had been in at the beginning of the myth; each woman was loved by her paternal uncle and had been placed by her father in a situation inaccessible to all suitors. In addition to the decomposition of the mother into Danae, Medusa, and Andromeda, paternal figures appear in this myth as a triple repetition of twin brothers in exactly similar structures (Acrisius and Proetus, Polydectes and Dictys, Phineus and Cepheus).

The same decompositional motive occurs in the myth of Oedipus, who overcomes the female monster Sphinx by solving her riddle and then is rewarded by receiving his mother Jocasta as his wife. This episode contains many levels of meaning, but it is not difficult to see that one of them is the split identity of the Sphinx and Jocasta. Other confrontations between a hero and a monster usually end with the hero killing the monster, but in this anomalous story the Sphinx commits suicide by jumping from a mountain (a puzzling choice of self-destruction for a winged creature). Similarly, Jocasta commits suicide after Oedipus has solved another problem, the question of her (and his) identity.

Examples of mythical decomposition could be multiplied indefinitely, but we may conclude by noting that this mechanism, essentially the differential representation of the ambivalent relationship between child and parents, is one of the major structural principles in Greek myth and in all (but especially polytheistic) religious systems.

A third mode of displacement important in myth is projection, the attribution of unpleasant or dangerous internal motives and emotions to some external agency. Primitive societies in general tend to assign much of what we would regard as internal causality, whether psychological or physical, to some outside force—gods, demons, or enemies who cause illness, death, aberrational behavior, or bad fortune—and it might be objected that when Homer, for example, describes someone's irrational act as the result of a deity's physical intervention, it is because Homer, like primitive people, lacked the knowledge and language to identify internal causality and motivation. This may be true concerning disease and death, but it is certainly not true about mental functioning; Homer is no different from us in attributing unwelcome or unexpected behavioral phenomena to a foreign source.

Of the many forms of projection in myth, the most obvious is the function of oracles, which regularly tell men of their unconscious wishes and fears. The most common reason for consulting an oracle in myth is the failure of a man to engender a son, or the birth of a daughter instead of a son. In the first instance, the man is told of his "counter-oedipal" fear: if he has a son, that son will kill him. In the second instance, he is told of his possessive incestuous wish and also of this fear: he should not let his daughter be married, for if she marries he will be killed by his son-in-law or grandson. Therefore, mythical fathers of marriageable daughters typically place some insurmountable barrier between their daughters and any suitor. The ostensible reason for this is the oracle's warning, but the internal motive is the father's desire to keep the daughter to himself; sometimes this is explicitly stated, as in the myth of Oenomaus and Hippodamia (Apollodorus *Epitome* 2.4), and often it is implied in the fact that the impossible task facing the suitor is competing with the father in something the father does better than anyone else. For example, to win Iole Heracles must win an archery contest against her father Eurytus, his own archery teacher (Apollodorus 2.4.10, 2.6.1); to win the Golden Fleece and Medea, Jason must perform the labors of the fire-breathing bulls and the dragon's teeth, tasks which Medea's father Aeetes himself can accomplish in a single day (Apollodorus 1.9.23); to win Hippodamia, Pelops must win a chariot race against her father Oenomaus, whose magical horses were a gift from the god Ares (Apollodorus *Epitome* 2.5).

Projection takes many other forms in myth, as when someone does something because of "fate" or "destiny" or "the will of the gods" or even "by chance" or "unintentionally." The action taken for any of these reasons invariably turns out to be the object or result of predictable unconscious wishes or fears. Bellerophon kills his brother "accidentally" and Oedipus kills his father "unwittingly"; the stranger killed by chance or ignorance always turns out to be not a stranger but the object of childhood aggression.

Projection may take the form of a complete reversal of the situation: "it is not I who desire her, it is she who desires me"; "I don't hate him, he hates me." This disguised expression of one idea by its opposite is natural for unconscious thought, which is oblivious of the law of contraries (that a quality and its contrary cannot both be predicated of the same object at the same time).[7] Freud defines the dream mechanism of reversal as follows: "An element in the manifest dream which admits of an opposite may stand simply for itself, or for its opposite, or for both together; only the sense can decide which translation is to be chosen"

(1916–17, 178). Reversal occurs frequently in symptom formation, most obviously in overcompensation; the compulsive assertion of innocence derives from hidden guilt, the obsessional display of masculinity betrays a hidden anxiety. Although a symbolic mode that allows "black" to represent "white" and "up" to stand for "down" may seem strange and puzzling, it is in fact this strangeness that makes it so appropriate for unconscious thought, since opposites are at the same time farthest apart from one another and most closely related to one another. As simultaneous affirmation and denial, representation by opposition lends itself to condensation, particularly in the portrayal of opposed emotions. A mythological example is the punishment of being turned to stone which Medusa inflicts on those she catches looking at her. The monster herself, like so many female monsters in Greek myth, represents the forbidden aspect of maternal sexuality, the simultaneously feared and desired object of the child's curiosity (which is why the myth portrays the hideous Medusa as having been once the most beautiful of women). Just as a prohibition could not exist without the desire to do what is prohibited, the punishment imposed on those Medusa sees looking at her requires a prior desire to see what is forbidden. The combination of fear and desire, ugliness and beauty, repulsion and attraction, reappears in the punishment of being turned to stone: the victim is dead, immobilized, impotent, but at the same time he is fixed forever in the act of looking, frozen in fascination and fixation before a scene from which he literally can never turn away.

More important than such individual examples, however, is the function of reversal as a kind of ironic principle throughout myth. When Oedipus, according to Sophocles, vows to avenge the dead king Laius as if he were his own father, or when the Player Queen in *Hamlet* speaks of her love for her husband (to which the real queen replies, "the lady doth protest too much, methinks"), this is dramatic irony; the truth is the opposite of what a character says or does. Mythological reversal, however, tends to constitute irony as a pervasive presence rather than as an occasional occurrence, and thus accounts, at least in part, for the mysterious and uncanny mood of myth. As the myths of Bellerophon and Oedipus suggest, the stranger is really the closest relation, and the one who seems most innocent is in fact most guilty.

The ideas that are most subject to repression (and, therefore, the ideas that figure most importantly and frequently in the content of the unconscious and in the latent content of dreams and myths) are typically ideas from early childhood, and especially ideas connected with prohibited, dangerous, and anxiety-provoking thought and behavior of childhood. During childhood the individual learns what he can and cannot do, should and should not do, in order to take his place as an accepted member of the family and the larger society.

Ideas enter the unconscious through repression (or through association with already repressed material), and since repression is simply one of the conditions of growing up in a given family and a given culture, the unconscious ideas of adults are chiefly a remnant of this maturational process. Not every stimulus received by the mind leaves a memory; when memories do occur, some remain preconsciously, some are repressed, and many disappear forever. Memories subject to repression tend to be those concerned with sexuality, as the developing individual learns that the ideas connected with his strongest feelings and desires are also the ideas that attract the prohibitions and strictures of his society. This does not mean that children below the age of six think only or mostly of sexual matters or that these are the most important concerns of children; it means only that sexuality is the area of childhood experience that is most likely to be affected by repression. Clearly children do many things, want many things, and are curious about many things that have nothing to do with sexuality; but these are not usually the areas of experience where repression is likely to occur.

The concept of childhood sexuality, one of the best-known and most controversial doctrines of psychoanalysis, has acquired much wider acceptance now than when Freud first began to speak of it. While it includes the activities and pleasures oriented toward a genital function, sexuality also refers in psychoanalysis to all activities, wishes, and fantasies that aim at producing a specific organic pleasure and that cannot be adequately explained in terms of a basic physiological need such as breathing, hunger, or excretion. Thus sexuality originally appears in the early life of the individual when a pleasurable activity carried on in the service of a biological function first continues to be engaged in after the biological need has been satisfied and is no longer present; the most obvious example is the infant who sucks his thumb or some other object not because he is hungry but for the pleasure of sucking. Even in this earliest manifestation, important characteristics of infantile sexuality are already apparent: the child can take his own body (or a part of his body such as the thumb) as a sexual object, the pleasure can occur in a nongenital location (the mouth in this instance), and the "plasticity" of the sexual impulse is evident from the start. That is, the same pleasure can be achieved by sucking at the breast, the bottle, the pacifier, the blanket, or the thumb; furthermore, since the last four items in this series seem to be substitutes for the first, it would seem that already a rudimentary kind of fantasy or symbolic thinking is taking place.

All of childhood sexual fantasy, the primary matrix of dreams and myths, may be viewed as successive stages and variations of an answer to the great question of children—"Where do babies come from?" In the first instance this question asks about the child's own identity, and reaches back to the first experiences of individuation and, even further, to memory traces of symbiotic fusion and the anxiety of separation. Subsequently the question's emphasis shifts from how the baby becomes separate from the mother to how it got inside her in the first place, from the mechanics of birth to the complications of sexual activity, gender roles, and the child's own role and status in the oedipal triangle.

For the first six months or so after birth, the infant lacks a stable perception of himself as a separate being surrounded by other separate beings. The technical term for this situation before the discovery of the difference between self and other is *symbiosis,* a biological metaphor referring to the infant's attachment and dependence upon the mother and her complementary involvement with her child, and also to a state of undifferentiation and fusion in which the "I" is not yet distinguished from the "not-I." [8] For the symbiotic infant, the self is the whole world (admittedly a tiny world, especially during the first weeks when unde-veloped eyesight can barely see beyond the confines of the crib), and the whole world consists essentially of the illusory fusion of two separate individuals, the child and the mother.

The symbiotic state is followed by the state of *individuation,* or *sepa-ration-individuation:* these terms refer to an emerging awareness of self, or individual identity, as a result of differentiation between self and other, subject and object. The symbiotic state ends, as Lacan (1949) has said, when the infant is first able to look in a mirror and recognize him-self. In reality, however, the mirror in which the infant first sees himself is not an actual mirror but rather another human being, usually the mother, and it is a result of his perception that the mother is a separate being that the infant begins to think of himself as separate. The begin-ning of individuation is due to innate maturational processes and a suf-ficiently helpful environment, but the infant knows nothing of these causes. For the child individuation is the occasion for feelings of depen-dence, aloneness, and loss, as he realizes for the first time that the person on whom he depends for the satisfaction of his basic needs and wishes is not part of himself but is a separate person who may leave the room and never return.

It is because of individuation, not physical birth, that the infant first experiences separation anxiety (the newborn infant does not cry when left alone or even know that he is alone). One half of what had been the symbiotic unity now becomes known as a separate person; this perception, on which subsequent awareness of the self as separate is based, is precipitated by the intermittent loss or absence of the other person, and thus we might say that the subject comes into existence through perception of the other as lost object.

The symbiotic infant is conscious, but his consciousness is like that of a dream, from which he is awakened by individuation. As mental faculties are separated into conscious and unconscious systems at the time of, and as a result of, individuation, memory traces of the symbiotic state become the first contents of a "primal" unconscious and the state of individuation itself serves to repress these memories, to bar them from consciousness. Symbiotic memories persist in the unconscious, however, and the first unconscious desires, based on these memories, will aim at regaining the lost part of the once all-inclusive self. The images that signify this lost and desired state, memories of a lost world, will be the standard against which later pleasurable experiences will be measured.

Although the desire for symbiosis is desire for a state, not an object, it is important to recognize that this desire first appears already focused on a symbolic object, the mother, and that symbiotic memories and desires become attached to, and influence, later relationships throughout childhood and throughout life. Symbiotic desire may appear connected with desire for the mother as lost object during the second year of life, with desire for the parent as incestuous object during the years of the Oedipus complex, or with desire for the sexual object in adulthood. The unconscious memory of symbiosis persists as the prototype of total gratification, and the unconscious desire for symbiosis remains as the prototype of desire as impossible, unsatisfiable, and total.

The difficulties involved in the observation and analysis of early childhood are obviously great, but it is not difficult to see the role that this desire plays in certain cultural projections. The goal of much Eastern mystical religion, for example, is virtually identical to a recovery of the symbiotic state: the overcoming of individuality through merger or dissolution into a cosmic whole, the attainment of a state of zero desire and perfect equilibrium, the absolute loss of the self.

The best-known and most widespread cultural representation of the symbiotic state occurs in mythical and religious fantasies, found throughout the world, of an original paradise in which the first humans lived for a time before exile to a life of loss, desire, time, suffering, alienation, and death. The Garden of Eden in Genesis 1–3, for example, portrays the first humans as living in a timeless and effortless Nirvana in which nothing is desired because nothing is lacking. The emergence of desire is equivalent to the loss of this state, and this loss appears as a primal prohibition. The inevitable fact of individuation, like the angel with the fiery sword at the gates of Eden, prohibits return to paradise and condemns mankind to a life of separation and lack. A similar situation appears in the Near Eastern epic of Gilgamesh (Sandars 1960; Pritchard 1955, 72–99), as Enkidu, the "savage-man" (Pritchard 1955, 75), is seduced from his solipsistic wilderness by a harlot who leads him "like a mother" (ibid., 77) to culture, strife, and death, while Gilgamesh in his search for immortality travels through a great expanse of impenetrable darkness (like the "abyss" of Genesis or the *chaos* of Hesiod's *Theogony*) before reaching the magical garden of the gods and the woman who tells him of life's inevitable limitation.

Memories of a symbiotic paradise lost in the past underlie Hesiod's myth of a "golden race" (*Works and Days* 110–27), and the impossible wish to regain this paradise appears in afterlife myths of the "islands of the blessed" (*Works and Days* 170), the "Elysian field" (Homer, *Odyssey* 4.564), or, in a derivative form, the garden of the Hesperides, where "springs of ambrosia flow" (Euripides, *Hippolytus* 748). Most striking, however, is the diagrammatic account of the beginning of individuated existence in Hesiod's description of the origin of the world (*Theogony* 116–21):

> First of all Chaos came into being; but next wide-breasted Ge, the always safe foundation of all the immortals who possess the peaks of snowy Olympus, and dim Tartarus in a recess of the wide-pathed earth, and Eros, most beautiful among the immortal gods.

Here the symbiotic state appears not as a paradise of effortless and total gratification, but as Chaos, whose primary meaning in Greek is a vast expanse of undifferentiated opacity. This amorphous totality is brought to an end by perception of the mother as separate (the emergence of Ge), but the price of this recognition is loss of the symbiotic mother. Primal loss and eternal frustration are represented by Tartarus (see pp. 000–000 below), and it is on the basis of this deprivation that desire (Eros) first comes into being.

Once the problem of the baby's manner of birth is solved, the child's curiosity turns to the question of how the baby got inside the mother in the first place and consequently to the second great problem of infantile sexual curiosity, the difference between the sexes. The urgency of this question, the natural outgrowth of the child's preceding concerns, is intensified by the fact that it typically arises at the beginning of the phallic phase, the period during which the child's fantasies of obtaining pleasure are centered on genital stimulation. It is difficult to say (in fact impossible outside of individual examples) whether sexual curiosity promotes interest in the genitals or vice versa, but in any case the combination of the two leads the child into the fantasy world of the Oedipus complex.

Far more important than physiological matters, however, are the child's fantasies concerning parental sexuality, just as the child's fantasies about the wishes and behavior of the parents are more important than the actual wishes and behavior around which fantasies are constructed. Along with the new importance attached to the difference between the sexes (or more specifically to that which constitutes this difference, the phallus), the child begins to wonder about the sexual behavior of his parents, especially that secret activity, from which he is excluded, which produces both pleasure and babies. Several factors—the emergence of the genitals as leading erogenous zone, fantasies about the origin of babies, curiosity about parental sexual organs and behavior (a curiosity whose intensity is only slightly modified by variations in parental openness or reticence)—combine to produce in the child the Oedipus complex, the phase during which the child wants the exclusive attention and affection of the parent of the opposite sex and views the parent of the same sex as a rival or enemy to be replaced.

Since by the time of the Oedipus complex repression has come to play a major and appropriate role in the child's mental life, oedipal phenomena rarely appear undisguised in the conscious memories of postoedipal individuals, and parents or other observers usually notice nothing more than occasionally excessive jealousy or possessiveness. But the unconscious fantasies of the oedipal phase, appearing later in more or less disguised fashion in symptoms, dreams, character, and imaginative creations, are exceedingly complicated and significant—so important, in fact, that Freud (1958, 14) called the Oedipus complex the "nuclear complex of the neuroses" and thought that the key to mental health or mental illness lay largely in the successful or unsuccessful resolution of this complex (Freud 1924).

Although psychoanalytic theory has undergone a considerable shift of emphasis in the years since Freud, from the Oedipus complex to preoedipal developments, the general tendency has been not so much to devalue the Oedipus complex as to realize that earlier phenomena are also, and perhaps equally, important. For example, if we define the essential basis of the Oedipus complex as the expression of a wish for union with a parental object and the ultimate failure of this wish because of an overwhelming prohibition, it is clear that the same definition describes exactly the earlier wish to return to symbiotic union with the mother and the impossibility of fulfilling this wish because of individuation, a prohibition given personal form in the figure of the father or stranger who interrupts the dyadic relation between child and mother. In the symbiotic situation, things happen for the first time and patterns are established that may affect much of what happens later, including the Oedipus complex. In the oedipal situation, however, things happen for the last time: the emotional dialectic of childhood is crystalized in a form that will define the individual's desires henceforth during his passage from the closed world of the family into the society outside. Furthermore, the Oedipus complex, which introduces the individual into society, has as its societal correlate the universal incest taboo, the basis of primitive social organization. The principle of exchange, then, which every individual learns in bargaining for parental affection, appears first at the beginning of human society in the agreement of men to exchange daughters as wives, and subsequently in the resolution of the individual Oedipus complex; the child is forced to give up the object of his desire within the family in order to receive later a substitute object from outside the family.

Freud gave the name "Oedipus complex" to this combination of love for one parent and hate for the other because of its famous and relatively undisguised representation in the Greek myth of Oedipus, who killed his father Laius and married his mother Jocasta. Writing to his friend Fliess in 1897, Freud said, "The Greek myth siezes on a compulsion which everyone recognizes because he has felt traces of it in himself" (Freud 1954, 223). The depiction of oedipal themes, however, is not confined to the Oedipus myth as an isolated instance but is a general and important characteristic of all heroic myth. We meet an oedipal situation wherever we find a triangular relationship between a hero, the forbidden object of his desire, and a prohibiting figure who denies the hero access to his own possession. Usually these mythical figures are not literally son, mother, and father, as they are in the Oedipus myth, and even when they are, one aspect of the triangle is generally missing or altered—Uranus marries his mother Ge, but doesn't overthrow his father (he doesn't have one), and both Cronus and Zeus overcome their fathers but then marry their sisters, not their mothers—but this brings myths closer to, not further from, the Oedipus complex and real life. The real significance of the Oedipus complex lies not in the child's family, but in its effect on his life beyond the family, and the significant characters in the complex are not so much the real mother and father as the parents of fantasy and other figures who inherit the function of the fantasized parents. In myth and in life, what matters is not the specific identity of involved parties, but rather the persistence of a specific structure and functions.

Freud (1924) believed that the male Oedipus complex came to an end

because of the child's fear that persistence in his wishes would bring him
into direct conflict with his father. In this contest the child could only
lose and the price of defeat would be castration (a conclusion reached
by the child on the basis of the importance of the phallas in this sexual
conflict, especially in light of his discovery that not all people possess
this organ). The anxiety caused by the child's fantasies of paternal revenge, whether general or specific, is called *castration anxiety,* and it is
this anxiety that compels the child to give up his oedipal desires and to
make his peace with the father (by a process which substitutes identification for rivalry and leads to the origin of the superego, or conscience).

The overthrow of the primal father Uranus by his son Cronus at the
beginning of Greek mythology is accomplished by a real rather than
symbolic castration; while still within his mother Ge, Cronus castrates
Uranus during the act of parental intercourse. This myth represents the
fulfillment of an oedipal wish, particularly since Cronus is aided by his
mother, who gives him the sickle with which he accomplishes his victory. In real life, however, this wish is countered by the fear that sexual
conflict, with castration as its ultimate outcome, will result in the defeat
of the son by his much more powerful father, and it is this fear, Freud
believed, that causes the boy to renounce his oedipal desires.

Freud (1931) thought that progress through the Oedipus complex is
quite different for the girl, for two main reasons: castration cannot be a
threat to her as to the boy, and she must change her primary love object
from mother to father while the boy keeps always the same object, the
mother. In fact, Freud believed, castration (threatened) ends the male
Oedipus complex but castration (perceived) begins the female Oedipus
complex; the discovery that she and her mother are "castrated" leads
the girl to transfer her principal love to the father, and her concomitant
wish to have a penis is transformed into a wish to have a child by her
father. "Penis envy," a notorious term in contemporary psychoanalysis,
means nothing more or less than the observable fact that little girls in a
male-dominated culture may feel deprived of something that boys have.
What matters, of course, is the effect this childhood perception has on
later life, an effect that may be significant or negligible, depending on
societal circumstances. Like the color of one's skin, the shape of one's
genitals is a neutral biological fact that acquires meaning from society,
which prizes or devalues certain biological differences.

We would expect the incidence of penis envy to be high in a strongly
patriarchal culture like ancient Greece, but the overvaluation of male
activity and attributes in that society results in the virtual absence from
historical records of any direct information about the psychological behavior of women. If we turn to Greek myth, we find that two of the five

Olympian goddessess, Artemis and Athena, reject the sexual and maternal roles of women and tend to adopt the activities and attitudes of men. The only occasion on which this facade is penetrated is when Athena the warrior and Artemis the huntress put aside their weapons and clothing to bathe (Apollodorus 3.4.4, 3.6.7). Before seeing these two goddesses, or the related myth of the Amazons, as examples of a feminine wish to be a man, however, we must remember that these myths, like virtually all of Greek myth, are presumably male fantasies. It is much more likely that Athena's masculine behavior is related to her general helpfulness to mythical heros than that it reflects a woman's desire to escape from femininity.

The male castration complex, on the other hand, does seem to appear frequently in Greek myth. In addition to the earlier examples, we might note the presence of monsters who threaten some kind of real or figurative castration, like the Harpies, Gorgons, or Furies. Here, however, we are presented with an obvious problem: if castration anxiety, as usually described by psychoanalysis, concerns the son's fear of his hostile father, why are these castrating monsters usually female? And why, in the stories of Tiresias's punishment for oedipal offenses (see below), is blindness inflicted not by a god but by the goddesses Athena and Hera? Or, to put the question in another form, can the male child's oedipal anxieties and fears center as much or more around the figure of the mother as that of the father?

A possible answer to this question is suggested by the Argive myth of Bellerophon, grandson of the oedipal criminal Sisyphus (Apollodorus 2.3.1–2). Having accidentally killed his brother, Bellerophon was forced to find a foreign figure of authority who would purify him for this deed. Proetus, king of Tiryns, agreed to perform the purification, but while Bellerophon was staying with him, Proetus's wife Stheneboea fell in love with their guest. When Bellerophon rejected her advances, she went to her husband and falsely told him that Bellerophon had tried to seduce her. Proetus believed his wife and was obliged to punish Bellerophon, but because of the special relationship now existing between purifier and purified he had to find an indirect means of vengeance. He therefore sent Bellerophon to his father-in-law Iobates, king of Lycia, with a sealed letter requesting Iobates to kill the bearer of the message. Iobates commanded Bellerophon to fight the terrible Chimaera, a flying female monster who combined the forms of a lion, a serpent, and a goat and breathed fire on her enemies. At first helpless, Bellerophon was aided by Athena, who gave him a magic bridle with which he was able to tame and ride the winged horse Pegasus. In the midair conflict between Bellerophon and Chimaera, the hero was ultimately victorious (in one version, by putting a lump of lead on the end of his spear and poking it into Chimaera's fiery mouth, causing the monster to swallow the molten metal and die of lead poisoning). Iobates then sent Bellerophon on a number of missions that, he was sure, would cause his death; Bellerophon was forced to fight, with the help only of Pegasus, against the Amazons, the Lycian army, and the king's own bodyguard. When Bellerophon, like Samson, singlehandedly defeated this multitude of foes, Iobates realized the futility of his intention and made Bellerophon his successor by giving him a share of his kingdom and marriage with his daughter Philonoe.

This myth is only one of many examples in Greek and other myth of what is called the "Potiphar's Wife" motif, named for the Old Testament story of the slander by the Egyptian Potiphar's lecherous wife against the innocent Joseph (Yohannan 1968). Whether the story concerns a husband, wife, and unrelated third party (as in the myths of Bellerophon and Joseph) or a father, son, and stepmother (as in the well-known Greek myth of Theseus, Hippolytus, and Phaedra), the triangular relationship clearly represents the oedipal situation of father, mother, and son. But why then would the son, whose primary oedipal wish is presumably to have his mother to himself, reject the mother's offer to gratify this wish and, furthermore, deny the existence of the wish itself? The obvious (and psychoanalytically orthodox) answer would be that he fears being punished by his father, even if the father were merely to learn of the existence of the wish. In every case the father does attempt to punish the supposedly innocent son, and in most instances he is successful.

Without denying the plausibility of this explanation, however, we might entertain the possibility of a different motive for Bellerophon's behavior and a different answer to the question of why he denies his oedipal desire. At the time of his stay with Proetus and Stheneboea, Bellerophon is hardly as yet a hero, although his causing the death of a brother does hint at oedipal aspirations. It is only after he receives Pegasus and triumphs in the exploits on which he is sent by Iobates that he becomes a great hero and receives in marriage the sister of Stheneboea. Now it might be argued that this outcome supports the view that oedipal renunciation results from fear of the father; through becoming a hero and defeating Iobates' armies Bellerophon overcomes both his fear and his paternal enemies. At first so inadequate and powerless that he had to deny his wishes, he now is invincible and receives from the father himself the double of the woman he had earlier rejected. The secret of his success, the difference between Tiryns and Lycia, is Pegasus, a doubly determined symbol of phallic superiority. In this grandiose wish fulfillment, the weak and helpless child becomes sexually powerful, conquers the world, and replaces the father.

Still this argument leaves certain aspects of the myth unexplained, in particular the role of the woman who represents the mother. While her sexual advances might be explained as a projection of the child's wishes, why is it that in all versions of the Potiphar's Wife story it is the mother who is principally responsible for the punishment of the son? If the myth is about father-son enmity, why are Proetus and Iobates essentially instruments of Stheneboea's desire for revenge? Why is it that the enemies Bellerophon and Pegasus must initially face are female, Chimaera and the Amazons?

A different interpretation (and perhaps a more persuasive one, since it takes all elements into account) would begin from the fact that everything happens in this myth because of the hostility of a maternal figure whose sexual demands are unfulfilled. We should then ask what sort of fantasy on the part of the male child would produce such a situation. Both before and during the Oedipus complex, the child's primary desire is to please his mother, and in order to do this he must first learn what his mother wants him to do. The child's desire is always a function of his mother's desire, or, more specifically, of the child's fantasy of what his mother's desires are. During the Oedipus complex, when the child wants to replace the father as his mother's sexual companion, he creates on the basis of his knowledge of that relationship (the primal-scene fantasy) a fantasy of maternal sexual expectations: What will he have to do if he takes his father's place? What is the nature of his mother's relationship with his father, and what will she therefore expect of him? How will he satisfy her sexual wishes and demands?

It seems entirely likely that this fantasy generates anxiety and fear concerning the child's inability to satisfy the mother, particularly as a result of comparison between his own size and abilities and those of his mother and father. How will he possibly be able to do whatever it is that his father does, and how will he be able to gratify the *imagined* needs of his mother? Antecedent to fear of punishment (castration anxiety), then, may be prior fear of inadequacy and inferiority (a kind of "performance anxiety") that is of earlier and perhaps greater significance.

When mythical and legendary heroes must overcome a terrible male adversary to win a princess, the psychology of the confrontation concerns castration anxiety and the rivalry between son and father (or brother, who often represents the father). But when the obstacle to be overcome is female, whether a female monster, as so often in Greek myth, or the inaccessibility or power of the desired woman herself, as in the Arthurian legends, we are dealing with performance anxiety and the child's feelings of impotence, inadequacy, and limitation.

Stheneboea, the unsatisfied woman in the myth of Bellerophon, and other versions of Potiphar's Wife would then represent the unsatisfiable woman, the mother whose sexual needs and wishes, as imagined by the oedipal son, are so overwhelming and frightening that he must deny his own wishes and project them onto the mother: it is not *I* who want her, it is *she* who wants me. But the father always believes his wife's lying accusation, and the reason is that it is not in fact a lie. The son really does desire the mother (although he cannot admit it), he really is guilty, and so he must be punished. In instances where the punishment is successfully carried out, we would suppose that a prime determinant of the myth is castration anxiety and fear of the father. In cases where punishment fails, it would seem that performance anxiety is uppermost; this is especially evident in the myth of Bellerophon, who marries Iobates' other daughter and replaces the father after demonstrating his phallic heroism.

The model of an impossible love, of a desire that cannot be realized, is the sexual love of a son for his mother, and the Oedipus complex, which brings childhood psychosexual development to a close, is the final childhood adaptation to reality. During the first years of life the child was forced by the fact of individuation to repress fantasies of symbiotic union. Subsequently he learned to deal with the world of others, and lost his illusions of omnipotence in the necessity of having to give something in order to acquire something. And now he learns from the Oedipus complex that there are some things he cannot give, and consequently that there are some things he can never acquire.

PSYCHOANALYSIS AND STRUCTURALISM

In the current renewal of interest in the study and interpretation of Greek myth, the favored methodology seems to be the structuralist model first proposed by Claude Lévi-Strauss and subsequently adopted and revised by scholars such as J.-P. Vernant, Marcel Detienne, Walter Burkert, and Geoffrey Kirk. Here I will limit myself to a brief comparison of structuralist and psychoanalytic approaches to myth,[9] and I will conclude with four practical (and elementary) examples of how structuralist and psychoanalytic methods can be combined in the analysis of several familiar and related myths.

The basic principles of the psychoanalytic approach to myth are strikingly similar to those of a structuralist methodology, whether one regards myth as an aspect of religion, as sociohistorical data, or as a form of narrative. This similarity is especially clear if we use as a structuralist model Lévi-Strauss's exemplary discussion of the Oedipus myth (1963). For both methods the meaning of a myth is unconscious, or latent—that is, not apparent on the surface level of sequential narrative. The motive that generates the myth is to be found in its latent meaning and generally takes the form of an attempt to resolve or mediate a conflict of some sort. For both methods all elements of a myth, no matter how apparently unimportant they may seem, should be regarded as at least potentially significant, and therefore not only all details, but also all variants, should be included in the investigation. The latent meaning of a myth, as well as of its component elements, is best seen by analyzing the myth synchronically as well as diachronically; that is, by isolating patterns of similarity and repetition that cut across the temporal narrative sequence.

The methodological tactics of structuralism would not seem at all strange to a practicing psychoanalyst, since they are virtually identical to the therapeutic strategy of free association; from the welter of data (including silences and omissions) generated by a patient, the analyst attempts to uncover meaningful repetition and significant patterns. The major differences between psychoanalysis and structuralism are found not in practice but in the underlying theories, as a few examples will show. The location of meaning at an unconscious level means to the psychoanalyst that repressed ideas and fantasies are involved, but Lévi-Strauss and other structuralists tend to use the term "unconscious" in a sense closer to what psychoanalysis would call "preconscious" (as when a native speaker is necessarily "unconscious" of the rules and even the linguistic operations themselves which he employs in his use of language). The latent conflicts that both methods believe to be the source of myths also differ from one another in accordance with theoretical assumptions: the structuralist conflict is an *intellectual* or *logical* contradiction (for example, life/death, male/female) just as the underlying linguistic theory emphasizes binary opposition (as in the binary differentiation of phonemes), whereas for psychoanalysis it is an *emotional* conflict that is the source of anxiety, repression, unconscious fantasy, and thus of myth.

The inclusion of all variants and the assumption that any element is potentially significant are justified for the structuralist again by reference to language and to Saussure's dictum that all linguistic signs are arbitrary, endowed with meaning only by reference to a structure of other signs. A psychoanalyst, on the other hand, would refer to the theory of displacement and to the slippage, or facile transfer, of both affect and signification in unconscious thinking. In fact, as all analysts know from their practical experience, it is precisely when a patient describes a detail in a dream as "unimportant" that the analyst should suspect the presence of something significant.

Synchronic analysis is emphasized by both structuralists and psychoanalysts because of a shared belief that meaning emerges from the repetition of similarity and contrast. Structuralists may point to the existence of a synchronic or "paradigmatic" dimension within every diachronic or "syntagmatic" linguistic phenomenon, while psychoanalysts may refer to the dream mechanism called "secondary elaboration." Since in a myth, as in a dream, the function of chronological sequence is to provide coherence, often at the expense of altering causal relationships and distorting the underlying pattern, disclosure of this pattern involves undoing the distortion caused by diachronic sequence and isolating synchronic similarities and contrasts.

It should be evident, from even this cursory comparison of the two methodologies, that the real difference between them is the priority structuralism attaches to language and to linguistic theory, the premise that primary linguistic processes are the basis of a wide spectrum of human mental and behavioral activities ranging from the formation and meaning of myths and social institutions to the ways we eat and clothe ourselves. Yet it is certainly possible and arguable that language is not that basic source of all other structures, but should rather be included among them as derived from the ontogenetically prior mechanisms of unconscious "primary process" structures. Structuralists (for example, Lévi-Strauss 1966, 204–8; Jakobson 1956, 81; Lacan 1957, 64) have often noted the equivalence of the dream mechanism condensation and displacement to the fundamental linguistic operations of metaphoric selection and metonymic combination, but it is wrong to assume that language must precede unconscious thought or that language is required for meaning. It may be true that language is the means by which we try to name our wishes and fears, but it is also true that a large text can be conveyed by a single scent, or color, or tone. In the development of the human individual the emergence of rudimentary language seems to coincide with the appearance of rudimentary consciousness, but infants know the meaning of many things before they know the words that denote them. It is this primal ordering of sensory data, it might be argued, that first constitutes thought, an original structure on which language is imposed from the outside and to which language conforms. Or, as N. O. Brown once said, "Language is a functional superstructure on an erotic base."

Although the myth of Oedipus is an obviously appropriate source from which to take our first example of a combined structural-psycho-analytic approach, I will spare the reader another critique of Lévi-Strauss's much-criticized analysis of this myth (1963, 214–16). Unlike Lévi-Strauss, I regard the myth, for the purpose of my analysis, as consisting of the three Labdacid generations (Oedipus, his parents, and his children) and as representing the viewpoint of the male members of each generation. By identifying important elements or events in the life of Laius and corresponding factors in the lives of his son and grandsons, we can arrange the following summary of the myth in a structural diagram that indicates both synchronic and diachronic relationships.

Labdacus, father of Laius, died when Laius was one year old. Forced into exile before he could assume the kingship of Thebes, Laius stayed with Pelops but, after raping Pelops's illegitimate son Chrysippus, was cursed by Pelops to the effect that he would either die childless or be killed by his own son. Having returned to Thebes and married Jocasta, Laius learned of the curse from the Delphic oracle and resolved not to have a sexual relationship with his wife. One night, however, overcome by drunkenness, madness, or lust, he entered the bed of Jocasta and she conceived a son, Oedipus. The infant was mutilated and exposed by Laius, but rescued by a servant and raised in the home of Polybus, king of Corinth. As a young man Oedipus wondered if Polybus and Merope were his true parents and consulted Delphi, where he was told he was fated to kill his father and marry his mother. Still believing that Polybus was his father, he decided never to return to Corinth, but in his journey he met and killed Laius (without recognizing him) and arrived at Thebes. Having solved the riddle of the Sphinx and freed Thebes from the affliction this monster imposed, he received the throne and marriage with the widowed queen, his mother. Oedipus and Jocasta had two sons and two daughters, but, when a plague struck Thebes and Oedipus was told by the oracle to find the unpunished murderer of Laius, he discovered his true identity. Jocasta committed suicide and Oedipus blinded himself, then went into exile (according to Sophocles) or remained as a helpless prisoner in Thebes (according to Euripides). He cursed his sons because they did not aid him in exile (or mistreated him in Thebes), to the effect that they would kill one another in a conflict over their inheritance. After Oedipus died, his sons Polynices and Eteocles tried to avoid the fate predicted by their father's curse and agreed to alternate rule. While Eteocles was king, Polynices went in exile to Argos, where he married Argeia, daughter of the king Adrastus. As a wedding present Adrastus gave Polynices an army with which to return to Thebes, defeat his brother, and secure the kingship permanently, but in the ensuing battle the Argive army was defeated and Eteocles and Polynices killed one another.

	I	II	III	IV
Laius	Labdacus dies when Laius is one year old.		Laius rapes Chrysippus.	
		Laius refuses sexual rela- tions with Jocasta.		Laius is killed by Oedipus.
Oedipus:	Oedipus is exposed as infant, later kills Laius.	Oedipus flees from Cor- inth, and comes to Thebes.		
			Oedipus de- feats Sphinx, marries Jo- casta.	Oedipus learns iden- tity, blinds himself.
Polynices and Eteocles:	They abuse Oedipus and are cursed by him.	They agree to alternate rule.	Polynices marries Ar- geia and re- turns to Thebes; Eteocles re- gards women as enemies.	They kill one another.

The common factor in column I is the absence of the father from the life of his son or sons in all three generations, a situation that accurately reflects the virtually nonexistent relationship between father and son in historical Greece (Ehrenberg 1943, 147; Flacelière 1965, 55, 67, 71, 89; Lacey 1968, 168–69). Where interaction does occur, it is marked by mutual hostility: Oedipus curses his sons because they have ignored or abused him (or, in one striking variant, because he thinks they have tried to seduce his wife and thus duplicated his crime [scholia on *Iliad* 4.376 and on Euripides, *Phoenissae* 53]); Oedipus and Laius meet on only two occasions, first when father tries to kill son and second when son kills father; even the death of Labdacus, a seemingly innocent occurrence, is the ultimate cause of Laius' exile and the curse of Pelops, another hostile father.

The second column is concerned, on a literal level, with the attempts made by all three generations to avoid the fate predicted for them by either a curse or an oracle that reveals the curse. If, however, we examine these responses to a predicted future (which are also responses to a malevolent father)[10] in light of how each response affects the individual's relationship with Jocasta or her symbolic equivalent, a clear dichotomy emerges within the literal similarity. Knowledge of Pelops's curse leads Laius to avoid contact with Jocasta, whereas the same knowledge leads Oedipus directly to Thebes, to the deadly encounter with Laius, and to marriage with Jocasta. In the next generation, knowledge of Oedipus's curse leads his sons to their abortive agreement concerning the kingship and consequently, by different paths, to their fratricidal conflict. The difference between Polynices and Eteocles, which appears in the third column, precisely mirrors the difference between Oedipus and Laius: Eteocles, who shuns the company of women and rails against the women of Thebes in Aeschylus's *Seven against Thebes,* is the counterpart of Laius, who refuses the company of Jocasta: Polynices, who leaves Thebes and acquires new kin in a foreign land, then returns to fight with his brother over the kingship, is like Oedipus, who is sent away because of a father's curse, receives a new family, and then returns to fight with his father in a conflict that decides who will be king of Thebes and husband of Jocasta. These parallels are most striking in Euripides' version (*Phoenissae*), which tells how Jocasta was still alive when her sons died and committed suicide over their corpses, but the Sophoclean version, in which Jocasta dies while her sons are still children, can be similarly interpreted. The prize won by Oedipus over Laius at the triple crossroad is not merely right of way, but is also his father's possessions, the kingship, and Jocasta; similarly Polynices and Eteocles fight and die over their inheritance, their father's possessions, and the land itself of Thebes, actual mother of the first Thebans (the Spartoi) and symbolic representative of Jocasta. While Oedipus and Polynices respond to knowledge of the future by leaving home (or, in Oedipus's case, what he regards as home) and then returning to Thebes to fight with father or brother for supremacy (i.e., the paternal prerogative), Laius and Eteocles choose to stay in Thebes and to avoid the female enemy within the home.

The central issue running through the attempts of all four men to avoid their fates is their ambivalent feelings about women, and ultimately the conflict between fear and desire that characterizes the oedipal son's relationship with his mother. In the case of Laius the fearful side of ambivalence is dominant, but for Oedipus desire is uppermost; the oracle and curse take Laius away from Jocasta and bring Oedipus to her. The scenario is then repeated by Oedipus's sons: Eteocles' mis-

ogyny replicates Laius's avoidance of Jocasta, and Polynices traces the
steps of his father, until the two brothers meet in mortal combat, as did
Laius and Oedipus, over possession of the motherland.

The third column portrays alternate possibilities in the response of
men to the woman who is both desired and feared. The fear of Laius
and Eteocles leads them to avoidant responses, and in addition explains
the homosexual rape of Chrysippus by Laius. By disregarding the causal
relationships imposed by the diachronic sequence of the myth, we can
see that Laius's homosexual act is not the cause of his flight from Jocasta; on the contrary, homosexuality, like misogyny, is a predictable
result of fearful and conflicted feelings about women (and, in addition,
an institutionalized component of actual Greek society, just as misogyny
figures largely in Greek literature from Hesiod and Homer on). The response of Oedipus is a familiar one in myth, employing the dream mechanism of decomposition; by separating the ambivalently regarded female into two representatives, one desired and the other feared,
Oedipus is able to overcome his fear in one instance and achieve his
desire in another. The split-off representation of Jocasta's feared (i.e.,
maternal) aspect is the Sphinx, and by defeating her Oedipus immediately wins Jocasta. The identity of Jocasta and Sphinx is evident, especially when we consider the peculiar circumstances of the Sphinx's demise. As we have seen, this confrontation between a hero and a monster
is unique in that the monster commits suicide, and even the form of
suicide she chooses is quite strange, as though to draw attention to itself; the winged, part-bird Sphinx dies by leaping from a height. Thus
both the Sphinx and Jocasta commit suicide after a riddle, the question
of identity, has been solved.

The response of Polynices to the ambivalent female seems at first to
be "normal": he marries the nonmaternal, nonthreatening princess Argeia. But immediately (and as a direct result of his marriage, since an
army is a wedding present) he leaves Argos to return to Thebes for combat with his brother over the maternal objective symbolized by the land
of Thebes and the paternal inheritance. The virgin bride is not an object
of fear since she is not sexual (that is, maternal), but the gratification of
desire necessarily sexualizes her. Having transferred her by marriage
into the equivalent of the woman for whom she is a substitute, Polynices
now leaves her to seek the original object of desire.

The fourth column is straightforward; the attempts made by all four
men to solve the problem of ambivalence, and to escape their predicted
destinies, end in failure. Laius, Eteocles, and Polynices die at the hands
of their familial rivals, while Oedipus, the only one to realize his failure
without dying, imposes on himself the punishment of blinding. The

emotional ambivalence that characterizes the oedipal project, the conflict between desire and fear in a single psyche, is distributed by decomposition among the four male descendants of Labdacus, and through the failure of these four the impossibility of the project is confirmed.

The blindness of Oedipus, structurally parallel to the deaths of his father and sons, is also related to the blindness of the Theban prophet Tiresias, an important figure in the Oedipus myth. One aspect of the myth of Tiresias, the variant accounts of how he came to be blind, shows how structural-psychoanalytic analysis can be applied to different versions of the same mythic episode. Three different variants of the blinding of Tiresias are summarized by the mythographer Apollodorus (3.6.7):

> Various stories are told about the blindness and prophetic ability of Tiresias. Some say that he was blinded by the gods because he revealed to men the secrets of the gods, but Pherecydes says that he was blinded by Athena. For Chariclo [Tiresias's mother] was a friend of Athena; when he saw her entirely naked, the goddess covered his eyes with her hands and made him blind. Chariclo begged her to restore his sight, but she could not do this. By cleansing his ears, she made it possible for him to understand every sound of the birds. . . . But Hesiod says that he saw snakes copulating on Cyllene and, having wounded them, was changed from a man into a woman. When he again saw the same snakes copulating, he was changed back into a man. Therefore, when Hera and Zeus were arguing over whether men or women derived greater pleasure from acts of sex, they asked Tiresias. He said that if sexuality were figured on a scale of ten, men would enjoy one part and women would enjoy nine. Therefore Hera blinded him, but Zeus gave him the gift of prophesying.

A structural diagram might look like this:

	I	II	III
A.	Tiresias reveals gods' secrets.	Gods blind Tiresias.	
B.	Tiresias sees Athena naked.	Athena blinds Tiresias.	Chariclo intercedes; Athena makes Tiresias prophet.
C1.	Tiresias wounds copulating snakes.	Tiresias changes to woman.	
C2.	Tiresias sees snakes again.		Tiresias changes to man.
C3.	Tiresias answers sexual question.	Hera blinds Tiresias.	Zeus makes Tiresias prophet.

On a literal level the first column lists the offenses of Tiresias, the second contains his punishments, and the third the compensation he received. From a psychological viewpoint, the first column is a record of oedipal wishes and incestuous curiosity, the second is a series of symbolic representations of castration, and the third shows the acquisition of a special knowledge and status inaccessible to ordinary mortals.

I.A. If we had nothing more than this bare mention, we might still suppose that the "gods" are parental figures, and that their secrets are those sexual components of parental behavior that attract curiosity and create anxiety in the child. This supposition, however, can be corroborated in several ways, both internal and external. Internally, we have the four other items in column I, each of them a representation of the child's confrontation with parental sexuality. Externally (although these also could be situated within the structural analysis), elements from other myths, or from elsewhere in the Tiresias myth, provide substantiation. For example, Sisyphus also is punished for revealing the gods' secrets, and the specific secret he reveals is Zeus's affair with Aegina, daughter of Asopus (see below). The forbidden observation of divine sexual activity, especially when it involves the paternal Zeus, represents a "primal-scene" fantasy, the child's imaginary version of parental intercourse, and a primal-scene revelation by Tiresias, similar to the crime of Sisyphus, is mentioned by Apollodorus (2.4.8): Tiresias disclosed to Amphitryon the secret of his wife's sexual relationship with Zeus.

I.B. As in the first variant, the object of "accidental" curiosity is parental sexuality, but this time the father is eliminated and the primal scene consists only of the mother's sexuality revealed. It may seem strange that Athena, the most resolutely virginal and antimaternal of goddesses, would represent the mother, but this conforms with the common mythical situation (and possessive childhood fantasy) in which the mother of a divine or favored child is a virgin; the child's proprietary jealousy is duplicated in the exclusion of a father from the scene. Furthermore the equation of the goddess with the mother appears in the relationship between Athena and Chariclo, Tiresias's actual mother. The ambiguity in Apollodorus's phrase, "He saw her naked" (who is "her," Athena or Chariclo?) is psychologically appropriate, but has led all editors to change this text so that "her" refers unequivocally to Athena. But in Callimachus's version of the event (*Bath of Pallas* 75–82, which apparently uses Pherecydes, the same source Apollordorus cites), Tiresias sees *both* Athena and his mother Chariclo naked together in the spring of Hippocrene.

I.C1–2. In this third primal-scene episode, parental sexuality is portrayed as the copulating serpents, and Tiresias's attempt to interfere (he "wounds" them [Apollodorus] by striking them with his staff or by kicking them [Hyginus, *Fab.* 75]) recalls Freud's remark (1918) that a regular feature of these fantasies is the spectator's attempt to interrupt the observed action. The frequent association of snakes with the older generation in myth, as well as in Greek funerary and hero cult, is probably due to the facts that snakes inhabit holes in the ground, like the dead, and achieve a kind of immortality by sloughing their skin. In addition snakes are preeminently bisexual symbols (swallowing and enveloping as well as penetrating) and therefore particularly appropriate for a primal-scene fantasy. It may be because they are phallic that snakes can penetrate into women's "secrets," but it is because of their intermediary position on the boundaries between life and death, male and female, that snakes are so often associated with the acquisition of special or prophetic knowledge (Slater 1968, 97–100).

I.C3. The sexual question put to Tiresias by Zeus and Hera may seem at first to concern an evaluation of sexual capability of the adult male and adult female, since this is presumably the literal subject of their argument. Nevertheless the fact that the other versions of Tiresias's blinding occur in a context of chidllhood sexual curiosity and desire suggests that the same is true also of this version, and that Tiresias's answer is primarily a comparison between the adult female and male child. In describing the sexual possibilities (or better, impossibilities) inherent in the child's oedipal relationship with his mother, Tiresias is answering on the basis of what he saw rather than what he has been, his transsexual experience itself having been a direct result of repeated primal-scene fantasies. As in the first variant, illicit observation is represented metonymically by the knowledge it imparts—revealing a "secret" or answering a "question."

II. Tiresias's change into a woman is equivalent to castration, not only because of the structuraal parallel with three instances of blinding, the most frequent mythic symbol of the castration that punishes sexual offenses, but also because Greek myth is a product of a patriarchal society in which the loss of manhood is presumably a major concern. But, just as the change of sex may be equivalent to blinding/castration, so also the three instances of blinding are equivalent to becoming a woman.

III. Although column II seems to equate blinding and becoming a woman with punishment by castration, column III implies that these punishments are in fact the signs of a new status achieved by Tiresias as a result of the episodes in column I. On a literal level Tiresias receives the gift of prophecy as compensation for blindness, but on a psychological level Tiresias is a prophet, the possessor of arcane knowledge, not because he has been blinded but because he has witnessed a forbidden sight. The secret knowledge acquired by Tiresias in the successive primal-scene episodes is what makes him a prophet, and blindness, the sign of his status, is external proof that he has seen and knows what is prohibited to other mortals.

This interpretation allows us to understand the anomalous episodes concerning Tiresias's double change of sex, II.C1 and III.C2, as the key to the meaning of columns II and III. Tiresias's becoming a woman is not so much a subtraction from his previous state as an addition, an opportunity not merely to look at, but actually to be, a woman. While in the structural parallelism of the three versions the change into a woman appears as a punishment, its aftermath in the third version shows that it is also the occasion for appropriation of new knowledge, the experiential knowledge of female sexuality. Similarly, blinding is not merely a punishment; it is also, by virtue of its equivalence with the loss of manhood, associated with becoming a woman and learning the secrets of women. The internal vision that replaces the lost organs of external sight (as the internal female genitals replace the external male organ) is the primal-scene fantasy, the prototype of secret and forbidden knowledge. The reverse change in column III, then, does not simply restore Tiresias to his previous state: he is now again a man, but a man who has acquired knowledge unavailable to other men and sought out even by the gods, and it is this knowledge that makes him a prophet.

The nature of prophetic knowledge is further specified by the answer Tiresias gives to the sexual question of Zeus and Hera, an answer that defines the sexual disproportion between child and mother. Having viewed the primal scene, seen the maternal genitals, and lived as both male and female, Tiresias knows that the fulfillment of oedipal desire is impossible and that an inescapable limitation is imposed on the son's greatest wish. Furthermore this limitation is due not to the threatening and forbidding father, who is hardly present in any of the versions, but to the imagined needs and demands of the mother (as in the Bellerophon myth). It is the goddesses Hera and Athena who blind Tiresias, just as in the nursery rhyme it is the farmer's wife, not the farmer, who cuts off the tails of the three blind (and thus doubly castrated) mice. The child's awareness of inadequacy and limitation is due to his fantasized perception of what his mother, not his father, wants and expects.

Knowledge of oedipal limitation and impossibility is the paradigm of that forbidden knowledge for possession of which Tiresias, like other wise men and seers, is blinded. On an infantile level the knowledge of the prophet is that the child cannot give what the mother wants. On an adult level it is the message of all prophets in all cultures: the absolute fact of human limitation, the inescapable discrepancy that must always exist between our fundamental desires and our ability to fulfill them.

A related structural pattern of oedipal crime and punishment can be seen in the myths of famous criminals given specific punishments in Tartarus. The four earliest occupants of Tartarus (other than Hesiod's cosmogonic losers, the Titans and Typhoeus) are Tantalus, Sisyphus, Tityus (Homer, *Odyssey* 11.576–600), and Ixion (Pindar, *Pythian* 2.21–48), whose crimes and punishments are as follows:

	I	II
A. Tantalus	1. reveals gods' secrets. 2. serves Pelops to gods. 3. steals ambrosia.	A. is forever hungry and thirsty.
B. Sisyphus	sees Zeus rape Aegina.	B. rolls boulder endlessly.
C. Tityus	tries to rape Leto.	C. is immobilized; liver is eaten by vultures.
D. Ixion	tries to rape Hera.	D. is tied to a fiery wheel.

Columns I and II are series of variations on a single theme: the first contains different representations of oedipal transgression, and the second, the familiar punishments suffered by the four criminals, is a record of frustration and impossible striving. The common characteristic of the crimes of all four of the inhabitants of Tartarus is that they attempted to satisfy a sexual desire for one of Zeus's mates or enacted a symbolic equivalent of this desire. Tityus tried to rape Leto, the sixth of Zeus's seven wives and mother of Apollo and Artemis, but was shot by her children before he could succeed. Ixion attempted to rape Hera, Zeus's seventh and last wife, but was deceived by Zeus, who substituted a phantom Hera made of cloud for his wife. In the cases of Tantalus and Sisyphus, however, straightforward oedipal assault is replaced by an infantile metaphoric equivalent: Tantalus is punished for having revealed to men the "mysteries of the gods" (Apollodorus, *Epitome* 2.1), and Sisyphus is punished for having revealed the "secret" that Zeus had carried off Aegina (Apollodorus 1.9.3). As in the myth of Tiresias, the secrets of the gods are the secrets of parental sexuality, the object of the child's curiosity. This is explicit in the case of Sisyphus, who witnesses

Zeus's rape of Aegina, but we are not told the content of the "mysteries" revealed by Tantalus. Nevertheless it seems reasonable to suppose that they must be similar to those revealed by Sisyphus and Tiresias, and this assumption is supported by the nature of the other crimes he was charged with. Both Apollodorus (*Epitome* 2.1) and Pindar (*Olympian* 1.59–64) say he stole the ambrosia of the gods, and Pindar (in the same poem) also mentions, but says he does not believe, the common story that Tantalus was so obsessed with proving himself superior to the gods that he cut up his son Pelops and served him to the gods for dinner. If any of the gods ate a piece of Pelops, Tantalus thought, this would prove that Tantalus knew something they did not know. All the gods recognized Pelops on their plates and refused to eat, with the exception of Demeter. Distraught because her daughter Persephone had disappeared, she paid no attention to her food and inadvertently ate Pelops's shoulder. The other gods, horrified at what had happened, punished Tantalus and put Pelops back together; substituting an ivory shoulder for his missing part, they restored him to life. The oedipal nature of Tantalus's slaughter of his son is evident; the very act by which he tries to prove himself superior to Zeus (who, in addition to his symbolic role, is the real father of Tantalus) simultaneously eliminates the potential threat of his own son. The cannibalistic nature of his crime is reminiscent of Cronus, who castrated his father Uranus and then swallowed his children in an ultimately futile attempt to prevent his own overthrow.

Tantalus's other crime, the theft of ambrosia, aims at replacing the father by usurping a paternal prerogative. Ambrosia is the food of the gods, the source of their immortality (the literal meaning of the Greek word *ambrosia* is "immortality"). Ambrosia is the sign of the difference between gods and mortals; it is what gods have but men want. From a psychological perspective, the wish of men (that is, children) to win the prerogative of the gods (that is, parents) is an oedipal desire; the paternal possession that the son wants, but fears he will be punished for wanting, is the mother (or, to put the same wish in other terms, the sexual power and freedom of the father). The oedipal nature of the theft of ambrosia is confirmed in three ways: (1) as a result of his crime Tantalus is punished in Tartarus, where his fellow prisoners are oedipal criminals; (2) ambrosia is the Greek analogue of various divine substances in Indo-European myth (most obviously the cognate *amrta* and related *soma* in Hindu myth [O'Flaherty 1975, 15]) which symbolize semen and paternal sexuality; (3) the crime of Tantalus is similar to the crime of the culture-hero Prometheus, who stole fire (another divine prerogative) and gave it to men (Freud 1932).

The crimes of the inhabitants of Tartarus all represent oedipal striving, the epitome of impossible desire, and their punishments combine frustration of appetite or endeavor with enforced immobilization. But at the same time that these punishments represent the inevitable frustration of impossible desire, desire itself is portrayed as never annulled. The perpetual frustration of desire leads only to its perpetual reemergence; Tantalus forever hungers and thirsts, Sisyphus begins again to roll his stone uphill, Ixion spins on forever without destination, and Tityus's liver grows back each month. The desire that led to punishment is reflected in the various modes of punishment, as though the desire itself must be continuously and vainly reenacted.

Before leaving this structural analysis (based on a simple listing of crimes and punishments), we might pause to note that this way of looking at a set of mythic data exemplifies the structuralist principle that any given element acquires meaning through its inclusion in a certain structure. The relationship among the different crimes of Tantalus, for example, or the meaning of Sisyphus's punishment, are clarified by reference to other elements, both within and outside the finite structure. Yet it may be misleading to speak of elements "outside" the structure, since our diagram could be extended almost indefinitely through the field of Greek myth (cf. Lévi-Strauss 1963, 229). Tiresias, for example, could easily be included, since his crimes and punishments are clearly parallel to those of the criminals in Tartarus, and so could the Titans and Giants, Typhoeus, Orion, the Aloadae, Endymion, Salmoneus, Ceyx, Theseus and Peirithous, and many others. Perhaps the most interesting example is Prometheus, whose crime is like that of Tantalus, while his punishment resembles that of Tityus. Both Prometheus and Tityus are immobilized in chains while birds (Prometheus's eagle and Tityus's two vultures) consume their livers, which grow back periodically (daily for Prometheus, monthly for Tityus). If similarity in punishment denotes similarity in crime, Prometheus's theft of fire (like Tantalus' theft of ambrosia) is equivalent to Tityus' oedipal attack on Zeus's wife.

The sexual significance of fire, which Prometheus steals from Zeus, is widespread and well attested in myth and folklore; in Hindu myth ambrosia and fire are practically interchangeable as objects representing paternal sexuality and stolen from the gods for men, and in Greek myth one need only think of the incineration of Semele by Zeus's sexual lightning (Apollodorus 3.4.3). The fire stolen by Prometheus is essentially this lightning, the emblem of Zeus's paternal power and sexual authority, and like the ambrosia stolen by Tantalus it is a jealously guarded prerogative.

The similarities between Tantalus and Prometheus, which could also be easily arranged in a structural diagram, extend beyond the obvious connection between their thefts and corroborate their roles as oedipal usurpers. In Hesiod's account (*Theogony* 507–616), the quarrel between Zeus and Prometheus began at Mecone, where gods and men met to make a decision concerning the distribution of sacrifices. Prometheus cut up a sacrificed ox and placed before men the meat covered by the skin and stomach, while before Zeus he put the bones "covered by shining fat." Angered at being deceived, Zeus withheld from men the gift of fire, but Prometheus again deceived him by stealing fire and carrying it to men in a hollow reed. As a result Zeus punished mankind by the creation of Pandora, the first woman, and condemned Prometheus to be tortured by the eagle eternally.

If we compare the episode at Mecone to another of Tantalus's crimes, his attempt to deceive the gods with the sacrifice of Pelops, another set of similarities emerges alongside the parallel thefts. Both Prometheus and Tantalus choose a communal meal for their crimes, and both conceal something beneath the surface of the food in an ambiguously successful attempt to deceive the gods; Zeus may recognize Prometheus's trick but chooses the wrong portion anyway, and the gods recognize Tantalus's trick except for Demeter, who eats a shoulder of Pelops. Prometheus and Tantalus are virtual doubles; each is punished for having stolen the sexual possession of the gods and also for having attempted to deceive the gods by a meal with hidden contents. The difference between them lies in the permanent punishment of the mortal Tantalus and the eventual victory of the god Prometheus, a victory moreover that consists precisely in reminding Zeus that only by a limitation of his sexual activity (in fact, by giving up a desired female to another male) will he avoid being overthrown by an oedipal rival, the son destined to be greater than his father.

My final example of a psychoanalytic-structural approach to myth illustrates how a structural outline of a large myth cycle may supplement or corroborate an answer to a single question arising from one point in the cycle. The myth I propose to examine, the story of the descendants of Tantalus, is connected both genealogically and, in a broad sense, structurally to those we have already considered. Beginning with a transgenerational myth, the history of the Labdacids, we next took up a single aspect of the myth of Tiresias, an important figure in both the plot and the thematic concerns of the Labdacid myth. We then looked at the crimes and punishments of the inhabitants of Tartarus and found a pattern quite similar to the crimes and punishments of Tiresias, especially in the case of Tantalus, whose son Pelops played an important role in the beginning of the Labdacid myth. Continuing now with Tantalus and turning to another transgenerational myth, the story of the Tantalids, we seem to have come full circle; the cycle culminates with Orestes, who kills his mother in order to avenge his father, and this myth appears to be diametrically opposed to that of Oedipus, who kills his father and marries his mother. Orestes is then an "anti-Oedipus," and his myth may be viewed as upholding the oedipal taboos against parricide and incest. Orestes and Oedipus, the focal points of two great mythic cycles, seem then to be situated at opposite poles of the series of transformations of familial relationships that constitute the basic system of Greek myth.

The specific question we will look to for a structural answer is the motive of Orestes' matricide: from the viewpoint of the structure of the entire myth, why does Orestes kill his mother Clytemnestra? Although the question of Orestes' motivation is a complex matter, our concern here will be only with his motive as defined in the general structure of the myth.

The mythic background of Orestes' matricide is complicated, but its chief structural components can be seen in the following paraphrase of Apollodorus's account (*Epitome* 2.4–6.25):

Oenomaus, the father of Hippodamia, was in love with his daughter (or had received an oracular warning that he would be killed by whoever married her). He therefore proposed to her suitors a contest, with marriage to Hippodamia as the prize. The contest was a chariot race between Oenomaus and the suitor, and twelve suitors had already lost both the race and their heads, which Oenomaus nailed to his house. When Pelops came to court Hippodamia, she fell in love with him and secured the assistance of Myrtilus, the charioteer of Oenomaus, who, like father and suitors, was also in love with her. While preparing Oenomaus's chariot for the race with Pelops, Myrtilus deliberately failed to insert the pins in the wheel naves; when the chariot crashed during the race, Oenomaus was entangled in the reins and dragged to death. As he was dying, Oenomaus realized the truth and cursed Myrtilus, to the effect that he would be killed by Pelops. Myrtilus, Hippodamia, and Pelops escaped together, and while Pelops was temporarily absent, Myrtilus tried to rape Hippodamia. She informed Pelops of this and he threw Myrtilus into the sea (cursing the descendants of Pelops as he fell).

The sons of Pelops were Atreus and Thyestes. Atreus was married to Aerope, daughter of Catreus, but Aerope and Thyestes were in love with one another and conspired against Atreus. When a golden lamb appeared in the flocks of Atreus, he killed it and hid it away, but Aerope found it and secretly gave it to her lover Thyestes. In a subsequent contest between the two brothers over the kingship of Mycenae, Thyestes told the people that whoever had the golden lamb should be king.

Atreus agreed, thinking that the lamb was still in his possession, but Thyestes produced it and became king. With the help of Zeus, however, Atreus recovered the kingdom and banished Thyestes. Learning later of the adultery, he invited Thyestes to a supposed reconciliation supper; cutting up and boiling the sons of Thyestes, he served them to their father, who unwittingly ate his own children.

The sons of Atreus were Agamemnon, king of Mycenae, and Menelaus, king of Sparta. The two brothers married sisters; Agamemnon married Clytemnestra, and Menelaus married Helen. Paris came from Troy to be the guest of Menelaus, and on the tenth day of his stay Menelaus went to Crete for the burial of his maternal grandfather. While Menelaus was gone, Paris persuaded Helen to run off with him; the result, of course, was the Trojan War. At the end of the war Paris was killed by Philoctetes, and Helen was recovered by Menelaus and Agamemnon.

While Agamemnon was off at war, Clytemnestra and Aegisthus, the son of Thyestes, became lovers. They sent away Orestes, the son of Agamemnon and Clytemnestra, and killed Agamemnon himself upon his return from Troy. Some years later Orestes returned from exile and killed both Aegisthus and Clytemnestra.

The following outline of the myth, arranged on both diachronic and synchronic axes, is basically an enumeration of positive and negative relationships in the myth, listed chronologically in such a way that instances of repetition are in vertical columns.

I	IIa	IIb	IIc	III	IV
Oenomaus loves Hippodamia.	Myrtilus loves Hippodamia.	Pelops loves Hippodamia.	Hippodamia loves Pelops.	Myrtilus and Hippodamia kill Oenomaus (and not Myrtilus).	Pelops kills Myrtilus (cursed by Oenomaus).
Atreus marries Aerope.	Aerope and Thyestes love one another.			Aerope and Thyestes deceive Atreus.	Atreus wins kingdom, kills sons of Thyestes.
Menelaus marries Helen.	Helen and Paris love one another.			Helen and Paris deceive Menelaus.	Menelaus wins Helen; Philoctetes kills Paris.

Agamem-non marries Clytemnes-tra.	Aegisthus loves Cly-temnestra.		Clytemnes-tra loves Aegisthus (and not Orestes).	Aegisthus and Cly-temnestra kill Aga-memnon.	Orestes kills Aegis-thus (to avenge Agamem-non).
		Orestes kills Cly-temnestra.			

Reading the myth diachronically, it appears as four miniature oedipal dramas, in each of which the desired woman is won from her father or husband by a hero, who is then punished for his deed. Reading synchronically, the paternal figures are Oenomaus / Atreus / Menelaus / Agamemnon; the maternal figures are Hippodamia / Aerope / Helen / Clytemnestra; and the representations of the son are Myrtilus / Thyestes / Paris / Aegisthus. None of these "sons" is in fact the real son of his respective "father" and "mother," but the oedipal drama, in myth as in life, is essentially played out with substitutes for the original figures; as Jacques Derrida said, "It is obvious that, if by *mother* one understands *real mother*, the oedipus complex no longer has any meaning" (Macksey and Donato 1970, 194).

Remembering then that the terms mother, son, and father are a kind of shorthand, or code, representing the object of desire, the one who desires the object, and the rival who possesses the object, we may examine the pattern of synchronic relationships. The first column contains the relationships between father and mother, the second contains those between mother and son, the third is the successful conspiracy of mother and son against the father, the fourth is the punishment of the guilty son. The pattern is quite straightforward, with these two complications: the variations of punishment in column IV, and the doubling of the son figure, with resultant complexity of column II, in the first and fourth horizontal series. To understand column IV, we should recognize that in each of the four instances the son is indirectly punished. In the first and fourth series (which the structural outline reveals as clearly opposed to the second and third series), the father is dead but still an effective agent; Myrtilus is killed in accordance with the curse of Oenomaus, Aegisthus is killed in order to avenge the murder of Agamemnon. In the second and third series, the father, having been only betrayed, lives on to regain his lost possession, but the son nevertheless is punished indirectly; someone other than the father kills the son, or the father himself kills not the son but the son's children. To continue the clear parallelism of the first and fourth series, in each the son (Myrtilus, Aegisthus) who has killed the father (Oenomaus, Agamemnon) and thus replaced him is killed by a second or alternate son (Pelops, Orestes) who, by acting on behalf of the father and eliminating the pretender to the father's position, wins the father's position for himself. Myrtilus and Aegisthus, then, are scapegoats: having killed the father at the instigation of the mother, they turn out to have done this on behalf of Pelops and Orestes, who now can replace the father without the taint of parricide. It may seem strange to connect Orestes with parricide, but since parricide is simply the necessary antecedent to incest, the real question is whether an incestuous element can somehow be present in Orestes' case.

A solution is found in the complexity of column II. Myrtilus and Aegisthus love Hippodamia and Clytemnestra, just as Thyestes and Paris love Aerope and Helen. But at this point the situation is complicated in the first and fourth series by the appearance of Pelops and Orestes, the alternate sons, who will play exactly identical roles in column IV but precisely inverted roles in column II. Pelops desires and wins Hippodamia, but Orestes kills Clytemnestra (IIb), and the reason is immediately given in IIc: Hippodamia loves Pelops but not Myrtilus (whom she accuses), while Clytemnestra loves Aegisthus but not Orestes (whom she exiles). The oedipal desire of Pelops is fulfilled in the reciprocal love of Hippodamia, but that of Orestes is frustrated by Clytemnestra's choice of Aegisthus. Myrtilus, despite his intentions, simply did Pelops's work for him, but Aegisthus did Orestes' work too well: by not only killing the father but winning the mother as well, he has usurped the oedipal project of Orestes. For this he is killed, and for this yet another cause is added to the overdetermined motivation of matricide: Clytemnestra chose to bestow her favors on the false rather than on the true son.

The possibility that jealousy and frustrated incestuous wishes may be present in the matricidal act of Orestes, suggested here through structural duplication (Orestes = Pelops), can be argued for other reasons as well: (1) Henry Bunker (1944) has collected a variety of matricidal myths, from different cultures, in which incestuous overtones are clearly apparent; (2) Philip Slater (1968, 187) has proposed that matricide is the product of ambivalence in a mother-son relationship so intense as to require an extreme solution; (3) if over compensation reveals an urge that is the opposite of the apparent emotion, the matricidal act may be seen as a compulsive denial of, or defense against, incestuous desire; (4) by the same principle, a defense against parricidal impulses or against guilt for such impulses in the past may be seen in Orestes' resolve to avenge his father (Freud 1910b; Abraham 1922); (5) like the seemingly

irrelevant details in a dream, apparently insignificant details in the retelling of a myth may sometimes hint at its repressed meaning. Parricide
is the last thing we would expect Orestes to be charged with, and yet in
one account of his trial he is charged not with the murder of Clytemnestra, as in Aeschylus's *Eumenides,* but with the killing of the father of
Erigone (the daughter of Aegisthus and Clytemnestra), whom he then
married (Apollodorus, *Epitome* 6.25, 28). A psychoanalytic interpretation would see in this account the thinly veiled presence of parricide
(displaced from the first husband of Clytemnestra to the second) and
incest (displaced from Clytemnestra to her daughter). Other examples
of the "return of the repressed" through displacement occur in several
variants of this myth: in one Pelops, not Myrtilus, is named as the slayer
of Oenomaus; in another Agamemnon has by Cassandra a son named
Pelops; in a third Agamemnon is said to have married Clytemnestra
only after killing her infant son and her first husband, who is named
Tantalus.

One way to summarize what the psychoanalytic and structuralist
methods of myth interpretation have in common is to regard both as
based on a *principle of redundancy.* For the psychoanalyst this means
that complex mythic structures will be generated by a kind of repetition
compulsion (as found clinically in children's play or in dreams during
traumatic neurosis). We should also note that the "overdetermination"
of an element in a myth or dream or symptom is virtually equivalent to
the technical notion of "redundancy" in information theory (Wilden
1972, 5, 35). For the structuralist, redundancy is implied in the emphasis on synchrony and in the location of meaning only in the relationship
between repeated and opposed events (or functions), never in the isolated event. This emphasis on the priority of structural relationships, on
the relation between relationships, is analogous to Freud's insistence
that the "meaning" of a dream element is not to be found in a "dream-
book," or one-to-one code, but rather must be sought as a function of
the complex of relationships in which the element occurs. As Freud says
of dream symbols, "as with Chinese script, the correct interpretation
can only be arrived at on each occasion from the context" (1900, 353).
And yet far more radical than this contextualism is a footnote in *The
Interpretation of Dreams* (1900, 506–7) that prophetically aligns
Freud's theory with structuralism by arguing that the "code" is to be
found not in symbols but in processes, not in the "dream-thoughts" but
in the "dream-work":

> I used at one time to find it extraordinarily difficult to accustom readers
> to the distinction between the manifest content of dreams and the latent

dream-thoughts. . . . But now that analysts at least have become reconciled to replacing the manifest dream by the meaning revealed by its interpretation, many of them have become guilty of falling into another confusion which they cling to with equal obstinacy. They seek to find the essence of dreams in their latent content and in so doing they overlook the distinction between the latent dream-thoughts and the dream-work. At bottom, dreams are nothing other than a particular *form* of thinking, made possible by the conditions of the state of sleep. It is the *dream-work* which creates that form, and it alone is the essence of dreaming—the explanation of its peculiar nature.

NOTES

a. Edmunds 1985.
b. Roazen 1971, 231, with reference 261.
c. For a concise statement of the problems, see Dundes 1984, 244–45.
d. On Campbell, see Segal 1984.
e. Edmunds 1988.
f. Lévi-Strauss 1958/1963; 1973/1976; 1985/1988.

1. Much of this essay is adapted from previously published work (Caldwell 1973, 1974, 1976a, 1976b, 1981, 1988). The chief reason why it is a demonstration rather than a review article is that, other than the works of Freud and his early circle and Philip Slater's brilliant *Glory of Hera* (1968), there is no book I could recommend wholeheartedly to someone wishing to learn about the psychoanalytic approach to Greek myth. None of Freud's books deal primarily with this subject, of course, although his collected works contain more than 750 references to classical subjects. Nevertheless, psychoanalytic interpretation should not be attempted (or criticized) without a thorough grounding in Freud's basic writings, especially those up to and including *Beyond the Pleasure Principle* (1920).

The most valuable and accessible works on this subject by Freud's early associates are Abraham (1955), Jones (1951), and Rank (1914). Rank's most important works (1919, 1926) have never been translated into English.

Slater's book has been unfairly criticized, on small methodological points, by classicists who have in general failed to recognize that what most offends them is in fact a theoretical, not a methodological, error: Slater's tendency to regard as pathological what are probably normal developmental factors. Despite this mistaken nomenclature, which has little effect on Slater's arguments and insights, his book remains the most important contribution to the subject since Freud.

I have omitted Jung and Jungian studies from consideration for the simple reason that Jungian psychology is not psychoanalysis. This is not to say that there are not individual points of interest, especially in Jung's earlier writings. Even these tend to be lost, however, in a mystical and mystifying theory, the necessary result of Jung's denial of the two fundamental psychoanalytic concepts, childhood psychosexual development and repression (which he replaces with his notorious "archetypes" and "collective unconscious").

More than seventy-five years ago, Freud (1958, 13) expressed the wish that "our studies on the content of the neuroses might be destined to solve the riddle of the formation of myths." If that wish is now any closer to being fulfilled, it is largely owing to the work of specialists in other fields (for example, the anthropologists Géza Róheim and George Devereux and the sociologist Slater). Classicists working on myth have for the most part ignored psychoanalysis or condemned it; Geoffrey Kirk's statement (1974, 75) that "[Freud's concept of the] 'Oedipus complex' has not, in the end, won many converts, and its interest from the point of view of specifically Greek myths is surprisingly slight" probably reflects the view of most classicists who have bothered to think about the subject.

2. "Preconscious" ideas are those capable of being brought to consciousness, while "unconscious" ideas are those barred from consciousness by the force of repression.

3. Although it has been showed that changes in chemical metabolism accompany dream deprivation, one should not assume, as does Kirk (1970, 272), that chemical and psychological processes are mutually exclusive.

4. The controversial notion that virtually all dreams have a sexual content has received an unexpected confirmation from empirical research on the physiology of dreaming, which has shown that dream states (REM) are regularly accompanied, in both sexes, by some degree of physically evident sexual arousal (Fisher, Gross, and Zuch, 1965).

5. Whenever possible I cite myths by their occurrence in the *Library* of Apollodorus. Section, paragraph, and line numbers follow the Loeb edition and translation of Frazer (1921).

6. Standard references on this subject are Rank (1914) and Freud (1919).

7. Tolerance of contradiction and opposition in unconscious thought has an analogy in the presence in some languages and scripts, especially ancient ones, of words and signs that can express either of two opposites. Citing examples in Old Egyptian (*Ken* is either "strong" or "weak") and Latin (*sacer* is either "sacred" or "accursed," *altus* is either "high" or "deep"), Freud (1910a) described reversal as an "archaic" characteristic of the dreamwork, one of several similarities between unconscious thinking and primitive forms of expression and writing.

8. Standard references are Mahler (1968) and Mahler, Pine, and Bergman (1975).

9. Psychoanalytic and structuralist methods are combined in an acute study of Greek tragedy by Segal (1978).

10. Both Laius and Oedipus consult an oracle, but the oracle merely transmits the curse of Pelops, a curse that is directed at Laius but affects Laius and Oedipus equally.

WORKS CITED

Abraham, Karl. 1922. "The Rescue and Murder of the Father in Neurotic Fantasy-Formations." *International Journal of Psycho-Analysis* 3: 467–74.

———. 1955. "Dreams and Myths: A study in folk-psychology." In *Clinical Papers and Essays on Psycho-Analysis*. London.

Bunker, Henry. 1944. "Mother-Murder in Myth and Legend." *Psychoanalytic Quarterly* 13: 198–207.

Burkert, Walter. 1979. *Structure and History in Greek Mythology and Ritual.* Berkeley-Los Angeles.

Caldwell, Richard. 1973. "The Misogyny of Eteocles." *Arethusa* 6: 197–231.

————. 1974. "The Blindness of Oedipus." *International Review of Psycho-Analysis* 1: 207–18.

————. 1976a. "Primal Identity." *International Review of Psycho-Analysis* 3. 417–34.

————. 1976b. "Psychoanalysis, Structuralism, and Greek Mythology." In H. Garvin, ed. *Phenomenology, Structuralism, Semiology*, 209–30. Cranbury, NJ.

————. 1981. "Psychocosmogony: The representation of symbiosis and separation-individuation in archaic Greek myth." In W. Muensterberger and L. Boyer, eds. *The Psychoanalytic Study of Society*. Vol. 9, 93–103. New York.

————. 1988. *The Origin of the Gods: A Psychoanalytic Study of Greek Theogonic Myth*. New York.

Dundes, Alan ed. 1984. *Sacred Narrative: Readings in the Theory of Myth*. Berkeley-Los Angeles.

Edmunds, Lowell. 1985. "Freud and the Father: Oedipus Complex and Oedipus Myth." *Psychoanalysis and Contemporary Thought* 8: 87–103.

————. 1988. "La sphinx Thébain et Pauk Tyaing, l'Oedipe Birman." In Claude Calame ed., *Métamorphoses du mythe en Grèce ancienne*, 213–27. Geneva.

Ehrenberg, Victor. 1943. *The People of Aristophanes*. Oxford.

Fisher, C., J. Gross, and J. Zuch. 1965. "Cycle of penile erection synchronous with dreaming (REM) sleep." *Archives of General Psychiatry* 12: 29–45.

Flacelière, Robert. 1965. *Daily Life in Greece at the Time of Pericles*. London.

Frazer, James, tr. 1921. *Apollodorus: The Library*. 2 vols. Cambridge.

Freud, Sigmund. 1953–74. *The Standard Edition of the Complete Psychological Works of Sigmund Freud*. Tr. and ed. James Strachey et al. 24 vols. London. The following works of Freud are cited by initial date of publication and volume number in the *Standard Edition*.

1900. *The Interpretation of Dreams*. Vols. 4–5.

1905. *Three Essays on the Theory of Sexuality*. Vol. 7.

1908. "Creative Writers and Day-Dreaming." Vol. 9, 141–53.

1910a. "The Antithetical Meaning of Primal Words." Vol. 11, 153–61.

1910b. "A Special Type of Choice of Object Made by Men." Vol. 11, 163–75.

1916–17. *Introductory Lectures on Psycho-Analysis*. Vols. 15–16.

1918. *From the History of an Infantile Neurosis*. Vol. 17, 1–122.

1919. "Preface to Reik's 'Ritual: psychoanalytic studies'." Vol. 17, 257–63.

1920. *Beyond the Pleasure Principle*. Vol. 18, 1–64.

1924. "The Dissolution of the Oedipus Complex." Vol. 19, 171–79.

1931. "Female Sexuality." Vol. 21, 221–43.

1932. "The Acquisition and Control of Fire." Vol. 22, 183–93.

————. *The Origins of Psycho-Analysis: Letters to Wilhelm Fliess, drafts and notes: 1887–1902*. Tr. E. Mosbacher and J. Strachey. New York.

————. 1958. "Letter to D. E. Oppenheim." In S. Freud and Oppenheim, eds. *Dreams in Folk-Lore*. New York.

Jakobson, Roman. 1956. "Two Fundamentals of Language and Two Types of Aphasia." In R. Jakobson and M. Halle, *The Fundamentals of Language*. The Hague.

Jones, Ernest. 1951. *Essays in Applied Psycho-Analysis*, Vol. 2: *Essays in Folklore, anthropology and Religion*. London.

Kirk, Geoffrey. 1970. *Myth: Its Meaning and Functions in Ancient and Other Cultures*. Berkeley.

———. 1974. *The Nature of Greek Myths*. Harmondsworth, UK.

Lacan, Jacques. 1949. "Le stade du miroir comme formateur de la fonction du Je." *Revue Française de Psychanalyse* 13: 449–55.

———. 1957. "L' instance de la lettre dans l' inconscient." *La Psychanalyse* 3: 47–81.

Lacey, William. 1968. *The Family in Classical Greece*. London.

Lévi-Strauss, Claude. 1958. *Anthropologie structurale*. Paris. Tr. 1963 by Claire Jacobson and Brook G. Schoepf. *Structural Anthropology*. New York.

———. 1973. *Anthropologie Structurale deux*. Paris. Tr. 1976 by Monique Layton, *Structural Anthropology*, vol. 2. Chicago.

———. 1985. *La potière jalouse*. Paris. Tr. 1988 by Bénédicte Chorier, *The Jealous Potter*. Chicago.

———. 1966. *The Savage Mind*. Chicago.

Macksey, Richard, and Eugenio Donato. 1970. *The Languages of Criticism and the Sciences of Man*. Baltimore.

Mahler, Margaret. 1968. *On Human Symbiosis and the Vicissitudes of Individuation*. New York.

———. F. Pine, and A. Bergman. 1975. *The Psychological Birth of the Human Infant*. New York.

O'Flaherty, Wendy. 1975. *Hindu Myths*. Baltimore.

Pritchard, James, ed. 1955. *Ancient Near Eastern Texts Relating to the Old Testament*, 2nd ed. Princeton, NJ.

Rank, Otto. 1914. *The Myth of the Birth of the Hero*. New York.

———. 1919. *Psychoanalytische Beiträge zur Mythenforschung.*. Leipzig.

———. 1926. *Das Inzest-Motiv in Dichtung und Sage*, 2nd ed. Leipzig.

Roazen, Paul. 1971. *Freud and His Followers*. New York.

Sandars, N., tr. 1960. *The Epic of Gilgamesh*. Harmondsworth, UK.

Segal, Charles. 1978. "Pentheus on the Couch and on the Grid: Psychological and Structuralist Readings of Greek Tragedy." *CW* 72: 129–48.

Segal, Robert A. 1984. "Joseph Campbell's Theory of Myth." In Dundes 1984: 256–69.

Slater, Philip. 1968. *The Glory of Hera: Greek Mythology and the Greek Family*. Boston.

Wilden, Anthony. 1972. *System and Structure*. London.

Yohannan, John. 1968. *Joseph and Potiphar's Wife in World Literature*. New York.

The references above are only those works mentioned in the essay and notes. For bibliographic studies see the following:

Arthur, Marylin. 1977. "Classics and Psychoanalysis." *CJ* 73: 56–68.

Caldwell, Richard. 1974. "Selected Bibliography on Psychoanalysis and Classical Studies." *Arethusa* 7: 115–34.

Glenn, Justin. 1972. "Psychoanalytic Writings on Greek and Latin Authors, 1911–1960." *CW* 66: 129–45.

———. 1976. "Psychoanalytic Writings on Classical Mythology and Religion, 1909–1960." *CW* 70: 225–47.

PART FOUR

GREEK MYTHOLOGY AND GREEK VASE PAINTING

8

ICONOGRAPHY

The main sources for the study of Greek mythology have been literary: first, the great works, epic, lyric, and tragic, of Greek literature; second, the mythographical tradition;[a] third, comparative evidence of various sorts, again textual—in short, the kinds of evidence that have been used and cited in the essays in this collection. Another rich source, still largely untapped, is Greek vase painting. It has been estimated that Greek painted vases and fragments number eighty thousand,[b] of which a large percentage have mythological scenes.[c] Although scholars of Greek vase painting never overlooked this subject matter, their agenda, until recently, did not include its interpretation or study from a strictly mythological standpoint. To take one example of the state of affairs, an authoritative handbook, R. M. Cook's *Greek Painted Pottery*, mentions mythology only in passing, and, in a forty-two-page chapter entitled, "The History of the Study of Greek Vase-Painting," not once.[d] The student of the subject was dedicated to classification—of shapes, style, painters, and workshops—and to dating and periodization. The study of iconography was at the service of these projects. The first departures from this historical-esthetic scholarship were in the direction of the potters and their patrons, the uses of the vases, and the vase trade as an element of economic history. Those scholars, a distinct minority, who addressed themselves to the mythological subject matter of Greek vase painting, typically understood it as illustration of the verbal myths.

For various reasons, new approaches are now in operation. First, the preliminary work of classification is, at least for the purposes of interpretation, sufficiently complete. Second, access to the major publication projects is more efficient.[e] Third, developments in perception theory,[f] semiotics,[g] and art history have affected the way scholars see Greek vase painting. Perhaps the most important principle emerging from these new approaches is that iconography should be understood not primarily with reference to attested or inferred verbal narratives but as an autonomous, self-sufficient form of mythology in itself, with its own kinds of signification, based in its own traditions. Likewise the interpretation of scenes of everyday life assumes that the primary relation is not between the vase painting and reality but between the vase painting and comparable imagery on other vases.[h] This principle entails new methodologies that can verbalize a nonverbal mythology in such a way as to bring it into the same discussion with analyses based on evidence from the other sources mentioned above.

The methodology proposed by Christiane Sourvinou-Inwood in the following chapter and in other publications in fact insists upon the separation of iconographic analysis from what she calls semantic analysis. The semantic field of an image is the set of meaning it expresses and invokes, and these can, in some cases, be established on the basis of textual evidence. As for iconography, Sourvinou-Inwood's approach is in fundamental respects Derridean.[i] She stresses the unfixed, differential character of the image, its polysemy, and the importance of the "trace" of images that might have been used but were not. The goal of this methodology is to establish not the vase painter's intentions but the process of signification. In explicit concern with methodology, Sourvinou-Inwood's closest scholarly kin are French and Swiss, though some British and American scholars have ventured into interpretation of vase paintings.[j]

Sourvinou-Inwood here focuses on a small group of fifth century Athenian vases showing Theseus, sword in hand, pursuing a woman. Although Theseus, as the Athenian national hero, is exceptionally well known in all the stages of his life, from both literature and art, the episode in question is rather obscure, and it is for this reason that interpretation of the vases has been so contradictory. Survinou-Inwood is able to identify the woman as Medea. The pursuit is hostile. Theseus is driving his murderous stepmother out of Athens. She would go east, and her son Medos would give his name to the Medes, the later enemies of Greece. In the semantic context, the scene expressed Athenian pride in the victories at Marathon, Thermopylae, and Salamis. This, however, is only part of the elaborate signification of which, as Sourvinou-Inwood shows, the vase paintings in question are capable.

Myths in Images: Theseus and Medea as a Case Study

CHRISTIANE SOURVINOU-INWOOD

The Greek world[1] was full of images, many of which represented mythological subjects. An attempt to consider how myths are articulated in images, and thus also how the representational evidence can contribute to the study of Greek myth, must begin with a central methodological question: how can we read these mythological representations as nearly as possible in the ways in which they were read by their contemporaries and avoid imposing on them our own assumptions, expectations, and preconceptions? A "common sense" approach is obviously unsatisfactory, since it is empirically demonstrable that perception and understanding (including, of course, "common sense" itself) are culturally determined; any "direct" reading involving an empirical confrontation with the ancient images inevitably deploys implicitly our own assumptions, which are culturally determined and thus vastly different from those of the ancient Greeks and which are therefore alien intrusions corrupting our reconstruction of the ancient meanings.

In this essay I set out the methodology I consider appropriate for the reading of ancient images and apply it to the solution of a particular problem, the reading and interpretation of a set of fifth century mythological scenes painted on Athenian vases. The iconographic theme on which this investigation is focused—though other themes will also be discussed—represents Theseus, drawn sword in his right hand, pursuing a woman, who is shown on the same or on the other side of the vase running away from him (cf. Plates 1–3). This theme (on which: Sourvinou-Inwood 1979; Kron 1981, 420, 422–23 429; Sourvinou-Inwood 1987b) will henceforth be referred to as "Theseus with a (drawn) sword." A section of this essay summarizes the results of the detailed iconographic and semantic analyses of "Theseus with a sword" conducted elsewhere (Sourvinou-Inwood 1979, 1987b). The fact that many of the technical analyses have been published elsewhere will allow me to cover a lot of ground without exhaustively setting out all parts of the argument in the detail necessary for methodological rigor. Here I first sketch out the arguments elaborated elsewhere on the basis of which I concluded that the images under consideration represent Theseus attacking his stepmother Medea, who had tried to poison him. Next, I answer certain objections. Finally, I further illustrate my methodology for reading Greek mythological representations by offering a sample reading of selected scenes that I have not considered before, and that, I shall argue, support my interpretation of the central series.

Investigations in different fields, from the psychology of perception to art history and literary criticism, have shown that we make sense of pictures and of texts through perceptual filters shaped by our culture-determined assumptions and expectations.[2] Thus, if our aim is to reconstruct the meanings particular ancient images had for people of the society in which they were produced, it is necessary first to reconstruct the relevant assumptions and expectations that shaped ancient perceptual filters in an attempt to reconstitute those filters and read the ancient pictures through them. Otherwise, we will implicitly wrench them from their historical context and read them as "floating pictures" by default because, unless they are blocked, our own perceptual filters, shaped by and bearing alien assumptions, naturally come into play and inevitably distort the original meanings. Of course, our own cultural determination cannot be completely eliminated from our reading and interpretation of texts and images; but it is possible to approximate the ancient realities to a considerable extent by using a methodology capable of preventing—as far as possible—our own assumptions from intruding and thus distorting the reading and interpretation of the ancient pictures. This is what I propose here.

I first set out the parameters governing the production of meaning as I see them.[3] No sign—in our case, no iconographic element—has a fixed meaning. Its value in any given signifier—in our case, image—is determined by a complex and dynamic process of interaction involving for each iconographic element, for example, the drawn sword: (1) that element as it appears in a given scene with its semantic field of functions, associations, connotations, and so on; (2) its syntactic relationships with other elements in the representation and their semantic fields; and (3) its relationships with semantically related elements that might have been, but were not, selected in its place. For example, the value of the drawn sword held in the left hand (represented in an image I will consider below) is in part determined by the fact that it is not a drawn sword held in the right hand.

An example of a whole iconographic schema without a fixed meaning but with a basic semantic core, which acquires its specific meanings with the help of and in interaction with the particular contexts in which it occurs (cf. also Bérard 1983, 112), is the iconographic schema I call "fleeing woman" (cf. Plates 1–3), which appears in the scenes at the center of this investigation. It shows a girl/woman[4] running away, head turned back (in the most frequent variant she is turning back toward a male who is pursuing her), making gestures of supplication or alarm. This schema is common. It is a codified sign[5] deployed in many different themes: in erotic pursuits, to represent the girl about to be abducted (Sourvinou-Inwood 1987a, especially 136–37); in scenes of attack in which she is the victim; and also in other contexts (Sourvinou-Inwood 1987a, 137, n. 36). The schema itself denotes "girl/woman fleeing in panic." This basic semantic core, and so also the iconographic sign "fleeing woman," is applicable to several different situations involving women. The particular contexts give it particular meanings. In some instances the "fleeing woman" schema itself is slightly modified to denote a particular context and set of meanings. For example, in some erotic pursuits the fleeing girl holds a flower, an element connected with girls' abductions (Sourvinou-Inwood 1987a, 137 and nn. 38–42). Even divine attributes do not have a fixed meaning but acquire value in context; the same attributes can be associated with different divinities, and it is the context that helps determine the divine identity (Metzger 1985, 173–78).

A second important characteristic of signs—again, in our case images—is that they are polysemic; they produce more than one meaning, and these meanings are often ambiguous and ambivalent. So for example, many scenes are both mythological and paradigmatic, sliding toward the generic. In the case of Greek images the distinction "mythological" and "nonmythological" is not always sharp and clearcut (cf. Touchefeu 1983, 21–23; Schnapp 1985, 74–75). In addition to the polysemy of all signs, Greek myths and their representations functioned also as paradigms. For example, the images showing Theseus's erotic pursuits did not only signify the mythological narrative in which Theseus pursued and abducted a girl. Theseus was, among other things, the Athenian ephebe par excellence. The chlamys, petasos, and spear that characterized him in erotic pursuits also characterized Athenian ephebes in general (cf. Sourvinou-Inwood 1987a, 135). Thus for the Athenians the elements "youth" combined with "chlamys," "petasos," and "spear(s)" made up the sign "ephebe" or "Theseus as ephebe." Consequently, the pursuer in "erotic pursuit" scenes was perceived to represent "ephebe" as well as "Theseus," especially since the context was of direct relevance to all ephebes because it articulated certain Athenian perceptions pertaining to marriage and the relations between the sexes (Sourvinou-Inwood 1987a especially 135, 152). Thus the representations depicting the mythological narrative of Theseus's pursuit of a girl were read at the same time as "Theseus as ephebe" and "any ephebe" pursuing a girl, with all the meanings that such representations carried.

Not all representations of erotic pursuit are mythological in the first instance. When the protagonist is a generic youth, the representation in the first instance is "generic," "emblematic"; it expresses certain perceptions about women and male-female relationships, though when read through fifth century Athenian eyes it would also refer to, and acquire its value through, the mythological paradigm of Theseus. The differences between fully mythological scenes and this type of "generic" scene are only a matter of emphasis. All representations of the theme carried both components, and many were probably not positively identified as one or the other, but belonged to an indeterminate part of the semantic spectrum from "Theseus as ephebe" to "generic youth."[6] The presence of an element such as a deity pushes the scene toward the mythological pole, though a deity is also compatible with the generic version. Many scenes were identified as, above all, mythological; a most potent element in this identification is inscriptions ascribing mythological names to the figures.

The assumptions and expectations we need to recover in order to reconstruct the perceptual filters through which images were inscribed and read in fifth century Athens are of two basic types: iconographic—the conventions, codifications, and modalities of the signifying system of Greek iconography—and semantic—the knowledge, ideas, assumptions, and mentality that constitute the semantic fields related to, inscribed in, and called up by, the signifiers under consideration in the two processes of meaning production, the inscription of meanings in the representations by the painters and the extraction of meaning, the making sense of the scenes, by the viewers. The iconographic assumptions can be recovered through formal analyses of various kinds (cf., e.g., Bérard 1976, 61–73; Durand and Lissarague 1980, 89–106) and the semantic assumptions through semantic analyses. Formal iconographic analyses alone are not sufficient. Though they appear to be objective, they are in fact subject to cultural determination. Since even the recognition of resemblance between an iconic sign and the represented object is culture dependent (Gombrich 1977, 73–78, 230–31; Culler 1981, 24; Eco 1976, 204–5), the process of comparison is clearly vulnerable to the intrusion of our own culturally determined notions of, for example, what constitutes a significant similarity or a significant difference. This type of cultural determination can be considerably reduced by making the formal analyses as exhaustive as possible. Also, cultural determination in the evaluation of the resulting data can be reduced considerably through preliminary sets of analyses that help define the concepts directly relevant to the investigation in fifth century Athenian terms (Sourvinou-Inwood 1987b, 42–43). Thus, for example, I tried to show that the study of the relationship between two iconographic themes can be grounded more securely by recovering the parameters of the concept "thematic differentiation" in fifth century Attic ceramic iconography by considering, first, the parameters of variability within one iconographic theme in the work of each artist and, second, the parameters of variability and the modalities of differentiation between different themes in the work of each artist. The second reason why the iconographic analyses must be complemented by semantic analyses is because the reading of an image is a complex process involving a continuous to and fro movement between the image and the reader's semantic universe, his knowledge and assumptions that were called up by it (Eco 1979, 3–43 on reading texts); thus the fifth century Athenians deployed their semantic assumptions in the very process of recognizing and organizing, reading, the iconographic elements that made up these images. For example, an operation such as the individuation of topic (Eco 1979, 24–27), which takes place as the viewer makes sense of the image, generates certain expectations and directs the reading in certain ways, highlights certain things, reduces the polysemy in certain directions, and so on.

Given that all reconstructions and interpretations are culturally determined, and given also the fragmentary state of our evidence, methodological rigor demands that the two sets of analyses, the iconographic and the semantic, be conducted separately and independently in order to prevent the interpenetration of assumptions and fallacies from one set of analyses to the other and consequent contamination, which would lead to fallacious conclusions. This procedure also does not allow, as its "synthetic" alternative does, unconscious adjustments to make the two types of evidence fit. Such adjustments can vitiate the evidence and corrupt the discourse. Finally, this strategy allows us to effect a control on our analyses by cross-checking their conclusions. If the results of the independently conducted iconographic and semantic analyses coincide, their validity is significantly confirmed. Thus, for example, in an earlier investigation of "Theseus with a drawn sword" prompted by Bérard's suggestion (1980, 619) that it may represent an erotic pursuit, I showed that the results of my two sets of analyses converge. The iconographic comparisons of "Theseus with a drawn sword" to the images of erotic pursuit by Theseus show that the former is a true attack, while the latter is not, and that the iconographic schema of erotic pursuit by a god, which includes elements of attack, is different from that of erotic pursuit by Theseus and other heroes, which does not include attack. These conclusions coincide with those of the semantic analyses showing that there are fundamental distinctions between "erotic pursuits by heroes" and "erotic pursuits by gods": the latter have seriously threatening connotations corresponding to the observed iconographic differences between the two erotic pursuit schemata. These conclusions entail that it is not legitimate to postulate that erotic pursuits by heroes could have been shown through the same schemata as erotic pursuits by gods and, consequently, that "Theseus with a drawn sword" does not show an erotic pursuit (Sourvinou-Inwood 1987b).

The overwhelming majority of the scenes representing Theseus with a drawn sword deploy the same basic iconographic schema, illustrated here in Plates 1–3, with or without additional elements, such as an altar at which the fleeing woman is taking, or is about to take, refuge (Sourvinou-Inwood 1979, 35–41, 42, nos. 4, 25, 33), or one or two additional figures—a king and/or female companions (Sourvinou-Inwood 1979, 43–45; Plate 3). None of these scenes depicting this schema is inscribed, though another one, painted by Macron, in which the two figures are differently arranged and Theseus is unsheathing his sword (Plate 4), is. Given the potential importance of apparently small divergences (Sourvinou-Inwood 1987b, 42–43), and thus the theoretical possibility that this apparently similar scene represents a different iconographic theme, we should prevent any prior (inevitably culturally determined) assumptions from corrupting the discourse by separating the uninscribed scene from the others and leaving it aside for the moment.

The detailed analyses of the iconographic schema under discussion, of the two figures, their gestures and stances, and of their relationships, and of the iconographic schema as a whole in all its variants (Sourvinou-Inwood 1979, 41, 42–43, 70, nn.147–50; 1987b, 44) demonstrate conclusively that these scenes represent a serious, life-threatening attack by a male youth against a woman. The identity of the youth as Theseus is incontrovertible. It does not depend on the inscription on the Macron cup. The youth with the sword is represented according to the iconographic schema used to represent Theseus; this occurs in different variants, found both in our scenes and in other, certain, representations of Theseus (Sourvinou-Inwood 1987a, 133–34). To be sure, this iconographic schema was used to represent other ephebes also; it was not confined to the Athenian ephebe par excellence that was Theseus. But the specific action depicted, and its nature, indicate that these scenes were in the first instance and above all mythological. The combination of chlamys, pilos, sword, and club on a cup in the Vatican (Sourvinou-Inwood 1979, 35, no. 4; Kron 1981 Pl. 330 Aethra I 38) confirms this conclusion and makes clear that the mythological figure depicted is Theseus (cf. also Kron 1981, 423). The identity of the mythological male protagonist can be recovered also in the other scenes. I submit that in the absence of a sign to identify him as a mythological figure other than

Theseus, the mythological male protagonist of this attack is Theseus. Theseus was the Athenian ephebe par excellence, and thus in the absence of iconographic elements that could have identified the youth as some other mythological ephebe, the schema under discussion would have been read as "ephebe attacking a woman with a sword" or "Theseus attacking a woman with a sword." It cannot be argued that the Athenians understood the scene differently because they possessed information we do not have, for there are no additional iconographic elements (in the ephebic schema) that may have signaled to them (but not to us, because we do not share their knowledge) that this was someone else, not Theseus. Nor can it be argued that the ephebe was identified by the Athenians as someone other than Theseus through the identification of the topic, for (even leaving aside the fact that Theseus was shown attacking a woman in some scenes) like the theme "erotic pursuit," the theme "attack against a woman" is too general to be attached to only one ephebic hero.

Orestes, Alcmaeon, Telephus are but three examples who spring to mind as alternative candidates (Sourvinou-Inwood 1979, 8–9, 13). Of course, the codification of the schema (Sourvinou-Inwood 1979, 4, 61, n.2) would have quite strongly attached an identity to the protagonists; but in Attic iconography if the hero were not Theseus, given that the schema was used to represent "Theseus attacking a woman" at least in the case of the Vatican cup, such a codification would have had to include an element identifying the protagonist as other than Theseus (cf. Sourvinou-Inwood 1987a, 133–35). That it is Theseus is confirmed by the fact that on more than one vase (Sourvinou-Inwood 1979, nos. 9, 11, 21) our theme is combined with an erotic pursuit by Theseus, and the semantic axis along which the connection is made is, as in the case of other, comparable combinations, the identity of the protagonist (Sourvinou-Inwood 1987a, 148–9; cf. 133–34). Since images are polysemic and ambiguous, and the same iconographic schema was also used to represent common ephebes, the possibility should be kept in mind that these scenes (or at least some of them) may also have had a paradigmatic facet of signification, that they could also be read, on a second level, "generically," with Theseus the paradigmatic Athenian ephebe symbolizing also something relevant to all ephebes. As we shall see, it is indeed possible to reconstruct a "paradigmatic" level of signification in Theseus's attack against his stepmother Medea.

The interpretation of this iconographic schema as a serious, life-threatening attack is confirmed by the fact it is iconographically very similar to certain other scenes known to represent a serious attack (Sourvinou-Inwood 1979, 41, 42–43, 70, nn.147–50; 1987b, 44). The basic elements in the stance of Theseus in "Theseus with a sword" can be paralleled in many other scenes of attack. The nearest iconographic parallels for the whole schema are representations of Odysseus attacking Circe and of Menelaus attacking Helen, two themes representing the "averted murder of a perfidious woman by a man whom she had wronged." This is of some importance, as is the fact that the closest parallel of the two, the one for which the same iconographic schema as that involving Theseus is used most consistently, is that depicting the averted murder of a perfidious sorceress. The similarity between these iconographic schemata suggests the possibility of a semantic similarity between the two represented subjects. On my interpretation of our scenes, they are indeed semantically similar.

The woman's iconography cannot help us identify her. She is shown, we saw, according to the schema "fleeing woman, which suits her situation, and according to the iconographic type suitable in Greek iconography for both girls of marriageable age and above and mature (albeit not elderly) women. Of the other elements that can appear in our scenes the figure of the king suggests a context in which one of the kings with whom Theseus came into contact would not have been out of place. Space prevents me from discussing all the scenes that are combined with representations of Theseus attacking a woman with a sword,[7] but I will mention briefly a group of seven vases by, or close to the style of, the Carlsruhe painter (Sourvinou-Inwood 1979, nos. 17–23). Four, possibly five, of these vases (Sourvinou-Inwood 1979, nos. 17–20; cf. no 22), all by the Carlsruhe painter, repeat the same decorative schema: on side A Theseus is attacking a woman with a sword, on B an identical woman is fleeing away from a king who is not pursuing her, and in the tondo a king is shown in the company of a Nike. It is not impossible that the same decorative schema may also have been repeated on the fragmentary stemless cup Barcelona 538 (ARV² 738.142). In addition, no. 23 has a related combination: it represents Theseus attacking a woman with a sword on the tondo and Nike and a fleeing woman on A. This suggests that there is a good possibility that all three scenes may have been connected in the eyes of the artist and his contemporaries who shared his assumptions. As we shall see, on my reading they can indeed be seen as connected, relating to the same event. The fact that this painter uses women, Nikai, and kings also elsewhere in his repertory, in different arrangements, is not, of course, an argument against this view. Through the manipulation of established, often polysemic, schemata different scenes and themes are created in an iconographic system with the economy and conventionality of Attic ceramic iconography. It is not inconceivable that the motif of the helmet, attached to Theseus (he is

Plate 1. Manchester III.1.41

Plate 2. Leningrad 777 (St. 1786)

Plate 3. London B.M. E 446

Plate 4. Cup Leningrad 1543 (649, St. 830), tondo

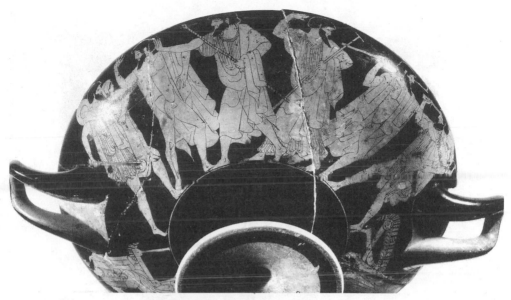

Plate 5. Cup Leningrad 1543 (649, St. 830), side A

Plate 6. Cup Leningrad 1543 (649, St. 830), side B

Plate 7. Leningrad W 205

Plate 8. Cup, Metropolitan Museum, New York 53.11.4, side B

Plate 9. Cup, Metropolitan Museum, New York 53.11.4, side A

Plate 10. Cup, Metropolitan Museum, New York 53.11.4, tondo

wearing it) on no. 19 and to Nike on the tondo (she is holding it) of no. 22 may confirm the connection and allusively relate both scenes to a military victory; again, the fact that the schema "Nike with a king holding a helmet" is not limited to vases with this particular combination of subjects (cf. e.g. the tondo of the stemless cup Villa Giulia 25048 [ARV² 738.139]) does not constitute an argument against this hypothesis, whether or not such scenes on other vases were sometimes seen as extracts from the "triptych" postulated here. On my reading such a connection with a military victory does indeed obtain, as we shall now see.

Semantic analyses of the Theseus myth show that (leaving aside the Amazons with their special iconography) the only woman with whom Theseus had been in conflict, and whom he had confronted in a way that could be iconographically articulated through the schema of the serious attack, was his stepmother Medea (Sourvinou-Inwood 1979, 22–25 and passim). When Theseus arrived in Athens from Troezen, Medea made two attempts to bring about his death, by persuading Aegeus, who was ignorant of Theseus's identity, first to send him to fight the Marathonian bull, and then, when he emerged victorious from this confrontation, to poison his drink; before Theseus could drink the poison, Aegeus saw the sword he had left for his son under a rock at Troezen and recognized his son and heir; Medea was expelled from Attica. This confrontation between Theseus and Medea was very important in Athenian myth and ideology, though it has attracted far less attention from scholars. It maps out in a condensed form the basic skeleton of the symbolic universe of fifth-century Athens. For when we consider the characteristics of, and the values and connotations associated with, each of the two figures in the Athenian perceptions and representations (through which images, stories, and plays were made sense of), it becomes clear that in their eyes it was inevitably perceived (at whatever points of the conscious-unconscious spectrum) as a confrontation between two figures in whom were condensed and crystallized, and structured hierarchically, a series of antitheses that in fact articulated the Greek semantic universe (Sourvinou-Inwood 1979, 53).

The first antithesis articulated in, and through, this myth is "male versus female"; the second is "Greek, especially Athenian, versus Oriental." The combination of these two antitheses has helped all the negative values associated with the female to drift to the figure of Medea in this context. The fact that she is a sorceress in opposition to Theseus, who is a benefactor of humanity, is a manifestation of, and a means of expressing in a polarized form, these negative characteristics. Medea is a murderous stepmother. She is not the only bad stepmother in Greek myth; there are many others who, in one way or another, seriously threatened the children of their husband's first marriage or liaison. An example of a "straightforward" murderous attempt is that of Ino, Athamas's second wife, against Phrixus (Apollod. i. 9.1). Phaedra destroyed Hippolytus via a different route (E. *Hipp.*), but the two mythological schemata are permeable to each other's motifs (cf. Pherecyd. *FrGHist* 3 frag 98). Such myths are articulated by the perception that a father's second wife threatens the interests, and may even conspire against the life, of the children of the first marriage (Sourvinou-Inwood 1988a, section 2).

The figure of the bad stepmother expresses more than this perception, however. It is also a mask for the figure of the bad mother, in the sense that the negative traits of the figure of the mother, the fear that she will not care for, and may even use her virtually unlimited powers to damage, her powerless small (male is what matters) children, have drifted to the figure of the stepmother. This can be seen in a variety of relationships between these two figures. First, in some myths the role of the destructive mother and the destructive stepmother are interchangeable in the different versions. Thus, the blinding of the Phineids is sometimes ascribed to their mother and sometimes to their stepmother—and in some other versions to their father, at the instigation of the stepmother (Sourvinou-Inwood 1988b). Second, in another type of myth a woman kills her own children by mistake, while trying to murder her stepchildren (as happened to Themisto [Nauck *TGF*² p. 482; Hygin. *Fab.* 4])—or nephews, as in the case of Aedon in one variant (Pherecyd. *FrGHist* 3 frag 124). Such myths express both the threat of the stepmother and a censored (inadvertently killed her children) representation of the "bad mother," itself a polarization of what were perceived as the negative traits of the mother and symbolized also through the figure of the stepmother. The combination of these two forms of censorship in such myths confirms that one representation articulating them is the "bad mother." Another modality of censorship of the "bad mother" underlies the figure of the mother who kills her children while in a state of madness (as in the version of Aedon's story in *Od.* 19.518–23, and in that of the Minyads [Plu. *Mor.* 299E–F]). Third, the behavior of the bad stepmother is the same as that of the much rarer figure of the unambiguously bad mother, such as Clytemnestra, who (unsuccessfully) threatened the life of her son Orestes, or Procne, who killed her son Itys (*TrGF* vol. 4 [Ratd ed.] p. 435). Fourth, Medea, the bad stepmother par excellence—because she threatened the life of the Athenian hero par excellence—becomes the bad mother par excellence in another myth in which she actually murders her children (E. *Med.*). In addition, the myth of Medea illustrates the fact that the schemata "unintentional killing by the mother" and "intentional murder by the mother" expressed closely related perceptions and can be seen as transformations of each other, and thus also that the former can be seen as being, among other things, a censored version of the latter; for in one major variant of her myth (almost certainly the earliest) Medea, who eventually was the murderous mother par excellence and the murderous stepmother par excellence, had killed her children unintentionally, while trying to make them immortal (Page 1938, xxii; Knox 1977, 194).

Let us return to the notion that Medea is a polarization of the negative traits of the female in the Greek collective representations. When the female is opposed (as a symbolic counter) to the male, she stands for the negative values in the Greek representations (Sourvinou-Inwood 1979, 9–10, 53). This is connected with, and reinforced by, the fact that women were perceived as biologically and socially inferior, in need of control, and potentially dangerous and treacherous. Men were most vulnerable to women in their family relationships, where women had some power that men could not always be certain of controlling. A bad wife can damage her husband in a variety of ways; for example, she can introduce someone else's children into his *oikos*, pretending they are his, or hurt or destroy his small sons (whether her own or some other woman's) while they are in her power. Thus she is always a potentially threatening mother and stepmother. (In the latter role she can always seduce her husband's sons and turn them into his sexual rivals [Sourvinou-Inwood 1988a, section 2]). She has also a partly comparable power as a daughter and sister. Medea condensed into herself all these negative traits in a polarized form subverting all family relationships. She subverted the father-daughter relationship by betraying her father, helping and running away with Jason, and, above all, by killing her brother, her father's son, thus also subverting the sister-brother relationship. She subverted the father-daughter relationship in another way by causing the Peliades to kill their father. Through the murder of her sons she subverted the wife-husband and the mother-son relationships. The former she subverted again in trying to kill the son of her next husband, Aegeus. In other words, she subverted the woman's role in the family in all possible ways. One particular facet of this subversion is manifested in Medea's exploitation of men's fatherhood (her father's, Pelias's, Jason's, Creon's, and Aegeus's desire for fatherhood) to gain her ends or defeat or punish her enemies (Hanson 1965, 57–60). This is another negative and polarized articulation of the notion that a man's fatherhood is in a woman's hands, and more generally of the male vulnerability to women in the family sphere and of the threat perceived to be represented by a bad woman.

Thus in the fifth century Athenian mythological universe[8] Medea is, among other things, a polarization of all the negative traits of the female. Consequently, Theseus's defeat of her expressed, among other things, the notion of victory of the male hero par excellence over the frightening female, the bad woman who threatens male power, and even male life, especially in the sphere of the family. One of the figures lurking under, and defeated in, her persona is the "bad mother." Theseus the ephebic hero par excellence defeats the par excellence bad mother, here crystallized into the figure of the stepmother.

Medea is, and she is not, like other women, and she both stands for, and is differentiated from, the figure "Greek woman." The complexity and ambivalence of this figure has been most subtly expressed in Euripides' *Medea*. Insofar as she is a woman abused by a man as well as a stranger in a foreign land, Medea arouses some sympathy as well as revulsion. The iconographic equivalent of this is the fact that in our scenes identified as "Theseus attacking Medea to punish her" she is represented through the schema of the fleeing woman, the normal schema used to represent women (passive and innocent as well as "wicked" women) who are fleeing to escape a man who either is attacking them or wants to force his sexual attentions on them, or otherwise threatens them. Insofar as Medea's vulnerable and abused situation (at least in Euripides' *Medea*) is a polarized version of all women's vulnerability, and insofar as she embodies in a polarized form all the negative characteristics, potentialities, and connotations associated with women in the Greek collective representations, she is perceived as being up to a point "like other women," as representing—among other things—a facet of "woman" (cf. also Knox 1977, 211, 218–25); women, being powerless and at the mercy of men, can only use perfidious means to defend themselves. But insofar as that facet is entirely negative, indeed an extreme and sharply polarized version of that negativity, correlative with, and expressed through, Medea's character as an Oriental and a sorceress, she was perceived as very different from ordinary Greek women (Eur. *Med.* 1339–43). Thus, this polarized negativity has drifted to the Oriental sorceress, and the representation of ordinary Greek women is protected from this negativity, which is, however, at the same time articulated, marginalized, and purged, defeated through the victory over Medea of the Athenian hero par excellence Theseus.

However, her expulsion from Athens and Greece was not the end of her story, and its sequel brings us to yet another level of signification in the myth and the images of the confrontation between Theseus and Medea. When Medea was expelled from Athens she went to the East, and there (Sourvinou-Inwood 1979, 49) she (Eust. *Comm.* on D.P. 1017.20;

Paus. 2.3.8) or her son Medus (sometimes, though not always, said to be Aegeus's son [cf. both versions in D.S. 4.55.5–56.2]), reigned in Media (according to one variant (D.S. 10.27) founded by Medus) and/or gave their name to the land. This story is already found in Herodotus (Hdt. 7.62). Given this pseudohistorical and thus also symbolic association between Medea and the Persians, it was inevitable that the myth under discussion would be perceived by the Athenians as "Theseus, the Athenian hero, defeating, and chasing out of Attica and Greece, Medea, an Oriental woman closely connected with the Medes, and thus in general with the Persian enemy." This myth, then, is clearly a mythological correlative of, and thus a mythological paradigm for, the Greek, and especially Athenian, victories over the Persians. The identification of Medea with the invading Persians was explicitly made at that time. At some point the story that Medea/Medus was associated with, and the ancestor of, (some of) the Medes was explicitly connected with the Persian Wars, and in particular with the battle of Marathon. It became part of the mythicohistorical discourse deployed as part of the historical and political discourse of the present. In Schol.Ar. *Pax* 289[9] Datis the Mede, the Persian general at Marathon,[10] is said to have claimed Attica by virtue of his descent from Medus, Medea's son from Aegeus. Diodorus Siculus 10.27 following Ephorus (Raubitschek 1957, 236) reports the same story and adds that the Athenian answer, given by Miltiades, was that since Medus the founder of Media was an Athenian, it was the Athenians that should lay claim to the land of the Medes and not vice versa. We do not know the date at which this story first appeared. However, the years following the Persian Wars are the most likely time both in terms of the general interest, and because this type of mythological discourse concerning common ancestry between Greeks and Persians had been articulated at that time (cf. Hdt. 7.150). Certainly Herodotus gives us the *terminus ante quem* for the connection between Medea and the Medes. Indeed, as Professor Burkert kindly pointed out to me, the unique form *(ho) Medeion (strategos)* in Ibycus 320 Page is thought to reflect already the etymology Medoi/Medeia. Another instance of this association between Medea and the Persians in the mythicohistorical discourse pertaining to the Persian Wars is found at the beginning of Herodotus's *Historiai* (1.1–5), where it is claimed that according to the Persians the origins of the Persian Wars (in the sense of being the causes of the enmity between Greeks and Asians) were the rape of Io, the rape of Europa, the abduction of Medea, the abduction of Helen and, above all, the Trojan War.

I hope to have shown (Sourvinou-Inwood 1979, 49–50) that the correspondence between, on the one hand, the mythical events of Theseus's career from his arrival at Athens from Troezen until Medea's expulsion and, on the other, the Persian Wars are extremely close, too close to be coincidental, and that therefore the career was reshaped to fit and function as a mythological paradigm for, and prefiguration of, the wars. Even if we leave aside the dates suggested by the vases—to avoid any hint of circularity—the best candidate for this manipulation is Pherecydes, in the context of the Cimonian promotion of the figure of Theseus (Sourvinou-Inwood 1979, 54–55). Incidentally, an additional "coincidence" that I had not noticed in my earlier discussions, which gives, I submit, strong support to the notion that the manipulation of the Theseus-Medea myth took place in Cimonian times and in a Cimonian milieu—where the notion that Cimon was "like" Theseus was promoted—is that Theseus's paternal half-brother Medus who went to the East—according to one version via Phoenicia (D.S. 4.556)—and became the ancestor of the Medes has an exact counterpart in Cimon's paternal half-brother Metiochus, who was captured by Phoenicians but then was given land and a Persian wife by Darius and whose children counted as Persians (Hdt. 6.41.2–4).

In these circumstances, it was inevitable that images representing Theseus attacking Medea would be seen as symbolizing, among other things, the Greek victory over the Persians. For, once created, the symbolic identification between Medea and the invading Persians was part of the assumptions through which the fifth century Athenians made sense of the scene. Moreover, the fact that at this time a series of other similar themes, the Trojan War, Amazonomachies, Centauromachies, came to be seen and to be used as mythological paradigms of and metaphors for the Persian Wars (cf. e.g. Thomas 1976, 40–6; Boardman 1982, 5–15; Gauer 1968, 18 and n. 48; Kebric 1983, 14–16) not only makes it very likely that this interpretation of the Theseus-Medea myth would have taken place at this time, but also entails a culturally conditioned reception especially geared to seeing (certain types of) myths also as mythological paradigms and metaphors for contemporary events, above all the central contemporary event, the Persian Wars, and to reading the images representing such myths as, among other things, symbolizing and articulating certain perceptions of that event—perceptions of the type "victory of the civilized and superior over the uncivilized and inferior." Indeed I would be inclined to go further and suggest that in the particular climate of reception of the second quarter of the fifth century (the two earliest scenes, which do not follow the schema, date from the 470s; the heavy concentration is between the 460s and the 440s) any representation of Theseus attacking a woman was likely to be interpreted as Theseus expelling Medea, seen as a paradigm for the defeat of the Persians, unless there were signs indicating otherwise.

Let us now consider how the conclusions of the semantic analyses of the myth "the confrontation between Theseus and Medea" compare to those of the iconographic analyses of the representations of Theseus attacking a woman, drawn sword in hand. I submit that there is a perfect match (cf. also Sourvinou-Inwood 1979, 42–43). The pattern of appearance of the scenes, both the chronological pattern and the number of scenes, which is large (Brommer 1982, 134, n. 21 s.v. no. 3), fits the expected pattern of the theme "Theseus confronting Medea" as we can reconstruct it in its main lines on the basis of its symbolic importance. I shall return to this. The woman's iconography fits that of Medea— another point to which I shall return. As for the other iconographic elements, the altar is also found in one of the two scenes depicting Theseus's recognition (Brommer 1982, Pl. 44; discussion: Sourvinou-Inwood 1979, 42). Of the two additional figures, a second woman is also represented in the second recognition scene (Plate 7), and thus was not out of place in that context. The king is clearly Aegeus, whose role in this scene is obvious; the rarity of his portrayal, like the absence of Attic ceramic scenes representing Theseus's recognition, is strongly motivated and will be discussed below. Most strikingly, the theme of Theseus and Medea as analyzed here fits the iconographic combinations so often repeated by the Carlsruhe painter: Medea running away from Aegeus after the discovery of her plot (symbolizing her role as bad wife), his revulsion at her action, and the fact that he as well as Theseus chased her out of Athens. The king with the Nike would be polysemic, signifying Aegeus's "victory" of ensuring a worthy heir and of having avoided his son's murder, and also Theseus's victories over the bandits, the bull, and Medea, and finally the Athenian victories over the Persians, to which the helmet held by Nike may allude.

The heavy clustering of scenes of "Theseus with the sword" in the years from the 460s to the 440s prompted me to suggest that interest in the theme of the confrontation between Theseus and Medea was sparked by a tragedy, and that this may have been Sophocles' *Aegeus*, of whose ending I offered a tentative reconstruction (Sourvinou-Inwood 1979, 55–56). I shall now consider a scene that I entirely overlooked when I put forward that hypothesis and that I have now come to believe was inspired by the end of this tragedy as I have reconstructed it. I do not mean that it is a re-presentation of it, but that it is an iconographic creation articulating (certain perceptions of) the events shown at the end of this tragedy. The systematic reading of this scene, through detailed iconographic analyses the results of which will be related to the conclusions of the semantic investigations, will now illustrate in concrete detail the methodology I am advocating here.

In his review of my book (Sourvinou-Inwood 1979) Bérard (1980, 620) suggested, not, I believe, entirely in earnest, that my proposed reconstruction of the end of Sophocles' *Aegeus* might be reflected in a scene on the cup New York 53.11.4 (Plate 8). This suggestion prompted me to attempt to read this scene systematically, on the basis of the methodology I am here advocating. I will now set out the relevant analyses. But first I will summarize my proposal concerning the end of Sophocles' *Aegeus* (Sourvinou-Inwood 1979, 56). I suggested that while Theseus was pursuing Medea sword in hand in order to punish her with death for her attempt on his life, Athena appeared as a *dea ex machina* and stopped the hero, urged him to let Medea go, and prophesied that on leaving Athens she would settle in the East in a land whose people would be called Medes after her, would come to Greece and try to subjugate it, and would be defeated.

The cup New York 53.11.4 (ARV² 406.7; Add 115) represents Theseus and Amphitrite in the tondo (Plate 10), Theseus, Triton, Poseidon, and the Nereids on A (Plate 9) and a scene described by Beazley (in ARV²) as "Theseus returning to Athens" on B (Plate 8). It is the last scene that concerns us here. The iconographic analyses show that the scene is located in Aegeus's palace. The spatial indicators are two columns with part of an entablature and an altar. The combination column + altar can, depending on the context, denote either "sanctuary" or "house"—the courtyard of a house in particular (Sourvinou-Inwood 1987a, 141–43). The two columns with entablature + altar are a grander version of the column with entablature + altar and here denote a palace; this is shown by the fact that on side A of this cup the same indicators, two columns with a part of an entablature and an altar (the altar represented under the handle is inescapably read into both scenes) denote Poseidon's palace, which in the tondo is denoted through the indicators "column with part of entablature + chair," which indicate generally "house" and in particular "courtyard of a house."

Theseus had been associated with three palaces apart from that of Poseidon: that of his grandfather Pittheus at Troezen, that of his father Aegeus at Athens, and that of Minos in Crete. The first can be excluded here for a combination of reasons. First, Pittheus is absent. Second, none of the women surrounding Theseus is represented as being more prominent that the others, as would befit Theseus's mother Aethra. Thus, if this were Pittheus's palace, the two crucial figures of Theseus's early life would be absent at an important moment in that life (so characterized by the presence of Athena and the crowning) that took place in their home. Furthermore, since the women crowning Theseus are undifferentiated (in status and prominence) and, among other things, remind us of the undifferentiated Nereids on A, they are likely to represent a group of undifferentiated women (such as "the women of Athens"). Finally, Theseus is here represented as someone who had won general acclaim, and it is unlikely that he would have been so represented when he left Troezen. It is true that Nike crowns him with a taenia for lifting the rock underneath which lay the *gnōrismata* on the scyphus Ferrara T971 (Brommer 1982, Pl. 18a). But this is simply an emblematic way of representing Theseus's achievement, which was, however, a "private" achievement marking his passage out of boyhood (Sourvinou-Inwood 1971, 99–100)—a perception articulated in some representations of Theseus lifting the rock through the depiction of Pittheus or Aethra (Sourvinou-Inwood 1971, 103–4, nos. 1, 2, 5). Minos's palace can also be excluded because of the context of popular acclamation and of the absence of Minos. Aegeus's palace fits the representation without any difficulty; it was, incidentally, also associated with a sanctuary, the Delphinion (Plu. *Thes.* xii.3; Graf 1979, 15), and thus fits both potential denotations of the spatial indicators. In addition, there is at least one scene set in Aegeus's palace representing Theseus's recognition (and thus, on my reading, immediately preceding this one) in which an altar is shown (Brommer 1982, Pl. 44). Moreover, Aegeus's palace is totally symmetrical to that of Poseidon on the other side—a selection that makes perfect sense if the scenes on the two sides were located in the palaces of the divine and the human fathers of Theseus. The absence of his human father from the scene does not, we will see, spoil this harmony.

Let us continue the comparison between the two scenes. The central group is different: Poseidon, Triton, and Theseus on A; Athena and Theseus on B. On B there are four female figures apart from Athena, three of which are about to crown Theseus with taeniae, while the fourth is turned away from the central group with her head looking back. On A three Nereids are present; the one near the altar is holding a jug and phiale for a libation, and another is holding a phiale. A fourth woman belonging to the context of Poseidon's palace is shown on the tondo: Amphitrite is offering Theseus the wreath mentioned by the literary sources (B. 17.113–16) which would help him in his Minotaur adventure (Isler-Kerenyi 1977, 22). As has been correctly remarked, the Nereids are about to pour the libation for Theseus's departure (Brommer 1982, 79) and for the success of his enterprise. On another vase, a Zurich pointed amphora (Isler–Kerenyi 1977, 20–24, Pl. 1b), the Nereids are crowning Theseus with taeniae in a schema very similar to that on side B of our cup, not on the occasion of a victory, but as part of their joyous reception and acknowledgment of Theseus as the son of Poseidon.

In our scene on B there is one woman, the figure next to the altar, who differs from the other women in this scene and also from the Nereids on A in two important respects. First, she is the only one of these figures whose body is turned away from the central group, though she turns her head back toward it. Her stance is a variation on the "fleeing woman" schema and appears to denote that she had been moving in the opposite direction from the central group and suddenly stopped. The gestures of her hands do not conflict with this; they are the gestures made by one particular iconographic variant of the "fleeing woman" schema used both in representations of erotic pursuit, to represent the pursued girl and/or her companion(s) (cf. e.g. the stamnos Oxford 1911.619 [ARV² 629.16; Sourvinou-Inwood 1987a Pl.IIIb]; the stamnos Krefeld Inv. 1034/1515 sides A and B, [ARV² 502.5; CVA Germany 49 pls. 37.1–4, 38.1–4]), and in representations of serious attacks, as, for example, in a representation of Menelaus's attack on Helen, which is in the process of coming to a halt as shown by the fact that Menelaus is dropping his sword (on the bell krater Louvre G 424 [ARV² 1077.5; 1682]). Thus, the gestures made by the woman on the right of the altar in our scene denote "alarm"; they are one particular version of the gestures of alarm and/or supplication that are part of the "fleeing woman" schema. Since meaning is created in context, this reading will be confirmed and further defined if the rest of the scene proves to provide an appropriate context for such a gesture, and indeed such a schema. As we shall see, this is in fact the case here. This woman's gestures constitute the second difference between her and all the other women on B and the Nereids on A: she is the only one among them whose gestures do not denote some form of benign activity toward Theseus.

At the center of the scene are Athena and Theseus. The identity of the youth is certain beyond doubt thanks to the combination of the iconographic schema through which he is depicted and the proximity to the incontrovertible representations of Theseus on the tondo and especially on A, where he is depicted according to what is virtually the same iconographic schema. In our scene he is holding the sword in his left hand and making a gesture toward Athena with his right. The meaning of this latter gesture can be identified with certainty: it is a gesture of adoration common in votive reliefs that are emblematic images of worship toward the deity who is shown as ideally present (cf. e.g. Neumann 1979, Pl. 46b; Petrakos 1981, 93, no. 73 [votive relief Athens NM 4466]; 104, no. 83 [votive relief Athens NM 1402]). It also occurs in other contexts (cf. the figure on the votary on the Niinnion tablet [Mylonas 1961, Pl. 88]). This gesture can also be made with the left hand, while the right hand is pouring a libation (cf. the cup Tarquinia RC 1918 [ARV^2 366.88]). The sword held in the left hand is rare, but not wholly unparalleled in Attic iconography (Prag 1985, 1, 61, 108, n. 11). In at least one case originating in the same milieu it is not a random variation of the normal "sword in the right hand" schema but carries specific connotations—in the particular context of the sacrifice of Iphigeneia, connotations of revulsion toward the act to be performed by the sword (Prag 1985, 61).

Moreover, I hope to have shown (Sourvinou-Inwood 1987b, 46) that in scenes of erotic pursuit the iconographic element "spears carried in the left hand" is part of the characterization of the spear as "not weapon used or about to be used in an attack." Thus we must not assume that the "sword in the left hand" here is a variant without significance of the common schema "sword in Theseus's right hand." On the contrary, the presumption must be that the variation is significant, especially since small divergences are more immediately obvious to the members of the cultural community in which the images were produced (Gombrich 1977, 53). Indeed, reversals of this type belong to a common modality through which the vase painters manipulated the established schemata to create different meanings. (A different but comparable manipulation is that of the *kanoun* carried during a sacrifice, which in representations of Heracles and Busiris is modified into the "fallen *kanoun*" because in them the "sacrifice" schema has been reversed to depict human sacrifice [Durand and Lissarague 1983, 153–67, especially 158, 166].) Because the sword in the right hand denotes attack and the spears in the left hand help denote "not attack," I suggest that the sword in the left hand may also signify some form of "not attack." It would be fallacious to think that "the sword in the left hand" was "not significant" because it was dependent on the fact that Theseus was making the gesture of adoration with his right. Whatever the factors that determined these selections, the arrangement carried certain meanings in the fifth century assumptions shared by the painters and their contemporary viewers through which the viewers made sense of the schema. Thus, they would have understood the sword to be directly significant to the scene's action; otherwise it would not be shown, or it would be in its scabbard, but at that particular moment not in use in an attack, with perhaps some emphasis on the connotation "not attack."

Theseus's gesture of adoration toward Athena shows that she is not simply ideally present, a symbolic representation of her protection, help, and encouragement to Theseus, but an actual participant in the action, visible to him. This is confirmed by the fact that this gesture (though not the rest of Theseus's stance) is closely paralleled on the hydria Berlin 2179 (ARV^2 252.52; Add 101), where Athena, toward whom Theseus is again making this gesture, is known to have been a participant in the action: she is ordering Theseus away from Ariadne, who is being led away by Dionysus. In this case (and therefore, conceivably also in ours), the gesture made by Theseus as he is obeying Athena and moving away denotes obedience as well as worship, the acceptance of Athena's command. This reading is also confirmed by the fact that Athena's gesture toward Theseus in our scene is similar to that made by Poseidon in the direction of Triton (and also Theseus) urging the action on, urging Triton to carry Theseus back to the surface (cf. von Bothmer 1972, 52–53, s.v. no. 22). Equally, Theseus's gesture toward Athena is very similar to, albeit not identical with, the gesture he makes with his right hand toward Poseidon on A. Athena, then, on B is depicted in epiphany, communicating with, and making a gesture toward, Theseus, who is making a gesture of adoration (with perhaps also connotations of obedience) toward her.

The gesture made by Athena is one made also by other divine beings (as well as humans, but it cannot be assumed that the significance of the gesture is the same whether made by gods or men [cf. Sourvinou-Inwood 1987b, 50–51]). A close parallel is the gesture made by the god whose identity is controversial on the astragalus London E 804 (ARV^2 765.20; Add 140). Another, very similar, but not identical, is that made by Hermes in another scene in which Theseus deserts Ariadne in obedience to divine command, the cup Tarquinia RC 5291 (ARV^2 405.1; Add 114). Zeus's gesture on the pelike London E 410 (ARV^2 494.1; Add 122) is also comparable. The significance of these gestures is not totally clear, because their contexts do not normally allow the unambiguous recovery of their meanings. In the case of Hermes, and probably in the case of Poseidon on side A of our cup, the gesture appears to signify that the deity is urging some course of action. The god on the astragalus is also urging some course of action with the gestures of both arms and hands; Neumann (1965, 23–24) takes them to signify beckoning. Zeus's gesture on the pelike Neumann (1965, 34) takes to be above all characteristic of the god, a power gesture that is also made by the statue, and thus emblematic representation, of Zeus from Artemisium (Ridgway 1970, Fig. 98), whose outstretched left hand and arm are very similar to Athena's outstretched right in our scene.

Gestures do not have a fixed meaning; they are defined by the context. It may be possible to see the two sets of meanings as part of the same "divine power" semantic field, within which the context some-times defines the gesture as an emblematic power gesture and other times, when addressed to humans, as a gesture urging a certain action, which in the circumstances is equivalent to a gesture of divine com-mand.

The fact that Theseus is holding the sword in his left hand probably signifies, we saw, some form of "not attack," evidently not in the sense that he is not attacking the goddess, for on fifth century Athenian as-sumptions, this alternative would be inconceivable, and no Athenian artist would have used it. One possible reading of this iconographic schema is that Theseus had been in the process of attacking someone and was interrupted by Athena's appearance. This reading gains sup-port from the presence of a figure, the woman on the right, who fits iconographically the role of victim of Theseus's attack. Thus, even if we leave aside Bérard's suggestion and my proposal concerning the end of Sophocles' *Aegeus*, the fact that this is a representation in which The-seus had been attacking a woman with a sword connects it with the main series that concerns us and suggests that it probably also belongs to the same theme. If this is correct, we gain a series of arguments in support of my reading of our main series. First, this vase places the scene of Theseus attacking a woman in the exact context in which both the textual and the iconographic tradition place Theseus's recognition and the attack on Medea: in Aegeus's palace, by an altar. Second, the con-text of the whole vase, the combination of the three scenes, and the not negligible iconographic similarities between A and B suggest very strongly a close semantic as well as iconographic connection between the two scenes such as is provided by my thesis that the scene on B pertains to the reception of Theseus by his human father and/or step-mother—in counterpoint to his reception by his divine father on A and his divine stepmother on the tondo. The reception of Theseus by his divine father and stepmother stands in a relationship of symmetry and reversal to that by his human father and stepmother (Sourvinou-Inwood 1979, 27–28). The emphasis on Theseus's good and helpful divine step-mother, who is represented alone on the tondo, would be thus ex-plained. It balances and counterpoints the bad human stepmother, who threatened the hero's life but was defeated—a defeat that is, on my reading, the focus of the scene on B. These two arguments strongly sup-port the view that "Theseus with a drawn sword attacking a woman" represents Theseus attacking Medea after the discovery of the poisoning attempt and his recognition by Aegeus.

Furthermore, I submit that the reading of the scene on side B of our cup produces meanings that correspond very closely to my reconstruction of the end of Sophocles' *Aegeus*.[11] For in this scene Theseus has just stopped his attack on a woman shown standing near an altar; people in fear of their lives took refuge at an altar and, we saw, some scenes show the woman attacked by Theseus fleeing to an altar. Theseus is responding to Athena's command by stopping the attack and making a gesture of worship indicating obedience. Of course, this scene would be an autonomous image, not a faithful re-presentation of the tragic scene. Athena is not shown as a *dea ex machina*, but as an actual divine presence; the scene is not articulated as a theatrical performance, but is located in the mythological time of which the tragic articulations present themselves as reflections. The women are crowning Theseus in joyful celebration of the recognition of this acclaimed hero (who had performed exploits on the road from Troezen to Athens and defeated the bull) as Aegeus' son and heir to the Athenian throne. Plutarch (*Thes.* 12.3) describes a grateful public acknowledgment by the Athenians of Theseus as heir to the throne. As we saw, we have a close iconographic parallel for the schema "women crowning Theseus in celebration of his being acknowledged as their lord's son" in the representation of Theseus being crowned by the Nereids on the Zurich pointed amphora. In this particular context the crowning also signified Theseus's salvation from Medea's murderous plot and, through it, the historical motif for which this confrontation between Theseus and Medea was the mythological paradigm, the Greek victories over Persia.

What, it may be asked, of Aegeus's absence? Would it not be surprising if he were absent from a scene representing an event that followed immediately after his recognition of Theseus and depicted the celebration of this recognition? Far from it. For when we take account of the assumptions and perceptions relevant to this scene and the vase as a whole, we see that the following considerations are correlative with, and can thus be seen to underlie, the absence of Aegeus: (1) the emphasis on the divine parentage of Theseus and at the same time on his Athenian nationality; (2) the emphasis on the symbolic focus of the story, the confrontation between Theseus, the Athenian hero, and Medea, the ancestress of the Persians, and its function as a mythological prefiguration of, and paradigm for, the victory against the Persians in this symbolic mode so common to Greek iconography, especially in this period; (3) finally, the fact that Aegeus's role in the plot against Theseus was not glorious and thus would not be stressed in images glorifying Theseus and Athens. This last consideration may explain why the only known ceramic representations of the recognition are on two Apulian kraters reflecting Athenian tragedy (Brommer 1982, Pl. 44 [the Adophseck vase]; Plate 7 [the Leningrad vase]), despite the fact that this episode

stressed Theseus's Athenian identity. Brommer (1982, 127) acknowledged that the complete absence of Attic ceramic representations of
Theseus's recognition of Aegeus is remarkable. My interpretation can
explain this oddity, by showing that the recognition nexus became symbolically focused on, and represented by, the moment of its conclusion,
Theseus's attack on Medea, which elided Aegeus's complicity and focused on a symbolically potent confrontation that also expressed highly
pertinent patriotic historical and ideological meanings.

On my reading, one scene conflates and articulates emblematically
the recognition of Theseus by Aegeus and Medea's defeat and ultimate
expulsion. On side A of a neck amphora in a German private collection
(Hornbostel 1977, 332–35) a youth is shown, depicted according to the
commonest iconographic schema used for Theseus, with petasos slung
at the back of his neck, chlamys and endromides and holding two spears
that rest on the ground vertically, spearheads upwards, his sword hang-
ing in its scabbard. He is facing a mature, bearded king holding a scepter resting on the ground vertically. The two figures are looking at each
other. On B a woman is represented according to the "fleeing woman"
schema also used for the woman attacked by Theseus. She is looking
back, as is normal in this schema, and this visually connects side B with
the scene on A. Even if we disregard this (it may, after all, be a culturally
determined perception), the reconstruction of the process of meaning
creation suggests that much of the debate about this vase and the relationship between its two sides, reported by Hornbostel (1977, 332,
335), is misplaced.

It is not the vase painter's intentions, which are in any case inaccessible, that we should be trying to determine, but the process through
which the vase painting's contemporaries, reading through perceptual
filters shaped by the iconographic and semantic assumptions they
shared with the vase painter, made sense of it. The fact that the fleeing
woman is a codified sign that occurs in a variety of contexts does not
make it meaningless; as we saw, this, like all other, signs acquires meaning in context. Given the existence of the established iconographic
schema "Theseus attacking a woman with a sword," which sometimes
includes the figure of a king (ascribed crucial importance in the story
through the activation of semantic knowledge), I submit that, even independently of my particular interpretation of the theme, the juxtaposition of the fleeing woman with a youth represented according to the
schema used for Theseus, including the sword, and a king would have
activated that iconographic schema as part of the assumptions through
which the topic of the image was identified; and this would have inevitably led the viewers to connect the two sides and make sense of them

as one image. If my reading of the theme "Theseus with a sword" is correct, this diptych image makes perfect sense: the juxtaposition of a fleeing Medea with Theseus activates the "poison attempt–recognition–Medea's expulsion" nexus and thus identifies the king as Aegeus and the scene on A as an emblematic image of the relationship between the two figures as it emerged as a result of the recognition, father and son, king and heir. For on side A the image of the two looking at each other articulates the notion of a close relationship between them, which in this context can be seen as an emblematic representation of Theseus's recognition by Aegeus as well as a more general representation of Theseus, the son of Aegeus and future Athenian king. The scene may also have had more generic meanings pertaining to the relationship between father and son, the latter's accession to manhood at the completion of the ephebeia, and prospective replacement of the father as a warrior and citizen.

The close correspondence between the image on side B of the New York cup and the end of Sophocles' *Aegeus* as I had tentatively reconstructed it (Sourvinou-Inwood 1979, 56) confirms, I submit, the validity of that reconstruction by showing that the action plot I had predicted (since I had taken no account of this scene until Bérard's suggestion drew my attention to it) is in fact articulated iconographically. Such a confirmation of a prediction is one of the strongest forms of validation.

I will now try to show that the other proposed interpretations of the scene, based on an empirical matching of what is depicted with Theseus's career as it is known from the texts, are unsatisfactory even independently of the case for the reading proposed here. The least unconvincing is the interpretation (von Bothmer 1972, 52–53; Brommer 1982, 79) that Theseus is greeted by Athena and some of the grateful mothers of the victims intended for the Minotaur and that he has unsheathed his sword as he tells the story of his slaying of the Minotaur. A first serious objection against this reading is that it cannot account for the woman on the right of the altar. A second is that, insofar as we can judge, Athena's gesture toward Theseus does not indicate greeting but urges a course of action. It should be added that in the representation of Theseus's victory over the Minotaur on the stamnos Leningrad 804 (ARV^2 484.16), where Athena is greeting the hero and/or expressing her pleasure while a woman is crowning him, the goddess's gestures are very different from the one under discussion.

Even if we leave aside these two arguments entirely, I submit that Theseus's stance, and in particular the way he holds the sword, disallows the interpretation here under consideration. To begin with, the sword in itself cannot be considered as particularly characteristic of the

Minotaur adventure and thus capable of conveying the meaning that the
victory for which Theseus is being crowned is the one against the Minotaur. Moreover, his way of holding the sword does not suggest that he
is or had been, displaying it while narrating his adventures—even assuming that an image showing Theseus giving an illustrated (with ges-
ticular reconstruction) talk to the mothers of his companions (in the
absence of the latter) is a representation likely to have been articulated
in fifth century iconography and not a culturally determined construct,
which I doubt. He is not displaying the sword or holding it in a way that
can be seen as a modification of the displaying schema. Nor is he holding it in the way he does (always in his right hand) in the scenes representing the moment after his victory over the Minotaur (cf. e.g. London
E 84 [Brommer 1982, Pl. 13]) and on the Leningrad stamnos mentioned
above, where he is being crowned in the presence of Athena and other
spectators. Since the schema "sword in the left hand" here is a reversal
of "sword in the right hand" in positions of attack, it suggests not "display" but "not attack," in this case probably "desisting from attack." A
final argument against the interpretation under discussion is that if it
were correct, the three sides of this cup would be the only example of a
coherent Theseus cycle that has nothing to do with his exploits on the
road from Troezen to Athens (Brommer 1982, 79). This argument cannot, obviously, invalidate this interpretation, but it does add a little
weight to the strong cumulative case against it.

The other main hypothesis concerning the interpretation of our scene
is that it represents Theseus's arrival at Athens from Troezen (Froning
1971, 47–48; cf. Shapiro 1982, 297 and no. 29). A most serious objection to this interpretation is, as Brommer (1982, 79) noted, the absence
of Aegeus. Also, unless the scene is situated after the recognition, which
would virtually equate it to my reading, the unsheathed sword not only
does not make sense, but is in fact in conflict with the development of
the story.

In these circumstances, I submit that there can be little doubt that the
reading of the scene under discussion that emerged at the conclusion of
the detailed analyses set out here must be correct; it accounts for all
elements and aspects of the scene without leaving any unanswered problems, and in addition, it articulates a dramatic situation that was independently reconstructed on the basis of other evidence.

Let us now return to the iconographic theme "Theseus with a sword"
and consider the inscribed scene painted on the tondo of the cup Leningrad 1543 (649, St.830) by Macron (Plate 4; ARV^2 460.13; Add 120;
Sourvinou-Inwood 1979, 35, no. 1; Kron 1981, 422, no. 25), which
names the figures "Theseus" and "Aethra." The iconographic analysis

of this scene, whose schema is different from that of the others, shows (Sourvinou-Inwood 1979, 3–6) that it represents a serious, life-threatening attack. This is demonstrated through the analyses of the individual gestures and of the iconographic schema as a whole. There is a close iconographic parallel to the Leningrad scene, painted by an artist whose work is related to Macron's, the Brygos painter, and it represents a serious attack, Odysseus's attack against Circe (Sourvinou-Inwood 1979, 5). The similarities between these representations acquire even greater significance when it is considered that, as we saw, the closest iconographic parallels for the scenes depicted according to the iconographic schema "Theseus attacking a woman sword in hand" are representations of the same theme, Odysseus's attack against Circe. In these circumstances, it is certain that the scene on the Leningrad tondo represents a serious attack and cannot be explained away as horseplay.

The interpretation put forward by Kron (1981, 429), that Theseus is trying to force his mother with the sword to disclose his father's name while she is begging him not to undertake the dangerous journey, is not as unsatisfactory as the horseplay thesis, but, I believe, also incorrect. First, since the schema articulating the Macron scene corresponds to, and denotes, the established schema "serious attack," a fifth century artist would not have used it for, and his viewers would not have understood it to be, a different subject, in which the attack was not serious and the supplication was about something else entirely. Second, in the story as we understand it from the surviving sources (Sourvinou-Inwood 1971, 100–101; 1979, 6) the recovery of the gnōrismata and the revelation of Aegeus's fatherhood were inextricably connected; there was no point to the first without the second. This makes sense in terms of logic, mythological and "ordinary." If Macron had wished to create a new variant in which Aethra showed Theseus the gnōrismata but would not reveal his father's name, he would not, I submit, have chosen to articulate it by means of an iconographic schema his viewers would have understood to denote serious attack and supplication in response to it.

It cannot be claimed that the characters' names would have made the meaning clear. I do not know of any case in which the iconographic schema denotes a particular action plot, X, and the inscriptions alone alter this to make the schema denote an entirely different action plot, Y. Even if this were possible, the meaning of the scene would not have been clear because the viewers could only have read it as a representation of a serious attack by Theseus on his mother. I do not deny that inscriptions can be used to "surdéterminer le sens de l'image, ... imposer une lecture qui n'allait pas de soi" (Schnapp 1985, 75), nor do I deny the possibility of "les jeux savants de la composition." But we have to be certain in each specific case that we do not overinterpret and import our own preconceptions. Because we do not share the ancient assumptions, we have to reconstruct them systematically before deploying them. It is not methodologically legitimate simply to choose to privilege the inscriptions, especially since fifth century Athenian vase painters did not privilege writing in the way that our (academic) culture does. Furthermore, as we saw, we must protect our analyses from cultural determination by conducting each set separately, thus preventing the iconographic analyses from being contaminated by assumptions and expectations generated by the inscriptions and the (conscious or unconscious) consequent attempt to reconcile the two in what appears to us a logically satisfactory way. Thus, we must first try to reconstruct what the schema in itself meant before the inscriptions came into play. Of course, for the Athenians this was an interactive process, but our limited access entails that the rigorous strategy is to separate the two in the first stage of the investigation in order to avoid unconscious adjustments in the reading.

We must, then, begin with the fact that the analyses of the gestures, stances, and overall schema show that this is a serious, life-threatening attack. I should mention that, since the significance of the schema is the same, and the male protagonist is the same, there is a case for considering this scene to represent the same subject as the main series discussed above, especially since the closest iconographic parallels for both schemata are in representations of the same theme, Odysseus's attack on Circe. However, if the inscriptions are to be seen as creating a different reading from that created by the schema, then it would not follow that Macron's scene represents the same subject as the others (of which the only other early example known to me is Myson's scene [Sourvinou-Inwood 1979, 35, no. 2]). In that case the inscriptions would differentiate Macron's scene from the rest.

A series of semantic analyses (Sourvinou-Inwood 1979, 18–28, cf. 8–17) shows conclusively that in the Athenian myth of Theseus there was no space in which a life-threatening attack by Theseus against Aethra could have been located—not simply that we have no evidence for it, though we do not, not a single, even ambiguous and controversial, trace of such a story in the literary sources—but also that the structures and mentality of the myth exclude such a possibility. As I hope I have shown (Sourvinou-Inwood 1979, 7–17, especially 17) in matricide and averted matricide (as in patricide) myths, the hostility consistently begins with the parent, and in the Athenian myth of Theseus there was no space in which such an act of hostility from Aethra to Theseus could have been located (Sourvinou-Inwood 1979, 18–28). Patterns such as matricide and averted matricide in mythological schemata are not random; they are constant within certain parameters because the myths are structured by, and express as "messages" the realities, perceptions, beliefs, and ideologies of, the society that produced them (Sourvinou-Inwood 1979, 8–17; 1988a, section 2). In the myth of Theseus the schema I call, conventionally, "hostility between parent and child" has gravitated to the figure of the father and the stepmother, both of whom initiated acts of hostility toward Theseus (Sourvinou-Inwood 1979, 21–28). Moreover, the structures that determined this state of affairs were not open to variability; for they were correlative with the mythopoeic "compromise" between Athens and Troezen concerning Theseus's homeland (Sourvinou-Inwood 1979, 20–27), which shaped, determined, and dominated at least the fifth century and later versions of the Attic myth of Theseus.

There are also further reasons against the notion that the Theseus myth could have included an averted matricide schema and that Theseus would be represented as attacking his mother Aethra. As we saw, the stepmother is also a censored version of the mother, so that the attack on the stepmother is a censored version of an attack on the mother. This representation "attack on the mother" does not only correspond to certain attitudes toward the mother; it is polysemic. Myths of matricide are also structured by, and relate to, the pattern of adolescent initiation marking the passage from boyhood to manhood. In Greece as in other societies, "killing the mother" is an image for separation from the world of women and children and integration into the world of men. Symbolically, every Athenian ephebe had to overcome and "defeat" the figure of the mother in order to become fully male and join the world of men (Zeitlin 1978, 149–84). The representation of Theseus, the paradigmatic Athenian ephebe (various episodes of whose saga reflect, and are connected with, initiatory institutions and representations) attacking and defeating the figure of the mother fits perfectly within that context. However, this mother could not be Theseus's mother Aethra for a variety of reasons. First, as we saw, there was no place in his myth for a life-threatening attack on Aethra—a "justifiable" attack, that is, one that (according to the established mythological mentality as it can be observed in a variety of myths) would not leave Theseus's reputation besmirched. Second, whatever the symbolic meanings of the theme, a hero's attack on his mother was not perceived as a praiseworthy feat to be advertised on vases, as witness the paucity of representations depicting matricide or averted matricide. On the one hand, matricide as a symbolic representation was significant and, as it were, "desirable." On the other, matricide was a deplorable and dangerous act. Thus, the representation "attacking/killing the mother" is censored (Sourvinou-Inwood 1979, 12–14; 16–17). Averted matricide is one form of censoring; another, and more potent one, is novercacide—or, in the case of Theseus, averted novercacide, a double censure, which in the negative figure of Medea transforms the notion "attack on the mother" to "attack on a hostile stepmother who also happens to be an Easterner, a sorceress, and the ancestor of the country's enemy": a perfect representation crystallizing the multifaceted and polysemic exploits of Theseus, the ideal ephebe, who was also the hero standing for the Athenian people, who won the victories over the Persians with his help (Plu. Thes. 35.5; cf. Paus. 1. 15.3). To put it differently, Theseus, the ideal ephebe and male in general, was a matrix in which to articulate male existence as perceived in the fifth century Athenian practices and representations in a paradigmatic form. Thus, with regard to the mother, he had to express both sides of the ambivalent representations: he had to be a loving son, acting out the ideology about, and prescriptive behavior toward the mother; and he had symbolically to kill his mother in order to act out symbolically the ephebic transition. This was articulated through a split, following an established censoring modality for the "killing the mother" motif, helped by the historical development of the Theseus myth that dictated certain roles for Aethra and for Aegeus (Sourvinou-Inwood 1979, 18–25): the positive traits and behavior drifted to the mother, the negative to the stepmother, who, in the case of the Athenian hero par excellence was the bad mother/bad stepmother par excellence, the bad woman par excellence, who also came to represent Greece's historical enemy.

In addition, there is, in my view, a further possible reason why a myth and representation of Theseus attacking his mother would not have been appropriate. I suggest that the figure of Aethra had a different significance in Athenian myth and iconography in the second quarter of the fifth century, which would have blocked the creation of an iconographic type depicting Theseus attacking his mother. One segment of Aethra's myth was popular in Athenian iconography in the years that concern us, the story of her liberation (cf. Kron 1981, 426–27, nos. 59–76, 430; Kron 1976, 152–56): Aethra, who was guarding the abducted Helen for Theseus, had been taken prisoner by the Dioscuri when they liberated their sister and went to Troy as Helen's servant; after Troy's sack she was liberated by her grandsons, Theseus's sons, Acamas and Demophon. In my view, this theme's Athenian connections do not adequately explain its popularity, and especially the fact that it was represented on one of the metopes of the Parthenon. Kron's explanation

(1976, 155, n. 731) that it was not considered to be humiliating because it was celebrated as a paradigm for behavior characterized by *pietas* is probably right, but not, in my view, sufficient to explain it.

In order to reconstruct the meanings this particular theme had in the eyes of its contemporary viewers we must consider it in its full context; its iconographic and mythical context was the sack of Troy, which was one of the themes that came to symbolize, in the years following the Persian Wars, the Greek victories, seen in terms of Greece and civilization defeating barbarism and the Eastern "other." Part of those victories pertained to, and affected, Greeks under Persian rule. The notion of the liberation of the Ionians, the Athenians' kinsmen, matched, and thus, I suggest, came to be symbolized by, the myth that among the enemy at Troy was a servant, Aethra, who was closely connected with Athens, and whose grandsons were fighting on the Greek side. Besides the match of historical and mythological event, Aethra herself was an appropriate figure to represent Ionia. Leaving aside her general connections with Asia Minor through her grandfather Pelops (E. *Med.* 683–84), she had been Poseidon's beloved, and Poseidon was the god of the Panionion at Mycale and thus most closely associated with the notion "Ionia." Moreover, the nexus Ionia-Poseidon-liberation of Ionia was inevitably brought symbolically together by an event particularly associated with the liberation of Ionia, the battle of Mycale (Hdt. 9.90.96–106), in which the Ionians revolted against the Persians; in Herodotus's report of this battle, incidentally, the contribution of the Troezenians as well as of the Athenians (and the Corinthians and Sicyonians) is stressed (Hdt. 9.105).

If this hypothesis about Aethra's symbolism is right, it would further strengthen the conclusion that in the case of Theseus, the ideal Athenian hero, all the positive values have drifted to the mother and all the negative ones to the stepmother. The former is pushed toward the positive pole at every dimension of signification because the fully negative stepmother fills the negative role. Whatever its significance, the theme of Aethra's rescue is a reversal of the theme of Medea's expulsion from Attica: Medea is expelled from the family and from Attica and Greece (by her stepson) and goes to the East, while Aethra is brought back from the East and reintegrated into the family, Attica, and Greece (by her grandsons).

A final reason why the woman attacked by Theseus should not be Aethra is that the most consistent parallels for our theme are representations of an averted attack against a perfidious woman, which creates a presumption that our theme may also represent such an attack. Aethra did not have, in Attic myth, any trait, or perform any act, that could characterize her as a "perfidious woman," while Theseus is indeed known to have confronted and defeated a perfidious woman, Medea. This argument cannot on its own prove that the woman is Medea, but it adds weight to an already strong cumulative case.

Consequently, an attack by Theseus on Aethra does not fit either the mythological or the ideological level of signification of their myth, and there are many reasons for thinking that it was not part of that myth. How, then, do we explain the inscriptions on Macron's cup? We must begin by acknowledging that there is a contradiction between representation and inscription. Two easy ways of eliminating this contradiction are both, I submit, fallacious. First, to assume that we have misread the scene is fallacious because the reading is based on a series of systematic analyses, the results of all aspects of which converge. Recovery of the iconographic assumptions through which Macron's contemporaries read the scene shows incontrovertibly that they would have read it as a serious, life-threatening attack.

The second easy way out is through rejection of the notion that we can reconstruct the structures of myths and mythological schemata in ways that allow us to determine whether a particular mythological schema (such as matricide or averted matricide) can have been part of a particular hero's myth. Such a rejection appears rigorous because it wears the mask of scepticism, and our own culturally determined mode of reception privileges the sceptical articulation, the "we cannot know" mode; but in fact it is fallacious because it relies on hidden assumptions that, when unraveled, appear questionable. It entails the implicit belief that mythological articulations and developments happened at random, that there were no constricting factors guiding their development. This belief is wrong; it ignores the nature of myth in general and Greek myth in particular. That Theseus was the Athenian hero par excellence, the paradigmatic ephebe, and the good king, and that Aegeus was his mortal father and Poseidon his divine one, had certain implications for the articulation of his myth. This myth did change, it generated new variants over the years, under the influence, and in response to, a variety of historical and other factors. But these developments were always determined by the parameters of what was appropriate to or compatible in the Greek mentality with these roles (with all their ambivalences and ambiguities, of course), in interaction with the parameters derived from the schemata that came into play (for example, that in matricide and patricide the hostility begins with the parent, determined by the "messages" articulating these schemata, which express the beliefs, practices, and ideologies of the society) and, of course, in interaction also with the main lines of the myth, which were themselves structured by the above factors and parameters.

Perversions of these established myths are possible in particular genres, such as comedy, but they have to be seen as they would have been perceived by their contemporary viewers, through the perceptual filters created by the conventions of the genre and the context of the articulation, a distortion of the norm deployed as an ad hoc creation to serve the comedian's comic purpose. A similar interpretation of Macron's cup as an ad hoc comic or parodic creation, a subversion of the norm, is not impossible, at least in theory. But this does not entail that there was a reference myth that the image reflected, nor that all the other scenes also represented this distortion. On the contrary, such a distortion could not have become as popular a theme in Attic iconography, especially between the 460s and 440s, as the theme "Theseus attacking a woman with a sword" was. In addition, since the confrontation between Theseus and Medea is a mythological fact, attested in the sources, whose meanings, we saw, inevitably included a symbolism pertaining to the victories over the Persians, representations of Theseus attacking a woman were bound to be interpreted as representations of that confrontation and victory, unless information was given to the contrary, and in all the other scenes it was not. Moreover, in order to make sense as a parody, Macron's creation would have needed to have been parasitic on a straightforward, established myth and/or its iconographic reflections, which in the circumstances would mean parasitic on the myth and representation "Theseus confronts and defeats Medea." This, then, is one possible explanation of the contradiction between, on the one hand, the iconographic schema that represents an attack and, on the other, the mythological relationship of the figures named by the inscription, which did not include the possibility of a serious attack.

The other possible explanation, which is the one I proposed (1979, 29–30), is that the inscription "Aethra" is the result of a slip of the pen. I must stress that the slip of the pen is an attested phenomenon in Attic red-figure vase painting. An interesting comparable example is seen on a lekane fragment in Leningrad representing an erotic pursuit, in which the youth is inscribed "Theseus" and the pursued girl "Thetis" (Sourvinou-Inwood 1987a, Pl. IIb). Beazley (1954, 81) took "Thetis" to be a slip, and indeed this is the most likely explanation; alternatively, the theme of Theseus's erotic pursuit may have been deliberately conflated with the semantically and iconographically closely related theme of the erotic pursuit of Thetis by Peleus—some kind of joke or play (Sourvinou-Inwood 1987a, 133, 134–35, 138–39). This undeniable example of what is either a slip of the pen or an "incongruity" of a different kind suggests that when two themes or figures are closely related there is the possibility of unconscious (slip) or conscious (conflation/joke) slippage. The figures of Medea and Aethra are very closely related in precisely the kind of relationship that is likely, and known to, generate such slips at a variety of levels, and through a variety of mechanisms, any one of which is sufficient to generate a slip. It can be called a textbook case of a slip of the pen (Sourvinou-Inwood 1979, 29–30, 69, nn. 112–18; Timpanaro 1976, 147–48 cf. 22, n. 4; Fowler 1982, 273–74, 278–79).

This slip, if it is a slip, would involve antonyms (the mother's name for the stepmother's). In addition, it can also be seen as a "Freudian" slip, in so far as it would decensor the censored version of the killing of the mother, since at one particular level of signification Medea is a transformation of Aethra, and the attack on the stepmother a transformation of the schema "killing the mother." This may have been explicated, whether unconsciously, as a slip of the pen, or consciously, as a result of a deliberate manipulation, through the creation of a variant iconographic schema without a mythological reference. Thus in a way the distinction between the two alternative possibilities is deconstructed. Finally, with regard to the possibility of a slip of the pen, there is a third type of propitious condition for the generation of such a slip; the context, the Trojan scene on the outside with Demophon and Acamas, may have called up Aethra's name and encouraged a contextually produced slip.

Since there are very good reasons for thinking that a life-threatening attack on Aethra could not have been part of Theseus's Attic myth, while it could make some sense as an ad hoc image created as a transformation of the "Theseus attacking Medea" theme, it follows that if the inscription "Aethra" on the Macron cup is not the result of a slip of the pen but of an intentional manipulation, the scene would not be the representation of a mythological theme, referring to a story about Theseus's relationship to Aethra, but an image pertaining to a symbolic aspect of Theseus's persona—especially to his persona as an ephebe. Let us now consider a related question, one that may help us approach the problem from another angle. If the "Aethra" inscription was the result of a slip, how would the Athenian viewers have made sense of the scene? After what has been said above, we can assert that they made sense of it through the filter, as a perversion, of Theseus's attack on Medea; either they would have identified the inscription as a mistake, or they would have read it as an image to be understood without a myth, functioning at the symbolic level of signification in connection with Theseus and in particular with the directly related myth and schema "Theseus attack-

ing Medea." That is, "Aethra attacked by Theseus" only made sense by
being parasitic on "Medea attacked by Theseus." It is possible to identify a context in which such a perversion of Theseus's confrontation
with, and victory over, Medea could be seen as a political parody.

First I shall consider an aspect of the reading of Macron's Leningrad
cup that I have hitherto neglected: the scenes on the outside. On side A
(Plate 5) are shown Diomedes and Odysseus, each holding a palladium,
quarreling, in the presence of Demophon and Acamas, Agamemnon
and Phoenix; all the figures are named.[12] On B Greek princes are shown
(Plate 6). Though the exact meaning of the scene is problematic, the
representation of the two palladia and the presence of Demophon and
Acamas next to each of the two litigants indicate that the variant articulated here was some variation of the story according to which the true
palladium ended up in Athens.[13] Thus A and B depict an episode from
the Trojan War that had a special reference, first, to the Greek victory,
since Troy could not be taken until the palladium was stolen from it,
and second, to Athens. Moreover, this image also created meanings at a
further level of signification. In the years following the Persian Wars the
Trojan War functioned as a mythological paradigm and symbolic representation of those wars, and in particular of the Athenian contribution, especially Cimon's aggressive campaigns against the Persians
(Gauer 1968, 19, 106–17; Thomas 1976, 65). At least by the time of
the Eurymedon victory (a decade or so later than our scene)[14] the palladium was an important element in that symbolic connection (Amandry
1954, 314–15; Thomas 1976, 62). Consequently, an important facet of
signification in the scenes on A and B referred to the Greek victories over
the Persians, with a special emphasis on Athens in general and Cimon
in particular. Given that Macron often painted connected scenes on the
tondo and the outside of a cup,[15] and that the tondo scene on the Leningrad cup does not involve a Trojan theme, this state of affairs suggests
that this tondo scene is likely to represent a mythological theme with a
symbolic meaning pertaining to the Greek, and especially Athenian, and
in particular Cimonian, victories over Persia. My interpretation of the
image as Theseus attacking Medea, a myth that also functioned as a
symbolic representation of, and paradigm for, the Greek and especially
Athenian, victories, fits this requirement precisely, and this is an important argument in its favor.

In that context, and given the very significant promotion of the figure
of Theseus by Cimon (Sourvinou-Inwood 1971, 108–9; 1979, 54–55)
and the consequent symbolic association between the two figures in the
semantic knowledge of the time, the viewers may have seen the Theseus
of the tondo also through the filter of Cimon. Cimon and his (and his

father's) Persian victories would have been connoted unproblematically if Theseus's antagonist and victim were Medea, but with Aethra in that role (and in the absence of a mythological reference) meaning becomes problematic, and the image could only function with reference to the "Theseus attacking Medea" theme, as a parody and a perversion of it. It cannot be totally excluded that this was, and was perceived to be, a perversion of the accepted schema used for "Theseus attacking Medea" scenes, here deployed to create a negative image of Theseus, and through him of Cimon. Theseus attacks, instead of his guilty stepmother, his own innocent mother. Could this be the expression of a negative view of Cimon's generalship of the Delian League (through a trope deploying the symbolic association between Aethra and the liberated Ionians [if the latter has been correctly identified])? I do not, personally, find this cartoon type of reading very convincing, nor do I find any other images in Macron's work that could be seen as allowing the space for comparable practices. But the possibility cannot be totally excluded.

In these circumstances, we conclude that, while all the other representations of "Theseus with a drawn sword" depict Theseus and Medea, Macron's, which also represents a serious attack by Theseus against a woman, depicts, as it now stands, something else: the woman here is his mother instead of his stepmother, named through an inscription that is either a slip of the pen or a tool through which Macron created an ad hoc iconographic articulation without a mythological reference, probably a parodic image, and certainly one parasitic on the theme "Theseus's confrontation with, and defeat of, Medea."

Before leaving this cup, I must consider very briefly the notion (which raises issues of great methodological importance) that there were other versions of the myth of Medea in Athens, unattested in the surviving literary sources but reflected in some representations on vases. The idiom of Attic red-figure inconography is not solely, or indeed above all, descriptive-narrative (Moret 1984, 154–55); it does not only represent (mythological and other) events and stories as they (were perceived to have) happened; it also articulates particular perceptions of those events and stories, and it weaves emblematic figures like Erotes into mythological and genre scenes.[16] In one particular modality of representation iconographic elements are juxtaposed which were heretofore separate in (the mythological or everyday) reality; they are deployed emblematically; thus, for example, a space is constructed that expresses certain symbolic values (Durand and Lissarague 1980, 103 and passim) and articulates iconographically particular perceptions of the theme represented without a (real or mythological) referent (Sourvinou-Inwood 1987a, 141–47). One version of this modality juxtaposes in the same scene figures who belonged to different periods. Thus, for example, in the representation of the birth of Erichthonius by the Codrus painter (who also painted one of the scenes relevant to our discussion, to which I will refer below) on the cup Berlin F 2537 (ARV² 1268.2; Add 177), Aegeus and his brother Pallas are shown present at the birth of Erichthonius, which according to mythological history took place long before they were born. Another juxtaposes figures who were not in the same place in the mythological "reality" (Raeck 1984, 22–23).

Consequently, it is not legitimate to assume that, unless the contrary is proved beyond doubt, all representations are "descriptive-narrative," represent figures interacting as they did at a particular moment in (mythical) time; therefore, it is not legitimate to consider the presence of a figure in a context from which, according to the extant versions of her story, she was absent as constituting evidence of unknown versions of her myth (cf. also Moret 1984, 153). The hidden presumption of which such notions rely implicitly is that if a descriptive narrative reading is possible it should be preferred, a presumption that has no epistemological or methodological basis. It is simply the unconscious result of our own culturally determined assumptions and expectations, based on an unarticulated assumption that "realism" or its nearest approximation, in this case the descriptive-narrative mode representing the events of one particular moment, is "natural" and everything else is an exception—a presumption that is wholly unjustified in a highly conventional idiom such as that of red-figure vase painting, in which the emblematic mode is demonstrably important. Thus, for example, the fact that on side A of the cup Bologna PU 273 by the Codrus painter (ARV² 1268.1; Add 177) Medea and Aethra are shown in the same scene, a representation of Theseus's departure for one of his adventures, does not suggest that there was a version of a myth that placed Medea and Aethra in Athens together.

Limitations of space force me to set out my detailed reading of the Bologna cup elsewhere. Here I will only mention that the analysis of the scenes on sides A and B and on the tondo of the cup shows that they do not re-present events as they were perceived to have taken place at a particular moment in the mythical past, but are emblematic scenes constructed to articulate certain representations of a mythical past, with direct and complex symbolic associations to the present. Therefore, this and other such scenes do not testify to the existence of unknown versions of the myth of Medea in Athens. I must stress that even if there were such unknown myths unattested in the surviving literary sources, my argument that there cannot have been a myth in which Theseus attacked his mother would not be affected; as I have tried to show, the parameters determining the developments of Theseus's myth did not allow a space in which such an attack could have been located.

To conclude this essay, I consider, and briefly answer, some objections against my interpretation raised by Brommer, because they involve serious methodological issues. His objections run as follows (Brommer 1982, 134, n. 21).

(1) *The subject I propose is not attested in the literary tradition* (Brommer 1982, 126, note; 134, n. 21). This is entirely incorrect, and the formulation of this objection exemplifies one of the flaws in Brommer's approach to the iconography of Greek myths. The reality is that what is not attested is a specific description of an attack of Theseus on Medea, sword in hand; the story of the confrontation between the two and of Medea's murderous plot and the story that Theseus threw her out of Attica are amply attested.[17] Whether or not Theseus had intended to kill her in the myth, we can reasonably conclude that the act of throwing her out of the country was not, in the circumstances, an amicable, friendly operation, but a hostile and violent act, whose iconographic articulation our scenes clearly are. But in any case, even leaving such reasonable conclusions aside, since the main confrontation and hostility and Theseus's defeat of Medea and her plots are unambiguously attested, the only way this objection can be taken to be correct is if we understand the notion "attested in the literary sources" to be equivalent to "precisely described."

For this notion to make any sense, let alone to be a valid argument against my thesis, it would be necessary to rely on an assumption that is in reality entirely fallacious: that vase painters were directly and narrowly dependent on texts, that they translated texts into pictorial images, and that they did not create their own iconographic versions, did not manipulate the schemata to create different versions of the same stories (cf. e.g. Sourvinou-Inwood 1987b, 44), did not condense action into symbolic crystallizations, did not use emblematic elements to articulate particular perceptions, constructions of the *imaginaire social* (Durand and Lissarague 1980, 89 and passim) because only in that case can a confrontation often referred to in the surviving texts be said not to be attested in the literary sources. This is a demonstrably erroneous view of Greek ceramic iconography, which had its own freedom of creation in the treatment of mythological and other subjects and did not necessarily depend closely on texts (Touchefeu 1983, 22–26; Moret 1984, 153–58) and which produced polysemic images articulating complex perceptions through the manipulation of conventional iconographic schemata. Theseus attacking Medea to kill her, or Theseus throwing Medea out of Attica, either or both could be represented through the iconographic schema under discussion; and either or both represented (inevitably, given the assumptions of the time), among other things, also the Greek victory over the Persians, with whom Medea was symbolically identified, a symbolic association that, we saw, is also mentioned in the literary sources.

As it happens, in this particular case, even if the erroneous perception of the relationship between text and image referred to above were right, Brommer would still have been wrong to use against my interpretation the argument that the story represented in these images according to that interpretation is not attested in the sources. For since the relevant tragedies have not survived, the story of Medea's attempt on Theseus's life and its aftermath is preserved only in mythographic summaries. Thus the nature of the surviving sources precludes the inclusion of a detailed description of the hostile violent act that followed Aegeus's recognition of Theseus and preceded and brought about Medea's expulsion; all that could be attested in any case is the core of the story of the confrontation, and this is indeed well attested. The story that is *not* attested is the alleged attack of Theseus against Aethra. Even the notion that a deity intervened to avert the killing of Medea and predict her future settlement in the land of the Medes is not without textual support. Theopompus's fragment 17K from the *Theseus* parodies an address to Medea (Herter 1939, 318, n. 389) in which she is told by a prophesying god (Herter 1973, 1083) that she will settle in the land of the Medes, which fits precisely my reconstruction of the tragedy (Sourvinou-Inwood 1979, 56–57), now, I submit, also supported by the reading of the New York cup.

In these circumstances, it is clear that Brommer's first objection against my hypothesis is invalid.

(2) *My interpretation is not attested through inscriptions on vases.* This is correct. But this state of affairs pertains also with respect to many other iconographic subjects, including, for example, another popular theme involving Theseus, his erotic pursuit of a girl (Sourvinou-Inwood 1987a 132–36). There is nothing odd about this, given that inscriptions played only a minor role in the construction and manipulation of iconographic schemata.

(3) *He, Brommer, knows at least twenty more representations of Theseus attacking a woman in addition to those I listed (Sourvinou-Inwood 1979, 35–41), so that this story would have been represented more often than any other Theseus story except for the Minotaur and the bull.* This alleged objection in fact provides very strong support for my interpretation. The popularity of the scene cannot be explained if it represented an unattested attack of Theseus against his mother which (even suppos-

ing I am mistaken, and it did exist in the myth of Theseus) did not arouse sufficient interest to leave any traces in the surviving literary sources. It does, on the other hand, make perfect sense, as does its concentration in the decades 460s to 440s, if it represents, as I suggested, Theseus's confrontation with and victory over Medea, a polysemic image that among other things was a symbolic representation of the Greek, and especially Athenian, victories against the Persians. Indeed, in my view, only this type of image can explain its popularity.

(4) *The woman is never shown in Oriental dress, as we would have expected her to be if she were Medea, and if the theme of Theseus attacking Medea symbolized the Greek victory over the Persians* (Brommer 1982, 134, n. 21; Bérard 1980, 620). The first argument against this objection pertains to the pattern of appearance of the scenes: the overwhelming majority of them were painted between the 470s and the 440s; only in the second half of the century is Medea given Oriental dress—and then, of course, not always. It follows then, first, that the iconographic schema under consideration had become firmly established by the time Oriental dress became an element that could be selected and, second, that Oriental dress was not an available iconographic choice for Medea in the period in which the schema was popular and symbolically most potent. But it can be asked why, if my reading is indeed correct, didn't they earlier invent Oriental costume, which would have made explicit the symbolic identification between Medea and the Persians?

Leaving aside the fact that the question is itself culturally determined—it relies on expectations formed after certain choices (that changed perceptions) had been made—there is a very good reason why Medea in this scene is never shown wearing Oriental costume. Myths and their images are polysemic. The fact that Medea came to stand for the Persian enemy did not entail that the meanings attached to her figure and to her confrontation with Theseus were limited to just this one—however important—semantic dimension. Medea was also a particular version of the figure of the mother, and this particular transformation of the schema "killing the mother" articulated, and was articulated by, important meanings in the eyes of fifth century Athenians. Thus the representations of Theseus attacking Medea were polysemic images, crystallizing the multifaceted exploits of Theseus as the ideal ephebe and the paradigm for the Athenian male, as well as the Athenian hero par excellence and a symbol of Athens. For these images to function in this complex way, the censored version of the mother whom Theseus was confronting had to be depicted as a generic woman/mother. The use of Oriental dress would have produced closure of a whole dimension of

meanings, blocked Medea's signification of "woman" and "mother" in
general, and thus also the production of the ephebic nexus of the scene's
meanings (which was not necessarily consciously articulated) and limited the scene's meanings to the historical/ideological ones. On my reading, Medea in these scenes is at the same time the mother, the (dangerous) female, and the symbol for the Persians, in a rich and polysemic
process of meaning production involving fundamental Athenian perceptions and ideas that operated at different levels of signification. It is because in the artists' perceptions Medea in this episode stood also for
"woman" and "mother" that the selection "Oriental dress" was
blocked for them.

(5) *The woman is never shown holding the vessels that Medea is
holding in other representations of the Theseus cycle.* This is factually
correct. (As Bérard 1980, 618–19 noted, the fragment of the left hand
with the jug in my no. 26 does not belong.) However, this is not an
argument against the Medea identification, for it makes perfect sense
that Medea in these scenes should not be characterized by the vessels
involved in the poisoning. First, as we saw, there were good reasons,
pertaining to one of the important facets of the scene's signification,
why she should be represented through as generic an iconographic
schema as possible, and this drift was underpinned by the fact that the
scene's high codification made the protagonists' identities unambiguous
(Sourvinou-Inwood 1979, 39). Second, the vessels' absence also makes
sense in purely narrative terms, for in the dominant articulations of the
myth Medea had not been holding any of her vessels at that particular
moment: in one representation inspired by tragedy, on the Adolphseck
krater depicting the recognition of Theseus (Brommer 1982, Pl. 44) she
drops the jug at the moment of the recognition in surprise and conster-
nation; in the second recognition scene, on the bell krater Leningrad W
205 (Plate 7; Cambitoglou and Trendall 1961, 27 pl., viii, Figs. 37–38)
she does not have a jug or other vessel. (Medea is probably the seated
woman, but in any case neither woman has any vessels.) This dissocia-
tion of Medea from the vessels is confirmed, and its importance enhanced, by the consideration that it is emblematically significant because it also denotes the failure of her plot and her transformation from
aggressor to hunted woman and eventually exile. Consequently, the fact
that the woman whom Theseus is attacking, sword in hand, is not holding the vessels associated in other scenes with Medea is not a valid objection to her identification as Medea. On the contrary, it makes perfect
sense at every level of signification.

This section of this discussion, then, demonstrates once again the
dangers of reading the ancient images through the distorting mirrors of

our own culturally determined assumptions and expectations, and thus also the need for a systematic methodology that can, as far as possible, block this process and allow us to reconstruct (however partially) the ways in which the images' contemporary viewers made sense of them. I hope to have shown that the methodology I have here advocated and illustrated meets these requirements.

NOTES

a. Beginning in the classical period, with the compilation and organization of myths. See the article, "Mythographers," in *The Oxford Classical Dictionary*, 2nd ed.

b. Scheibler 1983, 9.

c. Brommer 1973 lists more than eight thousand vases. The first sentence of the preface to Brommer 1980 states: "It surpasses the power of a single person to collect and to make an orderly presentation of all the representations of groups of divinities on Greek vases." Indexes of mythological subjects in ABV, 723–28, ARV², vol. 3:1720–32, and Beazley 1971, 531–35.

d. Cook 1977.

e. Keuls 1988 on data bases.

f. Moret 1984, 153–62.

g. Bérard 1983b, 5–12.

h. See *La cité des images*.

i. See her methodological discussion in Sourvinou-Inwood 1987.

j. For the French and Swiss, see, in addition to *La cité des images* and the works of Moret and Bérard already cited, Bérard, Bron, and Pomari 1987. For British and American ventures, see, for example, Moon 1983.

I am indebted to Dr. I. Saverkina and the Hermitage Museum, Leningrad, for Plates 2 and 4–7, to Dr. J. Prag for Plate 1, to the Trustees of the British Museum for Plate 3, and to the Metropolitan Museum, New York, for Plates 8–10.

1. My focus here is the classical world. I take account of the preceding archaic age but do not consider the Hellenistic period.

2. A few references to discussions of cultural determination in sensory perception and in the perception of pictorial representations: Gregory 1966, 204–28; Gombrich 1977, 76–77, 170–203, 231; Gombrich 1971, 158. On perceptual controls in general cf. e.g. Douglas 1982, 1–8.

3. On signs and signification: cf. e.g. Derrida, 1972, 29–46; 105–30; Derrida, 1974–76, 11–15, 44–73; Derrida 1973, 129–60; Derrida 1967, 311–14; Culler 1981, 41–42.

4. Girls and women are represented through the same iconographic type in fifth century iconography (cf. Sourvinou-Inwood 1988c, Pt. 1, Section i).

5. On codification: Guiraud 1975, 24–25.

6. On this type of indeterminacy see also Schefold 1975, 27; Krauskopf 1977, 28.

7. The consideration of such combinations can offer some support for a proposed identification of a subject, but because there is not always a thematic connection between the scenes on a vase, they cannot invalidate it (cf. Sourvinou-Inwood 1987a, 148–50).

8. We are here concerned with the versions dominant in the Athenian mythological representations, not those in which the murder of her children had cultic connections and different connotations (Brelich 1969, 356–65; Page 1938, xxi-xxv). Ideally, we should consider each text and each image separately; but the limitations of space make this impossible. (On the history of her myth and its chronology see Simon 1954, 203–27; Page 1938, xxi-xxxix; Sourvinou-Inwood 1979, 53). Though each articulation of the myth was autonomous, the fact that the main lines of her story and persona appear to be constant makes the procedure followed here legitimate, especially since the semantic knowledge pertaining to Medea activated by our images is made up of precisely such a conflation.

9. I owe this reference to Professor W. Burkert.

10. On Datis: Raubitschek 1957, 234–42; Lewis 1980, 194–95.

11. I believe this cup was painted in the 460s; this date would fit with the date of production I proposed for Sophocles' *Aegeus* (Sourvinou-Inwood 1979, 57).

12. On the scene: Moret 1975, 71–73; Kron 1976, 149–51; Scheibler 1960, 83.

13. On the myths pertaining to the Trojan palladium cf. Nilsson 1967, 435–36; Kron 1976, 149–51.

14. I would date this cup somewhere in the 470s. Others think Macron's career stopped at 480. Chronological precision is not, in my view, possible at this particular moment in Attic vase painting.

15. Cf. e.g. Louvre G 153 (ARV² 460.14; Add 120): on the tondo the ransom of Hector, on A-B the sacrifice of Polyxena; Athens Acr. 327 (ARV² 461.23): Athena and Giant on the tondo, on A-B Gigantomachy; Orvieto Faina 36 (ARV² 461.39): I. Maenad, A-B satyrs and Maenads; cf. also ARV² 462 nos. 41–45, 47–48; ARV² 463.50–53; 464.76, and many others.

16. Cf. e.g. in a mythological scene by Macron: on side A of the scyphus Boston 13.186 (ARV² 458.1; Add 119). Cf. also in a "genre" wedding scene: loutrophoros Boston 10.223 (ARV² 1017.44; Oakley 1982, 115, Fig. 2). Cf. also Shapiro 1986, 3–23.

17. For the testimonia cf. Sourvinou-Inwood 1979, 22–24; 49; cf. also above on the story that she went to the land of the Medes. The version in which it is stated that Theseus cast her out is Apollod. *Epit.* 1.5–6 (on which cf. Sourvinou-Inwood 1979, 52, 55).

WORKS CITED

ABV = Beazley, J. D. 1956. *Attic Black-Figure Vase Painters*. Oxford.

Add = Burn, Lucilla, and Ruth Glynn, eds. 1982. *Beazley Addenda. Additional References to ABV, ARV² and Paralipomena*. Oxford.

Amandry, Pierre. 1954. "Notes de topographie et d'architecture delphiques." *BCH* 78:295–315.

ARV² = Beazley, J. D., 1963. *Attic Red-Figure Vase-Painters*. 2nd ed. Three vols. Oxford.

Beazley, J. D. 1954. In Caskey, Lacy D., and J. D. Beazley, *Attic Vase Paintings in the Museum of Fine Arts, Boston*. Pt. II. Boston.

———. 1971. *Paralipomena*. Oxford.

Bérard, Claude. 1976. "Axie taure." In *Mélanges d'histoire ancienne et d'archéologie, offerts à Paul Collart*. Lausanne.

———. 1980. Review of Sourvinou-Inwood 1979. *Gnomon* 52: 616–20.

———. 1983a. "Héros de tout poil. D'Héraklès imberbe à Tarzan barbu." In Lissarague and Thelamon 1983: 111–18.

———. 1983b. "Iconographie-Iconologie-Iconologique." *EL* 4: 5–37.

———, C. Bron, and A. Pomari, eds. 1987. *Images et société en Grèce ancienne*. Lausanne.

Boardman, John. 1982. "Herakles, Theseus and Amazons." In Donna C. Kurtz and Brian Sparkes, eds. *The Eye of Greece: Studies in the Art of Athens* (Festschrift for C. M. Robertson, 1–28. Cambridge.

Bothmer, Dietrich von. 1972. *Bulletin of the Metropolitan Museum of Art, New York* 31: 32 33.

Brelich, Angelo. 1969. *Paides e parthenoi*. Rome.

Brommer, Frank. 1982. *Theseus. Die Taten des griechischen Helden in der antiken Kunst und Literatur*. Darmstadt.

Cambitoglou, A., and A. D. Trendall. 1961. *Apulian Red-figured Vase-Painters of the Plain Style*. Rutland, VT.

La cité des images: Religion et société en Grèce antique. 1984. Lausanne.

Cook, R. M. 1977. *Greek Painted Pottery*. 2nd ed. London.

Culler, Jonathan. 1981. *The Pursuit of Signs, Semiotics, Literature, Deconstruction*. London.

Derrida, Jacques. 1967. *L'écriture et la différence*. Paris.

———. 1972. *Positions*. Paris.

———. 1973. *Speech and Phenomena and Other Essays on Husserl's Theory of Signs*. Evanston, Il.

———. 1974–76. *Of Grammatology*. Baltimore.

Douglas, Mary. 1982. "Introduction to Grid/Group Analysis." In M. Douglas, ed. *Essays in the Sociology of Perception*, 1–8. London.

Durand, Jean-Louis, and François Lissarague. 1980. "Un lieu d'image? L'espace du loutérion." *Hephaistos* 2: 89–106.

——— and ———. 1983. "Héros cru ou hôte cuit: histoire quasi cannibale d' Héraklès chez Busiris." In Lissarague and Thelamon 1983, 153–67.

Eco, Umberto. 1976. *A Theory of Semiotics*. Bloomington, IN.

———. 1981. *The Role of the Reader. Explorations in the Semiotics of Texts*. London.

Fowler, Carol A. 1982. Review of V. Fromkin, ed. 1980. *Errors in Linguistic Performance: Slips of the Tongue, Ear, Pen and Hand*. In Anne Cutler, ed. *Slips of the Tongue and Language Production*, 265–86. Berlin.

Froning, Heide. 1971. *Dithyrambos und Vasenmalerei in Athen*. Würzburg.

Gauer, Werner. 1968. *Weihgeschenke aus den Perserkriegen*. Tübingen.

Gombrich, Ernst H. 1971. *Meditations on a Hobby Horse and Other Essays on the History of Art*. 2nd ed. London.

———. 1977. *Art and Illusion. A Study in the Psychology of Pictorial Representation*. 5th ed. Oxford.

Graf, Fritz. 1979. "Apollo Delphinios." *MH* 36:2–22.

Gregory, Richard L. 1966. *Eye and Brain: The Psychology of Seeing*. London.

Guiraud, P. 1975. *Semiology*. London.

Hanson, J. O. de G. 1965. "The Secret of Medea's Success," *G&R* 12: 54–61.

Herter, Hans. 1939. "Theseus der Athener." *RhM* 88: 244–86; 289–326.

———. 1973. "Theseus." *RE* Supplementband 13: 1045–1238.

Hornbostel, Wilhelm. 1977. *Kunst der Antike. Schätze aus Norddeutschem Privatbesitz*. Mainz.

Isler-Kerenyi, Cornelia. 1977. *Lieblinge der Meermädchen. Achilleus und Theseus auf einer Spitzamphora aus der Zeit der Perserkriege*. Zurich.

Kebric, Robert B. 1983. *The Paintings in the Cnidian Lesche at Delphi and their Historical Context*. Leiden.

Keuls, Eva. 1988. "The *Corpus Vasorum Antiquorum,* the *Lexicon Iconographicum Mythologiae Classicae,* and the Beazley Archive Project: Different Data Bases for the Study of Ancient Greek Iconography." *Modern Greek Studies Yearbook,* 4:213–34.

Knox, Bernard M. W. 1977. "The *Medea* of Euripides." *YCS* 25: 193–25.

Krauskopf, Ingrid. 1977. "Eine attisch schwarzfigurige Hydria in Heidelberg." *AA* 1977: 13–37.

Kron, Uta. 1976. *Die zehn attischen Phylenheroen, Geschichte, Mythos, Kult und Darstellungen*. Berlin.

———. 1981. "Aithra I." *Lexicon Iconographicum Mythologiae Classicae* I, 420–31. Zurich.

Lewis, David L. 1980. "Datis the Mede." *JHS* 100: 194–95.

Lissarague, François, and Thelamon, Françoise, eds. 1983. *Image et céramique grecque. Actes du Colloque de Rouen*. Rouen.

Metzger, Henri. 1985. "Sur le valeur de l'attribut dans l'interprétation de certaines figures du monde éleusinien." In *Eidolopoiia. Actes du Colloque sur les problèmes de l' image dans le monde méditerranéen classique*. Rome.

Moon, Warren G., ed. 1983. *Ancient Greek Art and Iconography*. Wisconsin Studies in Classics. Madison.

Moret, Jean-Marc. 1975. *L'Ilioupersis dans la céramique italiote. Les mythes et leurs expression figurée au IVe siècle*. Rome.

———. 1984. *Oedipe, la Sphinx et les Thébains. Essai de mythologie iconographique*. 2 vols. Rome.

Mylonas, George E. 1961. *Eleusis and the Eleusinian Mysteries*. Princeton, NJ.

Neumann, Gerhard. 1965. *Gesten und Gebärden in der griechischen Kunst*. Berlin.

———. 1979. *Probleme des griechischen Weihreliefs*. Tübingen.

Nilsson, Martin P. 1967. *Geschichte der Griechischen Religion*. Vol. I, 3rd ed. Munich.

Oakley, John H. 1982. "The Anakalypteria." *AA* 1982: 113–18.

Page, Denys L. ed. 1938. *Euripides: Medea*. Oxford.

Petrakos, Basil. 1981. *National Museum, Sculpture–Bronzes–Vases*. Athens.

Prag, John (A. J. N. W.). 1985. *The Oresteia. Iconographic and Narrative Tradition*. Warminster, UK.

Raeck, Wulf. 1984. "Zu Erzählweise archaischer und klassischer Mythenbilder." *JDAI* 99: 1–25.

Raubitschek, Anthony E. 1957. ""Das Datislied." In Konrad Schauenburg, ed. *Charites. Studien zur Altertumswissenschaft (Festschrift for E. Langlotz)*. Bonn.

Ridgway, Brunilde S. 1970. *The Severe Style in Greek Sculpture*. Princeton, NJ.

Scheibler, Ingeborg. 1960. *Die symmetrische Bildform in der frühgriechischen Flächenkunst*. Kallmunz, FRG.

Schefold, Karl. 1975. *Wort und Bild. Studien zur Gegenwart der Antike*. Basel.

Schnapp, Alain. 1985. "Des vases, des images et de quelques uns de leurs usages sociaux." *DArch* 3: 69–75.

Shapiro, Alan. 1982. "Theseus, Athens, and Troizen." *AA* 1982: 291–97.

——. 1986. "The Origins of Allegory in Greek Art." *Boreas* 9: 4–23.

Simon, Erika. 1954. "Die Typen der Medeadarstellung in der antiken Kunst." *Gymnasium* 61: 203–27.

Sourvinou-Inwood, Christiane. 1971. "Theseus Lifting the Rock and a Cup Near the Pithos Painter." *JHS* 91: 94–109.

——. 1979. *Theseus as son and stepson. A tentative illustration of the Greek mythological mentality*. BICS Supplement 40. London.

——. 1987a. "A Series of Erotic Pursuits: Images and Meanings." *JHS* 107: 131–53.

——. 1987b. "Menace and Pursuit: Differentiation and the Creation of Meaning." In Bérard, Bron, and Pomari 1987.

——. 1988a. ""Myth" and History: On Herodotos iii.48 and 50–53." *OAth* 17: 167–82.

——. 1988b. "Le mythe dans la tragédie, la tragédie à travers le mythe: Sophocle, *Antigone* vv. 944–87." In Claude, Calame, ed., *Métamorphoses du mythe en Grèce antique*, 167–83. Geneva.

——. 1988c. *Studies in Girls' Transitions. Aspects of the Arkteia and Age Representation in Attic Iconography*. Athens.

Thomas, Eberhard. 1976. *Mythos und Geschichte. Untersuchungen zum historischen Gehalt griechischer Mythendarstellungen*. Cologne.

Timpanaro, Sebastiano. 1976. *The Freudian Slip. Psychoanalysis and Textual Criticism*. London.

Touchefeu, Odette. 1983. "Lecture des images mythologiques. Un exemple d'images sans texte. La mort d'Astyanax." In Lissarague and Thelamon 1983, 21–27.

Zeitlin, Froma I. 1978. "The Dynamics of Misogyny: Myth and Myth-making in the Oresteia." *Arethusa* 11: 149–84.

CONTRIBUTORS

Carlo Brillante is Researcher in Greek Literature at the University of Venice. He is the author of *La leggenda eroica e la civiltà micenea* (Rome 1981). His main interests are in historical and anthropological approaches to archaic Greek poetry and culture. His recent publications concern the function of dreams in ancient Greece.

Claude Calame is Professor of Greek Language and Literature at the University of Lausanne. He is the author of *Les choeurs de jeunes filles en Grèce archaïque* (Rome 1977), a commentary on the poems of Alcman (Rome 1984), and of *Le récit en Grèce ancienne* (Paris 1986). He has edited the collections *L'amore in Grecia* (Rome-Bari 1983) and *Métamorphoses du mythe en Grèce antique* (Geneva 1988).

Richard Caldwell is Professor of Classics at the University of Southern California. He is the author of articles on the psychoanalytic interpretation of Greek myths and of *The Origin of the Gods: A Psychoanalytic Study of Greek Theogonic Myth* (New York 1989).

Lowell Edmunds is Professor of Classics and Director of the Graduate Program in Classics at Rutgers University. He is the author of *Chance and Intelligence in Thucydides* (Cambridge MA 1975) and of *Cleon, Knights, and Aristophanes' Politics* (Lanham MD 1987). He has edited a collection of Oedipus folktales, *Oedipus: The Ancient Legend and its Later Analogues* (Baltimore 1985), and, with Phyllis Culham and Alden Smith, *Classics: A Discipline and Profession in Crisis?* (Lanham MD 1989).

William Hansen is Professor of Classical Studies and Fellow of the Folklore Institute at Indiana University (Bloomington IN). He is the author of *The Conference Sequence: Patterned Narration and Narrative Inconsistency in the* Odyssey (Berkeley 1972) and *Saxo Grammaticus and the Life of Hamlet: A Translation, History, and Commentary* (Lincoln NB 1983).

Robert Mondi is Associate Professor of Classics at Randolph-Macon's Woman's College. His other publications in the area of mythology include articles on the Cyclopes, Chaos, and the Titanomachy. He is completing a book on Hesiodic myth.

Joseph Falaky Nagy is Associate Professor of English at the University of California, Los Angeles. He is the author of *The Wisdom of the Outlaw: The Boyhood Deeds of Finn in Gaelic Narrative Tradition* (Berkeley, Los Angeles, and London 1985) and various articles on Indo-European mythologies.

Christiane Sourvinou-Inwood is a former Lecturer in Classical Archaeology at the University of Liverpool and is an Honorary Research Fellow at University College, London. She is the author of *Theseus as Son and Stepson: A Tentative Illustration of the Greek Mythological Mentality* (1979) and *Studies in Girls' Transitions: Aspects of the Arkteia and Age Representation in Attic Iconography* (1988) and has published many articles on Greek religion, mythology and iconography.

H. S. Versnel is Professor of Ancient History at the University of Leiden (the Netherlands). He is the author of *Triumphus* (Leiden 1970) and of *Ambig.iities in Greek and Roman Religion* I–II (Leiden 1990–91). He has edited *Faith, Hope and Worship* (Leiden 1981).